A CASEBOOK ON THE **Roman Law**

A CASEBOOK ON THE
Roman Law of Contracts

Bruce W. Frier

OXFORD
UNIVERSITY PRESS

OXFORD
UNIVERSITY PRESS

Oxford University Press is a department of the University of Oxford. It furthers
the University's objective of excellence in research, scholarship, and education
by publishing worldwide. Oxford is a registered trade mark of Oxford University
Press in the UK and certain other countries.

Published in the United States of America by Oxford University Press
198 Madison Avenue, New York, NY 10016, United States of America.

© Oxford University Press 2021

Library of Congress Cataloging-in-Publication Data
Names: Frier, Bruce W., 1943– author.
Title: A casebook on the Roman law of contracts / by Bruce W. Frier.
Description: New York, NY : Oxford University Press, [2021] |
Includes bibliographical references and index.
Identifiers: LCCN 2020052633 (print) | LCCN 2020052634 (ebook) |
ISBN 9780197573211 (hardback) | ISBN 9780197573228 (paperback) |
ISBN 9780197573242 (epub)
Subjects: LCSH: Contracts (Roman law) | LCGFT: Casebooks (Law)
Classification: LCC KJA2544 .F75 2021 (print) | LCC KJA2544 (ebook) |
DDC 346.3702/2—dc23
LC record available at https://lccn.loc.gov/2020052633
LC ebook record available at https://lccn.loc.gov/2020052634

DOI: 10.1093/oso/9780197573211.001.0001

9 8 7 6 5 4 3 2 1

Paperback printed by Marquis, Canada
Hardback printed by Bridgeport National Bindery, Inc., United States of America

Contents

Preface for Students   xvii

Acknowledgments   xxiii

Major Jurists Cited in This Casebook (in Rough Chronological Order)   xxv

Introduction to Roman Contract Law   1

Part A. The Praetor's Edict and the *Iudex*   1
Part B. Two Legal Remedies: The *Condictio* and the Actions on Sale/Purchase   2
Part C. The Juristic Development of Contract Law   5
Part D. The Concept of Agreement (*Consensus*)   7
Part E. The Concept of Good Faith (*Bona Fides*)   9
Part F. The Theory of "Cause" (*Causa*)   12
Part G. Obligation and Debt   14
Part H. Roman Contract Law and the Economy   17
Part I. From the Jurists to Justinian   22

Chapter I. Capacity to Contract   27

Case 1: Mental Capacity (Gaius, *Inst.* 3.106–109)   28
Case 2: Protecting Creditors of Wards (Paul, D. 18.5.7.1)   30
Case 3: The Creditor's Position after Performing (Ulpian, D. 26.8.5 pr.-1)   32
Case 4: The Contracts of Young Adults (Ulpian, D. 4.4.1)   34
Case 5: The Tutelage of Adult Women (Gaius, *Inst.* 1.190–191)   36

Chapter II. Stipulation: A Formal Contract   39

Part A. Making a Stipulation   41

Case 6: The Challenge of Formalism (Gaius, *Inst.* 3.92–93; Ulpian, D. 45.1.1 pr.-2)   42
Case 7: Altering the Promise (Ulpian, D. 45.1.1.3–5)   46
Case 8: The Role of Agreement (Venuleius, D. 45.1.137.1; Paul, D. 45.1.83.1)   49
Case 9: The Weight of a Written Stipulation (Severus and Caracalla, C. 8.37.1; Ulpian D. 2.14.7.12)   51
Case 10: Stipulations to the Benefit of Third Parties (Gaius, *Inst.* 3.103–103a)   53

Part B. Interpreting a Stipulation   56

Case 11: General Principles (Ulpian, D. 50.17.34)   57
Case 12: Interpretation against the Stipulator (Celsus, D. 45.1.99
    pr.-1)   59
Case 13: Preserving the Transaction (Ulpian, D. 45.1.80, and
    D. 45.1.41 pr.)   61
Case 14: "Women's Clothing" (Pomponius, D. 45.1.110.1)   63
Case 15: Broad Construction (Pomponius, D. 45.1.111)   64
Case 16: Like-Named Farms (Javolenus, D. 45.1.106)   65
Case 17: Mistake about a Characteristic (Paul, D. 45.1.22)   66

Part C. Conditional Stipulations and the Theory of Cause (*Causa*)   67

Case 18: Impossible Conditions (Gaius, *Inst.* 3.98)   68
Case 19: Immoral Conditions (Celsus, D. 45.1.97.2; Javolenus,
    D. 45.1.107)   69
Case 20: Implied Conditions (Ulpian, D. 23.3.21, 23; Paul,
    D. 23.3.22)   71
Case 21: A Condition and a Deadline (Paul, D. 45.1.8)   73
Case 22: Obstructing a Condition (Ulpian, D. 50.17.161, 22.2.8)   75

Part D. Execution and Impossibility   76

Case 23: Definite and Indefinite Stipulations (Ulpian, D. 45.1.75
    pr.-2, 5)   77
Case 24: Initially Impossible Stipulations (Gaius, *Inst.* 3.97–97a, 99;
    Venuleius, D. 45.1.137.4)   79
Case 25: Ensuing Legal Impossibility (Paul, D. 45.1.83.5)   81
Case 26: Ensuing Physical Impossibility (Paul, D. 45.1.37; Pomponius,
    D. 45.1.33)   84
Case 27: The Promissor's Responsibility (Paul, D. 45.1.91 pr., 2)   85
Case 28: Persistence of the Obligation (Paul, D. 45.1.91.3)   87
Case 29: Early Payment (Ulpian, D. 12.6.17; Paul, D. 12.6.10; Pomponius,
    D. 12.6.16 pr.)   89
Case 30: Liability after Default (Proculus, D. 45.1.113.1; Ulpian,
    D. 45.1.114)   90
Case 31: Default and Partial Performance (Proculus, D. 45.1.113 pr.)   92
Case 32: A Building Contract (Venuleius, D. 45.1.137.3)   95
Case 33: A Bottomry Loan (Scaevola, D. 45.1.122.1)   96

Part E. Defenses against Liability under a Stipulation   99

Case 34: The Action on the Stipulation (Gaius, *Inst.* 4.136–137)   100
Case 35: The Defense of Deceit and the Theory of Cause (Ulpian,
    D. 44.4.2.3)   102

Case 36: A Loan Not Provided; A Subsequent Pact
(Gaius, *Inst.* 4.115–116b)   104
Case 37: Obstruction by the Promisee (Javolenus, D. 45.1.105)   106
Case 38: The Defense of Non-Payment of Money (Caracalla,
C. 4.30.3)   107

Part F. Some Special Types of Stipulation (Novation, Suretyship, etc.)   109

Case 39: Novation of Debt (Gaius, *Inst.* 3.176–177)   110
Case 40: A Secondary Stipulator (Gaius, *Inst.* 3.110–111)   112
Case 41: Suretyship (Justinian, *Inst.* 3.20 pr.-3)   113
Case 42: Accessory Nature of Suretyship (Ulpian, D. 46.1.8.7)   115
Case 43: Availability of Defense of Deceit to a Surety (Julian, D. 46.1.15
pr.)   116
Case 44: Liability of a Co-Surety (Gaius, *Inst.* 3.121–122)   117
Case 45: Recourse of the Surety against the Debtor (Ulpian,
D. 17.1.6.2)   118
Case 46: Cession of Actions by the Creditor to the Surety (Paul,
D. 46.1.36)   119
Case 47: Warranty in a Sales Agreement (Ulpian, D. 21.2.31)   120
Case 48: Penalty Clause for Not Executing a Contract (Venuleius,
D. 46.5.11; Julian, D. 19.1.28)   122
Case 49: A Penalty Clause with a Tacit Condition (Paul,
D. 19.2.54.1)   124

Part G. Other Types of Formal or Unilateral Promises   125

Case 50: Two Formal Oral Promises (Gaius, *Institutionum Epitome*
2.9.3–4)   126
Case 51: The "Literal" Contracts (Gaius, *Inst.* 3.128–130, 134)   128
Case 52: Informal Promises to Municipalities (Ulpian, D. 50.12.1
pr.-2, 4)   130
Case 53: Reward for Information on a Thief (*Pauli Sententiae* 2.31.24)   132

Chapter III. Contracts Created through Delivery ("Real Contracts")   133

Part A. Gratuitous Loan for Consumption (*Mutuum*)   135

Case 54: Loan of Fungibles (Paul, D. 12.1.2 pr.-2; Justinian, *Inst.*
3.14.2)   136
Case 55: Loan via Third Parties (Ulpian, D. 12.1.15)   139
Case 56: Loan through Sale of an Object (Ulpian, D. 12.1.11 pr.)   141
Case 57: Stipulation to Give a Loan (Paul, D. 45.1.68)   143
Case 58: Agreement to Pay Back More than Was Lent (Ulpian,
D. 12.1.11.1)   145

Case 59: The *Condictio* and Over-Claiming (Gaius, *Inst.* 4.53–53b) 147
Case 60: Supplying Terms for Repayment (Julian, D. 12.1.22) 148
Case 61: The Senatus Consultum Macedonianum (Ulpian,
      D. 14.6.1 pr.) 149

Part B. Gratuitous Bailment: Deposit and Loan for Use (*Commodatum*) 151

Case 62: The *Formulae* for Deposit and Loan for Use (*Commodatum*)
      (Gaius, *Inst.* 4.47) 152
Case 63: Possession of the Object (Gaius, *Inst.* 4.153) 155
Case 64: Liability of the Holder (The Benefit Principle) (Ulpian,
      D. 13.6.5.2–3) 156
Case 65: Protecting against Damage by a Third Party (Ulpian,
      D. 19.2.41) 159
Case 66: The Depositary's Duty to Restore (Ulpian, D. 16.3.1.23–25) 160
Case 67: Expenses by the Holder (Modestinus, *Collatio* 10.2.5, = D.
      16.3.23) 162
Case 68: Conversion of a Deposit into a *Mutuum* (Ulpian,
      D. 12.1.9.9, 10) 164
Case 69: Irregular Deposit (Papinian, D. 16.3.24) 165
Case 70: Loan and Holding on Sufferance (*Precarium*) (Ulpian,
      D. 43.26.1) 168

Part C. Pledge (*Pignus*) 169

Case 71: Pledge as a Real Contract (Justinian, *Inst.* 3.14.4) 170
Case 72: Recovery of the Pledge (Ulpian, D. 13.7.9.3, 5; Gaius,
      D. 13.7.10) 172
Case 73: Agreement on Sale of the Pledge (Ulpian, D. 13.7.4) 174
Case 74: The Counterclaim (Ulpian, D. 13.7.25) 175
Case 75: Pledge and Hypothec (Justinian, *Inst.* 4.6.7) 177
Case 76: Mortgage (*Fiducia*) (Isidore, *Etym.* 5.25.21–24;
      Gaius, *Inst.* 2.60) 178

Chapter IV. Sale: A Contract Created through Informal Agreement 181

Part A. Formation of a Sale 182

Section 1. Agreement on the Basic Elements of a Sale 183

Case 77: The Origins of Sale (Paul, D. 18.1.1 pr.) 184
Case 78: The Nature of Agreement (Gaius, *Inst.* 3.135–137, 139) 185
Case 79: Sale and Barter (Paul, D. 18.1.1.1) 188
Case 80: Mixed Sales (Javolenus, D. 18.1.79) 190

Case 81: Definiteness of Price (Ulpian, D. 18.1.7.1–2)   191
Case 82: Reality of Price (Ulpian, D. 18.1.38)   193
Case 83: Fairness of Price (Paul, D. 19.2.22.3; Hermogenianus,
   D. 19.2.23)   195
Case 84: Saleable Objects (Paul, D. 18.1.34.1)   197
Case 85: Object Made by Seller (Pomponius, D. 18.1.20)   198
Case 86: Future Objects (Pomponius, D. 18.1.8)   200
Case 87: Sale from Stock (Gaius, D. 18.1.35.5–6)   202

Section 2. Defects in Agreement   204

Case 88: Mistake on a Basic Element of Sale (Ulpian, D. 18.1.9 pr.-1)   205
Case 89: Mistake on a Characteristic (Ulpian, D. 18.1.9.2, 11)   208
Case 90: Shared Mistake (Ulpian, D. 18.1.14)   211
Case 91: The Buyer's Alertness (Paul, D. 18.1.15.1)   212
Case 92: Fraud (Ulpian, D. 4.3.9 pr.)   213

Section 3. Impossibility   214

Case 93: Sale of Objects Not in Commerce (Modestinus,
   D. 18.1.62.1)   215
Case 94: Sale of a Free Man or a Stolen Object (Paul,
   D. 18.1.34.2–3)   216
Case 95: Sale of an Object Already Destroyed (Papinian,
   D. 18.1.58)   218

Section 4. Interpreting Agreements of Sale   219

Case 96: The Course of Negotiations (Labeo, D. 18.1.80.2)   220
Case 97: Interpreting a Condition (Julian, D. 18.1.41 pr.)   222
Case 98: Reasonability (Javolenus, D. 18.1.77)   223
Case 99: Interpretation against the Seller (Paul, D. 8.3.30)   224
Case 100: Supplying Reasonable Terms (Celsus, D. 19.1.38.2)   225
Case 101: Dispositive Provisions (Ulpian, D. 19.1.13.10–11, 13)   227

Section 5. Associated Pacts and Modification   228

Case 102: Pacts Incorporated into the Sale (Ulpian, D. 2.14.7.5)   229
Case 103: Pacts Made after the Sale (Papinian, D. 18.1.72 pr.)   231
Case 104: Rescinding or Modifying a Sale (Ulpian, D. 2.14.7.6)   232
Case 105: Reserving Seller's Right to Accept a Better Price (Ulpian,
   D. 18.2.2)   234
Case 106: Calling Off Sale If Price Is Not Paid (Pomponius, D. 18.3.2)   236
Case 107: Sale on Approval (Ulpian, D. 19.5.20 pr.-1)   237
Case 108: Condition of Tasting Wine (Ulpian, D. 18.6.4.1)   239
Case 109: Restricting Use of Object of Sale (Paul, D. 18.1.56)   240

Part B. Execution of a Sale   241

Section 1. Risk of Damage or Destruction Prior to Delivery   243

Case 110: Passage of Risk (Paul, D. 18.6.8 pr.)   244
Case 111: Explaining the Passage of Risk (Justinian, *Inst.* 3.23.3)   247
Case 112: Risk in a Conditional Sale (Gaius, D. 18.1.35.7)   249
Case 113: The Seller's Duty to Protect Object of Sale (Gaius,
    D. 18.1.35.4)   250
Case 114: Seller's Fair Use of a Purchased Slave (Labeo, D. 19.1.54
    pr.)   252
Case 115: Buyer's Liability before Delivery (Ulpian, D. 19.1.13.22)   253

Section 2. Buyer's Default and Remedies   254

Case 116: Determining Default (*Mora*) (Marcian, D. 22.1.32 pr.-2)   255
Case 117: Buyer's Failure to Take Delivery (Ulpian, D. 18.6.4.2)   257
Case 118: Buyer's Failure to Fulfill a Condition (Ulpian, D. 18.6.1.3)   258
Case 119: Buyer's Failure to Pay Price (Hermogenianus, D. 18.6.20)   260
Case 120: A Penalty Clause (Papinian, *Fragmenta Vaticana* 11)   261
Case 121: Seller's Right to Reclaim Object (Pomponius, D. 18.1.19)   262

Section 3. Seller's Default and Remedies   263

Case 122: Seller's Failure to Deliver (Ulpian, D. 19.1.1 pr.)   264
Case 123: Measuring the Buyer's Interest (Paul, D. 19.1.21.3)   266
Case 124: Failure to Deliver Wine (Pomponius, D. 19.1.3.3–4)   268
Case 125: Effects of Seller's Default on Risk (Gordian, C. 4.48.4)   270
Case 126: Purging Default (Pomponius, D. 18.6.18)   271

Section 4. Seller's Warranties for Lack of Right   272

Case 127: No Duty to Convey Ownership (Ulpian, D. 18.1.25.1)   273
Case 128: Delivery of Quiet Possession (Ulpian, D. 19.1.11.13)   275
Case 129: Liability Absent an Express Warranty (Javolenus,
    D. 21.2.60)   277
Case 130: Measuring Damages after Eviction (Julian, D. 21.2.8)   278
Case 131: Concealment, Warranties, and Disclaimers (Ulpian,
    D. 19.1.1.1)   280
Case 132: Liability Prior to Eviction (Africanus, D. 19.1.30.1)   282
Case 133: The Stipulation for Undisturbed Possession (Ulpian,
    D. 19.1.11.18)   283
Case 134: The Stipulation for Double (Pomponius, D. 21.2.16.1)   285
Case 135: The Express Warranty and Regional Custom (Gaius,
    D. 21.2.6)   287

Case 136: Requiring the Stipulation for Double (Ulpian, D. 21.2.37 pr.-1)   288
Case 137: Implying the Warranty (*Pauli Sententiae* 2.17.1–2)   289

Section 5. Seller's Warranties for Defects   291

Case 138: Puffery and Express Warranties (Florentinus, D. 18.1.43)   292
Case 139: Concealment and Express Warranties (Gaius, D. 18.6.16)   294
Case 140: Remedies for Violating an Express Warranty (Ulpian, D. 19.1.13.3–4)   295
Case 141: Non-Disclosure of a Beneficial Servitude (Pomponius, D. 18.1.66.1)   297
Case 142: Express and Implied Warranties (Pomponius, D. 19.1.6.4)   298
Case 143: Liability under the Aediles' Edict (Ulpian, D. 21.1.1.1–2)   300
Case 144: The Soundness of Slaves (Ulpian, D. 21.1.1.8, 4.4)   303
Case 145: Implied Warranty of Merchantability (Ulpian, D. 19.1.13 pr.-2)   304
Case 146: Mistake and the Implied Warranty (Paul, D. 19.1.21.2)   306

Chapter V. Other Consensual Contracts: Problems in Execution   307

Part A. Lease/Hire (*Locatio Conductio*)   309

Section 1. Lease of a Dwelling   310

Case 147: Grounds for Expelling the Tenant (Caracalla, C. 4.65.3)   310
Case 148: Damages for Unjustified Expulsion (Labeo, D. 19.2.28.2)   313
Case 149: Justified Abandonment Because of Fear (Alfenus, D. 19.2.27.1)   314
Case 150: Tenant Remedies If Dwelling Deteriorates (Gaius, D. 19.2.25.2)   316
Case 151: Deduction from Rent (Alfenus, D. 19.2.27 pr.)   317
Case 152: The Tacit Pledge of Furnishings (Ulpian, D. 43.32.1 pr-1; Neratius, D. 20.2.4)   318
Case 153: Tenant's Liability for Damaging the Dwelling (Marcian, D. 20.2.2)   320
Case 154: Mitigation of Damages (Ulpian, D. 19.2.9 pr.)   322

Section 2. Lease of a Farm   324

Case 155: Duties of the Landlord (Ulpian, D. 19.2.15 pr.-1)   324
Case 156: Justified and Unjustified Expulsion (Gaius, D. 19.2.25.1)   326

Case 157: Duties of the Tenant (Gaius, D. 19.2.25.3–5)   328
Case 158: Useful Expenses (Scaevola, D. 19.2.61 pr.)   330
Case 159: Remission of Rent (Ulpian, D. 19.2.15.2–3, 5, 7)   332
Case 160: Holdover (Ulpian, D. 19.2.13.11)   334

Section 3. Lease of a Movable Object or a Slave   336

Case 161: Lessor's Warranty against Defects (Ulpian, D. 19.2.19.1)   336
Case 162: Leasing a Slave as a Muleteer (Ulpian, D. 19.2.60.7,
    9.2.27.34)   338

Section 4. Performance of a Job; Employment   340

Case 163: Duties of the Contractor (Javolenus, D. 19.2.51.1)   340
Case 164: Moving a Column; Cleaning Clothes (Gaius,
    D. 19.2.25.7–8)   342
Case 165: Timely Completion (Labeo, D. 19.2.58.1)   344
Case 166: Approval and Risk (Labeo, D. 19.2.62; Florentinus,
    D. 19.2.36)   345
Case 167: Cost Overruns (Labeo, D. 19.2.60.4)   348
Case 168: "Lease" of One's Own Labor (Paul, D. 19.2.38 pr.-1)   350

Part B. Partnership (*Societas*)   352

Case 169: Contributions, Profit, and Loss (Gaius, *Inst.* 3.148–150)   354
Case 170: The Common Fund (Ulpian, D. 17.2.58 pr.-1)   357
Case 171: The Standard of Conduct for Partners (Ulpian,
    D. 17.2.52.1–3)   359
Case 172: Liability for One's Slaves (Ulpian, D. 17.2.23.1)   362
Case 173: Compensation for Partnership Debts (Paul, D. 17.2.27)   363
Case 174: Compensation for Expenses (Ulpian, D. 17.2.52.4)   365
Case 175: Ending a Partnership (Gaius, *Inst.* 3.151–154)   367
Case 176: Untimely Renunciation (Paul, D. 17.2.65.3–5)   369

Part C. Mandate (*Mandatum*)   372

Case 177: "On the Mandator's Behalf" (Gaius, *Inst.* 3.155–156, 162)   373
Case 178: The Duty to Perform the Mandate (Ulpian,
    D. 17.1.6.1–2)   376
Case 179: The Standard of Performance (Ulpian, D. 17.1.8.9–10)   378
Case 180: Overstepping the Mandate (Gaius, *Inst.* 3.161)   380
Case 181: Claims of the Mandatary (Ulpian, D. 17.1.12.9)   382
Case 182: Limits on the Mandatary's Claims (Paul, D. 17.1.26.6–7)   384
Case 183: Training a Slave (Paul, D. 17.1.26.8)   386
Case 184: The Honorarium (Ulpian, D. 11.6.1 pr., 50.13.1.10)   388

Chapter VI. Filling in the Gaps: Contracts Created Through One Party's Performance 391

Part A. Boundary Problems in Roman Contract Law 392

Case 185: Sale or Lease? (Gaius, *Inst.* 3.145–147) 392
Case 186: Brokerage (Ulpian, D. 19.3.1) 395

Part B. Half-Executed Contracts of Exchange 397

Case 187: Exchange and the Theory of *Causa* (Ulpian,
D. 2.14.7 pr.-2, 4, 5) 397
Case 188: Excavating Clay; Sowing a Field (Pomponius, D. 19.5.16
pr.-1) 400
Case 189: Approval; Sharing Oxen (Ulpian, D. 19.5.17.2–3) 402
Case 190: A Complex Loan (Africanus, D. 19.5.24) 404
Case 191: Alternative Remedies (Paul, D. 19.5.5.1) 406
Case 192: Standards of Performance (Paul, D. 19.5.5.1–2, 19.4.2) 407

Chapter VII. Third-Party Rights and Responsibilities 409

Part A. Sons and Slaves 410

Case 193: Liability of Sons for Their Contracts (Ulpian, D. 5.1.57) 411
Case 194: Transactions Ordered by the *Paterfamilias*
(Gaius, *Inst.* 4.70) 412
Case 195: The Nature of an Order (Ulpian, D. 15.4.1.1–2, 6) 413
Case 196: The *Peculium* (Justinian, *Inst.* 4.6.10) 415
Case 197: The Action on the *Peculium* (Gaius, *Inst.* 4.72a–73) 417
Case 198: Liability Despite a Prohibition to Contract (Paul,
D. 15.1.47 pr.) 419

Part B. The Manager of a Business (*Institor*) 421

Case 199: Liability for Contracts of an *Institor* (Gaius, *Inst.* 4.71; *Pauli Sent.*
2.8.1–2) 422
Case 200: Liability of the Manager (Ulpian, D. 14.1.1 pr.) 424
Case 201: Contracts within the Scope of Authorization (Ulpian,
D. 14.3.5.11–15) 425
Case 202: Liability of Third Parties to the Principal (Ulpian, D. 14.3.1;
Gaius, D. 14.3.2) 428

Part C. The Supervisor (*Procurator*) 430

Case 203: The *Procurator* (Ulpian, D. 3.3.1 pr.-1) 431

Case 204: Acquiring Property for the Principal (Neratius, D. 41.1.13;
Ulpian, D. 41.2.42.1)   434
Case 205: Contracting for the Principal (Papinian, D. 14.3.19 pr.,
3.3.67)   436
Case 206: Liability of Third Parties to the Principal (Ulpian,
D. 19.1.13.25)   438
Case 207: Compensation (Papinian, D. 17.1.7; Ulpian, D. 17.1.10.9)   439
Case 208: Extension of the Theory (Papinian, D. 3.5.30 pr.)   441

Part D. Transfer of Contract Rights and Duties to Third Parties   442

Case 209: Ordering My Debtor to Pay My Creditor (Paul, D. 46.3.64)   443
Case 210: Mandate to My Banker to Pay My Debt (Scaevola,
D. 2.14.47.1)   445
Case 211: Delegating Obligation for a Debt Owed by Me (Ulpian,
D. 46.2.11; Gaius, *Inst.* 2.38–39)   448
Case 212: Appointing a *Procurator* for a Lawsuit (Gaius, *Inst.* 4.84)   450
Case 213: Assigning a Debt to Your *Procurator* (Ulpian,
D. 3.3.55, 2.14.16 pr.)   452
Case 214: Delegation vs. Mandate to a Creditor (Gordian, C. 8.41.3)   454
Case 215: Cession of Actions against Co-Sureties (Julian, D. 46.1.17;
Modestinus, D. 46.1.39)   456

Chapter VIII. Quasi-Contract   459

Part A. Unauthorized Administration of Another's Affairs (*Negotiorum Gestio*)   460

Case 216: The Invention of Quasi-Contract (Gaius, D. 44.7.5 pr., 3;
Justinian, *Inst.* 3.27 pr.)   461
Case 217: The Reason for the Actions on Unauthorized Administration
(Ulpian, D. 3.5.1; Gaius, D. 3.5.2)   464
Case 218: Benefit to the Recipient (Ulpian, D. 3.5.9.1; Celsus,
D. 17.1.50 pr.)   467
Case 219: Benefit the Recipient Does Not Want (Justinian,
C. 2.18.24)   470
Case 220: Mistake as to the Beneficiary (Ulpian, D. 3.5.44.2)   472
Case 221: Benefit to Oneself (Ulpian, D. 3.5.5.5)   474
Case 222: The Intent to Seek Compensation for Expenses (Alexander,
C. 2.18.11)   476
Case 223: Standards of Care in Administering Another's Affairs
(Pomponius, D. 3.5.10)   477
Case 224: Administering the Affairs of a Deceased Debtor (Paul,
D. 3.5.12)   479

Part B. Unjustified Enrichment (The *Condictio*)   481

    Case 225: Payment by Mistake (Gaius, *Inst.* 3.91)   482
    Case 226: Requirements: Mistake (Ulpian, D. 12.6.1.1; Paul,
        D. 22.3.25 pr.-1)   485
    Case 227: Requirements: A Transaction and the Transfer of Property
        (Julian, D. 12.6.33)   487
    Case 228: Requirements: Absence of a Basis for Retention of Benefit
        (Papinian, D. 12.6.66; Ulpian, D. 12.7.1)   489
    Case 229: Subsequent Failure of Cause (Ulpian, D. 12.7.2; Ulpian,
        D. 19.1.11.6)   491
    Case 230: Misunderstanding about the Basis of a Transaction (Ulpian,
        D. 12.1.18)   494
    Case 231: Frustration of Purpose (Celsus, D. 12.4.16)   496
    Case 232: Dowry for an Incestuous Marriage (Papinian, D. 12.7.5)   497
    Case 233: Extent of Recovery and Change of Position (Paul,
        D. 12.6.65.5–8)   499
    Case 234: Unowed Services by a Freedman (Ulpian, D. 12.6.26.12)   501
    Case 235: Tracing the Benefit (Diocletian and Maximian, C. 4.26.7
        pr.-1, 3)   503

Glossary   505

Short Biographies of the Jurists   513

Suggested Further Reading   519

Index of Passages Cited   525

Preface for Students

This Casebook introduces an area of Roman private law that has had enormous influence on subsequent legal systems. Contracts have long been perceived as vital to any economy advanced beyond primitive systems of exchange. They allow for individuals or groups of individuals, even governments, to plan systematically for the future, in a way that accords protection to their promises.

A Casebook such as this one relies on direct use of primary sources in order to convey a clear understanding of what legal sources are like and how legal thinkers work. For Roman law, the primary sources are above all the writings of the late Republican and early imperial jurists. Almost all their writings date to what is commonly termed the Classical period of Roman law, from approximately 100 BCE to 235 CE. Justinian's Digest, promulgated as law at Constantinople in 533 CE, collects more than 9,000 lightly edited excerpts (totaling over 800,000 words) that derive mainly from Classical juristic writings. The excerpts vary in length from a few words to several pages. Modern knowledge of Classical Roman Law rests chiefly on the Digest and a few other sources, most prominent of which is the *Institutes* of Gaius, an elementary textbook written about 160 CE. This is the sole work of the Classical jurists that has survived to us more or less intact; it later served as the basis for the *Institutes* of Justinian.

Legislation also contributed to the development of Roman contract law. The original form of such legislation took the form of laws (*leges* or *plebiscite*) passed by the Roman legislative assemblies from the early Republic onward. But in the early Empire decrees of the Senate (*Senatus consulta*, abbreviated SC), passed by the Roman Senate usually after they had been moved by the emperor or his agent, tended to replace popular legislation. Further, a large amount of imperial lawmaking also takes the form of direct imperial proclamations, especially "rescripts" (*rescripta*), answers to questions of law addressed by officials or private citizens to the emperor. These rescripts, which became increasingly numerous and important starting in the second century CE, were somewhat haphazardly accumulated, but many were collected in the Codex of Justinian, the final edition of which was promulgated as law at Constantinople in 534 CE.

For the most part, however, the 235 Cases in this book derive from the writings of the Classical jurists. These jurists were not judges in our sense, nor were they quite like modern lawyers or law professors. They were, instead, a tiny elite of legal professionals who were charged with conserving and developing the law, especially the private law that Romans used in lawsuits between themselves. Although the Cases often describe fact situations at least loosely drawn from real life, they are, with few exceptions, not judicial opinions on real legal disputes. Rather, the jurists write about hypothetical and simplified, but nonetheless realistic situations as part of their effort to discuss and develop law among themselves. The jurists' writings were originally intended, in the main, for reading by their fellow jurists or other skilled legal scholars, not by laypersons. However, the legal rules that the jurists created through their writings were then applied directly to actual cases arising in Roman courts, in order to settle questions of law.

The course of Roman trials and the relationship of civil procedure to the development of Roman contract law are discussed in the Introduction to Roman Contract Law. The important take-away is that when significant questions of law arose at any stage of an actual trial, they were quite commonly settled through reference to the opinions of the jurists. Thus the Roman jurists, although they usually played no formal role in the judicial system, had a pivotal role in determining law within Roman courts.

The "Case-Law" Approach

In this Casebook, students are exposed to the working methods of the Roman jurists, to their internal debates, and to the principles and values that underlay their law. One important area, contract law, has been chosen to illustrate these points. The basic framework of Roman contract law derives from two sources: statutes (legislation in its various forms) and a crucial procedural document, the Edict of the Urban Praetor. But in most Cases the jurists range well beyond this basic framework into broader legal issues associated with contracts, and most of Roman contract law is in fact the jurists' own creation, not the result of straightforward statutory or edictal interpretation.

I have often used such a Casebook as the basic text for semester-long undergraduate, graduate, and law school courses in Roman law. The course is organized around classroom discussion of the individual Cases—usually about four to six Cases each hour. By delving into the Cases, students develop their own ability to examine legal rules and to assess them critically. For undergraduates, the improvement in their legal skills over a semester is usually remarkable. Further, all law is to a large extent a seamless cloth, and this is no less true of Roman law; so students soon pick up a good deal of Roman law in areas outside contract law, as well as some sense of the rules in their own legal system.

In order to encourage a deeper understanding of the Cases, I require students to purchase a general handbook on Roman law, such as Barry Nicholas's *An Introduction to Roman Law* (revised ed., 1962). I also recommend that undergraduates purchase Edward Levi's *An Introduction to Legal Reasoning* (revised ed., 2013) or Frederick Schauer's *Thinking like a Lawyer* (2012). Students who not only participate in classroom discussion but also read these books come away from the course with a good grasp on the nature of legal thinking more generally, as well as an appreciation of the general operating methods of both Roman and modern law.

Students in my law classes in Roman law need no such introduction, of course, and can make much speedier use of the Cases. They still use them, nonetheless, to organize their understanding of Roman contract law.

This Casebook is modeled after the format of Herbert Hausmaninger's highly successful German casebooks on Roman obligations and property law, as well as my earlier published casebooks on delict and on family law (with Thomas A. J. McGinn). To my mind, this format offers the best available method to communicate to modern students the content and character of Classical Roman Law. Direct exposure to original sources is far more intellectually stimulating than lectures or a reading of a modern synthetic account; students also learn much more about law from the original sources than they could possibly learn from a summary. I believe that students are best advised to avoid the crabbed formalism of elementary works such as the *Institutes* of Gaius or Justinian, and instead to plunge as quickly as possible into the actual working texts of the jurists.

How to Use This Casebook

The presentation of the Cases is invariable: first, the Latin text with the appropriate citation; second, an English translation of the text; third, discussion of the elements of the Case to orient students regarding the main legal problems raised, along with questions to encourage deeper reflection on the Case and its ramifications.

The Cases are grouped by subject matter and presented in a definite order, usually so that legal questions can be explored on a progressively deeper basis. It is important to think about the interrelationship between the Cases and the various approaches that the jurists take within them.

The discussion questions have several forms. Some encourage accurate understanding of the Case itself, others involve application of the Case to different situations, and still others raise open-ended problems that invite a response based on broader considerations, including morality and public policy. For this reason not all of the questions have clear and specific answers. Some, in fact, are intended mainly to stimulate thought and classroom discussion, and these questions may have no "correct" answer at all. Roman law, like all law, tends to raise difficulties on several levels simultaneously; students should quickly learn to think about the connection between broad and narrow legal issues.

Frequent reference is made to other legal texts, including many not quoted in this Casebook. Although it is not necessary to look up these references in order to understand the discussion, students who wish to learn more about Roman law are urged to consult these texts and the works mentioned in the "Suggested Further Reading" at the end of the book. To assist readers in becoming familiar with some of the more common technical terms of Roman law, a Glossary has been provided that contains definitions of key Latin words and some unfamiliar English words.

Finally, students should remember that the writings of the Roman jurists span more than three centuries and accordingly display a development in legal ideas. The chronological list of jurists in the front matter should make it easier to observe this development. An appendix to the Casebook contains short biographies of the major Roman jurists. Fortunately, they are few in number, and students who look up the biographies will soon become familiar with their names.

In reading this Casebook, students should think about not only the particular problems raised by the Cases, but also the larger issues they concern. On what principles does a civil society attempt to structure institutions as fundamental as contracts? How, and to what extent, is law used to protect not only the existence of the contract but also the independent interests of the parties to it and of third parties? The jurists' thought on these matters is in some respects similar to our own and in other respects sharply different. What explains the differences? Do they result chiefly from the relative social and economic "underdevelopment" of the Roman world, or from deeper disagreements about the way in which societies should be organized and governed? To what extent is the development of Roman law affected by accidents of its history or the conservatism of the jurists, and to what extent by the conscious or unconscious efforts of the jurists to achieve a socially beneficial body of rules? How close is the "fit" between Roman law and the social needs of Roman society? These are difficult questions, concerning which modern scholars often disagree.

A Note on Translation

Throughout this Casebook, "D." stands for the Digest (*Digesta*) of Justinian, "C." for the Codex of Justinian, and *Inst.* for the Institutes (*Institutiones*) of Gaius or Justinian, as indicated. Several Cases also come from postclassical collections or epitomes of juristic sources: the *Collatio*, a "comparison of Roman with Mosaic law"; the *Fragmenta Vaticana*, a collection of excerpts from Roman jurists and imperial rescripts; and the *Sentences of Paul* (*Pauli Sententiae*) deriving in part from the jurist Paul but with much later law. Although these late imperial sources all derive much of their substance from earlier Classical sources, all have been subjected to postclassical abbreviation or alteration. A few Cases are also taken from non-legal works.

In handling texts, I have adopted a few special editorial conventions: square brackets ([ ]) indicating letters or words in the transmitted Latin text that I believe are not authentic and that I therefore do not translate, and angle brackets (< >) indicating letters or words that I have inserted into the Latin text. In both cases, I am almost always following earlier editors. Within the English translations (whether or not a Latin text is also printed), parentheses always indicate my editorial insertions that are intended to clarify or explain the translation. Finally, readers unfamiliar with the Latin originals of Justinianic sources may wish to know that "pr." in a citation (e.g., Case 3: D. 26.8.5 pr.-1) refers to the *principium*, or "beginning," of the Latin fragment, before the numbered sections start. This rather awkward numbering system originated in the Renaissance.

The translations in this Casebook are intended to render the original Latin into clear and comprehensible English, even at the cost of wordiness. Where the Latin text is disputed or its meaning ambiguous, I have opted for what I feel is the best solution; and this has often meant making small changes in the transmitted text. All translations are my own, but I have often been influenced by the renderings in *The Digest of Justinian* (a four-volume English translation edited by Alan Watson, 1985); J. B. Moyle, *The Institutes of Justinian* (5th ed., 1913); *The Codex of Justinian* (a three-volume English translation edited by me, 2016); Francis de Zulueta, *The Institutes of Gaius* (2 vols. 1946); and other standard translations.

For reasons that should become clear, I have occasionally left untranslated some important technical terms, since any English translation of these terms might fatally prejudice understanding of them. It is preferable that students learn the meaning of these words from the contexts in which they appear. However, the glossary at the end of the volume should help with unfamiliar vocabulary.

I have created a password-protected companion website with Teacher's Notes that may assist instructors in presenting this Casebook to students (https://global. oup.com/us/companion.websites/9780197573228/). Instructors may request permission to access the website by writing either Profs. Bruce Frier (bwfrier@umich. edu) or Thomas McGinn (thomas.a.mcginn@vanderbilt.edu).

Acknowledgments

I am happy to thank the Cook Research Fund of the University of Michigan Law School, which supported my work on this book over one summer; as well as Arthur S. Rodrigues, a J.D. student who assisted mightily in my research. Profs. Thomas McGinn of Vanderbilt and Dennis Kehoe of Tulane were kind enough to read my drafts and send me their corrections or suggestions. Dr. William Sullivan, who taught from a casebook draft at Boston College Law School, offered much useful advice as well.

I would also like to thank Stefan Vranka, Oxford University Press's Executive Editor for Classics, Ancient History, and Archaeology, for his considerable help in getting this book into print; and also the press's anonymous readers and its editors, especially Dorothy Bauhoff, for their close work on my manuscript.

Major Jurists Cited in This Casebook (in Rough Chronological Order)

Jurist	Roman Emperor
Late Republican (100–30 BCE)	
QUINTUS MUCIUS Scaevola	
C. Aquilius GALLUS	
SERVIUS Sulpicius Rfus	
P. ALFENUS Varus	
Early Classical (30 BCE–90 CE)	
M. Antistius LABEO	Augustus (31 BCE–14 CE)
Massurius SABINUS	Tiberius (14–37)
C. CASSIUS Longinus	Claudius (41–54)
PROCULUS	Nero (54–68)
PLAUTIUS	Vespasian (69–79)
High Classical (90–180 CE)	Domitian (81–96)
L. JAVOLENUS Priscus	Trajan (98–117)
L. NERATIUS Priscus	
P. Juventius CELSUS	Hadrian (117–138)
P. Salvius JULIANUS (JULIAN)	
Ulpius MARCELLUS	Antoninus Pius (138–161)
VENULEIUS Saturninus	
Sextus Caecilius AFRICANUS	Marcus Aurelius (161–180)
GAIUS	
Sextus POMPONIUS	
Q. Cervidius SCAEVOLA	
Late Classical (180–235 CE)	
Aemilius PAPINIANUS (PAPINIAN)	Septimius Severus (193–211)
CALLISTRATUS	
Julius PAULUS (PAUL)	Caracalla (211–217)
Domitius ULPIANUS (ULPIAN)	
Herennius MODESTINUS	Alexander Severus (222–235)

Note: The Latin name by which each jurist is referred to in the text is capitalized. The Biographies appendix contains further information on these and other jurists mentioned in the text.

Introduction to Roman Contract Law

Roman contract law is of enduring interest not only as a body of law in its own right, but also because of its enormous historical influence. Although this law developed over almost a millennium, from the Twelve Tables of 449 BCE down to Justinian's codification in 530–534 CE, most attention has centered on a middle period, from about 100 BCE to about 235 CE, during which the Roman jurists refined and developed contract law to an extraordinary level: Classical Roman Law, as scholars have long called it. This casebook retains that traditional focus. Still, the earlier period left strong marks on the later law, and, in addition, our sources were powerfully shaped by the transmission and abbreviation (and in some cases the alteration) of Classical sources during the later Roman Empire up to Justinian.

Part A. The Praetor's Edict and the *Iudex*

Most Classical Roman contract law takes as its starting point the Edict of the Urban Praetor at Rome, although in reality the legal history of Roman contract law reaches still further back than the creation of this office in 367 BCE.[1] The praetorship was a regular annual magistracy, elected by the Centuriate Assembly, invested with the power of command (*imperium*), and second in rank after the two Consuls. The Urban Praetor (by the late Republic, selected by lot from among several elected Praetors) had, among a great many other duties, the charge of presiding over the initial stages of trials between Roman citizens. His court was set up on an open-air tribunal in the vicinity of the central Forum at Rome.

In order to regulate the litigation being channeled through his court, each Praetor, at the start of his year in office, set up an Edict that listed the causes of action he would accept. Some of these actions derived from statutes, but most were devised by successive Praetors, in an incremental process that each year could mean additions or subtractions, or just changes in existing wording. While successive Praetors usually took over much of the content from the Edicts of their predecessors, they also appear to have prided themselves on making small or occasionally large changes. Over centuries, what resulted from this slow accumulation was an intricate listing of causes of action: over four hundred, on the authoritative reconstruction by Otto Lenel in the late nineteenth century.[2] This accretion continued, although probably at a slowly diminishing pace, until under Hadrian the jurist Julian prepared a final edition of it ca. 135 CE.

The Urban Praetors were usually members of the Roman upper class with considerable prior administrative experience, but often little specifically legal

---

[1] For a concise summary of Roman civil procedure, see David Johnston, *Roman Law in Context* (1999): 112–132; Ernest Metzger, "Litigation," in David Johnston, ed., *Companion*, 272–298. Scholarship that is included in the appendix of Suggested Further Reading is cited in abbreviated form.

[2] Otto Lenel, *Das Edictum Perpetuum* (1883), third edition (1927).

A Casebook on the Roman Law of Contracts. Bruce W. Frier, Oxford University Press. © Oxford University Press 2021. DOI: 10.1093/oso/9780197573211.003.0001

knowledge, and their innovations came, it may be assumed, on advice from friends and colleagues who had such knowledge—including, at times, the Roman jurists. As laypersons, they may also have relied on such advice in granting trials to plaintiffs. The central issue in such a trial was embodied in a short statement, called the *formula*, appointing a judge for the case and summarizing the matter in question (see the following section for two examples).

At that point, however, the Praetor's involvement in trials largely ended. He consigned each trial for a hearing and determination by a single *iudex* (or at times a small panel of judges) who took responsibility for reaching a verdict after listening to both sides. The *iudex* was also almost always a layperson selected either through agreement between the parties or, doubtless most frequently, from the Praetor's *album*, a long list of persons whom the Praetor named each year to act in this role gratuitously, as a public service. A *iudex* also usually had little or no specific legal knowledge. Indeed, the entire system of civil procedure was clearly designed to be run by laypersons at little cost to the state.

At the end of the trial, the *iudex* was called upon to issue a verdict: either condemnation or absolution of the defendant. This verdict was neither appealable nor reviewable except in extraordinary circumstances, and the defendant's condemnation almost always involved an award of money to the plaintiff (*condemnatio pecuniaria*).

Classical Roman contract law is largely based upon this structure of civil procedure, called the formulary system. Most juristic works are, in fact, organized around the Praetor's Edict, even though, by the late Classical period, the Praetor's formulary system was gradually being displaced by imperial courts that in some respects began to resemble more modern judicial systems; see Part H of this Introduction.

Part B. Two Legal Remedies: The *Condictio* and the Actions on Sale/Purchase

The details of Roman civil procedure can be intricate and often baffling. At the cost of very considerable simplification, it may help to begin by looking at two model *formulae* that illustrate very different approaches to the issues of contract law.

The first is the *condictio*, a *formula* with ancient origins (an archaic version is known from the Twelve Tables). The Classical wording of a model *condictio* is given by Gaius, *Inst.* 4.49–50.

> Iudex esto. Si paret Numerium Negidium Aulo Agerio sestertium decem milia dare oportere, iudex Numerium Negidium Aulo Agerio sestertium decem milia condemnato; si non paret, absolvito.
>
> Let X be the *iudex*. If it appears that the defendant ought to give ten thousand sesterces to the plaintiff, let the *iudex* condemn the defendant

to the plaintiff for ten thousand sesterces; it this does not appear (to be true), let him absolve.

We will come upon the *condictio* repeatedly throughout this Casebook. In its form, as you can see, it appoints the *iudex* and gives him minimal instructions on what to do. The *formula* itself does not provide even a bare bones account of the plaintiff's claim, beyond stating that the defendant allegedly owes a specified sum of money (*condictio certae pecuniae*).[3] In time there developed a closely parallel *condictio* for a specific object (*condictio certae rei*). The abstract nature of the claim remains, however, the most outstanding characteristic of *condictiones*. For instance, a plaintiff who overstates his claim will often lose his lawsuit altogether (Gaius, *Inst.* 4.53–60, see Case 59). Nor does the *formula* itself provide any indication of how the defendant is expected to respond, beyond a simple denial that money is owed. In all these ways, this action is said to be "strict law" (*stricti iuris*).[4] If the defendant has any legal defenses (*exceptiones*), he or she will need to get them inserted into the *formula* at the preliminary stage before the Praetor.

Despite its rigidity, the *condictio* might have developed into a generalized contract action, rather as, many centuries later, the writ of *assumpsit* did in Common Law. But for a very long period it seems to have remained frozen as a demand for a specified sum or quantity or an object. Only in the late Classical period do the jurists begin to speak of a *condictio* for an indefinite amount (*condictio incerti*). By then, the need was so obvious that Roman law had previously developed a special *formula* for a central Roman contract, the stipulation, when a promise required a judicial estimation of value (Case 34).

However, in the meantime, and long before the *condictio* was generalized, a large number of actions for individual types of contracts had grown up, of which the actions on purchase and sale (*actio empti, actio venditi*), introduced before the end of the third century BCE, can stand as an early but not atypical example. On Lenel's reconstruction (*EP*[3] 299), the Edict's model *formula* for the action on purchase, brought by the buyer, ran:

Quod Aulus Agerius de Numerio Negidio hominem quo de agitur emit,
qua de re agitur, quidquid ob eam rem Numerium Negidium Aulo Agerio

---

[3] In a *formula* for a trial in the port city of Puteoli, however, the language of the *condictio* has a prefatory statement (*praescriptio*) stating the basis of the lawsuit.

[4] This term is not technical, but see Ulpian, D. 13.6.3.2; Marcian, D. 12.3.5 pr. and 4; Justinian, *Inst.* 4.6.28. It is basically used to bring out the contrast with actions *ex fide bona*; see later discussion.

dare facere oportet ex fide bona, eius iudex Numerium Negidium Aulo Agerio condemnato; si non paret, absolvito.

Whereas the plaintiff purchased the slave in question from the defendant, this being the matter under litigation, whatever on this account the defendant ought to give to or do for the plaintiff in accord with good faith, let the *iudex* condemn the defendant to the plaintiff for this; if it does not appear, let him absolve.

The *formula* for the action on sale, brought by the seller, was identical except for a change in the initial clause: "Whereas the plaintiff sold the slave in question to the defendant, . . ."

Although the "legalese" of the *formulae* can make this initially hard to understand, these two actions are very different from the *condictio*. First, the foundation of the plaintiff's claim is clearly stated in the *formula*: an alleged sale or purchase (in this model, of a slave). Second, the claim is not for a definite sum or thing, but for an amount to be determined by the *iudex*; this opened the way to a much broader evaluation of the plaintiff's claim. Third, and much the most important point, what the defendant owes must be evaluated "in accord with good faith" (*ex fide bona*). Although originally good faith may have explained why the claim itself was actionable, eventually the phrase became the basis for the development of much Roman contract law; see Part E of this Introduction.[5]

Not all Roman contract actions can be neatly divided into categories resembling these two *formulae*, but the contrast between them is useful because it helps to describe the general development of early Roman contract law. In brief, the Romans began, as early as the fifth century BCE, with a procedural structure, built around actions like the *condictio*, which might have permitted them to generalize a unified law of contract.[6] But this did not happen. Instead, successive Urban Praetors began recognizing, and developing procedural mechanisms for, individual contract types that they deemed worthy of protection. The chronology and details of this process are hard to discern, and scholars have debated for centuries. Still, the overall result is clear enough: no general contract claim, but instead a multiplicity of contract types.[7] (On a broad level, Roman contract law resembles, in this respect, the Common Law of torts, with its proliferation of distinct causes of action.)

[5] On *bonae fidei iudicia*, see Max Kaser and Karl Hackl, *Das Römische Zivilprozessrecht* (2nd ed., 1996), 153–157. The *formulae* for the actions on sale are reconstructed by Lenel, *EP*³ 299.

[6] This was observed by John P. Dawson, *Unjust Enrichment* (1951), 42: "The condiction was the Roman general assumpsit."

[7] The distinction should not be overdrawn, since, of course, much modern contract law centers on individual contracts; see F. H. Lawson, in W. W. Buckland, *Roman Law and Common Law: A Comparison in Outline* (2nd ed., revised by Lawson; 1965) 265–270.

Part C. The Juristic Development of Contract Law

Although Urban Praetors were still regularly modifying their annual Edicts in the first century BCE (the Edict would not be finally frozen until about 135 CE), the Roman jurists, as they began to work more systematically in the late Republic, are likely to have perceived the opportunities for legal development that the maze of recognized contracts offered.

The jurists[8] were largely self-appointed experts in Roman private law (*iuris periti*), and later in law more generally. The privileged inner circle of jurists at Rome—never more than ten to twenty at any one time, so it seems—were mainly responsible for preserving and developing legal rules, but played no formal role in the Roman judicial system until late in the Classical period. It is their extensive writings that are sampled in Justinian's Digest. Their influence on trials stemmed rather from their general reputation, which was recognized, during the early Empire, by an imperial grant of the right to give "responses" backed by the emperor's warrant (*ius respondendi ex auctoritate principis*). These jurists stemmed almost invariably from the empire's upper classes. Before 150 CE most of them pursued careers within the Senate, but thereafter they were increasingly absorbed into the imperial bureaucracy.

When it came to contracts, the initial task of the jurists was to create a credible typology of the various contracts. This they did on the basis of how these contracts were formed: as Gaius says (*Inst.* 3.88), "An obligation is contracted either by (delivery of) a thing, or by (formal) words, or by writing, or by agreement" (*aut . . . re . . . aut verbis aut litteris aut consensu*). With one variation, this Casebook follows Gaius' typology. Contracts may be divided as follows:

1. Those created by the formal pronouncement of prescribed words (*verbis*), above all the stipulation but also some minor binding promises (Chapter II);

2. The two formal bookkeeping contracts created through entries in account books (*litteris*; see Case 51);

3. The four so-called real contracts created by informal agreement followed by the delivery of property (*re*; Chapter III); and

4. The four consensual contracts created by informal agreement alone (*consensu*), which are the most important from the standpoint of commerce: sale, lease, partnership, and mandate (Chapters IV–V).

Although this typology is not meant to describe a chronological or evolutionary development, it should be noted that the first two categories, plus one of the real contracts, were most frequently actionable by the ancient *condictio*, while the remaining seven were actionable, at least eventually, through actions *ex fide bona*.

---

[8] A. Arthur Schiller, "Jurists' Law," *Columbia Law Review* 58 (1958): 1226–1238, and *Roman Law*, 269–401; Barry Nicholas, *Introduction*, 28–38.

With the aid of this typology, juristic writings began to develop the signal rules and characteristics of each contract. They drew upon their experience as individuals and as sometime participants in trials, but also upon the common and diverse features within each type. Particularly in the case of the consensual contracts, the jurists' handling went well beyond the simple issue of their initial enforceability, into deeper questions of contract formation, interpretation, standards of performance, remedies, and so on. In particular, the jurists strove for ways to make the Praetor's contracts more serviceable to an increasingly complex society and economy; and contract types founded on archaic principles of gratuitous performance (such as the "real" contracts and mandate) underwent general remodeling. In all these respects, the concept of *bona fides*, discussed in Part E, dramatically expanded, until it finally emerged as the central social principle in the Roman legal understanding of most informal contracts.

Despite these efforts, the developed typology brought vividly to light the more fundamental problems with the Urban Praetor recognized contracts. Altogether too frequently, the praetorian scheme allowed contracts that were clearly worthy of enforcement to fall through the cracks. Where feasible, the jurists tried to interpret the contractual categories as broadly as possible, in an effort to catch the maximum number of deserving contracts. But in the end they were often obliged to resort to makeshifts, particularly as it became clear that Praetors were averse to multiplying the actions available in the Edict. The result is somewhat tentative, but still interesting (Chapter VI). The jurists also steadily developed contract law as it applied to parties other than those making the contract, although Roman law never quite accepts legal agency in the modern sense (Chapter VII).

Finally, the jurists began, rather tentatively, to explore instances where, despite no valid contract being in play, the law nonetheless gives remedies that can be broadly described as contract-like, *quasi ex contractu* (Chapter VIII).

In sum, the contract law of the jurists, although certainly not perfect even within ancient social and economic conditions, is still a considerable achievement, particularly in its intelligence and thoroughness. From a modern perspective, it may seem disappointing that the jurists were unable to devise more than the rudiments of a generalized contract law. But, by way of compensation, the jurists' law displays great sensitivity to the details of particular contracts, and particularly to potential points of deeper conflict between parties. Although the jurists had important, and historically highly influential, things to say about general principles of contract law, the real glory of their thinking is in the details—an outstanding example of the virtues of thinking inside the box.

In the following four sections, the basic concepts the jurists employed are further explored.

Part D. The Concept of Agreement (*Consensus*)

Is it possible to articulate a broad requirement that will hold good for all enforceable agreements?[9] The preceding discussion might suggest that, in the case of Roman contract law, this was impossible, or at any rate undesirable; the factual situations that may be referred to under the broad heading "contract" were simply too various to permit fruitful generalization.

Nonetheless, the jurists did attempt to find such a requirement. At least by the mid-second century CE, the jurists seem to have accepted that the essence of contract lay in a requirement of "mutual agreement" (*consensus*) producing "an agreement" (*conventio*). The late Classical jurist Ulpian (4 *ad Ed.*) D. 2.14.1.3, explains the concept thus:

> Conventionis verbum generale est ad omnia pertinens, de quibus negotii contrahendi transigendique causa consentiunt qui inter se agunt: nam sicuti convenire dicuntur qui ex diversis locis in unum locum colliguntur et veniunt, ita et qui ex diversis animi motibus in unum consentiunt, id est in unam sententiam decurrunt. Adeo autem conventionis nomen generale est, ut eleganter dicat Pedius nullum esse contractum, nullam obligationem, quae non habeat in se conventionem, sive re sive verbis fiat: nam et stipulatio, quae verbis fit, nisi habeat consensum, nulla est.
>
> *Conventio* (literally, "coming together") is a general word covering all things agreed to by those who deal with one another in order to contract and transact affairs. People who are gathered and come from different places to one place are said to "come together" (*convenire*), and they resemble those who from different mental impulses agree on one thing, i.e., come to one way of thinking (*sententia*). To such an extent is *conventio* a general word that, as (the jurist) Pedius elegantly expressed it, there is no contract, no obligation, which does not have an agreement (*conventio*) within it, whether it is created by an act or by formal words; for even stipulation, which is created by formal words, is void unless it has agreement (*consensus*).

Ulpian's argument employs a bold metaphor: persons gathering together in one place form a "convention"; their physical coalescence resembles the mental coalescence of persons who arrive at a "meeting of the minds" on a common purpose or undertaking. Further, this agreement is seen as fundamental to the validity of their contract.

[9] See W. W. Buckland, *Text-Book* (1966), 412–422; Fritz Schulz, *Classical Roman Law* (1951), 524–526; Reinhard Zimmermann, *Obligations* (1996), 561–565; Cosimo Cascione, *Consensus* (2003); Giuseppe Falcone, "Riflessioni sulla Conventio in D. 2.14.1.3," *Annali del Seminario Giuridico Univ. Palermo* 62 (2019): 195–218.

Ulpian's metaphor is not completely convincing, however, at least not in the absence of much further explication. First of all, just what is meant by a "meeting of the minds"? Is Ulpian requiring that the parties reach actual mental agreement, so that their intentions are in fact united on a common end (so-called subjective agreement)? Or is he only requiring that they appear to agree, or might reasonably think that they agree, even if in fact they do not do so (so-called objective agreement)? The distinction between subjective and objective agreement can make a large difference in particular cases. Suppose, for instance, that a party promises something through a formal stipulation, without fully appreciating the apparent content of the promise; should the words be enforced as they were spoken, or should consideration be given to the actual meaning that either the promissor or the promisee attached to the words? Or what if a seeming agreement is vitiated by a defect such as misunderstanding or mistake?

The jurists never attempted a definitive answer to these questions. Whereas modern legal systems have generally favored an objective concept of agreement (this resonates with the impersonality of the modern marketplace), the jurists seem to have given appreciably greater weight to actual, subjective intentions, particularly in the case of informal contracts, but to a more limited extent also in the case of stipulation. Still, in general they quite reasonably used an objective concept at least as a starting point for evaluating and interpreting individual contracts. Many Cases, as we shall see, serve to illustrate this basic ambiguity.

Second, while Ulpian plainly holds that *consensus* on a *conventio* is a necessary requirement for any binding contract, he is not also holding it to be a sufficient requirement. That is, he is not adopting what is termed a "voluntaristic" theory holding that parties have a generalized freedom, through their "wills" (*voluntates*), to make their agreements enforceable at law. For one thing, the Roman contract types did not really allow for such freedom; the valid contract types all had additional requirements of form (as in the case of stipulation) or delivery ("real" contracts) or content (consensual contracts), and these requirements also had to be met. Therefore agreement alone was never enough; for a contract to be enforceable at law, it had to occur within the preexisting framework of the recognized contract types. In this respect, freedom of contract was far more restricted among the Romans than in modern law.

Third, the jurists regularly envisage the "meeting of the minds" as occurring instantaneously between two individuals who are in one another's presence. Although the jurists refer to the possibility of arranging an informal contract through an exchange of letters, they do not discuss at any length the complex problems of offer-and-acceptance that long-distance communications can create. Further, the jurists have difficulty with the type of offer that is normally accepted by acting, as for instance when someone broadcasts the offer of a reward for finding a lost pet. To the jurists, since the parties do not reach personal agreement with one another, such an offer is in principle not binding on the offeror even after someone acts in reasonable reliance on the offer, and thus the promised reward need not be paid.

Within these limits, the concept of *consensus* serves as a good organizing principle in evaluating Roman contract law, particularly the law as to the formation and interpretation of informal contracts. Since the Romans do not adopt a voluntaristic theory of contract, *consensus* plays a more limited role in juristic discussion of the execution of contracts.

Part E. The Concept of Good Faith (*Bona Fides*)

The second central concept of developed Roman contract law is good faith (*bona fides*).[10] The concept apparently entered Roman law as a means whereby Praetors explained why some informal agreements, such as sale, were legally enforceable simply as a result of agreement. The Praetor's *formulae* for these actions typically require the defendant to pay the plaintiff the value of whatever he or she is obligated to do "in accord with good faith" (*ex fide bona*). As it seems, this phrase originally designated just the reason for enforcing the obligation; as Javolenus puts it (D. 19.2.21), "*Bona fides* requires that what was agreed be done." In time, *formulae* based on *bona fides* were created for most of the "real" contracts as well; but not for the obligations such as stipulation and other contracts enforceable through the *condictio*, which are commonly described as enforced through "strict law" actions (*actiones stricti iuris*).

If *bona fides* was originally used only to explain why a person could be legally obliged to execute a promise, by the late Republic the phrase had come to be used far more widely, in order to establish the full legal implications of a promise. Suppose, for example, that I promise to give you a horse in exchange for you paying me its price; *bona fides* can explain why I must execute this promise, but it can also serve to establish what the promise means: when and how I must deliver the horse, whether I must make you its owner, whether the horse must be free of defects, and so on. In this respect, *bona fides* came to serve as a powerful quasi-ethical principle in the jurists' further development of contract law. *Bona fides* had become not just a reason for enforcement, but also an independent source of obligation.

This broadening seems initially to have occurred within the Roman judicial system itself, as *iudices* struggled to implement the jejune *formulae* for trials by acting on the basis of their socially formed consciousness to determine how plaintiffs and defendants ought to have acted toward one another. Thus, as the statesman Cicero reports (*de Officiis* 3.70), the great early jurist Q. Mucius Scaevola was accustomed to say, ca. 100 BCE, that:

[10] Still helpful are Fritz Schulz, "Fidelity," in *Principles* (1936), 223–238; Luigi Lombardi, *Dalla Fides alla Bona Fides* (1961).

. . . summam vim esse dicebat in omnibus iis arbitriis, in quibus adderetur EX FIDE BONA, fideique bonae nomen existimabat manare latissime, idque versari in tutelis, societatibus, fiduciis, mandatis, rebus emptis, venditis, conductis, locatis, quibus vitae societas contineretur; in iis magni esse iudicis statuere, praesertim cum in plerisque essent iudicia contraria, quid quemque cuique praestare oporteret.

. . . the greatest force attached to all trials in which was added *ex fide bona*, and the phrase *bona fides* extended very far; it was employed for guardianships, partnerships, *fiduciae*, mandates, sales, leases—matters on which the social relations of life depend. In these, especially since counterclaims were admitted in many, it was the job of a great *iudex* to determine what each person ought to do for another.

By the late Republic, however, *bona fides* was more commonly the province of the jurists themselves, who gradually transformed broad social feelings into specific legal norms against which the conduct of plaintiffs and defendants could be more objectively measured. At the end of his life, in 44 BCE, Cicero acknowledges this (*Topica* 66):

In omnibus igitur eis iudiciis, in quibus ex fide bona est additum, ubi vero etiam ut inter bonos bene agier oportet, in primisque in arbitrio rei uxoriae, in quo est quod eius aequius melius, parati eis esse debent. Illi dolum malum, illi fidem bonam, illi aequum bonum, illi quid socium socio, quid eum qui negotia aliena curasset ei cuius ea negotia fuissent, quid eum qui mandasset, eumve cui mandatum esset, alterum alteri praestare oporteret, quid virum uxori, quid uxorem viro tradiderunt.

In all the trials in which *ex fide bona* has been added . . . they (the jurists) should be on hand. They have given us (the concepts of) deceit (*dolus malus*), good faith (*bona fides*), the right and the good (*aequum bonum*), what a partner must do for a partner, what one who takes care of another's affairs for the person whose business this is, what a giver of a mandate and a mandatary, each to the other; what a husband for a wife and a wife for a husband.

Bona fides is, in this respect, an aggressive concept, more far-reaching than the corresponding concept of "good faith" in Anglo-American law. Not only does it require that parties abstain from deceit and fraud, it also requires, to some extent, that they actively cooperate with one another; and it often does so by imposing duties that the parties may not have envisaged in forming their agreement. As the jurist Tryphoninus puts it (9 *Disp.*) D. 16.3.31 pr., "The *bona fides* that is demanded in contracts requires the highest fairness (*aequitas summa*)." The extensive contractual rules that the jurists created through reference to *bona fides* were frequently "dispositive" in character, in that the parties could eliminate or vary them through mutual agreement. However, there is little evidence that Romans generally made much use of lengthy written contracts, so that the default rules that law provided were almost always binding.[11]

More puzzling is the question of whether *bona fides* should be looked upon as primarily an interpersonal legal value between two contracting parties, or rather as a broader social value. This question is raised by Tryphoninus (9 *Disp.*), D. 16.3.31 pr.), who starts from the following problem: A defendant on a criminal charge deposits a large sum of money with me, and is then condemned in his trial to forfeiture of his estate. Does contractual *bona fides* require me to return the deposit to the depositor, or instead to surrender it to the State? Tryphoninus (9 *Disp.*), D. 16.3.31 pr.-1, reasons:

> Si tantum naturale et gentium ius intuemur, ei qui dedit restituenda sunt: si civile ius et legum ordinem, magis in publicum deferenda sunt: nam male meritus publice, ut exemplo aliis ad deterrenda maleficia sit, etiam egestate laborare debet.
>
> 1. Incurrit hic et alia inspectio. Bonam fidem inter eos tantum, quos contractum est, nullo extrinsecus adsumpto aestimare debemus an respectu etiam aliarum personarum, ad quas id quod geritur pertinet? Exempli loco latro spolia quae mihi abstulit posuit apud seium inscium de malitia deponentis: utrum latroni an mihi restituere seius debeat? si per se dantem accipientemque intuemur, haec est bona fides, ut commissam rem recipiat is qui dedit: si totius rei aequitatem, quae ex omnibus personis quae negotio isto continguntur impletur, mihi reddenda sunt, quo facto scelestissimo adempta sunt. Et probo hanc esse iustitiam, quae suum cuique ita tribuit, ut non distrahatur ab ullius personae iustiore repetitione. . . .
>
> . . . If we consider only the Law of Nature and of Nations (*naturale et gentium ius*), they (the coins) must be restored to the giver; if (we consider) Civil Law and the legal order, they should rather be delivered to the State. For a person deserving ill of the State ought to suffer even in poverty so that he be an example to others, to deter misdeeds.
>
> 1. And here is a further observation. Should we evaluate *bona fides* only between those who are parties to a contract, with no third party

---

[11] Be warned, however, that "good faith" is not a magic elixir capable of solving all contract problems. When the jurists assign rights and duties, their reasoning (or, if it is unknown, their likely reasoning) should be subjected to thorough interrogation as to its practicality and its fairness to both sides.

considered, or with regard also to other persons whom the matter concerns? For example, a bandit deposits what he stole from me with Seius, who is unaware of the depositor's wrongdoing; should Seius restore it to the bandit or to me? If we consider the giver and recipient by themselves, it is *bona fides* that the giver receive the entrusted property. If (we consider) the fairness of the whole matter, which is comprised from all the persons affected by this business, it should be returned to me from whom it was taken by a most wicked act. And I consider this to be Justice that accords to each his own, such that it is not removed from the more just claim of anyone. . . .

If we act in good faith, where should our contractual loyalties lie? Tryphoninus inclines toward the broader view, which suggests that he sees *bona fides* as having at least a substantial social component. A contract party's duty of *bona fides* is directed not just toward a contractual partner, but also toward society and the state, as well as toward vitally interested third parties. The impact of such social content is important in evaluating the decisions the jurists make on particular contractual questions.

On the other hand, the interpersonal aspect of *bona fides* is also certainly of enormous significance. In an action based on *bona fides*, the plaintiff is not allowed to restrict the suit only to those claims he or she might have against the defendant; by virtue of *bona fides*, the *iudex* was supposed to evaluate and offset any counterclaims of the defendant, so long as they arise from the same transaction. Thus the *iudex* must examine the entire transaction from the standpoint of both parties. For the most part, this offset of claims occurs automatically; the defendant simply raises counterclaims in the course of pleading before the *iudex*.

Bona fides has little direct application to contracts such as stipulation, which were in principle governed by "strict law" rules; the promissor was obliged to do exactly what he or she had promised. However, this principle was gradually somewhat loosened in Classical law. In particular, the defense of deceit (*exceptio doli*) allowed defendants to raise important collateral issues about the origin and enforceability of promises.

Part F. The Theory of "Cause" (*Causa*)

A third common theme, of substantially lesser significance, is *causa*.[12] The word *causa* has numerous meanings, both in Latin generally and, more particularly, in legal contexts. But here we are interested in a particular meaning: the reason why a promise was made. The existence of such a *causa* was not ordinarily a requirement for contractual validity in Roman law; a *iudex*, confronted with a common sale, was under no

---

[12] See Reinhard Zimmermann, *Obligations*, 549–559, who also outlines the difference from Anglo-American consideration.

immediate obligation to inquire further into the reasons for the sale. But *causa* nonetheless becomes important in a number of specific areas. Among them are:

- A stipulation, as a formal promise, may frequently have an abstract or absolute form ("Do you promise to pay me one hundred sesterces?" "I promise."). Ostensibly, such a promise seems binding irrespective of the reasons why it was given. But the jurists allow a defendant, by way of a defense, to argue in various ways that a *iudex* must probe the factual background of the promise being given. If the promise was given contingent on some anticipated event that is not mentioned in the spoken words, or if the promise was for an immoral or illegal purpose, that may be relevant to the trial's outcome. See Chapter II.C and E.

- Somewhat similarly, the Roman law of unjustified enrichment, which is made actionable by the strict-law *condictio*, is heavily dependent on the theory of *causa* for determining both why a plaintiff bestowed a benefit on a recipient and whether the recipient is justified in retaining that benefit. See Chapter VIII.B.

- A somewhat narrower usage of *causa* occurs in the law concerning bilateral exchanges that fall outside the recognized contract types (Chapter VI.B). When one party has performed his promise and the other has not, in later Classical law the performing party is often allowed to claim his interest in the other party performing. The requirement that there be bilaterality can be expressed using *causa*.

In these three instances, but rarely elsewhere, *causa* appears as a handy jurisprudential tool for opening up alleged promises to wider judicial inspection. Use of this tool is, however, markedly less sweeping than in later Western (especially French) law, where *causa* (or *cause*) will have a rich and not altogether salubrious career.[13]

In particular, it must be stressed that in Roman law *causa* was not an independent requirement for a contract's validity. The original concept has no strong kinship at all with ideas like the Anglo-American requirement of "consideration" (a bargained-for exchange making a promise enforceable). Many of the recognized Roman contract types are not contracts of exchange at all, and a promise made with donative intention—a more or less pure act of altruism—possesses in Roman law the same validating *causa* as a strongly bilateral exchange of promises such as sale or lease, so long as intent is present.

---

[13] See Ernest G. Lorenzen, "Causa and Consideration in the Law of Contracts," *Yale Law Journal* 28 (1919): 621–645; F. H. Lawson, "Excursus: Cause and Consideration," in W. W. Buckland, *Roman Law and Common Law* (2nd ed., revised by Lawson; 1965), 228–236; B. S. Markesinis, "*Cause* and Consideration: A Study in Parallel," *Cambridge Law Journal* 37 (1978): 53–75.

Part G. Obligation and Debt

Finally, it should be observed that the jurists treat contract law not as a largely discrete area of law, but rather under the broader heading of "obligations" (*obligationes*), which also include delicts (*delicta*, civil wrongs analogous to torts).[14],[15] "Obligation" (*obligatio*) derives from the Latin verb *obligare*, meaning "to bind or fasten." The Emperor Justinian (*Inst.* 3.13 pr.) expands on the metaphor: "An obligation is a legal bond (*iuris vinculum*) whereby we are inescapably constrained to perform some act in accord with the law of our State." (*Obligatio est iuris vinculum, quo necessitate adstringimur alicuius solvendae rei, secundum nostrae civitatis iura.*) As this definition indicates, the primary source of the compulsion is not, in the case of a contract, the will of the parties, but rather the force that Roman law attaches to their specific agreement, its form and its substance.[16]

An obligation creates debt (*debitum*), defined by Ulpian as follows: "Debt (*aes alienum*) is what we owe to other people" (D. 50.16.213.1). A person who owes a debt is a debtor (*debitor*), "one from whom money can be exacted despite resistance" (Modestinus, D. 50.16.108: *is a quo invito exigi pecunia potest*). Creditors are "not just those who have lent money, but all to whom it is owed for whatever reason" (Gaius, D. 50.16.11).

The chief characteristic of an obligation is therefore that it creates a claim that is actionable *in personam*, against a particular individual. For example, in the bilateral contract of sale, the seller has, as an immediate result of the contract, an *in personam* claim against the buyer for performance, and vice versa; and nothing but this *in personam* claim arises directly from the agreement itself. A broadly similar *in personam* claim would arise in delict if, for instance, one person wrongfully damaged another's property; the injured party could then sue the injurer for the penalty set by the Lex Aquilia for wrongful damage to another's property.

This integration of contract and delict has five important implications for contract law:

1. Privity of Contract. All agreements, except for the very simplest immediate performances, give rise to the possibility of credit and debt. The party with a claim is the creditor; the other party is the debtor. (In strongly bilateral contracts such as sale, each party is at the outset both a creditor and a debtor.) The creditor/debtor relationship lies at the core of *in personam* liability, since the relationship is thought of as an intensely personal

[14] On obligations, see Max Radin, "Fundamental Concepts of the Roman Law," *California Law Review* 12 (1924): 481–495; Reinhard Zimmermann, *Obligations*, 1–67; Peter Birks, *Obligations* (2014), 1–25.

[15] Gaius, *Institutes* 3.88: "Let us now proceed to obligations. These are basically divided into two species: for every obligation arises either from contract or from delict." (*Nunc transeamus ad obligationes, quarum summa diuisio in duas species diducitur: omnis enim obligatio uel ex contractu nascitur uel ex delicto.*)

[16] For an exhaustive analysis of the imagery in this sentence, see Birks, *Obligations*, 2–5.

one. It follows that the Romans have some difficulty envisaging the use of a contract to create legal rights or duties in a third party, someone who is extraneous to the contractual relationship. Although the jurists found ways around this problem, there is often a definite clumsiness to the legal mechanisms they devised. See Gaius, *Inst.* 3.163–167.

2. Debt. Second, the Roman jurists tend to treat the law of debt as a unity. In particular, they develop complex, but reasonably well-unified rules on how debt can be satisfied. These rules do not require detailed exposition. Basically, if a debt demands a performance or payment, the debtor can normally discharge the debt by making or tendering the required performance, either to the creditor or to a person authorized by the creditor. A third party could also discharge the debt, even against the debtor's will, unless the performance was inseparably bound up with the debtor's person. In general, the performance must correspond exactly to the debt, including any specifications as to the time or place of performance. Although full performance would ordinarily discharge the debtor, there were some exceptions; one was stipulation, for which performance was often accompanied by a formal release (*acceptilatio*).

Absent full performance, a debtor could also be effectively released by an informal agreement (*pactum*) to that effect, or by a compromise (*transactio*) of the claim, or by other less commonly used legal devices such as offset of claims (*compensatio*). Roman law also recognized the possibility of novation of debt (*novatio*), the transformation of an obligation into a new one, normally through a stipulation; and, to a more limited extent, the delegation of duty (*delegatio*) or assignment of right by one person to another. See generally Gaius, *Inst.* 3.168–181.

3. Standards of Performance. The assimilation of contract and delict within a single category of obligation also led to some influence of delict law on contract. For instance, in the late Republic the jurists began to articulate what was meant by "wrongfulness" (*iniuria*) under the Lex Aquilia governing wrongful damage to property. The jurists developed two main measures of the duty of care: *dolus*, deliberate infliction of harm; and *culpa*, "fault," including also non-deliberate carelessness. These standards, although originally developed for delict, were also widely applied in contract law, as individual situations required.

4. Damages. The fourth consequence of the unified category of obligation is that contract and delict share much theory for assessing compensation for "loss" (*damnum*). In contracts, the plaintiff is frequently allowed to sue for the full extent of his or her "interest" (*id quod interest*) in the defendant's misdeed or failure to perform, although the exact definition of this "interest"

varies considerably. This "interest" is, however, always measured in money (*condemnatio pecuniaria*), since the rather weak Roman judicial system did not allow for the judge to order specific performance of a promise.[17] As an alternative to "interest," both contract and delict often allow a "penalty" (*poena*), punitive damages calibrated to the severity of a defendant's offense; in contract, such punitive damages can arise either as a result of the parties' agreement or through operation of law. These concepts will be frequently encountered in the Cases. It should be noted that when parties provide for penalties in their contract, they need not always attempt to estimate actual or likely damages from a breach. Finally, Roman law does not award victorious plaintiffs with litigation costs.

5. Separation of Obligations from Property Law. In a famous passage, Paul (2 *Inst.*) D. 44.7.3 pr., observes: "The essence of obligations does not lie in making some object or a servitude our own, but (rather) in binding another person to give or do or provide something for us." (*Obligationum substantia non in eo consistit, ut aliquod corpus nostrum aut servitutem nostram faciat, sed ut alium nobis obstringat ad dandum aliquid vel faciendum vel praestandum.*) Although, in the aftermath of a contract or a delict, property rights do often pass from one party to another (as when the parties to a sale exchange money for the object of sale, or a promisee performs under a stipulation), particularly in the case of contract the agreement itself does not, in principle, automatically transfer a property right, but only, to the extent that it is binding, an actionable claim to performance. As we shall see, this rather awkward idea resonates profoundly in Roman law: a buyer receives a property claim simply by virtue of a sales agreement; a lessee, during the term of the lease, has no defensible property right in the leased object; and so on.

Finally, in some cases, even though the law imposes no immediate liability on a promissor, there may still be legal consequences of a promise. This is true, for instance, of "contracts" made by a slave or by a daughter in her father's power, both of whom lack the legal capacity to contract independently. Although such

[17] The content of an obligation is often expressed in terms of a performance, as in the *formula* for the sales actions discussed earlier: "whatever on this account the defendant ought to give to or do for the plaintiff in accord with good faith." However, as Gaius, *Inst.* 4.48, observes, "The *condemnatio*, in all *formulae* that have one, is expressed as an estimate of money. So, even if we sue for some physical thing like a farm, a slave, clothing, gold, or silver, the *iudex* condemns the defendant not for this thing itself, as was once the practice, but for the money at which the thing is evaluated." See Heinrich Honsell, *Quod Interest* (1969); Reinhard Zimmermann, *Obligations*, 770–773, 824–833.

"contracts" were not legally enforceable, a valid real or personal security could be given for such a "debt"; further, performance in fulfillment of the promise could not be recovered; and so on. To this extent, the transaction could have legal consequences even though it was in principle unenforceable. In order to distinguish such obligations from ordinary enforceable obligations, the jurists refer to them as "natural obligations" (*obligationes naturales*), in the sense that they create at least a moral or social duty to perform. The concept of a "natural obligation" will occur from time to time throughout this Casebook.

Part H. Roman Contract Law and the Economy

A principal function of contract law, now as in antiquity, is to facilitate individuals in the conduct of their daily lives: not only for their immediate dealings (e.g., the exchange of cash for groceries), but also in their structured planning for the future.[18] Contract law does this through mechanisms that, in relation to a specific social and economic context, make these transactions both easier to arrange and more predictable in their unfolding. The previous sections have centered on how the jurists contributed conceptually to building such mechanisms for the Roman world.

Unfortunately, much about the Roman economy remains deeply uncertain and shrouded in controversy.[19] Despite some heroic efforts at quantification,[20] we have no reliable information about basic economic statistics such as the size of the empire's population, its geographical distribution and structure, the empire's domestic product and its sectors, the empire's per capita income, and so on; and other measures of social welfare, such as mortality and literacy rates, are likewise disputed. For want of better alternatives, historians have frequently turned to indirect techniques such as modeling and using comparative data, with discrepant and unverifiable results.[21]

---

[18] Stephen A. Smith, *Atiyah's Introduction to the Law of Contract* (2005), 3–5.

[19] On the Roman economy generally, see the works cited in the Suggested Further Reading, especially Jean Andreau, *Economy* (2016); Walter Scheidel, ed., *Cambridge Companion to the Roman Economy* (2012); and Giuseppe Dari-Mattiacci and Dennis P. Kehoe, eds., *Roman Law and Economics* (2020); also Hans-Joachim Drexhage, Heinrich Konen, and Kai Ruffing, *Die Wirtschaft des Römischen Reiches (1.–3. Jahrhundert): Eine Einführung* (2002). Scholarship on the Roman economy has burgeoned in recent years; citations in this section are mainly suggestions for further reading.

[20] Richard Duncan-Jones, *The Economy of the Roman Empire: Quantitative Studies* (2nd ed., 1982), and *Structure and Scale in the Roman Economy* (1990); Alan Bowman and Andrew Wilson, eds., *Quantifying the Roman Economy: Methods and Problems* (2009).

[21] See just Walter Scheidel and Steven J. Friesen, "Size of the Economy and the Distribution of Income in the Roman Empire," *Journal of Roman Studies* 99 (2009): 61–91.

By their nature, Roman legal sources throw only an oblique light on these disputes. By and large, juristic sources correspond with a common qualitative understanding of what the Roman economy must have looked like and how it probably developed. For purposes of this Casebook, such a broad-stroke understanding probably suffices.

Early Rome, as represented especially in the Twelve Tables that laid the foundations of later contract law, had a sturdily agrarian economy, with numerous smallholders raising crops and livestock. Agricultural production, channeled primarily through the family members of individual households as the basic unit of production, remained imperfectly integrated with larger markets, some of which already existed at the margins. Although class structures, along with unequal distribution of income and wealth, already clearly existed, Rome's relative poverty seems to have promoted a degree of offsetting democratic egalitarianism at least in the political arena.[22]

The early economy of Rome deeply influenced the subsequent development of its contract law. The influence can be seen above all in the surprisingly large number of Roman contract types that were, at least originally, gratuitous: not only the "real" contracts and mandate, but also, in a different sense, the unilateral stipulation. These contracts are suggestive of a weak market economy, in which individuals, even those of means, were habitually obliged to rely upon the kindness of friends and neighbors, albeit against a background of anticipated reciprocity and, to a certain extent, redistribution through socially expected euergetism.[23] This also helps to explain why Roman law came to place such heavy emphasis on *consensus* and *bona fides* as fundamental contractual conceptions, rather than on a market-oriented idea of bargained-for exchange.

Much of this early economy survived, even flourished, throughout Rome's later history. Agriculture and agricultural products are pervasively present in the juristic sources: the sale of farms (*fundi*) with attendant rights and duties both express and implied; the lease of farms to tenants (Chapter V.2); the harvesting and distribution of agricultural products, especially wine (e.g., Cases 23, 25, 54, 87, 108, 112, 117–118, 123–124, 139, 229), but also, for instance, olive oil and grain (e.g., Cases 23, 54, 87, 123, 201, 233), livestock and timber (Cases 96, 145),

---

[22] See A. Drummond, "Rome in the Fifth Century I: The Social and Economic Framework," in F. W. Walbank et al., eds., *The Cambridge Ancient History* vol. 7.2 (2nd ed., 1990), 113–171; also Christopher John Smith, *Early Rome and Latium: Economy and Society c. 1000 to 500 BC* (1996).

[23] See, of course, Karl Polanyi, *The Great Transformation* (1945), who, however, considerably underestimated the spread of markets and market thinking in the ancient economy. See also Filippo Carlà and Maja Gori, eds., *Gift Giving and the "Embedded" Economy in the Ancient World* (2014), esp. Koenraad Verboven, "'Like Bait on a Hook': Ethics, Etics, and Emics of Gift-Exchange in the Roman World," 135–153.

ceramic containers for agricultural goods (Cases 12, 142); and so on. The jurists regularly treat the *fundus* as the archetypal example of real estate, rather in the way that Common Lawyers refer to Blackacre.[24] By and large, Classical jurisprudence tries to foster agricultural development.[25]

Nonetheless, Rome's expansion during the later Republic, and above all its conquest of the Mediterranean, resulted in both a dramatic upsurge in urbanism and massive infusions of new capital, inevitably aggravating the prior social discord but also encouraging economic advances that partially displaced or reorganized the older economy.[26]

The first of these developments was the far broader and deeper monetization of the Roman economy, especially as a consequence of Rome's systematic introduction of its own silver-backed currency from ca. 211 BCE.[27] As David Daube observed a half-century ago, when social relationships come to be measured in monetary terms, legal systems gain considerably greater leverage in determining responsibility and damages, while the previously non-monetized relationships tend to decline correspondingly in their efficacy.[28] The insistence of Classical legal procedure that remedies must be measured in money (*condemnatio pecuniaria*) may be taken as emblematic of that change, with various markets used when possible (Cases 123–124); and so too, the curious debate among the jurists about whether barter, the exchange of goods for goods, can be considered a form of sale (Cases 77, 79, 191). Unsurprisingly, juristic sources appear to pay greater attention to monetized transactions, perhaps exaggerating their actual weight within an economy that still was significantly non-monetized. (The jurists likewise often assume widespread literacy, see Case 201; this may also be exaggerated.[29])

---

[24] E.g., D. 50.16.60 (Ulpian), 115 (Javolenus), 211 (Florentinus); see also D. 30.34.15 (Ulpian).

[25] See Dennis P. Kehoe, *Investment, Profit, and Tenancy: The Jurists and the Roman Agrarian Economy* (1997), and *Law and the Rural Economy* (2007); also Robert J. Buck, *Agriculture and Agricultural Practice in Roman Law* (1983).

[26] Jean-Paul Morel, "Early Rome and Italy," in Walter Scheidel et al., eds., *Cambridge Economic History of the Greco-Roman World* (2007), 487–510; also Philip Kay, *Rome's Economic Revolution* (2014); Saskia T. Roselaar, *Italy's Economic Revolution: Integration and Economy in Republican Italy* (2019).

[27] Sitta von Reden, "Money and Finance," in Walter Scheidel, ed., *Cambridge Companion to the Roman Economy* (2012), 260–286.

[28] David Daube, "Money and Justiciability," *Zeitschrift der Savigny-Stiftung für Rechtsgeschichte, Rom. Abt.* 96 (1979) 1–16, reprinted in *Collected Studies in Roman Law*, vol. 2 (1991), 1341–1356. See now Neil Coffee, *Gift and Gain: How Money Transformed Ancient Rome* (2016).

[29] See just William V. Harris, *Ancient Literacy* (1991); this issue is highly controversial.

The second development was the mass importation of slaves, which, as the institution became endemic, had enduring effects on the economy of Rome. Although slavery was well known in Rome long before the second century BCE, the wars of conquest hugely increased the presence and importance of slaves in Roman business operations.[30] Durable slave systems like Rome's, in which ownership of labor involves long-term capital investment, require considerable rationalization of resources.[31] It seems evident, for instance, that widespread use of slave labor permitted intensification of agriculture on larger *fundi*, most of which became dedicated to a single cash crop such as wine or olive oil; and slave labor was also widely utilized in other productive businesses such as mining, transport, and light manufacture. The implied market warranties for slaves established under the Edict of the Curule Aediles (Cases 143–144) are telling: what buyers wanted, primarily, was healthy slaves capable of heavy labor, in a market where buyers were often adversely affected by an imbalance of information.[32] However, the Romans also soon found ways to employ some slaves—assuredly, a small portion of the total number—on a more advanced level as managers or quasi-agents, a possibility that the jurists actively fostered (Chapter VII.A–B).[33]

Third, the gradual imperial unification of the Mediterranean during the late Republic also occasioned a considerable growth in patterns of production, distribution, and consumption, a sort of economic "boom" that, while it certainly never displaced the predominantly agrarian character of the empire, gave it nonetheless a visibly more lively and commercial aspect.[34] Much of this

[30] See Walter Scheidel, "Slavery," in Scheidel, ed., *Cambridge Companion to the Roman Economy* (2012), 89–113; John Bodel, "Slave Labour and Roman Society," in Keith Bradley and Paul Cartledge, eds., *The Cambridge World History of Slavery*, vol. I: *The Ancient Mediterranean* (2014), 311–336.

[31] Still worth reading is Gavin Wright, *The Political Economy of the Cotton South* (1978). See also Alan Bowman and Andrew Wilson, eds., *The Roman Agricultural Economy: Organization, Investment, and Production* (2013).

[32] Bruce W. Frier and Dennis P. Kehoe, "Law and Economic Institutions," in Walter Scheidel et al., eds., *Cambridge Economic History of the Greco-Roman World* (2007), 113–143, at 119–122 ("Asymmetrical Information and Adverse Selection").

[33] Richard Gamauf, "Slaves Doing Business: The Role of Roman Law in the Economy of a Roman Household," *European Review of History* 16 (2009): 331–346, and "Slavery: Social Position and Legal Capacity," in D. Plessis et al., eds., *Oxford Handbook of Roman Law and Society* (2016), 386–401. For the favorable economic implications, see Barbara Abatino, Giuseppe Dari-Mattiacci, and Enrico Perotti, "Depersonalization of Business in Ancient Rome," *Oxford Journal of Legal Studies* 31 (2011): 365–389.

[34] See Peter Temin, *The Roman Market Economy* (2017); Andrew Wilson and Alan Bowman, eds., *Trade, Commerce and the State in the Roman World* (2018). See also David J. Mattingly and John Salmon, eds., *Economies beyond Agriculture in the Classical World* (2011).

"boom" is readily apparent in juristic sources on contract. For instance, the Discussion to Case 199 describes numerous large and small businesses operated by managers who had been appointed by the owner; slaves figure prominently as these managers, in what has been described as a Roman retail revolution.[35] Again, Case 33 describes an elaborate marine insurance contract for transport of goods between a Syrian and an Italian port. The Digest teems with bankers and moneylenders and brokers; quarriers of stone and clay; traders in grain, wine, and olive oil in bulk; sellers of slaves, of livestock and teams of horses, of ceramic containers; sellers of luxury goods such as jewelry, goblets, and citron wood tables; the makers and menders and cleaners of clothing; ship captains and muleteers and movers of heavy columns; suppliers of gladiators for sale or lease; construction contractors; operators of storage facilities and granaries; artisans in metals and precious stones; doctors, advocates, surveyors, and teachers; even prostitutes and tightrope walkers—so many occupations that an accurate census is nigh unto impossible, but all of them bound within a latticework of contracts.

At least insofar as law is concerned, it would not be amiss to describe this world of trade and commerce as an overlay on the older agrarian economy. The spirit of the new world is magnificently captured in Case 83 ("Fairness of Price"), where the jurist Paul candidly states that in sale and lease "it is by Nature (*naturaliter*) allowed (for parties) . . . in turn to cheat one another. . . ."

But the new world placed considerable stress on preexisting legal institutions, many of which were ill-adapted to a sophisticated urban economy. The jurists reacted in various ways. One of the most evident was their effort to adapt the gratuitous contract types (especially mandate and the "real" contracts: Chapters II.A–B and V.C) to take account of situations where the flow of "benefit" was less one-sided; the belated creation of "irregular deposit" (Case 69) is one example, the awkward incorporation of the *procurator* within the contract of mandate (Chapter VII.C) is another. At times, and with limited results, the jurists encouraged the development of new contract types (Case 186), but more usually they attempted at least to accommodate the interests of parties who fell outside the web of contract types, as by recognizing half-executed exchange agreements (Chapter VI.B) or different forms of sophisticated credit arrangements such as suretyship (Cases 41–46), or their provision of buyer protection through implied warranties of title and merchantability (Chapter IV.B.4–5).[36]

---

[35] Andrew Wilson, ed., *Urban Craftsmen and Traders in the Roman World* (2016); Steven J. R. Ellis, *The Roman Retail Revolution: The Socio-Economic World of the Taberna* (2018).

[36] See also Hendrik L. E. Verhagen, "Secured Transactions in Classical Roman Law," in Dari-Mattiaci and Kehoe, eds., *Roman Law and Economics*, vol. II (2020), 113–156.

But clearly there were limits on such developments, and especially so when it came to economic organizations. As recent research has made clear, most Roman businesses were quite small: a handful of persons, with little vertical integration.[37] The frailty of the law governing partnerships (Chapter V.B), as well as the reluctance of the jurists to fully recognize agency (Chapter VII.A–C), can perhaps be explained through the high transaction costs associated with the conduct of most businesses in the Roman world.[38] Or perhaps forestalling concentration of commercial wealth was a matter of public policy in view of the political turmoil caused by the *publicani* in the latter years of the Roman Republic.[39] In any case, as Max Weber observed,[40] "none of the characteristic legal institutions of modern capitalism are derived from Roman law, such institutions being annuity bonds, bearer securities, shares, bills of exchange, trading companies (in their modern, capitalistic form), mortgages (as capital investment), direct agency."

Part I. From the Jurists to Justinian

The so-called Classical period of Roman law—perhaps better styled "The Age of the Jurists"—lasted for almost three and a half centuries, from ca. 100 BCE to ca. 235 CE. The great bulk of what we know about Roman contract law (and about Roman private law in general) derives from the writings of the jurists during this period. However, with the major exception of Gaius' *Institutes* (ca. 160 CE, known almost entirely from a single palimpsest discovered in 1816), their work does not survive intact, but mainly through the mediation three centuries later of the Roman Emperor Justinian (reigned 527–565 CE).

At the beginning of his reign, as part of his efforts to revive the Roman State now relocated to Constantinople, Justinian authorized the creation of what has come to be known as the *Corpus Iuris Romani*, literally "the Body of Roman Law." This

[37] Andreas M. Fleckner, *Antike Kapitalvereinigungen*, and "Roman Business Associations," in Dari-Mattiaci and Kehoe, eds., *Roman Law and Economics*, vol. I (2020), 233–272. See also Bruce W. Frier and Dennis P. Kehoe, "Law and Economic Institutions," in Walter Scheidel et al., eds., *Cambridge Economic History of the Greco-Roman World* (2007), 113–143, at 126–134 ("Firms").

[38] See Dennis Kehoe, "Contracts, Agency, and Transaction Costs in the Roman Economy," in Kehoe, David M. Ratzan, and Uri Yiftach, eds., *Law and Transaction Costs in the Ancient Economy* (2015), 231–252; Barbara Abatino and Giuseppe Dari-Mattiacci, "Agency Problems and Organizational Costs in Slave-Run Businesses," in Dari-Mattiaci and Kehoe, eds., *Roman Law and Economics*, vol. I (2020), 273–306.

[39] Ernst Badian, *Publicans and Sinners* (1972).

[40] Max Weber, *Wirtschaftsgeschichte* (2nd ed., 1924), 292 (translation by Marguerite Wolff).

vast compendium aimed to restate all Roman law in a revised and updated form, and thereby to replace previous authorities. The original compilation consisted of three works: the *Institutiones*, an elementary text in four books nominally written by Justinian himself; the *Digesta*, a 50-book assemblage of excerpts from the writings of the Roman jurists; and the *Codex*, a 12-book collection of still valid proclamations of law by Roman emperors. The first two were promulgated as law in 533 CE, the *Codex* (in its final version) in 534. To these three works were eventually appended the *Novellae Constitutiones*, a collection of Justinian's major legislation after 534.

In promulgating the Digest as law, Justinian states that he had expressly instructed his compilers to distill and modernize their sources (*Constitutio Tanta* 10; 533 CE):

> Tanta autem nobis antiquitati habita est reverentia, ut nomina prudentium taciturnitati tradere nullo patiamur modo: sed unusquisque eorum, qui auctor legis fuit, nostris digestis inscriptus est: hoc tantummodo a nobis effecto, ut, si quid in legibus eorum vel supervacuum vel imperfectum aut minus idoneum visum est, vel adiectionem vel deminutionem necessariam accipiat et rectissimis tradatur regulis. Et ex multis similibus vel contrariis quod rectius habere apparebat, hoc pro aliis omnibus positum est unaque omnibus auctoritate indulta, ut quidquid ibi scriptum est, hoc nostrum appareat et ex nostra voluntate compositum. . . .
>
> We had such veneration for the past that We in no way allowed the names of the jurists to pass into silence. Each of those who wrote on law is entered in Our Digest. The only thing done by Us was that, if something in their legal rules seemed either unnecessary or defective or less suitable, it receive either the necessary amplification or abbreviation and be transmitted with the most correct rules. Also, from many similar or conflicting (rules), that which appeared more correct was set down in place of all the rest, and a single authority was accorded to all, so that whatever was written there would appear as Ours and written in accord with Our will. . . .

There is every reason to believe that the compilers took these instructions seriously. Particularly in the case of the Digest, this meant, above all, a process of "simplifying," as the countless controversies among the jurists were resolved by eliminating divergent views and superfluous argument. Juristic fragments from the Digest often provide evidence for such condensation, particularly when, on rare occasions, its text can be directly compared with parallel pre-Justinianic texts that survive in a scattering of other works. Although the Digest purports to quote jurists directly, it therefore frequently gives a modified version of what they wrote.[41]

But the work of the compilers did not stop there. In the three centuries since the disbanding of the Roman jurists, the elaboration and development of their jurisprudence had continued, rather haltingly, in the Western Empire (which was in a slow process of disintegration), but far more vigorously in the law schools of the Eastern Empire: above all at Berytus (Beirut) perhaps already by 200 CE, and later at Constantinople (Istanbul) where in 425 the Emperor Theodosius II endowed two professorships of law at his newly founded university. Late imperial legal thinking, which was intermittently influenced also by Greek philosophy and Christianity, found its way into the Justinianic codification. A particularly rich area of postclassical influence had to do with standards of liability, which were developed with numerous gradations reflecting degrees of moral blameworthiness.

These textual changes, referred to collectively (and rather misleadingly) as "interpolations," are often difficult to spot and have been the subject of centuries of scholarly debate; but, mercifully, for contract law they do not appear to be especially numerous or significant. Here is an example of possible change, a passage that has bedeviled Roman law scholars. The jurist Celsus (11 *Dig.*) D. 16.3.32, is discussing the liability of a person who receives another's property as a deposit, for its safekeeping.

> Quod Nerva diceret latiorem culpam dolum esse, Proculo displicebat, mihi verissimum videtur. Nam et si quis non ad eum modum quem hominum natura desiderat diligens est, nisi tamen ad suum modum curam in deposito praestat, fraude non caret: nec enim salva fide minorem is quam suis rebus diligentiam praestabit.
>
> Nerva's view that more serious fault (*latior culpa*) is deceit (*dolus*) was dissatisfying to Proculus, but seems exactly right to me. For also if someone is not diligent to the degree that human nature requires, still, unless he provides care for the deposit up to his own standard, he is not free of fraud (*fraus*); for, if he is true to his word, he will not provide less watchfulness than for his own property.

On its face, this passage of Celsus tries to increase the depositary's liability to the depositor, first by equating deliberate misconduct (*dolus*) with what we would probably call "gross negligence" (*latior culpa*), and then by further imposing the even

---

[41] On the compilation and interpolations, see, briefly, David Johnston, *Roman Law in Context* (1999), 14–29. At greater length: A. Arthur Schiller, *Roman Law* (1978), 29–41, 62–83; Wolfgang Kaiser, "Justinian and the Corpus Iuris Civilis," in David Johnston, ed., *Cambridge Companion to Roman Law* (2015), 119–148.

higher standard of care equivalent to what he shows toward his own property. Legal historians have gone back and forth in trying to determine whether this fragment accurately reports Celsus' views; the modern consensus is that it does, but in reality there is no foolproof way to settle the question, and the fragment might be, entirely or at least in part, a Justinianic creation.

Finally, it should be observed that already in the later Classical period the Praetor's formulary system of civil procedure, around which most juristic writing had been organized, was being supplanted by a decidedly more modern-looking (although by no means modern) procedural system centered on imperial courts and, commonly, professional judges, with an appellate system, especially over questions of law, that ultimately could reach the emperor. Although the Digest compilers accepted from juristic writings the great bulk of substantive contract law, they necessarily stripped away much of the associated procedural law that was based on the Praetor's Edict and court—what were now only relics of a bygone legal regime. For us, this loss of procedural detail is considerable, but, fortunately, the fourth book of Gaius' *Institutes* gives at least an elementary introduction to Roman civil procedure, and it can be supplemented from other surviving sources.

Although the Justinianic changes were not inconsequential, the compilers left the body of juristic opinions on contract law fundamentally intact, even if considerably abbreviated. From time to time in this Casebook, likely alterations by the compilers are signaled. But Roman contract law survived in good condition until its revival, in Western Europe, during the eleventh and twelfth centuries—a revival out of which modern Civil Law eventually emerged in various forms. In the Eastern Roman Empire, Justinianic contract law remained essentially in force until the Ottoman capture of Constantinople in 1453, but this law has also left considerable traces on subsequent Islamic law, particularly in the Near East.[42]

---

[42] See generally the early chapters of Franz Wieacker, *A History of Private Law in Europe* (transl. Tony Weir, 1993), and Zachary Chitwood, *Byzantine Legal Culture and the Roman Legal Tradition, 867–1056* (2017). On the (limited) influence of Roman law on Islamic law, see, e.g., Aayesha Rafiq, "Borrowings, Influences, and Comparability: The Case of Islamic Law," *Islamic Studies* 55 (2016): 113–129.

Capacity to Contract

The sources on Roman contract law, if read in isolation, can present a misleadingly modern impression of individuals freely contracting with one another. However, many Romans, even of adult age, faced considerable legal constraints on their ability to make contracts. This Chapter sketches those constraints.

The Roman law of status divided free Romans into two groups: those *sui iuris*, possessing full personal rights because they were not under the power of a *paterfamilias* (usually the person's father or paternal grandfather; this power is called *patria potestas*); and persons *alieno iuri subiecti*, subject to the power of a *paterfamilias*. In this Chapter only the legal capacity of *sui iuris* individuals is described. (Contracts made by children under the power of a *paterfamilias* and by slaves are dealt with in Chapter VII.A.)

In Roman law, *sui iuris* persons, both male and female, normally had full legal capacity to enter contracts unless they were classified as lacking understanding (the insane; very young children). Older children, if below the age of adulthood (conventionally, twelve for girls and approximately fourteen for boys), could obligate themselves contractually only with the authorization of their legal guardian, their *tutor*. The other party to their contracts, nevertheless, could become obligated to them, a situation that resulted in potential problems of fairness. After reaching adulthood, both males and females had full contractual capacity (provided they were sane). However, until they reached age twenty-five, the Praetor provided some protection when they entered disadvantageous contracts or other transactions.

In principle, adult *sui iuris* women remained subject to lifelong guardianship (*tutela*), and their guardian's authorization was required for certain formal transactions. This guardianship had little consequence, it is believed. However, women were also legally restricted in various ways from full participation in commerce and public life.

The rules as to contractual capacity apply to Roman citizens. Insofar as Roman law was concerned, other free residents of the empire had somewhat diminished capacity until 212 CE when the Emperor Caracalla enacted nearly universal citizenship within the empire.

A Casebook on the Roman Law of Contracts. Bruce W. Frier, Oxford University Press. © Oxford University Press 2021.
DOI: 10.1093/oso/9780197573211.003.0002

CASE 1: Mental Capacity

Gaius, *Institutiones* 3.106–109

106. Furiosus nullum negotium gerere potest, quia non intellegit, quid agat. 107. Pupillus omne negotium recte gerit, ut tamen, sicubi tutoris auctoritas necessaria sit, adhibeatur, uelut si ipse obligetur; nam alium sibi obligare etiam sine tutoris auctoritate potest. 108. Idem iuris est in feminis, quae in tutela sunt. 109. Sed quod diximus de pupillo, utique de eo uerum est, qui iam aliquem intellectum habet; nam infans et qui infanti proximus est non multum a furioso differt, quia huius aetatis pupilli nullum intellectum habent. sed in his pupillis propter utilitatem benignior iuris interpretatio facta est.

Gaius in the third book of his *Institutes*:

106. A mad person (*furiosus*) cannot conduct any business since he does not understand what he is doing. 107. A ward (*pupillus*) properly conducts all business, provided that the authorization of his guardian (*tutor*) is obtained whenever necessary, e.g., if he obligates himself; for he can obligate another to himself even without his guardian's authorization. 108. The rule is the same for women who are under guardianship.

109. But what we said about a ward is at least true for one who already has some understanding. An infant (*infans*), and someone close (in age) to an infant, does not differ much from a mad person, since wards of this age have no understanding (*intellectus*). But in the case of these latter wards (those close to infancy), for practical reasons (*propter utilitatem*) a more liberal interpretation of the law has been adopted.

Discussion

1. Mad Persons. In 106, Gaius states the general rule: those classified as insane (*furiosi*) cannot make contracts or wills, nor commit delicts. Is this rule entirely convincing? What if the mad person gives no outward sign of being insane, particularly to third parties who are unacquainted with him? On intermittent madness, see, e.g., *Pauli Sent.* 3.4a.5. No text deals with other mental impairments that might affect contractual capacity, e.g., drunkenness.

2. Wards. Again, Gaius gives general rules for *sui iuris* children under the age of adulthood, i.e., fatherless orphans. (On women, see Case 5.) At what age does a child cease being a legal infant? The Emperors Theodosius and Valentinian set seven as an appropriate age, see C. 6.30.18 pr. (426 CE); previously it may have been even younger. What age do you think is appropriate?

   Slightly older children (say, age eight or nine) also originally could not make contracts without a guardian's authority, the ground being lack of understanding; see Paul, D. 29.1.9. Eventually, as Gaius suggests (see also Justinian, *Inst.* 1.21 pr.), they were permitted to contract without a guardian provided that they benefited from the transaction, a rule eventually extended to all wards (as in section 107 in the preceding text).

As to the age of adulthood, when this form of guardianship comes to an end, see Gaius, *Inst.* 1.196; *Tituli Ulp.* 11.28.

CASE 2: Protecting Creditors of Wards

D. 18.5.7.1 (Paulus libro quinto Quaestionum)

Si pupilli persona intervenit, qui ante sine tutoris auctoritate, deinde tutore auctore emit, quamvis venditor iam ei obligatus fuit, tamen quia pupillus non tenebatur, renovata venditio efficit, ut invicem obligati sint: quod si ante tutoris auctoritas intervenerit, deinde sine tutore auctore emit, nihil actum est posteriore emptione. Idem potest quaeri, si sine tutoris auctoritate pactus fuerit, ut discedatur ab emptione: an proinde sit, atque si ab initio sine tutoris auctoritate emisset, ut scilicet ipse non teneatur, sed agente eo retentiones competant. Sed nec illud sine ratione dicetur, quoniam initio recte emptio sit contracta, vix bonae fidei convenire eo pacto stari, quod alteri captiosum sit, et maxime, si iusto errore sit deceptus.

Paul in the fifth book of his *Questions*:

If it happens that a ward (*pupillus*) makes a purchase first without his guardian's authorization and subsequently with it, even though (by the first sale) the seller was already obligated to him (the ward), nonetheless since the ward was not (then) liable, the renewal of the sale brings it about that they are reciprocally obligated. But if the guardian's authorization occurs first and he (the ward) subsequently buys without his guardian's authorization, nothing is transacted through the second sale.

The same question can arise if, without his guardian's authorization, he makes an informal agreement (*pactum*) to abandon the sale. Is it then (the same) as if he had initially purchased without his guardian's authorization, so that he himself is not liable, but, if he sues, (the right to) retention is available (to the seller)? However, not without reason it will be held that, since at the outset the sale was validly contracted, it hardly accords with good faith (*bona fides*) to uphold an agreement that is fraudulent for one party, particularly if he was deceived through a legitimate mistake.

The Problem

A *sui iuris* thirteen-year-old boy purchases a chariot without his guardian's authorization. He takes delivery, but then refuses to pay the seller. Is he liable, and, if so, for what? Does it matter if he misrepresented his age?

Discussion

1. A Guardian's Authorization. The guardian (*tutor*) was, among other things, broadly responsible for protecting his young ward from unwise transactions. His authorization had to be given orally during the course of a transaction, and a subsequent or written authorization was ineffective; see Gaius, D. 26.8.9.5. To what extent does Paul create exceptions to this rule when authorization is not given? He initially discusses two situations: an initial sale without authorization, followed some time later by an apparently

identical sale of the same object but with authorization; and then an initial authorization followed by an unauthorized sale. Is the other party adequately protected in both cases?

2. **Unilateral Obligation in a Bilateral Contract.** Paul goes on to discuss a situation in which a tutor authorizes a sale, and the ward later rescinds it by an informal pact, without the guardian's consent; is the pact effective between the seller and the ward? Paul suggests this situation is similar to one in which, without authorization, a ward contracts to buy a slave; the jurists say that the seller (presumably an adult) is then obligated, but the minor buyer is not, see Ulpian, D. 19.1.13.29; Justinian, *Inst.* 1.21 pr. Does this mean that the minor can sue for delivery of the slave without paying the price? In the second half of the present Case, Paul speaks of the seller's right of retention; this means that the seller can refuse to deliver the slave unless the price is tendered. More difficult is what happens when the seller has delivered and then seeks the price; see the following Case. As Paul states, a minor cannot even discharge a contractual obligation without authorization. This rule applies even when the creditor performs, although equitable protection is then available (Gaius, *Inst.* 2.84); see the following Case.

CASE 3: The Creditor's Position after Performing

D. 26.8.5 pr.-1 (Ulpianus libro quadragesimo ad Sabinum)

pr. Pupillus obligari tutori eo auctore non potest. Plane si plures sint tutores, quorum unius auctoritas sufficit, dicendum est altero auctore pupillum ei posse obligari, sive mutuam pecuniam ei det sive stipuletur ab eo. Sed et cum solus sit tutor mutuam pecuniam pupillo dederit vel ab eo stipuletur, non erit obligatus tutori: naturaliter tamen obligabitur in quantum locupletior factus est: nam in pupillum non tantum tutori, verum cuivis actionem in quantum locupletior factus est dandam divus Pius rescripsit. 1. Pupillus vendendo sine tutoris auctoritate non obligetur sed nec in emendo, nisi in quantum locupletior factus est.

Ulpian in the fortieth book *On Sabinus*:

pr. A ward cannot be obligated to his own guardian through the latter's authorization. Clearly, if there are several guardians and authorization from one of them is enough, it should be held that with one's authorization the ward can be obligated to another, whether he (the guardian) lends him money or stipulates from him. But if there was (only) one guardian and he lent money to his ward or stipulated from him, he (the ward) will not be obligated to the guardian.

Still, he will have a natural obligation (*naturaliter obligabitur*) to the extent of his (unjustified) enrichment. For, by a rescript of the deified (Antoninus) Pius, an action against the ward for the extent of his enrichment should be granted not only to a guardian, but to anyone. 1. A ward is not obligated if he sells without his guardian's authorization, nor if he buys, except to the extent of his enrichment.

Discussion

1. **Liability for Enrichment.** The first half of this Case, dealing with a ward's liability to a guardian, is largely self-explanatory. The second half is of more interest. A ward enters an unauthorized transaction, and the other party performs. The Emperor Antoninus Pius (reigned 138–161 CE) allows the other party at least to recover the amount by which the ward is enriched by the performance, although the contract itself remains fundamentally unenforceable; see also Ulpian, D. 3.5.3.4, 26.8.1 pr. Note that it took an imperial rescript to bring about even this result. Problems could still arise in defining enrichment, e.g., if the minor damaged the object of sale. What outcome if the ward had also performed?

2. **Natural Obligations.** A natural obligation is one that cannot be enforced by an action, so the creditor is unable to use law to bring about performance. But it still may have effect to the extent that, if the debtor performs, this

performance, or its value, cannot be legally undone. It appears, however, that recovery under Antoninus Pius' rescript looked rather to the undoing of unjustified enrichment, either through a claim for recovery of property (Paul, D. 44.7.46; Ulpian, D. 13.6.3 pr.) or one for restitution of the enrichment itself, as in this Case; see Chapter VIII.B.

CASE 4: The Contracts of Young Adults

D. 4.4.1 (Ulpianus libro undecimo ad Edictum)

pr. Hoc edictum praetor naturalem aequitatem secutus proposuit, quo tutelam minorum suscepit. Nam cum inter omnes constet fragile esse et infirmum huiusmodi aetatium consilium et multis captionibus suppositum, multorum insidiis expositum: auxilium eis praetor hoc edicto pollicitus est et adversus captiones opitulationem. 1. Praetor edicit: "Quod cum minore quam viginti quinque annis natu gestum esse dicetur, uti quaeque res erit, animadvertam." 2. Apparet minoribus annis viginti quinque eum opem polliceri: nam post hoc tempus compleri virilem vigorem constat. 3. Et ideo hodie in hanc usque aetatem adulescentes curatorum auxilio reguntur, nec ante rei suae administratio eis committi debebit, quamvis bene rem suam gerentibus.

Ulpian in the eleventh book *On the Edict*:

pr. In accord with Natural Fairness (*naturalis aequitas*), the Praetor established this edict whereby he protected the young. For since it is universally agreed that the prudence of (people at) this age is weak and unsteady, and vulnerable to many frauds and exposed to many people's traps, by this edict the Praetor promised them help and assistance against frauds. 1. The Praetor's edict runs: "Regarding what is alleged to have been transacted with a person less than twenty-five years of age, I will take notice as each case will require." 2. He evidently promises aid (only) to those less than twenty-five years old; for after that time it is agreed that adult alertness is fully attained.

3. And so today youths up to this age are restrained by the help of curators (*curatores*); nor before this (age) should administration of their own affairs be entrusted to them, even if they conduct their affairs well.

Problem

A twenty-two-year-old *sui iuris* Roman purchases a statue at well above its usual market price. Can he or she undo the sale after later discovering the statue's true value?

Discussion

1. Curatorship of Young Adults. The Romans realized that children did not obtain adult judgment upon reaching puberty. But instead of raising the age of adulthood, the Praetor instituted a special protection for those under age twenty-five against transactions clearly to their disadvantage: the Praetor could set aside the transaction through a process called *restitutio in integrum*, roughly "restoration of the status quo ante." Since this made it potentially difficult for young adults to obtain credit, it became usual for them to request from the Praetor a *curator* to give them advice, and indeed potential

creditors often required this. Transactions entered into with the assent of a *curator* were considered presumptively not disadvantageous, absent evidence of the *curator*'s misconduct, see Scaevola, D. 4.4.39.1.

The question that arises is whether the Romans, by setting the age of adulthood so low and then providing protections until so late an age, managed to get it wrong twice. What do you think?

CASE 5: The Tutelage of Adult Women

Gaius, *Institutiones* 1.190–191

190. Feminas uero perfectae aetatis in tutela esse fere nulla pretiosa ratio suasisse uidetur: nam quae uulgo creditur, quia leuitate animi plerumque decipiuntur et aequum erat eas tutorum auctoritate regi, magis speciosa uidetur quam uera; mulieres enim, quae perfectae aetatis sunt, ipsae sibi negotia tractant, et in quibusdam causis dicis gratia tutor interponit auctoritatem suam; saepe etiam inuitus auctor fieri a praetore cogitur. 191. Unde cum tutore nullum ex tutela iudicium mulieri datur: at ubi pupillorum pupillarumue negotia tutores tractant, eis post pubertatem tutelae iudicio rationem reddunt.

Gaius in the first book of his *Institutes*:

190. No credible reason seems to favor women of adult age being in guardianship (*tutela*). The common view, that they are frequently deceived because of their mental inconstancy and that it was (therefore) fair that they be restrained by their guardians' authorization, seems more specious than true. Adult women transact their business for themselves; although in certain cases, for form's sake, the guardian interposes his authorization, the Praetor often forces him to authorize, even against his will.

191. So a woman is granted no action against her guardian; by contrast, when guardians conduct the affairs of wards (*pupilli*) of either sex, through the action on guardianship they give them an accounting after (their wards reach) puberty.

Discussion

1. Permanent Tutelage for Adult Women. Originally, the function of these guardians (*tutores muliebres*) was to protect the property of adult *sui iuris* women mainly in the interest of their intestate heirs. In Classical law this function had largely disappeared, and the authorization of a woman's guardian was required chiefly for certain formal transactions; the guardian had no authority to act on behalf of the woman (*Tituli Ulp.* 11.25), and accordingly, as Gaius observes, no duty to account for his actions. In practice, the guardianship of women had little consequence, since women could compel authorization judicially and could also apply to change guardians, see Gaius, *Inst.* 1.173. Still, the institution lingered throughout Classical law, despite the obvious reservations expressed by Gaius. The contractual capacity of adult women is largely unrestricted; for one exception, see Gaius, 2.80 (a *sui iuris* woman cannot convey title to *res mancipi* without her tutor's authorization; Gaius apparently refers to the ceremony of mancipation, used for land, slaves, large farm animals, and certain other property). This limitation might restrict a woman's ability to operate freely in the market. For another, more important constraint, see the Discussion on Case 44: women prohibited from assuming liability for others (e.g., through suretyship).

A woman who met statutory requirements for number of childbirths was released altogether from a guardian's care: *Pauli Sent.* 4.9.1–9 (e.g., 1: "For mothers, both freeborn and freedwomen if they are Roman citizens, it is enough to have given birth three or four times (respectively) in order to be held entitled to the right of children (*ius liberorum*), so long as they bear them alive and in full term.").

By and large, however, adult *sui iuris* women seem to possess considerable legal independence, at least by pre-modern standards.

CHAPTER II

Stipulation: A Formal Contract

To modern lawyers who are instilled with an understanding of contracts as bargained-for exchanges, and who therefore instinctively resist the formal requirements associated with one-sided promises, it may come as a surprise that the Romans relied heavily, for a millennium or more, on a formal contract in which, through an oral question-and-answer, one party (called the stipulator) received from the other (the promissor) a promise that was, in most circumstances, legally enforceable.

Stipulation is the very simplest of forms. The *stipulatio* takes its name from the verb *stipulari*, meaning "to exact a solemn promise or guarantee." (The modern English verb "stipulate" has a quite different import.) The stipulator puts the wording of the promise in question form, for instance, "Do you promise to pay me 5,000 sesterces on July 1?" The promissor answers by repeating the verb, "I promise." It's as easy as that.

Stipulation is a unilateral contract, as a result of which, in very large measure, one party acquires rights and the other acquires duties. ("Unilateral" is used differently in Anglo-American contract law.) The Romans employed stipulations in a huge variety of situations. As a stand-alone contract, a stipulation could, for instance, make enforceable the informal promise of a gift or a marriage dowry or a loan, where the informal promise by itself would have been unenforceable prior to its execution; it could transform a preexisting debt into a new debt through a process called novation; and it could cede to another party a claim the promissor had. As a complement to other contracts, it could expand a gratuitous loan by making it interest-bearing; it could establish a penalty for failure to perform; in the transfer of property as a result of a contract or a bequest, it could guarantee title or quiet possession, or that possession would be returned at some point in the future; it could guarantee the sale of an estate or the transfer of a universal testamentary trust; it could create warranties and other guarantees; and it could be used to establish suretyship for another's debt. Indeed, both legal and documentary sources indicate that stipulations were often employed also to reinforce contracts, such as sale or mandate, that were already enforceable under Roman contract law. Finally, stipulation also has a very wide use in Roman civil procedure, when one party is obliged to make a binding promise to the other.

Historically, many legal systems (including Anglo-American law) have made available some type of formal contract. They are thought to serve several interrelated purposes. First, formal contracts are useful in clearly separating any pre-contractual bargaining from the conclusion of a binding contract. In Rome, when the binding words were spoken, there could no longer be doubt about whether bargaining continued. Second, formal contracts help to clearly separate promises that parties wish to be enforceable from those they do not; thus, they provide good evidence of a promissor's intent to be legally bound. Third, because the form acts to make enforceable only what is expressed through the form, it encourages both parties to

A Casebook on the Roman Law of Contracts. Bruce W. Frier, Oxford University Press. © Oxford University Press 2021.
DOI: 10.1093/oso/9780197573211.003.0003

ensure that the promise's content is stated precisely; the parties must approach the act of promising in a serious and deliberate manner. Fourth, because of a formal contract's generality and its more or less ready availability, it actually encourages the making of promises; the parties can rely on the form if they wish their promises to be enforceable.

On the other hand, formal contracts have obvious and serious disadvantages. Above all, they are intrusive; in many situations, promissors may justifiably resent being asked to express their promises through a formal legal mechanism, as if their word alone was insufficient. Further, there is always the risk that a formal promise may not exactly capture the intended content of the promise, or that its wording may be inadvertently obscure or misleading, or that it may fail to provide for unforeseen situations. If so, severe injustice can result. Finally, particular formal contracts may have traps that are largely hidden from contracting parties.

Stipulation makes use of a prescribed oral ceremony. As a formal contract, it can be contrasted with the contract under seal, which once played a similar role in Common Law. The contract under seal was obligatorily a written form, in which (originally) the promissor had the promise inscribed on a parchment or paper to which the promissor's seal was affixed; the document was then delivered to the promisee, who could later bring suit on it if the promise was not fulfilled. It is worth considering the relative advantages and disadvantages of a written as against a purely oral formal contract.

While the jurists deal in the main with relatively simple, highly stylized promises, surviving stipulations (on papyrus or wooden tablets) frequently have many terms and show clear evidence of professional drafting by notaries or lawyers. In some respects, these documents anticipate the lengthy standard-form contracts so familiar in the modern world, although the jurists do not deal directly with the issues of fairness that bedevil contemporary lawyers in handling such "boilerplate."

PART A

Making a Stipulation

Stipulation is thought to be older than Roman law itself; the form may have originated simply as a social convention, to which law subsequently gave recognition. In any event, it is already referred to in the Twelve Tables of 449 BCE. Its purely oral form may point back to a time when literacy was at least still uncommon in Rome. Various other legal rigidities with regard to the making of stipulations are discussed in the following Cases; they too point to the archaic nature of the contract.

Still, the simplicity of the stipulation made it extremely appealing; even persons new to Roman law could quickly learn how to form stipulations. Further, the stipulation is psychologically quite shrewd. Both parties had to be present when the stipulation was made. The party to whom the promise would be rendered (the stipulator, or promisee) was the one who stated its content; while the other party was expected to listen carefully, and then to assent if the content was acceptable. As Fritz Schulz observed in *Classical Roman Law* (1951) 474, "Psychologically the binding force of a formal oral promise given in the presence of the other party is (at least for Romans) much greater than that of a formal document which the promisor might sign without having fully read or understood it."

Although the Romans stuck with the stipulation for a surprisingly long time, their insistence on strict adherence to the form gradually weakened. In the Classical period, the oral stipulation became more problematic as ordinary promises increased in complexity and problems of evidence became more salient. Witnesses, of course, if available could always be summoned; but memory vacillates or fades. In time, the oral stipulation was, it appears, more and more frequently accompanied by a written record documenting the content of the promise, and this record slowly but surely supplanted the oral ceremony.

Further, the other requirements for making stipulations were also gradually eased, presumably in response to "hard cases" where formal strictures set traps for the unwary. Despite the effortlessness with which a stipulation could be created, it was not without certain snares. As the following Cases demonstrate, the Roman jurists wrestled with these problems, at times by introducing equitable "reforms" that may gradually have eroded the efficacy of the original strict procedure.

CASE 6: The Challenge of Formalism

Gaius, *Institutiones* 3.92–93

92. Verbis obligatio fit ex interrogatione et responsione, uelut "dari spondes? spondeo" "dabis? dabo," "promittis? promitto," "fidepromittis? fidepromitto," "fideiubis? fideiubeo," "facies? facio." 93. Sed haec quidem uerborum obligatio "dari spondes? spondeo" propria ciuium Romanorum est; ceterae uero iuris gentium sunt, itaque inter omnes homines, siue ciues Romanos siue peregrinos, ualent. et quamuis ad Graecam uocem expressae fuerint, . . . etiam hae tamen inter ciues Romanos ualent, si modo Graeci sermonis intellectum habeant; et e contrario quamuis Latine enuntientur, tamen etiam inter peregrinos ualent, si modo Latini sermonis intellectum habeant. . . .

D. 45.1.1 pr.-2 (Ulpianus libro quadragesimo octavo ad Sabinum)

pr. Stipulatio non potest confici nisi utroque loquente: et ideo neque mutus neque surdus neque infans stipulationem contrahere possunt: nec absens quidem, quoniam exaudire invicem debent. Si quis igitur ex his vult stipulari, per servum praesentem stipuletur, et adquiret ei ex stipulatu actionem. Item si quis obligari velit, iubeat et erit quod iussu obligatus. 1. Qui praesens interrogavit, si antequam sibi responderetur discessit, inutilem efficit stipulationem: sin vero praesens interrogavit, mox discessit et reverso responsum est, obligat: intervallum enim medium non vitiavit obligationem. 2. Si quis ita interroganti "dabis?" responderit "quid ni?," et is utique in ea causa est, ut obligetur: contra si sine verbis adnuisset. Non tantum autem civiliter, sed nec naturaliter obligatur, qui ita adnuit: et ideo recte dictum est non obligari pro eo nec fideiussorem quidem.

Gaius in the third book of his *Institutes*:

92. A "verbal" obligation (*verbis obligatio*) is created by a question and a reply, e.g., "Do you swear to deliver?" "I swear"; "Will you give?" "I will give"; "Do you promise?" "I promise"; "Do you promise on your honor (*fides*)?" "I promise on my honor"; "Do you order on your honor?" "I order on my honor"; "Will you do?" "I will do."

93. But the wording: "Do you swear to pay?" "I swear" (*dari spondes? spondeo*) is reserved for Roman citizens; the others belong to the Law of Nations (*ius gentium*), and so are valid among all persons, whether citizens or (resident free) aliens (*peregrini*). And even when they are expressed in Greek, . . . these are still valid even among Roman citizens, provided they understand the Greek language. Conversely, although they are spoken in Latin, they are still valid among aliens, provided they understand Latin.

Ulpian in the forty-eighth book *On Sabinus*:

pr. A stipulation cannot be brought about unless both parties speak; and so neither a mute nor a deaf person nor an infant can contract a stipulation. Nor, indeed, (can) someone absent, since they should listen in turn. So if one of these wishes to put a stipulation, he does so through a slave who is present and who acquires the action on stipulation for him.

1. A person who was present and put the question, if he departed before receiving the reply, makes an ineffective stipulation; but if he was present and put the question, but soon departed and received the reply on his return, he obligates (the other party), since a short break does not vitiate the obligation.

2. If someone, on being asked: "Will you give?" replies "Why not?" he too is undoubtedly in the position of being obligated. But the reverse (is true) if he had wordlessly nodded. A person who nodded in this way is obligated neither by Civil nor by Natural Law; and so it is correctly held that not even a surety is obligated for him.

Discussion

1. Accepted Words. Gaius appears to indicate that the question and answer can be expressed by any corresponding exchange of identical verbs, except that the unusually solemn verb *spondere* ("to swear") was reserved for Roman citizens. One of his examples, *facies?* ("Will you do (something)?") is not overtly promissory at all, and it appears that in general the obligation arises mainly from the parties' deliberately using the repeated verb (though Latin lacks any other commonly used way to say "yes"). At least by convention, however, the list of verbs was restricted; for instance, the parallel list in *Pauli Sent.* 2.3 (ca. 300 CE, but with much earlier law) varies little from that of Gaius. What advantages or disadvantages are there in restricting the list of acceptable verbs? Is there any real danger that persons might inadvertently commit themselves to promises in the course of ordinary conversation? On this ground alone, you may be justly skeptical about Ulpian's suggestion that "Why not?" (*Quid ni?*) was an adequate reply; scholars think this observation is a much later insertion, probably by the Digest compilers. In later Roman law the outward form of the stipulation had become much freer. See Leo, C. 8.37.10 (472 CE); Justinian, *Inst.* 3.15.1.

2. Language. By the second century CE, as more and more residents of the Greek-speaking Eastern Mediterranean received Roman citizenship, the jurists accepted the idea that stipulations might be in Greek as well as Latin. Ulpian, D. 45.1.1.6, though he allows for an interpreter, expresses doubt whether stipulations could also be formed in other languages, such as Punic or Assyrian; why might he have been uneasy on this score? Perhaps the issue here is related to the degree to which the stipulation had been adopted as a legal device in non-Roman cultures. Since the stipulation is legally

enforceable only on the basis of its form, why does Gaius insist that the persons making a stipulation must understand the language they are using?

3. Seriousness of Intent. Related to the issue of understanding language is that of seriousness of contractual intent: do questioner and replier actually wish to form a contract? What legal result would you anticipate, and why, if two parties go through the form of a stipulation while both are acting in a play, or as a joke, or in order to show off their cleverness? See Paul, D. 44.7.3.2. Requiring seriousness of intent—an obvious element of all contractual regimes—could seem hard to reconcile with strict formalism.

4. Deaf Persons, Mutes, and Infants. The oral nature of stipulation may be adequate to explain why deaf persons and mutes cannot use the form. Is the situation of infants exactly the same? Gaius, *Inst.* 3.105–106, adds that the mentally incompetent (*furiosi*) also cannot make stipulations, even though, of course, they may be able to speak. How is the situation of the mentally incompent related to that of infants?

5. Absent Persons. Stipulation requires that both parties be present. How much does this limit the utility of stipulation as a contract-making device? In the case of absent persons (as also in that of those mentioned in the previous note), the Romans got around this requirement by using slaves (as well as free dependents) as "agents" through whom obligations could be acquired or created; see Chapter VII.A. Is this device a wholly effective substitute?

6. Continuity. Ulpian, whose text the compilers may have confusingly altered, requires that question and reply be continuous, but allows for a "small break" (*intervallum medium*) between them. How "short" it can be is unclear, but Justinian, C. 6.23.28.1–3, permits a similar break when a legal formality, such as the execution of a will, is interrupted because one of the participants urgently needs to use the lavatory. About a century before Ulpian, Venuleius, D. 45.1.137 pr., insists on continuity, "save only that a natural interval (of time) can intervene. . . . But if, after the question, he (the promissor) begins to do something else, it will be invalid even if he had promised on the same day." So Ulpian may be describing a relaxation of the rule, right?

The problem becomes more difficult when several stipulations are being made more or less simultaneously. Julian, D. 45.2.6.3, discusses a situation in which two persons are jointly obligating themselves through stipulation, and a third party is obligating himself as their surety (guarantor of performance; see Part F in this Chapter): "If a surety, to whom the question has been put, gives his answer between the responses of the two co-debtors, he cannot be held to prevent the debtors' obligation, because no long space of time intervenes nor is there a transaction contrary to the obligation." How does this ruling follow from the general rule requiring continuity?

So what is the purpose of continuity? That the question be as fresh as possible in the promissor's mind before a reply is given?

CASE 7: Altering the Promise

D. 45.1.1.3–5 (Ulpianus libro quadragesimo octavo ad Sabinum)

3. Si quis simpliciter interrogatus responderit: "si illud factum erit, dabo," non obligari eum constat: aut si ita interrogatus: "intra kalendas quintas?" responderit: "dabo idibus," aeque non obligatur: non enim sic respondit, ut interrogatus est. Et versa vice si interrogatus fuerit sub condicione, responderit pure, dicendum erit eum non obligari. Cum adicit aliquid vel detrahit obligationi, semper probandum est vitiatam esse obligationem, nisi stipulatori diversitas responsionis ilico placuerit: tunc enim alia stipulatio contracta esse videtur. 4. Si stipulanti mihi "decem" tu "viginti" respondeas, non esse contractam obligationem nisi in decem constat. Ex contrario quoque si me "viginti" interrogante tu "decem" respondeas, obligatio nisi in decem non erit contracta: licet enim oportet congruere summam, attamen manifestissimum est viginti et decem inesse. 5. Sed si mihi Pamphilum stipulanti tu Pamphilum et Stichum spoponderis, Stichi adiectionem pro supervacuo habendam puto: nam si tot sunt stipulationes, quot corpora, duae sunt quodammodo stipulationes, una utilis, alia inutilis, neque vitiatur utilis per hanc inutilem.

Ulpian in the forty-eighth book *On Sabinus*:

3. If someone is asked unconditionally and responds, "I will pay if this occurs," it is agreed that he is not obligated. Or if the question was: "(Will you pay) by the fifth Kalends" and the reply is "I will pay on the Ides," likewise he is not obligated, since he does not reply as he was asked. And conversely if he is asked under a condition and replies without one, it must he held he is not obligated. When he adds to or subtracts from the obligation, judgment must always be that the obligation is vitiated unless the stipulator (promisee) at once approves the different reply, for then another stipulation is held to have been contracted.

4. If I stipulate for "ten (thousand sesterces)" and you reply "twenty," it is agreed that an obligation is not contracted except for ten. Conversely also, if I ask for "twenty" and you reply "ten," no obligation is contracted except for ten; for although the amount ought to match, still it is wholly obvious that ten is contained in twenty.

5. But if I stipulate for (the slave) "Pamphilus" and you swear "Pamphilus and Stichus," I think the addition of Stichus should be deemed superfluous; for if there are as many stipulations as objects (of them), in a sense there are two stipulations, one effective (*utilis*) and the other ineffective (*inutilis*), nor is the effective one vitiated by the ineffective one.

The Problem

You put the question, "Do you promise to pay me 5,000 sesterces?" I respond, "I promise to pay you 2,000 sesterces." Am I obligated through this stipulation?

Discussion

1. **Correspondence.** Gaius, *Inst.* 3.102, states flatly that: "A stipulation is also ineffective (*inutilis*) if someone does not answer what he is asked," without noting the exceptions listed by Ulpian—whose text, it is widely supposed, the Digest compilers once again altered in the interests of reducing formal requirements. The notion that the stipulator can form a new stipulation by simply approving a non-corresponding answer (a process that we would characterize as offer/counteroffer/acceptance) is unique to this fragment.

2. **The Lesser and the Greater.** Ulpian's exception in section 4 is a good deal less plausible than it may seem. The non-correspondence here between stipulator and promissor goes to quantity, a basic element of a great many contracts. Gaius, *Inst.* 3.102, maintains, for instance, that a stipulation is ineffective "if I stipulate that ten thousand sesterces be given by you and you promise five thousand sesterces." If the parties have a fundamental disagreement on how much should be promised, how can a binding obligation result? Can you come up with a reason why the stipulator might not be content with the promise of the lesser sum?

3. **Obligations Expressed in the Alternative.** Related to this question is the problem of stipulations that are expressed so as to give the promissor alternatives, one of which may obviously be less onerous than the other. For example: "Do you promise to pay ten thousand sesterces on the first of either January or February?" or "Do you promise to pay me either five or ten thousand sesterces?" If the promissor answers: "I promise," what obligation results? See Pomponius, D. 45.1.12, 109; Paul, D. 45.1.83.3. Do such problems help to explain why the jurists moved toward the "lesser/greater" rule?

   Paul, D. 45.1.83.2, puts the case where the stipulator asks for delivery of "either Stichus or Pamphilus," and the promissor replies by promising delivery of "Stichus." Is the stipulation binding? Paul says not, even though the promissor, had the reply been "either Stichus or Pamphilus," would have had the choice as to which slave to deliver; see Case 15. The possible reasons for Paul's holding will become clearer when you look at the Cases on execution of stipulations (Part D in this Chapter).

4. **Severance.** Much the oddest and most important of Ulpian's exceptions is the one in section 5, where the stipulator asks for Pamphilus and the promissor promises both Pamphilus and Stichus. Here, the rule in the previous section (the less is contained in the greater) is no longer applicable; still, the promissor has answered positively to at least part of the stipulator's question, and the jurists may have been reluctant to declare the entire stipulation void. But the device they create (two stipulations, one effective and

one ineffective, with the former not vitiated by the latter) means severing the promise into good and bad parts and enforcing only the good parts, a distinctly dicey process when the stipulation is supposed to be originating from the two parties and not from a court.

This outcome is assisted, however, by the legal maxim that "there are as many stipulations as there are subjects" (*tot stipulationes quot res*), see Ulpian, D. 45.1.29 pr., 86; Paul, D. 45.1.140 pr. For instance, if the stipulation is that money be paid in three installments, this is, says Paul, D. 45.1.140 pr. 1, three separate stipulations, so that, if the promissor defaults on the first payment, suit can be brought only on the first installment and not on the entire amount due. (Is this result good law? Paul admits the question had been debated among earlier jurists.) The maxim helped to break down the ostensible unity of the stipulation when it later came to interpreting and enforcing it, but it is not uncontroversial.

CASE 8: The Role of Agreement

D. 45.1.137.1 (Venuleius libro primo Stipulationum)

Si hominem stipulatus sim et ego de alio sensero, tu de alio, nihil acti erit: nam stipulatio ex utriusque consensu perficitur.

D. 45.1.83.1 (Paulus libro septuagensimo secundo ad Edictum)

Si Stichum stipulatus de alio sentiam, tu de alio, nihil actum erit. Quod et in iudiciis Aristo existimavit: sed hic magis est, ut is petitus videatur, de quo actor sensit. Nam stipulatio ex utriusque consensu valet, iudicium autem etiam in invitum redditur et ideo actori potius credendum est: alioquin semper negabit reus se consensisse.

Venuleius in the first book of his *Stipulations*:

If I put a stipulation for a slave, and I thought of one person and you of another, nothing was accomplished, since a stipulation is brought about from the agreement (*consensus*) of both parties.

Paul in the seventy-second book *On the Edict*:

If I stipulate for (a slave) Stichus, and I think of one person and you of another, nothing has been accomplished. Aristo thought this also (true) for trials. But here (in trials) the better view is that the person in the plaintiff's mind is held to be the one sought. For a stipulation is valid from the agreement of both parties, but a trial is granted also against an unwilling person, and so the plaintiff must rather be believed; otherwise the defendant will always deny he agreed.

Discussion

1. *Consensus*. As we saw in the Introduction to this book, the jurist Pedius had insisted on the importance of agreement in understanding this formal contract: "even stipulation, which is created by formal words, is void unless it has agreement (*consensus*)"; Ulpian, D. 2.14.1.3. But the overt role of agreement seems to be limited mainly to this situation, where stipulator and promissor (like ships that pass in the night) have a mutual misunderstanding when they make the stipulation. The opposite result would obtain (says Ulpian, D. 45.1.32) if the parties merely made a mistake about the name of the slave, but both intended the same slave.

2. What Kind of Agreement? Even within this narrow ambit, it is unclear what the jurists meant by: "I think (*sentiam*) of one person and you of another": actual mental agreement (what we would describe as a unity of subjective intents), or just the objective appearance of agreement. This problem will continue to plague us in later Cases, but the absence of juristic discussion about how, in cases such as this, the mutual misunderstanding arose, or about how a party's intent can be proved, or about what happens when one party was responsible for the misunderstanding or at least aware

of the other's interpretation, could indicate that the jurists were generally requiring subjective agreement. How can a subjective misunderstanding be proved?

3. A Messy Problem. A woman whose dowry was 100,000 sesterces divorced her husband and stipulated from him for return of 200,000. How much does he owe her on his promise? Does it matter whether she was aware of the correct amount? See Javolenus, D. 24.3.66.4.

CASE 9: The Weight of a Written Stipulation

C. 8.37.1 (Impp. Severus et Antoninus AA. Secundo)

Licet epistulae, quam libello inseruisti, additum non sit stipulatum esse eum cui cavebatur, tamen si res inter praesentes gesta est, credendum est praecedente stipulatione vocem spondentis secutam.

D. 2.14.7.12 (Ulpianus libro quarto ad Edictum)

Quod fere novissima parte pactorum ita solet inseri "rogavit Titius, spopondit Maevius," haec verba non tantum pactionis loco accipiuntur, sed etiam stipulationis: ideoque ex stipulatu nascitur actio, nisi contrarium specialiter adprobetur, quod non animo stipulantium hoc factum est, sed tantum paciscentium.

The Emperors Severus and Caracalla to Secundus (206 CE):

Although, onto the letter that you included in your complaint (*libellus*), it was not (expressly) added that the person who received the guaranty had (also) stipulated (for it), nonetheless, if the transaction took place between persons who were (both) present, it should be presumed that the promissor's voice followed upon a preceding stipulation.

Ulpian in the fourth book *On the Edict*:

The words customarily inserted in the final portion of agreements (*pacta*), "Titius asked, Maevius swore," are interpreted as forming not just an agreement, but also a stipulation. And so the action on stipulation arises unless the opposite is specifically shown, (i.e.,) that this was done not with their intent (*animo*) to stipulate, but only to agree.

Discussion

1. Rescripts. Unlike most of the Cases in this book, the first source in Case 9 is a "rescript" issued in the emperor's name; it attempts to settle a question of law that a petitioner has raised. By the end of the Classical period of Roman law, rescripts were a common way to declare or make law. Here, the petitioner Secundus has asked about the probative value of a written document attesting that a promissor made a promise, but not specifically stating that the promisee first put a question to the promissor. Why might the petitioner have been in doubt about the document's validity? How do the co-emperors handle his question?

2. Documentation. It had long been usual for stipulations to be reduced to writing, which could then be used to prove the stipulation's content— one way around the problems of an oral transaction. What is interesting in these sources is the process whereby the written promise gradually supplanted the oral ceremony. Already in the late Republic, Cicero (*Topica* 96) describes stipulations as primarily written documents, a view that the

jurists eventually recognized. In late Classical law, the written transcription was presumptive proof of a stipulation's existence—an irrebutable presumption unless it was proven that the oral proceedings had not taken place; see Paul, D. 24.1.57, 45.1.134.2; also *Pauli Sent.* 5.7.2 (postclassical); Justinian, C. 8.37.14 (531).

The practice described by Ulpian (appending "Titius asked, Maevius swore" to a statement of the promise) is often found in surviving documents. Paul, D. 17.2.71 pr. describes an equally valid alternative in which the terms were spelled out and then followed by words such as: "Do you promise that the things written above will be so given and done, and nothing done against them?" See also Case 33, and Paul, D. 45.1.140 pr. To what extent does it seem likely that, by the early third century CE, the oral stipulation was largely a decorative appendage to the written document?

CASE 10: Stipulations to the Benefit of Third Parties

Gaius, *Institutes* 3.103–103a

103. Praeterea inutilis est stipulatio, si ei dari stipulemur, cuius iuri subiecti non sumus. unde illud quaesitum est, si quis sibi et ei, cuius iuri subiectus non est, dari stipuletur, in quantum ualeat stipulatio. nostri praeceptores putant in uniuersum ualere et proinde ei soli, qui stipulatus sit, solidum deberi, atque si extranei nomen non adiecisset. sed diuersae scholae auctores dimidium ei deberi existimant; pro altera uero parte inutilem esse stipulationem. 103a. Alia causa est, si ita stipulatus sim: "mihi aut Titio dari spondes?" quo casu constat mihi solidum deberi et me solum ex ea stipulation agree posse, quamquam etiam Titio solvendo liberaris.

Gaius in the third book of his *Institutes*:

103. Further, a stipulation is ineffective if we stipulate for performance to a person to whose power we are not subject. Hence this question arose: If someone stipulates for performance to himself and to a person to whose power he is not subject, to what extent is the stipulation valid? Our (Sabinian) teachers think it is completely valid, and so the entire performance is owed only to the stipulator, as if he had not added the name of a third party. But the authorities of the other (Proculian) school think that half is owed to him (the stipulator), while the stipulation for the other half is ineffective.

103a. The situation is different if I stipulate in this way: Do you swear that (something) be given to me or to Titius?" In this case it is settled that the entirety is owed to me and that I alone can sue on this stipulation, but you will be discharged also if you pay Titius.

The Problem

Titius owes money to me, and I owe the same amount of money to Sempronius. If I stipulate from Titius that he pay the money to Sempronius and Titius promises this, can Sempronius sue Titius for it?

Discussion

1. Third Parties and Interest. Why is it that, in principle, a stipulation cannot be used to create contractual rights in a third party? Note that Gaius appears to say that the stipulation is completely ineffective, meaning that neither the third party nor the stipulator can sue in order to obtain performance. Why should this be so, particularly as to the stipulator? Ulpian, D. 45.1.38.17, attempts an explanation: "Obligations of this type were created so that each person might acquire for himself what was of benefit to him; but I have no interest in performance to someone else." So the crucial missing element is the promisee's interest, right? Is Ulpian thinking mainly of donative stipulations?

But is it always the case that such interest is missing? Suppose, for instance, that I owe money to Titius and want to use the stipulation so that the promissor, who is my debtor, will pay Titius rather than me. See Ulpian, D. 45.1.38.22: "If someone stipulated when it was in his interest that it be delivered to a third party, he will be in a position such that the stipulation is valid"; compare Ulpian, D. 45.1.38.20, 23; Paul, D. 45.1.126.2; Diocletian, C. 8.38.3 pr. (290). Note that only the stipulator (and not the promise's beneficiary) had an action, and the former had to demonstrate his interest.

2. **A Way Around: Penalties.** As Ulpian, D. 45.1.38.17, goes on to say, another way of avoiding the difficulty was to stipulate for a penalty (*poena*) in the event the promissor did not render performance to the third party; e.g., "Do you promise to pay ten to Titius, and to pay ten to me if you do not pay ten to Titius?" The stipulator can enforce the penalty clause, but not Titius. Ulpian explains: "For when someone stipulates for a penalty, it is not his interest that is examined, but rather the amount and conditions of the stipulation." In other words, the promisee's interest is presumed. Is this wholly convincing? On penalties, see Cases 48–49.

3. **"And"/"Or."** Gaius next discusses stipulations calling for performance to "me and Titius," or to "Titius or me." Try to follow the legal argument that Gaius develops on how such stipulations ought to be interpreted. The former type was the subject of controversy between the two early Classical "schools" of jurists, the Sabinians and the Proculians (named after their putative founders); Justinian, *Inst.* 3.19.4, eventually resolved the dispute in favor of the Proculians (who severed the promise). Do you agree?

4. **Performance by a Third Party.** Suppose that the stipulation runs: "Do you promise that Titius will pay me ten?" Is it enforceable by the promisee? Justinian, *Inst.* 3.19.3, 21, states flatly that it is not, although he adds that the stipulation would be enforceable if it ran: "Do you promise to get Titius to pay me ten?" Is this distinction remotely convincing? In any case, even in stipulations of the first type, the promisee might have an interest in performance by the third party, and this could make the stipulation enforceable despite the absence of an attached penalty; e.g., Ulpian, D. 45.1.81 pr.-1, citing Celsus.

5. **Privity of Contract.** The modern doctrine of privity of contract holds that a contract can create obligation only between the participants in the contract, but not either for or against a party who is not "privy" to the contract. The doctrine, which was general and of early date in Roman contract law (Q. Mucius, D. 50.17.73.4), seems to rest on a vague moral sense that parties can create rights and duties between themselves through a personal relationship, but cannot implicate others; however, although this proposition

still has a degree of intuitive appeal, there are numerous exceptions. To what extent does Roman law appear to observe this principle? Note that Gaius already admits one major exception: a stipulation to the exclusive benefit of a third party is enforceable by the third party if the promisee is subject to that person's power, i.e., if the third party is either the master or *paterfamilias* of the promisee. This exception, which became the basis for extensive contract law, arises from the nature of the Roman household (*familia*); see Chapter VII.A. Other exceptions are discussed in the remainder of that Chapter, and occasionally throughout this book. Keep an eye out for them!

PART B

Interpreting a Stipulation

Stipulation is, in principle and also, within broad limits, in practice, a means for making a promise that is binding because of its form and irrespective of its content. Therefore, if the content of the promise is clear, the promisee can usually bring suit if the promise is not faithfully executed. (The legal mechanisms for enforcing stipulations are discussed later in this Chapter.)

Unfortunately, in many cases the wording of a stipulation (or, indeed, of any other contract and of legal documents generally) may lead to dispute. Sometimes such problems arise because, either at the time it was made or afterward, the parties to the stipulation had differing ideas about what the promise meant. At other times the wording itself may be at fault: it may be inherently ambiguous, capable of yielding two or more quite different meanings. In still other circumstances the wording may fail to express what one party believes to be the full content of the promise. Such difficulties are commonplace in human attempts to use language as a device for precise expression, especially in the legal arena.

The Cases that follow are typical of the jurists' efforts to deal with such difficulties for stipulation. In general, Roman interpretation of stipulations is less strict than might have been anticipated: considerable attention is given to "what was transacted," what the parties did, if this can be determined on the basis of, presumably, extrinsic evidence beyond the contract language itself. But failing such evidence, the jurists tend to limit stipulations to their "plain meaning." Still, on some occasions they give a broader reading that takes into account what the parties are likely to have intended. In any case, the starting point is always the words themselves.

Related to the issue of interpretation is the role played by "agreement" (*consensus*) in creating stipulations; see Case 8. This broad notion receives fairly little overt play in interpreting stipulations, at any rate by comparison with the role that *consensus* has in informal contracts. The reason is not hard to find: if *consensus* had a larger role, the foundations of stipulation as a formal contract would have been gradually undermined.

CASE 11: General Principles

D. 50.17.34 (Ulpianus libro quadragensimo quinto ad Sabinum)

Semper in stipulationibus et in ceteris contractibus id sequimur, quod actum est: aut, si non pareat quid actum est, erit consequens, ut id sequamur, quod in regione in qua actum est frequentatur. Quid ergo, si neque regionis mos appareat, quia varius fuit? Ad id, quod minimum est, redigenda summa est.

Ulpian in the forty-fifth book *On Sabinus*:

In stipulations and other contracts, we always follow what was transacted (*id quod actum est*); or, if it is unclear what was transacted, the next step is that we follow usage in the region where the transaction took place. What if regional custom is also uncertain because it varies? The entire (obligation) should (then) be reduced as much as possible.

Discussion

1. The Process of Interpretation. Ulpian describes a three-step sequence for interpreting stipulations:

    i. Discovering "what was transacted" (*quod actum est*). This presumably means an individualized approach to the particular stipulation: its wording as seen in light of extrinsic evidence as to the relationship between the parties and their intent in making the stipulation. (Since the jurists regarded this largely as a "question of fact," *quaestio facti*, that was reserved for the *iudex*, they laid down no hard and fast rules; but in any case, parol evidence was not excluded.)

    ii. Applying "regional custom." Again, a concept broad enough to embrace not only the "plain meaning" of the stipulation as it would appear to a reasonable person in the region, but also, for instance, local trade usage.

    iii. Giving a narrow interpretation of the words. This is the last resort, which the following Case also addresses.

    Does this sequence seem sound to you? What other means of interpretation would you add? (Some possibilities are discussed in the following Cases.) In any case, the Roman jurists do not stick closely to formulations such as Ulpian's, and there are numerous variations.

2. Incorporation of Pacts. One aspect of interpretation that causes difficulty is when a stipulation's "plain meaning" is altered by an informal agreement (*pactum*) between the parties. For instance, Paul, D. 2.14.4.3 (citing Julian), discusses a hypothetical in which the promisee, a prospective groom, stipulated for dowry payment from the bride's family; the stipulation was absolute ("Do you promise to pay ten?"), but the parties informally agreed

that the groom would not claim the principal so long as he was paid the interest on it. Paul holds that this condition is part of the stipulation even if it was not expressed. (So evidence of the pact is not excluded by any sort of legal device like the Statute of Frauds.) This decision is evidently based on "what was transacted"; to what extent does this undermine stipulation as a formal contract?

CASE 12: Interpretation against the Stipulator

D. 45.1.99 (Celsus libro trigensimo octavo Digestorum)

pr. Quidquid adstringendae obligationis est, id nisi palam verbis exprimitur, omissum intellegendum est: ac fere secundum promissorem interpretamur, quia stipulatori liberum fuit verba late concipere. Nec rursum promissor ferendus est, si eius intererit de certis potius vasis forte aut hominibus actum. 1. Si stipulatus hoc modo fuero: "si intra biennium Capitolium non ascenderis, dari?," non nisi praeterito biennio recte petam: nam etsi ambigua verba sunt, sic tamen exaudiuntur, si immutabiliter verum fuit te Capitolium non ascendisse.

Celsus in the thirty-eighth book of his *Digests*:

pr. Anything making an obligation harsher is construed as omitted unless it is expressed in plain words; and we virtually interpret in favor of the promissor, since the stipulator was free to formulate the words broadly. Nor, on the other hand, should the promissor be listened to if it will be in his interest that, e.g., specific containers or slaves were rather involved.

1. If I stipulated as follows: "delivery (of something) if you do not climb the Capitoline Hill within two years," I may not properly sue before the two years are over. For although the words are ambiguous, still they are given attention only if is unalterably true that you have not climbed the Capitoline.

Discussion

1. **Restrictive Interpretation.** Although Ulpian, in the previous Case, regards interpretation against the stipulator as a last resort, many other sources suggest that restricting the content of an ambiguous promise was a common practice; see, e.g., Celsus, D. 34.5.26; Ulpian, D. 45.1.38.18. Evaluate this form of narrow interpretation as it relates to the nature of stipulation as a formal contract. Should this principle (in modern law, *contra proferentem*, "against the drafter") be generally regarded as a sound method for interpreting standard-form contracts? What ambiguity does Celsus detect in the stipulation in section 1?

2. **An Example.** One specialized type of stipulation (called the Aquilian stipulation after the late Republican jurist Aquilius Gallus) was used to discharge all existing and future debts owed by one party to another. It has the form: "Do you promise to pay me whatever, on any cause whatsoever, you are obliged to give me or to do for me or will owe me at present or at a future date?" After the promissor accepts, all other debts are eliminated through novation (see Case 39); the promisee can then formally acknowledge receipt under the Aquilian stipulation, and the result is that the account is cleared. What if, however, the parties have only certain debts in mind, but not others? Papinian, D. 2.15.5, writes: "When the Aquilian stipulation is

interposed, since it is governed by agreement (*consensus*), lawsuits that were not under consideration remain as they were, since the jurists' interpretation defeats deceitful squandering." How straightforward is this as an application of the rule in the present Case?

CASE 13: Preserving the Transaction

D. 45.1.80 (Ulpianus libro septuagensimo quarto ad Edictum)

Quotiens in stipulationibus ambigua oratio est, commodissimum est id accipi, quo res, qua de agitur, in tuto sit.

D. 45.1.41 pr. (Ulpianus libro quinquagensimo ad Sabinum)

Eum, qui "kalendis Ianuariis" stipulatur, si adiciat "primis" vel "proximis," nullam habere dubitationem palam est: sed et si dicat "secundis" vel "tertiis" vel quibus aliis, aeque dirimit quaestionem. Si autem non addat quibus Ianuariis, facti quaestionem inducere, quid forte senserit, hoc est quid inter eos acti sit (utique enim hoc sequimur quod actum est), easque adsumemus. Si autem non appareat, dicendum est quod Sabinus, primas kalendas ianuarias spectandas. Plane si ipsa die kalendarum quis stipulationem interponat, quid sequemur? Et puto actum videri de sequentibus kalendis.

Ulpian in the seventy-fourth book *On the Edict*:

Whenever the language in stipulations is ambiguous, the most convenient course is that it (an interpretation) be accepted which preserves the matter being litigated.

Ulpian in the fiftieth book *On Sabinus*:

If someone stipulates for (payment on) "the Kalends of January," there is clearly no doubt if he adds "the first (Kalends)," or "the next." But also if he says "the second" or "the third" or something else, he equally removes question.

But if he does not add on which (Kalends of) January, he raises a question of fact as to what he meant, i.e., what was transacted between them (*quid inter eos acti sit*), since in any case we always follow what was transacted; and we shall adopt that date. But if this is unclear, Sabinus' ruling must be upheld, that the first Kalends of January should be looked to. Obviously, if he interposes a stipulation on the very day of the Kalends, what will we do? I think the transaction apparently concerned the following Kalends.

The Problem
The stipulator (the promisee) says, "Do you promise to pay me 10,000 sesterces on January 1?" and the promissor answers, "I promise." When can the promisee sue for payment?

Discussion
1. The Principle. Why is the general rule in the first fragment a desirable one? How does it fit with the process of interpretation described in Case 11?

2. Application. A stipulation states that money is due "on New Year's Day (the Kalends of January)," without indicating which New Year's Day. How does

Ulpian propose to deal with the problem? Here is a good instance where figuring out "what was transacted" may be the best solution. But if this cannot be determined, what real alternative is there to Sabinus' rule?

3. Extension. What should be done if the stipulation gives no date at all for the proposed payment? Would it matter if the parties were in Rome and payment was to be made in far-off Alexandria? See Ulpian, D. 45.1.41.1–2.

CASE 14: "Women's Clothing"

D. 45.1.110.1 (Pomponius libro quarto ad Quintum Mucium)

Si stipulatus fuero de te: "vestem tuam, quaecumque muliebris est, dare spondes?," magis ad mentem stipulantis quam ad mentem promittentis id referri debet, ut quid in re sit, aestimari debeat, non quid senserit promissor. Itaque si solitus fuerat promissor muliebri quadam veste uti, nihilo minus debetur.

Pomponius in the fourth book *On Quintus Mucius*:

If I stipulate from you: "Do you swear to give all the women's clothing you have?" reference should be made to the stipulator's intent rather than to the promissor's, so that evaluation should be made of what is (actually) involved, not what the promissor thought. And so if the promissor (although male) commonly wore some women's clothing, nevertheless this (clothing) is owed.

Discussion

1. **Plain Meaning**. In this Case, the promissor presumably wants to give only such women's clothing as he did not wear himself (a restrictive interpretation), while the promisee wants everything that can reasonably be classed as women's clothing in ordinary usage (a broader interpretation). Why does Pomponius prefer the second view? Can his holding be reconciled with Celsus' view in Case 12? Note especially the final sentence of the *principium* in that Case, but also the different interpretation in Case 13. Can this stipulation be reasonably regarded as entirely unambiguous?

2. **Contrast with Wills**. The problem in this Case is that the promissor doubtless did not think of the clothing which he himself wore as "women's clothing." But would the situation be different if, in his will, he left "all my women's clothing" as a legacy to someone? Pomponius, D. 34.2.33 (citing Q. Mucius), holds that it would: "if he were to legate women's clothing, he would not be held to have expressed an intention concerning what he himself used as male clothing." Why is probable intent held to be important in the case of a testator, but not in that of a promissor? An important underlying principle is in play.

CASE 15: Broad Construction

D. 45.1.111 (Pomponius libro quinto ad Quintum Mucium)

Si stipulatus fuero "per te non fieri, quo minus mihi illa domo uti liceat," an etiam, si me non prohibeas, uxorem autem meam prohiberes, vel contra uxore mea stipulata me prohibeas, an committatur stipulatio? Et latius est haec verba sic accipi. Nam et si stipulatus fuero "per te non fieri, quo minus mihi via itinere actu uti liceat," etsi non me, sed alium nomine meo ingredientem prohibeas, sciendum erit committi stipulationem.

Pomponius in the fifth book *On Quintus Mucius*:

If I stipulated "that you not be responsible for obstructing me in my use of this house," is the stipulation violated also if you prevent, not me, but my wife? Or conversely, (what if) my wife stipulates (for the same thing) and you prevent me? And the broader view is that these words be construed in this way (i.e., that our spouses are included). For also if I stipulate "that you not be responsible for limiting my use of a right of way," it should be recognized that the stipulation is violated even if you prevent, not me, but a third party entering in my name.

Discussion

1. Reasonable Interpretation. This type of stipulation would most commonly be given during the course of a land transfer. The problem is to decide whether "obstructing me in my use" refers only to me, or also to my spouse as well. On what basis does Pomponius establish a more generous interpretation of the stipulation? Can his decision be reconciled with earlier Cases? Would he take the same line if, for instance, the stipulator demanded free use for his children? His slaves? His visitors? Local contractors?

2. Example. I promise you by stipulation that another person will appear in court on the day of a trial; but no penalty clause is attached to my promise. Is it implied that, if this person does not appear, you can sue me for your interest in the promise having been kept? See Ulpian, D. 45.1.81 pr., citing Celsus.

3. Another Example. Venuleius, D. 45.1.138 pr., discusses an early imperial school controversy about a stipulation for payment "at a market fair" that lasts for several days. Sabinus holds that the promisee can claim payment on the first day of the fair. Proculus (with whom Venuleius agrees) takes the view that payment is due only when the fair comes to an end. Using the principles developed in the preceding Cases, determine which side has the better interpretation.

CASE 16: Like-Named Farms

D. 45.1.106 (Iavolenus libro sexto Epistularum)

Qui ex pluribus fundis, quibus idem nomen impositum fuerat, unum fundum sine ulla nota demonstrationis stipuletur, incertum stipulatur, id est eum fundum stipulatur, quem promissor dare voluerit. Tamdiu autem voluntas promissoris in pendenti est, quamdiu id quod promissum est solvatur.

Javolenus in the sixth book of his *Letters*:

Out of several farms bearing the same name, someone stipulated for one farm without specifically indicating (which one he wanted). He stipulates for an indefinite thing (*incertum*); that is, he stipulates for the farm the promissor wishes to give. The promissor's intention remains in suspense until what was promised is fulfilled (by him).

The Problem
The stipulator asks, "Do you promise to give me the Cornelian farm?" without specifying which of several Cornelian farms is meant. If the promissor answers, "I promise," what is he or she liable for?

Discussion
1. **Definite and Indefinite Stipulations.** This case is based upon an important procedural distinction that is further discussed in Case 23. Briefly, had the stipulation been for a specific, identifiable farm, it could be sued for directly through a *condictio* for a definite thing (*certa res*). However, if it is not immediately apparent which farm is meant, the suit is for an indefinite thing (*incertum*) through what is called an action on the stipulation (*actio ex stipulatu*) in which the *iudex* determines its value. In the present Case, this action can be used to force the promissor to decide which farm he wishes to give.

2. **Latent Ambiguity.** The promissor has several farms named "the Cornelian farm"; the promisee stipulates for "the Cornelian farm" without expressly indicating which one. Why does the promissor get to choose? Does Javolenus' rule presume that there is no other evidence indicating what the parties intended in this regard?

CASE 17: Mistake about a Characteristic

D. 45.1.22 (Paulus libro nono ad Sabinum)

Si id quod aurum putabam, cum aes esset, stipulatus de te fuero, teneberis mihi huius aeris nomine, quoniam in corpore consenserimus: sed ex doli mali clausula tecum agam, si sciens me fefelleris.

Paul in the ninth book *On Sabinus*:

If I stipulated from you for something I thought was gold but was (actually) bronze, you will be liable to me for this bronze since we agreed on the object. But I may sue you on the (Praetor's) edict governing deceit (*dolus malus*) if you knowingly deceived me.

Discussion

1. **The Promisee's Mistake.** The stipulation was for delivery of an object that the promisee believed to be made of gold; in fact, it was made of bronze, which is, of course, far less valuable. The material from which an object is made is a characteristic. Why does Paul hold that the promisee's mistake does not affect the validity of the stipulation? Is it irrelevant whether both parties share the false belief (a bilateral mistake), or is only the promisee's (unilateral) mistake relevant? The hard question starts to arise if the promisee mistakenly thought the object to be gold while the promissor knew it to be bronze, but neither side was aware of the other's belief. How is this different from misunderstanding about the object of the promise (Case 8)?

   Would it matter if the situation was the other way around; could the promissor escape from the stipulation if he or she thought the object was made of bronze when in fact it was made of gold? Apparently not; so long as the two parties agree on the physical object to be transferred, it does not matter whether one or both is mistaken about a characteristic. For stipulation, how can this position be justified? As we will see (in Chapter IV.A.2), the law concerning the consensual contract of sale was different.

2. **Deceit (*Dolus*).** This is a delict, a private wrongdoing that gives rise to an action. The deceit must be intentional and result in loss to the plaintiff, who can sue for compensation from the person responsible. Paul allows the promisee to sue if the promissor knowingly led him or her to make a mistake regarding an important characteristic, for instance by deliberately misrepresenting the object; but no suit would be available if the promisee's mistake arose otherwise, for instance through a third party's deception. Is this remedy sufficient?

PART C

Conditional Stipulations and the Theory of Cause (*Causa*)

A condition (*condicio*) can make a promise legally binding if and only if a specified event occurs; the promise is "suspended" until the event occurs, at which time it becomes fully effective. Within very broad limits, Roman law allows parties to make a stipulation conditional if they wish.

Frequently a condition will state the reason why a promise was made. Compare the following three stipulations:

- "Do you promise to pay me ten (thousand sesterces)? (*Decem dari spondesne?*)

- "Do you promise to pay me ten because of a dowry?" (*Decem dari spondesne propter causam dotis?*)

- "If I marry you, do you promise to pay me ten?" (*Si tibi nupsero, decem dari spondesne?*)

The first promise is formulated absolutely, without any condition or indication of a reason for the payment; it is, as scholars put it, "abstract." The second states a reason for the payment. The third makes the promissor's performance expressly conditional on the occurrence of the marriage, but does not mention dowry as the payment's purpose.

If a stipulation, in any of these three forms, is in fact meant to constitute a dowry, then the intended dowry can be described as the reason, or "cause" (*causa*), for the stipulation. *Causa* (unlike consideration in Common Law) is not a necessary condition for legally enforcing a stipulation, since that reason is provided already by its legitimate form. So *causa* is broad enough to embrace, for instance, a purely altruistic gift.

When the *causa* (e.g., marriage) is expressed in the form of a condition, the stipulation is simply unenforceable if the planned wedding does not take place, since the condition has failed. Likewise, although by a more extended interpretation, if the stipulation expressly states that the promise is intended "for a dowry" (*propter causam dotis*).

But what if the stipulation is formulated absolutely? In theory, the promise is enforceable on the basis of its wording, whether or not the marriage occurs. But the jurists readily recognized that stipulations are seldom if ever made in a void; they are usually tied up with something that the promissor is anticipating or seeking to bring about, some goal (even a gift) that the promissor wants to achieve through the promise. This idea is articulated through the concept of *causa*. In addition, the jurists used the concept in order to monitor the legal acceptability of stipulations, which were unenforceable if their *causa* was illegal or immoral.

In Part E of this Chapter, we will see how the jurists applied the theory of *causa* in order to prevent absolute promises from being enforced when the underlying reason for a promise was legally unacceptable or defective.

The rules on conditions are generalized in Roman contract law, but it is mainly in stipulation that they are related to the theory of *causa*.

CASE 18: Impossible Conditions

Gaius, *Institutiones* 3.98

Item si quis sub ea condicione stipuletur, quae existere non potest, uelut "si digito caelum tetigerit," inutilis est stipulatio. sed legatum sub inpossibili condicione relictum nostri praeceptores proinde deberi putant, ac si sine condicione relictum esset; diuersae scholae auctores nihilo minus legatum inutile existimant quam stipulationem. et sane uix idonea diuersitatis ratio reddi potest.

Gaius in the third book of his *Institutes*:

Likewise, if someone stipulates under a condition that cannot occur, e.g., "if he touches the sky with his finger," the stipulation is ineffective.

But our (Sabinian) teachers hold that a bequest left under an impossible condition is due exactly as if it had been left unconditionally, while the authorities of the other (Proculian) school think that (such) a bequest is just as ineffective as a stipulation (of this sort). No wholly convincing explanation of the (Sabinian) distinction can be provided.

Discussion

1. **Impossibility.** The stipulation takes the form: "Do you promise to pay me fifty if I touch the sky?" The envisaged performance itself, namely payment of fifty, is entirely possible. However, this performance is not legally due unless a physically impossible condition (in this case, a patently ridiculous one) first occurs. Hence the entire stipulation is ineffective. Is this simply a matter of common sense? Suppose, for instance, the condition is not utterly impossible, but just very, very unlikely, for instance: "if I broadjump fifteen feet." (The world record is just over twelve feet.)

2. **Legacy.** A legacy (*legatum*) is a bequest from a testator's estate. Suppose that it takes the form: "I leave fifty to Gaius if he touches the sky." Which of the two solutions proposed by the jurists seems to you the best? Can you think of a reason why legacies should not be treated the same as stipulations? Justinian ultimately decided in favor of the Proculians: *Inst.* 2.14.10.

3. **Legal Impossibility.** What if a stipulation is subject to a condition that is not legally possible, for instance: "if I sell a public building" or something else that cannot be sold (see Case 84)? Venuleius, D. 45.1.137.6, holds that this stipulation is also ineffective even though the public building might be privatized and become saleable at some time in the future, since "a stipulation should be assessed by the law of the present, not of the future." What if the public building is in the process of being sold off by a city, but the sale has not yet been completed?

CASE 19: Immoral Conditions

D. 45.1.97.2 (Celsus libro vicensimo sexto Digestorum)

"Si tibi nupsero, decem dari spondes?" causa cognita denegandam actionem puto, nec raro probabilis causa eiusmodi stipulationis est. Item si vir a muliere eo modo non in dotem stipulatus est.

D. 45.1.107 (Iavolenus libro octavo Epistularum)

Utrum turpem talem stipulationem putes an non, quaero. Pater naturalis filium, quem Titius habebat in adoptionem, heredem instituit, si patria potestate liberatus esset: pater eum adoptivus non alias emancipare voluit, quam si ei dedisset, a quo stipularetur certam summam, si eum manumisisset: post emancipationem adiit heres filius: petit nunc pecuniam pater ex stipulatione supra relata. Respondit: non puto turpem esse causam stipulationis, utpote cum aliter filium emancipaturus non fuerit: nec potest videri iniusta causa stipulationis, si aliquid adoptivus pater habere voluerit, propter quod a filio post emancipationem magis curaretur.

Celsus in the twenty-sixth book of his *Digests*:

"If I marry you, do you swear to pay ten (thousand sesterces)?" I think that an action should be denied (by the Praetor only) after investigating the case; it is not unusual that the cause (*causa*) of such a stipulation is acceptable. Similarly, if a man stipulated in this way from a woman not for her dowry.

Javolenus in the eighth book of his *Letters*:

I ask whether you think a stipulation like the following is immoral. A natural father named as heir his son whom Titius had adopted, provided he was freed from his father's power (*patria potestas*). The adoptive father did not wish to emancipate him except if he (the son) had given to him a specified amount (of money) on the basis of a stipulation (for payment) if he had manumitted him. After the emancipation the son accepted the inheritance. Now the (adoptive) father sought the money on the basis of the stipulation given above.

He (Javolenus) responds: I do not think the cause (*causa*) of the stipulation is immoral (*turpis*), seeing that he would not emancipate the son otherwise. Nor can the cause be held illegal (*iniusta causa*) if the adoptive father wishes to have something on the basis of which he is better cared for by his son after the emancipation.

Discussion

1. Immorality. Stipulations are ineffective if the promise itself is contrary to law or morality, "for instance, if someone promises to commit murder or sacrilege" (Pomponius, D. 45.1.27 pr.). Does it logically follow that a stipulation should also be ineffective if a promise is conditional on an immoral or illegal act?

2. Procuring Marriage. Stipulations for payment of money if a marriage occurs, or payment of a penalty if it does not occur, are usually ineffective, "since it has been held improper that present or future marriages be constrained by a penalty" (Paul, D. 45.1.134 pr.). The idea is that marriage should be freely undertaken. The stipulation described by Celsus seems at first sight to violate this rule. Why does Celsus nonetheless hold that the *causa* of the stipulation might be acceptable? It appears that a woman is receiving this promise from a man. What innocent purpose might she have? Was his motive just to make her a gift in anticipation of the wedding?

3. Purchasing Emancipation? In the situation described by Javolenus, the promissor was the "natural son" (probably the offspring of sexual relations between a free man and a slave woman) who was named heir to his biological father on the condition that he be emancipated (released from paternal power) by a third party who had adopted the boy, probably after procuring his freedom. In effect, the adoptive father now wants a share of his son's inheritance, and to that end extracts a promise of money payable after the emancipation; but the emancipated son then refuses to pay. Here, too, Javolenus searches for a way to avoid judging the *causa* immoral before first examining extrinsic evidence as to the stipulation's background.

4. A Promise to Make Someone Heir. Julian, D. 45.1.61, considers a stipulation to this effect: "If you do not make me your heir, do you promise to give me some specified amount of money?" Promises of payment to be made at or after the promissor's death were controversial and often void on their face in Classical law; see Gaius, *Inst.* 3.100; Justinian, C. 8.37.11 (528 CE). But Julian holds that: "This (particular) stipulation is contrary to good morals, *contra bonos mores*." Why?

5. Performance of Immoral or Illegal Stipulations. Money paid (not just promised) under an illegal or immoral stipulation could often be reclaimed by the payer through a *condictio* (see D. 12.5 and Case 232).

CASE 20: Implied Conditions

D. 23.3.21 (Ulpianus libro trigesimo quinto ad Sabinum)

Stipulationem, quae propter causam dotis fiat, constat habere in se condicionem hanc "si nuptiae fuerint secutae," et ita demum ex ea agi posse (quamvis non sit expressa condicio), si nuptiae <fuerint secutae>, constat: quare si nuntius remittatur, defecisse condicio stipulationis videtur.

D. 23.3.22 (Paulus libro septimo ad Sabinum)

Et licet postea eidem nupserit, non convalescit stipulatio.

D. 23.3.23 (Ulpianus libro trigesimo quinto ad Sabinum)

Quia autem in stipulatione non est necessaria dotis adiectio, etiam in datione tantundem ducimus.

Ulpian in the thirty-fifth book *On Sabinus*:

If a stipulation is made because of a dowry (*propter causam dotis*), it is agreed that it contains the condition "if the marriage then follows"; and therefore, although the condition is not express, it is agreed that action can be brought on it (only) if the marriage follows. So, if a messenger is sent back (by the bride, to call off the marriage), the stipulation's condition is held to have failed.

Paul in the seventh book *On Sabinus*:

And even though she later marries the same man, the stipulation does not revive.

Ulpian in the thirty-fifth book *On Sabinus*:

But since in a stipulation for dowry this addition (an explicit reference to the dowry) is unnecessary, we hold the same for the (executed) gift (of a dowry).

The Problem
A bridegroom asks a bride, "Do you promise to pay me 20,000 sesterces?" and she promises. Both parties understand that a dowry is being arranged, although the promise does not mention dowry. If the marriage is then called off, can the stipulation nonetheless be enforced?

Discussion
1. Dowry. A dowry is property given or promised to the groom by a bride or by someone else (most commonly, her *paterfamilias*) in anticipation of a marriage; the groom becomes the property's effective owner, but in many circumstances must return it if the marriage comes to an end. Dowries were frequently promised by stipulation before the marriage, as in this Case. Here, however, the bride or groom backed out of the marriage before it was

finalized. The situation would be the same if the proposed marriage turned out to be legally impossible.

2. Failure of Cause. The problem in this Case probably arose because the stipulation was expressed absolutely: "Do you promise to pay me 100?" The underlying *causa* for the stipulation was a dowry, but the parties did not include the *causa* in their wording. Note that *causa* is being used here differently than in the previous Case; the purpose of the stipulation was not immoral or illegal, nor is it likely that the promise lacked a valid *causa* at the time it was made, but obstacles still arise because the original purpose was not realized. Ulpian tries to incorporate the *causa* into the stipulation by means of a theory of implied condition, where establishing the condition will require some extrinsic evidence. Is this maneuver legitimate? See further Case 35 for how such problems were handled procedurally. What is it that prevents the promise from reviving once it has failed?

3. Postclassical Law. In the later Roman Empire, written stipulations became all but universal. Where a written document failed to state a *causa* for a promise, at that date the promisee was required, in suing, to prove the existence of the underlying reason for the promise. The Digest compilers altered Paul, D. 22.3.25.4, in order to reflect this development.

CASE 21: A Condition and a Deadline

D. 45.1.8 (Paulus libro secundo ad Sabinum)

In illa stipulatione: "Si kalendis Stichum non dederis, decem dare spondes?" mortuo homine quaeritur, an statim ante kalendas agi possit. Sabinus Proculus exspectandum diem actori putant, quod est verius: tota enim obligatio sub condicione et in diem collata est et licet ad condicionem committi videatur, dies tamen superest. Sed cum eo, qui ita promisit: "Si intra kalendas digito caelum non tetigerit," agi protinus potest. Haec et Marcellus probat.

Paul in the second book *On Sabinus*:

In the case of this stipulation: "If you do not convey (the slave) Stichus on the Kalends, do you promise to pay ten," it is asked whether, if the slave dies, suit can be brought at once, before the Kalends. Sabinus and Proculus thought that the plaintiff must await the deadline (*dies*), which is more correct, since the entire obligation was placed under (both) a condition and a deadline (*dies*), and although the condition is deemed to be fulfilled, the deadline still remains. But with a person who promised in this way: "If within the Kalends he does not touch the sky with his finger," suit can be brought immediately (i.e., before the Kalends). Marcellus also approves this.

Discussion

1. **Waiting for the Deadline.** In this Case, the stipulation is for a penalty to be paid if the slave is not conveyed "on the first of the next month." (On penalty clauses, see Case 48.) Because of the slave's death, the condition can no longer be met. So why must the promisee wait until the Kalends before suing? The rule here clearly demonstrates exaggerated respect for the deadline as independent from the condition, and the same respect shows up in Paul, D. 2.11.10.1: "A slave whose appearance in court was promised perishes before the deadline (*dies*) through the promissor's deliberate act (*dolus*); we have the fixed rule that a penalty cannot be sought before the deadline comes, since the entire stipulation is held to refer to the deadline." It's worth comparing Celsus, D. 45.1.99.1 (Case 12), as well as Case 32. On severing stipulated promises, see Discussion 4 on Case 7.

   Paul concedes that the ruling of Sabinus and Proculus (leaders of the two early imperial "schools") was contested; see "more correct" (*verius*). How would you frame the opposing view? Why does Paul think it would matter if the promise had been unfulfillable from the outset?

2. **Anticipatory Breach of Contract.** In the Case, the promissor could not physically have delivered Stichus. Suppose, instead, that the promissor had repudiated the promise by clearly stating, before the Kalends, his intention not to convey Stichus, or that he simply conveyed Stichus to a third

party, thereby rendering his performance impossible. Would the outcome be any different? Surely not, right? There is no clear evidence that the jurists recognized anticipatory breach for any contract. In modern law, legal recognition of anticipatory breach permits the aggrieved promisee to terminate the contract immediately and, if he wishes, arrange for substitute performance, thereby often mitigating the amount of loss he sustains from the breach.

CASE 22: Obstructing a Condition

D. 50.17.161 (Ulpianus libro septuagesimo septimo ad Edictum)

In iure civili receptum est, quotiens per eum, cuius interest condicionem non impleri, fiat quo minus impleatur, perinde haberi, ac si impleta condicio fuisset. Quod ad libertatem et legata et ad heredum institutiones perducitur. Quibus exemplis stipulationes quoque committuntur, cum per promissorem factum esset, quo minus stipulator condicioni pareret.

D. 22.2.8 (Ulpianus libro septuagesimo septimo ad Edictum)

Servius ait pecuniae traiecticiae poenam peti non posse, si per creditorem stetisset, quo minus eam intra certum tempus praestitutum accipiat.

Ulpian in the seventy-seventh book *On the Edict*:

D. 50.17.161. In the Civil Law, the received view is that, whenever a person with an interest in this happening is responsible for a condition not being fulfilled, it is treated as if the condition is fulfilled. This rule is extended to grants of freedom, bequests, and the naming of heirs. On these models, stipulations also are binding when the promissor is responsible for the stipulator's not complying with a condition. . . . 22.2.8. Servius says that the penalty on (repayment of) a bottomry loan cannot be claimed if the creditor was responsible for his not receiving it (repayment) within the predetermined fixed time.

Discussion

1. **Penalty on a Bottomry Loan.** A bottomry loan is a form of marine insurance that was widely used in the ancient world because of the large risks inherent in sea travel; see Case 33, where the loan is more fully described. Quite commonly, repayment of the loan was secured by a stipulation for a penalty in the event that the loan was not repaid on time. See Labeo, D. 22.2.9; Africanus, D. 44.7.23. In this case, the creditor has obstructed repayment, and therefore the borrower can make a late repayment without incurring the penalty.

2. **Extending the Rule.** These two fragments were originally part of a single text, as in the translation. The various rules on conditions are much the same in contract law generally, and even beyond. For sale, take Ulpian, D. 18.1.50: "Labeo writes that, if you sell me a library on the condition that Capua's town councilors have (first) sold me a site on which I can place it, and I am responsible for not procuring this from the Capuans, . . . I think there can also be an action on the sale as though the condition was fulfilled since the buyer was responsible for its not being fulfilled." As these examples illustrate, conditions frequently contain a promissory element: the party that will be advantaged if the condition is not fulfilled not only must not obstruct its fulfillment, but may even be obliged to assist in carrying it out.

PART D

Execution and Impossibility

A promise expressed in the form of a stipulation must in principle be executed exactly as it is stated, subject to any necessary interpretation. If the promissor fails to carry out the promise, then the promisee will usually be able to bring suit: either a *condictio* for a specified sum of money or a specified thing, or an action on the stipulation for an indeterminate amount. So, for instance, if the promise was to provide a service (such as a promise to construct a building), then the promisee must sue on the stipulation itself (*ex stipulatu*) and the *iudex*, during the trial, will determine the promise's value to the plaintiff.

Particularly in the case of such indefinite stipulations, problems can arise in deciding whether promissors have fulfilled their legal duties. For instance, a promise may be impossible to perform at the outset (e.g., a promise to deliver a slave who, unknown to the parties, is already dead), or it may become impossible to perform (a promise to deliver a slave who dies of natural causes after the stipulation but before delivery). Again, it is necessary to determine the extent of the promissor's duty to carry out the promise; what if, for instance, the promissor is responsible for the slave's death? What are the legal consequences if the promissor has failed to execute and is in "default," or what the jurists call "delay" (*mora*)? All these questions are discussed the following Cases.

Problems of execution are of great importance in contract law, since they go to the heart of what is meant by making a promise. Because stipulations are promises in "strict law" (*stricti iuris*, not a technical term), the jurists can sometimes seem rather harsh when discussing their execution. As we will see in subsequent Chapters, they display considerably greater flexibility when handling informal contracts in "good faith" (*bona fides*).

CASE 23: Definite and Indefinite Stipulations

D. 45.1.75 pr.-2, 5 (Ulpianus libro vicensimo secundo ad Edictum)

pr. Ubi autem non apparet, quid quale quantumque est in stipulatione, incertam esse stipulationem dicendum est. 1. Ergo si qui fundum sine propria appellatione vel hominem generaliter sine proprio nomine aut vinum frumentumve sine qualitate dari sibi stipulatur, incertum deducit in obligationem. 2. Usque adeo, ut, si quis ita stipulatus sit "tritici Africi boni modios centum" "vini Campani boni amphoras centum," incertum videatur stipulari, quia bono melius inveniri potest: quo fit, ut boni appellatio non sit certae rei significativa, cum id, quod bono melius sit, ipsum quoque bonum sit. At cum optimum quisque stipulatur, id stipulari intellegitur, cuius bonitas principalem gradum bonitatis habet: quae res efficit, ut ea appellatio certi significativa sit. . . . 5. Sed qui vinum aut oleum vel triticum, quod in horreo est, stipulatur, certum stipulari intellegitur.

Ulpian in the twenty-second book *On the Edict*:

pr. When it is unclear what is contained in the stipulation—(e.g.,) what quality and how much—it must be held the stipulation is indefinite (*incerta*). 1. So if someone stipulates for delivery to him of a farm without its proper name, or a slave generically (and) without his or her proper name, or wine or grain without (specifying) its quality, his obligation is for an indefinite thing.

2. This rule holds up to the point that if someone stipulated for "one hundred bushels of good African wheat" (or) "one hundred amphoras of good Campanian wine," he is held to stipulate for an indefinite thing since something better than "good" can be found; the result is that the term "good" does not designate a definite thing, since what is better than good is also itself good. But when someone stipulates for "the best," he is construed to stipulate for the highest level of quality; the result is that this term designates a definite thing. . . .

5. But if he stipulates for the wine or olive oil or wheat that is in a storehouse, he is construed as stipulating for a definite thing.

Discussion

1. **Definiteness.** What is the difference between stipulating for delivery of "a farm," and stipulating for delivery of "this farm"? What problems does the first stipulation raise that the second does not? As you sort through Ulpian's examples, try to discover the principles he uses in classifying stipulation in one or the other category. As to "good African wheat," would it matter if this was the grade of wheat most commonly used by merchants? Can "the best Campanian wine" be established as a definite thing just by looking at prices? In any case, note that definiteness is determined as of when the stipulation is made.

2. Procedure. The main reason for distinguishing between the two categories is procedural. Definite stipulations are actionable under a *condictio* for a definite thing or a definite amount of money. By contrast, indefinite stipulations are actionable under an action on the stipulation (which, in later law, may have been generalized into a *condictio incerti*); for its model wording, see Case 34. This second *formula* demands more discretion from the *iudex* in estimating the amount due to the plaintiff.

3. Vagueness. If a stipulation is for a performance so vague that its value cannot be reasonably estimated even as an *incertum*, then the stipulation is ineffective. Marcellus, D. 45.1.94, gives as an example a stipulation for "wheat," without express specification of quantity or quality. Marcellus writes: "If he (the stipulator) was thinking about certain wheat of a definite kind and quantity, this will be treated as an express term (*pro expresso*); but if he did not do so because he wished (later) to decide on the kind and quality, he is held to stipulate for nothing, not even a single measure." How can it be determined what the stipulator "was thinking about"? Must the promissor be aware of what the stipulator had in mind? This could be an example of interpretation following "what was transacted" (*id quod actum est*); see Case 11. In general, the jurists seem inclined to uphold indefinite stipulations wherever possible; see, for instance, section 1 of this Case. Whether omitted terms can be supplied by interpretation is largely a question of fact for the *iudex*, after hearing extrinsic evidence.

CASE 24: Initially Impossible Stipulations

Gaius, *Institutiones* 3.97–97a, 99

97. Si id, quod dari stipulamur, tale sit, ut dari non possit, inutilis est stipulatio, uelut si quis hominem liberum, quem seruum esse credebat, aut mortuum, quem uiuum esse credebat, aut locum sacrum uel religiosum, quem putabat humani iuris esse, dari stipuletur. 97a. Item si quis rem, quae in rerum natura esse non potest, uelut hippocentaurum, stipuletur, aeque inutilis est stipulatio. . . . 99. Praeterea inutilis est stipulatio, si quis ignorans rem suam esse dari sibi eam stipuletur; quippe quod alicuius est, id ei dari non potest.

D. 45.1.137.4 (Venuleius libro primo Stipulationum)

Illud inspiciendum est, an qui centum dari promisit confestim teneatur an vero cesset obligatio, donec pecuniam conferre possit. Quid ergo, si neque domi habet neque inveniat creditorem? Sed haec recedunt ab impedimento naturali et respiciunt ad facultatem dandi. Est autem facultas personae commodum incommodumque, non rerum quae promittuntur. . . . Et generaliter causa difficultatis ad incommodum promissoris, non ad impedimentum stipulatoris pertinet, ne incipiat dici eum quoque dare non posse, qui alienum servum, quem dominus non vendat, dare promiserit.

Gaius in the third book of his *Institutes*:

97. If what we stipulate for is such that it cannot be delivered, the stipulation is ineffective, e.g., if someone stipulates for delivery of a free person whom he believed to be a slave, or a dead (slave) whom he believed to be alive, or a sacred or religious place that he thought was subject to human law. 97a. Likewise, if someone stipulates for an object that cannot exist, like a centaur, the stipulation is also ineffective. . . . 99. Further, a stipulation is ineffective if someone unknowingly stipulates that his own property be delivered to him; clearly, what belongs to a person cannot be delivered to him.

Venuleius in the first book of his *Stipulations*:

It must be examined whether a person who promises delivery of 100 (thousand sesterces) is liable immediately, or the obligation is postponed until he can collect the money. What if he does not have it at home and finds no one to lend it? But these matters involve no natural obstacle; they look (only) to ease of payment. Ease (of payment) concerns the convenience or inconvenience of an individual, not of the things that are promised. . . . Generally, difficulty of performance is a burden for the promissor, not an obstacle for the stipulator; otherwise, it would be held that someone who promises (delivery of) another person's slave is unable to deliver if the (slave's) owner won't sell.

Discussion

1. Legal and Factual Impossibility. Except for the centaur (an imaginary creature), the examples cited by Gaius relate to legal impossibility. The situation is different when the promissor can legally perform the promise, but in fact lacks the means to execute it, as in the Venuleius fragment. Study carefully the difference between the situations in the two fragments. See also Gaius, D. 45.1.141.4 (a stipulation made in Rome for payment "today" in far-off Carthage).

2. A Slave in the Enemy's Hands. I promise by stipulation to deliver to you a slave who is presently being held by the armed forces of Rome's enemies, and so cannot be delivered. What outcome? See Pomponius, D. 19.1.55.

CASE 25: Ensuing Legal Impossibility

D. 45.1.83.5 (Paulus libro septuagensimo secundo ad Edictum)

Sacram vel religiosam rem vel usibus publicis in perpetuum relictam (ut forum aut basilicam) aut hominem liberum inutiliter stipulor, quamvis sacra profana fieri et usibus publicis relicta in privatos usus reverti et ex libero servus fieri potest. Nam et cum quis rem profanam aut Stichum dari promisit, liberatur, si sine facto eius res sacra esse coeperit aut Stichus ad libertatem pervenerit, nec revocantur in obligationem, si rursus lege aliqua et res sacra profana esse coeperit et Stichus ex libero servus effectus sit. <Celso tamen contra visum est:> Quoniam una atque eadem causa et liberandi et obligandi esset, quod aut dari non possit aut dari possit: nam et si navem, quam spopondit, dominus dissolvit et isdem tabulis compegerit, quia eadem navis esset, inciperet obligari. Pro quo et illud dici posse Pedius scribit: si stipulatus fuero ex fundo centum amphoras vini, exspectare debeo, donec nascatur: et si natum sine culpa promissoris consumptum sit, rursum exspectare debeam, donec iterum nascatur et dari possit: et per has vices aut cessaturam aut valituram stipulationem. Sed haec dissimilia sunt: adeo enim, cum liber homo promissus est, servitutis tempus spectandum non esse, ut ne haec quidem stipulatio de homine libero probanda sit: "illum, cum servus esse coeperit, dare spondes?" item "eum locum, cum ex sacro religiosove profanus esse coeperit, dari?" quia nec praesentis temporis obligationem recipere potest et ea dumtaxat, quae natura sui possibilia sunt, deducuntur in obligationem. vini autem non speciem, sed genus stipulari videmur et tacite in ea tempus continetur: homo liber certa specie continetur. Et casum adversamque fortunam spectari hominis liberi neque civile neque naturale est: nam de his rebus negotium recte geremus, quae subici usibus dominioque nostro statim possunt. Et navis si hac mente resoluta est, ut in alium usum tabulae destinarentur, licet mutato consilio perficiatur, tamen et perempta prior navis et haec alia dicenda est: sed si reficiendae navis causa omnes tabulae refixae sint, nondum intercidisse navis videtur et compositis rursus eadem esse incipit: sicuti de aedibus deposita tigna ea mente, ut reponantur, aedium sunt, sed si usque ad aream deposita sit, licet eadem materia restituatur, alia erit. Hic tractatus etiam ad praetorias stipulationes pertinet, quibus de re restituenda cavetur et an eadem res sit, quaeritur.

Paul in the seventy-second book *On the Edict*:

If I stipulate for a sacred or religious thing, or for something devoted to permanent public use, e.g., a forum or a basilica, or for a free man, this is ineffective even though the sacred object can be secularized, what was left for public use can revert to private, and a free person can be made a slave. Likewise, if someone promised delivery of (either) a secular object or Stichus, he is discharged if, through no act of his own, the object becomes sacred or Stichus achieves liberty; nor does the obligation revive if by some statute the sacred thing once again becomes secular and Stichus loses freedom and is made a slave.

<But Celsus thought the opposite,> since there is one and the same reason for both the discharge and the obligation, namely what either can or cannot be delivered. For likewise, if the owner takes apart a ship he had promised (to deliver), and (then) joins it together with the same planks, he begins to be obligated (once more), since it is the same ship. Pedius says that a further point can be made for this view: if I stipulate for one hundred amphoras of wine from a farm, I must wait until it (the wine) comes into existence; and if it comes into existence and is (then) consumed without the promissor's fault (*culpa*), I would have to wait once more until it comes into existence again and can be delivered. So the stipulation will in turn either lapse or be valid.

But these situations are different. For when a freeman has been promised, we should not await the time of his servitude, so that we not have to approve the following stipulation about a free man: "Do you swear to deliver him when he becomes a slave?" Or: "(Do you promise) delivery of this place when it becomes secular instead of being sacred or religious?" For the thing cannot at present be subject to an obligation, and only things that are possible by their nature are part of an obligation. But we appear to stipulate not for specific wine, but for a kind of wine, and time is implicitly contained in this (stipulation); (whereas) a free man is a definite thing. And it is neither Civil nor Natural (*neque civile neque naturale*) to wait for chance and the bad luck of a free person (becoming a slave); we properly conduct business (only) about those things that can at present be subject to our use and ownership.

And if the ship were taken apart with the intent that the planks be put to some other use, although plans change and it is remade, nonetheless the earlier ship is gone and this should be held to be a new one. But if all the planks were detached to reconstruct the ship, the ship is held not yet to have perished, and it begins to be the same (ship) after its reconstruction. Similarly, timbers that are taken from a building with the intent of replacing them belong to the building; but if they are taken to a (different) site, although the same material is (later) restored, it will be different. . . .

The Problem
I stipulate that you deliver to me a piece of land that is public property. The stipulation is unenforceable now. But if the land is subsequently made private, does the stipulation then become enforceable?

Discussion
1. **Legal Reasoning.** Examine this (highly unusual) extended passage as an example of Roman legal reasoning. How clear are Paul's arguments as he proceeds step by step? Do his points and categories seem realistic? Celsus' contrary view appears in D. 32.79.3 and 46.3.98.8 (from Paul); scholars

assume that the Digest compilers deleted his name from this passage when abbreviating the text.

The ship that Celsus describes as having been disassembled and then reassembled is similar to the famous metaphysical "ship of Theseus" problem that had been discussed by philosophers since Heraclitus and Plato.

CASE 26: Ensuing Physical Impossibility

D. 45.1.37 (Paulus libro duodecimo ad Sabinum)

Si certos nummos, puta qui in arca sint, stipulatus sim et hi sine culpa promissoris perierint, nihil nobis debetur.

D. 45.1.33 (Pomponius libro vicensimo quinto ad Sabinum)

Si Stichus certo die dari promissus ante diem moriatur, non tenetur promissor.

Paul in the twelfth book *On Sabinus*:

If I stipulated for specific coins, e.g., those in a strongbox, and they perished without the promissor's fault (*culpa*), nothing is owed to me.

Pomponius in the twenty-fifth book *On Sabinus*:

If Stichus was promised for delivery on a specific day and dies before the day, the promissor is not liable.

Discussion

1. The Problem of Risk. This is an important (and rather surprising) principle. By stipulation, you promise to me "the coins in your strongbox" (clearly, a definite thing); thereafter, before you can deliver them to me, they are somehow destroyed without your fault (see Cases 28–29). Are you liable? The jurists hold that you are not; but what reason can be given for this holding? Why should I, and not you the promissor, bear the risk that the object of the stipulation might be accidentally destroyed? Is it that the stipulation is ostensibly a unilateral promise made subject to the tacit condition that it can be performed? How realistic is the Roman view? Note that, in any case, this principle is inapplicable to an indefinite stipulation, since the object of such a promise cannot perish.

2. Reciprocal Stipulations. Suppose that, by an exchange of stipulations, I promise you the 100,000 sesterces in my strongbox and you promise me your farm, and the strongbox is then stolen or destroyed without my fault. Curiously, no surviving Roman source addresses exactly this point, but it can be supposed that suit on the second stipulation, which was really given in exchange for the first, can be obstructed by the defense of deceit, *exceptio doli* (Case 35)—a result that would make the two promises interdependent, as Common Law would hold. The Roman law for sale, however, is different: see Chapter IV.B.1.

CASE 27: The Promissor's Responsibility

D. 45.1.91 pr., 2 (Paulus libro septimo decimo ad Plautium)

pr. Si servum stipulatus fuero et nulla mora intercedente servus decesserit: si quidem occidat eum promissor, expeditum est. Sin autem neglegat infirmum, an teneri debeat promissor, considerandum est: utrum, quemadmodum in vindicatione hominis, si neglectus a possessore fuerit, culpae huius nomine tenetur possessor, ita et cum dari promisit, an culpa, quod ad stipulationem attinet, in faciendo accipienda sit, non in non faciendo? Quod magis probandum est, quia qui dari promisit, ad dandum, non faciendum tenetur. . . . 2. De illo quaeritur, an et is, qui nesciens se debere occiderit, teneatur: quod Iulianus putat in eo, qui, cum nesciret a se petitum codicillis ut restitueret, manumisit.

Paul in the seventeenth book *On Plautius*:

pr. I stipulate for a slave and the slave dies prior to the occurrence of default (*mora*). If the promissor kills him, this is actionable. But if he neglects a sick slave, we must consider whether the promissor should be liable, i.e., whether, just as in the vindication of (the ownership of) a slave the possessor is liable for fault (*culpa*) if he neglected (the slave), so too (the promissor is liable) when he promised delivery; or whether, instead, insofar as a stipulation is concerned, *culpa* should be construed (to occur) in acting, not in not acting? And this (latter) is the better view, since the person who promised delivery is liable to deliver, not to act. . . .

2. Question arises about whether a person is also liable if he kills (a slave) while unaware that he owes (him). Julian thinks this (is correct) for a person who manumitted (a slave) while unaware that his restitution was being claimed from him owing to the codicils (to a will).

Discussion

1. **The Promissor's Duties.** Examine the first paragraph of this opinion closely. A slave was promised to the stipulator; the slave then died before his delivery was legally due, i.e., before "default" (*mora*). Under what circumstances is the promissor liable? Paul holds that the promissor is liable if he himself kills the slave, but is not liable if the slave falls sick and he fails to provide adequate medical care, "since the person who promised delivery is liable to deliver, not to act." That is to say, the stipulation does not impose on the promissor any positive duty to take action ensuring that delivery occurs. Does Paul's distinction make sense? Does it result from an overly literal interpretation of the stipulation?

   Compare Ulpian, D. 4.3.7.3 (citing Labeo): a promissor who was obliged to hand over a slave administered a (slow acting?) poison before transferring him; unless the stipulation provided against such misconduct, the promisee has no action on the stipulation and must sue directly on the promissor's deceit (*de dolo*). Had the slave been sold, by contrast, the law of sale would allow for action on purchase despite there being no special provision against deceit; see Cases 113–114.

2. *Culpa.* Paul concedes that the promissor is held to a standard of care for the slave that is termed *culpa*, meaning "fault"; this includes not just deliberate causing of harm (what the jurists call *dolus*), but also carelessness. Paul's rule is in accord with Pomponius, D. 46.3.107, who says that a stipulation is fulfilled in four circumstances: (i) by payment (carrying out the stipulation); (ii) "when the object of the stipulation ceases to exist without the promissor's *culpa*"; (iii) by a formal release (called an *acceptilatio*), whether or not delivery actually occurs; (iv) when through other events, for instance, inheritance, the roles of promissor and stipulator coalesce in the same person. Although in other areas of law the jurists may interpret the *culpa* standard as imposing a duty to act, they draw back from that view for stipulation. Why?

3. Knowledge. Even more unusual is the discussion in section 2, which appears to hold that the promissor is liable for killing a promised slave even if he was unaware that the slave was owed under a stipulation. (The same would also presumably be true if the promissor had unknowingly manumitted the slave, thus making delivery impossible.) Paul reasons by analogy from the rules governing testamentary trusts (*fideicommissa*); the same rule for trusts is stated by Justinian, *Inst.* 2.20.16, where the high authority of Julian is once again invoked. But in other passages concerning trusts, Paul seems to require knowledge (*scientia*) for liability: D. 12.6.65.8 (Case 233) and 39.6.39. Therefore it may be that in the original form of this passage Paul went on to reject Julian's view, and his contrary opinion was edited out by the Digest compilers. In any case, which view seems to you in better accord with the general nature of stipulation?

4. Alternative Stipulations. Julian, D. 46.3.33.1, sets the following problem: A person promises by stipulation that either Stichus or Pamphilus (two slaves) will be given to the promisee. The promissor then seriously wounds Stichus. Can he escape liability under the stipulation by tendering Stichus?

CASE 28: Persistence of the Obligation

D. 45.1.91.3 (Paulus libro septimo decimo ad Plautium)

Sequitur videre de eo, quod veteres constituerunt, quotiens culpa intervenit debitoris, perpetuari obligationem, quemadmodum intellegendum sit. Et quidem si effecerit promissor, quo minus solvere possit, expeditum intellectum habet constitutio: si vero moratus sit tantum, haesitatur, an, si postea in mora non fuerit, extinguatur superior mora. Et Celsus adulescens scribit eum, qui moram fecit in solvendo Sticho quem promiserat, posse emendare eam moram postea offerendo: esse enim hanc quaestionem de bono et aequo: in quo genere plerumque sub auctoritate iuris scientiae perniciose, inquit, erratur. Et sane probabilis haec sententia est, quam quidem et Iulianus sequitur: nam dum quaeritur de damno et par utriusque causa sit, quare non potentior sit qui teneat, quam qui persequitur?

Paul in the seventeenth book *On Plautius*:

Next consider how to understand the rule established by Republican jurists, that the obligation persists whenever the debtor's fault (*culpa*) intervenes. Indeed, if the promissor brought it about that he could less easily perform, the rule is readily applicable; but if he only delayed (in paying), there is doubt whether his earlier default (*mora*) is purged if he is not in default later.

The younger Celsus writes that a person who had promised to deliver Stichus and was in default (*mora*) can purge this default by later tendering (Stichus); for this is a question of what is right and proper (*bonum et aequum*); in this area, he says, many destructive mistakes are made under the authority of legal science. And this is clearly the acceptable view, which Julian also follows. For when it is it is a question of loss and each party has an equal case, why shouldn't the party who defends prevail over the one who sues?

The Problem
Seius has promised by stipulation to deliver the slave Stichus by January 1, but Stichus dies of natural causes before delivery. Is Seius liable under the stipulation if he had not made a timely delivery and thereby fallen into default (*mora*)?

Discussion
1. Persistence. The Republican rule on persistence of the obligation can best be understood as a fiction. *Pauli Sent.* 5.7.4, puts the fiction this way: "When the object of a stipulation perishes by the promissor's act, action can then be brought on the stipulation as if the object (still) existed." Why was such a fiction necessary?

2. The Effect of Default. When performance becomes impossible after default, the promissor is liable even if he or she is not at fault. Ulpian, D. 45.1.82.1: "If a slave dies after default (*mora*), he is nonetheless liable as if the slave lived." Another fiction, but this time with no reference to the promissor's act. Why? On default, see Case 30, where purging default is also discussed.

CASE 29: Early Payment

D. 12.6.17 (Ulpianus libro secundo ad Edictum)

Nam si cum moriar dare promisero et antea solvam, repetere me non posse Celsus ait: quae sententia vera est.

D. 12.6.10 (Paulus libro septimo ad Sabinum)

In diem debitor adeo debitor est, ut ante diem solutum repetere non possit.

D. 12.6.16 pr. (Pomponius libro quinto decimo ad Sabinum)

Sub condicione debitum per errorem solutum pendente quidem condicione repetitur, condicione autem existente repeti non potest.

Ulpian in the second book *On the Edict*:

For if (by stipulation) I promised delivery "when I die" and I pay before then, Celsus says I cannot recover (my payment); this opinion is correct.

Paul in the seventh book *On Sabinus*:

A debtor under a deadline (for payment) is (nonetheless) a debtor to the extent that he cannot recover what is paid before the deadline.

Pomponius in the fifteenth book *On Sabinus*:

A debt subject to a condition, if paid by mistake while the condition is (still) pending, is recoverable; but when the condition occurs, it cannot be recovered.

Discussion

1. Early Payment of a Debt. You owe me 50,000, due in two years on July 1. You mistakenly believe that your debt is due in one year and you pay me then. When you realize that you paid early, you want your money back so you can make use of it in the meantime; and so you sue using a *condictio* for a mistaken payment (see Case 225). Why will you lose?

2. Conditional Debt. The result is different if you mistakenly pay a debt while a condition is pending. This may help to explain the more usual rule on early payment. Do you see the logic, and does it make sense to you?

CASE 30: Liability after Default

D. 45.1.113.1 (Proculus libro secundo Epistularum)

Cum venderet aliquis, promisit emptori fideiussores praestari et rem venditam liberari: quae ut liberetur, nunc desiderat emptor: in mora est is, qui ea stipulatione id futurum promisit: quaero quid iuris sit. Proculus respondit: tanti litem aestimari oportet, quanti actoris interest.

D. 45.1.114 (Ulpianus libro septimo decimo ad Sabinum)

Si fundum certo die praestari stipuler et per promissorem steterit, quo minus ea die praestetur, consecuturum me, quanti mea intersit moram facti non esse.

Proculus in the second book of his *Letters*:

A seller promised to provide the buyer with sureties and that the object of sale be freed (from third-party claims). Now the buyer seeks that it be freed (from possible claims), and the person who promised that this would be done is in default (*mora*). I ask what the law is. Proculus responds: The lawsuit should be evaluated for the amount of the plaintiff's interest (*quanti actoris interest*).

Ulpian in the seventeenth book *On Sabinus*:

If I stipulate for delivery of a farm on a specified day and the promissor is responsible for non-delivery on that day, (a jurist holds) that I will obtain the amount of my interest in default not occurring.

Discussion

1. **Defining Default.** A debtor's default (*mora*) occurs when he does not perform in response to the creditor's legitimate demand (so, at least, *Pauli Sent.* 3.8.4). Marcian, D. 22.1.32 pr. = Case 116), observes that: "Default depends not on the matter (*res*) but on the person (of the defaulter), i.e., if when called upon (to do so) he does not pay at a suitable place. This will be investigated by the *iudex* . . . since it is more a matter of fact than of law." This is much easier when the contract itself has a fixed date for performance (*dies*), as in the present Case; unexcused failure to perform by the fixed date is quite commonly default and hence breach of contract.

2. **Purging Default.** As Case 28 indicates, the promissor may purge default by tendering performance even after default. This raises two problems. First, can the promisee reject performance and then sue on the total default? The answer, as it seems, is no. Why would the jurists take this position, which in some cases may well be harmful to the promisee—for instance, if the promisee has in the meantime contracted for a substitute performance from someone else? (But see also Case 32.) Second, although the promissor performs after default, the promisee may still seek damages based on the late performance. As this Case indicates, the measure of damages is the

promisee's "interest" (*quanti mea interest*) in the breach not having occurred. Ulpian does not define this measure, but Paul, D. 46.8.13 pr., suggests: "as much as I lose or was able to gain," indicating at least some consequential damages. How clear is this as a measure? The concept of "interest" is an important measure of damages in Roman contract law; try to clarify its definition in subsequent Cases throughout the Casebook.

CASE 31: Default and Partial Performance

D. 45.1.113 pr. (Proculus libro secundo Epistularum)

Cum stipulatus sim mihi, Procule, si opus arbitratu meo ante kalendas Iunias effectum non sit, poenam, et protuli diem: putasne vere me posse dicere arbitratu meo opus effectum non esse ante kalendas Iunias, cum ipse arbitrio meo aliam diem operi laxiorem dederim? Proculus respondit: non sine causa distinguendum est interesse, utrum per promissorem mora non fuisset, quo minus opus ante kalendas Iunias ita, uti stipulatione comprehensum erat, perficeretur, an, cum iam opus effici non posset ante kalendas Iunias, stipulator diem in kalendas Augustas protulisset. Nam si tum diem stipulator protulit, cum iam opus ante kalendas iunias effici non poterat, puto poenam esse commissam nec ad rem pertinere, quod aliquod tempus ante kalendas iunias fuit, quo stipulator non desideravit id ante kalendas Iunias effici, id est quo non est arbitratus ut fieret quod fieri non poterat. Aut si hoc falsum est, etiam si stipulator pridie kalendas Iunias mortuus esset, poena commissa non esset, quoniam mortuus arbitrari non potuisset et aliquod tempus post mortem eius operi perficiendo superfuisset. Et propemodum etiam si ante kalendas Iunias [futurum] <certum> esse coepit opus ante eam diem effici non posse, poena commissa est.

Proculus in the second book of his *Letters*:

Dear Proculus: I stipulated for a penalty (*poena*) payable to me if in my judgment a job was not completed before the Kalends of June. I (later) extended the deadline. Do you think I can say that in my judgment the job was not completed before the Kalends of June since I chose to give another, more extended deadline for the job?

Proculus responds: Not without reason a distinction should be made as to whether the promissor was not responsible for the default (*mora*) preventing completion of the work before the Kalends of June as provided in the stipulation; or whether, when the job could not be done before the Kalends of June, the stipulator extended the deadline to the Kalends of August. For if the stipulator extended the deadline at a time when the job could not be completed before the Kalends of June, I think the penalty falls due; nor is it relevant that there was a period of time before the Kalends of June during which the stipulator did not demand completion before the Kalends of June, i.e., during which he did not judge that the impossible could be done.

If this (view) is false, (then) the penalty would not be due even if the stipulator died on the day before the Kalends of June, since a dead man could not make a judgment and some time would remain after his death for completing the job. And it is virtually the case that the penalty was due even if before the Kalends of June it became certain the job could not be completed by that date.

Discussion

1. A *Responsum*. This fragment has the literary form of a question put to Proculus by a petitioner, followed by the jurist's reply (*responsum*), a mode frequently employed by the jurists for discussing legal problems in an abstract but user-friendly way (somewhat like the illustrations in modern Restatements of the law). Since arguably extraneous details are mostly omitted, it is usually impossible to tell whether real cases or inquiries underlie such juristic discussions.

2. **Penalties.** In this Case, someone who contracted out for performance of a construction job (probably under the contract of *locatio conductio*; see Chapter V.A.4) also took a stipulation from the contractor for a penalty payable if the job was not completed by June 1. Within wide limits this was possible; the penalty need not be the parties' estimate of "liquidated damages," that is, it need not bear any close relationship to damages actually suffered or likely to be suffered, and so it could be used, in effect, to compel performance (*in terrorem*). In general, the penalty would not become due until the set date, even if performance was obviously impossible; see Paul, D. 2.11.10.1, quoted earlier in the Discussion on Case 21. The last sentence of the present Case was probably not meant to suggest otherwise. On penalty stipulations, see Cases 48–49.

3. **The Reasons for Delay.** The promisee in this Case was concerned because he had postponed the contractual completion date after the delay in completion arose. Proculus makes a distinction. First, the contractor may not have been responsible for the delay; for instance, building materials may have arrived late because of a storm. If so, what result? Would the promisee have been able to invoke the penalty clause had he not voluntarily extended the deadline?

   Second, however, if the contractor was responsible for the delay, such that timely completion had become impossible, then the promisee can invoke the penalty even though he extended the deadline. What, then, was the purpose of the extension? Perhaps because the promisee placed priority on getting the building completed before settling any accounts? What if it had not been entirely clear whether the job could not be completed before the deadline?

4. **Partial Performance and Penalties.** It appears that the promissor in this Case had at least partially performed before June 1. Does that affect the amount of the penalty? Paul, D. 19.1.47, discusses the following problem: A seller of building materials gave a stipulation for a money penalty if they were not delivered in good condition; the seller then died after partial delivery. Paul rules that the seller's heir can be sued for the entire penalty (plus interest if the suit is brought in sale). Is this decision justified?

5. Penalties Without Time Limits. A stipulation runs: "If you do not deliver (the slave) Pamphilus, do you solemnly promise to pay 100,000 sesterces?" When does this stipulation fall due? Papinian, D. 45.1.115.2, reports an earlier school controversy; Pegasus had held that it falls due only when performance becomes impossible, while Sabinus argued "from the parties' intention" (*ex sententia contrahentium*) that the promisee could sue on the stipulation as soon as the slave could be conveyed but was not, with a delay only for as long as the promissor was not responsible for non-delivery. Papinian's discussion is worth reading in its entirety.

CASE 32: A Building Contract

D. 45.1.137.3 (Venuleius libro primo Stipulationum)

Item qui insulam fieri spopondit, non utique conquisitis undique fabris et plurimis operis adhibitis festinare debet nec rursus utroque aut altero contentus esse, sed modus adhibendus est secundum rationem diligentis aedificatoris et temporum locorumque. Item si non inchoetur opus, id tantum aestimetur, quod in illo intervallo effici potuit. Transactoque tempore, quo insulam consummare oportuerit, si postea aedificetur, liberetur reus, sicut liberatur, qui se daturum spopondit, si quandoque tradit.

Venuleius in the first book of his *Stipulations:*

Likewise, a person who promised by stipulation to build an apartment building need not, in any case, rush by gathering craftsmen from all over and employing numerous laborers, nor again (should he) be satisfied with one or two. A middle ground should be sought, in accordance with the standards of a careful builder (*diligens aedificator*) as well as the time and the place. So if the job is not begun, evaluation (at trial) is of what could be completed in that space of time. Even after the time has passed in which he should finish the building, the defendant will be discharged if he constructs thereafter, just as a person who promised delivery is discharged if he hands (it) over at some time.

Discussion

1. **Absence of a Time Limit.** If a stipulation for a performance of long duration does not contain a deadline, how should law construct one? In D. 45.1.137.2 (the fragment preceding this Case), Venuleius discusses a stipulation for money to be paid in a distant city, with no deadline. He argues that: "we should refer the whole matter to a *iudex*, i.e., to a reasonable man (*vir bonus*), who will estimate in how much time a careful *paterfamilias* could do what he promised he would do"; extraordinary measures (traveling night and day, etc.) are not required. How is that theory applied in the present Case? How would Venuleius define "the standards of a careful builder"? What evidence might be available?

2. **Purging Delay: A Qualification.** Like Cases 28 and 30, this Case appears to suggest that the builder has unlimited time, after default, to perform. However, Paul, D. 45.1.84, adds an important qualification: the customer can end the "grace period" by bringing suit, and performance after judicial "joinder of issue" (*litis contestatio*) then does not help the builder. In terms of the practical dynamics between the two parties, what is the effect of this qualification? By bringing suit, the customer effectively terminates the contract. Shouldn't he previously have had the power to refuse performance?

CASE 33: A Bottomry Loan

D. 45.1.122.1 (Scaevola libro vicensimo octavo Digestorum)

Callimachus mutuam pecuniam nauticam accepit a Sticho servo [Seii] <Lucii Titii> in provincia Syria civitate Beryto usque Brentesium: idque creditum esse in omnes navigii dies ducentos, sub pignoribus et hypothecis mercibus a Beryto comparatis et Brentesium perferendis et quas Brentesio empturus esset et per navem Beryto invecturus: convenitque inter eos, uti, cum Callimachus Brentesium pervenisset, inde intra idus septembres, quae tunc proximae futurae essent, aliis mercibus emptis et in navem immissis ipse in Syriam per navigium proficiscatur, aut, si intra diem supra scriptam non reparasset merces nec enavigasset de ea civitate, redderet universam continuo pecuniam quasi perfecto navigio et praestaret sumptus omnes prosequentibus eam pecuniam, ut in urbem Romam eam deportarent: eaque sic recte dari fieri fide roganti Sticho servo Lucii Titii promisit Callimachus. Et cum ante idus supra scriptas secundum conventionem mercibus in navem impositis cum Erote conservo Stichi quasi in provinciam Syriam perventurus enavigavit: quaesitum est nave submersa, cum secundum cautionem Callimachus merces Berytum perferendas in navem imposisset eo tempore, quo iam pecuniam Brentesio reddere Romam perferendam deberet, an nihil prosit Erotis consensus, qui cum eo missus erat, cuique nihil amplius de pecunia supra scripta post diem conventionis permissum vel mandatum erat, quam ut eam receptam Romam perferret, et nihilo minus actione ex stipulatu Callimachus de pecunia domino Stichi teneatur. Respondit secundum ea quae proponerentur teneri. Item quaero, si Callimacho post diem supra scriptam naviganti Eros supra scriptus servus consenserit, an actionem domino suo semel adquisitam adimere potuerit. Respondit non potuisse, sed fore exceptioni locum, si servo arbitrium datum esset eam pecuniam quocumque tempore in quemvis locum reddi.

Scaevola in the twenty-eighth book of his *Digests*:

At Berytus in the province of Syria, (a freedman named) Callimachus received from Stichus, the slave of <Lucius Titius>, a bottomry loan for (a voyage to) Brundisium. The loan was for the entire two hundred days of the voyage, with real securities (*pignora et hypothecae*) in the goods bought from Berytus for transport to Brundisium, as well as in what he would buy at Brundisium and convey by ship (back) to Berytus. They agreed that after Callimachus reached Brundisium, he would buy other goods, put them on board the ship, and travel by sea to Syria before the upcoming Ides of September (Sept. 13); or, if he did not repurchase goods and sail from that city before the above date, he would at once pay the entire amount (of the loan) as if the voyage was ended, and also pay all costs to those who recovered the money for transport to Rome. Stichus, the slave of Lucius Titius, asked that these things be thus properly done, and Callimachus promised on his honor (*fides*).

In accord with the agreement, the goods were loaded on board (at Brundisium) before the above mentioned Ides (of September), and then he (Callimachus), together with Stichus' co-slave Eros, set sail intending to reach the province of Syria. The ship sank when Callimachus, in accord with the stipulation, had loaded onto the ship the goods to be carried to Berytus at a time when he ought (instead) to have paid the money at Brundisium for its transport to Rome. It was asked whether he was helped by the agreement of Eros who had been sent with him and who had no further authorization or instruction concerning the above mentioned money except that he receive it and transport it to Rome after the date in the agreement, and notwithstanding (Eros' assent) Callimachus is liable for the money to Stichus' master in an action on the stipulation.

He (Scaevola) responds that, according to the facts as proposed, he is liable.

Likewise, if Eros, the above-mentioned slave, agreed to Callimachus' sailing after the above-mentioned date, I ask whether (by doing so) he can take away an action his master had once acquired. He (Scaevola) responds that he cannot, but there will be grounds for a defense if it was in the slave's discretion at what time and to what place the money should be returned.

The Problem

Callimachus, evidently a freedman, borrowed money at Beirut from Stichus, the slave of a certain Lucius Titius. The loan was secured by the cargo Callimachus was shipping to the Italian port of Brindisi. Stichus stipulated for repayment of the loan. Under ordinary circumstances, the loan was to be repayable, with hefty interest, when the ship reached Brindisi; but if the cargo was lost, Callimachus would owe nothing. However, this bottomry loan also included a renewal provision for the return voyage with a new cargo to Beirut, under the condition that the ship had to set sail by 13 September, near the end of the normal Mediterranean sailing season. Callimachus got a second cargo on board by that date, but evidently did not set sail until later, with the apparent consent of Eros, another slave of Lucius Titius, who may or may not have had the legal authority to waive this contract provision. (The fragment is a bit discombobulated, but this is the likeliest interpretation.)

Discussion

1. Bottomry Loans. A bottomry loan (*faenus nauticum*) is a complex marine insurance device in which the owner of a ship or of its cargo takes a loan at the point of departure, with the property as security for the loan; if the ship reaches its destination, the loan is repayable at what looks like a high rate of interest, but actually takes account of the risk since the loan is forgiven in the event of shipwreck. The loan is effectively repaid out of profits at the point of arrival, either on the charge for transport or on resale of the goods.

Follow as best you can Scaevola's efforts to interpret the stipulation in light of the subsequent shipwreck. The crucial issues are as follows: Is Callimachus (or his master) liable if the goods were aboard by September 13, but the ship did not leave until after that date, and does it make any difference if the lender's apparent agent gave permission for the delayed departure? Do you find Scaevola's responses convincing? How does Scaevola handle the issue of Eros' authority to allow a late departure? The "defense" referred to at the end of the Case is the defense of deceit (*exceptio doli*); see Cases 35–36.

PART E

Defenses against Liability under a Stipulation

In principle, as we have seen, a stipulation results in liability if the promissor fails to execute the promise. In archaic law, this logic was perhaps inescapable. A stipulation in the form, "Do you promise to pay fifty?" resulted in liability for fifty if the promise went unfulfilled.

Classical law did not entirely reject this principle. However, at least by the late Republic there had evolved several procedural "defenses" (*exceptiones*) that a defendant could use to escape liability in particular circumstances. Suppose, for instance, that the stipulation to pay fifty had been extorted through force: the defendant was allowed to insert into the trial *formula* a "defense of duress" (*exceptio metus*) ordering the *iudex* to reject the plaintiff's claim if it could be shown that the promise had come about through extortion. Note, however, that the defendant had to claim any such defenses from the Praetor at the outset of the trial. Failure to do so resulted in loss of the defense. To this extent, the strict logic of stipulations still prevailed.

By far the most important of these defenses is the "defense of deceit" (*exceptio doli*) ordering the *iudex* to reject the plaintiff's claim if it is irreparably tainted by the plaintiff's deliberate past or present "deceit" (*dolus*). In practice, this defense was used in order to enable judicial examination of the underlying "cause" (*causa*) for the stipulation. (The theory of *causa* was discussed earlier in Part C.) If, for example, a promissor gave an absolute stipulation to "pay fifty" in the expectation of receiving a loan of fifty from the promisee, it would plainly be "deceitful" for the promisee to sue for the fifty without first making the loan. The "cause" for the stipulation has clearly not been realized.

The defense of deceit and other defenses therefore could help to expose for judicial review the circumstances in which a stipulation had been made, but at the undeniable cost of undermining the reliability of the stipulation as a formal contract.

CASE 34: The Action on the Stipulation

Gaius, *Institutiones* 4.136–137

136. Item admonendi sumus, si cum ipso agamus, qui incertum promiserit, ita nobis formulam esse propositam, ut praescriptio inserta sit formulae loco demonstrationis hoc modo: "Iudex esto. Quod Aulus Agerius de Numerio Negidio incertum stipulatus est, cuius rei dies fuit, quidquid ob eam rem Numerium Negidium Aulo Agerio dare facere oportet," et reliqua. 137. At si cum . . . fideiussore agatur, praescribi solet . . . in persona uero fideiussoris: "Ea res agatur, quod Numerius Negidius de Lucio Titio incertum fide sua esse iussit, cuius rei dies fuit"; deinde formula subicitur.

Gaius in the fourth book of his *Institutes*:

136. We must further be warned that, when we are suing someone who promised an indefinite thing (*incertum*), the *formula* that is declared for us has a preamble inserted in the *formula* in place of the statement of cause (*demonstratio*), like this: "Let X be the *iudex*. Whereas the plaintiff stipulated for an indefinite thing from the defendant, the deadline for performance (*dies*) now having passed, whatever on this basis the defendant ought to give to or do for the plaintiff," etc. 137. But in an action with a surety (*fideiussor*) the usual preamble in the surety's case is: "Let the issue be that the defendant gave a guarantee on his honor (*fideiussio*) for Lucius Titius for an indefinite amount, the deadline having passed"; then the *formula* is added.

Discussion

1. **The *Formula*.** Book 4 of Gaius' *Institutes* is the only surviving lengthy discussion of civil procedure in the Classical period of Roman law; it was written ca. 160 CE. Here Gaius gives the *formula* to be used when suit is brought on a stipulation for an indefinite thing, an *incertum*, which can mean any performance that does not involve conveyance of a particular object or a definite sum of money (or other fungible, such as wheat). For *incerta*, the *condictio* was initially unavailable, and so an action straightforwardly on the stipulation was devised. Gaius' model *formula* uses "John Doe" names for the plaintiff (Aulus Agerius, from *agere*, "to sue") and the defendant (Numerius Negidius, from *negare*, "to deny").

   Note especially that the *formula* (which will be forwarded to the *iudex* after the actual names of the litigants are substituted and the Praetor grants a trial) envisages a sort of strict liability arising from the stipulation, with no defense. Therefore a defendant must be alert, during the first stage of the trial before the Praetor, about getting the relevant defenses into the *formula*, or these defenses will be forfeited. Note also that the exact nature of the *incertum* is not specified in the *formula*; in this respect it resembles the *condictio*.

Several sources from the late Classical period indicate that by then a new action, called the *condictio incerti*, had been introduced for cases where the amount of damages had to be estimated by the judge.

2. **The Surety**. Section 137 gives the *formula* when a personal surety is sued on a promissor's debt that he has guaranteed. On sureties, see Cases 41–46.

CASE 35: The Defense of Deceit and the Theory of Cause

D. 44.4.2.3 (Ulpianus libro septuagensimo sexto ad Edictum)

Circa primam speciem, quibus ex causis exceptio haec locum habeat, haec sunt, quae tractari possunt. Si quis sine causa ab aliquo fuerit stipulatus, deinde ex ea stipulatione experiatur, exceptio utique doli mali ei nocebit: licet enim eo tempore, quo stipulabatur, nihil dolo malo admiserit, tamen dicendum est eum, cum litem contestatur, dolo facere, qui perseveret ex ea stipulatione petere: et si cum interponeretur, iustam causam habuit, tamen nunc nullam idoneam causam habere videtur. Proinde et si crediturus pecuniam stipulatus est nec credidit et si certa fuit causa stipulationis, quae tamen aut non est secuta aut finita est, dicendum erit nocere exceptionem.

Ulpian in the seventy-sixth book *On the Edict*:

Regarding the first type of cases where this defense (of deceit, the *exceptio doli*) is relevant, the following matters can be examined. If someone stipulated from another without cause (*sine causa*) and then sued on this stipulation, the defense of deceit will generally bar him (from winning). For even if he committed no *dolus malus* when the stipulation was made, still it must be ruled that at joinder of issue (*litis contestatio*) he acts with *dolus* by continuing to sue on this stipulation.

Likewise, if he had a legitimate cause (*iusta causa*) when the stipulation was taken but is held to lack good cause now. Accordingly, if a person who was going to lend money took a stipulation (for repayment) and then did not make the loan, and if there was a specific cause for a stipulation that was either not pursued or not carried out, it will be ruled that the defense harms (the plaintiff).

The Problem

Aulus, who mistakenly believed that Seius owed him money, stipulated for its payment; if Aulus sues on the stipulation, does Seius have a defense? What if Seius actually did owe Aulus the money when the stipulation was made, but not when Aulus sued? What if Aulus made his promise in the belief that Seius would lend him money, but Seius reneged on the loan?

Discussion

1. Two Kinds of Deceit. The defense of deceit (*exceptio doli*) is inserted into the middle of the *formula* for the trial. The model *formula* reads: "if in this matter nothing has been done or is being done through the plaintiff's deceit" (*si in ea re nihil dolo malo Auli Agerii factum sit neque fiat*). As Gaius, *Inst.* 4.119, comments, this makes condemnation conditional on a finding that no deceit by the plaintiff was present either at the time of the transaction or at the time of the trial. Give examples of both types of deceit. How does Ulpian relate the defense to the theory of *causa*? Would the defense also be available in the case of an "immoral" *causa*?

2. Failure of Cause. When a stipulation was made for repayment of a loan that was not then forthcoming, why do the jurists not simply hold that since the *causa* of the stipulation has failed, the stipulation is unenforceable? See Case 37.

CASE 36: A Loan Not Provided; A Subsequent Pact

Gaius, *Institutiones* 4.115–116b

115. Sequitur, ut de exceptionibus dispiciamus. 116. Conparatae sunt autem exceptiones defendendorum eorum gratia, cum quibus agitur. saepe enim accidit, ut quis iure ciuili teneatur, sed iniquum sit eum iudicio condemnari. 116a. Velut si stipulatus sim a te pecuniam tamquam credendi causa numeraturus nec numerauerim. Nam eam pecuniam a te peti posse certum est. dare enim te oportet, cum ex stipulatu tenearis; sed quia iniquum est te eo nomine condemnari, placet per exceptionem doli mali te defendi debere. 116b. Item si pactus fuero tecum, ne id, quod mihi debeas, a te petam, nihilo minus id ipsum a te petere possum dari mihi oportere, quia obligatio pacto conuento non tollitur; sed placet debere me petentem per exceptionem pacti conuenti repelli.

Gaius in the fourth book of his *Institutes*:

115. Next, let us look at defenses (*exceptiones*). 116. Defenses were devised to protect those who are sued. For it often occurs that someone is liable at Civil Law (*iure civili*), but it would be unfair that he be condemned in a trial.

116a. For instance, if I stipulated from you for money (as repayment) on the pretext that I was about to provide it (to you) as a loan, and I did not provide it, it is settled that this money can be claimed from you, for you ought to pay since you are liable on the stipulation; but because it is unfair that you be condemned on this account, it is held that you should be protected through the defense of deceit (*dolus malus*).

116b. Likewise, if I (informally) arranged with you that I not claim from you what you owe me (because of a stipulation), I can still claim from you that this must be delivered to me, since an obligation is not discharged by informal agreement; but it is held that if I sue, I am defeated by the defense of an informal agreement (*exceptio pacti conventi*).

Discussion

1. Two Defenses. Gaius clearly sets out the theory behind the defenses he describes. The stipulated debt remains binding at Civil Law (why?), but in some instances a claim based on the stipulation can be defeated by an *exceptio* inserted into the trial *formula*. How does the defense of deceit (*exceptio doli*) differ from the defense of an informal agreement (*exceptio pacti conventi*)? Some jurists (e.g., Gaius, *Inst.* 3.179) indicate that the defense of deceit was also available in the case of a later informal agreement waiving a claim.

2. Payment Where a Defense Is Available. What happens if the promissor pays money owed under a stipulation, in circumstances when a claim brought on the stipulation could have been defeated by a defense? Ulpian,

Frag. Vat. 266 (= D. 12.6.26.3): "We construe a payment as not due not only if it is not owed at all, but also if it cannot be claimed because of some defense that is permanent. Therefore this too can be recovered if someone pays when protected by a permanent defense." (The Digest version adds that this would be untrue if the payer knew of the defense and paid anyway; the idea seems to be that otherwise the debtor paid mistakenly, forgetting about the subsequent pact.) In this Case, the agreement in 116b that the promisee would not press a claim gives rise to a permanent defense. But if the parties had informally agreed that, for instance, payment would not be claimed before January 15, payment before that date would not be recoverable (compare Case 29). On the *condictio indebiti* (claim for restitution of a payment not owed), see Chapter VIII.B.

3. Counter-Defenses. Gaius, *Inst.* 4.126, raises the following problem: You owe money to me, e.g., under a stipulation. Subsequently, we informally agree that I will not claim the money; but later we again informally agree that I can, in fact, claim the money. I then bring suit for non-payment, and you raise the defense of an informal pact. This defense will succeed unless I have a counter-defense (a *replicatio*) also inserted into the *formula*, in a sort of point-counterpoint fashion. The substance of the counter-defense is that your defense is invalid if we subsequently agreed that suit could in fact be brought. How does Gaius' discussion illustrate the formalism of Roman judicial procedure?

4. Contemporaneous Agreements. What if the parties reduce their agreement to a stipulation, but also simultaneously make a side agreement not included in the stipulation? Can the promisee use the *condictio* to sue on the side agreement, as if it were part of the stipulation? The original answer was surely no, since the *condictio* is narrowly confined to the stipulation's wording. But in the late Classical period this rule was probably relaxed so as to allow the pact to be incorporated into the stipulation. See Discussion 2 on Case 57.

CASE 37: Obstruction by the Promisee

D. 45.1.105 (Iavolenus libro secondo Epistularum)

Stipulatus sum Damam aut Erotem servum dari: cum Damam dares, ego quo minus acciperem, in mora fui: mortuus est Dama: an putes me ex stipulatu actionem habere? Respondit: secundum Massurii Sabini opinionem puto te ex stipulatu agere non posse: nam is recte existimabat, si per debitorem mora non esset, quo minus id quod debebat solveret, continuo eum debito liberari.

Javolenus in the second book of his *Letters*:

I stipulated for delivery of a slave, (either) Dama or Eros. When you tendered Dama, I was in default (*mora*) in accepting him, and Dama died. Do you think I have an action on the stipulation (for Eros)?

He (Javolenus) replied: In accord with the opinion of Massurius Sabinus, I think that you cannot sue on the stipulation. For he correctly thinks that if the debtor's default was not the cause for his not paying what he owed, he is immediately released from the debt.

Discussion

1. Delay by the Promisee. In Roman law generally, when a creditor unjustifiably delays in accepting performance from a debtor, the latter is then liable only for deliberate harm (*dolus*), but no longer for carelessness: Case 126, and also Paul, D. 18.6.5 (sale); Pomponius, D. 24.3.9 (dowry). In this case, however, after the promisee delayed in taking delivery, the death of the tendered slave Dama (apparently with no fault on the promissor's part) raised a question as to whether the promissor, who had tendered Dama, now had a duty to deliver Eros instead. Sabinus and Javolenus free the promissor from further liability. Do you agree with this outcome?

2. Losing Money. Marcellus, D. 46.3.72 pr., sets a more complex problem. Suppose that a debtor offers repayment to a creditor who refuses it "without legitimate cause" (*sine iusta causa*), and the debtor then loses the money "through no fault of his own" (*sine sua culpa*). The creditor then sues on the debt. Can the debtor defend himself by interposing the defense of deceit? Marcellus says yes, arguing that: "It is unfair that he be liable for the lost money since he would not be liable if the creditor had wanted to accept it." Marcellus relies on the analogy of the ruling in the present Case; but money is a fungible and arguably different from a promised slave. How should this problem be resolved?

CASE 38: The Defense of Non-Payment of Money

C. 4.30.3 (Imp. Antoninus A. Demetriae)

Si ex cautione tua, licet hypotheca data, conveniri coeperis, exceptione opposita seu doli seu non numeratae pecuniae compelletur petitor probare pecuniam tibi esse numeratam: quo non impleto absolutio sequetur.

The Emperor Caracalla to Demetria (215 CE):

If you come to be sued on your guarantee (*cautio*, for repaying a debt), although a security (*hypotheca*) was given, the plaintiff must prove the money was paid to you if there is interposed a defense of deceit (*dolus*) or of non-payment of money (*pecunia non numerata*). If this (payment) was not made, your exoneration (from the claim) will follow.

Discussion

1. The Defense. Several late Classical sources mention the defense of non-payment of money. It applies when a person seeking credit promises re-payment to the creditor before receiving the loan; should suit be brought on this stipulation, the defense can be raised that the loan was never actu-ally paid to the defendant. Gaius (in the previous Case) gives the defense of deceit in such a situation, and it is not entirely clear how the defense of non-payment of money differs, if at all, in result; but the most prob-able difference is that, whereas a defendant who used the plaintiff's deceit (*dolus*) as a defense was obliged to prove the deceit, a defendant who used non-payment as a defense forced the plaintiff to prove that payment had actually been made—presumably through witnesses or account books. (If this is right, the compilers altered the constitution.) What is the significance of this shift in the burden of proof? Why might it have been desirable? Alexander, C. 4.30.7, also allows the promissor in these circumstances to sue to have the stipulation declared void.

2. Security. In this Case, the promissor had used property in order to secure performance of the stipulation, a common Roman practice; if the debtor failed to perform, the creditor could seize and sell the property. As the parties agreed, the debtor's security (called a hypothec, *hypotheca*) might or might not be initially placed in the creditor's control. If the security is already in the creditor's hands, Septimius Severus and Caracalla, C. 4.30.4 (= 8.32.1; 197 CE), allow the pledger to reclaim it if the creditor had not made the payment on which the stipulation had been based.

3. The Defense of Non-Delivery of Goods. This is the reciprocal. Julian, D. 19.1.25, puts a case in which the owner of grapes that are still on the vine sells them to a buyer, who is to harvest them himself. Although this would normally be an informal contract of sale (see Chapter IV), the buyer

in this Case promised payment through a stipulation. The stipulator then forbade the buyer from gathering the grapes, but brought suit on the stipulation for the price. If the informal contract of sale had been the basis of the lawsuit, a special defense would not have been necessary, since the contract would be governed by the rules of *bona fides*. But in stipulation the problem is more difficult; why? Julian gives the buyer a defense for non-delivery of the goods.

The possible intersection between formal stipulation and informal contracts raises some interesting problems. Suppose, in Julian's case, that after the terms of the sale had been arranged, the buyer of the grapes had refused to answer the seller's stipulation; would the agreement still be valid as an informal contract of sale? Paul, D. 45.1.35.2, indicates that it would. Do you agree? Was it part of the seller's terms that the buyer promise payment by stipulation? Why might the seller have wanted this?

PART F

Some Special Types of Stipulation (Novation, Suretyship, etc.)

Stipulations were commonly used for particular legal purposes, not infrequently as annexes to larger agreements. These specially designed stipulations, which are often intricately worded, could be used to transform an existing debt into a new form (novation, *novatio*) or to provide for a subsidiary creditor (*adstipulatio*); but their most important use was for creating personal suretyship, in which one person (usually called a "guarantor," *fideiussor*) assures performance by another person, the principal debtor. Today, such a personal guarantee is considerably less common than real security (the pledge of property, as in a mortgage), but the Romans made heavy use of *fideiussio*.

The Roman law of suretyship has a long and complex history; the Cases that follow offer no more than the most cursory introduction to the institution. Normally, suretyship arises when a creditor, or a potential creditor, lacks confidence in a debtor's ability to pay a debt or otherwise to perform (as in a construction contract). The surety is a third party who, usually at the debtor's request (through the contract of mandate, *mandatum*), guarantees to the creditor that the debt will be paid. The creditor then has the option of suing the surety for payment, while the surety, in turn, is forced to look to the debtor for recovery of anything that he or she has paid to the creditor. This is a delicate and risky relationship, in which it is often very difficult to protect the legitimate interests of all three parties.

This Part concludes by examining two other situations in which stipulations were regularly used to back up other contracts, through express warranties and through penalty clauses.

CASE 39: Novation of Debt

Gaius, *Institutiones* 3.176–177

176. Praeterea nouatione tollitur obligatio ueluti si quod tu mihi debeas, a Titio dari stipulatus sim; nam interuentu nouae personae noua nascitur obligatio et prima tollitur translata in posteriorem, adeo ut interdum, licet posterior stipulatio inutilis sit, tamen prima nouationis iure tollatur, ueluti si quod mihi debes, a Titio post mortem eius uel a muliere pupilloue sine tutoris auctoritate stipulatus fuero; quo casu rem amitto; nam et prior debitor liberatur, et posterior obligatio nulla est. non idem iuris est, si a seruo stipulatus fuero; nam tunc prior proinde adhuc obligatus tenetur, ac si postea a nullo stipulatus fuissem. 177. Sed si eadem persona sit, a qua postea stipuler, ita demum nouatio fit, si quid in posteriore stipulatione noui sit, forte si condicio uel dies aut sponsor adiciatur aut detrahatur.

Gaius in the third book of his *Institutes*:

176. Further, an obligation is discharged by novation, e.g., if I stipulated that what you owe to me be given (to me) by Titius (instead). Through the intervention of a different person, a new obligation arises and the earlier one is discharged by being transformed into the later one, to such an extent that sometimes the earlier one is legally discharged even though the later stipulation is ineffective, e.g., if I stipulate that what you owe me (is to be paid) by Titius after his death, or (that it be paid) by a woman or a ward without a guardian's authorization. In this case I lose the obligation, since the earlier debtor is released and the later obligation is void. The law is different if I stipulate from a slave, since then the prior (debtor) remains still obligated, just as if I had not subsequently stipulated from anyone.

177. But also if the person from whom I later stipulated is the same person, a novation occurs if there is something new in the later stipulation, e.g., if a condition or a deadline or a guarantor (*sponsor*) is added or removed.

Discussion

1. Novation. The parties to a novation aim to extinguish an existing obligation and substitute another in its place. The prior obligation must, of course, be a real one, and it must be referred to in the novating stipulation; but, as Gaius indicates, the novation is also required to effect a partial change in this prior obligation, either as to its form (e.g., a stipulation that replaces a debt owed from a sale; see Marcellus, D. 13.5.24), or its terms (the addition or removal of a deadline), or its parties (substitution of a new debtor). Note that the prior obligation is extinguished even if the new one turns out to be void, so care is required. Why might a creditor seek to novate a debt? Usually in two situations: A owes money to B, and B owes the same amount to C, so that novation creates a debt from A to C (delegation of the debtor, see Case 211); or, doubtless much more frequently, the creditor may prefer the relative security of a formal stipulation.

2. Intent to Novate. Ulpian, D. 46.2.2, requires that the parties intend to novate, a requirement not mentioned by Gaius. Usually this would be obvious enough on the face of the stipulation; see, for instance, Ulpian, D. 46.2.6 pr. (there is no novation if the stipulation is "to pay whatever I do not recover from my debtor Titius"). But in some instances it would be hard to tell a novation from the stipulation for a surety; see Case 41.

3. Addition of a Condition. Gaius, *Inst.* 3.179, notes a difficulty when the novating stipulation adds a condition not present in the prior obligation. If the condition fails or (more weakly) has not yet come to pass, does the prior obligation still remain in force? Gaius thought that it did, though he cites authority to the contrary; nonetheless, Gaius apparently allows the debtor under this novation to insert a defense (see Cases 34–36) if the creditor sues on the prior obligation. But there are difficult questions here. For instance, Marcellus, D. 46.3.72.1, discusses a debtor who had defaulted in delivering a slave, and then novated subject to a condition; the slave then died while the condition was still pending. Does the novation purge the debtor's prior default (*mora*)? Marcellus thought it did. Why so?

4. Consolidation of Debts. All existing debts owed by a debtor to a creditor can be consolidated through an Aquilian stipulation, a device invented by the late Republican jurist Aquilius Gallus. Its form was given earlier in Case 12. Does this stipulation have a novating effect?

5. Release from Debt (*Acceptilatio*). A stipulation could also be used to discharge a debt arising from a stipulation; see Gaius, *Inst.* 3.169–172 ("What I promised to you, have you received it?" "I have."). This is effective whether or not actual payment has been received. If the debt was based on other than a stipulation, it could be recast as a stipulation through a novation, and then discharged by a release. Formalism! See also the Discussion on Case 209.

CASE 40: A Secondary Stipulator

Gaius, *Institutiones* 3.110–111

110. Possumus tamen ad id, quod stipulamur, alium adhibere, qui idem stipuletur, quem uulgo adstipulatorem uocamus. 111. Et huic proinde actio conpetit proindeque ei recte soluitur ac nobis; sed quidquid consecutus erit, mandati iudicio nobis restituere cogetur.

Gaius in the third book of his *Institutes*:

110. But for what we stipulate, we can bring in a second person to stipulate for the same thing; he is commonly called a secondary stipulator (*adstipulator*). 111. He has the action (on the stipulation) and, like us, can properly receive payment; but through the action on mandate he must restore to us whatever he may obtain.

Discussion

1. *Adstipulatio*. An *adstipulator* is not a co-creditor, but rather a convenient stand-in for the primary creditor, to whom he is bound by a contract of mandate (*mandatum*: Chapter V.C). As Gaius, *Inst.* 3.117, notes, the institution was especially useful in one situation: "Because a stipulation that something be given to us after our death (i.e., to our heir) is void, an *adstipulator* is summoned so that he can sue after our death; if he recovers anything, he is liable to our heir, in an action on mandate, to restore it." As you should be able to see, this is a work-around.

2. Co-Creditors or Co-Debtors. Stipulation could also be used to create fully shared debt. The mechanism is described by Justinian, *Inst.* 3.16: several creditors would simultaneously put the question, and the debtor would answer all of them at once; or one creditor would put the question, and several debtors would simultaneously answer. (All parties must be present. Formalism!) The parties are then jointly and severally entitled or bound for the entire debt; and if one co-creditor releases the debt, or one co-debtor pays it, the debt is extinguished; see Javolenus, D. 45.2.2. Similar types of fully shared debt are occasionally attested for other contracts, although the jurists generally do not favor them.

CASE 41: Suretyship

Iustinianus, *Institutiones* 3.20 pr.-3

pr. Pro eo qui promittit solent alii obligari, qui fideiussores appellantur, quos homines accipere solent dum curant ut diligentius sibi cautum sit. 1. In omnibus autem obligationibus adsumi possunt, id est sive re sive verbis sive litteris sive consensu contractae fuerint. ac ne illud quidem interest, utrum civilis an naturalis sit obligatio cui adiciatur fideiussor, adeo quidem ut pro servo quoque obligetur, sive extraneus sit qui fideiussorem a servo accipiat, sive ipse dominus in id quod sibi naturaliter debetur. 2. Fideiussor non tantum ipse obligatur, sed etiam heredem obligatum relinquit. 3. Fideiussor et praecedere obligationem et sequi potest.

Justinian in the third book of his *Institutes*:

pr. Third parties called sureties (*fideiussores*) are often obligated on behalf of a promissor. People generally take (sureties) to ensure better protection for themselves. 1. They can be taken for all obligations, i.e., whether they are contracted by a delivery (*re*) or by (formal) words or in writing or by agreement. Nor indeed does it matter whether the obligation to which a surety is added is Civil or Natural, to such an extent that he can be obligated also on behalf of a slave, whether it is an outside party who receives from the slave, or from the master himself, for the amount of the Natural debt to him (the creditor). 2. A surety is not just obligated himself, but also leaves his heir obligated. 3. A surety can both precede and follow an obligation (made by the principal debtor).

Discussion

1. *Fideiussio*. The type of suretyship discussed in this Case is the latest in date of three types that had varying forms and distinct effects; Justinian's discussion derives from Gaius, *Inst.* 3.115–126, where the three types are discussed, but *fideiussio*, the most expansive, is the only one that survives in Justinian's compilation. Gaius, *Inst.* 3.116, gives the stipulation's wording: "Do you order on your honor the same thing (as the primary debtor has promised)?" The effect is to make the surety liable for the principal's debt; but the surety, if the debtor has requested him to act, can then usually collect from the principal through the action on mandate (Case 45). As Justinian states, suretyship is especially useful in reinforcing the so-called Natural obligations undertaken by slaves, since these obligations were not actionable at law. However, the primary debt must be a least a Natural one; thus, a suretyship taken after the principal has been ordered deported (and hence is beyond judgment) is void; see Papinian, D. 46.1.47 pr.

2. False Debts. Celsus, D. 12.6.47, considers a case in which you mistakenly promise to repay money you do not owe, and your surety on this promise then pays the money to the promisee on your account (*nomine tuo*); result: the stipulator (creditor) owes the money to you (unjustified

enrichment; see Chapter VIII.B), and you in turn owe it to the surety (mandate), so everything comes out even, at least in theory.

However, suppose that the surety had paid on his own account what in fact he did not owe by consequence of your mistaken promise. "He can reclaim it from the stipulator (the promisee) since he paid money not owed by the Law of Nations (*ius gentium*). But to the extent he can obtain less (than the full payment) from the person to whom he paid it, he will obtain it from you in an action on mandate, provided that, because he was unaware, he did not defeat the claimant by (utilizing) a defense." Sort this one out, if you can.

CASE 42: Accessory Nature of Suretyship

D. 46.1.8.7 (Ulpianus libro quadragensimo septimo ad Sabinum)

Illud commune est in universis, qui pro aliis obligantur, quod, si fuerint in duriorem causam adhibiti, placuit eos omnino non obligari: in leviorem plane causam accipi possunt, propter quod in minorem summam recte fideiussor accipietur. Item accepto reo pure ipse ex die vel sub condicione accipi potest: enimvero si reus sub condicione sit acceptus, fideiussor pure, non obligabitur.

Ulpian in the forty-seventh book *On Sabinus*:

Common to all who obligate themselves on behalf of others is the rule that if they are subjected to harsher terms (than their principals are), in the prevailing view they are not obligated at all. Obviously, they can be accepted on lighter terms; thus, a surety is properly accepted for a smaller amount (than the principal debtor owes). Likewise, if the principal debtor is accepted unconditionally, he (the surety) can be accepted as from a date or under a condition; but if the principal debtor was accepted under a condition and the surety unconditionally, he (the surety) will not be obligated.

Discussion

1. Harsher Terms. This curious rule seems to result from the rigidity of stipulations: it is not possible simply to roll back the harsher terms that the surety has accepted. So if the principal was obligated for fifty, and the surety took on liability for sixty, the surety's stipulation was entirely void. The same rule is applied if the surety promises something completely different from the principal, e.g., a thousand pecks of grain instead of 10,000 sesterces; see Javolenus, D. 46.1.42. But here the rule makes more sense. The rule is applied in reverse to an *adstipulator*; see Gaius, *Inst.* 3.113, 126.

2. Extinction of Suretyship. In principle, the surety's duties automatically lapse if the primary debt ceases to exist, either because the basis of the debt vanishes or it is satisfied; this follows from suretyship's accessory nature. Likewise, if the creditor "elects" to bring suit against the principal, the suretyship ends; see *Pauli Sent.* 2.15.16. Most probably, the same is true if the creditor first sues a surety: Caracalla, C. 8.40.5 (214 CE). (However, it is defamation of character if the creditor seeks payment by a surety in a malicious effort to bring the principal's credit rating into question; see Gaius, D. 47.10.19.) But if, for instance, the principal is deported or dies without an heir, so that the debt is not collectible from him or her, the surety remains bound: Severus and Caracalla, C. 8.40.1 (200 CE).

CASE 43: Availability of Defense of Deceit to a Surety

D. 46.1.15 pr. (Iulianus libro quinquagensimo primo Digestorum)

Si stipulatus esses a me sine causa et fideiussorem dedissem et nollem eum exceptione uti, sed potius solvere, ut mecum mandati iudicio ageret, fideiussori etiam invito me exceptio dari debet: interest enim eius pecuniam retinere potius quam solutam stipulatori a reo repetere.

Julian in the fifty-first book of his *Digests*:

If you stipulated from me without a cause (*sine causa*) and I gave a surety, and I wanted him not to use the defense (of deceit, *exceptio doli*) but rather to pay and then sue me by the action on mandate, the defense should (nonetheless) be given to the surety even against my will, since it is in his interest to keep his money rather than to reclaim from the principal debtor what was paid (by him) to the stipulator.

Discussion

1. Defenses. The general rule, stated by Marcian, D. 44.1.19, is that any defense available to a principal debtor is also available to the surety, regardless of the principal's wishes. For example, if the creditor subsequently promises the debtor not to sue on the debt, the surety can normally use the defense of a pact (Case 36), see, e.g., Paul, D. 2.14.21.5; unless the creditor intended that only the debtor himself benefit, Ulpian, D. 2.14.22.

   The latter holding is part of an important exception to the general rule: possible defenses do not avail the surety if they are "personal" (*in personam*) to the principal, in the sense that he or she alone can claim them. For example, if the creditor is a freedman and the primary debtor is his or her patron (former master), the patron is entitled to a defense that limits liability to as much as he or she can afford; but this defense is not available to a surety on the patron's debt; see Paul, D. 44.1.7 pr. This exception is obviously necessary if sureties are to be held liable for "Natural" obligations.

CASE 44: Liability of a Co-Surety

Gaius, *Institutiones* 3.121–122

121. . . . [F]ideiussores uero perpetuo tenentur, et quotquot erunt numero, singuli in solidum obligantur. itaque liberum est creditori, a quo uelit, solidum petere. sed nunc ex epistula diui Hadriani compellitur creditor a singulis, qui modo soluendo sint, partes petere. . . . 122. . . . [I]taque si creditor ab uno totum consecutus fuerit, huius solius detrimentum erit, scilicet si is, pro quo fideiussit, soluendo non sit. sed ut ex supra dictis apparet, is, a quo creditor totum petit, poterit ex epistula diui Hadriani desiderare, ut pro parte in se detur actio.

Gaius in the third book of his *Institutes*:

121. . . . But sureties are permanently liable, and, however many there are, each is obligated for the entire debt. So the creditor is free to claim the entirety from whom he wishes. But now, under a letter of the deified Hadrian, the creditor is forced to claim (only) shares from each, provided they are solvent. . . .

122. . . . So, if the creditor obtains the entire debt from one (surety), the loss will be his (the surety's) alone, assuming that the person for whom he gave his guarantee is insolvent. But, as appears from what was said above, when the creditor claims the entire debt from one (surety), he (the surety) can demand, in accord with the letter of the deified Hadrian, that the action against him be given (only) for a share.

Discussion

1. **Co-Sureties**. Creditors frequently took several sureties for the same debt. Originally, the liability of each surety was unlimited up to the entire amount of the debt. But Hadrian (117–134 CE) changed the rule, as Gaius indicates, so as to limit liability to shares where co-sureties are solvent. The surety is not automatically entitled to this; as usual with actions on stipulations, the surety had to request the defense when sued by the creditor; see Gaius, D. 46.1.26; Paul, D. 46.1.28. But if one surety becomes insolvent, the others must pick up the load.

2. **Legal Limits on Suretyship**. Gaius, *Inst.* 3.124–125, discusses the Lex Cornelia, of uncertain date, which limited to 20,000 sesterces the amount by which any surety could become liable, in one year, to one creditor for one debtor. What is the public policy underlying this statute? The law might explain why co-sureties were common for larger debts. A few exceptions were permitted: promises of dowry, of debt owed under a will, of judicial debt, and of the tax owed on a will. How should these exceptions be explained?

   Of more contemporary interest is the SC Velleianum (more correctly: Vellaeanum: 46 CE), which prohibited women from assuming liability for others (Paul, D. 16.1.1; Marcian, D. 12.6.40 pr.). It is likely that the SC was motivated by overt paternalism.

CASE 45: Recourse of the Surety against the Debtor

D. 17.1.6.2 (Ulpianus libro trigensimo primo ad Edictum)

Si passus sim aliquem pro me fideiubere vel alias intervenire, mandati teneor et, nisi pro invito quis intercesserit aut donandi animo aut negotium gerens, erit mandati actio.

Ulpian in the thirty-first book *On the Edict*:

If I allowed someone to be a surety on my behalf or otherwise to guarantee (my performance), I am liable on mandate, and there will be an action on mandate unless someone intervened on behalf of a (debtor who was) unwilling, or (did so) with the intent to make a gift or to administer affairs (without the debtor's authorization).

Discussion

1. Contractual Relation between Surety and Principal. Ulpian distinguishes between two types of sureties: those who act pursuant to a request (*mandatum*) from the principal, and those who act without such a request. The former can recover any expenses from the principal through the contractual action on mandate (see Chapter V.C). This is presumably the normal situation, but who bears the burden of proof that a mandate exists? See Ulpian, D. 50.17.60: "A person who does not stop another from intervening (as a surety) on his behalf is considered to give a mandate. But also if he (subsequently) ratifies what was done, he is bound by the action on mandate." This suggests a strong presumption in favor of mandate. (See also Case 178.)

   In addition to the action on mandate, a surety had a special statutory claim against the debtor for double damages if the latter failed to pay recompense within six months (Gaius, *Inst.* 3.127, 4.22). But, of course, such a remedy will work only against a solvent debtor.

2. Unauthorized Sureties. In principle, an unauthorized surety cannot recover in contract if the surety acted against the principal's wishes or with donative intent (but see the following Case). However, Ulpian's reference to unauthorized administration of affairs (*negotia gesta*) points to the possibility of a suit on "quasi-contract"; see Chapter VIII.A. As with the mandatary, this administrator would be liable for misconduct.

CASE 46: Cession of Actions by the Creditor to the Surety

D. 46.1.36 (Paulus libro quarto decimo ad Plautium)

Cum is qui et reum et fideiussores habens ab uno ex fideiussoribus accepta pecunia praestat actiones, poterit quidem dici nullas iam esse, cum suum perceperit et perceptione omnes liberati sunt. Sed non ita est: non enim in solutum accipit, sed quodammodo nomen debitoris vendidit, et ideo habet actiones, quia tenetur ad id ipsum, ut praestet actiones.

Paul in the fourteenth book *On Plautius*:

A person who has both a principal debtor (*reus*) and sureties, if he receives the money from one surety, presents (him with) the actions (against the principal debtor and his co-sureties). It could indeed be held that they (the actions) are now void, since he (the creditor) receives his debt and all (parties) are discharged by this receipt. But this is not so, since he does not (really) receive payment; rather, in a sense, he sells the debtor's account. Therefore he (still) has the actions, since he is himself liable to present the actions (to the surety).

Discussion

1. Cession of Actions (*Cessio Actionum*). Even when the surety is not protected by the action on mandate against the principal, the jurists construct an equitable protection by requiring the creditor to cede actions against the principal debtor; so too Julian in Case 215. As Paul observes, this necessitates constructing a legal fiction, since the creditor, once paid by the surety, no longer can sue the principal debtor and in theory has nothing to cede; so the creditor is construed as "selling the debtor's account." Presumably, however, the surety must insist on cession of actions prior to paying the creditor. The Emperors Severus and Caracalla, C. 8.40.2 (207 CE), allow the surety to have not only a lawsuit on the principal debt itself, but also any claims to real securities that the principal had given for the debt. Presumably, however, the surety must insist on cession of action prior to paying the creditor.

2. Co-Sureties. In the present Case, one of the sureties has paid the entire debt instead of requesting its division among his co-sureties. See Case 215 on how the law handled this situation.

CASE 47: Warranty in a Sales Agreement

D. 21.2.31 (Ulpianus libro quadragesimo secundo ad Sabinum)

Si ita quis stipulanti spondeat "sanum esse, furem non esse, vispellionem non esse" et cetera, inutilis stipulatio quibusdam videtur, quia si quis est in hac causa, impossibile est quod promittitur, si non est, frustra est. Sed ego puto verius hanc stipulationem "furem non esse, vispellionem non esse, sanum esse" utilem esse: hoc enim continere, quod interest horum quid esse vel horum quid non esse. Sed et si cui horum fuerit adiectum "praestari," multo magis valere stipulationem: alioquin stipulatio quae ab aedilibus proponitur inutilis erit, quod utique nemo sanus probabit.

Ulpian in the forty-second book *On Sabinus*:

If someone swears to a stipulator that "(a slave) is healthy, not a thief, not a grave robber" and the like, to some the stipulation seems ineffective because if a person (the slave) is in this position, what is promised is impossible; if not, it accomplishes nothing. But I think it more correct that this stipulation—"he is not a thief, not a grave robber healthy"–is effective since it expresses his (the buyer's) interest in these things being so or not being so. But also if (the word) "provide" was added to any of these (promises), (I think) the stipulation would be much stronger; otherwise, the stipulation put forward by the Aediles will be useless, a view no rational person will approve.

Discussion

1. Express Warranties. In concluding an informal contract of sale, the seller frequently gave warranties, in the form of a stipulation, guaranteeing the title or the quality of the object of sale; and at times he was also legally obliged to do this. (See Chapter IV.B.4–5 for a fuller discussion.) Such warranties have a promissory form. However, as the "some" whom Ulpian is here criticizing pointed out, when the warranty simply affirms a characteristic (such as that a slave is not a grave robber) it is stating a fact, not a promise about the future; and this fact is either true or false. If true, no liability; if false, the stipulation is for something impossible (like stipulating for delivery of a slave who, unbeknownst to the promissor, is dead). Is this position absurd? What does it seem to be missing? How does Ulpian go about refuting it, and how does his suggested language for the stipulation eliminate the problem?

2. Example. A number of actual sales warranties have survived on papyrus or wooden tablets. Typical is this papyrus recording the sale of a seven-year-old Mesopotamian slave boy to a Roman naval adjutant in 166 CE (FIRA III no. 132); the sale took place in Seleucia Pieria, the seaport of Antioch. The bill of sale reads, in part: "That this boy is healthy in accord with the Edict (of the Curule Aediles, see Case 143); and, if anyone (as a true owner)

takes away this boy or any share in him, duly to give a refund without a lawsuit: Fabullius Macer (the buyer) stipulated, Q. Julius Priscus (the seller) swore. C. Julius Antiochus, a soldier of trireme Virtus, ordered that this be on his honor and authority (*fide sua et auctoritate*)." The regularity of language in such documents indicates that they were drafted by local notaries who kept abreast of the law.

CASE 48: Penalty Clause for Not Executing a Contract

D. 46.5.11 (Venuleius libro octavo Actionum)

In eiusmodi stipulationibus, quae "quanti ea res est" promissionem habent, commodius est certam summam comprehendere, quoniam plerumque difficilis probatio est, quanti cuiusque intersit, et ad exiguam summam deducitur.

D. 19.1.28 (Iulianus libro tertio ad Urseium Ferocem)

Praedia mihi vendidisti et convenit, ut aliquid facerem: quod si non fecissem, poenam promisi. Respondit: venditor antequam poenam ex stipulatu petat, ex vendito agere potest: si consecutus fuerit, quantum poenae nomine stipulatus esset, agentem ex stipulatu doli mali exceptio summovebit: si ex stipulatu poenam consecutus fuerit, ipso iure ex vendito agere non poterit nisi in id, quod pluris eius interfuerit id fieri.

Venuleius in the eighth book of his *Actions*:

In the kind of stipulation that has a promise for "as much as the matter is worth," it is more convenient to include a specific amount (of money), since it is often difficult to prove the extent of one's interest and this results in a small amount (being awarded).

Julian in the third book *On Urseius Ferox*:

You sold property to me and we agreed that I do something; I promised a penalty (*poena*) if I did not do it. He (Urseius) responds: The seller can sue on the sale before he seeks the penalty on the stipulation. If he (then) obtains as much as he had stipulated for as a penalty, the defense of deceit will prevent his suing on the stipulation. If he has obtained a penalty on the stipulation, by the same rule he will be able to sue on the sale only for his additional interest in the act being done.

Discussion

1. Subjective Interest. In marked contrast to Common Law, Roman jurists are not averse to liquidated damages clauses in contracts. As Venuleius indicates, such clauses can serve to assist plaintiffs in getting damages when ordinary "objective" standards may be inadequate or difficult to apply, as when the plaintiff has a subjective interest in a particular performance that cannot be evaluated by usual market measurements. Julian goes on to describe the interaction between damages in the action on sale and those in the action on stipulation; here my agreement to "do something" (e.g., build a house) is annexed to the sale (see Case 102), but the penalty clause relates only to this side agreement.

2. *In Terrorem*. Neither Venuleius nor Julian indicates any concern over excessively high penalties, out of all relation to anticipated or actual damages (even subjective ones) that the promissor may suffer. Such penalties seem

intended to coerce the promissor into performing. Other sources fairly explicitly endorse this position; e.g., Caracalla, C. 2.55.1 (213 CE). At its most extreme, penalty clauses can be used to enforce promises that are otherwise unenforceable, such as stipulations to pay money to third-party beneficiaries; see Case 10. Should we have reservations about this practice?

3. Two Stipulations? Suppose one stipulation is for construction of a ship, and a second for payment of one hundred if this ship is not constructed. Can a disappointed promisee sue for both damages on the first stipulation and the penalty? See Paul, D. 44.7.44.6.

CASE 49: A Penalty Clause with a Tacit Condition

D. 19.2.54.1 (Paulus libro quinto Responsorum)

Inter locatorem fundi et conductorem convenit, ne intra tempora locationis Seius conductor de fundo invitus repelleretur et, si pulsatus esset, poenam decem praestet Titius locator Seio conductori: vel Seius conductor Titio, si intra tempora locationis discedere vellet, aeque decem Titio locatori praestet: quod invicem de se stipulati sunt. Quaero, cum Seius conductor biennii continui pensionem non solveret, an sine metu poenae expelli possit. Paulus respondit, quamvis nihil expressum sit in stipulatione poenali de solutione pensionum, tamen verisimile esse ita convenisse de non expellendo colono intra tempora praefinita, si pensionibus paruerit et ut oportet coleret: et ideo, si poenam petere coeperit is qui pensionibus satis non fecit, profuturam locatori doli exceptionem.

Paul in the fifth book of his *Responses*:

The lessor and lessee of a farm agreed that, during the term of the lease, Seius the lessee would not be unwillingly ejected from the farm and, if he were to be ejected, Titius the lessor would owe a penalty of ten (thousand sesterces) to Seius the lessee; conversely, Seius the lessee should likewise pay ten to Titius if he wished to depart within the term of the lease. They stipulated for this in turn. I ask, when Seius the lessee does not pay the rent for two straight years, whether he can be ejected without fear of the penalty (falling due)?

Paul responds: Although nothing was stated in the penalty stipulation about payment of rent, still it is likely they agreed in this way about not ejecting the tenant farmer within the specified time (only) if he complied with the rent payments and cultivated properly; so, if the one who did not satisfy the rent payments then tries to sue for the penalty, the defense of fraud will benefit the lessor.

Discussion

1. Solve the Problem! Consider this fragment a sort of graduate course in stipulations. The parties to this farm lease (*locatio conductio fundi*; see Chapter V.A.2) have chosen to supplement their informal contract with reciprocal penalty stipulations. Only the lessor's promise against ejecting the tenant during the lease term is in play. You need to know that under the basic lease a tenant farmer has an implied duty to cultivate seasonably, take good care of the property and not damage it, avoid quarrels with neighbors, and so on (Case 157); payment of rent is also obviously on the list (Case 147). How do these implied duties intersect with the penalty stipulation? What interpretative theory is Paul relying on?

PART G

Other Types of Formal or Unilateral Promises

The final Part of this Chapter deals with some other ways in which Roman law allowed obligation to arise through formal or unilateral promises, outside of stipulation. All are of relatively minor legal significance in Classical Roman Law.

Case 50 discusses the only two instances in which obligation can arise from a formal oral promise without the preceding question that is required for a stipulation. Both these oral contracts appear to be of archaic origin. Case 51 concerns the "literal contract," a formal written contract that is accomplished through an authorized entry in the creditor's account books. Most unfortunately, very little is known about this type of contract, since it fell out of use after the Classical period and Justinian's compilers eliminated most references to it from the Digest.

Although generally speaking a unilateral donative promise (*pollicitatio*) could not lead to contractual liability in Roman law, Case 52 describes one exception: a promise to benefit a municipality. In many instances the municipality could enforce the promise, apparently because public policy favored such generosity.

Much more unusual is Case 53, the informal offer of a reward for information leading to capture of a thief. It is usually supposed that such a unilateral promise was not enforceable in Roman private law even if a third party, acting in reliance on the offer, provided the requested information. One reason is that, at the time of the act, there was no "agreement" (*consensus*) between the offeror and the third party, who are usually also unknown to each other. But the enforceability of such reward offers is so clearly in the public interest that a way may have been found to make an exception in some instances.

CASE 50: Two Formal Oral Promises

Gaius, *Institutionum Epitome* 2.9.3–4

3. Sunt et aliae obligationes, quae nulla praecedenti interrogatione contrahi possunt, id est, ut si mulier siue sponso uxor futura, siue iam marito, dotem dicat. Quod tam de mobilibus rebus, quam de fundis fieri potest. Et non solum in hac obligatione ipsa mulier obligatur, sed et pater eius, et debitor ipsius mulieris, si pecuniam, quam illi debebat, sponso creditricis ipse debitor in dotem dixerit. Hae tantum tres personae nulla interrogatione praecedente possunt dictione dotis legitime obligari. Aliae uero personae, si pro muliere dotem uiro promiserint, communi iure obligari debent, id est, ut et interrogata respondeant, et stipulata promittant. 4. Item et alio casu, uno loquente et sine interrogatione alii promittente, contrahitur obligatio, id est, si libertus patrono aut donum aut munus aut operas se daturum esse iurauit. In qua re supradicti liberti non tam uerborum solemnitate, quam iniurandi religione tenentur. Sed nulla altera persona hoc ordine obligari potest.

Gaius in the second book of *The Epitome of his Institutes*:

3. There are other (formal oral) obligations as well, which can be contracted with no preceding question, i.e., if without (a guardian's) authorization a woman promises a dowry to her future or present husband. This rule applies both to movables and to farms. And this form of obligation obligates not only the woman herself, but also (if he promises) her father, and (likewise) a debtor of this woman if the debtor, with her authorization, promises as a dowry the money he owes to her. Only these three persons can be legally obligated by a (unilateral) promise of a dowry, with no preceding question. But if other persons promise a dowry to her husband on a woman's behalf, they must be obligated by the general rule (for stipulations), i.e., that they respond to questions and promise what is stipulated for.

4. Likewise, an obligation is contracted in another case when one party speaks and promises to another without having been asked a question, i.e., if a freedman swore that he would give his patron either a gift or (performance of) a duty or services. In this situation the above mentioned freedmen are liable less through the formality of words than through the sanctity of their oath. But no other person can be obligated in this way.

Discussion

1. Promise of Dowry. Dowry was usually arranged through the question-and-answer exchange of a stipulation (e.g., Case 20). However, in specific circumstances it sufficed if the promissor gave a formal promise without a complete stipulation. Such a promise of dowry (*dotis dictio*) could only be given by the bride-to-be, her debtor acting on her order, or her father; *Tituli Ulp.* 6.2 adds her paternal grandfather. This institution is probably a fossil from archaic law, as is suggested by the narrow interpretation as to who can make it; but formal stipulations may also be very awkward

in the intimate family context of an impending marriage. (Common Law has similar problems with such prenuptial promises.) Originally the *dotis dictio* probably had a prescribed wording, but even an informal promise is allowed in Classical law; see, e.g., Paul, D. 23.3.25. However, promise of a dowry must be given orally in the presence of the promisee; see Gaius, *Inst.* 3.96 (with *Epit. Gai* 2.9.4). The institution vanishes from Justinianic law.

2. **Promise of Services by a Freedman.** When slaves were manumitted, their owners often required them to provide a fixed number of annual workdays of service (*operae*). The slave normally took an oath before manumission, and then renewed the oath after manumission; see Ulpian, D. 38.1.7.2. The Praetor provided an action to enforce this oath, but also to regulate it against undue severity; see Ulpian, D. 38.1.2, and Paul, D. 38.1.37 pr. Again, this promise is given in an intimate household context where a stipulation might have been awkward; and the promise of a slave to his or her master was anyway not normally enforceable after manumission. The Romans found it easier to make a special provision.

CASE 51: The "Literal" Contracts

Gaius, *Institutiones* 3.128–130, 134

128. Litteris obligatio fit ueluti in nominibus transscripticiis. fit autem nomen transscripticium duplici modo, uel a re in personam uel a persona in personam. 129. A re in personam transscriptio fit, ueluti si id, quod tu ex emptionis causa aut conductionis aut societatis mihi debeas, id expensum tibi tulero. 130. A persona in personam transscriptio fit, ueluti si id, quod mihi Titius debet, tibi id expensum tulero, id est si Titius te pro se delegauerit mihi. . . . 134. Praeterea litterarum obligatio fieri uidetur chirografis et syngrafis, id est, si quis debere se aut daturum se scribat, ita scilicet, si eo nomine stipulatio non fiat. quod genus obligationis proprium peregrinorum est.

Gaius in the third book of his *Institutes:*

128. An obligation is created through writing (*litterae*), e.g., in transcriptive entries of debt. But a transcriptive entry of debt occurs in two ways, either from a transaction to a person, or from a person to a person. 129. There is a transcription from a transaction to a person if, e.g., I enter (in my account books) as paid out to you what you owe me because of a sale or a lease or a partnership. 130. There is a transcription from (one) person to (another) person if, e.g., I enter (in my account books) as paid out to you what Titius owes to me, that is, if Titius delegates you to me (as a substitute debtor) for him. . . .

134. Further, an obligation through writing is held to occur through promissory notes (*chirographa*) and bonds (*syngraphae*), i.e., if someone writes that he owes or will deliver (something), assuming of course that no stipulation is made on this account. This type of obligation is special to resident aliens (*peregrini*).

Discussion

1. Bookkeeping Contracts. This is another formal contract that disappeared in Justinianic law; accordingly, little is known of it apart from stray mentions in pre-Justinianic sources. The form described in section 129 involves a preexisting debt; in his account books, the creditor, apparently with the debtor's presence and consent, enters a record that the debt has been paid, and then a record that an equivalent amount has been paid out to the debtor. The creditor can then bring suit through a *condictio* on the account record instead of on the original debt. The second form, described in section 130, is broadly similar, but it brings about the transfer of the same debt from one debtor to another, apparently with the consent of both debtors. In either case, the effect is virtually that of novation, see Case 39. While it is likely that such bookkeeping contracts were often used by bankers, they are not obviously confined to financial institutions.

2. Chirographic Debt. A promissory note (*chirographum*) had the form of an unwitnessed, handwritten, and signed acknowledgment of debt by the debtor. Although it was of Greek origin, Roman citizens actually used it fairly widely, as also the bond (*syngraphe*), a witnessed document narrating the debt and signed by both parties, then deposited with an official. In Greek law, such documents were enforceable on their face; in Roman law, it appears they may have been only evidence of debt, although surely very good evidence. (Note that Roman law does not directly treat such chirographs as negotiable instruments.)

CASE 52: Informal Promises to Municipalities

D. 50.12.1 pr.-2, 4 (Ulpianus libro singulari *De Officio Curatoris Rei Publicae*)

pr. Si pollicitus quis fuerit rei publicae opus se facturum vel pecuniam daturum, in usuras non convenietur: sed si moram coeperit facere, usurae accedunt, ut imperator noster cum divo patre suo rescripsit. 1. Non semper autem obligari eum, qui pollicitus est, sciendum est. Si quidem ob honorem promiserit decretum sibi vel decernendum vel ob aliam iustam causam, tenebitur ex pollicitatione: sin vero sine causa promiserit, non erit obligatus. Et ita multis constitutionibus et veteribus et novis continetur. 2. Item si sine causa promiserit, coeperit tamen facere, obligatus est qui coepit. . . . . 4. Sed si non ipse coepit, sed cum certam pecuniam promisisset ad opus rei publicae contemplatione pecuniae coepit opus facere: tenebitur quasi coepto opere.

Ulpian in the monograph *On the Duties of the Overseer of a Municipality*:

pr. If someone promises that he will construct something for, or give money to, a community, he will not be sued for interest (on any unpaid debt). But if he begins to be in default (*mora*), interest will accrue, in accord with the rescript of our Emperor (Caracalla) and his deified father (Septimius Severus).

1. It must be understood that a person who made (such) a promise is not always obligated. If someone made the promise because of an office decreed to him, or one about to be decreed, or for some other legitimate cause (*iusta causa*), he will be liable for the promise; but if he promises without cause (*sine causa*), he will not be obligated. It is so provided in numerous imperial constitutions both old and new.

2. Likewise, if he promises without cause (*sine causa*) but begins performance, he is obligated after he starts. . . . . 4. But if he does not start, but after his promise of a specific amount of money the community began construction in expectation of (receiving) the money, he will be liable as if he had started the work.

Discussion

1. Promises to Municipalities. Largely through imperial enactment, charitable promises to municipalities (*pollicitationes*) became often enforceable in later Classical law. Although they are not contracts in the strict sense, the present Case shows that elements of contract thinking are applied to them: the concept of *causa* for the gift, or reliance by the donee, as the basis for enforceability; and default (*mora*) as a ground for awarding interest on the promise (see Case 116). However, the jurists do not discuss the municipality's acceptance of the gift terms as a condition for its enforceability; thus, for instance, burdensome conditions imposed on promises (as,

that no tax be collectible on donated land) were treated as void; see Papirius Justus, D. 50.12.13.1, citing a rescript of Marcus Aurelius and Verus. What elements of public policy favor making charitable promises enforceable?

2. Vows. Also theoretically enforceable, although under sacred law, are vows (*vota*) made to temples and gods; see Ulpian, D. 50.12.2.

CASE 53: Reward for Information on a Thief

Pauli Sententiae 2.31.24

Ob indicium comprehendendi furis praemium promissum iure debetur.

The second book of the *Sentences of Paul*:

A reward promised for evidence to apprehend a thief is legally payable.

Discussion

1. **Rewards.** This text (from a postclassical treatise written perhaps ca. 300 CE) is the sole evidence for the enforceability of offers of reward. From a formalistic perspective, such offers to the world at large face the challenge that the person responding to the offer (and usually acting in reliance on the offer) is generally unknown to the offeror when the offer is made, and no agreement (*consensus*) is therefore possible, at least in the subjective sense. But such a result is very hard. If offers of reward ever became legally enforceable, it was probably through imperial enactment; but prior performance in reliance on the offer was presumably required.

2. **Classical Law.** In a fascinating fragment that casts a bitter light on Roman social norms, Ulpian, D. 19.5.15, sketches out the alternatives for handling a reward for return of a runaway slave. If a third party knows where runaway slaves are hidden and points them out to their owner, this is not theft even if a reward for the information is demanded and paid in advance, "because he receives (the money) for a reason that is not unworthy." (Why?) But what if owner and third party only agreed on a reward, with no payment in advance? Even here the third party can sue for the agreed-upon reward, using the mechanism described in Chapter VI.B, since their agreement "has a bit of reciprocal transaction in it." However, in neither of these cases is a generally broadcast offer of a reward involved.

3. **A Slave Collar.** An iron slave collar of late imperial date, probably from central Italy, has a bronze tag reading: "I have run away, seize me. When you return me to my master Zoninus, you get a gold coin." *CIL* 15.2.7194, which is discussed, along with other such collars, by Jennifer Trimble, *American Journal of Archaeology* 120 (2016) 447–472. If someone found the slave and consulted you (as a lawyer) about what she should now do, what would you advise under Classical law?

CHAPTER III

Contracts Created through Delivery ("Real Contracts")

A stipulation arises from using a legally prescribed form in which a promise is cloaked with solemn spoken words. By contrast, the four contracts discussed in this Chapter are informal; they can be arranged without using any set words or ceremonies. They do all require, however, what has sometimes been called a "natural formality": the delivery of an object (*res*) from one party to the other. Without such delivery, no contractual obligation arises. Thus they are called "real" contracts because of this delivery.

The four real contracts originally involved situations that most frequently occur between friends who, in many instances, are not dealing at arm's length or expecting direct payment: one person lends another money interest-free (*mutuum*), or lends something for the other's gratuitous use (*commodatum*), or entrusts an object to another's uncompensated safekeeping (*depositum*), or gives an object as security for a debt (*pignus*). The parties intend that the object (or, in the case of *mutuum*, its equivalent in kind) be returned at some point in the future; and they may also impose other restrictions on, for instance, the object's use in the meantime. But the delivery is essentially not a calculated bargain from which both parties expect to profit, but rather a friendly and gratuitous gesture from which only one party normally profits: either the recipient (in the case of *mutuum* and *commodatum*) or the giver (in the case of *depositum*). Pledge (*pignus*), to be sure, is more complex in that both parties benefit from the transaction, but it too is at least nominally gratuitous. In all four cases, the aim of the legal procedures supporting the contracts originally concentrated on return of the delivered object or its value.

If we look at these contracts analytically, they each involve three elements: first, the agreement (*consensus*) as to the purpose and conditions of the delivery; second, the delivery itself; and third, the basically gratuitous and unilateral nature of the transaction. These elements were originally interlinked. Agreement was necessary to define the transaction and to create the expectation of return or restitution, but agreement does not become legally binding until delivery occurs; and the underlying reason for this second requirement is that the transaction is unilateral in its benefit. Thus, an informal promise to loan someone money, or to receive a deposit, has no force in Roman law until the object is actually delivered, even if in the meantime the benefiting party has relied on the promise. It requires insight into the nature of promising in order to understand why Roman law adopted this position, which is not at all obvious.

However, as time passed, the jurists made strenuous efforts to broaden this basic conceptual framework and loosen its strictures, in order to incorporate a broader variety of potential social and economic uses for all four contracts.

A Casebook on the Roman Law of Contracts. Bruce W. Frier, Oxford University Press. © Oxford University Press 2021.
DOI: 10.1093/oso/9780197573211.003.0004

The Roman real contracts (except for *pignus*) have marginal significance in the modern world, but were considerably more important in the ancient world where the various markets for credit, goods, and services were poorly developed, and relations between friends were therefore often of great practical value.

PART A

Gratuitous Loan for Consumption (*Mutuum*)

The simplest of the four "real contracts" is *mutuum*, the gratuitous loan of money or some other fungible (such as wine, grain, and the like) with the expectation of return not of the exact object lent, but rather its equivalent in kind. Thus, for instance, a lender gives money to a borrower; both parties tacitly understand that the borrower will take ownership of the money and repay an equivalent amount in the future. If the borrower fails to repay, the lender can sue for this amount through a *condictio*, a claim for an exact sum. There are parallel actions for loans of fungibles.

Moneylending, in particular, runs up against social and political inhibitions in many societies. Although Roman law itself is not necessarily hostile to charging (non-usurious) interest on loans, it does adopt the position that, in principle, interest on a simple loan cannot arise from informal agreement, but must be arranged through a formal stipulation—a ritual that was perhaps thought to guarantee gravity of intent. Thus, the only beneficiary in a purely informal *mutuum* is the borrower who can use the lender's money for an interval; the lender is essentially extending temporary credit to the borrower. Another example of such inhibitions is the curious restraint on the validity of loans to sons in the power of a *paterfamilias* (Case 61).

More interesting are the jurists' efforts to extend the concept of delivery, above all by gradually asserting the importance of agreement (*consensus*) in the formation of a loan. It is essential to the idea of a *mutuum* that the borrower becomes owner of the borrowed sum, and hence can dispose of it as he or she wishes, with full assumption of risk as to the eventual return of an equivalent. But must the lender deliver ownership directly? In a line of decisions, the jurists argue about the possibility of indirect delivery, which can occur when, for instance, a lender does not have immediately available cash, but instead asks a third party (often the lender's debtor) to pay the money to the borrower.

On the whole, nonetheless, and despite these efforts, *mutuum* is not very successful as an example of Roman contract jurisprudence. For the most part, the procedural system proved intractable when it came to direct loans of money, although otherwise it largely tolerates informal arrangements for interest-bearing debts.

CASE 54: Loan of Fungibles

D. 12.1.2 pr.-2 (Paulus libro vicensimo octavo ad Edictum)

pr. Mutuum damus recepturi non eandem speciem quam dedimus (alioquin commodatum erit aut depositum), sed idem genus: nam si aliud genus, veluti ut pro tritico vinum recipiamus, non erit mutuum. 1. Mutui datio consistit in his rebus, quae pondere numero mensura consistunt, quoniam eorum datione possumus in creditum ire, quia in genere suo functionem recipiunt per solutionem quam specie: nam in ceteris rebus ideo in creditum ire non possumus, quia aliud pro alio invito creditori solvi non potest. 2. Appellata est autem mutui datio ab eo, quod de meo tuum fit: et ideo, si non faciat tuum, non nascitur obligatio.

Iustinianus, *Institutiones* 3.14.2

. . . Et is quidem qui mutuum accepit, si quolibet fortuito casu quod accepit amiserit, veluti incendio, ruina, naufragio aut latronum hostiumve incursu, nihilo minus obligatus permanet.

Paul in the twenty-eighth book *On the Edict*:

pr. We give a loan for consumption (*mutuum*) when we will get back not the same specific thing we gave—otherwise, it would be a loan for use (*commodatum*) or a deposit—but (something of) the same generic type; for if (we give to get back) a different type, e.g., that we get back wine for wheat, this will not be a *mutuum*. 1. The giving of a *mutuum* occurs for those things that are reckoned in weight, number, or measure. By giving them we can become (generic) creditors, since through payment they operate within their generic type, not by their specific identity. In the case of other objects, we cannot become (generic) creditors, for, unless he is willing, a creditor cannot be paid one object in discharge of another. 2. The giving of a *mutuum* was named from the fact that what was my property becomes yours (*de meo tuum*); and so, if he does not make it your property, no obligation arises.

Justinian in the third book of his *Institutes*:

. . . And, indeed, a person who has received a *mutuum*, should he lose what he received by some unavoidable accident (*fortuitus casus*), e.g., by conflagration, shipwreck, or the incursion of bandits or enemies, nonetheless remains obligated.

Discussion

1. Fungibles are interchangeable goods, frequently sold or delivered in bulk, with any one of them as good as another. The archetypal example of a fungible, as Paul defines it, is money as a measure of value; but wine or wheat can also serve as fungibles, although in their case a measure of quality is also usually present; see Pomponius, D. 12.1.3. Any fungible may also be, in particular circumstances, a non-fungible. For example, the coins in a

coin collection may still be legal tender, but it is unlikely that their lender would be satisfied with return of other than the exact same coins.

2. Credit. Ulpian, D. 12.1.1.1, defines "credit" (*creditum*) in terms of reliance upon another person's honor (*fides*). The concept is a general one in most of Roman contract law outside of formal contracts: "Whatever we agree to in reliance on another's honor and with the expectation of receiving something in the future, from this contract we are said to extend credit." The concept receives a simple application in the case of a gratuitous *mutuum*: you ask me for $50 until payday, and I hand the money over to you with the expectation of its repayment without interest. I am your creditor, and you are my debtor.

3. The Role of Agreement. Paul, D. 44.7.3.1: "For an obligation to arise, it is not enough that money is the giver's and becomes the recipient's; to constitute an obligation, it must also be given and received with this intent (*animus*)." Thus, delivery alone is insufficient without mutual agreement on the nature of the delivery, an idea that becomes increasingly prominent in later Classical law. But from this simple principle some hard cases arose. Suppose I give you money as a gift, and you receive it as a *mutuum*. Ulpian, D. 12.1.18 pr. (= Case 230), holds that this is neither gift nor *mutuum*, and that therefore no ownership passes; but the giver is prevented by the defense of deceit (see Cases 35–36) from reclaiming the money. So what if the situation were reversed: I think I'm lending you money, and you think it's a gift? Other such hard cases are discussed in Chapter VIII.B dealing with unjustified enrichment.

4. Conveying Ownership. Paul gives a folk etymology for *mutuum*, but his rule is general, and Justinian bluntly states the consequence: all risk of its loss is borne by the borrower. (See also Diocletian and Maximian, C. 4.2.11 [294 CE]: "A conflagration does not exempt a debtor from owing money.") But ownership itself can only be conveyed by the coins' owner. If a thief uses stolen money to make a *mutuum*, is the borrower under any obligation to repay? Ulpian, D. 12.1.13 pr.-1, holds that there is no initial liability since the lender cannot convey ownership, but the borrower is liable for restitution, apparently in quasi-contract (Chapter VIII.B: unjustified enrichment), assuming that the money has been used. Is this holding correct? Similarly, Julian, D. 12.1.19.1 (a ward lends money without a guardian's authorization; the ward cannot convey ownership without this authorization); Paul, D. 46.1.56.2 (loan of coins belonging to a third party; is the borrower's surety liable on this loan?). As Paul comments, D. 12.1.2.3, "Likewise it cannot be a *mutuum* unless the money 'travels' (*profiscatur*)" from the lender to the borrower.

5. Promising to Give a Loan. This point may seem obvious by now, but deserves emphasis once again for modern lawyers. Suppose that you ask a friend for a loan "until payday," and the friend says she doesn't have the money now, but promises to have the money for you tomorrow morning. Is this promise enforceable in Roman law? Does it matter whether, in the meantime, you have relied on her promise to your detriment (for instance, by overdrawing your bank account)? *Mutuum* is a real contract that requires delivery by the lender. An informal promise to lend money in the future (called a *pactum de mutuo dando*, a pact on giving a loan) is therefore unenforceable without delivery; such a promise becomes enforceable only if expressed formally as a stipulation (Case 57). The same idea is applicable to the other "real contracts" as well, but the consequences are likely to be more dire in the case of *mutuum*. So you're out of luck unless your friend has acted deliberately (with *dolus*) to cause you loss—in which case an action on the delict of deceit (*dolus*) may be available, but no contractual action.

CASE 55: Loan via Third Parties

D. 12.1.15 (Ulpianus libro trigensimo primo ad Edictum)

Singularia quaedam recepta sunt circa pecuniam creditam. Nam si tibi debitorem meum iussero dare pecuniam, obligaris mihi, quamvis meos nummos non acceperis. Quod igitur in duabus personis recipitur, hoc et in eadem persona recipiendum est, ut, cum ex causa mandati pecuniam mihi debeas et convenerit, ut crediti nomine eam retineas, videatur mihi data pecunia et a me ad te profecta.

Ulpian in the thirty-first book *On the Edict*:

Some special rules have been established for the lending of money. For if I order my debtor to give money to you, you are obligated to me even though you do not receive my coins.

What is established for two persons should hold also for the same person, so that, if you owe me money as a result of a mandate and we agree that you hold it on credit (as a loan), the money seems to me to have been given (back to me) and to have (then) passed back from me to you.

Discussion

1. Delegation of a Debtor. You request a *mutuum* from me; I tell my debtor to pay you, and he does (thereby also paying off all or part of his debt to me). At what point do you become indebted to me: when I give the order, or when my debtor pays the money? Presumably the latter, because of the nature of *mutuum* as a real contract. Is this an exception to the rule cited in the previous Case, and, if so, what explains it? Ulpian, D. 12.1.9.8, citing Aristo and Julian, notes that such delegation was common practice; but this situation contains some difficulties. Suppose the third party is not my debtor, but, without my knowledge, lends money to you as if it were mine. Ulpian holds that I can then claim it through a *condictio*, but how can this be? Is the third party to be construed as making a gift to me? In short, how essential is the order to the existence of a *mutuum*? (On delegation in a stricter contractual sense, see Chapter VII.D.)

   Note that in this type of a loan, the borrower receives ownership of the money from the lender's debtor. The requirement that the lender transfer ownership is solved for movables by a legal fiction called *traditio longa manu*, "handover by a long hand": Javolenus, D. 46.3.79 (ownership is construed as passing from the debtor first to the lender, thereby extinguishing all or part of the debt, and then to the borrower).

2. Transformation of a Debt into a *Mutuum*. More troublesome is the second part of this Case. Ulpian uses a legal fiction in order to convert the debt owed from a mandate into a *mutuum*; the money "fictionally" passes to me and then back to you. This fiction (called *traditio brevi manu*, "handover

with a short hand"; see Case 68), which circumvents the requirement of the lender's physically handing over the *res*, has one awkward consequence: because of the law regarding *mutuum*, the loan cannot bear interest without a stipulation, see Case 58. Ulpian, citing Papinian, draws this consequence in D. 17.1.10.4 (Titius asks for a loan from X, who gives a mandate to Titius to collect the loan from X's slave managers [*actores*]; the loan cannot bear interest without a supplementary stipulation). But Julian, cited by his student Africanus, D. 17.1.34 pr., has a long discussion in which he permits the loan to remain within the perimeter of the *bona fides* contract of mandate (see Chapter V.C); in this contract the parties can agree informally on payment of interest. A better solution, no?

CASE 56: Loan through Sale of an Object

D. 12.1.11 pr. (Ulpianus libro vicensimo sexto ad Edictum)

Rogasti me, ut tibi pecuniam crederem: ego cum non haberem, lancem tibi dedi vel massam auri, ut eam venderes et nummis utereris. Si vendideris, puto mutuam pecuniam factam. Quod si lancem vel massam sine tua culpa perdideris prius quam venderes, utrum mihi an tibi perierit, quaestionis est. Mihi videtur Nervae distinctio verissima existimantis multum interesse, venalem habui hanc lancem vel massam nec ne, ut, si venalem habui, mihi perierit, quemadmodum si alii dedissem vendendam: quod si non fui proposito hoc ut venderem, sed haec causa fuit vendendi, ut tu utereris, tibi eam perisse, et maxime si sine usuris credidi.

Ulpian in the twenty-sixth book *On the Edict*:

You asked me to lend you money; since I had none, I gave you a platter or a gold ingot for you to sell and use the money. If you sold it, I think a loan of money was made.

But if, through no fault (*culpa*) of your own, you lost the platter or ingot (before selling it), it is questionable whether you or I bear the loss. Nerva's distinction seems to me exactly right; he thought it mattered greatly whether I (already) had this plate or ingot up for sale. If I (previously) had it up for sale, the loss is mine, just as if I had given it to another person to sell. (But) if it was not my intention to sell it, but the reason (*causa*) for selling it was that you use (the proceeds), its loss is yours, especially if I lent without interest.

Discussion

1. A Problem. When does the *mutuum* arise: when the lender delivers the plate, or when the borrower sells it, or when the borrower receives the price? Use the discussion in this text to solve the following problem, which is posed by Ulpian, D. 12.1.4 pr.: You want to buy property and ask Titius for a loan; but you will need this loan only when the sale is finally arranged. Since Titius is about to depart on a journey, he arranges to leave the money on deposit with you, with the understanding that you can use the money if the sale is completed, and that you will then be liable for a *mutuum* (see Case 68). If the money is then stolen before the sale, are you liable? Would it make any difference if Titius was a professional moneylender? The jurists have some difficulty with this kind of situation; compare Case 186.

2. Imaginative Solutions. It seems clear that both ordinary Romans and their lawyers struggled to surmount the awkwardness of the law in this area. After the Classical period, the Emperors Diocletian and Maximian, C. 4.2.8 (293 CE), consider a case in which a certain Proculus asked for a loan of money; but the lender gave him instead some silver at an appraised value on which the parties had agreed. The silver was, in fact, worth appreciably

less than the appraisal, but this rescript nonetheless allows the lender to sue for return of the loan at the appraised value. This enables the parties to, in effect, arrange for interest on the loan, right? Say the object is worth fifty but is appraised at sixty; the borrower can sell the object to get the desired cash, but is liable to the lender for more than he is likely to obtain through the sale. Such roundabouts become a common theme in later law.

CASE 57: Stipulation to Give a Loan

D. 45.1.68 (Paulus libro secundo ad Edictum)

Si poenam stipulatus fuero, si mihi pecuniam non credidisses, certa est et utilis stipulatio. Quod si ita stipulatus fuero: "pecuniam te mihi crediturum spondes?," incerta est stipulatio, quia id venit in stipulationem, quod mea interest.

Paul in the second book *On the Edict*:

I stipulated for a penalty (*poena*) if you had not lent me money. The stipulation is definite and effective (*certa et utilis*). But if I stipulated in this form: "Do you swear that you will lend me money?" the stipulation is indefinite because at issue in the stipulation is (the extent of) my interest (in the loan being given: *quod mea interest*).

Discussion

1. Promise to Give a Loan. A bare promise to give a *mutuum* is unenforceable before delivery, whether or not the promisee relies upon the promise. For this reason, the borrower in this Case had to use a stipulation to make a bare promise enforceable. As Paul states, the stipulation may take the form of a penalty if the *mutuum* is not forthcoming, or a promise with the promisee's "interest" being collectible; but the latter is much more difficult to prove. Why does Roman law require the cumbersome apparatus of a stipulation in the case of a gratuitous contract like *mutuum*? The Romans never solved the problem of how to integrate into a single informal contract a promise to loan, the actual loan itself, and a promise of interest payable on the loan.

2. Use of Stipulations to Uphold Loans. Stipulations could also be used to arrange terms for repayment of loans and for interest on loans. Indeed, it seems to have been common to incorporate the loan itself into a stipulation: e.g., Pomponius, D. 46.2.7; Paul, D. 45.1.126.2; Ulpian, D. 12.1.9.4, 46.2.6.1 ("When someone lent money without a stipulation and immediately made a stipulation (as well), there is one contract. The same should be said also if the stipulation was made first and the money counted out soon thereafter."); Modestinus, D. 44.7.52 pr., 3.

   Paul, D. 12.1.40, gives a particularly interesting report of a real case heard by his teacher Papinian as Praetorian Prefect. The case centered on a document in which: (i) a borrower acknowledged receipt of 15,000 sesterces; (ii) by stipulation, the borrower promised repayment of this amount by the first of the upcoming month; (iii) by a second stipulation, the borrower promised to pay one percent interest per month (the maximum allowable interest under usury laws) as a penalty if the first stipulation was breached; (iv) the parties informally agreed that the borrower would in that event repay 1,200 sesterces per month until the whole debt was paid. The borrower did not repay the entire loan by the first deadline, and also defaulted on several monthly payments. The informal agreement has at least the effect of making the first stipulation ineffective. (Why? See Case 36.) But how does it affect the second stipulation? Does interest accrue on the entire principal after the initial failure to repay it, or only on the unpaid monthly amounts? Work out your answer, and then look at the source.

CASE 58: Agreement to Pay Back More than Was Lent

D. 12.1.11.1 (Ulpianus libro vicensimo sexto ad Edictum)

Si tibi dedero decem sic, ut novem debeas, Proculus ait, et recte, non amplius te ipso iure debere quam novem. Sed si dedero, ut undecim debeas, putat Proculus amplius quam decem condici non posse.

Ulpian in the twenty-sixth book *On the Edict*:

If I give you ten (thousand sesterces) in order that you owe (me) nine, Proculus says, quite rightly, that your legal debt is no more than nine. But if I give (ten) in order that you owe (me) eleven, Proculus things that a *condictio* cannot lie for more than ten.

Discussion

1. Gratuitous Loans. As Ulpian states, agreement can operate to diminish the debt, but not to increase it; see also Paul, D. 2.14.17 pr. The more general rule is that a *mutuum*, concluded by bare agreement and delivery, cannot bear interest even if the borrower defaults in repaying; the parties must use a stipulation; see the Emperor Severus, C. 4.32.3 (200 CE). Does this rule result from the procedural *formula* used to reclaim a *mutuum*, or does it rather reflect a deeper prejudice against moneylending? Contrast the more liberal attitude in *bona fides* contracts; see Case 102.

   But the issue continued to rankle. In Case 190, a dispute arises over interest income when, on one understanding of the facts, a borrower invests a *mutuum* with the lender's consent.

2. Inadvertent Payment of Interest. Titius took a *mutuum* and promised, by stipulation, to pay five percent interest per year. He made payments on the loan for several years, but then inadvertently began paying as if the interest rate were six percent. Can Titius reclaim the overpayments? Scaevola, D. 46.3.102.3, states that the overpayments should be applied to the principal; would this also be true if the lender knew of the overpayments when they were made? What if the interest payments had not been based on a stipulation, but only on an unenforceable agreement? Severus and Caracalla, C. 4.32.3 (200 CE), hold that, in such a case, the payments do not go to reduce the principal and also cannot be reclaimed (in quasi-contract), so that they constitute a sort of gift to the lender. Is this consistent with Scaevola's holding? See also Ulpian, D. 12.6.26 pr. and 46.3.5.2 (both citing rescripts of Severus and Caracalla).

3. Interest on Loan of Other Fungibles. Curiously, when fungibles such as grain and olive oil are lent, a lender could collect interest on the basis of an informal agreement: Alexander, C. 4.32.11 (223 CE), and Diocletian and Maximian, C. 4.32.23 (294 CE). The second constitution justifies this on the

basis of the uncertain price of such fungibles (*incerti pretii ratio*), but this exception should indicate that the obstacle in the case of money was not insurmountable, right?

4. Bottomry Loans. This form of marine insurance, called *fenus nauticum*, is an exception to the general rules on interest, since it was fundamentally not a loan but a form of insurance. See Case 33.

CASE 59: The *Condictio* and Over-Claiming

Gaius, *Institutiones* 4.53–53b

53. Si quis intentione plus conplexus fuerit, causa cadit, id est rem perdit, nec a praetore in integrum restituitur, exceptis quibusdam casibus, in quibus . . . praetor non patitur [. . . *2 lines missing* . . .] 53a. Plus autem quattuor modis petitur: re, tempore, loco, causa. re, uelut si quis pro X milibus, quae ei debentur, XX milia petierit, aut si is, cuius ex parte res esset, totam eam aut maiore ex parte suam esse intenderit. 53b. Tempore, ueluti si quis ante diem uel ante condicionem petierit. . . .

Gaius in the fourth book of his *Institutes*:

53. If a person over-claims in his statement of claim (*intentio*), his case fails, i.e., he loses his (right to the) matter. Nor does the Praetor restore the prior status quo, except in some cases in which the Praetor does not allow (substantial forfeiture?) . . .

53a. Over-claim occurs in four ways: in substance, time, place, or *causa* (basis of the claim). In substance, for instance, if someone claims twenty thousand (sesterces) for the ten thousand that are owed to him; or if someone is a co-owner of property and claims as his own the entirety or a larger share. 53b. In time, for instance, if someone claims before a deadline or before a condition (occurs). . . .

Discussion

1. The *Formula*. This Case describes an important procedural complication. As you may recall from the Introduction, the model *condictio* runs: "If it appears that the defendant ought to give ten thousand sesterces to the plaintiff, let the iudex condemn the defendant to the plaintiff for ten thousand sesterces; if this does not appear (to be true), let him absolve." The "if" clause is technically a general statement of claim, the *intentio*, and it is adhered to fairly strictly; here, a specific sum is claimed, and over-claiming has a catastrophic result for the plaintiff: not only is the case lost, but also, as a result of how Roman civil procedure operates, his right to the claim. Gaius lists four types of over-claim; the other two are place (the promise was for conveyance at Rome, and this is omitted in the *intentio*) and *causa* (the promise was to convey ten thousand or Stichus, and the option is omitted). (The text of Gaius is plagued by gaps at this point, but can be restored with some confidence from Justinian, *Inst.* 4.6.33.) Most trial *formulae* are framed so as to avoid this problem.

2. Under-Claiming. If the plaintiff claims less than is owed, the *iudex* will award only the lesser amount, and the plaintiff cannot bring a claim for the remainder before the same Praetor: Gaius, *Inst.* 4.56.

CASE 60: Supplying Terms for Repayment

D. 12.1.22 (Iulianus libro quarto ex Minicio)

Vinum, quod mutuum datum erat, per iudicem petitum est: quaesitum est, cuius temporis aestimatio fieret, utrum cum datum esset an cum litem contestatus fuisset an cum res iudicaretur. Sabinus respondit, si dictum esset quo tempore redderetur, quanti tunc fuisset, si dictum non esset, quanti tunc fuisset, cum petitum esset. Interrogavi, cuius loci pretium sequi oporteat. Respondit, si convenisset, ut certo loco redderetur, quanti eo loco esset, si dictum non esset, quanti ubi esset petitum.

Julian in the fourth book *From Minicius*:

Wine given on loan (*mutuum*) was claimed through a *iudex*. Question arose as to what date the evaluation (of the judgment) is made: whether for when it (the wine) was given, or when the issue was joined (*litis contestatio*), or when the matter was adjudged. Sabinus responded that if a time was stated at which it should be returned, (judgment should be) for as much as it was worth at that time; if this was not stated, for as much as it was worth when it was claimed.

I asked what place's price should be followed. He responded that if its return at a set place was stated, (judgment should be) for its value at that place; if this was not stated, for its value where it was claimed.

Discussion

1. **Terms Added by the Parties.** Except for interest, the parties have considerable freedom to agree informally on the terms of a *mutuum*; see Ulpian, D. 12.1.7. For example, the lender can advance money subject to a condition that it only becomes a *mutuum* if some subsequent event occurs; see Pomponius, D. 12.1.8. Correspondingly, it is possible to make a present *mutuum* that will become a gift upon a condition being realized; see Julian, D. 39.5.1 pr. Agreement may also set terms for repayment and the like.

2. **Implied Terms.** Where the parties fail to set terms for repayment, problems arise of the sort discussed in this Case. Unlike money, wine may have a widely varying market value, so that the time of evaluation is important. How good is the Roman solution? If, in a rising market, the lender demands repayment and the borrower defaults, how long can the lender wait before bringing suit? Can the lender pick a place to sue in which the value of the wine is abnormally high? Gaius, D. 13.3.4, gives the same rules as this Case. Florentinus, D. 2.14.57 pr., and Ulpian, D. 44.4.2.6, push a bit further: if the lender had accepted interest for a future date from the borrower, it is implicitly agreed that no suit for the principal will be brought before that date; Ulpian thinks that to do this would be deceit, *dolus*.

CASE 61: The Senatus Consultum Macedonianum

D. 14.6.1 pr. (Ulpianus libro vicensimo nono ad Edictum)

Verba senatus consulti Macedoniani haec sunt: "Cum inter ceteras sceleris causas Macedo, quas illi natura administrabat, etiam aes alienum adhibuisset, et saepe materiam peccandi malis moribus praestaret, qui pecuniam, ne quid amplius diceretur incertis nominibus crederet: placere, ne cui, qui filio familias mutuam pecuniam dedisset, etiam post mortem parentis eius, cuius in potestate fuisset, actio petitioque daretur, ut scirent, qui pessimo exemplo faenerarent, nullius posse filii familias bonum nomen exspectata patris morte fieri."

Ulpian in the twenty-ninth book *On the Edict*:

The words of the Senatus Consultum Macedonianum are as follows: "Whereas, among the other causes of crime to which his nature predisposed him, Macedo also went into debt; and (whereas) bad habits often obtain the means for their wrongdoing from persons who lend money on accounts that are, to say the least, dubious: it is decided (by the Roman Senate) that no action or claim is to be given to anyone who lent money to a son in his father's power (*filius familias*) even after the death of the parent in whose power he was, so that those who perniciously lend at interest may know that the account of a son in his father's power cannot become good by waiting for the father's death."

Discussion

1. Macedo's Crime. Macedo, a son in the power of a wealthy Roman *paterfamilias*, borrowed money and was then pressed by the lenders for repayment; but Macedo had no assets of his own (see Chapter VII.A) and so, in response to his creditors' demands, he murdered his father to obtain the inheritance. (Or so the story goes, at any rate.) The Senate responded by invalidating moneylenders' claims on loans of money to a son in his father's power even after the father's death. A claim on such loans can be defeated by the Praetor denying the action or, in more ambiguous circumstances, by a defense based on the SC. However, the claim could be ratified by the *paterfamilias* or by the son after he became *sui iuris*, and money paid on the claim by anyone other than the son could not be recovered (since it is a "natural obligation"); and even partial payment by the son counts as ratification; see Ulpian, D. 14.6.7.15.

2. Statutory Interpretation. The words of the statute are given in the preceding extract. The jurists were at pains to interpret them in hard cases. Is the lender's claim enforceable in the following circumstances?

1. The loan is made to a grandson, see Julian, D. 14.6.14; or to a daughter, see Ulpian, D. 14.6.9.2.

2. The loan is not of money but of wine; see Ulpian, D. 14.6.7.3. Would it matter if the son was going to sell the wine and use the price as a loan (see Case 56)?

3. The son makes a purchase and promises an interest-bearing payment by stipulation; see Severus, C. 4.28.3 (198 CE), and Ulpian, D. 14.6.3.3.

4. The son takes a loan after falsely stating that he is *sui iuris*; see Pertinax, C. 4.28.1 (193 CE). Or the lender reasonably supposes that the borrower is *sui iuris*; see Ulpian, D. 14.6.3 pr.

5. A third party goes surety for a loan to the son. Does it matter whether the surety has already paid the lender? See Ulpian, D. 14.6.9.3-4, 11.

6. A son goes surety on a loan to a third party. Does it matter if this arrangement is a cover, and that the third party intends to convey the loan to the son? See Ulpian, D. 14.6.7 pr.-1.

PART B

Gratuitous Bailment: Deposit and Loan for Use (*Commodatum*)

As the Romans recognized, these two contracts mirror one another in many ways. In deposit (*depositum*), one person gives an object to another for gratuitous safekeeping; in loan for use (*commodatum*), one person lends an object to another for that person's gratuitous use. In both contracts, the primary duty of the temporary holder (in Common Law, the contractual bailee[1]) is to return the object upon demand. But, at least in general, deposit is for the exclusive benefit of the depositor, whereas loan for use is for the benefit of the borrower.

Although these two contracts appear initially straightforward, in practice they cause difficulties not present in *mutuum*. These difficulties led the Urban Praetor to supplement (and largely replace) the original restitutionary *formulae* for each with more complex *formulae* based on good faith (*bona fides*). Above all, in Roman law the giver retained legal ownership and possession of the object while it was in the recipient's hands. But rules were required to determine, for instance, the recipient's rights and duties in safeguarding and maintaining the giver's property. The jurists may originally have solved such problems through intuition; but in time they articulated a general theory of the flow of benefit (*utilitas*) within each contract type. The theory then provided a more secure framework for allocating rights and duties when the parties had not done so themselves, as is frequently the case in informal contracts between friends.

On the basis of the theory of *utilitas*, the jurists were also able to deal with some unusual forms of deposit or *commodatum*, in which the flow of benefit was not the ordinary one. Cases 68–69 deal with a difficult distinction between ordinary deposit and the deposit of money in a bank—a problem the jurists never satisfactorily resolved.

---

[1] Bailment in Common Law occurs when possession but not ownership of the personal property of one party, the bailor, is transferred to another, the bailee, for a limited time or specified purpose. The Roman contracts discussed here and in the following are analogous but not identical; for instance, legal possession is not transferred in deposit and loan for use, but it is transferred in pledge.

CASE 62: The *Formulae* for Deposit and Loan for Use (*Commodatum*)

Gaius, *Institutiones* 4.47

Sed ex quibusdam causis praetor et in ius et in factum conceptas formulas proponit, ueluti depositi et commodati. illa enim formula, quae ita concepta est: "Iudex esto. Quod Aulus Agerius apud Numerium Negidium mensam argenteam deposuit, qua de re agitur, quidquid ob eam rem Numerium Negidium Aulo Agerio dare facere oportet ex fide bona, eius, iudex, Numerium Negidium Aulo Agerio condemnato. Si non paret, absolvito," in ius concepta est. at illa formula, quae ita concepta est: "Iudex esto. Si paret Aulum Agerium apud Numerium mensam argenteam deposuisse eamque dolo malo Numerii Negidii Aulo Agerio redditam non esse, quanti ea res erit, tantam pecuniam, iudex, Numerium Negidium Aulo Agerio condemnato. Si non paret, absolvito," in factum concepta est. similes etiam commodati formulae sunt.

Gaius in the fourth book of his *Institutes*:

But for some causes of action the Praetor gives *formulae* framed both in law (*in ius*) and on the facts (*in factum*), e.g., for deposit and loan for use (*commodatum*).

A *formula* is framed *in ius* if framed as follows: "Let X be the *iudex*. Whereas the plaintiff deposited a silver table with the defendant, which is the issue in question, whatever on this account the defendant ought to give to or do for the plaintiff in accord with good faith (*ex fide bona*), let the *iudex* condemn the defendant to the plaintiff for this amount; if it does not appear, let him absolve."

But a *formula* is framed *in factum* if framed as follows: "Let X be the *iudex*. If it appears that the plaintiff deposited a silver table with the defendant, and it was not returned to the plaintiff because of the defendant's deceit (*dolus malus*), let the *iudex* condemn the defendant to the plaintiff for this amount; if it does not appear, let him absolve."

There are similar *formulae* also for *commodatum*.

Discussion

1. The *Formulae*. Closely examine the two *formulae* for deposit. The second one is undoubtedly the older; it looks to straightforward recovery of the silver table (or its value); see "not returned." The first *formula*, "framed in law," by contrast, calls upon the *iudex* to examine the larger contractual context. Although its wording seems to accept the truth of the plaintiff's assertion that there actually was a deposit ("Whereas"), in fact the defendant could raise this question too. The evolution of the *formulae* for *commodatum* was apparently similar, except that the earlier *formula* for such loans did not restrict the defendant's liability to acts of deceit (*dolus*).

2. Gratuitous Contracts. Both deposit and *commodatum* are ordinarily thought of as purely gratuitous acts between friends; see, e.g., Ulpian, D. 13.6.5.12, holding that a loan for a fee is lease (see Chapter V.A.3). The rules of both contracts are largely constructed on this assumption; the contractual element is clearly supplied by agreement and delivery (implying reliance on the agreement). However, as we shall see later, in some circumstances there may be a more complex flow of benefit between the parties even though the bailment itself remains nominally gratuitous. The jurists were then obliged to create special rules for such exceptions.

3. Infamy. We normally think of contract as not involving moral censure of a defendant who is found to have breached a contract. Roman law is in accord; but the Praetor marked with "infamy" (*infamia*) those condemned in certain contract actions that were regarded as having a strongly fiduciary aspect; see Julian, D. 3.2.1 (quoting the Edict, which also listed partnership and mandate); Gaius, *Inst.* 4.182. Deposit was one of these. Modestinus, *Collatio* 10.2.4: "A person condemned on deposit is infamous; but one condemned on *commodatum* is not infamous. For the former is condemned for deceit (*dolus*), the latter for fault (*culpa*)." *Infamia* is primarily a social stigma for "betrayal of trust," but the Praetor restricted the infamous from appearing as advocates for other persons, or being represented themselves. Other contract actions resulting in *infamia* for condemned defendants are partnership and mandate (Chapter V.B–C). It is worth thinking about this use of moral concepts in contract law.

4. Special Cases. Roman law recognized a few forms of deposit that required special rules. They are:

i. Deposit of property in emergency situations, for instance, conflagration, shipwreck, civil disturbance, and so on. Since the depositor was obliged to act swiftly with little ability to choose the best depositary, the latter was liable for double damages: Modestinus, *Collatio* 10.2.7; Paul, *Collatio* 10.7.3.

ii. Deposit with a stakeholder (*sequester*), normally used when parties are litigating over property. The stakeholder is responsible for the property's protection and its return to the appropriate person when the controversy is resolved: Ulpian, D. 16.3.5.1–2; Paul, D. 16.3.6. Because of the uncertainty, the stakeholder takes legal possession of the property: Florentinus, D. 16.3.17.1. Odd borderline cases are discussed by Ulpian, D. 4.3.9.3, 19.5.18.

iii. A developed form of deposit used for banking (called *depositum irregulare*) is discussed in Case 69.

5. Immovables. Finally, although both deposit and *commodatum* are usually thought of in relation to movables, the jurists were divided on whether, for instance, allowing someone to live in a dwelling for free was actionable as *commodatum*: Ulpian, D. 13.6.1.1. In Roman law, which lacks a doctrine of estates in land, the dividing line between movables and immovables is often weak.

CASE 63: Possession of the Object

Gaius, *Institutiones* 4.153

Possidere autem uidemur non solum, si ipsi possideamus, sed etiam si nostro nomine aliquis in possessione sit, licet is nostro iuri subiectus non sit, qualis est colonus et inquilinus. per eos quoque, apud quos deposuerimus aut quibus commodauerimus aut quibus gratuitam habitationem praestiterimus, ipsi possidere uidemur. et hoc est, quod uolgo dicitur retineri possessionem posse per quemlibet, qui nostro nomine sit in possessione. . . .

Gaius in the fourth book of his *Institutes*:

We are held to possess not only if we possess ourselves, but also if someone is in possession in our name even though he is not subject to our power, e.g., the tenant of a farm or dwelling. We are also held to possess through those with whom we deposit, or to whom we make a loan for use (*commodatum*), or to whom we offer a free dwelling. And this is the basis of the common saying, that possession can be retained through anyone who is in possession in our name. . . .

Discussion

1. Detention. A frequent result of contracts is that one party holds, for a time, the other party's property, under some form of bailment or lease. Roman property law develops the idea that in these situations the contractual bailee (the physical holder) or lessee is not a legal possessor, but only "in possession in our name," as a sort of surrogate of the other party. The immediate practical consequence is that the temporary holder has no property rights conferred through the contract. As this Case shows, this is true no less for the lease of immovables (such as farms or dwellings) than for the deposit or loan of movables. The holder is said only to "detain" the property (*detinere*), or to be the "Natural possessor" of it; see Julian, D. 41.5.2.1. This legal rule is not obvious and demands some thought. What awkwardness could it cause?

2. Bailment of Another's Property. Can you lend or deposit an object that does not belong to you, or that you have even stolen? Since, in Roman law, no property right is being transferred through the contract, the answer is yes, meaning that even the thief, so long as he possesses the property even unjustly, has the resulting actions against an intruder. Compare Africanus, D. 16.3.16: "You deposit an object with someone and he (then) deposits it with a third party. If that person is guilty of deceit (*dolus*), your depositary is liable (only) to provide you the actions on the deceit of the subsequent depositary." Africanus obviously assumes that both contracts are valid, and that the re-deposit is not necessarily a deceitful breach of contract; is he correct?

CASE 64: Liability of the Holder (The Benefit Principle)

D. 13.6.5.2–3 (Ulpianus libro vicensimo octavo ad Edictum)

2. Nunc videndum est, quid veniat in commodati actione, utrum dolus an et culpa an vero et omne periculum. Et quidem in contractibus interdum dolum solum, interdum et culpam praestamus: dolum in deposito: nam quia nulla utilitas eius versatur apud quem deponitur, merito dolus praestatur solus: nisi forte et merces accessit (tunc enim, ut est et constitutum, etiam culpa exhibetur) aut si hoc ab initio convenit, ut et culpam et periculum praestet is penes quem deponitur. Sed ubi utriusque utilitas vertitur, ut in empto, ut in locato, ut in dote, ut in pignore, ut in societate, et dolus et culpa praestatur. 3. Commodatum autem plerumque solam utilitatem continet eius cui commodatur, et ideo verior est Quinti Mucii sententia existimantis et culpam praestandam et diligentiam et, si forte res aestimata data sit, omne periculum praestandum ab eo, qui aestimationem se praestaturum recepit.

Ulpian in the twenty-eighth book *On the Edict*:

2. Now let us examine what is at issue in the action on loan for use (*commodatum*): whether deceit (*dolus*), or also fault (*culpa*), or indeed also all risk (*periculum*)?

In contracts we are sometimes liable just for *dolus*, sometimes also for *culpa*. But because the depositary receives no benefit (*utilitas*), he is rightly liable for *dolus* alone, unless perhaps a fee is also paid—for then, as the emperor has also ruled, he is liable as well for *culpa*—or if the parties agreed at the outset that the depositary be liable for both *culpa* and the risk (*periculum*).

But when the benefit (*utilitas*) of both parties is involved, as in sale, lease, dowry, pledge (*pignus*), and partnership, there is liability for both *dolus* and *culpa*.

3. *Commodatum* regularly involves only the borrower's benefit (*utilitas*), and so the view of Quintus Mucius is more correct. He thought that there was liability for both *culpa* and safekeeping (*custodia*), and if perchance an appraised object was given, the person who undertook to provide the appraised value is liable for all risk (*periculum*).

Discussion

1. The Principle of Benefit (*Utilitas*). Ulpian seeks to provide a theoretical framework for default rules, which are often vital especially in contracts between friends. The main device he uses, one that appears frequently in Roman contract law, is the principle of "benefit" (*utilitas*)—the flow of benefit between the two parties. This flow determines the level of care that must be maintained by a person holding another's property under each form of bailment. Three main levels are utilized:

    i. liability just for deceit or deliberate misconduct (*dolus*);

ii. liability also for fault (*culpa*), including carelessness; and

iii. liability for what is called *custodia*, safekeeping, which extends to all loss except what the bailee could not prevent. (This is the standard applied in section 3.)

As to deposit and *commodatum*, examine Ulpian's argument closely. How convincing is it? Scholars still debate about the extent to which Classical texts on these liabilities were altered by Justinian's compilers. See also Modestinus, *Collatio* 10.2.1, discussing the principle of advantage in a pre-Justinianic text.

2. **Depositary's Liability for *Dolus*.** This is the least demanding level of care, which derives also from the original *formula* for deposit (see Case 62). As Ulpian notes, the level can be varied by agreement, although liability for *dolus* cannot be excluded.

Since *dolus* covers only intentional acts, the jurists seem sometimes uneasy with so low a level. Gaius, D. 44.7.1.5, upholds the general rule for a depositary who carelessly loses a deposited object; but Celsus, D. 16.3.32 (possibly interpolated), favors classifying more serious fault (*latior culpa*, roughly gross carelessness) as *dolus*, and he also argues that the depositary should at least be liable for care equivalent to that which he gives to his own property. Does this subjective standard seem plausible? In any case, some of the difficulties in the Roman position emerge from Ulpian, D. 16.3.1.8: "If clothes are given to a bathkeeper for safekeeping and they perish, provided he takes no fee to guard them, I think him liable on deposit, but only for *dolus*." Assuming that the bathkeeper operates a commercial establishment, is this standard too narrow? Contrast Ulpian, D. 16.3.1.35: "But also if someone solicits a deposit, Julian writes that he assumes the risk of the deposit, but such that he is liable not only for *dolus* but also for *culpa* and *custodia*, although not for unavoidable accidents (*fortuiti casus*)." Can a banker be described as someone who "solicits a deposit"? (See Case 69.)

3. **Borrower's Liability for *Custodia*.** Again, for *commodatum* this was the usual level of care in Roman law; see Gaius, *Inst.* 3.206, and Ulpian, D. 13.6.5.5–7 (noting an exception for borrowed slaves), although the level is occasionally described only as *culpa*; see Modestinus, *Collatio* 10.2.1 (a pre-Justinianic source). However, once again some exceptional cases may arise. Gaius, D. 13.6.18 pr.: "But if (a *commodatum* benefits) both parties, e.g., if we invite a common friend to dinner and you undertook to arrange it while I lend you silver, I find it written by some jurists that you should be liable only for *dolus*; but consider whether liability should not also be for *culpa*. . . ." Here both parties benefit from the loan, although the benefit seems to be mainly social. Compare Ulpian, D. 13.6.5.10: "Sometimes the

borrower will clearly be liable just for *dolus* toward the borrowed object, e.g., if someone so agreed; or if he lent only for his own benefit, as to his fiancée or wife so that she be dressed more respectably for the marriage; or if a Praetor who is putting on games lent (clothing) to the actors, or someone voluntarily lent to the Praetor." In Ulpian's last example, is the lender seeking favor from the Praetor? Note that the jurists repeatedly stress the ability of the parties to vary the default rules.

Suppose a catastrophic fire in which the borrower faces a choice between saving his own property or that of the lender. *Pauli Sent.* 2.4.2 (postclassical) says that, if the borrowed object perishes, the borrower will not be liable unless he could have saved it and preferred to save his own property. Realistic?

Again, suppose that the lender sends his slave to get property back from the borrower, and the slave then takes it and flees instead of returning home. Is the borrower liable to the owner? Should it matter whether the owner had ordered the slave to retrieve the property, or instead only to remind the borrower? See Ulpian, D. 13.6.12.1.

4. Overstepping the Contract. The situation changes if the bailee uses the property other than as arranged with the bailor. It is theft (*furtum*) to use a deposit without permission (Gaius, *Inst.* 3.196–198), and the depositary also becomes liable for any ensuing loss; see the following Case. Similarly for *commodatum* if the object is used other than as agreed: Ulpian, D. 13.6.5.8.

CASE 65: Protecting against Damage by a Third Party

D. 19.2.41 (Ulpianus libro quinto ad Edictum)

Sed de damno ab alio dato agi cum eo non posse Iulianus ait: qua enim custodia consequi potuit, ne damnum iniuria ab alio dari possit? Sed Marcellus interdum esse posse ait, sive custodiri potuit, ne damnum daretur, sive ipse custos damnum dedit: quae sententia Marcelli probanda est.

Ulpian in the fifth book *On the Edict*:

But regarding loss (*damnum*) inflicted by another person, Julian says there can be no lawsuit against him (the borrower or lessee); for through what safekeeping (*custodia*) could he ensure that loss not be wrongfully inflicted by a third party? But Marcellus says this is sometimes possible if he could safeguard it against loss being inflicted, or if the guardian himself inflicted the loss. This opinion of Marcellus should be approved.

The Problem
You lent property to me, and, while it was in my control, a third party damaged it. Can I be held liable to you for this loss?

Discussion

1. A Dispute among Jurists. Julian's view, which we also have in his own words (D. 13.6.19) but Ulpian accurately captures, was that *custodia* liability did not extend to protecting the lender's or lessor's property against wrongful damage by third parties. Such damage was generally actionable as a delict (*damnum iniuria datum*) under the Lex Aquilia. Julian elsewhere is cited as arguing that the owner of borrowed property, but not the borrower, has an Aquilian action against the wrongdoer: Ulpian, D. 9.2.11.9. But the wrongdoer may be impossible to locate, or insolvent and hence judgment-proof. So the possibility of a contractual action against the borrower arises. Examine the conflict between Julian and his student Marcellus. How does Marcellus try to reinterpret the duty of safekeeping?

2. Innkeepers and Shipowners. Long-distance travel was risky business in antiquity; thieves and bandits were a constant threat. A special liability, called *receptum*, was imposed on innkeepers and shipowners to provide safekeeping for property that was entrusted to them by passengers or guests. This liability closely resembles *custodia*, so the same issues as in the present Case arise. Are shipowners and innkeepers obliged to protect entrusted property against theft or wrongful loss by third parties? See Gaius, D. 4.9.5.1.

CASE 66: The Depositary's Duty to Restore

D. 16.3.1.23–25 (Ulpianus libro trigensimo ad Edictum)

23. Hanc actionem bonae fidei esse dubitari non oportet. 24. Et ideo et fructus in hanc actionem venire et omnem causam et partum, dicendum est, ne nuda res veniat. 25. Si rem depositam vendidisti eamque postea redemisti in causam depositi, etiamsi sine dolo malo postea perierit, teneri te depositi, quia semel dolo fecisti, cum venderes.

Ulpian in the thirtieth book *On the Edict*:

23. There must be no doubt that this (the action on deposit) is an action in good faith (*bona fides*). 24. And so it must be held that fruits and all accessories and off-spring are at issue in this action; it is not (just) the bare object that is at issue.

25. If you sold a deposited object, and subsequently bought it back because of the deposit, then (a jurist held that) you are liable on the deposit even if it afterward perished without your deceit (*dolus malus*).

The Problem
You left a cow as a deposit with me, and, while it was in my control, the cow gave birth. I then caused the death both of the cow and her calf. For what am I liable?

Discussion
1. **The Depositary's Duty.** With section 24, compare Ulpian, D. 16.3.1.5: "The accessories of deposited things are not deposited. E.g., if a clothed slave is deposited, the clothing is not deposited; likewise for a horse with a halter, for only the horse is deposited." Can this fragment be reconciled with the present Case? In section 25, does Ulpian assume that the repurchased object perished as even an indirect result of the deceitful sale? Is the depositary simply unable to purge his *dolus*?

2. **The Borrower.** A borrower also must return the object and account for any profits derived from it. Pomponius, D. 13.6.13.1, gives as an example farm animals that the borrower leases to a third party; the borrower must transmit this rent to the lender. Ulpian, D. 13.6.5.14, discusses an interesting case: you are giving dinner parties on two successive days, and ask me for the loan of silver on both days; I agree, but decide to leave the silver with you overnight because I find it inconvenient to take it back. During the night the silver is stolen. Are you liable for its loss? The answer seems to turn on whether this is one continuous contract of *commodatum*, or two contracts interrupted by a deposit, with the recipient's liability varying accordingly. Which seems the better solution?

3. **Theft of the Bailed Object.** If a deposited object is stolen by a third party, the depositor normally can sue the thief through the delictual action on

theft (provided, of course, that identification is possible and the thief is solvent). But if a borrowed object is stolen, it is the borrower who normally can bring the action against the thief; see Modestinus, *Collatio* 10.2.6 (apparently assuming a borrower's liability for *custodia*). Is this a straightforward application of the varying rules on the bailee's care for the object and duty to return it?

CASE 67: Expenses by the Holder

Collatio 10.2.5, = D. 16.3.23 (Modestinus libro Differentiarum secundo sub titulo de deposito vel commodato)

Actione depositi conventus cibariorum nomine apud eundem iudicem utiliter experitur; at is cui res commodata est inprobe cibariorum exactionem intendit. Inpensas tamen necessarias iure persequitur, quas forte in aegrum vel alias laborantem inpenderit.

Modestinus in the second book of *Distinctions*, in the title on deposit and *commodatum*:

When one is sued by an action on deposit, expenses for board (of a slave) are effectively claimed before the same judge. By contrast, a borrower wrongly claims payment for board. Still, he has a right to obtain expenses that have to be made, e.g., those he spent on a sick or otherwise ailing (slave).

Discussion

1. Counteractions and Offset. The actions on deposit and *commodatum* both start from the bailor's right to recover (see Case 62), and hence are available to the bailor alone. However, at times the bailee (depositary or borrower) may have valid counterclaims against the bailor, and these he can assert as plaintiff through a separate counteraction (*actio contraria*). He can also raise them as a defendant through offset within the context of a lawsuit based on *bona fides*; see Gaius, D. 13.6.18.4. Reread Case 62 on the *formulae* framed in law: the plaintiff's claim is potentially limited by the phrase "in accord with good faith," *ex fide bona*. How does this limitation prepare the way for offset? Finally, the bailee can refuse to return the object until the bailor satisfies a valid counterclaim; see Julian, D. 47.2.60; this reinforces the bailee's bargaining position.

2. Expenses. Modestinus discusses two kinds of expenses: ordinary upkeep such as food for a slave, which the depositary can claim but the borrower cannot; and urgent expenses such as medical care, which both depositary and borrower can claim. You should be able to relate this distinction to the principle of advantage discussed in Case 64. Gaius, D. 13.6.18.2–3, notes that urgent expenses include the costs of recovering a borrowed slave who runs away; and, of medical expenses, only larger ones, not day-to-day costs. Gaius adds that the borrower can recover losses if the lender had knowingly lent an object that is defective for its intended purpose, e.g., wine containers that leak. Somewhat similarly, Africanus, D. 13.7.31: counterclaim if a borrowed or deposited slave steals from the borrower, and the lender knew the slave was a thief. What logic ties these various cases together?

3. **Justinian's Changes.** The Digest version of this fragment (D. 16.3.23) omits all but the first sentence (up to *experitur*), but adds, after the first clause, the words *servo constituto*, "after the slave has been restored (*restituto?*)." This is typical of many changes the compilers make in earlier juristic texts—in this case, a text that by chance was independently transmitted in a collection of excerpts from the early fourth century CE. Have the compilers substantially altered the original holding by Modestinus?

CASE 68: Conversion of a Deposit into a *Mutuum*

D. 12.1.9.9 (Ulpianus libro vicensimo sexto ad Edictum)

Deposui apud te decem, postea permisi tibi uti: Nerva Proculus etiam antequam moveantur, condicere quasi mutua tibi haec posse aiunt, et est verum, ut et Marcello videtur: animo enim coepit possidere. Ergo transit periculum ad eum, qui mutuam rogavit et poterit ei condici.

D. 12.1.10 (Ulpianus libro secundo ad Edictum)

Quod si ab initio, cum deponerem, uti tibi si voles permisero, creditam non esse antequam mota sit, quoniam debitu iri non est certum.

Ulpian in the twenty-sixth book *On the Edict*:

I deposited ten (thousand sesterces) with you, and later permitted you to use them. Nerva and Proculus say that even before they are moved (from the place of deposit), a *condictio* can be brought for them as if they were on loan to you; for he (the borrower) began to possess by intent (*animo*). Therefore the risk (*periculum*) passed to the person who requested the loan, and a *condictio* can lie against him.

Ulpian in the second book *On the Edict*:

Wherefore if from the outset, when I made the deposit, I allow you to use it if you wish, (a jurist held that) it is not loaned before it is moved (by you), since it is uncertain that debt will arise.

Discussion

1. Conversion to a *Mutuum*. Study this Case closely. For Ulpian, the issue is not just the parties' ability to convert a deposit into a loan for consumption (a *mutuum*), but also when the *mutuum* arises, i.e., at what point ownership of the money passes to the borrower, who then assumes all risk. Ulpian outlines two distinct situations: deposit followed by later agreement on a *mutuum*; and deposit accompanied by agreement that the depositary may use the money at will. In the first situation, Paul, *Collatio* 10.7.9, appears to give the same result. In the second, Ulpian, D. 16.3.1.34, holds that, before use, the depositary is liable on the deposit; but what is the extent of that liability? Ulpian, D. 12.1.4 pr. (discussed in Case 56), holds that the depositary bears all risk when the deposit is made at his or her request, e.g., so that the money be on hand if the depositary wishes to use it later.

CASE 69: Irregular Deposit

D. 16.3.24 (Papinianus libro nono Quaestionum) "Lucius Titius Sempronio salutem. Centum nummos, quos hac die commendasti mihi adnumerante servo Sticho actore, esse apud me ut notum haberes, hac epistula manu mea scripta tibi notum facio: quae quando voles et ubi voles confestim tibi numerabo." Quaeritur propter usurarum incrementum. Respondi depositi actionem locum habere: quid est enim aliud commendare quam deponere? Quod ita verum est, si id actum est, ut corpora nummorum eadem redderentur: nam si ut tantundem solveretur convenit, egreditur ea res depositi notissimos terminos. In qua quaestione si depositi actio non teneat, cum convenit tantundem, non idem reddi, rationem usurarum haberi non facile dicendum est. Et est quidem constitutum in bonae fidei iudiciis, quod ad usuras attinet ut tantundem possit officium arbitri quantum stipulatio: sed contra bonam fidem et depositi naturam est usuras ab eo desiderare temporis ante moram, qui beneficium in suscipienda pecunia dedit. Si tamen ab initio de usuris praestandis convenit, lex contractus servabitur.

Papinian in the ninth book of his *Questions*:

"Lucius Titius (sends) greetings to Sempronius. By this letter written in my hand, I make known to you so that you have notice: I have the hundred coins that you .commended to me, counted out by your slave representative Stichus. I will pay these to you immediately when and where you wish."

Question arises about the growth of interest (on this money).

I responded that the action on deposit lies; for what is it "to commend" if not to deposit? But this is so if the transaction was that the same physical coins be returned; for if they agreed that an equivalent amount be paid, this oversteps the well-known boundaries of deposit. In this matter, if the action on deposit should not lie when they agreed that an equivalent and not the same thing be returned, it is not easy to decide that account be taken of interest.

And indeed, insofar as interest (on a deposit) is concerned, it is settled that in good faith actions the discretion of a judge is as good as a stipulation. But it is contrary to good faith and the nature of deposit to claim interest for the period before default (*mora*) from someone who confers a benefit by taking the money.

However, if from the outset they agreed on paying interest, the terms of the contract will be enforced.

Discussion

1. Bank Deposits. The document Papinian discusses undoubtedly originated from a banker. It acknowledges receipt of a sum of money (paid in by a slave) and promises return upon demand. Papinian discusses three interlocked questions: (i) whether the resulting contract is a *depositum* within the meaning of the Roman legal term; (ii) assuming that the contract is a

deposit, whether interest is payable on it if the banker defaults in repaying; (iii) again assuming it is a deposit, whether interest is payable even before default if the two parties have informally agreed on this. Implied in Papinian's discussion is the alternative, that the transaction might in fact be a *mutuum*, on which no interest is payable either by informal agreement or after default. This is a famous and very difficult Case, on which scholars have long disagreed. Make up your own mind about just how Papinian answers his three questions.

2. **Open Deposits.** Although deposit normally involves return of the same object (see Case 66), the jurists were prepared to concede that some deposits might involve return of an equivalent amount of money. E.g., Papinian, D. 16.3.25.1: "A person takes a deposit of money that is not under seal, for return of an equivalent. If he turns it to his own uses, after default he should be condemned, in an action on deposit, for interest as well." This concept of an "open deposit" is discussed as early as the late Republic; see Alfenus, D. 19.2.31 (grain from different owners is deposited in a pile in a ship's hold). Modern scholars usually refer to such a deposit as "irregular" (*depositum irregulare*). But how can an "open deposit" be distinguished from a *mutuum*? See, e.g., Paul, *Collatio* 10.7.9: "If I deposit money and allow you (to use) it, it seems to be lent rather than deposited; hence it will be at your risk." So can a distinction be drawn, depending upon whether it is the recipient who is the primary beneficiary of the transfer of money (as with most *mutua*), or rather the giver (as in an ordinary bank deposit, where the depositor is seeking both safety and liquidity)? Is it not the case that we "lend" money to our friends, but "deposit" money in our bank account, without ever thinking about the difference between the two?

3. **Banking and Bankruptcy.** Despite the obvious conceptual problems, most late classical jurists seem willing to treat bank deposits, not as *mutua*, but rather under the more flexible rules of deposit, which permit informal arrangements for interest; see Scaevola, D. 16.3.28, and Paul, D. 16.3.26.1, both quoting bank documents. (See also the Discussion on Case 102.) But problems remain. Ulpian, D. 16.3.7.2–3 and 42.5.24.2, discussing bank failures, state that depositors whose money does not bear interest receive preferred treatment in allocating the bank's assets after bankruptcy. But those with interest-bearing accounts are classed lower, with ordinary creditors of the bank. In the first passage Ulpian argues that depositors who receive interest effectively "renounce" (*renuntiare*) their deposits (thereby converting them into loans); in the second passage, that their transaction is properly a loan rather than a deposit. Is either argument persuasive? Note that for Ulpian the crucial issue seems to be whether a deposit can be interest-bearing prior to the bank's failure; while for his teacher Papinian,

in the present Case, the crucial issue is whether this is a deposit at all. If the transaction can in fact be classified as a deposit, Papinian has no difficulty with informally arranged interest. What do all these sources suggest about the flexibility of Roman law in handling banking and other commercial affairs? In any case, surviving sources make it crystal clear that Roman bankers were paying interest on at least some "deposits," obviously in an effort to attract them.

4. Gratuitous Deposit Revisited. Implicit in the sources we have been examining is an evolution in Roman contract law that can be closely correlated with a corresponding social evolution. The early law on deposit presumed a relatively non-commercial society: a world dominated, perhaps, by wealthy landowners with close personal interrelationships. Deposit described a typical social interaction between "friends" who are usually also social equals. But as the Roman world developed toward greater commercial sophistication, there emerged new types of transactions that were difficult to describe in terms of traditional legal categories.

Ordinary bank deposits are one example. The jurists slowly adapted Roman law to meet these new situations. In principle, deposit is gratuitous; if the depositor pays a fee for guard of the object, then the contract is lease. But Ulpian, D. 47.8.2.23, describes a deposit in which the depositor does not pay a fee (*merces*), but does pay what is described as a "charge for the deposit" (*pretium depositionis*). The transaction is still apparently treated as a deposit, but now the depositary is liable if the object is stolen, although still entitled to bring suit against the thief (see the discussion on Case 67). Ulpian reasons that because of the "charge," the depositary has an interest in the contract that would not exist if the deposit were purely gratuitous. Can it be presumed that this arrangement arose in the context of banking, in order to deal with "safety deposit boxes" or the equivalent? By the late Classical period, is anything really left of the older legal regime for deposit?

CASE 70: Loan and Holding on Sufferance (*Precarium*)

D. 43.26.1 (Ulpianus libro primo *Institutionum*)

pr. Precarium est, quod precibus petenti utendum conceditur tamdiu, quamdiu is qui concessit patitur. 1. Quod genus liberalitatis ex iure gentium descendit. 2. Et distat a donatione eo, quod qui donat, sic dat, ne recipiat, at qui precario concedit, sic dat quasi tunc recepturus, cum sibi libuerit precarium solvere. 3. Et est simile commodato: nam et qui commodat rem, sic commodat, ut non faciat rem accipientis, sed ut ei uti re commodata permittat.

Ulpian in the first book of his *Institutes*:

pr. A holding on sufferance (*precarium*) is something granted, for as long as the grantor allows this, to a petitioner who asks for its use. 1. This type of generosity originates in the Law of Nations (*ius gentium*). 2. It differs from gift in that a donor gives with no aim of recovering (the gift); but the grantor of a *precarium* gives with the expectation of recovery when he wishes to dissolve the *precarium*. 3. It is also similar to a loan for use (*commodatum*); for the lender of an object lends not to make the object the recipient's property, but to allow him use of the borrowed object.

Discussion

1. *Precarium*. This Case vividly illustrates the social presumptions upon which Roman contract law was constructed. A *precarium* (from *precari*, "to beseech") is not a contract at all, but a property arrangement in which one party, the superior, grants to another the use of his property, subject to recall at will. The grantee takes legal possession, which he or she can defend against everyone except the grantor. But the relationship is one of fairly stark social dependence. By contrast, *commodatum* is a gratuitous contract between persons presumed to be social equals; the borrower does not have possession, but does enjoy a bilateral contractual relationship with the lender. In practice, the two transactions are difficult to tell apart except through reference to the social background of the parties. A typical *precarium* is for land granted to, e.g., a dependent peasant, but such grants could also be for movables. See, in general, D. 43.26.

PART C

Pledge (*Pignus*)

The final "real" contract, pledge (*pignus*), is somewhat anomalous. It arises when one person secures a debt owed to his creditor by giving the creditor an object as a "pledge." If the debt is not paid, the creditor is usually entitled to sell the pledge. Although the contract of *pignus* is nominally gratuitous, in fact the relationship is accessory to the principal debt, and both parties benefit from its delivery: the debtor, by obtaining credit, and the creditor, by securing repayment. Therefore the flow of benefit (*utilitas*) is best described as bilateral (see Case 64), and the legal allocation of rights and duties largely follows from this presumed bilaterality.

Like other "real" contracts, *pignus* was originally actionable through a praetorian *formula in factum* (compare Case 62), which the pledger could use in order to recover the object after the debt had been paid or otherwise satisfied. The Praetor may later have provided a more developed *formula in ius* based on *bona fides*, although this is not certain. A corresponding counteraction protected the creditor's interests in the pledge.

As a "real" contract, *pignus* may at first have been effective only when the pledged object was delivered into the creditor's possession. However, the contract of *pignus* became entangled, in Classical law, with the further development of real security. This law eventually allowed the parties to arrange informally that an object be a security for a debt whether or not it was delivered into the creditor's possession; and the creditor was also given wide-ranging property rights in the pledge. An unpossessed pledge is conventionally called a "hypothec" (*hypotheca*), although the jurists frequently use this term almost interchangeably with *pignus*. By the end of the Classical period, the possessed pledge was only a special case of the more general law of real security. Since unpossessed pledges create a property interest in the creditor, they are most commonly dealt with in Roman property law, even though their formation has affinities with contract law.

CASE 71: Pledge as a Real Contract

Iustinianus, *Institutiones* 3.14.4

Creditor quoque qui pignus accepit re obligatur, qui et ipse de ea ipsa re quam accepit restituenda tenetur actione pigneraticia. sed quia pignus utriusque gratia datur, et debitoris, quo magis ei pecunia crederetur, et creditoris, quo magis ei in tuto sit creditum, placuit sufficere, quod ad eam rem custodiendam exactam diligentiam adhiberet: quam si praestiterit et aliquo fortuito casu rem amiserit, securum esse nec impediri creditum petere.

Justinian in the third book of his *Institutes*:

Likewise, a creditor who receives a pledge (*pignus*) is obligated by its delivery, and is also liable, by the action on pledge, to restore the object he received. But since a pledge is given in both parties' interest—both the debtor's, to obtain readier credit, and the creditor's, that he be safer in extending credit—the prevailing view is that it is enough that he (the creditor) show great carefulness (*exacta diligentia*) in guarding the object. If he provides this, and by some unavoidable accident (*fortuitus casus*) loses the object, he is protected and is not hindered from (nonetheless) suing for the debt.

Discussion

1. A Real Contract. Ordinarily, a pledge only became valid when the object was handed over into the creditor's possession; the Praetor then provided an *in factum* action whereby the debtor could recover the pledge when the debt had been paid. Later, this action may have been supplemented by a *bona fides* action, following the pattern in Case 62, since the range of problems arising from one party's property being held by another are similar for pledge. But note that, in early Roman law, the debtor's agreement to provide a pledge would usually not have been enforceable prior to delivery, at any rate if the debt was an informal *mutuum*; this defect was later solved through development of a wider law of real security; see Case 75.

2. The Creditor's Level of Care for the Pledge. Justinian describes the level of care as "great carefulness" (*exacta diligentia*). This is evidently a *custodia* standard, i.e., liability for all but unpreventable loss; see Ulpian, D. 13.7.13.1, on *pignus* ("This action involves both *dolus* and *culpa*, as in *commodatum*, and *custodia* as well, but not higher force, *vis maior*."). However, Justinian's argument, that both parties benefit from the contract, resembles that in Case 75, where, in fact, Ulpian says that the pledge-holder is liable for *dolus* and *culpa*, i.e., for deliberate harm and fault (including carelessness), but not for more exacting *custodia*. Some scholars therefore

suppose that Justinian raised the creditor's level of liability; others, that the matter was already disputed in Classical law, with some pre-Justinianic sources (above all, Gaius, *Inst.* 3.204–205) clearly pointing in the direction of *custodia*. Does the theory of benefit really help to solve the problem? In any case, what is the optimal default level?

CASE 72: Recovery of the Pledge

D. 13.7.9.3, 5 (Ulpianus libro vicensimo octavo ad Edictum)

3. Omnis pecunia exsoluta esse debet aut eo nomine satisfactum esse, ut nascatur pigneraticia actio. Satisfactum autem accipimus, quemadmodum voluit creditor, licet non sit solutum: sive aliis pignoribus sibi caveri voluit, ut ab hoc recedat, sive fideiussoribus sive reo dato sive pretio aliquo vel nuda conventione, nascitur pigneraticia actio. Et generaliter dicendum erit, quotiens recedere voluit creditor a pignore, videri ei satisfactum, si ut ipse voluit sibi cavit, licet in hoc deceptus sit. . . . 5. Qui ante solutionem egit pigneraticia, licet non recte egit, tamen, si offerat in iudicio pecuniam, debet rem pigneratam et quod sua interest consequi.

D. 13.7.10 (Gaius libro nono ad Edictum Provinciale)

Quod si non solvere, sed alia ratione satisfacere paratus est, forte si expromissorem dare vult, nihil ei prodest.

Ulpian in the twenty-eighth book *On the Edict*:

3. For the action on pledge to arise, all money ought to be repaid, or satisfaction be given on its account. We construe satisfaction to mean whatever the creditor wants, even though there is no (actual) payment; the action on pledge arises if, in exchange for giving up this (pledge), he wished to be protected by other pledges, or by sureties, or by a new debtor, or by some price (given in payment), or by bare agreement. As a general rule, whenever the creditor wishes to give up the pledge, it should be held that satisfaction was given to him if he made provision for himself as he wanted, even though he was deceived in the matter. . . . 5. A person who brought the action on pledge before payment, although he did so incorrectly, still should obtain the pledged object and his interest if he offers the money during the trial.

Gaius in the ninth book *On the Provincial Edict*:

But if he was ready, not to pay, but to give satisfaction otherwise, e.g., if he wished to give a co-promissor, this is of no use to him.

Discussion

1. Repayment or Satisfaction. The debtor can end the pledge either by repaying the entire debt or by giving some other "satisfaction" acceptable to the creditor; in fact, the creditor can end the pledge more or less at will, even by forgiving the debt. Repayment can be to the creditor or to some other person expressly or tacitly authorized to receive it; see Ulpian, D. 13.7.11.5, who notes that it is also enough if the creditor is "enriched" by the payment. Generally, as this Case indicates, the jurists try to construe the rules on repayment fairly liberally, with consideration for both sides. Thus, for example, if the debt is "novated" (see Case 39), the creditor loses

claim to the pledged security unless continuation of his prior claim was provided for; see Ulpian, D. 13.7.11.1. Likewise, if the creditor is in default (*mora*) in accepting payment; see Paul, D. 13.7.20.2.

2. **Extent of the Claim for Recovery.** Suppose that a slave woman is given to the creditor as a pledge, and she then dies while giving birth to a child; is the child pledged, and upon payment can the debtor recover the child by suing on pledge? It is clear that the parties can make an agreement to this effect; see Papinian, D. 20.1.1.2; and Paul, D. 20.1.29.1, indicates that the "fruits" of a pledged object (such as the child of a slave woman, or rent from a pledged farm) would also come tacitly under the pledge even in the absence of an agreement. But *Pauli Sent.* 2.5.2 (postclassical but pre-Justinianic) states flatly that this would not be true unless the parties expressly agreed. What is the best solution of this problem? Late Classical jurists also recognize an agreement (called *antichresis*) allowing a creditor to keep the fruits in lieu of interest on a debt; see Marcian, D. 20.1.11.1.

3. **Collateral Claims.** A debtor has given an object as a pledge for a debt, and pays this debt, but still owes money on other debts to the same creditor. Can the creditor keep the pledge until the other debts are also satisfied? The Classical jurists would probably have said no; but the Emperor Gordian, C. 8.26.1.2–3 (239 CE), permits the practice, which was probably borrowed from Greek law. Discuss the pros and cons of this ruling. Is it consistent with general principles of Roman contract law?

CASE 73: Agreement on Sale of the Pledge

D. 13.7.4 (Ulpianus libro quadragensimo primo ad Sabinum)

Si convenit de distrahendo pignore sive ab initio sive postea, non tantum venditio valet, verum incipit emptor dominium rei habere. Sed etsi non convenerit de distrahendo pignore, hoc tamen iure utimur, ut liceat distrahere, si modo non convenit, ne liceat. Ubi vero convenit, ne distraheretur, creditor, si distraxerit, furti obligatur, nisi ei ter fuerit denuntiatum ut solvat et cessaverit.

Ulpian in the forty-first book *On Sabinus*:

If, either initially or later, the parties agree on sale of the pledge, not only is the sale valid, but the buyer becomes owner of the object. But even if they do not agree on selling the pledge, nonetheless we use this rule: it is permitted to sell provided they did not agree that this is not permitted. But when they agree that it is not to be sold, the creditor is liable for theft if he sells, unless he (the debtor) was given three formal warnings to pay and has not responded.

Discussion

1. **Agreement on Sale.** Originally, the pledge may have been a sort of "hostage" to force repayment of the debt; but in Classical law it is more frequently regarded as an alternative means for the creditor to seek recovery of what is owed. Still, this Case raises many questions. Does an agreement against its sale have any actual effect? See the Emperor Alexander, C. 8.27.4 (225 CE), who requires notice to the debtor in any event. How does the buyer at auction acquire ownership? Gaius, *Inst.* 2.64, says that the debtor is construed as having given tacit assent to a sale through the creditor's agency; but is this true in the case of a pact forbidding sale? Can the creditor purchase the pledge himself, either directly or through an intermediary? See *Pauli Sent.* 2.13.4 (no, if the debtor is unwilling; why? what are the dangers here?); but the debtor can sell it to the creditor; see Papinian, *Frag. Vat.* 9. If the sale price was more than the debt, the debtor could sue to recover the surplus; see Diocletian, 8.27.20 (294 CE).

2. **Foreclosure.** The parties could also agree that the pledge would become the creditor's property if the debt was not paid by a deadline: Marcian, D. 20.1.16.9 (citing a rescript of Severus and Caracalla), who also stresses that it must be evaluated at a "just price" (*iustum pretium*). In late Classical law, the creditor could apply to an imperial court for ownership, which passed to him if the pledge had not been redeemed within a year; but the creditor lost any claim on the underlying debt and had to return any surplus in appraised value to the debtor; see Alexander, C. 8.33.1 (229 CE), and Gordian, C. 8.33.2 (238 CE).

CASE 74: The Counterclaim

D. 13.7.25 (Ulpianus libro trigensimo primo ad Edictum)

Si servos pigneratos artificiis instruxit creditor, si quidem iam imbutos vel voluntate debitoris, erit actio contraria: si vero nihil horum intercessit, si quidem artificiis necessariis, erit actio contraria, non tamen sic, ut cogatur servis carere pro quantitate sumptuum debitor. Sicut enim neglegere creditorem dolus et culpa quam praestat non patitur, ita nec talem efficere rem pigneratam, ut gravis sit debitori ad reciperandum: puta saltum grandem pignori datum ab homine, qui vix luere potest, nedum excolere, tu acceptum pignori excoluisti sic, ut magni pretii faceres. Alioquin non est aequum aut quaerere me alios creditores aut cogi distrahere quod velim receptum aut tibi paenuria coactum derelinquere. Medie igitur haec a iudice erunt dispicienda, ut neque delicatus debitor neque onerosus creditor audiatur.

Ulpian in the thirty-first book *On the Edict*:

If the creditor teaches skills to pledged slaves, there will be a counteraction (against the debtor) if they were previously being trained or the debtor wanted this. But if neither circumstance obtains, there will (still) be a counteraction provided the skills were needed; but not to the extent that the debtor must give up the slaves because of the size of the expenses. Just as the deceit (*dolus*) and fault (*culpa*) for which the creditor is responsible do not allow him to be careless, so (he ought) not to make the pledged object such that the debtor is burdened in recovering it. For example, a large tract of land is given by a man who can hardly pay for, much less cultivate it; you cultivate the pledge and so make it very valuable. For the rest, it is unfair that I (as a debtor) either seek out other creditors, or am forced to sell what I recover and wish (to keep), or because of poverty am forced to abandon (it) to you. The *iudex* must look for a middle way, listening neither to a fussy debtor nor to an overreaching creditor.

The Problem
The debtor gave his creditor a slave as a pledge for the debt, and the creditor then had the slave trained in a new and valuable skill. If the debtor then pays the debt and reclaims the slave, must he compensate the creditor for the cost of the training?

Discussion
1. Creditor's Counterclaims. As with other real contracts (see Case 67), the creditor could claim compensation for some expenses. This claim could be advanced either through a special counteraction or by refusing to return the object until a valid claim had been met; see Pomponius, D. 13.7.8 pr. Urgent expenses are compensable; Pomponius' example is medical expenses for a pledged slave (even if the slave then dies), or repairs to a building (even if it later burns down). But what of educating a slave or bringing a tract under cultivation? The concern in this Case appears to be

that the benefit will accrue to the pledge-debtor, and so he or she should pay for it; but the debtor may not have the means to do so, and thus the *iudex* should seek an equitable solution, perhaps by splitting the costs. Here and elsewhere, the jurists emphasize the role of the *iudex* as an intermediary between inflexible legal rules and the facts of particular cases. How easy will it be to fulfill that role?

2. **Misconduct by a Pledge-Debtor.** The creditor can also use the counteraction if, for instance, the debtor unknowingly pledges property belonging to a third party (see Paul, D. 13.7.16.1; it is a criminal offense if he knows), or knowingly pledges a bronze object that he tells the creditor is made of gold (Ulpian, D. 13.7.1.1–2, 36 pr.). If the debtor pledges a slave that he or she knows to be a thief, and the slave then steals from the creditor, the counteraction also lies; Africanus, D. 13.7.31.

3. **The Pledge-Debtor Steals or Damages a Pledge.** Pomponius, D. 13.7.3, sets the following problem: A creditor, misguidedly believing that his debtor was about to pay up, handed back the pledge; the debtor then threw the pledge out a window into the hands of an accomplice waiting below. Since the creditor has a substantial property interest in the pledge, this is the delict of theft; but can the creditor also bring a counteraction on the pledge? Pomponius says yes (but how would damages be measured?); and if the debtor raises the defense that the creditor voluntarily returned the object, the creditor can interject a counter-defense that the "voluntary return" was induced by the debtor's deceit. Presumably the counteraction would also be available if the debtor wrongfully damages the pledge. In both these cases, note that the creditor's present security interest supersedes the debtor's ownership interest.

CASE 75: Pledge and Hypothec

Justinianus, *Institutiones* 4.6.7

. . . Inter pignus autem et hypothecam quantum ad actionem hypothecariam nihil interest: nam de qua re inter creditorem et debitorem convenerit ut sit pro debito obligata, utraque hac appellatione continetur. sed in aliis differentia est: nam pignoris appellatione eam proprie contineri dicimus quae simul etiam traditur creditori, maxime si mobilis sit: at eam quae sine traditione nuda conventione tenetur proprie hypothecae appellatione contineri dicimus.

Justinian in the fourth book of his *Institutes*:

Insofar as the action on hypothec (*hypotheca*) is concerned, there is no difference at all between pledge (*pignus*) and hypothec. For when a creditor and debtor agree that an object be obligated for a debt, either one is included under this name (*hypotheca*). But in other respects they differ: for by the name pledge we properly include what is also handed over to the creditor at the same time, especially if it is movable. But by the name hypothec we properly include what is held (only) by bare agreement without a handover.

Discussion

1. **Unpossessed Securities.** The law of real security undergoes extraordinary development during the late Classical period. Creditor and debtor now become able to create a security interest in property by informal agreement alone, even though there is no delivery and both ownership and possession of the property remain with the debtor. What they create is a "charge," effectively an *in rem* right accruing to the creditor and enforceable against both the debtor and third parties; this right is realized through an action on the hypothec (*actio hypothecaria* or *Serviana*), which authorizes recovery even from third parties. Although the creditor's right is treated as part of property law, its creation is through a formless agreement, in effect a contract accessory to the principal debt. Although jurists often respect the terminological distinction in this Case between *pignus* and *hypotheca*, they also frequently do not. The resulting law, which is very complex, draws heavily on rules already worked out for possessed pledges.

CASE 76: Mortgage (*Fiducia*)

Isidorus, *Etymologiae* 5.25.21–24

21. . . . Item inter pignus, fiduciam et hypothecam hoc interest. 22. Pignus enim est quod propter rem creditam obligatur, cuius rei possessionem solam ad tempus consequitur creditor. Ceterum dominium penes debitorem est. 23. Fiducia est, cum res aliqua sumendae mutuae pecuniae gratia vel mancipatur vel in iure ceditur. 24. Hypotheca est, cum res commodatur sine depositione pignoris, pacto vel cautione sola interveniente.

Gaius, *Institutiones* 2.60

Sed cum fiducia contrahitur aut cum creditore pignoris iure aut cum amico, quo tutius nostrae res apud eum essent, si quidem cum amico contracta sit fiducia, sane omni modo conpetit usus receptio; si uero cum creditore, soluta quidem pecunia omni modo conpetit, nondum uero soluta ita demum competit, si neque conduxerit eam rem a creditore debitor neque precario rogauerit, ut eam rem possidere liceret; quo casu lucratiua usus capio conpetit.

Isidore of Seville in the fifth book of his *Etymologies*:

21. . . . This is the difference between pledge (*pignus*), *fiducia*, and hypothec. 22. A pledge is property obligated on account of extended credit; the creditor has possession of it only temporarily. 22. A *fiducia* is when property is either mancipated or ceded in court (*in iure cessio*) for the purpose of taking a money loan. 23. A hypothec is when property is furnished without transfer of the pledge, by means only of an agreement or formal promise (*cautio*).

Gaius in the third book of his *Institutes*:

But when a *fiducia* is contracted either with a creditor through the law of pledge (*pignus*) or with a friend to ensure safer keeping with him, if indeed *fiducia* has been contracted with a friend, recovery of ownership by continuous possession (*usureceptio*) occurs without condition. But if (*fiducia* was contracted) with a creditor, it (recovery) occurs without condition if the money has been paid; but if it has not yet been paid, then this occurs only if the debtor has not hired the object from the creditor nor asked for permission to possess the object on sufferance (*precarium*). In that case (where neither condition is true) a profitable acquisition by continuous possession (*usucapio*) occurs.

Discussion

1. The Fifth Real Contract? This security arrangement (broadly like a mortgage) existed alongside pledge, and later hypothec, for the entire of the Classical period, but it is little known because it fell between the cracks of Classical jurisprudence (neither wholly property law nor contract) and had also disappeared by Justinian's time. Isidore, a Christian scholar writing

ca. 625 and, though not himself a lawyer, still with extensive access to and knowledge of ancient sources including legal writings, isolates some major differences between the three forms of real security. The main characteristic of *fiducia* is that the debtor formally surrenders ownership of the security to the creditor, who promises to restore title to the debtor upon payment of the debt. Can you develop any hypotheses on how this institution arose and why it might then have gone extinct? (Recovery of the details of *fiducia* has been a major achievement of modern scholars.)

Gaius discusses a fairly narrow question, whether a debtor who has given property as a *fiducia* can reacquire ownership of it not through the creditor's formal conveyance back to him, but rather through informally receiving the property and simply holding it for the period of time required for usucapion (two years for land, one year for movables); this means of acquisition is called usucapion.

CHAPTER IV

Sale

A Contract Created through Informal Agreement

A Casebook on the Roman Law of Contracts. Bruce W. Frier, Oxford University Press. © Oxford University Press 2021.
DOI: 10.1093/oso/9780197573211.003.0005

PART A

Formation of a Sale

Unlike stipulations, which require the prescribed formality of solemn words, and "real" contracts, which require the "natural formality" of delivery, the four consensual contracts require only informal agreement (*consensus*) in order to be fully effective between the two parties to the contract. This Chapter deals with sale (*emptio venditio*), the most important and in many ways the most representative of these consensual contracts. The other three are considered more briefly in Chapter V.

In sale, the flow of benefit (*utilitas*) is almost always strongly bilateral; in this sense, it is much more like a typical modern contract than stipulation or the real contracts. The parties to a sale are each seeking advantage (usually, direct material advantage) from the sale of the object, and the agreement thus results from a genuine, bargained-for exchange between them. This is the real underlying reason why a sale becomes effective when agreement is reached, even though neither party may yet have begun to carry out the agreement or even to rely on it in preparation for performance. Their agreement is therefore often wholly executory, an exchange of promises that are to be carried out in the future. The Roman jurists, to be sure, explain the effectiveness of consensual contracts somewhat differently: the parties are obligated by good faith (*bona fides*) to carry out their agreement. Although this argument is illusory since *bona fides* has such a legal effect only in specific circumstances, nonetheless the jurists' argument opens the way to a more social interpretation of the process of making and executing contracts.

As the Cases will show, much more substantial problems arise in defining *consensus* itself. It is not always clear what the jurists mean by *consensus*: a true mental (subjective) agreement between the parties, or rather an apparent and objective agreement that may even be contrary to one or both parties' actual intentions. The Cases on mistake and interpretation throw limited light on this issue, but it is ultimately unclear how the jurists resolved the fundamental question.

SECTION 1. Agreement on the Basic Elements of a Sale

The Urban Praetor's Edict contained two *formulae* for sale: one for the seller (*actio ex vendito*), and one for the buyer (*actio ex empto*). Their wording is discussed in the Introduction to this book; it is almost laconically brief, giving no detailed instructions to the *iudex* beyond a description of the object of sale and an injunction to determine liability on the basis of good faith (*ex fide bona*), a phrase that became the starting point for most Roman law surrounding this contract.

Although, on their face, the *formulae* seem to declare the fact of the sale, even this could be contested before the *iudex*. Most importantly in this respect, the two *formulae* gave no clue even as to how "sale" itself should be defined. This was a "question of law" (*quaestio iuris*) that was, at least eventually, the domain of the jurists. Plainly, the *formulae* required the *iudex* to identify a transaction as a sale, and also to identify the seller and the buyer. In most instances, this would not be difficult, since ordinary language would suffice. But not infrequently contracts could be more complicated or ambiguous. The problem of identification is, of course, basic to all the Roman contract types, but the answers the jurists give in the case of sale are not always obvious and in some instances are highly debatable. These answers imply, as we shall see, a conception of sale that differs in important respects from the modern conception; and the reason for the differences may perhaps be related to the underdeveloped character of the Roman economy.

The Cases in this section explore a number of interrelated issues concerning the distinction between sale and barter, the nature of "price," and the sorts of property that qualify as objects of sale. It should be noted that, although our own law lays considerable stress on the difference between sale of goods and sale of land, Roman law, for the most part, does not, so the rules for sale are, to that extent, more generalized.

CASE 77: The Origins of Sale

D. 18.1.1 pr. (Paulus libro trigensimo tertio ad Edictum)

Origo emèndi vendendique a permutationibus coepit. Olim enim non ita erat nummus neque aliud merx, aliud pretium vocabatur, sed unusquisque secundum necessitatem temporum ac rerum utilibus inutilia permutabat, quando plerumque evenit, ut quod alteri superest alteri desit. Sed quia non semper nec facile concurrebat, ut, cum tu haberes quod ego desiderarem, invicem haberem quod tu accipere velles, electa materia est, cuius publica ac perpetua aestimatio difficultatibus permutationum aequalitate quantitatis subveniret. Eaque materia forma publica percussa usum dominiumque non tam ex substantia praebet quam ex quantitate nec ultra merx utrumque, sed alterum pretium vocatur.

Paul in the thirty-third book *On the Edict*:

Purchasing and selling (*emptio venditio*) took its origin from barters (*permutationes*). For at one time there was no coinage, nor was one thing called goods (*merx*) and the other the price (*pretium*). Rather, as time and circumstance dictated, each person bartered what was not needed for what was needed, since it is often the case that one party has in abundance what the other party lacks. But it did not always nor easily turn out that when you have what I want, I have in turn what you wish to take. Therefore a material was chosen, the public and enduring value of which overcame the problems with barter through the evenness of its amount. This material, struck with a public symbol, provided use and ownership less from its substance than from its amount; nor are both (the items exchanged) called goods, but one is called the price.

Discussion

1. Legal Anthropology. Reconstruct Paul's account of the origins of sale. It seems plausible, doesn't it? How does the invention of money fit into Paul's scheme? The theory of economic development in this passage can be traced back at least to Greek philosophers such as Aristotle, who argued that money, as a neutral measurement of the value of other goods, had to have an intrinsic value of its own, be durable and portable, and finally be divisible into precise units (*Politics* 1.8–10); and he too advances the idea Paul expresses, that money was devised to make exchanges easier. In this understanding, money is still largely metallic: for the most part, gold or silver bullion secured by official minting and with a face value something close to its value as bullion, or bronze supported by the precious metals.

2. Barter and Sale. Does this passage provide any clear grounds for distinguishing barter (*permutatio*) from sale? As the following Cases will suggest, this was a major problem for the jurists, who eventually held that barter was not actionable through the *formulae* for sale (see Case 79).

CASE 78: The Nature of Agreement

Gaius, *Institutiones* 3.135–137, 139

135. Consensu fiunt obligationes in emptionibus et uenditionibus, locationibus conductionibus, societatibus, mandatis. 136. Ideo autem istis modis consensu dicimus obligationes contrahi, quod neque uerborum neque scripturae ulla proprietas desideratur, sed sufficit eos, qui negotium gerunt, consensisse. unde inter absentes quoque talia negotia contrahuntur, ueluti per epistulam aut per internuntium, cum alioquin uerborum obligatio inter absentes fieri non possit. 137. Item in his contractibus alter alteri obligatur de eo, quod alterum alteri ex bono et aequo praestare oportet, cum alioquin in uerborum obligationibus alius stipuletur alius promittat et in nominibus alius expensum ferendo obliget alius obligetur. . . . 139. Emptio et uenditio contrahitur, cum de pretio conuenerit, quamuis nondum pretium numeratum sit ac ne arra quidem data fuerit. nam quod arrae nomine datur, argumentum est emptionis et uenditionis contractae.

Gaius in the third book of his *Institutes*:

135. Obligations are created through agreement (*consensus*) in the case of (the contracts of) purchase and sale, lease and hire, partnership, and mandate. 136. We say that these kinds of obligations are contracted by agreement because no formality of words or writing is required; it is enough that the persons who make the transaction agree. So such transactions are contracted also between absent parties, e.g., through a letter or by messenger, whereas a verbal obligation (a stipulation) cannot be made between absent persons.

137. Likewise, in these contracts one party is obligated to the other for what each ought to provide the other in accord with what is right and proper (*bonum et aequum*), whereas in verbal obligations one party stipulates and the other promises. . . . 139. Purchase and sale are contracted when there is agreement on a price, even if the price is not yet paid, nor even an earnest (*arra*) given. For what is given as an earnest is (only) evidence that a sale was contracted.

The Problem

Seius and Titius agree orally on Seius' sale of a Greek vase to Titius for 50,000 sesterces. Is anything further required in order to make their sale legally binding?

Discussion

1. **Stipulation and Sale.** According to Gaius, how do sale and the other consensual contracts differ from stipulation? He seems to lay emphasis on the absence of formality in forming a consensual contract: the parties need not be in one another's presence (although sources suggest this was normal), nor must they employ any legally prescribed words, whether oral or written. Think about the pros and cons of informality. How easy will it be, for instance, to recognize a sale agreement when it has been made?

The second difference is the content of the resulting contractual obligation: in stipulation, focus is on the wording of the promise, whereas in
consensual contracts the debtor is liable "in accord with what is right and
proper (*bonum et aequum*)." This concept of obligation in good faith (*ex fide
bona*) comes, of course, from the procedural *formulae* for sales, which are
discussed in the introduction to this section. But is Gaius implying that
there is some deeper relationship between the informality of a sale and the
obligation that results? Think about this question as you read later Cases.

2. **The Characteristics of Agreement.** What does Gaius mean by *consensus*?
This problem figures large in subsequent Cases, but it is worth considering even at this early point. For instance, Scaevola, D. 21.2.12, gives the
following problem: A man was named heir to half of an estate, with his
co-heirs receiving the other half. The principal heir then sold the entire
estate to a buyer. The co-heirs attended the sale and received their share of
the purchase price, but at the time they sat poker-faced, saying and doing
nothing to indicate their approval or disapproval of the sale. The estate's
buyer later lost a lawsuit brought by a third party who claimed that some or
all of the estate belonged to him. Can the buyer sue the co-heirs as sellers,
on the grounds of breach of warranty of title (see Part B.4 in this Chapter)?
Scaevola says yes, because their presence and failure to object makes them
effectively sellers of their shares. But in what sense did the co-heirs actually
agree to sell? (The answer, you should be warned, is important.)

3. **Bilaterality of Obligation.** In a stipulation, one party is a promissor and
the other a promisee. Sale is more complex in that it always involves an
exchange, so both parties are, at the conclusion of a sale agreement and before each begins to execute it, both promissors and promisees who are each
bound to the other. In Roman law, there is an important consequence: neither party can legally enforce the sale against the other unless he or she first
tenders performance. For instance, Ulpian, D. 19.1.13.8: "When bringing
an action on purchase, the buyer should offer the price, and therefore, even
if he offers part of the price, there is still no action on purchase; for the
seller can retain the object of sale as a sort of security (for the buyer's full
payment)." This is a central rule that, by making their promises interdependent, protects each party from having to perform when the other may
be unwilling or unable to perform. But the parties can still vary this rule by
express agreement; e.g., Gaius, *Inst.* 4.126a.

4. **Earnest Money.** An earnest (*arra* or *arrha*, ultimately from Hebrew)
resembles a deposit by the buyer. It was sometimes popularly thought of
as "cementing the deal," as if the parties' bare agreement was not enough.
The Romans also used the custom of having the buyer give the seller a ring

as a kind of symbolic earnest. Such customs look like formalities, but the jurists treat them only as evidence of agreement on the sale; e.g., Gaius, D. 18.1.35 pr.: "The practice of giving an earnest does not mean that agreement without earnest is ineffective; it simply makes clearer that there was agreement on the price." Accordingly, if the sale went through, the earnest was applied to the price; but if the sale failed, the earnest could be recovered by the buyer; see Case 229. Why do you think that the popular custom of giving an earnest nonetheless persisted?

5. Agreement on Price. Gaius says that sale is concluded when there is agreement on price. Clearly price is a most important term, but there must also be agreement at least on the object of sale and the fact of the exchange; see Case 88.

CASE 79: Sale and Barter

D. 18.1.1.1 (Paulus libro trigensimo tertio ad Edictum)

Sed an sine nummis venditio dici hodieque possit, dubitatur, veluti si ego togam dedi, ut tunicam acciperem. Sabinus et Cassius esse emptionem et venditionem putant: Nerva et Proculus permutationem, non emptionem hoc esse. Sabinus Homero teste utitur, qui exercitum Graecorum aere ferro hominibusque vinum emere refert, . . . Sed verior est Nervae et Proculi sententia: nam ut aliud est vendere, aliud emere, alius emptor, alius venditor, sic aliud est pretium, aliud merx: quod in permutatione discerni non potest, uter emptor, uter venditor sit.

Paul in the thirty-third book *On the Edict*:

But it is doubtful that sale without money can still be spoken of today, e.g., if I gave you a toga to receive a tunic. Sabinus and Cassius think that this is sale; Nerva and Proculus, that it is barter, not sale. Sabinus cites as evidence Homer (*Iliad* 7.472–475), who reports that the Greek army "buys" wine with bronze, iron, and slaves. . . . But the more correct view is the opinion of Nerva and Proculus. For just as selling is one thing and buying another, and a buyer is different from a seller, so the price (*pretium*) is one thing and goods (*merx*) another. In barter it is impossible to distinguish which is the buyer and which the seller.

Discussion

1. Barter Again. This Case (a continuation of Case 77) describes an early imperial "school controversy" between the Sabinians and Proculians. The issue is whether an agreement on barter is actionable under the *formulae* for sale. In your opinion, which side had the better argument, and which side should have won? Eventually the Proculian position prevailed. (On the Classical rules for handling barters, see Chapter VI.B.) The Proculian position requires that if the transaction is a "sale," we must be able to identify one party as promising to pay a money price (*pretium*). Does their difficulty stem mainly from the procedural problem of having to sue either on the purchase or on the sale (*ex empto* or *ex vendito*)? Ulpian, D. 18.1.37, gives an illustration of the rule's application: As the heir of Titius, I agree to sell you a farm "for as much as Titius paid for it." But it turns out that Titius had received the farm as a gift. The sale is void; why?

2. An Exception? According to Gaius, *Inst.* 3.141, the Flavian jurist Caelius Sabinus, apparently attempting to circumvent the Proculian objection, argued that if you advertise a farm for sale, and I offer you a slave for the

farm, then the slave should be regarded as a "price" even though our arrangement is essentially a barter; hence the actions on sale are applicable. Does this argument get around the problems noted by the Proculians? On the whole, it is hard to imagine a better example of the jurists' "pigeonhole" mentality in handling contract law.

CASE 80: Mixed Sales

D. 18.1.79 (Iavolenus libro quinto ex Posterioribus Labeonis)

Fundi partem dimidiam ea lege vendidisti, ut emptor alteram partem, quam retinebas, annis decem certa pecunia in annos singulos conductam habeat. Labeo et Trebatius negant posse ex vendito agi, ut id quod convenerit fiat. Ego contra puto, si modo ideo vilius fundum vendidisti, ut haec tibi conductio praestaretur: nam hoc ipsum pretium fundi videretur, quod eo pacto venditus fuerat: eoque iure utimur.

Javolenus in the fifth book *From Labeo's Posthumous Writings*:

You sold half of a farm with the provision that the buyer lease the other half, which you kept, for ten years at a fixed amount per year. Labeo and Trebatius deny that suit can be brought on sale to enforce what was agreed upon (regarding the lease). I think the opposite, provided that you sold me the farm at a lower price in order to obtain this lease; for it is construed as the price of the farm that it was sold with this provision. And this is the rule we use.

Discussion

1. **Price Partially in Money.** The jurists display unease with the narrowness of the rule on money price, and so they try to expand it somewhat. How far are they willing to go? Pomponius, D. 19.1.6.1–2, discusses the sale of land for a price that includes a sum of money plus an undertaking to perform (in his hypothetical, either to repair a building, or to erect a building half of which is then to be conveyed to the original seller). In both cases, the seller can enforce the undertakings as an integral part of the sale. Does Javolenus, in the present Case, also presuppose that at least part of the price is a money payment? Is this the essence of his disagreement with the earlier jurists Trebatius and Labeo? Compare Paul, D. 19.1.21.4: sale of land, conditional on it being leased back to the seller for a fixed rent; the seller can enforce the lease "as though it were part of the price" of the sale (*quasi in partem pretii*).

2. **Exchange of an Object for a Performance.** On the other hand, it is not sale if an object is exchanged solely for an undertaking to perform, e.g., if I sell you a building in exchange for your repairing another building (see Neratius, D. 19.5.6). How can this instance be distinguished from those described in the previous question? Would it be sale if the buyer had also promised the repair plus some token sum of money? That is, how significant must the money component be? There is no real answer in our sources, but see Chapter VI.B.

CASE 81: Definiteness of Price

D. 18.1.7.1–2 (Ulpianus libro vicensimo octavo ad Sabinum)

1. Huiusmodi emptio "quanti tu eum emisti," "quantum pretii in arca habeo," valet: nec enim incertum est pretium tam evidenti venditione: magis enim ignoratur, quanti emptus sit, quam in rei veritate incertum est. 2. Si quis ita emerit: "est mihi fundus emptus centum et quanto pluris eum vendidero," valet venditio et statim impletur: habet enim certum pretium centum, augebitur autem pretium, si pluris emptor fundum vendiderit.

Ulpian in the twenty-eighth book *On Sabinus*:

1. A sale is valid when it takes this form: "as much as you bought him for" or "as much money as I have in my strongbox." The price is not indefinite in such an obvious sale; there is doubt more about how much it was bought for than about the reality of the transaction.

2. If someone buys (as follows): "Let the farm be bought by me for one hundred (thousand sesterces) and for as much beyond as I sell it for," the sale is valid and effective immediately; for there is a definite price of one hundred, but the price will increase if the buyer sells the farm for more.

Discussion

1. **Definiteness.** In section 1, the price is in fact determinable at the time of the sale, even though its amount may be then unknown to both parties. In section 2, a large portion of the price is fixed at the time of sale, but the remainder is determined only by a subsequent event (the buyer's resale of the farm). In what sense can the price be described as definite in both situations?

2. **Price to Be Determined.** The jurists hold that a sale is void if the price is set at "as much as you wish, as much as the buyer thinks fair, as much as you estimate" (see Gaius, D. 18.1.35.1), presumably because the buyer could set the price at nothing. But what if the price is "as much as Titius (a designated third party) thinks fair"? Gaius, *Inst.* 3.140, reports an early Classical controversy, with some jurists considering the transaction void and others upholding it as a sale. Gaius does not tell us the outcome of the controversy, but Justinian, *Inst.* 3.23.1, also upholds the sale, provided that the third party is named and then makes the evaluation. (Each party can also sue to revise the resulting price if the third party acts unfairly.) Does it seem likely that the jurists would have gone further and accepted a price determined by "the prevailing market price next January"? Would

they have felt differently about "the prevailing market price last January 1"? What about "your standard price"? Would they ever have been willing (as modern courts often are) to imply a "fair" price if the parties had neglected to specify one, or if they "agreed to agree later" and then couldn't arrive at one?

CASE 82: Reality of Price

D. 18.1.38 (Ulpianus libro septimo Disputationum)

Si quis donationis causa minoris vendat, venditio valet: totiens enim dicimus in totum venditionem non valere, quotiens universa venditio donationis causa facta est: quotiens vero viliore pretio res donationis causa distrahitur, dubium non est venditionem valere. Hoc inter ceteros: inter virum vero et uxorem donationis causa venditio facta pretio viliore nullius momenti est.

Ulpian in the seventh book of his *Disputations*:

If someone sells for less (than market value) in order to make a gift, the sale is valid. For we say that the sale is completely invalid whenever the entire sale was made as a gift; but whenever an object is sold at a lower price in order to make a gift, there is no doubt that the sale is valid. This is the general rule. But between husband and wife a sale at a cheaper price to make a gift is of no effect.

Discussion

1. A Gift Element in the Price. Especially in sales between family members or close friends, it is not unusual for the price to be less than market value. How clearly can the line be drawn between a price that is partially a gift and one that is an outright gift? By and large, this is a question of fact for the *iudex* to decide; but the jurists would hold that there is no sale if the price was set at "one sestertius" (a nominal amount); compare Paul, D. 19.2.20.1, and Ulpian, D. 19.2.46. Since the transaction would then be essentially a gift, the promise would not be irreversible until the donor executed it, as in Common Law. Likewise, if the parties set what would be an acceptable price, but the seller had no intention to collect it; see Ulpian, D. 18.1.36. Note that the problem here is not "adequacy of consideration," but the identification of the transaction as a contract of sale.

2. Husbands and Wives. To the rule just stated, Ulpian makes an exception for husbands and wives, who are not allowed to make effective gifts to one another during their marriage and hence must pay a reasonable price if one spouse sells property to the other: Ulpian and Paul, D. 24.1.1–3 pr. But the jurists do not always apply the rule as harshly as it is stated by Ulpian; here and elsewhere, a transaction the jurists describe as "void" may actually just be voidable. For example, a husband sells property worth 15,000 sesterces to his wife for 5,000; however, when the transaction is later challenged, the property is worth only 10,000. According to Ulpian, D. 24.1.5.5 (citing Neratius), the wife may keep the property provided she pays a further 5,000, the difference between the price paid and the fair price when the transaction is challenged; but in effect the sale is upheld. Somewhat similar

problems can arise in modern tax law. Is the Roman solution the best one? (To a certain extent, this problem also surfaces when a creditor sells property that a debtor has given as security: Marcian, D. 20.1.16.9, requiring a *iustum pretium*.)

CASE 83: Fairness of Price

D. 19.2.22.3 (Paulus libro quarto ad Edictum)

Quemadmodum in emendo et vendendo naturaliter concessum est quod pluris sit minoris emere, quod minoris sit pluris vendere et ita invicem se circumscribere, ita in locationibus quoque et conductionibus iuris est;

D. 19.2.23 (Hermogenianus libro secundo Iuris Epitomarum)

Et ideo praetextu minoris pensionis, locatione facta, si nullus dolus adversarii probari possit, rescindi locatio non potest.

Paul in the fourth book *On the Edict*:

Just as, in buying and selling, it is by Nature (*naturaliter*) allowed (for parties) to buy what is worth more for less, or to sell a thing worth less for more, and so in turn to cheat one another, this also is the rule for leases;

Hermogenianus in the second book of his *Epitomies of Law*:

And so when a lease is made, it cannot be rescinded on the basis of the rent being too low unless the other party's deceit (*dolus*) can be proven.

Discussion

1. Freedom of Contract. Paul and Hermogenian are writing about lease, but draw on sales law by analogy. The rule established by this Case is the Classical rule: within wide limits, the parties have unrestricted freedom to determine the price for themselves, and inequalities of bargaining power are not recognized except when one party deceives the other into a bad deal. (For an example, see Ulpian in Case 92.) As in the present Case, Ulpian there says that the action on a fraudulent sale can be used to rescind the sale.

2. *Laesio Enormis*. In early postclassical law, however, the Emperor Diocletian upset the Classical view at least in one particular situation: C. 4.44.2 (285 CE), 8 (293). Both constitutions were written during an economically turbulent era, and both are addressed to sellers who received a grossly low price for purchased land. The first rescript, so historically influential that it deserves quotation in full, is addressed to Aurelius Lupus, evidently a private citizen.

   "If you or your father sold property worth more for a lesser price, the humane course is that either you restore the farm to the buyers and recover the price under the authority of a *iudex*; or, if the buyer prefers, you recover the difference from the just price (*iustum pretium*). A price is deemed lesser if not even half of the true price (*verum pretium*) is paid."

The rescript bristles with problems; for instance, is a "just price" the same as a "true price," and how is each one related to a market price? But the fundamental point (brought out even more clearly in the later constitution) is that the seller need not prove any defect in contract formation, such as fraud by the buyers, in order to obtain relief. The excessively low price is enough in itself. Even though these two imperial rescripts ostensibly benefit only the sellers of land, they clearly look at sale from a much different viewpoint than did the Classical jurists, and they set the stage for later discussions of the possible substantive unconscionability of contracts—their fundamental unfairness—as a basis for wholly or partially undoing them. Think carefully both about the broader contractual implications of Diocletian's change in the law, and about the form of the remedy he devised. Is Diocletian's approach preferable to Classical Roman Law? At least as a general rule, should inequality of exchange provide a ground for attacking the validity of a bilateral contract?

CASE 84: Saleable Objects

D. 18.1.34.1 (Paulus libro trigensimo tertio ad Edictum)

Omnium rerum, quas quis habere vel possidere vel persequi potest, venditio recte fit: quas vero natura vel gentium ius vel mores civitatis commercio exuerunt, earum nulla venditio est.

Paul in the thirty-third book *On the Edict*:

Sale is properly made for all things that one can own or possess or sue for. But there is no sale of things that Nature or the Law of Nations or community usage exclude from commerce.

Discussion

1. Saleability. This text sets the ground rule: subject to a few exceptions, anything that private individuals can have a property right in, they can also sell. This includes not only tangible property, but also intangibles like debts, inheritances, personal servitudes, and so on. But there is no sale of things "excluded from commerce" (*extra commercium*) by the Law of Nature (e.g., the ocean or the air), or by a general or particular public law (e.g., the Brooklyn Bridge), except, of course, that the government or a municipality can normally sell its own property. This rule somewhat overlaps with other rules against immoral or illegal sales; for instance, in principle a free person cannot be sold; see Case 94. Certain other prohibitions also stem from public policy; e.g., a guardian may not purchase property of his ward; see Paul, D. 18.1.34.7. Gaius, D. 18.1.35.2, has an interesting discussion of the sale of poison: it is valid only if the poison can conceivably serve some acceptable purpose.

   It should be stressed that the sale itself does not immediately create any property right in the buyer. In the most usual case, possession and ownership of the object of sale are subsequently conveyed to the buyer not by the sale itself, but in the execution of it. See Part B.3 in this Chapter.

2. Effect of a Void Sale. What happens if someone does sell the Brooklyn Bridge to a gullible buyer? Although the sale may be void, the buyer still often has an interest in its performance, especially if he or she has already paid the price. Section 3 of this Chapter discusses how Roman law handled the resulting problems.

CASE 85: Object Made by Seller

D. 18.1.20 (Pomponius libro nono ad Sabinum)

Sabinus respondit, si quam rem nobis fieri velimus etiam, veluti statuam vel vas aliquod seu vestem, ut nihil aliud quam pecuniam daremus, emptionem videri, nec posse ullam locationem esse, ubi corpus ipsum non detur ab eo cui id fieret: aliter atque si aream darem, ubi insulam aedificares, quoniam tunc a me substantia . proficiscitur.

Pomponius in the ninth book *On Sabinus*:

Sabinus responds that it is regarded as sale also if we want something made for us, like a statue or a container or clothing, provided we give nothing but money (in exchange). There can be no lease (of a job) where the materials are not provided by the person for whom it is made.

It is different if I give a site where you are to build an apartment building, since then the substance comes from me.

Discussion

1. Movables. Although an object of sale usually exists at the time of the sale, the jurists also allow sale of movable objects to be made by the seller, provided that the latter also supplied the materials. For example, Gaius, *Inst.* 3.147 (= Case 185), holds that it is sale if a goldsmith makes rings for me out of his own gold, but lease (of a job, see Chapter V.A.4) if I furnish the gold. How plausible is this distinction? Javolenus, D. 18.1.65, applies the same rule to the manufacture of roof tiles. But would it also be sale if I commissioned you to paint my portrait on your canvas, or to prepare a legal document on your own parchment? These cases (usually discussed by the jurists as aspects of acquiring owner-ship, e.g., Gaius, *Inst.* 2.77–79) raise difficulties because the value of the materials is usually insignificant in relation to the value of the finished product. It is unclear how the jurists would have solved the problem for sale.

2. Immovables. A different rule is applied when, for instance, I contract with you to build a building with your materials on my land. What does Pomponius mean by "the substance comes from me"? Paul, D. 19.2.22.2, sheds some light: by the rules of property law, what is constructed on my land becomes my property, and ownership of your materials passes to me as they are incorporated into the structure (by a principle called *superficies solo cedit*, still widely in use today). Hence the contract is a lease (of a job), not a sale of the materials. Is this logic entirely convincing? Note that Roman

law has no statutory "mechanic's lien" if the customer is then unwilling or unable to pay for the completed structure; the contractor's remedy is solely contractual unless the parties have expressly agreed on a security arrangement.

CASE 86: Future Objects

D. 18.1.8 (Pomponius libro nono ad Sabinum)

pr. Nec emptio nec venditio sine re quae veneat potest intellegi. Et tamen fructus et partus futuri recte ementur, ut, cum editus esset partus, iam tunc, cum contractum esset negotium, venditio facta intellegatur: sed si id egerit venditor, ne nascatur aut fiant, ex empto agi posse. 1. Aliquando tamen et sine re venditio intellegitur, veluti cum quasi alea emitur. Quod fit, cum captum piscium vel avium vel missilium emitur: emptio enim contrahitur etiam si nihil inciderit, quia spei emptio est: et quod missilium nomine eo casu captum est si evictum fuerit, nulla eo nomine ex empto obligatio contrahitur, quia id actum intellegitur.

Pomponius in the ninth book *On Sabinus*:

pr. Neither purchase nor sale can be understood to exist without an object of sale. Still, future produce and offspring are legally bought, such that when the offspring is born, the sale is construed as having been made from when the transaction was contracted. But if the seller acts to prevent birth or crop growth, (a jurist holds) that suit can be brought on purchase (*ex empto*).

1. Nevertheless, sometimes sale is understood to exist even without an object (of sale), e.g., when it is purchased as if on a chance (*quasi alea*). This occurs when the catch of fish or of birds or of scattered largesse is bought. For the purchase is contracted even if nothing results, since it is the purchase of a hope (*emptio spei*). In the case of scattered largesse, if there is eviction from what was caught, no obligation on sale is contracted on this account, since this is construed as what the parties transacted.

The Problem

Seius, a farmer, sells to Titius the grapes from his vineyard, which are now on the vine and will be ripe in three months. Is this sale binding on the two parties, and what are their respective duties before the grapes are harvested?

Discussion

1. Two Kinds of Future Objects. In the *principium*, the seller sells an object that does not now exist, but may come into existence in the future, e.g., the future child of a slave woman. The sale is construed as conditional on the future event's occurring, but takes effect retroactively when the event occurs. (In the meantime, the contract seems to exist in pendency.) By contrast, in section 1 the sale is of an opportunity, e.g., for whatever a fisher may land by casting his net; here the sale is valid immediately, and the price is due even if the net lands nothing. What is the basic difference between these two forms of sale? How is it possible, in practice, to tell the difference between them? In section 1, the scattering of largesse refers to the Roman custom of having the emperor throw out prize tokens from a balcony to a

crowd; whoever caught the token got the prize. The parties have evidently contracted for one to act on behalf of the other. Comparable would be selling the proceeds of a lottery ticket prior to the drawing: the sale of a chance.

2. Obstruction of the Sale by the Seller. In the conditional sale of a future object, there is an action on sale if the seller acts to prevent the object from coming into existence; why, and for what? A similar problem may arise in the case of the sale of an opportunity. Suppose, for instance, that a fisher sells the catch from a future cast of his net, and then refuses to cast the net; Celsus, D. 19.1.12, allows the buyer to sue for the speculative value of the cast, calculated, perhaps, as the average return from prior casts.

3. A Problem. Julian, D. 18.1.39.1, sets the following hypothetical: Someone purchases olives that are still growing on the seller's trees. The sale price is a fixed amount for ten pounds of olive oil. In fact, the olives produce only five pounds of oil. What is the price? The Latin text is doubtful, but apparently the price is scaled back by half. Is this decision sound?

4. Sale of an Inheritance. Heirs occasionally sold their claim to an inheritance, that is, all their future rights in the estate. Problems could arise that are similar to those in sale of future objects. For example, must there actually be an inheritance in order for the sale to be valid? Normally this is true; see Paul, D. 18.4.7; the sale is construed as conditional on the existence of the inheritance. (Similarly for sale of a debt: Hermogenian, D. 21.2.74.3.) On calculation of damages, see Javolenus/Paul, D. 18.4.8–9. But it is also possible to sell an inheritance "if there is one"; in that case, the sale is valid as the sale of an opportunity, even if there is no inheritance; see Javolenus, D. 18.4.10 (noting that the risk is on the buyer). The same issues arise in the case of sale of a debt; must the debt actually exist? However the actual sale is construed, special provision must also be made against fraudulent sellers; see, for instance, Gaius, D. 18.4.12.

CASE 87: Sale from Stock

D. 18.1.35.5–6 (Gaius libro decimo ad Edictum Provinciale)

5. In his quae pondere numero mensurave constant, veluti frumento vino oleo argento, modo ea servantur quae in ceteris, ut simul atque de pretio convenerit, videatur perfecta venditio, modo ut, etiamsi de pretio convenerit, non tamen aliter videatur perfecta venditio, quam si admensa adpensa adnumeratave sint. Nam si omne vinum vel oleum vel frumentum vel argentum quantumcumque esset uno pretio venierit, idem iuris est quod in ceteris rebus. Quod si vinum ita venierit, ut in singulas amphoras, item oleum, ut in singulos metretas, item frumentum, ut in singulos modios, item argentum, ut in singulas libras certum pretium diceretur, quaeritur, quando videatur emptio perfici. Quod similiter scilicet quaeritur et de his quae numero constant, si pro numero corporum pretium fuerit statutum. Sabinus et Cassius tunc perfici emptionem existimant, cum adnumerata admensa adpensave sint, quia venditio quasi sub hac condicione videtur fieri, ut in singulos metretas aut in singulos modios quos quasve admensus eris, aut in singulas libras quas adpenderis, aut in singula corpora quae adnumeraveris. 6. Ergo et si grex venierit, si quidem universaliter uno pretio, perfecta videtur, postquam de pretio convenerit: si vero in singula corpora certo pretio, eadem erunt, quae proxime tractavimus.

Gaius in the tenth book *On the Provincial Edict*:

5. For objects reckoned by weight, number, or measure—e.g., grain, wine, olive oil, and silver—sometimes the same rules are observed as for other things, namely that the sale is held complete as soon as they agree on the price. At other times, even if they agree on the price, the sale is not held complete unless the objects are (subsequently) measured, weighed, or counted. For if all the wine or oil or grain or silver, as much as there is, is sold for a single price, the rule is the same as for other objects.

But if wine is sold at a fixed price for each amphora, or oil for each container, or grain for each bushel, or silver for each pound, question arises as to when the sale is held complete. But a similar question obviously arises about things determined by number, if a price is set (per unit) for a number of items. Sabinus and Cassius think that the sale is complete when the objects are counted, measured, or weighed; for the sale is treated as being made under the condition that it is contracted for each amphora, container, or bushel that you have measured, or for each pound you have weighed, or for each item you have counted.

6. Therefore also, if a herd is sold in its entirety for a single price, it is held to be complete after agreement is reached on a price; but if with a set price for each animal, the rule will be the same as just discussed.

Discussion

1. **Four Types of Sale from Stock.** Sale of an entire stock ("all the wine in my wine cellar") at a fixed price presents no difficulties; this is an ordinary sale. The other two types raise more problems: sale of a stock at a fixed price per measure, where the exact measure is presently unknown ("all my wine at 200 sesterces per amphora"); or sale of a stock at a price per unit, where the number of units is presently unknown ("my herd of cows at 500 sesterces per animal"). The same problem would arise in another way if the measures or units were to be selected out of an existing stock (e.g., "30 sheep from my flock"; see, e.g., Case 112). Gaius states that the sale is not "complete" (*perfecta*) until the measurement is taken, the units are counted, or the object of sale is isolated from the stock (i.e., identified). What exactly does he mean? Is he construing the sale as conditional, rather like the sale of a future object in the previous Case? Where is the problem in these various types of sale from stock: that the price is not presently certain, or that the object of sale is not identified? In any case, the main legal issue in sales from stock is the point at which risk of accidental destruction passes to the buyer; see Part B.1 in this Chapter.

2. **Generic Sale.** Pomponius, D. 18.1.8 pr. (Case 86), states flatly: "Without an object of sale, no sale can be construed." In the types of sale described earlier, although the exact object of sale is not always isolated when the contract is made, there is at least an existing stock from which the object of sale will eventually be drawn. Is it a requirement of Roman sales law that the physical object of sale be identifiable, at the time of the sale, at least to this extent? At any rate, our sources present no clear case in which the object of sale is identified, not by some existing or future object, but instead only by a set of specifications ("5,000 widgets of the following description"), where it is presumably often immaterial to the buyer where the seller obtains the conforming widgets. (Modern business relies heavily on sale of goods by description or specifications.) Look again at Case 85: the seller is to make a statue for the buyer; would the seller satisfy the contract by obtaining and tendering a conforming statue made by a third party? The sources on stipulation make it clear that the Romans did recognize generic promises. See, for instance, Case 23 (a stipulation for "one hundred bushels of good African wheat"). Why might the jurists have been more hesitant in the case of sale? (For one possible exception to the rule against generic sales, see Papinian, *Frag. Vat.* 16, discussed in Case 112.)

SECTION 2. Defects in Agreement

Even though two parties may believe that they have reached agreement on a sale, in some instances their *consensus* may prove illusory. Roman law identified three main ways in which apparent agreement can nonetheless be fatally defective: it may be induced by duress (*metus*), or by deceit (*dolus*), or it may be somehow based on a fundamental mistake of fact (*error*). Of these three, mistake is undoubtedly the commonest and most difficult, and what survives of juristic discussion is in any case a good deal less than satisfactory.

One way of looking at the problem is to ask: did the parties reach agreement on what can be identified as a complete sale? Granted the importance of identification to Roman contract types, an irreconcilable difference between the parties as to the price, the object of sale, or the exchange of object for price must usually be fatal to the existence of sale. For instance, if one party thought that the sale was of the slave Stichus, and the other that the sale was of a completely different slave Pamphilus, then it is possible to conclude that a sale never took place; misunderstanding or mistake (*error*) vitiates agreement (*consensus*), in the limited sense that the transaction cannot be conclusively identified as a sale. But even here it matters whether we require the parties to mentally agree on the object of sale, or only to ostensibly agree.

If this were the end of the doctrine of mistake, it would be comparatively innocuous. But mistake can also occur over some important characteristic of the object of sale; and here the parties may not simply differ in what they each individually believe, they may also both share the mistake. Suppose, for instance, that a table is sold which one or both parties believe to be of solid silver, when in fact it is made of lead. Note that if both parties are mistaken, there is no absence of *consensus*; and in any case it cannot be held that the object of sale is not identified. Nonetheless, the jurists (or some of them) hold that the sale may be invalid because of the mistake, provided at least that the buyer is reasonably mistaken, and also (as it seems) regardless of whether or not the seller is also mistaken.

This is a primitive and somewhat cumbersome form of buyer's protection that the jurists apparently devised at a time when the buyer would have been unprotected if the sale were upheld. In late Classical law, by contract, the buyer was better protected even when the sale was upheld; see Part B.5 in this Chapter. The doctrine of mistake on a characteristic had therefore been cut back to cover only a few, rather improbable cases—of which, reasonably mistaking a lead table for a silver one is certainly an example.

CASE 88: Mistake on a Basic Element of Sale

D. 18.1.9 pr.-1 (Ulpianus libro vicensimo octavo ad Sabinum)

pr. In venditionibus et emptionibus consensum debere intercedere palam est: ceterum sive in ipsa emptione dissentient sive in pretio sive in quo alio, emptio imperfecta est. Si igitur ego me fundum emere putarem Cornelianum, tu mihi te vendere Sempronianum putasti, quia in corpore dissensimus, emptio nulla est. Idem est, si ego me Stichum, tu Pamphilum absentem vendere putasti: nam cum in corpore dissentiatur, apparet nullam esse emptionem. 1. Plane si in nomine dissentiamus, verum de corpore constet, nulla dubitatio est, quin valeat emptio et venditio: nihil enim facit error nominis, cum de corpore constat.

Ulpian in the twenty-eighth book *On Sabinus*:

pr. In sales and purchases it is obvious that agreement (*consensus*) must occur. But the sale is incomplete if they disagree on (the fact of) the purchase itself, or on the price, or on something else. Therefore, if I thought that I bought the Cornelian farm and you thought that you sold the Sempronian, there is no sale because we disagreed on the object of sale (*in corpore*). Likewise, if I thought (I purchased) Stichus, and you that you sold the absent (slave) Pamphilus; for since there is disagreement on the object of sale, there is clearly no sale.

1. Clearly, if we disagree (merely) on the name but agree on the object, there is no doubt that the sale is valid; for mistake (*error*) on the name is not relevant if there is agreement on the object.

Discussion

1. Mutual Misunderstanding. A contract of sale is created through the agreement of seller and buyer; as we have seen in the previous section, this agreement must extend at least to the price, the object of sale, and their exchange. One problem that sometimes arises is that the parties think they have reached agreement when they have not. The classic example is mutual misunderstanding: we talk of sale of "the farm," but each of us has a different farm in mind, and neither of us knows or has reason to know the other's understanding. (In our law, this is the famous "Peerless" problem in *Raffles v. Wichelhaus*, 1864.) Is it clear that at least this situation is being discussed by Ulpian? How is mutual misunderstanding on the object of sale different from misunderstanding on the name of the object? Is it right in this situation simply to throw in the towel and declare the sale void for want of agreement, without examining how the misunderstanding arose?

2. Unilateral Mistake. This type of mistake differs from mutual misunderstanding. We both talk of sale of "the farm," and again each of us has a different farm in mind; but in conversation I seem (both to you and to an objective external observer) to accept the farm that you are thinking

of, even though this is not in fact the farm I want. A situation of this sort is much more common, and much more difficult to handle, than mutual misunderstanding. Essentially, law has two choices: either to hold me to what I seemed to say, on an "objective" theory of agreement that treats me as responsible for what I seem to say because the other party may have been misled by my mistake; or to let me escape from the contract on a "subjective" theory of agreement that requires genuine mental agreement (not just the external appearance of agreement) in order for a contract to come into existence. Which choice does Ulpian make? Although the answer is less than clear, note the way he words his opinion: "I *thought* (*putarem*) that I bought the Cornelian farm and you *thought* (*putasti*) that you sold the Sempronian." This wording seems to look toward a subjective theory of agreement. Do you think a subjective theory is correct, or at least defensible? What sorts of difficulties does it cause? In modern law, an objective theory is usually preferred because of the impersonal nature of the modern marketplace, although most authorities concede at least that a court must not impose on parties a contract that neither party wants.

3. **Mistake and Identification.** In discussing mistake theory, it is important to keep in mind the purpose of the analysis in relation to particular cases. One purpose in Roman law is to identify the transaction as a sale: it must have the required elements (price, object of sale, exchange) for properly classifying it. This purpose relates to the procedural needs of Roman law, with its intricate pigeonholes for various contracts. Another quite different purpose is judicial fairness with respect to the parties: are they each getting what they wanted from the contract, or, if not, what is the most equitable way for the court to proceed? Which of these two purposes does Ulpian have in mind in the present Case?

4. **Mistake on the Price.** Pomponius, D. 19.2.52, discusses what happens in the contract of lease if two parties disagree on the rent: "If I lease a farm to you for ten (thousand sesterces), but you think you hired it for five, the transaction is void. But again, if I think I lease for less, and you that you hire for more, the lease will not be for more than what I thought it to be." This text apparently establishes an option; the party that thought the rent was higher can nonetheless enforce the lease at the other party's lower amount, presumably even if the other party is no longer willing to be bound by this figure. It is unclear whether a similar option is available in sale; should it be?

5. **Mistake on an Accessory.** Paul, D. 18.1.34 pr., sets this problem: In the sale of a farm, the parties agree that "the slave Stichus" will be part of the farm, but it later emerges that they were thinking of different slaves of that

name. The sale remains valid. As to the slave, Paul appears to approve Labeo's holding that the Stichus meant by the seller is owed, and he adds that it makes no difference what the value of the "accessory" turns out to be in relation to the main object, "for at times we buy many things because of their accessories, as when a house is purchased because of its marbles and statues and paintings." Can such a holding be justified? Is the question here more one of contractual interpretation than of misunderstanding? If so, what rule would seem to be in play?

6. **Mistake on a Party's Identity.** What happens if one party is mistaken about the other party's identity (the buyer is not Seius, as I thought, but Titius)? No surviving text on sale discusses this problem, but elsewhere in the Digest mistake on identity is held to void a contract; e.g., Celsus, D. 12.1.32 (stipulation for a loan). The question can be important if, for instance, the other party's credit rating is important to the transaction.

CASE 89: Mistake on a Characteristic

D. 18.1.9.2, 11 (Ulpianus libro vicensimo octavo ad Sabinum)

9.2. Inde quaeritur, si in ipso corpore non erratur, sed in substantia error sit, ut puta si acetum pro vino veneat, aes pro auro vel plumbum pro argento vel quid aliud argento simile, an emptio et venditio sit. Marcellus scripsit libro sexto digestorum emptionem esse et venditionem, quia in corpus consensum est, etsi in materia sit erratum. Ego in vino quidem consentio, quia eadem prope οὐσία est, si modo vinum acuit: ceterum si vinum non acuit, sed ab initio acetum fuit, ut embamma, aliud pro alio venisse videtur. In ceteris autem nullam esse venditionem puto, quotiens in materia erratur. 11 pr. Alioquin quid dicemus, si caecus emptor fuit vel si in materia erratur vel in minus perito discernendarum materiarum? In corpus eos consensisse dicemus? Et quemadmodum consensit, qui non vidit? 11.1. Quod si ego me virginem emere putarem, cum esset iam mulier, emptio valebit: in sexu enim non est erratum. Ceterum si ego mulierem venderem, tu puerum emere existimasti, quia in sexu error est, nulla emptio, nulla venditio est.

Ulpian in the twenty-eighth book *On Sabinus*:

9.2. Next, question arises if there is no mistake on the object itself, but there is a mistake on its substance (*error in substantia*). E.g., if vinegar is sold as wine, bronze as gold, or lead or something silver-like as silver, is there a purchase and sale? Marcellus wrote, in the sixth book of his *Digests*, that there is a sale because there was agreement on the object even if there was a mistake on the material (*in materia*).

I agree (with Marcellus) concerning the wine, since it is virtually the same substance (οὐσία), provided the wine turns sour. But if the wine did not turn sour, but was vinegar from the start, like vinegar sauce, one object appears to have been sold for another. As for the rest, I think there is no sale whenever there is a mistake on the material.

11 pr. Otherwise what will we say if the buyer was blind, or in the case of a person less skilled in judging materials, if there is an error on the material? Will we say they agreed on the object of sale? And how has a person agreed if he does not see (the object)?

11.1. But the sale is valid if I thought I was buying a virgin when she was already a (sexually experienced) woman; for there was no mistake on the sex (of the woman). But if I sold a woman and you thought you bought a boy, there is no sale because there is a mistake on the sex.

Discussion

1. Mistake on a Characteristic. In this famous and difficult text (which Justinian's compilers probably abbreviated), the situation differs from the previous

Case. Here the two parties agree on the object of sale, but there is a possible mistake concerning some characteristic or quality that it has or is supposed to have, with significant effects on the equality of the exchange. Note that, at least as Ulpian phrases the Case, it is the buyer who is most likely to be mistaken: a lead object is sold as silver, or vinegar as wine, or a male slave as female. In each instance, the object is doubtless considerably less valuable to the buyer than he or she had thought it was. (Does it matter whether the seller was mistaken as well? What if only the seller is mistaken, e.g., in selling gold as bronze?)

Ulpian says nothing about how the buyer came to be mistaken. The mistake could result from the seller's misrepresentation, but also the buyer may simply be self-deluded, or acting on erroneous information from a third party. In any case, the basic problem is: when should a mistake be regarded as so fundamental that the sale should be entirely void, or at least voidable by the mistaken party? How do the issues raised here differ from those in the previous Case? The jurists obviously disagreed on how to handle this problem. Marcellus favored abolishing the doctrine of mistake on a characteristic altogether (and so too did Paul: Case 146), while Ulpian retained and perhaps even somewhat enlarged it. Who is right? Does your answer depend, at least in part, on what protection is afforded the buyer if the sale is preserved?

2. **Other Contracts.** As stated by Ulpian, the doctrine of mistake on a characteristic, as a basis for voiding a sale, is confined to a narrow set of circumstances. The doctrine is also not available for other contracts such as stipulation (Case 17) and *pignus* (Ulpian, D. 13.7.1.1–2). Why might the jurists have been reluctant to extend the doctrine beyond sale?

3. **Sale of a Virgin.** In section 11.1, the buyer is looking for a virgin slave, evidently with the (exceptionally disagreeable) intent of exploiting her sexually. The likelihood of this buyer being mistaken on this point is obviously considerably greater than his being mistaken on the slave's sex. Ulpian, D. 19.1.11.5, gives the mistaken buyer a remedy in sale for damages in some circumstances; see the Discussion on Case 140. How does the existence of this remedy affect a legal decision about whether to void the sale on the basis of the buyer's mistake about virginity?

4. **Mistake and Misrepresentation.** Ulpian speaks, e.g., of "bronze (sold) as gold." It is undoubtedly tempting in this context to suppose that the seller is misrepresenting the truth, even inadvertently. But in that event it is curious that Ulpian lays no stress on this possibility. Instead, his ruling goes off

on the buyer's mistake, which, as section 11 pr. suggests, must usually be reasonable granted the buyer's general capacities. The answers to Ulpian's three questions in 11 pr. have apparently been stripped away by the Digest compilers; but see Case 91 on the risk taken by "indolent" buyers. A blind buyer is, of course, not "indolent."

CASE 90: Shared Mistake

D. 18.1.14 (Ulpianus libro vicesimo octavo ad Sabinum)

Quid tamen dicemus, si in materia et qualitate ambo errarent? Ut puta si et ego me vendere aurum putarem et tu emere, cum aes esset? Ut puta coheredes viriolam, quae aurea dicebatur, pretio exquisito uni heredi vendidissent eaque inventa esset magna ex parte aenea? Venditionem esse constat ideo, quia auri aliquid habuit. Nam si inauratum aliquid sit, licet ego aureum putem, valet venditio: si autem aes pro auro veneat, non valet.

Ulpian in the twenty-eighth book *On Sabinus*:

But what will we hold if both parties are mistaken on the material and a characteristic (*materia et qualitas*)? For example, if I thought that I sold, and you that you bought, gold, when it was (in fact) bronze? For instance, co-heirs sold to one heir, for a substantial price, a bracelet said to be of gold, and it was (subsequently) found to be mostly bronze? It is settled that there is a sale because it had some gold. For, if something is gilded, the sale is valid even if I thought it (solid) gold; but if bronze is sold as gold, it is not valid.

Discussion

1. Both Parties Make a Mistake. This Case also illustrates the narrowness of Ulpian's views on mistake concerning a characteristic: the sale is void only if the bracelet contains no gold whatsoever. (But see later discussion.) In this text, however, both the seller and the buyer are mistaken about the characteristic. This is still a different type of mistake than those discussed in Case 88; here, the seller and buyer agree on the characteristic (so that their transaction cannot be void or voidable for want of *consensus*), but both are mistaken, and their fundamental mistake is held sufficient alone to render the sale invalid. Is Ulpian correct to treat this case as similar to the situations in the previous Case? If so, then it rather looks as if the seller's mistake is irrelevant, so long as the buyer is mistaken. Can the doctrine of mistake on a characteristic be plausibly regarded as a form of buyer's protection, allowing the buyer to void the sale if the object is fundamentally different from what he or she expected it to be?

2. Gilding. Ulpian holds that the sale is valid if the object is gilded or contains some admixture of gold. This holding appears to overrule Julian, D. 18.1.41.1: "You unknowingly sold me, also unaware, a silver-plated table as a solid one: there is no sale and money paid on this account can be recovered by a *condictio*." Does the contradiction illustrate the late Classical constriction of the doctrine of mistake on a characteristic, or can the two texts be distinguished?

CASE 91: The Buyer's Alertness

D. 18.1.15.1 (Paulus libro quinto ad Sabinum)

Ignorantia emptori prodest, quae non in supinum hominem cadit.

Paul in the fifth book *On Sabinus*:

Ignorance is of use to the buyer (only) if it is not that of an indolent person.

Discussion

1. Buyer's Ignorance. This tiny fragment (nine words!) states an important principle. If the buyer can avoid a sale because of his or her mistake, we are bound to ask whether the buyer has any countervailing duty to be reasonably careful in inspecting the object of sale. Although the context of Paul's remark is uncertain, he appears to indicate that buyers do have such a duty; they cannot be "indolent" (literally, "prostrate"). Look back at Case 89; in section 11 pr., Ulpian speaks of buyers who are blind or inexperienced in distinguishing metals. Unfortunately, Ulpian does not answer the questions he asks in that fragment (the Digest compilers presumably stripped away his answers), but it appears that Ulpian is worried about the relative capacity of various buyers. Presumably he would hold a sighted or an experienced buyer to a higher standard of alertness than one who was blind or inexperienced. Is this sensible? What does this apparent rule suggest about the purpose of the doctrine of mistake as to a fundamental characteristic?

2. Seller's Mistake. It is also possible, of course, for a seller to be mistaken about a characteristic. We have all read, for instance, about art dealers who inadvertently sell a Van Gogh for a tiny fraction of its real value, to a buyer who may or may not know the truth, or who may just suspect the truth. In surviving texts, the jurists say nothing about this situation. Do they assume that sellers should bear the risk of their own mistakes with regard to characteristics? Could such a legal position be justified?

CASE 92: Fraud

D. 4.3.9 pr. (Ulpianus libro undecimo ad Edictum)

Si quis adfirmavit minimam esse hereditatem et ita eam ab herede emit, non est de dolo actio, cum ex vendito sufficiat.

Ulpian in the eleventh book *On the Edict*:

If someone affirmed that an inheritance was of slight value and so bought it from the heir (for a low price), there is no action on deceit (*dolus*) since the action on sale suffices.

Discussion

1. The Action on *Dolus*. In this Case, the seller has purchased an estate from its heir after deceiving the heir into believing the estate was not worth much. In Roman law, the Urban Praetor provided an action on deceit (*dolus*), whereby those who are deceived into financial loss by someone can recover the loss from the deceiver; but the action is available only if there is no other remedy. Ulpian says that "the action on sale suffices," but does not indicate what the remedy in sale would be. Can the seller sue on purchase to force the buyer to pay a higher price, or is he limited to seeking rescission of the sale and restitution? Probably the latter, but there is no certain text.

2. Another Example. Papinian, D. 19.1.41, discusses a case in which the buyer of land discovers, after the sale, that he is obliged to pay an annual fee to a neighbor for conveying water through the neighbor's property. The seller presumably knew of this payment and did not inform the buyer when the sale was concluded. If the buyer is sued for the price, should the *iudex* take account of the unforeseen fee when assessing damages? Papinian says yes. This case illustrates the general duty of *bona fides* in the making of contracts; see also especially Case 131. Could the buyer escape the sale altogether if the fee was too burdensome?

3. Duress. In addition to mistake and fraud, it is likely that duress (*metus*) could also be used to void a sale. Although no juristic text survives on this point, it is presumed by early postclassical rescripts of Gordian, C. 2.19.3–5 (238–239). In Roman law, duress usually involves fear of death or serious physical injury (Ulpian, D. 4.2.1: "a mental alarm because of a present or future danger"). The fear must be objectively reasonable (Gaius, D. 4.2.6: "the fear not of a weak-minded person, but one that rightly befalls also a highly resolute person"). It is not clear that the Romans recognized undue influence as vitiating contractual consent, but they do support fairly high standards of conduct for the guardians of children.

SECTION 3. Impossibility

A stipulation is usually invalid if it is impossible to perform from the outset, or its performance subsequently becomes impossible without the promissor's fault (see Cases 18–21). In the law of sale, by contract, only initial impossibility is a bar to a contract's validity; subsequent impossibility to deliver the object of sale is instead treated largely under the theory of risk; see Part B.1 in this Chapter.

Problems of initial impossibility arise mainly with regard to the object of sale, if the object does not exist at the time of the sale (e.g., a purchased slave has previously died) or cannot be sold because it is not in commerce (see Case 84). One's initial intuition might be that such sales are entirely void. But here the doctrine of *bona fides* begins to affect the law on the formation of sale. If the buyer is unaware that the physical or legal condition of the object makes the sale impossible, in many circumstances the jurists hold that the buyer has a defensible legal interest in the sale; accordingly, they often award the buyer an action on purchase to recover this interest, even though the sale itself is void. The theory of impossibility thus seems to be used as a form of buyer protection, since the seller's knowledge of the sale's impossibility is often held to be immaterial.

In any case, physical or legal impossibility should be carefully distinguished from personal circumstances that prevent a party from performing. Suppose that a farm's seller incorrectly but justifiably believes that the farm belongs to her, or that a slave's buyer incorrectly assumes that he has the ready cash to pay for the slave. Although this party may then find it "impossible" to perform, the sale is nonetheless valid and binding, since otherwise the other party would have to bear the risk for a problem over which he or she has little control. The issue of proper risk allocation is fundamental not just for this problem, but in general for the entire law governing the formation and execution of contracts; it is almost always worthwhile to evaluate legal rules in terms of the allocations of risk they presuppose.

CASE 93: Sale of Objects Not in Commerce

D. 18.1.62.1 (Modestinus libro quinto Regularum)

Qui nesciens loca sacra vel religiosa vel publica pro privatis comparavit, licet emptio non teneat, ex empto tamen adversus venditorem experietur, ut consequatur quod interfuit eius, ne deciperetur.

Modestinus in the fifth book of his *Rules*:

If someone unknowingly bought sacred or religious or public areas as (if they were) private, then, although the purchase does not hold, he will still sue the seller on purchase (*ex empto*) in order to obtain his interest in not being deceived.

The Problem

Calpurnia sells to her neighbor Julia land on which sits a public temple to Jupiter. If Julia then incurs losses because of this sale, can she recover them from Calpurnia, and, if so, how?

Discussion

1. **Sale of the Brooklyn Bridge Revisited.** Note how Modestinus phrases his holding: the sale is invalid, but the unknowing buyer can still sue "on the purchase" (*ex empto*). Is this view inconsistent? The jurists vary somewhat in how they analyze situations of this type; but some uphold the sale, e.g., Licinius Rufinus, D. 18.1.70 (sale of a free man, see the following Case). Why is only an unknowing buyer protected? Would it matter if the buyer should have known that an object was unsaleable, but failed to exercise due care? Does the seller's knowledge make any difference? Discussion continues in the following Cases.

2. **Measure of Damages.** Modestinus says that the buyer can obtain "his interest in not being deceived." What is this interest? Is it the value to the buyer of the contract if it could have been carried out (somewhat similar to the expectation interest), or rather the losses the buyer sustains as a result of the contract being invalid (the reliance interest)? Probably the latter, but Modestinus does not express this very clearly. What measure would be appropriate? As you should see, the answer could depend on whether we regard the deception as negating the sale from the outset (in which case, most logically, only the would-be buyer's losses should be compensated), or as bringing about a subsequent breach of a contract (which allows the buyer to recover his or her "interest" in the contract being valid).

CASE 94: Sale of a Free Man or a Stolen Object

D. 18.1.34.2–3 (Paulus libro trigensimo tertio ad Edictum)

2. Liberum hominem scientes emere non possumus. Sed nec talis emptio aut stipulatio admittenda est: "cum servus erit," quamvis dixerimus futuras res emi posse: nec enim fas est eiusmodi casus exspectare. 3. Item si et emptor et venditor scit furtivum esse quod venit, a neutra parte obligatio contrahitur: si emptor solus scit, non obligabitur venditor nec tamen ex vendito quicquam consequitur, nisi ultro quod convenerit praestet: quod si venditor scit, emptor ignoravit, utrimque obligatio contrahitur, et ita Pomponius quoque scribit.

Paul in the thirty-third book *On the Edict*:

2. We cannot knowingly buy a free man. But neither is it allowed to make a sale or stipulation (with a condition) like this one: "when he will be a slave," even though we hold that future objects can be sold; for it violates religious law (*fas*) to await an event of this sort.

3. Likewise, if both buyer and seller know that the object of sale was stolen, an obligation is contracted by neither party. If the buyer alone knows, the seller is not obligated nor does he obtain anything by suing on sale unless he voluntarily tenders what was agreed on. But if the seller knows and the buyer was unaware, an obligation is contracted on either side; and Pomponius also writes this.

Discussion

1. Sale of a Free Person. Compare Case 25 on stipulation, particularly as to a contract that speculates on future enslavement. Although Celsus, cited by Pomponius, D. 18.1.6 pr., had ruled it "impossible" (*non posse*) to knowingly sell a free man, Paul considers the sale valid if the seller is aware of the truth and the buyer is not; so he would presumably also hold the sale valid if both parties are unaware; see Licinnius Rufinus, D. 18.1.70. Pomponius, D. 18.1.4, also indicates that only the buyer's knowledge or ignorance is relevant. What this means is that the unknowing buyer can recover damages. Does the rule function as a form of buyer protection?

2. Measure of Damages. Paul states that, in the case of an unknowing buyer, "an obligation is contracted on either side"; this could mean that the buyer must pay the price, but can then claim from the seller his or her entire expectation interest. Would that be appropriate? Why might the outcome here be different from the previous Case? Paul, D. 18.1.5, observes the inherent difficulty of telling a free man from a slave (Roman slavery did not depend much on ethnicity, for instance); is this problem then more salient than in the case of public property?

3. Sale of Property Already Owned by the Buyer. Pomponius, D. 18.1.16 pr., states that the sale of property to someone who already owns it is always

void, regardless of whether or not the buyer is aware of this fact; and if the sale has been executed, the unknowing buyer can recover the price. As stated, this rule is too broad. For example, Marcellus, D. 18.1.61, notes that the buyer can purchase his or her own property in order to quiet a possible claim on ownership by the seller; in that case, would it matter if the claim was patently frivolous? Must the buyer actually believe in the possible validity of the claim? (Similar problems arise in Common Law concerning the "reality" of consideration.) See also Paul, D. 18.1.15.2, who posits a buyer who unknowingly purchases his own property and then orders its delivery to a third party; does the buyer lose his ownership upon its delivery?

4. **Sale of a Third Party's Property.** It is usually possible to sell someone else's property, with the seller taking the risk that the third party may be unwilling to sell (Ulpian, D. 18.1.28). Still, often the owner may have preauthorized the sale; see, for instance, Case 186 (brokerage). However, in the case of stolen property, section 3 of the present Case applies most of the usual rules as to legally impossible sales. If both parties know that the property is stolen (e.g., in a typical fencing operation), the sale is void; if only the seller is aware, "an obligation is contracted on either side," presumably meaning that the buyer must pay and the seller must deliver. (Is the seller then liable in sale if the true owner reclaims the object? Surely yes, see Part B.4 in this Chapter.) More interesting is Paul's treatment of the situation where the buyer is aware and the seller is not: the seller incurs no obligation, but can claim the price upon delivery of the object. Is the seller liable if the true owner reclaims the object from the buyer? The answer is uncertain, but probably yes.

CASE 95: Sale of an Object Already Destroyed

D. 18.1.58 (Papinianus libro decimo Quaestionum)

Arboribus quoque vento deiectis vel absumptis igne dictum est emptionem fundi non videri esse contractam, si contemplatione illarum arborum, veluti oliveti, fundus comparabatur, sive sciente sive ignorante venditore: . . .

Papinian in the tenth book of his *Questions*:

Also when trees were blown down by wind or destroyed by fire, it was held that a sale of the farm was not contracted if the farm was bought with a view to those trees, e.g., an olive orchard; (and this is true) whether the seller knew (of their destruction) or was unaware. . . .

Discussion

1. **Physical Impossibility.** The jurists hold that there can be no sale without an object of sale; see Pomponius, D. 18.1.8 pr. (Case 86). Hence they find it easy to hold that when the object of sale has perished before the sale was agreed upon, there is no sale; see Paul, D. 18.1.15 pr.; Marcian, D. 18.1.44 (two slaves are bought for one price; if one was already dead, there is no sale also for the other). In this Case, the trees (presumably a major asset in determining the farm's value) had apparently been destroyed before the conclusion of the sale. The question that arises is whether there is still a sale at least of the land. Is Papinian's solution convincing? Ostensibly, the issue is one of physical impossibility, but the buyer's expectations take center stage in evaluating the destruction. Is this another form of buyer protection?

2. **Another Example.** Paul, D. 18.1.57 pr., discusses a more complex case, although this text was probably rewritten by the Digest compilers. A buyer has purchased a house that had been wholly or partially destroyed by fire before the sale. In the text as preserved, two issues are considered: the state of knowledge of the two parties, and the degree of destruction. If the buyer is unaware, the contract is void if the destruction is total or nearly total; but the contract is valid if the house is only partially destroyed, although the buyer may then seek a reduction in price. Where the buyer is aware and the seller is not, the contract is good and the buyer must pay full price. If both parties are aware, the sale is held void because of their mutual fraud. These rules (particularly the last one) may not be Classical. Try to devise better ones.

SECTION 4. Interpreting Agreements of Sale

We saw that the jurists normally interpret stipulations fairly closely, in accord with their "plain meaning" when a more case-specific understanding cannot be achieved (Chapter II.B). Such fairly narrow interpretation follows from the nature of a formal contract. By contrast, sales often receive a more generous interpretation that *bona fides* would appear to require, but the difference is not so great as one might have anticipated, and the jurists can occasionally be quite rigid.

However, there is one respect in which the contrast between stipulation and sale is especially instructive. At least in principle, every stipulation can be interpreted in its own right, since stipulation is theoretically only a form; the parties themselves determine the wording and thereby the content of each promise, even if they adhere to general patterns. But sale, as a contract type, has a predefined content; further, unlike stipulation, sale is subject to the overarching norm of *bona fides*. These two characteristics of sale made it much easier for the jurists to establish many general rules that were applicable to all sales. Some of these rules could not be varied by the parties, but most were enforced only if seller and buyer did not provide otherwise for a particular sale.

Rules of this second type are today often called "dispositive" or "default" rules, in the sense that they provide a structure that relieves individual parties from the necessity of elaborate bargaining over every contract. The touchstones for measuring the success of such dispositive rules is the perception of their general fairness and efficiency. In Part B of this Chapter, many of these dispositive rules will be more closely examined.

CASE 96: The Course of Negotiations

D. 18.1.80.2 (Labeo libro quinto *Posteriorum* a Iavoleno Epitomatorum)

Silva caedua in quinquennium venierat: quaerebatur, cum glans decidisset, utrius esset. Scio servium respondisse, primum sequendum esse quod appareret actum esse: quod si in obscuro esset, quaecumque glans ex his arboribus quae caesae non essent cecidisset, venditoris esse, eam autem, quae in arboribus fuisset eo tempore cum haec caederentur, emptoris.

Labeo in the fifth book of his *Posthumous Writings*, as Epitomized by Javolenus:

Timber rights (on a piece of land) had been sold for five years. Question arose as to whom the fallen acorns belonged. I know that Servius responded that the first thing to be followed is what it appears the parties transacted (*quod appareret actum esse*). But if this is unclear, then the seller owns whatever acorns fell from trees that were not felled, and the buyer, those that were on the trees at the time they were felled.

Discussion

1. The Felling of Timber. Although at the time of sale the timber is still attached to the seller's land, this arrangement is considered a normal sale in Roman law. By the contract, the buyer is presumably entitled to enter the seller's land and fell the trees. Compare sale of olives still on the trees: Julian, D. 18.1.39.1; also Julian, D. 19.1.25 (although a stipulation may be involved here). It would apparently make no difference if the seller contracted to fell and deliver the trees himself. Rather more startling is Labeo, D. 18.1.80.1: a buyer purchases the use of portions of his own building that project over the seller's property, with the projections to remain in place.

2. The Process of Interpretation. With this Case compare Case 11 on stipulation. How, if at all, is the interpretation of a sales contract different? The acorns could often be of some value as human and animal feed. Since the present contract made no provision at all for acorns, it is not ambiguous but defective; nonetheless, the *iudex* is allowed to fill in the missing term by surmise or by taking testimony from the parties and their witnesses. If this testimony is inconclusive (as it usually will be), the jurists supply the term. Compare Pomponius, D. 18.1.6.1: "In sales, what should be enforced is what was transacted (*id quod actum sit*), rather than what was said." Roman law appears to have no "parol evidence rule" restricting admission of evidence on the course of negotiations when it contradicts or at times even supplements or explains a written agreement; see Case 102. Is

this wise? What interest might the parties have, for instance, in preserving the "sanctity" of a written contract? Ulpian, D. 21.1.31.20, indicates that "practice and custom" (*mos et consuetudo*) were also used as tools in interpreting sales contracts; this is not far off from "plain meaning" as informed by "trade usage."

CASE 97: Interpreting a Condition

D. 18.1.41 pr. (Iulianus libro tertio ad Urseium Ferocem)

Cum ab eo, qui fundum alii obligatum habebat, quidam sic emptum rogasset, ut esset is sibi emptus, si eum liberasset, dummodo ante kalendas Iulias liberaret, quaesitum est, an utiliter agere possit ex empto in hoc, ut venditor eum liberaret. Respondit: videamus, quid inter ementem et vendentem actum sit. Nam si id actum est, ut omni modo intra kalendas Iulias venditor fundum liberaret, ex empto erit actio, ut liberet, nec sub condicione emptio facta intellegetur, veluti si hoc modo emptor interrogaverit: "erit mihi fundus emptus ita, ut eum intra kalendas Iulias liberes," vel "ita ut eum intra kalendas a Titio redimas." Si vero sub condicione facta emptio est, non poterit agi, ut condicio impleatur.

Julian in the third book *On Urseius Ferox*:

A certain person sought to buy a farm from someone who had obligated it (as a security) to a third party, under the condition that it be purchased by him if he (the seller) freed it (from the encumbrance) before the Kalends of July. It was asked whether he can effectively sue on the purchase to make the seller free it.

He (Julian) responded: Let us examine what the buyer and seller transacted. For if their transaction was that the seller free the land in any case before the Kalends of July, there will be an action on purchase in order that he free it, nor is the sale construed as being made under a condition—e.g., if the buyer made the following offer: "The farm will be bought by me such that you free it before the Kalends of July," or "such that you redeem it from Titius before the Kalends." But if the sale was made under a condition, he will not be able to sue for fulfillment of the condition.

Discussion

1. The Problem. In this contract, the meaning of the condition is ambiguous: is the seller actually undertaking to clear the farm of the third party's security interest, or is he merely promising to sell the farm if the security interest is (somehow) removed? In the former case (which is decidedly more likely), the buyer can bring action on purchase to enforce the "promissory condition," or at least to get damages for breach. How does Julian think that a *iudex* should resolve the problem? Does he seem to favor one solution over the other? What if the testimony from the parties is inconclusive as to the condition?

2. Another Example. In the sale of a farm, a contract stated that the farm had 18 acres and set a price per acre "as it may be measured." A survey later revealed that the farm had 20 acres. Must the buyer pay for all 20 acres? Paul, D. 18.1.40.2, says yes; is this outcome defensible?

CASE 98: Reasonability

D. 18.1.77 (Iavolenus libro quarto ex Posterioribus Labeonis)

In lege fundi vendundi lapidicinae in eo fundo ubique essent exceptae erant, et post multum temporis in eo fundo repertae erant lapidicinae. Eas quoque venditoris esse Tubero respondit: Labeo referre quid actum sit: si non appareat, non videri eas lapidicinas esse exceptas: neminem enim nec vendere nec excipere quod non sit, et lapidicinas nullas esse, nisi quae apparent et caedantur: aliter interpretantibus totum fundum lapidicinarum fore, si forte toto eo sub terra esset lapis. Hoc probo.

Javolenus in the fourth book *From Labeo's Posthumous Writings:*

In the terms for sale of a farm, rock quarries were reserved (for the seller) wherever they were on the farm; after considerable time, (new) quarries were opened on the farm. Tubero responded that they too belonged to the seller. Labeo (said) that it mattered what the parties transacted (*quid actum sit*); if this should be unclear, these (new) quarries should not be understood as reserved, since no one sells or reserves what does not exist, and there are no quarries unless they were obvious and (already) being mined. On the opposed interpretation, (Labeo said) that the entire farm would be a quarry if rock happened to lie everywhere beneath the earth. I approve this view.

Discussion

1. **Imposing a Reasonable Solution.** If the course of negotiations is unclear, the jurists often resort to plausible guesses about what the parties intended. In this Case, the issue is whether the seller would have wanted to reserve for himself just the existing quarries, or all present and future quarries. Is Tubero following the literal meaning of the contract? How reasonable is Labeo's opposing interpretation?

2. **Other Examples.** Paul, D. 18.1.40.1, 3, gives two other examples. (i) By an express term, the seller of a farm gave the buyer water rights in a neighboring farm that the seller retained; does the buyer also have a right of way to approach the water? (ii) The seller of a farm reserved the grain that had been sown by hand on the farm; can the seller claim grain that grows from thatch, or that grows from seed that accidentally falls from the sower's bag, or that grows from seed dropped by birds?

CASE 99: Interpretation against the Seller

D. 8.3.30 (Paulus libro quarto Epitomarum Alfeni Digestorum)

Qui duo praedia habebat, in unius venditione aquam, quae in fundo nascebatur, et circa eam aquam late decem pedes exceperat: quaesitum est, utrum dominium loci ad eum pertineat an ut per eum locum accedere possit. Respondit, si ita recepisset: "Circa eam aquam late pedes decem," iter dumtaxat videri venditoris esse.

Paul in the fourth book of his *Epitomies of the Digests of Alfenus*:

A person owned two (adjacent) properties. In selling one, he reserved (for himself) the water that sprang on the farm, as well as ten feet around this water. It was asked whether he has ownership of this area, or (only a property right) that he be able to approach through the area. He (Alfenus?) responded that if the reservation was worded: "ten feet around the water," the seller is held to have only a right of way (*iter*).

Discussion

1. **Against the Seller.** Paul, D. 18.1.21: "Labeo wrote that ambiguities in the agreement should harm the seller who stated it, rather than the buyer, since he (the seller) could state the matter more clearly in entering the transaction." This principle, which recurs in other texts, seems to apply the theory of interpretation against the stipulator; see Case 12. How convincing is its analgous application to sale? Is the seller likely in fact to have written most terms of the sale, particularly reservations of rights? Is the rule easier if the underlying principle is that ambiguous promises should be interpreted narrowly? Is the present Case an application of the rule?

2. **A Second Example.** The seller of a house reserved for himself the right either to live in the house for his lifetime, or, in lieu thereof, to receive 10,000 sesterces per year (its presumed rental value). The buyer interpreted this reservation to mean that the choice was his: he offered the seller the money for the first year, occupancy for the second, i.e., the seller would have to move in and out at the buyer's request. Paul, D. 19.1.21.6 (citing Trebatius), upholds the buyer's interpretation. Do you agree?

3. **And a Third.** The sale agreement states that the water flows and eave run-off are to remain as they now are, without specifying which ones. Pomponius, D. 18.1.33: "First we should examine what was transacted; if this is unclear, then we adopt the interpretation disadvantaging the seller, since the language is ambiguous."

CASE 100: Supplying Reasonable Terms

D. 19.1.38.2 (Celsus libro octavo Digestorum)

Firmus a Proculo quaesiit, si de plumbeo castello fistulae sub terram missae aquam ducerent in aenum lateribus circumstructum, an hae aedium essent, an ut ruta caesa vincta fixaque quae aedium non essententiarum. Ille rescripsit referre, quid acti esset. Quid ergo si nihil de ea re neque emptor neque venditor cogitaverunt, ut plerumque in eiusmodi rebus evenisse solet, nonne propius est, ut inserta et inclusa aedificio partem eius esse existimemus?

Celsus in the eighth book of his *Digests*:

Firmus asked Proculus: If underground water pipes bring water from a lead cistern into a cauldron built into the walls, are they part of the building, or (instead) like "things dug, cut, bound, and attached," which are not part of the building?

He wrote back that it matters what the parties transacted (*quid acti esset*). But what if neither buyer nor seller thought about this matter, as is often the case in matters of this sort? Is it not more fitting that we regard things implanted or inserted in the building as part of it?

Discussion

1. Conveyancing. A good deal of legal interpretation inevitably accumulated around the sale and subsequent conveyance of land, as to what is or is not reserved for the seller. One category that is reserved, in the absence of express agreement otherwise, is "things dug, cut, bound, and attached" (*ruta caesa vincta fixaque*), which are not part of the land; see Pomponius, D. 18.1.66.2. The jurists give many examples. According to Ulpian, D. 19.1.17 pr., the seller must deliver to the buyer the door bars, keys, and locks, but may keep crops and their receptacles even if buried. The buyer gets dung heaps and straw beds if they were not collected for later sale; the seller can take woodpiles. Paintings inserted as wall decorations go to the buyer; but netting around columns, awnings, and cupboards on walls belong to the seller. And so on. The distinctions seem to be mainly customary, though ultimately based on function.

2. Water Pipes. In the present Case, the underground water pipes feed a cauldron fixed in the walls. Note how Celsus (a great expert on interpretation) treats the problem. By contrast, Ulpian, D. 19.1.13.31 and 15, simply assumes that pipes and water receptacles are part of the building and belong to the buyer. Where the parties have not expressed themselves, is it worth inquiring into the course of their negotiations?

_____

_____

Earlier, Labeo, D. 18.1.78 pr., had examined another case in which the contract specified that pipes would accede to a purchased building; is the reservoir to which the pipes are connected also part of the sale? Labeo rules favorably to the buyer: "Apparently, what was transacted was that this too accede, although the writing omits this." Note that he does not seem to reach this conclusion on the basis of extrinsic evidence as to the parties' intent.

CASE 101: Dispositive Provisions

D. 19.1.13.10–11, 13 (Ulpianus libro trigesimo secundo ad Edictum)

10. Si fructibus iam maturis ager distractus sit, etiam fructus emptori cedere, nisi aliud convenit, exploratum est. 11. Si in locatis ager fuit, pensiones utique ei cedent qui locaverat: idem et in praediis urbanis, nisi si quid nominatim convenisse proponatur. . . . 13. Item si quid ex operis servorum vel vecturis iumentorum vel navium quaesitum est, emptori praestabitur, et si quid peculio eorum accessit, non tamen si quid ex re venditoris.

Ulpian in the thirty-second book *On the Edict*:

10. If farmland was sold when crops were already ripe, the settled view is that the crops also fall to the buyer unless they agreed otherwise. 11. If the farmland was leased, the rent in any case goes to the person who leased it. So too for urban properties, unless it is alleged that they expressly agreed on something (different). . . . 13. Likewise, if some profit resulted from the work of slaves or from fares for (using) beasts of burden or ships, it will be owed to the buyer; and also (in the case of slaves) if there was an increase in their *peculium*, but not what (comes) from the seller's property.

Discussion

1. **Default Rules.** Often it is helpful to the parties if law simply provides default rules for handling doubtful matters; the parties can then, if they wish, vary these rules by express agreement. This Case discusses several instances. The general rule is that the buyer takes any "fruit" (*fructus*) accruing to the object of sale after the contract is arranged, including, e.g., crops, rent, and profits from the lease of slaves, animals, and ships. Is this sensible? Keep watch for other dispositive rules in Roman sales law. How does the law of sale differ, in this respect, from stipulation? On the tenants, see Case 156.

2. **Sale of Slaves with Their *Peculia*.** A *peculium* is a separate account that for practical purposes is controlled by a slave, although it ultimately belongs to the slave's owner; see Case 196. When a slave is sold, his or her *peculium* is kept by the seller unless the parties provide otherwise; see, e.g., Ulpian, D. 18.1.29. But, as this Case indicates, the buyer of a slave with a *peculium* keeps most increases in it after the sale.

SECTION 5. Associated Pacts and Modification

Most sales involve the straightforward exchange of money for an object of sale. But some (such as the sale described in Case 80) are much more complex, the exchange being only one crucial element in a larger transaction. The Roman theory of contract types requires the ability to recognize the larger transaction as a sale so that it can be "pigeonholded" in its proper procedural category, but it is then also necessary to adapt or expand the law of sale so that it can take account of the larger transaction as well.

Roman law accomplishes this through a theory of "pacts" (*pacta*), informal agreements more or less contemporaneous with the central sale and, in effect, incorporated into it, so that they too become actionable as constituent parts of the sale. By contrast, subsequent pacts that modify the original bargain have a more limited effect: as a general rule, they can be used to narrow, but not to expand, one party's duties under the original sale. Roman law is, however, still fairly generous in permitting such modifications, at any rate by comparison with Common Law.

The Romans frequently used pacts in order to create specially tailored forms of sale, such as sale on approval. These special forms often raise delicate legal problems that the jurists found difficult to resolve, particularly when the form had implications for property law. Nonetheless, the jurists seem generally to have tried to give the parties the widest legally possible latitude to form sales as they wished. In a very few instances the parties could even impose covenants restricting future use of the object of sale by the seller and all subsequent owners; interestingly, in Roman law such permissible covenants invariably concern the use of slaves, not (as with us) the use of land.

CASE 102: Pacts Incorporated into the Sale

D. 2.14.7.5 (Ulpianus libro quarto ad Edictum)

Quin immo interdum format ipsam actionem, ut in bonae fidei iudiciis: solemus enim dicere pacta conventa inesse bonae fidei iudiciis. Sed hoc sic accipiendum est, ut si quidem ex continenti pacta subsecuta sunt, etiam ex parte actoris insint: si ex intervallo, non inerunt, nec valebunt, si agat, ne ex pacto actio nascatur. . . . Et si in tutelae actione convenit, ut maiores quam statutae sunt usurae praestentur, locum non habebit, ne ex pacto nascatur actio: ea enim pacta insunt, quae legem contractui dant, id est quae in ingressu contractus facta sunt. Idem responsum scio a Papiniano, et si post emptionem ex intervallo aliquid extra naturam contractus conveniat, ob hanc causam agi ex empto non posse propter eandem regulam, ne ex pacto actio nascatur. Quod et in omnibus bonae fidei iudiciis erit dicendum. Sed ex parte rei locum habebit pactum, quia solent et ea pacta, quae postea interponuntur, parere exceptiones.

Ulpian in the fourth book *On the Edict*:

But sometimes it (a pact, *pactum*) gives rise to an action itself, as in the actions on good faith (*bona fides*); for we usually hold that informal pacts are incorporated in good faith actions.

But this rule is understood to mean that if the pacts followed immediately (upon the contract being made), they are also incorporated in the plaintiff's case; if (they are made) after a space of time, they will not be incorporated, nor will they be valid if he sues, so as to prevent an action from arising out of a pact (alone). . . . I know Papinian gave the same response, that if, some time after a sale, they agreed on something outside the nature of the contract, no suit on sale can be brought for this reason, on account of the same rule that an action may not arise from a pact. This must be held in all good faith lawsuits. But on the defendant's side the pact is good, since even pacts that are later interposed generally provide defenses.

Discussion

1. Contracts and Pacts. As Ulpian indicates, in forming a consensual contract the parties have fairly wide latitude to make agreements (*pacta*) that are accessory to the contract. In the case of sale, such agreements are then actionable through the *formulae* on sale; that is, they become part of the sale. Case 80 provides a good example of this latitude: sale of half of a farm, accompanied by the buyer's ten-year lease of the other half: the lease is actionable through the sale provided it has a demonstrable effect on the sale price. Presumably it must be clear that the sale is the central transaction, and also that the accessory pact is in some way integrally connected with it. The jurists require that the pact be closely temporally connected to the sale; see also the Emperor Maximinus Thrax, C. 2.3.13 (236 CE).

In good faith contracts, one common use for pacts was to make interest payable on outstanding debts: Scaevola, D. 16.3.28. This device was often used for interest-bearing bank deposits; see Case 69.

2. Pacts Later Modifying the Sale. A different rule is adopted in the case of later agreements altering the original terms of the sale. Here, as Ulpian says, such an informal agreement has, in principle, no legal force (as the jurists put it, no action can arise from a bare agreement); but the agreement does give rise to a legal defense (*exceptio pacti*). The effect of this rule can be illustrated by two examples. First, sometime after the sale the parties agree that the buyer will pay interest on the price until it is paid; his agreement increases the duties of the buyer, so the seller cannot sue to enforce it: *Pauli Sent.* 2.14.1 (a subsequent agreement imposing interest on money due). (We might say the agreement fails for want of consideration; the jurists approach the question differently. In Roman law, the parties can, of course, make their subsequent agreement actionable through a stipulation.) Second, sometime after the sale the parties agree that the buyer pay no interest on the price; if the seller then sues for interest as provided in the original agreement, the buyer can use the pact as a defense (Case 36). To put this in the parlance of our time, the pact is a shield but not a sword. What reasons can be given for this lopsided rule? Is an agreement to raise the price more suspect (perhaps because of the possibility of duress) than one to lower the price?

CASE 103: Pacts Made after the Sale

D. 18.1.72 pr. (Papinianus libro decimo Quaestionum)

Pacta conventa, quae postea facta detrahunt aliquid emptioni, contineri contractui videntur: quae vero adiciunt, credimus non inesse. Quod locum habet in his, quae adminicula sunt emptionis, veluti ne cautio duplae praestetur aut ut cum fideiussore cautio duplae praestetur. Sed quo casu agente emptore non valet pactum, idem vires habebit iure exceptionis agente venditore. An idem dici possit aucto postea vel deminuto pretio, non immerito quaesitum est, quoniam emptionis substantia constitit ex pretio. Paulus notat: si omnibus integris manentibus de augendo vel deminuendo pretio rursum convenit, recessum a priore contractu et nova emptio intercessisse videtur.

Papinian in the tenth book of *Questions*:

Informal pacts that are made later and reduce some (duty) from the sale are regarded as contained in the contract; but those that increase (a duty) we regard as not incorporated. This applies to those (pacts) that support the sale, e.g., that the stipulation for double not be provided (against eviction), or that the stipulation for double be provided with a surety (*fideiussor*). But in this (latter) case (where the pact does support the sale), the pact is invalid if the buyer sues; but by the rule on defenses it operates if the seller sues. It is properly questioned whether the same can be held if the price is later increased or diminished, since the essence of the sale is the price.

Paul notes: If, while everything is still fresh (i.e., neither party has performed), they reach a new agreement on reducing the price, they (are understood to) back off from the earlier contract, and a new sale is held to have intervened.

Discussion

1. **Three Issues.** This Case is complicated because Papinian (in his usual irritating fashion) seems to discuss three issues at once: first, the distinction between pacts that increase or decrease a party's duty; second, the requirement that, in any case, a later pact must "support" (or supplement) the original contract, and cannot be entirely unrelated; third, Papinian's doubt, which he seems to be alone in expressing, as to whether a pact can modify an essential term such as the price. Try to clarify the discussion, if possible. The stipulation for double (*cautio duplae*) is a formal promise by the buyer that he or she will repay double the price if a true owner successfully claims the object from the buyer (see Case 134); and the seller's promise may be guaranteed by a surety as well.

CASE 104: Rescinding or Modifying a Sale

D. 2.14.7.6 (Ulpianus libro quarto ad Edictum)

Adeo autem bonae fidei iudiciis exceptiones postea factae, quae ex eodem sunt contractu, insunt, ut constet in emptione ceterisque bonae fidei iudiciis re nondum secuta posse abiri ab emptione. Si igitur in totum potest, cur non et pars eius pactione mutari potest? Et haec ita Pomponius libro sexto ad edictum scribit. Quod cum est, etiam ex parte agentis pactio locum habet, ut et ad actionem proficiat nondum re secuta, eadem ratione. Nam si potest tota res tolli, cur non et reformari? Ut quodammodo quasi renovatus contractus videatur. Quod non insuptiliter dici potest. Unde illud aeque non reprobo, quod Pomponius libris lectionum probat, posse in parte recedi pacto ab emptione, quasi repetita partis emptione. Sed cum duo heredes emptori exstiterunt, venditor cum altero pactus est, ut ab emptione recederetur: ait Iulianus valere pactionem et dissolvi pro parte emptionem: quoniam et ex alio contractu paciscendo alter ex heredibus adquirere sibi potuit exceptionem. Utrumque itaque recte placet, et quod Iulianus et quod Pomponius.

Ulpian in the fourth book *On the Edict*:

In *bona fides* lawsuits, subsequent pacts arising from the same contract are incorporated to such an extent that it is settled that in purchase and other *bona fides* trials, if nothing has yet been done, rescission of a sale is possible.

So, if this is possible for all of it, why can't a part of it also be changed by a pact? And in his sixth book on the Edict, Pomponius writes that this is so (i.e., that a part can be changed). In light of this, a pact is effective also for the plaintiff, so he too can enter an action by the same reasoning so long as nothing has yet been done. For if the entirety can be rescinded, why can't it also be modified? Such that the contract is held somehow to be almost recreated.

This position is subtly taken. Hence equally I will not reject what Pomponius affirms in his books of *Readings*, that by a pact a rescission in part is possible from a purchase, as though the purchase of part is reconsidered.

But when there are two heirs to the buyer, and the seller makes a pact with one to rescind the purchase, Julian says the pact is valid and the purchase is rescinded in part, since also from (some) other contract one heir could acquire a defense for himself. So each view, that of Julian and that of Pomponius, is correct.

Discussion

1. Counteragreement. Now a major complication. Since a sale (like other good-faith contracts) is created by agreement (*consensus*), the jurists hold that the parties can also dissolve it by bilateral counteragreement (*contrarius consensus*), at any rate so long as the sale is still completely executory, with neither side having yet performed. (The jurist Aristo permitted voluntary

rescission even after the contract was partially executed; see Neratius, D. 2.14.58; but this seems to have been a minority view.) The effect of such a counteragreement is to end the contract completely; neither side can enforce it. But the implication of this rule is that, so long as the contract is wholly executory, the parties have the power to substitute a new contract modifying the terms of the original contract; see, besides Ulpian in this Case and Papinian/Paul in the previous Case, Pomponius, D. 18.5.2, and Paul, D. 18.5.3. This possibility substantially undermines the rule on pacts in the two prior Cases. Why should the situation then change after one or both parties have begun to perform?

CASE 105: Reserving Seller's Right to Accept a Better Price

D. 18.2.2 (Ulpianus libro vicensimo octavo ad Sabinum)

pr. Quotiens fundus in diem addicitur, utrum pura emptio est, sed sub condicione resolvitur, an vero condicionalis sit magis emptio, quaestionis est. Et mihi videtur verius interesse, quid actum sit: nam si quidem hoc actum est, ut meliore allata condicione discedatur, erit pura emptio, quae sub condicione resolvitur: sin autem hoc actum est, ut perficiatur emptio, nisi melior condicio offeratur, erit emptio condicionalis. 1. Ubi igitur secundum quod distinximus pura venditio est, Iulianus scribit hunc, cui res in diem addicta est, et usucapere posse et fructus et accessiones lucrari et periculum ad eum pertinere, si res interierit.

Ulpian in the twenty-eighth book *On Sabinus*:

pr. When a farm is sold subject to rescission within a stated time (*addictio in diem*), there is a question whether the sale is unconditional but resolved under a condition, or the sale is instead conditional. I think it better to hold that it makes a difference what the parties transacted (*quid actum sit*). For if they arranged that it be called off when better terms are offered (by a third party), the sale will be unconditional but resolved under the condition. But if they arranged that the sale be complete unless better terms are offered, the sale will be conditional.

1. So when, according to this distinction, the sale is unconditional, Julian writes that the person who buys under such a provision can both usucapt and profit from its fruits and accessions, and that he bears the risk (*periculum*) if the object perishes (before the contract is resolved).

Discussion:
   1. *Addictio in Diem*. This clause allows the seller to accept a better offer before a specified date. The issue is whether, in the meantime, the sale is valid but can later be rescinded if the seller receives a better offer; or, instead, the sale is not presently valid but will become valid if no better offer is accepted. Ulpian treats this as entirely a matter of contractual interpretation. The issue is important because it affects especially the passage to the buyer of the risk for accidental destruction of the object prior to delivery; see Part B.1 in this Chapter. (Note that, in Roman law, a contract is said to be "conditional" only if it does not become valid except upon occurrence of a condition—what we would call a suspensive condition or a condition precedent. If a contract becomes valid at once but can be resolved upon occurrence of a condition—what we would call a resolutive condition or a condition subsequent—the jurists describe the contract as unconditional but resoluble.)

   2. Better Offers. An offer is considered "better" if, e.g., a higher price is offered, or faster payment, or sturdier credit; see Ulpian, D. 18.2.4.6. A *iudex* could

evidently review whether the second offer is in fact better. If it is, the original buyer has the option to meet the new offer; see Ulpian, D. 18.2.6.1; and, if the buyer fails to do so, the buyer must surrender the object back to the seller, although he may keep the fruits if the sale was unconditional in the interim.

3. The Effect of Annulling the Contract. Suppose that the sale is unconditional, and the buyer receives the object and pays the price; thereby the buyer will usually acquire ownership. What happens if a better offer is then made before the deadline? Clearly the sale is annulled retroactively, but does the buyer's ownership automatically revert to the seller? The answer is not completely certain. Ulpian, D. 18.2.4.3 (citing Marcellus), puts the case where a buyer in an unconditional sale has then used the property as a real security to a third party; if the seller subsequently accepts a better offer, the security interest in the property is automatically withdrawn, which would imply that the buyer no longer owns the object. (See also Ulpian/Marcellus, D. 20.6.3.) If these and similar texts mean what they seem to mean, then the buyer's ownership, in the interim before the deadline, is not absolute but only provisional; the seller is protected by the possible reversion of ownership. Although this would seem to be a reasonable solution, many scholars believe it was imposed on the texts by the Digest compilers. If that is so, the jurists themselves may have restricted the seller to a suit on the contract—a very harsh rule. Much the same problem arises with the other types of sale discussed in subsequent Cases.

CASE 106: Calling Off Sale If Price Is Not Paid

D. 18.3.2 (Pomponius libro trigensimo quinto ad Sabinum)

Cum venditor fundi in lege ita caverit: "Si ad diem pecunia soluta non sit, ut fundus inemptus sit," ita accipitur inemptus esse fundus, si venditor inemptum eum esse velit, quia id venditoris causa caveretur: nam si aliter acciperetur, exusta villa in potestate emptoris futurum, ut non dando pecuniam inemptum faceret fundum, qui eius periculo fuisset.

Pomponius in the thirty-fifth book *On Sabinus*:

When a farm's seller provides in the terms of sale as follows: "that, if the money is not paid by the due date, the land be unsold," this is taken to mean that the farm is not sold if the seller wishes it not to be sold, since the provision is for the seller's benefit. For were it otherwise interpreted, (a jurist held) that if the farmhouse burned down, it would be in the buyer's power to undo the farm's sale by not paying the money; but this was at his risk (*periculum*).

Discussion

1. *Lex Commissoria.* This clause allows the seller to rescind the sale if the buyer does not pay the price (or at least tender payment) by a deadline; note that the option to rescind is entirely with the seller. The present Case gives the standard formulation of the clause, which is regularly taken to mean that the sale is valid but can be resolved in the event of non-payment. However, it is also possible to make the validity of the sale dependent upon payment, though this seems to have been uncommon. Normally the buyer sought to have the object at once and pay for it later. If the buyer failed to pay by the deadline, the seller had to decide at once whether to call off the sale, and was obliged then to stick to this choice; see Papinian, *Frag. Vat.* 3–4; Ulpian, D. 18.3.4.2; Hermogenian, D. 18.3.7. Why is the seller required to choose promptly?

2. **Seller's Remedies.** Although the sale is rescinded, the seller is allowed to sue the buyer on sale; see Ulpian, D. 18.3.4 pr. The state of our texts makes it unclear whether ownership reverted to the seller, who could then bring a property law vindication to recover the object; for instance, consecutive rescripts of the Emperor Alexander (C. 4.54.3–4) contradict one another on this point. It is thought that in Classical law the seller did not automatically recover ownership if it had passed to the buyer; but such a rule may work hard consequences if, for instance, the buyer is insolvent.

3. Other Special Terms. The parties may also agree that the seller has the right to repurchase the object if the buyer later decides to sell it, or that the seller can repurchase it within a specified time.

CASE 107: Sale on Approval

D. 19.5.20 pr.-1 (Ulpianus libro trigesimo secundo ad Edictum)

pr. Apud Labeonem quaeritur, si tibi equos venales experiendos dedero, ut, si in triduo displicuissent, redderes, tuque desultor in his cucurreris et viceris, deinde emere nolueris, an sit adversus te ex vendito actio. Et puto verius esse praescriptis verbis agendum: nam inter nos hoc actum, ut experimentum gratuitum acciperes, non ut etiam certares. 1. Item apud Melam quaeritur, si mulas tibi dedero ut experiaris et, si placuissent, emeres, si displicuissent, ut in dies singulos aliquid praestares, deinde mulae a grassatoribus fuerint ablatae intra dies experimenti, quid esset praestandum, utrum pretium et merces an merces tantum. Et ait Mela interesse, utrum emptio iam erat contracta an futura, ut, si facta, pretium petatur, si futura, merces petatur: sed non exprimit de actionibus. Puto autem, si quidem perfecta fuit emptio, competere ex vendito actionem, si vero nondum perfecta esset, actionem talem qualem adversus desultorem dari.

Ulpian in the thirty-second book *On the Edict*:

pr. In Labeo it is asked: If my horses are for sale and I give them to you on approval, with the condition that you return them within three days if they displease you, and you (then) ride them in an acrobatic contest and win, and then decline to buy them, is there an action on sale against you? I think the better view is that suit must be by a special preamble (*actio praescriptis verbis*), since what we transacted was that you have a free trial, not that you also compete (with them).

1. Likewise, in Mela it is asked: If I give mules to you on approval, with the condition that you buy them if they please you and pay something for each day (before their return) if they displease you, and the mules are then stolen by brigands within the trial period, what should be owed: the price, or just the rent? Mela says that it matters whether or not the sale had yet been contracted, so that, if it was made, the price is claimed; if it was (still) in the future, (only) the rent is owed. But he does not speak about the actions. I think that if the sale was complete, an action lies on sale; if it was not yet complete, an action is given like that against the acrobat (in the case described earlier).

Discussion

1. Approval. This clause gives the buyer a virtually unrestricted right to reject the object after a trial period. The parties would normally specify this period, but a sixty-day limit was imposed if they did not; see Ulpian, D. 21.1.31.22–23. The parties were also free to determine that their arrangement would become a valid sale only if the buyer expressed agreement (a suspensive condition), or that the sale would be valid forthwith but resolved if the buyer rejected the object (in our law, a resolutive condition). The latter seems to have been more common; why?

2. Misuse of the Object on Trial. In the *principium* of this Case, the buyer has received the horses on trial and then used them in an acrobatic contest; this goes considerably beyond what would normally be considered fair use during a trial period, particularly because the buyer rejected the horses after winning the contest. The buyer's right to reject is apparently not questioned; but some remedy must be found for the seller. Labeo considered an action on sale; Ulpian prefers a special action, which probably did not exist in Labeo's time, that will presumably allow the seller to recover at least the fair rental value of the horses. (On the *actio praescriptis verbis*, see Chapter VI.B; but the applicability of this suit is unclear, and restitution of the benefit would seem more appropriate.) In this case, the sale appears to be subject to what we would call a resolutive condition; see Ulpian, D. 18.1.3; in such a sale, ownership would not automatically revert to the seller upon the buyer's rejection; see Ulpian, D. 20.6.3.

3. Destruction in the Interim. In section 1, a more elaborate arrangement is described: the prospective buyer pays rent for the trial period if he later rejects the mules, or the price if he accepts them. But the mules have been stolen before the buyer reached his decision on buying. As Fabius Mela and Ulpian indicate, the problem seems to hinge on how the arrangement is to be construed. If the sale was subject to a resolutive condition, then the sale was already in force and the buyer is liable in sale for failure to return the mules; but if the condition was suspensive, then the buyer needs to pay the rent and the seller bears the risk of the mules' loss. Which seems the better outcome?

4. Good Faith? Can it be presumed that the would-be buyer is acting honestly when accepting or rejecting the object? We might compare the decision on the horses or mules to a painting commissioned on approval; in the latter case, must the buyer at least look at the painting before rejecting it? What result if the approval is dishonest?

CASE 108: Condition of Tasting Wine

D. 18.6.4.1 (Ulpianus libro vicesimo octavo ad Sabinum)

Si aversione vinum venit, custodia tantum praestanda est. Ex hoc apparet, si non ita vinum venit, ut degustaretur, neque acorem neque mucorem venditorem praestare debere, sed omne periculum ad emptorem pertinere: difficile autem est, ut quisquam sic emat, ut ne degustet. Quare si dies degustationi adiectus non erit, quandoque degustare emptor poterit et quoad degustaverit, periculum acoris et mucoris ad venditorem pertinebit: dies enim degustationi praestitutus meliorem condicionem [emptoris] <venditoris> facit.

Ulpian in the twenty-eighth book *On Sabinus*:

If wine is sold for a lump sum, only safekeeping (*custodia*) is owed (by the seller). From this it is clear that if wine was not sold with a condition of tasting, the seller should not be liable for acidity or mustiness, but all risk (of the wine going bad) falls on the buyer. But it is hard (to believe) that anyone would buy on a condition of not tasting.

So if a deadline is not set for the tasting, the buyer can taste when he likes, and until he tastes, the risk of acidity and mustiness will lie on the seller; setting a deadline on tasting thus improves the position of the seller.

Discussion

1. Tasting. The sale of wine was a risky business in the Roman world, since wine often went bad before it could be marketed. Ulpian strongly recommends that the buyer insist on the right to taste the wine before accepting it, and that the seller insist in turn on a deadline for tasting. Unlike with a trial period (in the previous Case), a condition of tasting does not give the buyer an arbitrary right to reject; the tasting must conform to the judgment of an upright person; see Ulpian, D. 18.1.7 pr. (*vir bonus*); and so the buyer's decision is reviewable by a *iudex*. The legal situation if no condition of tasting is agreed upon is described in Case 139.

2. Preventing Tasting. Ulpian, D. 18.6.4 pr., deals with a case in which the seller sets a deadline for tasting and then obstructs the buyer from tasting before the deadline. The question is whether the seller thereby bears the risk if the wine goes bad after the deadline. Ulpian states that this depends on interpreting the agreement between the parties (*quid actum sit*), but, if the matter is unclear, then the seller bears this risk because of his obstruction. "Bearing the risk" presumably means, in this context, at least that the buyer can back out of the sale; should the buyer also be able to recover damages?

CASE 109: Restricting Use of Object of Sale

D. 18.1.56 (Paulus libro quinquagensimo ad Edictum)

Si quis sub hoc pacto vendiderit ancillam, ne prostituatur et, si contra factum esset, uti liceret ei abducere, etsi per plures emptores mancipium cucurrerit, ei qui primo vendit abducendi potestas fit.

Paul in the fiftieth book *On the Edict*:

If someone sells a slave woman under a pact that she not be prostituted, and that, if this be violated, he be permitted to take her back, (then) even if the slave passes through many (subsequent) buyers, the person who first sold her has the power to take her back.

Discussion

1. Covenants on Use. In a limited number of situations (all concerning sale of slaves), Roman law allows a seller to impose a covenant restricting future use: that the slave be sold abroad, that the slave be manumitted (or not be manumitted), or that a slave woman not be prostituted. Some of these covenants are intended to punish slaves, others to protect them. What is unusual about the covenants is that they have limited "real" effects. In this Case, for example, the original seller can take back the slave woman if she is prostituted not only by the original buyer, but even by a much later one (who may not know about the covenant). It was also possible to impose a covenant that the slave woman be free if she was prostituted: e.g., Paul, D. 18.7.9. Why did the Romans recognize such covenants? Why did they restrict the list of possible covenants?

2. Imperial Implementation. The Emperor Alexander, C. 4.56.1 (223 CE), citing a constitution of Hadrian, allows imperial officials to intervene and order a slave woman to be freed if she is prostituted against a covenant, even where the original owner tolerates the violation. This might be a humanitarian measure, but the emperors also enforce covenants requiring export of a slave; see Septimius Severus and Caracalla, C. 4.55.1–2 (200).

PART B

Execution of a Sale

After a sale has been successfully arranged, the two parties must execute it. The vast majority of sales are executed immediately: the seller hands over the object, the buyer pays its price. Even in such cash sales, it is helpful to keep in mind the agreement that underlies the transfer, since it is the agreement that explains not only why the transfer occurs, but also why in most circumstances it is legally irreversible once completed. Further, the agreement may have important subsequent repercussions, if, for instance, the object of sale turns out to be defective in some serious way.

More interesting, however, are sales that do not involve immediate exchange, but instead envisage the unfolding of performance over a period of time following the agreement. Here the interaction of the seller's and buyer's respective rights and duties can result in a richly textured law, a sort of intricate counterpoint with many possible variations. Suppose, for example, the seller retains the object for subsequent delivery, and the object is then destroyed before the buyer receives it. Clearly there is a loss; the difficult legal problem is to determine which party will bear the loss.

As they articulated the rules for executing sales, the jurists appear to have kept in mind the ultimate double goal of all sales: that the buyer receive the object, and the seller its price. This implies that the rights and duties of seller and buyer are not theoretically independent, but instead interlinked and inseparable; the implicit model remains the cash sale with its immediate exchange. As the following Cases will demonstrate, this model has many important legal implications.

There are two important subjects, related to execution of sales, that you need to keep your eye on. First, Roman law has a rather underdeveloped theory of breach, particularly as it relates to the rights of the aggrieved party; the jurists often seem to tie breach too closely to the concept of default (*mora*), or improper delay in performance, which is really just one type of breach. The issue here becomes more important in modern law, where the complexity of sales (think especially of installment sales) often makes it important for an aggrieved party to take action even before default.

Second, our sources are also surprisingly slender as regards remedies. As usual in Roman law, a plaintiff's remedy is normally expressed in money (*condemnatio pecuniaria*). So, too, in our law, except that we allow somewhat more access to court-ordered (specific) performance of the contract. But the Roman jurists are not especially clear on the amount of damages, beyond often defining them vaguely in terms of the plaintiff's "interest" (*id quod interest*). It may help to break damages down into two broad categories: direct damages (e.g., the plaintiff bought for 500 an object worth 600 on the market, and is now entitled to the difference) and consequential damages (e.g., the plaintiff loses a downstream contract because of the defendant's breach). Our sources seem to recognize both categories, but do not exhaustively analyze them, much less indicate when each form of damages is available. For the most part, the *iudex* seems to have been left on his own, to do the best he could.

Besides damages, other Cases provide for remedies such as rescission and restitution, essentially undoing the sale.

SECTION 1. Risk of Damage or Destruction Prior to Delivery

A sale is complete (*perfecta*) when the parties have agreed on all its basic terms and no condition bars its execution. The direct result of a completed sale is that each party has a contractual action for damages if the other party fails to perform. However, this liability is purely *in personam*; unlike in older Common Law, no property right in the object of sale passes to the buyer as an immediate consequence of the sale, regardless of whether or not specific property has been "identified" as the object of sale. Accordingly, if the seller then fails to deliver the object, the buyer can sue on purchase only to obtain damages from this breach.

In cases where the seller does not make immediate delivery, but instead retains the object for a time, it is possible that the object may be destroyed or damaged before delivery. In the law of sale, the resulting legal problem is handled through the doctrine of risk (*periculum*). This doctrine holds that the seller is liable for all physical damage to the object that he or she could conceivably prevent—what is called a liability for "safekeeping" (*custodia*). However, the risk falls on the buyer if the object is damaged or destroyed by a cause that is regarded as entirely beyond the seller's control—what the Romans term a "higher force" (*vis maior*), or a pure accident (*casus fortuitus*). This means that the buyer may have to pay for the destroyed object even though he or she does not receive it, and, what is more, even though no property right (title or possession) has yet passed from the seller to the buyer.

The Roman doctrine of risk is not obvious and has often attracted criticism. It may be hard to justify theoretically, but it makes eminent practical sense. Simply as a result of the sale, the buyer already has a limited legal interest in the object, and the seller's preexisting interest is correspondingly reduced. Both parties are likely to want the sale's execution in as short a time as is feasible, and the doctrine of risk encourages this result.

CASE 110: Passage of Risk

D. 18.6.8 pr. (Paulus libro trigesimo tertio ad Edictum)

Necessario sciendum est, quando perfecta sit emptio: tunc enim sciemus, cuius periculum sit: nam perfecta emptione periculum ad emptorem respiciet. Et si id quod venierit appareat quid quale quantum sit, sit et pretium, et pure venit, perfecta est emptio: quod si sub condicione res venierit, si quidem defecerit condicio, nulla est emptio, sicuti nec stipulatio: quod si exstiterit, Proculus et Octavenus emptoris esse periculum aiunt: idem Pomponius libro nono probat. Quod si pendente condicione emptor vel venditor decesserit, constat, si exstiterit condicio, heredes quoque obligatos esse quasi iam contracta emptione in praeteritum. Quod si pendente condicione res tradita sit, emptor non poterit eam usucapere pro emptore. Et quod pretii solutum est repetetur et fructus medii temporis venditoris sunt (sicuti stipulationes et legata condicionalia peremuntur), si pendente condicione res exstincta fuerit: sane si exstet res, licet deterior effecta, potest dici esse damnum emptoris.

Paul in the thirty-third book *On the Edict*:

It must be known when a sale is complete (*perfecta*), since we will then know who bears the risk (*periculum*); for when the sale is complete, the risk falls on the buyer. If the object of sale is clear, what and of what sort and how much it is, and what the price is, and the sale is unconditional, then the sale is complete. But if the object is sold under a condition, there is no sale if the condition fails, just as there is no stipulation (if a condition fails). But if it (the condition) is realized, Proculus and Octavenus say that the buyer (then) bears the risk; Pomponius approves this view in his ninth book.

But if the buyer or seller dies while the condition is pending, it is settled that, if the condition is realized, the (decedent's) heirs are also obligated, on the theory that the sale's effects now reach into the past. But if the object was handed over while the condition is pending, the buyer cannot usucapt it as buyer.

If the object of sale perishes while the condition is pending, any price paid will be recovered and the fruits for the interim belong to the seller, just as stipulations and conditional legacies fail. However, if the object remains but becomes worse, it can be said that the buyer bears the loss.

The Problem

Sempronia sells a cow to Titius, but the cow dies of natural causes before Sempronia can deliver it. Is Titius obliged to pay for the cow?

Discussion

1. Completion of the Sale. Paul relies on a distinction between the making of the contract through agreement on its essentials, and the contract's

"completion." Usually these occur more or less simultaneously with no further action required, but completion may be delayed, especially if the agreement involves a condition, such as that the object of sale be measured (Case 87) or come into existence (Cases 85–86). Even before completion, however, the agreement has consequences; neither party may unilaterally back out of the sale or obstruct the occurrence of the condition (see Case 86). Also, as Paul says, the obligations are already inheritable on either side. Paul's rule on the object's destruction or deterioration during a condition's pendency looks peculiar as it stands; his thought is perhaps that the sale cannot become complete without an object of sale, but surely the seller should at least bear contractual liability for any loss that he or she is responsible for. How would you rephrase Paul's rule?

2. **Performance before Completion.** The parties may begin to perform even before the sale is complete. If they do, as Paul says, their performance has limited effect: the buyer acquires no property rights in the object of sale, and may presumably recover any price that has been paid, so long as the condition is pending. If the object is destroyed through *vis maior* before the condition is realized, the seller "bears the risk" only in the sense that the contract is effectively nullified; the seller has no liability to the buyer. However, the parties can agree that the buyer bears the risk during pendency: Ulpian, D. 18.6.10.

3. **Effects of Completion: Passage of Risk.** Completion of a sale has two main consequences. First, the parties each become contractually liable to perform according to the terms of their agreement; note that this liability is solely contractual. Second, however, as Paul says, risk of the accidental destruction of the object passes to the buyer. This means that if before its delivery the object of sale is destroyed through circumstances over which the seller has no control (e.g., through *vis maior*), the buyer bears the loss and must pay the price regardless. Passage of risk is discussed in the Cases that follow, but Paul, D. 18.1.34.6, gives a hypothetical that may serve to illustrate it. Sale is of one of two slaves, Stichus or Pamphilus, with either the seller or the buyer to choose. Presumably without the seller's fault, one slave dies before choice can be made; then the other slave dies before delivery. Paul holds that the death of the first slave is at the seller's risk (in the sense that the possibility of choice is eliminated), but the death of the second is at the buyer's. Do you follow the logic? Paul goes on to note that the result is the same if the slaves die simultaneously, "since at least one lived at the buyer's risk." (Note that natural death of slaves and animals is deemed a form of *vis maior*.)

4. Deterioration of the Object. In the last sentence of this Case, Paul indicates that the buyer bears the loss if an object loses value after or even before completion of the sale. It is unclear what kind of loss in value he is thinking of. See Case 112 with Discussion 2, on wine that goes acetic. How widely should Paul's rule be applied? Ulpian, D. 19.1.13.12, indicates that if an object of sale is harmed by a third party, the seller must cede to the buyer any resulting actions against the wrongdoer; this probably indicates that the seller is not himself liable to the buyer for the damage. Compare Ulpian, D. 47.2.14 pr., on seller's cession of the action of theft; and see Case 113.

CASE 111: Explaining the Passage of Risk

Iustinianus, *Institutiones* 3.23.3

Cum autem emptio et venditio contracta sit . . . , periculum rei venditae statim ad emptorem pertinet, tametsi adhuc ea res emptori tradita non sit. itaque si homo mortuus sit vel aliqua parte corporis laesus fuerit, aut aedes totae aut aliqua ex parte incendio consumptae fuerint, aut fundus vi fluminis totus vel aliqua ex parte ablatus sit, sive etiam inundatione aquae aut arboribus turbine deiectis longe minor aut deterior esse coeperit, emptoris damnum est, cui necesse est, licet rem non fuerit nactus, pretium solvere. quidquid enim sine dolo et culpa venditoris accidit, in eo venditor securus est. sed et si post emptionem fundo aliquid per alluvionem accessit, ad emptoris commodum pertinet: nam et commodum eius esse debet cuius periculum est.

Justinian in the third book of his *Institutes*:

When a sale has been contracted . . . , the risk (*periculum*) for the object of sale falls at once on the buyer, even if the object is not yet handed over to the buyer. So if a slave died or was wounded somewhere on his body, or if all or part of a building was consumed by fire, or if all or part of a farm was destroyed by the force of a river or even lost considerable value through a flood or when its trees were blown down by a gale, (in all these circumstances) the buyer bears the loss and must pay the price even though he does not obtain the object. The seller is protected regarding whatever occurs without his deceit (*dolus*) and fault (*culpa*). But also if the farm is increased by alluvial soil after the sale, the benefit falls to the buyer; for he ought to have the benefit since he bears the risk.

Discussion

1. Why Does Risk Pass to the Buyer? This Case is, of course, not Classical but Justinianic (the omitted clause refers to one of the emperor's innovations). But by and large Justinian reproduces Classical sources (e.g., Paul, D. 18.6.7 pr.). The problem is to explain why the buyer must pay the price even though he or she has not received the object and does not even have title to it. The final sentence gives a clue: after completion of the sale, the buyer is entitled to any natural (or other) increase in the object of sale. In fact, the rule is still broader. For instance, Neratius, D. 19.1.31.1, holds that the seller must deliver any acquisitions made through a purchased slave. Justinian explains this as compensation to the buyer for bearing the risk; but he may reverse the true relationship. The buyer's entitlement to the "fruits" suggests the existence of an economic interest in the object, and it is this interest that justified passage of risk. In any event, as we will see in Case 114, the risk that the buyer assumes is not for all destruction of the object, but only for destruction beyond the seller's control. The question, then, is

which of two innocent parties should bear the loss when such destruction occurs. Work out the answer for yourself.

2. **Hard Cases under the Roman Rule.** You can easily imagine instances in which passage of risk is overly generous to the seller. Suppose, for example, that the sale is of an object not belonging to the seller, and the object perishes through *vis maior* before the seller can acquire it; or that the seller inadvertently sells the same object to two buyers and it then perishes through *vis maior* before delivery to either one. In both cases, the seller can apparently collect the price; and, in the latter case, twice! But a *iudex* would presumably take note if the seller was in bad faith; see Case 113. More generally, it may be objected to the Roman rule that before delivery the seller is in a better position to assess risk and to account for it in the contract price, and may also spread the expected or actual cost of any losses to other buyers.

3. **Passage of Title and the Buyer's Position.** Because Roman law holds that the buyer does not acquire property rights in the object of sale until it is conveyed, the buyer faces at least two further dangers. First, if the seller goes bankrupt before delivery, the buyer has no *in rem* rights and must line up with other creditors; but since the buyer would then have to tender the price, in many instances a buyer would probably prefer to avoid the contract altogether, rather than pursuing a remedy. Second, if a seller sells to two buyers separately and then conveys the object of sale to the second buyer, the first buyer has no property rights to the object and is limited to contract remedies against the seller. These examples help to explain modern criticism of the Roman rules on risk, don't they? Would you be inclined to regard the Roman rule as "an instinct surviving from primitive sale"? Or does it in fact correspond to "commercial convenience"?

4. **An Example.** An apartment building is sold; before it is conveyed to the buyer, the seller's slaves carelessly set fire to it and burn it down. Does the buyer bear this risk? Alfenus, D. 18.6.12, makes the seller liable in sale only for failure to show care in protecting the property, a responsibility that would perhaps include choosing careful slaves. Is this result correct?

5. **Variation by Contract.** Gaius, in Case 113, presumes that by an express agreement the parties can vary the dispositive rule on risk. However, little evidence suggests that the Romans commonly did so. Why might that be?

CASE 112: Risk in a Conditional Sale

D. 18.1.35.7 (Gaius libro decimo ad Edictum Provinciale)

Sed et si ex doleario pars vini venierit, veluti metretae centum, verissimum est (quod et constare videtur) antequam admetiatur, omne periculum ad venditorem pertinere: nec interest, unum pretium omnium centum metretarum in semel dictum sit an in singulos eos.

Gaius in the tenth book *On the Provincial Edict*:

But if part of the wine from a wine cellar is sold, e.g., one hundred containers, it is quite correct, and is also apparently agreed, that the seller bears all risk (*periculum*) before measurement. Nor does it matter whether one price is set for all hundred containers, or (a price) for each (container).

Discussion

1. Sale from Stock. In this Case, one hundred container-measures (nearly 4,000 liters) of wine from a cellar have been sold, but not yet measured out. Completion of the sale is held to be conditional on measurement; see Case 87. Gaius states that "the seller bears all risk before measurement"; what does he mean? That if the wine cellar is totally destroyed, the sale is off and the seller does not get the price? See also Case 77.

2. Spoilage. The situation is different, however, if the wine goes bad. Papinian, *Frag. Vat.* 16: "The buyer bears the risk of wine changing even though this occurs before the date for paying the price or the fulfillment of a condition of sale." This corresponds with Paul's rule in Case 110; the risk of wine going bad is generally regarded as beyond human control. (The most common cause, unknown to the Romans, was bacterial.) However, Papinian goes on to say: "But if he sold 1,000 amphoras at a fixed price, without physically defining (the wine), the buyer bears no risk in the meantime." If the text is right (this has been doubted), the sale looks to have been generic; the buyer does not bear the risk until the wine, or at least the stock of wine, is physically identified to the sale. But most scholars doubt the possibility of generic sale in Roman law; see Case 87.

3. Sale of a Slave. Two parties agree on sale of a slave; but until the price is paid, the buyer is to hold the slave under lease, i.e., evidently the seller retains ownership until he is paid, in a lease/purchase agreement. According to Javolenus, D. 18.6.17, the slave is not regarded as delivered to the lessee/buyer; but, under this arrangement: "The buyer bears the risk for whatever happens to the slave except through the seller's intentional misconduct (*dolus*)." Can this result be explained? It is hard to reconcile with the ordinary rules for lease; see Case 153.

CASE 113: The Seller's Duty to Protect Object of Sale

D. 18.1.35.4 (Gaius libro decimo ad Edictum Provinciale)

Si res vendita per furtum perierit, prius animadvertendum erit, quid inter eos de custodia rei convenerat: si nihil appareat convenisse, talis custodia desideranda est a venditore, qualem bonus pater familias suis rebus adhibet: quam si praestiterit et tamen rem perdidit, securus esse debet, ut tamen scilicet vindicationem rei et condictionem exhibeat emptori. Unde videbimus in personam eius, qui alienam rem vendiderit: cum is nullam vindicationem aut condictionem habere possit, ob id ipsum damnandus est, quia, si suam rem vendidisset, potuisset eas actiones ad emptorem transferre.

Gaius in the tenth book *On the Provincial Edict*:

If the object of sale is lost through theft, the first thing to examine is what the parties agreed to regarding the safekeeping (*custodia*) of the object. If what they agreed is unclear, then the degree of safekeeping (*custodia*) required from the seller is that which an upright *paterfamilias* would use for his own property. If he provided this and lost the object nonetheless, he should be protected, provided, of course, that he conveys to the buyer (the right to) vindicate the object and (also) the *condictio* (on theft).

Next we consider someone who sells another person's property. Since he can have no vindication or *condictio*, he should be condemned (in an action on purchase) for this very fact, since, if he had sold his own property, he would have been able to transfer these actions to the seller.

The Problem

Seius sells an antique vase to Aurelia; however, before he can deliver it to her, an unknown person steals it. Is Aurelia still liable for the price of the vase? Does the answer depend on how carefully Seius was safeguarding it?

Discussion

1. Liability for Safekeeping. In general, the seller is held to a very high standard of care in safeguarding the object: what is called a *custodia* liability, meaning that he is liable unless he can show that no possible care could have avoided the loss; see Paul, D. 18.6.3. But the jurists relax this requirement somewhat when a third party damages or steals the object; here it is enough if the seller took due care to prevent this from happening and surrenders the appropriate delictual actions to the buyer; see also Neratius, D. 19.1.31 pr. Is this relaxation justified?

2. Expropriation. The buyer bears the risk if the object is destroyed by an irresistible "higher force" (*vis maior*). But what if the state expropriates the object of sale prior to its delivery? Africanus, D. 19.2.33, holds that the

seller bears the risk; the sale is at an end, and the buyer can recover any of the price that has been paid. By contrast, in similar circumstances, Paul, D. 21.2.11 pr., allows the seller to obtain the full price despite failure to deliver because of expropriation. Which solution is better? Should it depend on the reasons for the expropriation (public need, as against criminal conviction)?

CASE 114: Seller's Fair Use of a Purchased Slave

D. 19.1.54 pr. (Labeo libro secundo Pithanon)

Si servus quem vendideras iussu tuo aliquid fecit et ex eo crus fregit, ita demum ea res tuo periculo non est, si id imperasti, quod solebat ante venditionem facere, et si id imperasti, quod etiam non vendito servo imperaturus eras. Paulus: minime: nam si periculosam rem ante venditionem facere solitus est, culpa tua id factum esse videbitur: puta enim eum fuisse servum, qui per catadromum descendere aut in cloacam demitti solitus esset. Idem iuris erit, si eam rem imperare solitus fueris, quam prudens et diligens pater familias imperaturus ei servo non fuerit. Quid si hoc exceptum fuerit? Tamen potest ei servo novam rem imperare, quam imperaturus non fuisset, si non venisset: veluti si ei imperasti, ut ad emptorem iret, qui peregre esset: nam certe ea res tuo periculo esse non debet. Itaque tota ea res ad dolum malum dumtaxat et culpam venditoris dirigenda est.

Labeo in the second book of *Plausible Views*:

If a slave whom you had sold (but not yet conveyed him to the buyer) did something on your order and as a result broke a leg, you do not bear the risk (*periculum*) for this, provided you ordered what he normally did before the sale, and that the order was one you would give also to a slave you had not sold.

Paul (comments): On the contrary. For if he (the slave) usually did something dangerous before the sale, this (his continuing to do it) will be held to occur by your fault (*culpa*); e.g., suppose he was a slave who usually walked a tightrope or was lowered into a sewer. The rule is the same if you usually ordered something that a cautious and careful *paterfamilias* would not order a slave to do. What if this right was reserved (by the seller)? He can still order the slave to do something new, which he would not have ordered had he (the slave) not been sold; e.g., if you ordered him to travel to the buyer who was abroad; this clearly should not be at your risk (as the seller). And so this entire matter should be reduced to just the seller's intentional deceit (*dolus*) and fault (*culpa*).

Discussion

1. Fair Use. To what extent can the seller continue using the slave before delivery to the buyer? Does Paul really differ from the views of the early Classical jurist Labeo? Note Paul's willingness to rely on a broader concept of *culpa* as defining the extent of the seller's obligation to the buyer. The "fair use" principle is closely linked to the seller's duty to deliver in good condition; see Case 127, and also Ulpian, D. 4.3.7.3 (the seller must not poison a slave prior to delivery).

CASE 115: Buyer's Liability before Delivery

D. 19.1.13.22 (Ulpianus libro trigesimo secundo ad Edictum)

Praeterea ex vendito agendo consequetur etiam sumptus, qui facti sunt in re distracta, ut puta si quid in aedificia distracta erogatum est: scribit enim Labeo et Trebatius esse ex vendito hoc nomine actionem. Idem et si in aegri servi curationem impensum est ante traditionem aut si quid in disciplinas, quas verisimile erat etiam emptorem velle impendi. Hoc amplius Labeo ait et si quid in funus mortui servi impensum sit, ex vendito consequi oportere, si modo sine culpa venditoris mortem obierit.

Ulpian in the thirty-second book *On the Edict*:

In an action on sale, he (the seller) also will recover his expenses on the object of sale, e.g., if there were some expenditures on buildings that were sold; for Labeo and Trebatius write that there is an action on sale for this. Likewise, if before delivery there were expenses on care for a sick slave, or if something (was spent) on instructing (the slave) that it was probable the buyer also wished to be spent. Furthermore, Labeo says that even if something was spent on the funeral of a dead slave, it should be recovered in an action on sale, provided that he met his death without the seller's fault (*culpa*).

Discussion

1. Expenses. Does Ulpian mean that the seller can recover all his or her expenditures on the object of sale, including, e.g., the costs of board? Or only those expenditures that are of an unusual and necessary kind, such as propping up a sagging building, or caring for a sick slave? The crucial example is the expense for instruction that the buyer would probably have wanted (and will also probably benefit from), but did not specifically request; how certain must it be that the buyer would want the instruction enough to pay for it? Roman law aside, what is the best rule regarding such incidental expenses?

2. Funeral for a Dead Slave. It should be noted that the buyer must pay the price for the dead slave, as well as the slave's funeral costs (consequential damages). Does this add insult to injury?

SECTION 2. Buyer's Default and Remedies

The buyer's principal duties under a sale are relatively straightforward: to make timely payment of the agreed price, and to take delivery of the object of sale.

In Roman law, the buyer is ordinarily obliged to remove the object of sale if it is movable. The jurists therefore commonly write of "taking delivery," rather than of "accepting delivery," and they make little of the buyer's inspecting the object upon delivery in order to spot any defects. Should the buyer delay unreasonably in taking delivery, the seller may even be entitled to destroy the object of sale; but the jurists make some effort to mitigate the harsh results of this rule. (For immovables, the rough equivalent is taking possession of the land by physically entering it with the intent to possess: e.g., Paul, D. 41.2.3.1. Title is transferred from seller to buyer most commonly by the formal ceremony of mancipation or, failing that, through usucapion, the buyer's uninterrupted possession of the land for two years. See Gaius, *Inst.* 2.18–22, 40–61.)

The parties may set a deadline (*dies*) for payment. Otherwise, the buyer must pay upon demand by the seller, this demand usually being accompanied by tender (or offer of tender) of the object of sale. If the buyer does not make timely payment, he or she is in default (*mora*, literally "delay"), and the seller who has tendered delivery is then entitled to sue for payment. However, once again, the jurists show considerable flexibility in allowing for particular circumstances to determine whether default has occurred.

They also make a crucial assumption: since the seller's damages are normally measurable by the agreed price, the condemnation of the buyer will usually be for this price alone, although the *iudex,* at his discretion, can also award interest from the time of *mora* onward. The only major apparent exception to this rule is when the object of sale has a readily calculable market value, such as generic wheat or wine; then the seller's damages are assessed at the prevailing price when suit is brought (see Case 123). The parties to a sale have sharply limited rights to increase this fundamental measure of damages, and consequential damages seem to be precluded. Besides the price, the buyer must also pay for many of the seller's expenses on the object before its delivery.

CASE 116: Determining Default (*Mora*)

D. 22.1.32 pr.-2 (Marcianus libro quarto Regularum)

pr. Mora fieri intellegitur non ex re, sed ex persona, id est, si interpellatus opportuno loco non solverit: quod apud iudicem examinabitur: nam, ut et Pomponius libro duodecimo epistularum scripsit, difficilis est huius rei definitio. Divus quoque Pius Tullio Balbo rescripsit, an mora facta intellegatur, neque constitutione ulla neque iuris auctorum quaestione decidi posse, cum sit magis facti quam iuris. 1. Et non sufficit ad probationem morae, si servo debitoris absentis denuntiatum est a creditore procuratoreve eius, cum etiam si ipsi, inquit, domino denuntiatum est, ceterum postea cum is sui potestatem faceret, omissa esset repetendi debiti instantia, non protinus per debitorem mora facta intellegitur. 2. In bonae fidei contractibus ex mora usurae debentur.

Marcian in the fourth book of his *Rules*:

pr. Default (*mora*) is construed as arising not from an objective fact (*res*) but from the person (of the defaulter), i.e., if he does not pay when called upon (to do so) at a suitable place. This will be investigated by the *iudex*, for, as Pomponius also writes in the twelfth book of his *Letters*, it is hard to define it. The deified (Antoninus) Pius, in a rescript to Tullius Balbus, wrote that whether default is held to have occurred cannot be determined by any imperial enactment or by asking the jurists, since it is more a matter of fact than of law.

1. To prove default, it is not enough if formal notice was given to the debtor's slave by the creditor or his *procurator*. For even if, he (Pomponius) says, he gave notice to the (slave's) owner himself, but later, when he had the chance to do so, he did not take the opportunity to reclaim the debt, the debtor is not automatically held to be in default.

2. In actions on good faith (*bona fides*), interest is owed after default.

The Problem
    Seius purchased from Titius a Greek wall painting, with payment due by January 1, but had not yet paid by that date. When can Titius bring suit against Seius for the price? Must Titius first demand payment from Seius? Would the answers change if there was no due date?

Discussion
    1. **Default in General.** Default (*mora*) is the failure to discharge a legal duty when its performance is demanded at a proper time and place. (On the effect of an express time limit, see the following Case.) The general definition of *mora* is a matter of law, as are the consequences that flow from it; but it is the province of a *iudex* to determine that any particular party is in *mora*, and the jurists uphold a case-by-case approach. Why? The jurists

hold that default occurs only if the defaulting party is "responsible" for *mora*; see, e.g., Pomponius, D. 19.1.3.4. At D. 12.1.5, Pomponius is more specific: the *iudex* must examine not only whether it was in the alleged defaulter's power to perform and whether the defaulter acted deceitfully to prevent performance, but also whether the defaulter has a legitimate excuse for non-performance. Ulpian and Paul, D. 22.1.21–24, suggest some possible excuses: the party was genuinely uncertain about the existence of the debt, or is unavoidably away on public business, and so on. The concept of *mora* is thus appreciably different from "default" in Common Law in that the alleged defaulter's state of mind and fault are considered judicially significant. Why does Roman law take this view? Note that the alleged defaulter must normally be notified that the other party regards his or her inaction as constituting *mora*; see Case 118. Why this requirement?

2. **Default by a Debtor.** This is the most common form of default: the debtor fails to perform or pay in a timely fashion. For example, a buyer fails to pay the price, or the seller fails to deliver the object. Details are discussed in subsequent Cases; but the main consequences in a *bona fides* contract such as sale are that a defaulting buyer becomes liable for interest on the money due (as Marcian states), while a defaulting seller becomes liable for virtually all loss to the object, i.e., the object is no longer at the risk of the buyer (Case 125).

3. **Default by a Creditor.** It is also possible for a creditor to be in default: for example, the buyer may fail to take delivery, or the seller may fail to accept payment. The main consequences are that a defaulting buyer becomes liable for all damage to the object except that intentionally done by the seller, and further must pay any costs for keeping the object. A defaulting seller loses interest on the price if the price is deposited with the court; see Marcellus and Ulpian, D. 26.7.28.1 (on tutelage).

4. **Purging Default.** One odd aspect of Roman law is that even default does not ordinarily have the consequence that the aggrieved party can terminate the contract. Rather, in general the aggrieved party continues only to be entitled to performance and can sue for damages if he or she is still willing to tender. But the defaulter can "purge delay" by tendering performance, although the aggrieved party can then sue for any damages owed as a result of the default. All this is very strange from a Common Law perspective; why shouldn't the aggrieved party have the option to look elsewhere for substitute performance in the event of default? This rule goes to the heart of the general Roman conception of obligation, and of contract in particular; why?

CASE 117: Buyer's Failure to Take Delivery

D. 18.6.4.2 (Ulpianus libro vicesimo octavo ad Sabinum)

Vino autem per aversionem vendito finis custodiae est avehendi tempus. Quod ita erit accipiendum, si adiectum tempus est: ceterum si non sit adiectum, videndum, ne infinitam custodiam non debeat venditor. Et est verius secundum ea quae supra ostendimus, aut interesse, quid de tempore actum sit, aut denuntiare ei, ut tollat vinum: certe antequam ad vindemiam fuerint dolia necessaria, debet avehi vinum.

Ulpian in the twenty-eighth book *On Sabinus*:

When wine is sold for a lump sum, the (duty of) safekeeping (*custodia*) ends with the time set for removal (by the buyer). This rule should be applied if a time was provided (by the contract); but if one was not provided, consider whether the seller owes permanent safekeeping. In accord with what we showed above, it is more correct (to hold) either that what the parties transacted about the time is decisive, or (if they set no deadline) that he (the seller) give notice to him (the buyer) to remove the wine. In any case, the wine ought to be removed before the vats are required for the (next) vintage.

Discussion

1. Buyer's Duty to Take Delivery. Pomponius, D. 19.1.9, sets a case where someone has purchased loose stones from a farm and then declines to remove them; the seller can sue on sale to force taking of delivery (through an award of money damages). Could the seller also make delivery himself and then sue for the delivery costs? Could the seller recover costs arising from the buyer's failure to take delivery? Would it matter if the buyer had refused to take delivery because, in the buyer's view, the object of sale did not conform to the contract specifications? (There are no specific surviving sources on these points.) See also Case 124.

2. Effect of Buyer's Default on Risk. Ulpian states that the seller no longer has a duty of safekeeping (*custodia*) after buyer's failure to remove the wine; default occurs upon expiration of a specified time limit, or upon reasonable notice if the contract contains no time limit. For the effects of buyer's default on risk, see Case 125; the seller is then liable only for *dolus*. Celsus, D. 19.1.38.1, discussing sale of a slave, holds that the buyer is liable for any expenses in maintaining the slave after *mora*. But both this text and the present Case simply assume that the seller will keep the object for the buyer, at least for a reasonable time. Is the seller required to do so?

CASE 118: Buyer's Failure to Fulfill a Condition

D. 18.6.1.3 (Ulpianus libro vicesimo octavo ad Sabinum)

Licet autem venditori vel effundere vinum, si diem ad metiendum praestituit nec intra diem admensum est: effundere autem non statim poterit, priusquam testando denuntiet emptori, ut aut tollat vinum aut sciat futurum, ut vinum effunderetur. Si tamen, cum posset effundere, non effudit, laudandus est potius: ea propter mercedem quoque doliorum potest exigere, sed ita demum, si interfuit eius inania esse vasa in quibus vinum fuit (veluti si locaturus ea fuisset) vel si necesse habuit alia conducere dolia. Commodius est autem conduci vasa nec reddi vinum, nisi quanti conduxerit ab emptore reddatur, aut vendere vinum bona fide: id est quantum sine ipsius incommodo fieri potest operam dare, ut quam minime detrimento sit ea res emptori.

Ulpian in the twenty-eighth book *On Sabinus*:

The seller may even pour out the wine if he set a deadline for measurement and it was not measured before the deadline. But he cannot pour out the wine immediately, before he gives formal notice (*denuntiatio*) to the buyer that he remove the wine or know that the wine will be poured out.

Nonetheless, if he did not pour it out when he could have, he is more praiseworthy. He can (then) also collect rent for the vats, but only if it was in his interest that the wine containers be empty—e.g., if he would have leased them out—or if he had to rent other vats. But it is more convenient that the containers be rented and the wine not returned (to the buyer) unless the buyer pays the amount of the rent, or (for the seller) to (re)sell the wine in good faith (*bona fides*), i.e., that to the extent he can, without inconvenience to himself, see to it that the buyer's loss from this be minimized.

Discussion

1. Seller's Right to Destroy the Object. Here the buyer has defaulted on a condition of measurement. Although Ulpian heartily urges the seller to take alternative measures (collect rent for the containers in the meantime, or resell the wine perhaps on a "distress" basis), the seller is not obliged to do so. Ulpian, D. 18.6.1.4, also allows for destruction of wine in the case of failure to take delivery; but Gaius, D. 18.6.2 pr., appears to permit destruction only as a last resort. Why do the jurists not oblige the seller to mitigate damages to the buyer, for instance by resale if possible?

   Would the outcome be different if the object of sale were not wine, but some imperishable? See Paul, D. 18.6.13: the seller makes beds for the buyer and then places them on the street, where an Aedile (a magistrate charged with keeping public streets clear) destroys them. The buyer is still liable for the price if he or she had previously taken delivery (although they remained with the seller), or was responsible for their prior non-delivery. Can we assume that the seller simply had no room for the beds in his shop? (Julian, D. 18.6.14, adds that if the Aedile was acting *ultra vires*, the seller would have a civil action against him for wrongful damage to property, *damnum iniuria datum*, and the buyer could then sue the seller on purchase to force cession of the action.)

CASE 119: Buyer's Failure to Pay Price

D. 18.6.20 (Hermogenianus libro secundo Iuris Epitomarum)

Venditori si emptor in pretio solvendo moram fecerit, usuras dumtaxat praestabit, non omne omnino, quod venditor mora non facta consequi potuit, veluti si negotiator fuit et pretio soluto ex mercibus plus quam ex usuris quaerere potuit.

Hermogenianus in the second book of his *Epitomies of Law*:

If the buyer is in default (*mora*) in paying the price to the seller, he will owe only interest (on the price), not everything that the seller could obtain had no default occurred, e.g., if he was a merchant and, if the price was paid, could profit more from the goods (he then purchased) than from the interest (on the price).

Discussion

1. **Interest If the Buyer Defaults on Payment.** The buyer must pay the price in timely fashion; this is interpreted to mean that the buyer must make the seller owner of the money paid; see, e.g., Ulpian, D. 19.1.11.1. But failure to pay results only in the buyer's liability for interest on the money due, not in consequential damages (such as the seller's lost profit on a possible resale); and even the reward of interest is subject to the discretion of the *iudex*; see Papinian, *Frag. Vat.* 2. Since the seller cannot make productive use of the unpaid price, loss of interest is the minimum loss that he or she sustains; but why should the *iudex* not consider other possible losses, at least if the probability of their occurrence was known to the buyer (as when a wholesaler purchases from a producer)? Roman law seems to lack a concept of the foreseeability, at the time the contract was made, of consequential losses in the event of a future breach (the rule in *Hadley v. Baxendale*).

2. **Buyer's Defenses.** The buyer can escape an action for the price by proving, e.g., that the seller has failed to deliver although delivery is still possible; or that the sale should be rescinded because of a serious latent defect in the object of sale, see Ulpian, D. 21.1.59 pr.; or that question has arisen whether a third party has title to the object of sale, so that the seller cannot deliver title, see Papinian, D. 18.6.19.1. (Papinian gives the last rule somewhat differently in *Frag. Vat.* 12.)

CASE 120: A Penalty Clause

Fragmenta Vaticana 11 (Papinianus libro tertio *Responsorum*)

Conuenit ad diem pretio non soluto uenditori alterum tantum praestari. quod usurarum centesimam excedit, in fraudem iuris uidetur additum. diuersa causa est commissoriae legis, cum in ea specie non fenus inlicitum exerceatur, sed lex contractui non inprobabilis dicatur.

Papinian in the third book of his *Responses*:

It was agreed that, if the price was not paid by the deadline, as much again (as the price) was owed to the seller. To the extent that this exceeds one percent interest, it is held to have been added as an evasion of the law (*in fraudem iuris*). Different is a *lex commissoria* (a clause rescinding the sale if the price is not paid), since in this case no illicit interest is sought; rather, a not unacceptable clause is provided in the contract.

Discussion

1. Penalties. Roman usury laws set the highest allowable interest at one percent per month, or twelve percent per annum; and compound interest was forbidden. This Case indicates that the parties are restricted in setting a penalty clause that effectively would exceed this rate, for non-payment of money. Why should this be so, at least in instances where the seller can demonstrate the importance to him or her of timely payment? (The jurists do not rely on a concept of a liquidated damages clause, as distinguished from a penalty.) The *lex commissoria* allows the seller to call off the sale if the price is not paid, see Case 106; although its purpose is similar to a penalty clause, it aims at simple rescission and restitution.

2. Evasion of Law. Papinian treats the contract clause as an attempt by the parties to dodge the usury statute; is this view correct? The jurists not infrequently enforce statutes beyond their face through this kind of interpretation. Their usual argument is either that, had they thought of this possibility, the legislators would have sanctioned the conduct in question; or (as here) that one or both parties are practicing a deceit to evade the statute (*fraus legis*). Both arguments result in an extension of the statutory norm, in much the same way that modern courts invoke a (judicially created) doctrine of illegality for contracts circumventing the law. Think about the pros and cons of this method of statutory interpretation.

CASE 121: Seller's Right to Reclaim Object

D. 18.1.19 (Pomponius libro trigensimo primo ad Quintum Mucium)

Quod vendidi non aliter fit accipientis, quam si aut pretium nobis solutum sit aut satis eo nomine factum vel etiam fidem habuerimus emptori sine ulla satisfactione.

Pomponius in the thirty-first book *On Quintus Mucius*:

What I sold does not become the recipient's property unless either the price is paid to me, or satisfaction is provided for it, or I extend credit (*fides*) to the buyer without (receiving) any satisfaction.

Discussion

1. Passage of Ownership to the Buyer. The principle stated in the Case is eminently sensible. Suppose, for instance, that the seller has delivered the object, but the buyer cannot pay for it because he or she has become insolvent; should the seller have to line up with the buyer's other creditors, rather than simply reclaiming the object? Justinian, *Inst.* 2.1.41, makes it clear that the rule stated in this Case was Byzantine law; but it is uncertain whether it was also the rule in Classical Roman Law. Archaic Roman law held that ownership of an important class of objects called *res mancipi* (principally land, slaves, and beasts of draft and burden) was conveyed, pursuant to a sale, through a formal ritual called mancipation, which is described by Gaius, *Inst.* 1.119; but Justinian notes that, under a rule of the Twelve Tables (VII.11; 449 BCE), ownership did not pass until payment of price or the giving of satisfaction. (On satisfaction, see Case 72; it usually involves alternative credit arrangements acceptable to the creditor.) Mancipation is a formal conveyancing procedure reserved for special objects; it is unclear whether the Classical jurists applied the same rule to sales in general, and the present Case may originally have referred to mancipation alone. If, for instance, the rule was general in Classical law, what would be the point of a *lex commissoria* such as is described in Case 106? Still, Gaius, D. 18.1.53, also supports the present Case: "For the object to become the buyer's, it makes no difference whether the price is paid or a surety is given on its account." Gaius indicates that some form of payment (even the attenuated form of providing a surety for payment) is required for ownership to pass.

2. Extending Credit. The force of the Justinianic rule is considerably vitiated, it appears, by the exception that ownership passes if the seller extends credit (*fides*) to the buyer. Doesn't a seller always extend credit by delivering before the price is paid? Perhaps Justinian's compilers had some more formal extension of credit in mind.

SECTION 3. Seller's Default and Remedies

The seller's legal duties are considerably more complex than the buyer's; indeed, most of the remainder of this Chapter is concerned with them. Leaving aside, for the moment, the seller's express and implied warranties as to legal title and the quality of the object (these are discussed in the next two sections), the seller must safeguard the object of sale until its delivery (see Part B, Section 1), and then allow the buyer to take delivery in timely fashion.

If the seller fails to allow timely delivery, the buyer is entitled to tender payment (see Ulpian, D. 19.1.13.8) and then sue for the extent of his or her "interest" (*id quod interest*). This measure is, in principle, considerably broader than the corresponding standard for seller's damages. It may include, besides a measure of the buyer's economic loss on the sale (so-called direct damages), also at least some of the consequential losses that the buyer has suffered because of the seller's default. The jurists do indicate that the buyer is not entitled to unlimited damages stemming from the seller's default, but the exact way in which the *iudex* was supposed to measure damages is not easy to work out.

CASE 122: Seller's Failure to Deliver

D. 19.1.1 pr. (Ulpianus libro vicesimo octavo ad Sabinum)

Si res vendita non tradatur, in id quod interest agitur, hoc est quod rem habere interest emptoris: hoc autem interdum pretium egreditur, si pluris interest, quam res valet vel empta est.

Ulpian in the twenty-eighth book *On Sabinus*:

If the object of a sale is not handed over, the action is for the extent of the (buyer's) interest (*id quod interest*), i.e., the buyer's interest in having the object. This sometimes exceeds the price if his interest is more than the object is worth or was purchased for.

Discussion

1. Delivery. Ulpian, D. 19.1.11.2: "The seller's primary duty is to tender the object itself, i.e., to hand it over." The object of sale must be delivered together with any accessories; see Ulpian, D. 19.1.13.10–18. For instance, in the case of an animal, under the Curule Aediles' Edict the seller must deliver the animal and the trappings in which it was displayed for sale; see Ulpian, D. 21.1.38 pr. (quoting the Aediles' Edict). Similarly, the seller must deliver any documents establishing title: Scaevola, D. 19.1.48 pr. However, the seller can recover anything that was delivered but not accessory to the object of sale; e.g., Paul, D. 21.2.3 (slave sold without his or her *peculium* takes something from it and is then delivered to the buyer). Delivery does not itself necessarily convey ownership to the buyer; for the seller's duties in this regard, see Section 4 of Part B.

2. Liability for Failure to Deliver. Ulpian sets the measure of damages as "the buyer's interest in having the object." *Id quod interest* means literally the buyer's "stake" in the transaction. This measure is explored in subsequent Cases, but obviously it is something different from the price. Could the measure also be less than the price, or does the price set a minimum measure of damages? The buyer can also collect some consequential damages as part of the "interest." See, for instance, Neratius, D. 19.1.31.1: "I (as seller of a slave) must provide not only what I acquired through him, but also that which the buyer would have acquired had the slave already been delivered to him." The former type of damages might include wages earned by the slave, or an inheritance that came to the seller through the slave, apparently only for the period after conclusion of the sale; the latter might include wages that the slave could have earned for the buyer. Is it right that the buyer should be able to claim both?

   Ulpian, D. 19.1.13.14 (citing Neratius), raises an odd problem: The seller of a 90-acre farm warrants that it has 100 acres. After the sale is concluded but before its handover, alluvial soil accumulates and adds 10 acres to the farm. If the original deficiency was an innocent error, the buyer has no action; but if the seller knew of the deficiency, the buyer can sue on purchase. This must mean that the buyer receives damages based on breach of warranty. But why, and how much?

3. Speculative Losses. I purchase the catch from the future cast of a fisherman's net (see Case 86). The fisherman refuses to cast his net, so the catch is purely speculative. Can I claim this speculative value? See Celsus, D. 19.1.12 (yes). How could the *iudex* estimate the value of the catch? (In our law of damages, this problem resembles the familiar "new business" difficulty.)

CASE 123: Measuring the Buyer's Interest

D. 19.1.21.3 (Paulus libro trigesimo tertio ad Edictum)

Cum per venditorem steterit, quo minus rem tradat, omnis utilitas emptoris in aestimationem venit, quae modo circa ipsam rem consistit: neque enim si potuit ex vino puta negotiari et lucrum facere, id aestimandum est, non magis quam si triticum emerit et ob eam rem, quod non sit traditum, familia eius fame laboraverit: nam pretium tritici, non servorum fame necatorum consequitur. Nec maior fit obligatio, quod tardius agitur, quamvis crescat, si vinum hodie pluris sit, merito, quia sive datum esset, haberem emptor, sive non, quoniam saltem hodie dandum est quod iam olim dari oportuit.

Paul in the thirty-third book *On the Edict*:

When the seller is responsible for not handing over the object, at issue in an evaluation is the buyer's entire benefit, provided that it is connected with the matter itself (*circa ipsam rem*). For if, e.g., he (the buyer) could trade with the wine and make a profit, this should not be evaluated, no more than if he buys grain and his household (then) starves because it was not delivered: he obtains the price of the grain, not that of the slaves killed by starvation. An obligation does not increase because it is executed late, although it does grow if wine is worth more now, and rightly so. For if it had been given (on time), I as buyer would have it; if it was not, what should be given now is what ought to have been given already previously.

Discussion

1. "Connected with the matter itself." The buyer's interest must be "connected with the matter (*res*) itself" (*circa ipsam rem*). *Res* is extremely ambiguous; it could mean "thing" (i.e., the object of sale) or "matter, affair" (i.e., the sale). Do the examples given by Paul clarify his ruling? What if the wine buyer had contracted to resell the wine before the present sale was arranged, and this fact was known to the seller? The most pathetic case is that of the householder who buys food for his slaves that is not then delivered. As the following Case shows, he can receive the so-called market difference (the current market price less what he paid, what we would think of as direct damages), and the jurists appear to assume that the buyer will always be able to purchase substitute goods. But what if this is untrue owing to the onset of a famine? In any case, Paul in this fragment is clearly eager to restrict the chain of "proximate cause" as much as possible, so as to bar most claims for consequential damages, at least for ordinary staples like wine and grain. What explains such a severe restriction? Did the Romans run into problems by their failure to develop a concept of foreseeability? See also Cases 119, 130.

2. Statutory Limits on Damages. Justinian, C. 7.47.1 (531 CE), conceding the problem in earlier attempts to define the buyer's "interest," set an upper limit on damages of double the price; the Digest compilers then inserted this limit into Africanus, D. 19.1.44. The Byzantine rule at least implies that earlier damage awards had occasionally been in excess of double the price.

CASE 124: Failure to Deliver Wine

D. 19.1.3.3–4 (Pomponius libro nono ad Sabinum)

3. Si per venditorem vini mora fuerit, quo minus traderet, condemnari eum oportet, utro tempore pluris vinum fuit, vel quo venit vel quo lis in condemnationem deducitur, item quo loco pluris fuit, vel quo venit vel ubi agatur. 4. Quod si per emptorem mora fuisset, aestimari oportet pretium quod sit cum agatur, et quo loco minoris sit. Mora autem videtur esse, si nulla difficultas venditorem impediat, quo minus traderet, praesertim si omni tempore paratus fuit tradere. Item non oportet eius loci pretia spectari, in quo agatur, sed eius, ubi vina tradi oportet: nam quod a Brundisio vinum venit, etsi venditio alibi facta sit, Brundisi tradi oportet.

Pomponius in the ninth book *On Sabinus*:

3. If a seller of wine is in default (*mora*) for non-delivery, he should be condemned for whatever time the wine was worth more, either when it was sold or when the lawsuit resulted in his condemnation; and (also) for whatever place it was worth more, either where it was sold or where suit was brought.

4. But if the buyer was in default (*mora*) (in taking delivery), the price should be evaluated for when suit is brought, in whichever place it is lower (i.e., where it was sold or where suit was brought). But default (by the buyer) is held to occur if no impediment prevents the seller's handing it over, especially if he was ready to hand it over at any time.

Likewise, (in some cases) we should examine not the prices in the place where the lawsuit is brought, but those where the wine should be delivered; thus, wine sold "as from Brundisium" should be handed over at Brundisium even if the sale is made elsewhere.

The Problem

Sempronius arranges with Claudia for the sale to her of 5,000 amphoras of wine, with delivery in Brundisium on the next February 1. If Sempronius fails to deliver by then, how should Claudia's damages be determined? If Claudia fails to accept delivery, how should Sempronius' damages be calculated?

Discussion

1. Measurement by Market Price: The Buyer. In determining the buyer's "interest" for highly marketable goods like wine, the jurists estimate direct damages mainly by relying on market prices as providing a base measurement. Pomponius, in section 3, gives the *iudex* a choice of market prices among which he can choose; the *iudex* is evidently expected to give the buyer the best of these prices. In any case, modern analysis would suggest that none of these market differences should be awarded (the place where suit was brought is particularly odd), and that the proper measure

is to place the buyer in the position he would have been in had the breach not occurred, i.e., the difference between the price and the time when the buyer learned of the breach, since it is then that the buyer will likely look for substitute goods as "cover." So far as Roman law in concerned, part of the problem undoubtedly lay in their overly quick identification of breach with *mora*, delay or default. Do you see why?

Suppose a contract, concluded on April 1, for delivery of 500 measures of wine on the coming October 1; in a sharply rising market, the seller then sells to a third party and repudiates the contract on September 1, and the buyer on that date either elects to buy substitute wine at a price much higher than the contract price, or to forgo cover and seek damages. If, as was true in Roman law (and would also probably be true in our law), the buyer cannot ask a court to compel delivery, and if, as was also true in Roman law (see Case 21; but not in our law), the buyer must await the contract deadline for delivery before seeking damages, it is not easy to see how any of Pomponius' standards is of much immediate relevance. You can vary the "facts" of this hypothetical to explore other possibilities. For instance, what if, in the hypothetical case, the wine was sold at Puteoli for delivery at Ostia, and suit was then brought at Rome in the Urban Praetor's court?

On the other hand, Pomponius is clearly right, in section 4, to emphasize the market at the point of delivery as better than the place where the lawsuit was brought or the sale was made.

2. **The Seller.** The situation in section 4 is unclear. It appears that, after the buyer's unjustified refusal to take delivery, the seller resold the wine at a loss and subsequently sued for the market difference. Pomponius' measurement resembles that for buyer's damages, except that now only the time of the lawsuit is relevant and the *iudex* is obliged to choose between only two market prices, whichever is lower.

CASE 125: Effects of Seller's Default on Risk

C. 4.48.4 (Imp. Gordianus A. Silvestro militi)

Cum inter emptorem et venditorem contractu sine scriptis inito de pretio convenit moraque venditoris in traditione non intercessit, periculo emptoris rem distractam esse in dubium non venit.

The Emperor Gordian to Silvester, a soldier (239 CE)

When the buyer and seller agreed on the price in an oral contract and the seller was not in default (*mora*) in handing over (the object of sale), there is no doubt that the buyer bears the risk for the object of sale.

Discussion

1. Risk after Seller's Default. The reasonable inference from this passage is that, after the seller defaults in making timely delivery, the buyer no longer bears the risk for the object's accidental destruction. This should mean that if the object is destroyed (no matter how), the buyer can then sue for his or her entire "interest" in the object of sale. See also Ulpian and Pomponius, D. 23.3.14–15; Paul, D. 18.4.21. This principle is broadly similar to "persistence of the obligation" in stipulation law, see Case 28. Is the rule sensible for sale?

2. Exception? Gaius, D. 16.3.14.1 (discussing deposit, not sale), discusses a case in which a plaintiff sues for a slave who then dies before a final judgment: "Sabinus and Cassius said that the defendant should be absolved because it is fair (*aequum*) that a natural loss fall on the plaintiff, especially since this property would perish even if it had been restored to the plaintiff." Although other texts suggest a generalization of the same rule (Ulpian, D. 4.2.14.11; Paul, D. 10.4.12.4), it is uncertain whether the rule is Classical, rather than a Justinianic innovation. In any case, a text of Ulpian (D. 6.1.15.3) makes an interesting modification of the rule, allowing for recovery in particular circumstances: "if the plaintiff might have sold it had he taken delivery, it (the price) ought to be paid to the person who experienced default; for if he had restored it to him, he would have sold it and profited from the price," obviously by shifting the inevitable loss onto a third party.

CASE 126: Purging Default

D. 18.6.18 (Pomponius libro trigesimo primo ad Quintum Mucium)

Illud sciendum est, cum moram emptor adhibere coepit, iam non culpam, sed dolum malum tantum praestandum a venditore. Quod si per venditorem et emptorem mora fuerit, Labeo quidem scribit emptori potius nocere quam venditori moram adhibitam, sed videndum est, ne posterior mora damnosa ei sit. Quid enim si interpellavero venditorem et non dederit id quod emeram, deinde postea offerente illo ego non acceperim? Sane hoc casu nocere mihi deberet. Sed si per emptorem mora fuisset, deinde, cum omnia in integro essent, venditor moram adhibuerit, cum posset se exsolvere, aequum est posteriorem moram venditori nocere.

Pomponius in the thirty-first book *On Quintus Mucius*:

It must be understood that when the buyer begins to be in default (*mora*), the seller is no longer liable for fault (*culpa*), but only for deceit (*dolus malus*).

But if both seller and buyer are in default, Labeo, to be sure, writes that default harms the buyer rather than the seller. But consider whether (only) subsequent default is harmful to him. For what if I gave notice to the seller and he did not deliver what I bought, and later he tenders and I do not accept? Clearly, in this case I should be harmed (by my subsequent default).

But if the buyer was in default, and then, while everything was fresh (i.e., before performance on either side), the seller was in default when he could perform, it is fair that his subsequent default harms the seller.

Discussion

1. Buyer's Default Revisited. In the first sentence of this Case, has the buyer defaulted by failing to pay the price or by not taking delivery? It appears to make no difference at least as to the issue discussed.

2. Default by Both Parties. With this Case, compare Labeo and Javolenus, D. 19.1.51, which handles two situations. In the first, both parties are responsible for delay in the tasting and delivery of wine; Labeo holds that the buyer alone should be treated as in default. In the second, the seller prevents payment of the price on the due date, but the buyer is then responsible for not paying at a later date; Javolenus allows seller's enforcement of a penalty clause against the buyer, provided that the seller was not acting dishonestly. Can these rulings be reconciled with each other and with this Case? Note the jurists' willingness to make the obligation persist beyond default.

SECTION 4. Seller's Warranties for Lack of Right

It might be anticipated that, simply because of the nature of sale, all sellers would be obliged to provide buyers with ownership (title) of the object of sale. However, for complex historical reasons, this was originally untrue in Roman law; the seller was obliged only to transfer what may be called "quiet possession," which meant that, after delivery, the seller was not liable on purchase unless and until the buyer was "evicted" from the object by its true owner who had successfully recovered the object through, e.g., a suit on ownership.

Since title was in itself often of considerable significance to buyers, it became common, particularly when more expensive items were sold, for the seller to provide an express warranty that offered the buyer additional protection. In Classical law, the usual form of the warranty was a stipulation that, in the event of the buyer's eviction, the seller would pay the buyer a multiple of the object's value—most commonly double, although the parties could determine the multiple for themselves. Such a stipulation was punitive, in the sense that it penalized a seller for failing to transfer valid title without requiring a proof of damages. The Edict of the Curule Aediles (magistrates slightly junior to the Praetors) required this stipulation for market sales of slaves and large farm animals; see Case 136.

The jurists, with considerable creativity, gradually extended the buyer's protections still further, for example by allowing the buyer to sue even before eviction when the seller knowingly sold another's property. By the end of the Classical period, it is likely that the seller was required to proffer a warranty of title, so that a buyer could sue on the purchase to obtain a warranty if none had been given. Some late sources even suggest that the warranty was being tacitly implied.

In examining the Cases in this and the following section, it is worthwhile to think about why the Roman jurists acted to provide increasing protection to buyers. From a modern perspective, a movement toward buyer protection is bound to seem desirable, but Rome had a much simpler economy in which the typical seller was not a large, anonymous corporation but a private individual often not very differently placed economically from the ordinary buyer. Why, therefore, were the jurists so solicitous of buyers? In any case, the toxic legal maxim *caveat emptor* ("Let the buyer beware") is entirely alien to Roman contract law.

CASE 127: No Duty to Convey Ownership

D. 18.1.25.1 (Ulpianus libro trigesimo quarto ad Sabinum)

Qui vendidit necesse non habet fundum emptoris facere, ut cogitur qui fundum stipulanti spopondit.

Ulpian in the thirty-fourth book *On Sabinus*:

A seller does not have to make the buyer owner of the (purchased) farm, unlike a person who promised a farm to a stipulator (the promisee).

Discussion

1. No Duty to Convey Ownership. This is the basic rule, often repeated in our sources. For example, Paul, D. 19.4.1 pr.: "For a buyer is liable on sale unless he makes the seller the owner of the coins (used in payment); but for the seller it is enough to oblige himself against eviction, hand over possession, and be free of deceit (*dolus malus*). Hence, he is not liable if the object is not evicted." Eviction is the removal of the object from the buyer by a true owner; before eviction, an innocent buyer of another's property is a "good faith possessor" (*bona fide possessor*). Why are the obligations of seller and buyer asymmetrical as to the duty to convey ownership?

2. Sale and Mancipation. For the seller, the sale creates an obligation to deliver possession of the object (if tangible; see the following Case); this can be accomplished by physically handing over the object (*traditio*). For most objects, handover pursuant to a sale would also transfer ownership if the seller was in fact the owner: Ulpian, D. 41.1.20 pr.; Paul, D. 41.1.31 pr. However, for a special class of objects called *res mancipi* (chiefly land, slaves, beasts of draft and burden), ownership is not conveyed by handover. Instead, for ownership of the property to pass, the seller must formally convey it through a ceremony called mancipation: Gaius, *Inst.* 1.119. It is clear that the buyer of a *res mancipi* can sue to obtain mancipation from the seller, see, e.g., Gaius, 4.131a; but in any case mancipation conveys ownership only if the seller is owner. If, without a valid mancipation, the buyer takes delivery from the owner of a *res mancipi*, he or she becomes a "bonitary owner" fully protected by the Praetor's Edict until possession ripens into ownership through usucapion (two years for land, one for other *res mancipi*). Note how carefully the Romans work out the distinction between the purely personal obligation created by the contract and the property consequences of its execution.

Under a provision of the Twelve Tables (VI.3; 449 BCE), if a *res mancipi* was delivered to the buyer and then evicted, the mancipator (seller), as implied guarantor (*auctor*) of title, was liable for double the price; Cicero, *Caec.* 54; *Pauli Sent.* 2.17.3.

3. Deceit in Delivery or Mancipation. The seller of a farm delivers it after deliberately or carelessly destroying buildings or cutting down trees, or imposes a servitude while formally mancipating it; can the buyer sue on the purchase? See Ulpian, D. 4.3.7.3, who says yes but indicates that the question had formerly been in doubt (why?). Compare Case 122 on the seller's duty to deliver, and Case 114 on seller's fair use of a purchased slave before delivery; and contrast Case 27 concerning stipulation.

CASE 128: Delivery of Quiet Possession

D. 19.1.11.13 (Ulpianus libro trigesimo secundo ad Edictum)

Idem Neratius ait venditorem in re tradenda debere praestare emptori, ut in lite de possessione potior sit: sed Iulianus libro quinto decimo digestorum probat nec videri traditum, si superior in possessione emptor futurus non sit: erit igitur ex empto actio, nisi hoc praestetur.

Ulpian in the thirty-second book *On the Edict*:

Neratius says that the seller, in handing over the object, ought to be liable to the buyer for his prevailing in a suit on possession. But Julian, in the fifteenth book of his *Digests*, states that it is not held to be handed over (at all) if the buyer would not prevail on possession; so there will be an action on purchase unless this is provided.

Discussion

1. **What Constitutes Delivery.** In the case of tangible property, delivery of possession (*tradition*) is obviously the minimum duty of the seller. The two jurists differ subtly in their interpretation of this duty: Neratius ca. 100 CE seems to make the seller's liability dependent on an adverse judgment in a lawsuit, while Julian (writing about fifty years after Neratius) indicates that there is liability if "the buyer would not prevail on possession," whether or not a suit has been brought by a true owner, so that the buyer can sue immediately, even before eviction, apparently for damages resulting from insecurity of title. Which jurist has the better of this dispute? In any event, Julian's view seems to have prevailed in late Classical law; see Pomponius, D. 19.1.3.1. Note that on neither view is failure to convey title in itself necessarily a breach. Titles were often cloudy for Roman property, which may help explain the rules in this Case.

2. **Delivery Itself.** Handover of possession (*traditio*), described in most handbooks, is governed by general rules of property law. On the part of the person taking possession, there is both a mental requirement (*animus*, the intent to take) and a close physical relationship to the object being taken (*corpus*): e.g., Paul, D. 41.2.3.1. The jurists, however, considerably attenuate these requirements in particular cases. For example, a buyer can take possession of heavy wooden beams by placing his seal on them even though they remain unmoved in the seller's lumberyard: Paul, D. 18.6.15.1. When goods stored in a locked warehouse are sold, it suffices if the seller gives the keys to the buyer; Papinian, D. 18.1.74, adds that both parties must also be present at the warehouse, but Gaius, D. 41.1.9.6, omits this requirement. (In any case, however, handover cannot ordinarily occur by simple agreement between the parties; a physical element must be present.) To some extent, delivery of possession is therefore a formal act that transfers to the

new possessor the protections that the Praetor's Edict provides for possession. The goods however, may remain with the seller even after handover of possession; see, e.g., Paul, D. 18.6.13 (beds made for and delivered to the buyer, even though the seller still has them in his shop).

CASE 129: Liability Absent an Express Warranty

D. 21.2.60 (Iavolenus libro secundo ex Plautio)

Si in venditione dictum non sit, quantum venditorem pro evictione praestare oporteat, nihil venditor praestabit praeter simplam evictionis nomine et ex natura ex empto actionis hoc quod interest.

Javolenus in the second book *From Plautius*:

If a sale does not provide for the extent of the seller's liability in the event of eviction, the seller will be liable, on account of eviction, for nothing but the simple value (of the object), plus, in accord with the nature of the action on purchase, the (buyer's) interest.

Discussion

1. **Implied Warranty against Eviction.** As Pomponius, D. 18.1.66 pr., notes, this warranty arises even if it is not express in the contract; it is based upon *bona fides*, the duty of protection that the seller owes the buyer. Labeo, D. 18.1.80.3, notes that it is simply not sale if the paries arrange that ownership not pass to the buyer; this idea presumably underlies the implied warranty. It can be excluded by express agreement, but this agreement is ineffective if the seller knows of a defect in title and the buyer is unaware; see Ulpian, D. 19.1.11.15–18, and Case 131. How effective is the implied warranty in protecting the buyer?

2. **Damages.** If the price has already been paid, the buyer is entitled at least to recover it upon eviction; if it has not been paid, the buyer can refuse payment until an impending lawsuit on eviction is decided; see Papinian, *Frag. Vat.* 12. The buyer may also claim "interest" as an addition; on measuring this, see the following Case.

3. **Sale of Intangibles.** A special problem arises in the case of the sale of intangible claims, as to a debt or to an inheritance. Provided that this is not the sale of a mere opportunity (Case 86), in the case of debt the seller must hand over the claim and warrant the debt's existence, but not the debtor's solvency (Ulpian, D. 18.4.4), unless the debt is expressly warranted to be of a certain amount (Paul, D. 18.4.5). Somewhat similarly for sale of an inheritance, see D. 18.4.7–13.

CASE 130: Measuring Damages after Eviction

D. 21.2.8 (Iulianus libro quinto decimo *Digestorum*)

Venditor hominis emptori praestare debet, quanti eius interest hominem venditoris fuisse. Quare sive partus ancillae sive hereditas, quam servus iussu emptoris adierit, evicta fuerit, agi ex empto potest: et sicut obligatus est venditor, ut praestet licere habere hominem quem vendidit, ita ea quoque quae per eum adquiri potuerunt praestare debet emptori, ut habeat.

Julian in the fifteenth book of his *Digests*:

The seller of a slave should provide the buyer with the extent of his interest in the slave having been the seller's. So if there is eviction either of a slave woman's offspring or of an inheritance the slave took up on the buyer's order, suit can be brought on the purchase. As the seller is obligated to provide the right to hold (*licere habere*) the slave he sold, so too he should be liable for the buyer's having what could have been acquired through him.

The Problem

Julia sells a slave woman to Tullius, and the slave, after Tullius takes delivery of her, gives birth to a child. The slave woman's true owner then asserts his ownership and, as is his right, reclaims both the woman and her child from Tullius. Is Julia liable to Tullius for the value of the child?

Discussion

1. Damages. The Cases on eviction supplement the discussion of the buyer's interest in Section 3. A slave woman who belongs to a third party was sold to an innocent buyer; the slave then gave birth and also received an inheritance. The true owner can use property rights to claim from the buyer the slave woman, her child, and the inheritance; but the buyer can then sue the seller for all three because of the breach of warranty against eviction. Paul, D. 19.1.43 and 45 pr., is broader still: A slave has a testamentary right to his manumission, but is sold without the buyer being notified; after several years (!), the slave successfully demands manumission. The buyer's interest includes even his own expenses in training the slave after the sale and before eviction. Limits are imposed only if the damages become wildly disproportionate to the slave's value at the time of the sale (e.g., a slave is sold for a small price and then becomes a highly successful charioteer or actor). Similarly, Paul, D. 19.1.45.1: land belonging to a third party is sold, and the innocent buyer then builds a house on it; after eviction, the buyer can sue on sale for the house's cost if the true owner does not pay compensation for it, even if the seller was also unaware of the defective title. Does this go too far?

2. Buyer's Duty to Resist Eviction. The buyer is expected to defend his or her property rights if a lawsuit is brought by a third party, and also to notify the seller about the claim; see, e.g., Ulpian, D. 21.2.55. Failure to do so results in loss of the warranty, see Paul, D. 21.2.53.1. Similarly, the buyer must be diligent in acquiring ownership by usucapion, if this is possible; see Paul, D. 21.2.56.3. This basically means that the buyer must remain in possession.

CASE 131: Concealment, Warranties, and Disclaimers

D. 19.1.1.1 (Ulpianus libro vicesimo octavo ad Sabinum)

Venditor si, cum sciret deberi, servitutem celavit, non evadet ex empto actionem, si modo eam rem emptor ignoravit: omnia enim quae contra bonam fidem fiunt veniunt in empti actionem. Sed scire venditorem et celare sic accipimus, non solum si non admonuit, sed et si negavit servitutem istam deberi, cum esset ab eo quaesitum. Sed et si proponas eum ita dixisse: "Nulla quidem servitus debetur, verum ne emergat inopinata servitus, non teneor," puto eum ex empto teneri, quia servitus debebatur et scisset. Sed si id egit, ne cognosceret emptor aliquam servitutem deberi, opinor eum ex empto teneri. Et generaliter dixerim, si improbato more versatus sit in celanda servitute, debere eum teneri, non si securitati suae prospectum voluit. Haec ita vera sunt, si emptor ignoravit servitutes, quia non videtur esse celatus qui scit neque certiorari debuit qui non ignoravit.

Ulpian in the twenty-eighth book *On Sabinus*:

If the seller concealed a servitude that he knew was owed (from purchased land), he will not escape the action on purchase, provided the buyer was unaware of it. For everything done contrary to good faith (*bona fides*) is included in the action on purchase. But we construe the seller as knowing and concealing not only if he did not warn (the buyer), but also if he was asked by him (the buyer) and denied that the servitude was owed.

But also, if you assume he spoke thus: "No servitude is owed, but I am not liable if one comes to light unexpectedly," I think he is liable on purchase because a servitude was owed and he knew it. But (also) if he acted to prevent the buyer's knowing that a servitude is owed, I think he is liable on purchase. I would hold generally that if he behaved reprehensibly in concealing a servitude, he should be held liable, but not if he (simply) wished to protect his own peace of mind.

These rules are correct if the buyer was unaware of the servitudes; but a person who knows of them is held not to be deceived, nor must he be informed if he was aware of them.

The Problem

Seius sells Julius a farm over which he knows that a neighboring property has a right of way. If Seius fails to disclose this fact, is he liable on the sale? Does it matter if he expressly disclaims liability? What if Julius knows of the servitude but Seius tries to conceal it?

Discussion

1. Servitudes. This Case concerns praedial servitudes (*servitutes praediales*), that is (in our parlance) easements, such as rights of way, that attach to a dominant property over an adjacent servient one. In sale of land, these

servitudes cause problems in two ways. First, servitudes may be owed to the purchased property. Papinian, D. 18.1.66 pr., states that, unlike with the implied warranty against eviction, the seller does not warrant existence of such a servitude unless he or she does so expressly; but see also Case 141 (the seller conceals a servitude that would benefit the buyer). Second, as in the present Case, the purchased property may be encumbered with a servitude to a neighboring property.

2. Concealment. If the seller was unaware of the servitude on the purchased property, Ulpian implies that there would be no liability absent an express warranty against servitudes. But there is liability on purchase if the seller knew of the servitude and the buyer did not. Who bears the burden of proof on this question? On the measure of damages if the seller is held liable, see Paul, D. 21.2.15.1: the buyer can recover the reduction in the value of the property. Should this reduction be measured subjectively (reduction in value to this particular buyer) or objectively (reduction in market value)? Similar rules are applied to other possible encumbrances on land: a prior security interest held by a third party (e.g., Pomponius, D. 19.1.6.9; Ulpian, D. 19.1.11.16); a public land tax (Paul, D. 19.1.21.1); or a fee for a public water channel running into the property (Papinian, D. 19.1.41). Should all such encumbrances lie outside the implied warranty against eviction?

3. Exclusion of Liability. Sellers had general freedom to exclude liability not only for encumbrances, but even for eviction; see, e.g., Ulpian, D. 19.1.11.15–18, and Papinian, D. 21.2.68 pr. In effect, the buyer, by thus assuming the risk, purchases an opportunity (as in Case 86). But such a disclaimer will not defeat a knowing seller who concealed the liability. Granted the difficulties in proving knowledge, are such disclaimers likely to be generally effective? Note Julian's attempt to diminish the effectiveness of such disclaimers in Case 133.

CASE 132: Liability Prior to Eviction

D. 19.1.30.1 (Africanus libro octavo *Quaestionum*)

Si sciens alienam rem ignoranti mihi vendideris, etiam priusquam evincatur utiliter me ex empto acturum putavit in id, quanti mea intersit meam esse factam: quamvis enim alioquin verum sit venditorem hactenus teneri, ut rem emptori habere liceat, non etiam ut eius faciat, quia tamen dolum malum abesse praestare debeat, teneri eum, qui sciens alienam, non suam ignoranti vendidit: id est maxime, si manumissuro vel pignori daturo vendiderit.

Africanus in the eighth book of his *Questions*:

If you knowingly sell another person's property to me, and I am unaware, he (Julian) thought that even before eviction I can effectively sue on purchase for the extent of my interest in it being mine. For although it is otherwise true that the seller is liable only for the buyer's right to hold (*habere licere*) the object, not also for his being made owner, nonetheless because he (the seller) ought to be liable for the absence of deceit (*dolus malus*), he is liable if he knowingly sells what is not his own property, but another's, to a person who is unaware of this. This is especially true if he sells to someone who wished to manumit (the slave) or use (him) as security (for a debt).

Discussion

1. The Knowing Seller. Although the seller has no direct duty to convey ownership to the buyer (Case 127), the jurists are sensitive to deliberate deceit (*dolus*) by the seller. Africanus, following the views of his teacher Julian, allows the knowing seller to be sued on purchase, even before eviction, for the buyer's interest in obtaining ownership. This presumes, of course, that the true ownership, as well as the seller's role in concealing it, has become known. How should the *iudex* measure the buyer's interest?

2. Intent to Manumit or Use as Security. The last sentence of this Case is curious. The buyer's intentions with regard to the object of sale are frustrated by failure of title to pass; he cannot manumit or use the slave as security. Does it matter whether these intentions were known to the seller? Do they affect the availability or extent of the buyer's remedy? Or is Africanus simply observing that the buyer may have intentions that are presently frustrated, even before eviction?

CASE 133: The Stipulation for Undisturbed Possession

D. 19.1.11.18 (Ulpianus libro trigesimo secundo ad Edictum)

Qui autem habere licere vendidit, videamus quid debeat praestare. et multum interesse arbitror, utrum hoc polliceatur per se venientesque a se personas non fieri, quo minus habere liceat, an vero per omnes. Nam si per se, non videtur id praestare, ne alius evincat: proinde si evicta res erit, sive stipulatio interposita est, ex stipulatu non tenebitur, sive non est interposita, ex empto non tenebitur. Sed Iulianus libro quinto decimo digestorum scribit, etiamsi aperte venditor pronuntiet per se heredemque suum non fieri, quo minus habere liceat, posse defendi ex empto eum in hoc quidem non teneri, quod emptoris interest, verum tamen ut pretium reddat teneri. Ibidem ait idem esse dicendum et si aperte in venditione comprehendatur nihil evictionis nomine praestatum iri: pretium quidem deberi re evicta, utilitatem non deberi: neque enim bonae fidei contractus hac patitur convenitone, ut emptor rem amitteret et pretium venditor retineret. Nisi forte, inquit, sic quis omnes istas supra scriptas conventiones recipiet, quemadmodum recipitur, ut venditor nummos accipiat, quamvis merx ad emptorem non pertineat, veluti cum futurum iactum retis a piscatore emimus aut indaginem plagis positis a venatore, vel pantheram ab aucupe: nam etiamsi nihil capit, nihilo minus emptor pretium praestare necesse habebit: sed in supra scriptis conventionibus contra erit dicendum. Nisi forte sciens alienum vendit: tunc enim secundum supra a nobis relatam Iuliani sententiam dicendum est ex empto eum teneri, quia dolo facit.

Ulpian in the thirty-second book *On the Edict*:

Let us examine what a person should be liable for if he sells (only) the right to hold (*habere licere*). I think it matters greatly whether he promises that the right to hold not be disturbed by himself and his heirs, or by anyone. For if (only) by himself, he is not held to provide against eviction by a third party; so, if the object is evicted (by a true owner), he will not be liable on stipulation if they concluded a stipulation, nor will he be liable on purchase (*ex empto*) if they did not conclude one.

But Julian writes, in the fifteenth book of his *Digests*, that even if he expressly affirms that the right to hold will not be disturbed by himself or his heir, it can be argued that (in the event of eviction by a third party) he is not liable on purchase for the extent of the buyer's interest, but he is nevertheless liable for return of the price. He goes on to say that the same should be held also if it is expressly included in the sale that there is no liability for eviction: after eviction (the return of) the price is owed, but the (buyer's) interest is not owed, since a contract in good faith (*bona fides*) does not permit an agreement that the buyer lose the object and the seller retain the price.

But perhaps, he says, someone might interpret all the agreements described above as similar to those in which the seller receives the money although the buyer does not get the object of sale (*merx*), e.g., when we buy from a fisherman the future haul of a net, or from a hunter his catch from setting nets, or from a fowler his entire catch. For even if he captures nothing, nevertheless the buyer must pay the price.

However, in the agreement described earlier the contrary view must be held, unless he knowingly sells another's property; for then, according to Julian's opinion given above (in the previous Case), it must be ruled that he is liable on purchase because he acted deceitfully.

Discussion

1. An Express Warranty of the Right to Hold. This is one common type of express warranty, which took the form of a stipulation; the seller promises that the buyer will be allowed to "have" the property. Such a stipulation is discussed at length by Ulpian, D. 45.1.38 pr.-5; the jurists tend to interpret it narrowly, since the seller cannot make a promise as to a third party's conduct; the stipulation only means that the seller binds himself and his heirs and successors not to prevent the buyer from "having" it. The stipulation itself provides no penalty upon eviction, and so that had to be separately arranged. The odd effect of the stipulation, therefore, was to exclude the seller's further liability for eviction by third parties. Was this interpretation inevitable?

2. Return of the Price. Julian is a bold and resourceful jurist, but never more so, perhaps, than in this passage. He argues that, even in the case of the seller's express disclaimer of liability for eviction, and (as it seems) regardless of whether the seller is knowing, the seller must refund the purchase price if the buyer is evicted; bona fides allows nothing else. The disclaimer is effective only to exclude liability for the buyer's "interest." Julian therefore rejects the analogy to sale of an opportunity (Case 86). In the final paragraph, Ulpian upholds the opposite view: in the face of a disclaimer, only a knowing seller has liability for eviction. Which jurist has the better of the argument?

CASE 134: The Stipulation for Double

D. 21.2.16.1 (Pomponius libro nono ad Sabinum)

Duplae stipulatio committi dicitur tunc, cum res restituta est petitori, vel damnatus est litis aestimatione, vel possessor ab emptore conventus absolutus est.

Pomponius in the ninth book *On Sabinus*:

The stipulation for double (in the event the buyer is evicted) is held to become due when the object has been surrendered to the claimant, or he (the buyer) has been condemned for the assessed worth of the lawsuit, or the possessor was sued by the buyer and absolved.

Discussion

1. Penalty for Eviction. By contrast with the warranty discussed in the previous Case, this form of warranty by stipulation provides that the seller pay the buyer double the price "if the object or part of it was evicted, preventing the right to enjoy, hold, and possess legally"; see Paul, D. 21.2.56.2. Double was the standard penalty, but the parties could set the multiplier at will. A penalty of double was also automatically available by statute if a mancipation was executed pursuant to a sale of a *res mancipi* (see Discussion on Case 127), and the buyer was then evicted; see *Pauli Sent.* 2.17.1–3. (This action, called the *actio auctoritatis*, was provided by the archaic Twelve Tables, VI.3; the Digest compilers removed most references to it from Classical texts.) The stipulation for double was often given when mancipation had not taken place or was not available because of the character of the object; see, e.g., Marcellus, D. 21.2.61; Ulpian, D. 21.2.33.

2. Violation of the Stipulation. This Case describes three instances in which the penalty comes due: the seller loses a suit on ownership and either surrenders the property to the true owner, or instead pays its condemned value (as was possible in a vindication); or the true owner takes possession and the buyer is unable to recover the property. If eviction is only of part of the object, the buyer's recovery is *pro rata* (see Ulpian, D. 21.2.1), provided that the stipulation also protected against partial eviction (Paul, D. 21.2.56.2). The buyer must, of course, have been vigilant in defending title against the true owner; otherwise, the stipulation is unavailable; see Ulpian, D. 21.2.55.

   Many sources (e.g., Paul, D. 21.2.18), indicate that the stipulation for double does not preclude a buyer from suing instead on the sale if that would yield him higher damages; i.e., double is not a damage limiter.

3. A Problem. A slave is sold with the proviso that, within thirty days, the seller undertakes to promise double, but will have no liability thereafter; the buyer fails to ask for the promise within the time limit, and is then evicted.

Under what circumstances can the buyer nonetheless claim damages from the seller? Is the buyer at least protected from interference by the seller as to the title to the object? See Ulpian, D. 19.1.11.15, citing Julian.

CASE 135: The Express Warranty and Regional Custom

D. 21.2.6 (Gaius libro decimo ad Edictum Provinciale)

Si fundus venierit, ex consuetudine eius regionis in qua negotium gestum est pro evictione caveri oportet.

Gaius in the tenth book *On the Provincial Edict*:

If a farm is sold, the undertaking against eviction should be given in accord with the custom of the region in which the transaction occurred.

Discussion

1. **Regional Custom.** At least in some areas of the Roman Empire, the giving of a stipulation became so normal that, as Gaius says, the seller's duty to give it was implied into the contract, so that the buyer could sue if he or she did not receive the stipulation. Probably only sales of considerable value were affected (see the following Case); in the present Case, for instance, Gaius rules only on sale of land. Note that Gaius is commenting on provincial law, which may have been more advanced in this respect than Roman law in the capital city.

2. **The Curule Aediles' Edict.** In Rome, the Curule Aediles had control over market sales of slaves and draft animals. They established some rules, separate from the ordinary rules for private sales, that regulate their markets. One of these rules is that, in a market sale, the seller is obligated to give the stipulation for double against eviction; see the following Case. What if the seller declined to do so? Ulpian, D. 21.1.31.20: "Since the stipulation for double is customary, it is further held that suit can be brought on purchase if the seller of a slave does not promise double; for matters of practice and custom should be included in *bona fides* actions." Ulpian envisages a suit in sale, within the Urban Praetor's court; what would the damages be? But the buyer could probably also sue in the Curule Aediles' court for rescission of the sale or recovery of the difference in value; see Case 143–144.

CASE 136: Requiring the Stipulation for Double

D. 21.2.37 pr.-1 (Ulpianus libro trigesimo secundo ad Edictum)

pr. Emptori duplam promitti a venditore oportet, nisi aliud convenit: non tamen ut satisdetur, nisi si specialiter id actum proponatur, sed ut repromittatur. 1. Quod autem diximus duplam promitti oportere, sic erit accipiendum, ut non ex omni re id accipiamus, sed de his rebus, quae pretiosiores essent, si margarita forte aut ornamenta pretiosa vel vestis serica vel quid aliud non contemptibile veneat. Per edictum autem curulium etiam de servo cavere venditor iubetur.

Ulpian in the thirty-second book *On the Edict*:

pr. Unless otherwise agreed, the seller must promise the buyer double (in the event of eviction); but (he must give only) a promise, not security, except if it is posited that this was specifically agreed to.

1. But as to our holding that double must be promised, this should be taken to mean not that we receive it for everything, but only for more valuable objects, e.g., pearls or precious jewelry or silk clothing or anything else of no small value.

But by the Edict of the Curule Aediles the seller is also ordered to give the undertaking for a slave.

Discussion

1. **Seller Must Give an Express Warranty.** The position taken in this Case appears first in late Classical sources. However, Ulpian, D. 19.1.11.8–9, cites the jurist Neratius (writing ca. 100 CE) as holding that the buyer has an action on purchase when the seller does not give a stipulation for undisturbed possession (see Case 133); and if the seller does not give security against eviction, the measure of damages is "the maximum a warranter of title (in a mancipation; an *auctor*) stands to lose," i.e., apparently double the price in the event of eviction. By about 150 CE, a *iudex* could impose on sellers a duty to give a stipulation for double; see Pomponius, D. 45.1.5 pr. Among late Classical jurists, this had probably become settled law, no longer discretionary. But Ulpian requires the stipulation only for sales of considerable value, and does not demand the seller give security against eviction; are such restrictions justified? The parties are also still permitted to exclude the stipulation.

2. **The Edict of the Curule Aediles.** Under their Edict, the Curule Aediles gave an action for rescission within two months, and an action for difference in price within six months, if the seller failed to give the stipulation for double: Gaius, D. 21.1.28; see also Ulpian, D. 21.2.37.1.

CASE 137: Implying the Warranty

Pauli Sententiae 2.17.1–2

1. Venditor si eius rei quam vendidit dominus non sit, pretio accepto auctoritatis manebit obnoxius: aliter enim non potest obligari. 2. Si res simpliciter traditae evincantur, tanto venditor emptori condemnandus est, quanto si stipulatione pro evictione cavisset.

The second book of the *Sentences of Paul*:

1. If the seller is not the owner of the property he sells, after receiving the price he will remain liable for authorization (*auctoritas*), but otherwise he cannot be obligated. 2. If there is eviction from objects that were simply handed over, the seller should be condemned for as much as if he had provided by stipulation against eviction.

Discussion

1. Implied Warranty. In this postclassical work (which, despite its title, may not directly derive from the writings of the Classical jurist Paul), the author is discussing only sales of *res mancipi*: especially land, slaves, and beasts of draft and burden. In section 1, it is assumed that the seller has mancipated them, as would normally be required for title in such property to pass; the ensuing liability for double in the event of eviction derives from the Twelve Tables (see the discussion on Cases 127, 134). But section 2 then posits that the objects were handed over without a mancipation, and the buyer has then been evicted by a true owner. In this situation, the author of this postclassical work finds it fairly easy to imply a promise of double damages, since the buyer was entitled to mancipation and would have been protected had it occurred. So too, probably, the "real" Paul: D. 21.2.2. If the stipulation for double is implied, the buyer no longer needs to sue in order to obtain it.

2. Warranties and the Action on Sale. Surviving sources make it difficult to reconstruct the final position of Classical Roman Law. The stipulation for double provides, in essence, for a sort of liquidated damages in the form of an enforceable penalty clause; the additional amount covers the buyer's anticipated consequential damages as well as the bother of things like court costs. By contrast, the stipulation for undisturbed possession permits the *iudex* to assess the buyer's interest (unliquidated damages) if the stipulation is violated; and this is also the natural position in the action on sale if no express warranty is either given or implied; see Cases 129–130. Further, under the action on sale the buyer can proceed immediately against a seller who knowingly sells another's property, see Case 132; the buyer need not wait for eviction. The action on sale lies even if the buyer acquires title otherwise than through the seller, e.g., by inheritance from the true owner

(Paul, D. 21.2.9); for instance, Julian, D. 19.1.29, lets the buyer recover the price if he is left the object by legacy and then unknowingly buys it from the heir. How well protected is the buyer's right to title in late Classical law? Have the jurists effectively undermined the rule in Case 127?

SECTION 5. Seller's Warranties for Defects

As with seller's warranties for lack of right, the seller's warranties for defects show a steady legal development in the direction of protecting buyers. By the end of the Roman Republic, a seller had two basic liabilities: for concealing from the buyer a fundamental latent defect in the object of sale, and for making an affirmative claim or promise about the object if this statement turned out to be untrue.

In the case of "market sales" of slaves and draft animals, the Curule Aediles established a set of remedies that were at first entirely distinct from, and additional to, those in the Urban Praetor's action on purchase. The Aediles imposed on the seller an obligation to reveal to the seller certain specified fundamental defects in the object of sale; further, this obligation was imposed even if the seller did not know of the defects, and the seller was also held liable for any affirmative claims about the object's quality. If the seller did not meet these obligations, the Aediles established two remedies: within six months after the sale the buyer could sue to rescind it (*redhibitio*), and within one year the buyer could sue for the difference in price (*quanto minoris*). However, buyers who used these remedies did not obtain their "interest" (*id quod interest*), as they did in a suit on the purchase.

By the mid-second century, the analogy of the Curule Aediles' remedies apparently led the jurists to strengthen the buyer's remedies in the action on purchase. In requiring the seller to reveal certain fundamental defects, the Curule Aediles had relied on the idea that these defects would render the object of sale "unmerchantable" unless the buyer was informed of them. Within the law of sale, the great jurist Julian picked up and extended this concept of merchantability: if an object of sale had a fundamental defect, an unknowing seller was liable for the difference in price (*quanto minoris*), while a knowing seller was liable for the buyer's full interest (*id quod interest*), potentially including some consequential damages. Julian's implied warranty of merchantability represents the high-water mark of buyer's protection in Roman law.

CASE 138: Puffery and Express Warranties

D. 18.1.43 (Florentinus libro octavo Institutionum)

pr. Ea quae commendandi causa in venditionibus dicuntur, si palam appareant, venditorem non obligant, veluti si dicat servum speciosum, domum bene aedificatam: at si dixerit hominem litteratum vel artificem, praestare debet: nam hoc ipso pluris vendit. 1. Quaedam etiam pollicitationes venditorem non obligant, si ita in promptu res sit, ut eam emptor non ignoraverit, veluti si quis hominem luminibus effossis emat et de sanitate stipuletur: nam de cetera parte corporis potius stipulatus videtur, quam de eo, in quo se ipse decipiebat. 2. Dolum malum a se abesse praestare venditor debet, qui non tantum in eo est, qui fallendi causa obscure loquitur, sed etiam qui insidiose obscure dissimulat.

Florentinus in the eighth book of his *Institutes*:

pr. In sales, statements intended to make (the object) attractive do not obligate the seller if they are readily apparent, e.g., if he says that a slave is handsome or a house is well built. But if he says that a slave is educated or a craftsman, he should provide this (to the buyer), since he sells for more on this basis.

1. There are also some promises that do not obligate a seller if the matter is so obvious that the buyer is not unaware of it, e.g., if someone buys a slave whose eyes are gouged out, and he stipulates concerning his health. For he is held to stipulate about the rest of the (slave's) body, rather than about that part where he deceives himself.

2. The seller should be liable that deceit (*dolus malus*) is absent; it occurs not only if he speaks obscurely in order to deceive, but also if he sneakily conceals (a defect).

Discussion

1. Puffery and Promises. Granted that warranties are enforceable, the problem is to distinguish real warranties from a seller's idle chatter in praise of the object. Ulpian, D. 21.1.19 pr.: "there is a large difference between words in praise of a slave, and a promise to provide what he (the seller) said." What criteria does Florentinus seem to use to separate the two? Consider, in particular, why it is puffery to say that a house is "well built." Is the seller obligated (and, if so, to what extent) if he says that a slave is hardworking? Loyal? A cook? A good cook? An excellent cook? Not a thief? See Gaius, D. 21.1.18; Ulpian, D. 21.1.17.20. When a warranty is given, the seller is liable on it regardless of whether he or she knew, or had reason to know, the truth concerning the quality warranted; see Case 140, where remedies are also discussed.

2. Warranties in Archaic Law. Even in archaic Roman law, the seller was liable for certain statements concerning the object of sale. For example, when the seller conveys purchased land by mancipation and describes it

as "in the best possible legal condition" (*optimus maximusque*), the seller is held to warrant against any undisclosed servitudes; see, e.g., Venuleius, D. 21.2.75. (This follows, however, from the terms of the mancipation, not from the sale itself.) Similarly, if the seller states that the purchased land has a specified acreage, the seller is liable by a special action if he or she overstates the actual acreage; see *Pauli Sent.* 2.17.4 (indicating that a *iudex* had discretion to award double damages, apparently even when parties had not specified this). Other warranties were often embodied in stipulations. But in Classical law even informal warranties could be incorporated into the sale by the doctrine on pacts; see Case 102.

3. Absence of Deceit. Whether or not a specific warranty is given, the seller is liable if he or she practices deceit (*dolus*) against the buyer; see also Case 131 (concealing a servitude). For significant defects, this normally means that the seller must reveal latent defects to the buyer unless they were already known. This rule was already in effect by the later Roman Republic. It suggests an early erosion of the maxim *caveat emptor* (not itself a Roman expression), doubtless under the influence of the general theory of *bona fides*.

CASE 139: Concealment and Express Warranties

D. 18.6.16 (Gaius libro secundo Cottidianarum Rerum)

Si vina quae in doliis erunt venierint eaque, antequam ab emptore tollerentur, sua natura corrupta fuerint, si quidem de bonitate eorum adfirmavit venditor, tenebitur emptori: quod si nihil adfirmavit, emptoris erit periculum, quia sive non degustavit sive degustando male probavit, de se queri debet. Plane si, cum intellegeret venditor non duraturam bonitatem eorum usque ad in eum diem quo tolli deberent, non admonuit emptorem, tenebitur ei, quanti eius interesset admonitum fuisse.

Gaius in the second book of *Everyday Matters*:

If wine in vats is sold and (then), before it is removed by the buyer, it is corrupted because of its nature, he (the seller) will be liable to the buyer if he in fact affirmed its quality. But if he made no affirmation, the buyer bears the risk (*periculum*), since if he did not taste, or he did taste and wrongly approved (the wine), he has himself to blame. Obviously, if the seller knew that its quality would not last until the day it was to be removed and did not warn the buyer, he will be liable for the extent of his (the buyer's) interest in having been warned.

Discussion

1. Wine Goes Bad after the Sale. This Case concerns wine that goes bad after the sale has been concluded but before delivery. Normally, the buyer bears the risk for this; see Ulpian, D. 18.6.1 pr. Gaius points out two exceptions: first, if the seller expressly warranted its quality; second, if the seller knew and did not reveal that it would go bad. Does this correspond to the seller's duties as outlined in the previous Case? The buyer is advised to insist on a condition of tasting; see Case 108.

2. The Duty to Reveal Defects. How far must the seller go in disclosing latent defects? The jurists do not consider this problem in the abstract, but some examples suggest that the duty was broadly construed. Gaius, D. 18.1.35.8: "The seller is liable if in selling property he conceals a neighbor and the buyer would not have purchased had he known of him." Does Gaius presume that the seller knew about the buyer's aversion to the neighbor? Would it matter if most buyers would not have minded the neighbor? Problems like this arise today when, for instance, the seller of a house conceals a grisly murder committed within it ten years before. Must sellers disclose (then or now) that a house is thought to be haunted?

CASE 140: Remedies for Violating an Express Warranty

D. 19.1.13.3–4 (Ulpianus libro trigesimo secundo ad Edictum)

3. Quid tamen si ignoravit quidem furem esse, adseveravit autem bonae frugi et fidum et caro vendidit? Videamus, an ex empto teneatur. Et putem teneri. Atqui ignoravit: sed non debuit facile quae ignorabat adseverare. Inter hunc igitur et qui scit <et tacuit non multum interest: nam qui scit> praemonere debuit furem esse, hic non debuit facilis esse ad temerariam indicationem. 4. Si venditor dolo fecerit, ut rem pluris venderet, puta de artificio mentitus est aut de peculio, empti eum iudicio teneri, ut praestaret emptori, quanto pluris servum emisset, si ita peculiatus esset vel eo artificio instructus.

Ulpian in the thirty-second book *On the Edict*:

3. But what if he (the seller) was unaware that he (the purchased slave) was a thief, but affirmed that he was of good character and honest, and (so) sold him at a high price? I would consider him liable even if he was unaware (of the truth): he ought not lightly to have asserted what he did not know. There is, thus, little difference between him and a person who knew and kept silent; the person who knew should have given warning that he was a thief, (while) the former should not be prone to rash assertion.

4. If the seller acted deceitfully (*dolo*) in order to sell property for more, e.g., by lying about a (slave's) skill or (the size of) his *peculium*, (a jurist holds) that he is liable in an action on purchase to provide the buyer with as much more as the slave would be worth if he had such a *peculium* or had been trained in this craft.

The Problem

In selling the slave Stichus to Decius, Calpurnia claims that the slave is honest. In fact, unknown to her, Stichus has stolen property from several persons. Is Calpurnia liable to Decius if she can show that there was no way she could have discovered this?

Discussion

1. Damages. As Ulpian indicates, the normal measure of damages is the same for both misrepresentation and a violation of an express warranty: the buyer can claim the reduction of value of the object as a result of the defect. That consequential damages might also be claimed is implied by sources awarding the buyer's "interest"; e.g., Gaius, D. 18.6.9 (seller of an orchard knows that the trees have been blown down, but does not reveal this). See also Case 145.

2. Rescission and Restitution. In some cases, as a result of the defect, a buyer
has no further desire for the object and may therefore wish to rescind the
sale altogether. The jurists allow this; e.g., Ulpian, D. 19.1.11.5 (the buyer
of a slave woman thought she was a virgin, but the seller knew otherwise),
see 3: "Both Labeo and Sabinus think that rescission (*redhibitio*) is also included in the action on purchase, and I agree."

CASE 141: Non-Disclosure of a Beneficial Servitude

D. 18.1.66.1 (Pomponius libro trigensimo primo ad Quintum Mucium)

Si cum servitus venditis praediis deberetur nec commemoraverit venditor, sed sciens esse reticuerit et ob id per ignorantiam rei emptor non utendo per statutum tempus eam servitutem amiserit, quidam recte putant venditorem teneri ex empto ob dolum.

Pomponius in the thirty-first book *On Quintus Mucius*:

If a servitude is owed to purchased land and the seller, instead of mentioning it, knowingly keeps silent, and for this reason the buyer, through ignorance of the facts, loses the servitude by not using it for the legally set period, some jurists rightly think that the seller is liable on purchase for deceit (*dolus*).

The Problem

Fabius sells a farm to Lavinia without telling her that the farm has a valuable right of way over a neighboring farm. Lavinia then takes possession and ownership of the farm, but, because she did not know of the right of way, she loses it through failing to use it for a long time. Can she sue Fabius on the sale if the farm's value is thereby decreased?

Discussion

1. Beneficial Servitudes. With this Case, compare Venuleius, D. 21.2.75: "But if the buyer (of land) sues for a right of way or of driving cattle, the seller cannot be held liable unless he expressly stated the right of way would accede (to the purchased property); for, if he did so state, he is liable." In the present Case, the buyer of the land would also ordinarily have obtained the servitude over the neighboring land, but lost it (through usucapion, failure to use) because the seller failed to inform her of its existence. It is easy enough to see why a seller would be liable for expressly warranting the existence of a servitude; but why should he be liable for knowingly concealing it? The buyer didn't rely on the existence of the servitude in purchasing the land, did she? How should the *iudex* go about measuring the buyer's interest? Should sellers generally be held liable for knowingly concealing potentially beneficial attributes of objects of sale, especially if these are generally counted as beneficial?

CASE 142: Express and Implied Warranties

D. 19.1.6.4 (Pomponius libro nono ad Sabinum)

Si vas aliquod mihi vendideris et dixeris certam mensuram capere vel certum pondus habere, ex empto tecum agam, si minus praestes. Sed si vas mihi vendidieris ita, ut adfirmares integrum, si id integrum non sit, etiam id, quod eo nomine perdiderim, praestabis mihi: si vero non id actum sit, ut integrum praestes, dolum malum dumtaxat praestare te debere. Labeo contra putat et illud solum observandum, ut, nisi in contrarium id actum sit, omnimodo integrum praestari debeat: et est verum. Quod et in locatis doliis praestandum Sabinum respondisse Minicius refert.

Pomponius in the ninth book *On Sabinus*:

If you sell me a container and you say it has a specified capacity or a specified weight, I may sue you on purchase if you provide less (than what was specified). But if you sell me a container with the promise that it is sound, you will also owe me what I lose on this account; however, if the agreement was not that you be liable for its soundness, (a jurist held) that you should be liable only for deceit (*dolus malus*). Labeo thinks the opposite, that the sole valid rule is that unless they arranged the opposite, a sound (container) should always be provided; and this is correct. Minicius reports Sabinus' response that this is owed also in the case of rented casks.

Discussion

1. Early Implied Warranties. This Case is an early attempt to break out of the pattern established by the previous Cases: seller's liability only for express warranties and deception. Containers are sold with no express warranty as to their soundness and no (demonstrable) deceit by the seller; they turn out to be unsound. An earlier jurist, whose name was doubtless removed by the Digest compilers, held to the established pattern; but the Augustan jurist Labeo develops an implied warranty of soundness, which can only be escaped by express agreement. Why might this situation have been especially appealing for the development of an implied warranty? Note that Labeo does not give the buyer's remedy; what should it be?

   To what extent is it important, for the effectiveness of such an implied warranty, that the buyer suffer actual economic loss (e.g., wine seeps out of the flawed container) as a result of the defect? What if the object was only less valuable because of it, perhaps because the defect was discovered before the container was put to use?

2. Containers as Accessories. Paul, D. 19.1.27: "Whatever the seller states will accompany (the object of sale) must be delivered whole and sound; e.g., if he said that storage jars would accompany a farm, he should provide ones that are sound, not broken." Does this simply extend the rule in the present Case?

3. Lease. For a further extension of Labeo's rule to lease, see Case 161.

CASE 143: Liability under the Aediles' Edict

D. 21.1.1.1–2 (Ulpianus libro primo ad Edictum Aedilium Curulium)

1. Aiunt aediles: "Qui mancipia vendunt certiores faciant emptores, quid morbi vitiive cuique sit, quis fugitivus errove sit noxave solutus non sit: eaque omnia, cum ea mancipia venibunt, palam recte pronuntianto. Quodsi mancipium adversus ea venisset, sive adversus quod dictum promissumve fuerit cum veniret, quod eius praestari oportere dicetur: emptori omnibusque ad quos ea res pertinet iudicium dabimus, ut id mancipium redhibeatur. Si quid autem post venditionem traditionemque deterius emptoris opera familiae procuratorisve eius factum erit, sive quid ex eo post venditionem natum adquisitum fuerit, et si quid aliud in venditione ei accesserit, sive quid ex ea re fructus pervenerit ad emptorem, ut ea omnia restituat. Item si quas accessiones ipse praestiterit, ut recipiat. . . .". 2. Causa huius edicti proponendi est, ut occurratur Fallaciis vendentium et emptoribus succurratur, quicumque decepti a venditoribus fuerint: dummodo sciamus venditorem, etiamsi ignoravit ea quae aediles praestari iubent, tamen teneri debere. Nec est hoc iniquum: potuit enim ea nota habere venditor: neque enim interest emptoris, cur fallatur, ignorantia venditoris an calliditate.

Ulpian in the first book *On the Edict of the Curule Aediles*:

1. The Aediles say: "Those who sell slaves must inform buyers concerning the disease or defect (*morbum vitiumve*) of each, and who is a runaway or a wanderer, or is not free from noxal liability; let them state all these things expressly and correctly when they sell slaves. But if a slave is sold in contravention of these rules, or contrary to what was stated or promised (by the seller) when he was sold, here is what he (the seller) must provide: to the buyer and all other concerned parties, we will give an action in order that the slave be restored (i.e., the action for redhibition). But if, after the sale and handover, a slave is worsened by the act of the buyer, his household, or procurator; and if, after the sale, anything is born to or acquired from him; and if any other thing acceded to him (the slave) in the sale, or if some fruit (*fructus*) came to the buyer from this thing: all these things he (the buyer) must restore (to the seller). Likewise, if he (the seller) provided any accessories, let him recover them. . . ."

2. This edict was proposed in order to check the deceptive practices of sellers and give aid to buyers who are deceived by sellers. But we should realize that the seller ought still to be liable even if he was unaware of those things the Aediles order him to provide. Nor is this unjust, since the seller could learn of them; it makes no difference to the buyer why he is deceived, whether by the seller's ignorance or by his guile.

Discussion

1. **Market Sales.** The Curule Aediles were elected magistrates (just lower than the Praetors) who had charge over the Roman markets where slaves and draft animals were commonly sold, often by sellers who were not previously known to their customers. The Edict of the Curule Aediles regulates this market to some extent; it provides remedies that are additional to any existing in the law of sale. As Ulpian suggests in section 2, deceptive practices may have been sufficiently common in such markets to warrant official regulation; but the Aediles intervened to protect all buyers, regardless whether the seller had been deceitful. Is Ulpian's argument in favor of this position entirely persuasive?

   The Aediles had a somewhat similar edict for animals: Ulpian, D. 21.1.38 pr.

2. **Seller's Duties.** According to the Edict, the seller must inform the buyer

   i.   if the slave has a disease or defect (*morbum vitiumve*; see the following Case);
   ii. if the slave has previously run away or shows a propensity to do so;
   iii. if the slave has committed a delict against a third party, who might bring suit against the slave's current owner.

   Other later provisions (not quoted here) require informing the buyer if the slave has committed a capital crime, attempted suicide, or fought wild animals in the arena. Why might all these things be considered defects? The seller's liability does not arise in the case of patent defects that the buyer should observe, see Ulpian, D. 21.1.14.10 (slave is blind, or has an obvious and dangerous scar on his head or elsewhere); and it may be excluded by express agreement, see Pomponius, D. 21.1.48.8.

3. **Buyer's Remedies.** The Curule Aediles' Edict establishes two remedies. The first, which is mentioned in section 1, is called redhibition and amounts to a rescission of the sale; the buyer must ask for it within six months of the sale. The second remedy, available within a year of the sale, is an action for reduction in the price (*actio quanti minoris*): the buyer claims the difference in value of the defective slave. The interrelationship between the two remedies is unclear. The buyer would presumably have a choice within six months, but perhaps redhibition was available only for defects that are more significant. In any case, characteristic of both remedies is, first, that they do not turn on seller's knowledge and hence are swift and relatively sure; second, that they do not provide any consequential damages to the buyer. Discuss the pros and cons of such a scheme of remedies. Would buyers always find the aedilician remedies attractive?

4. **Warranties.** The seller of a slave was also expected to give a stipulation against eviction (see Case 134) and against latent defects. Failure to do so

could result in redhibition within two months, and the action for difference in value within six months; see Gaius, D. 21.1.28. The Edict also established liability for any other express warranties; see Ulpian, D. 21.1.17.20.

CASE 144: The Soundness of Slaves

D. 21.1.1.8, 4.4 (Ulpianus libro primo ad Edictum Aedilium Curulium)

1.8. Proinde si quid tale fuerit vitii sive morbi, quod usum ministeriumque hominis impediat, id dabit redhibitioni locum, dummodo meminerimus non utique quodlibet quam levissimum efficere, ut morbosus vitiosusve habeatur. Proinde levis febricula aut vetus quartana quae tamen iam sperni potest vel vulnusculum modicum nullum habet in se delictum, quasi pronuntiatum non sit: contemni enim haec potuerunt. Exempli itaque gratia referamus, qui morbosi vitiosique sunt. . . .
4.4. In summa si quidem animi tantum vitium est, redhiberi non potest, nisi si dictum est hoc abesse et non abest: ex empto tamen agi potest, si sciens id vitium animi reticuit: si autem corporis solius vitium est aut et corporis et animi mixtum vitium, redhibitio locum habebit.

Ulpian in the first book *On the Edict of the Curule Aediles*:

1.8. So if there is any defect or disease that impedes the slave's usefulness and service, this is a basis for redhibition, provided we remember that is not just anything however slight that leads to his being considered diseased or defective (*morbosus vitiosusve*). Hence a mild fever or an old case of malaria that can now be disregarded, or a slight wound, result in no liability if not declared; for they could be ignored. So let us give some cases of slaves who are diseased and defective. . . .

4.4. In sum, if the defect is only mental, there can be no redhibition, except if it was stated not to be present when (in fact) it was; but there can be an action on purchase if he (the seller) knowingly kept silent about a mental defect. However, if there was a purely physical defect, or a mixed physical and mental defect, redhibition is available (under the Curule Aediles' Edict).

Discussion

1. **Defect or Disease.** The jurists eventually decided that only physical defects should be considered; see Ulpian, D. 21.1.1.7. Presumably, most buyers were looking for physically sound laborers; mental qualities were of smaller importance. But the jurists discuss many hard cases. Is a slave defective if he or she is a moron? A lunatic? A religious fanatic? An alcoholic? A gambler? A chronic liar? Unable to speak? Unable to speak intelligibly? If the slave lacks a tooth, or has a wart on the nose, or is a bed wetter? If a female slave regularly has stillborn issue? These and numerous other questions are discussed in D. 21.1. The answers paint a vivid picture of the expectations of slave buyers in the Roman world.

CASE 145: Implied Warranty of Merchantability

D. 19.1.13 pr.-2 (Ulpianus libro trigesimo secundo ad Edictum)

pr. Iulianus libro quinto decimo inter eum, qui sciens quid aut ignorans vendidit, differentiam facit in condemnatione ex empto: ait enim, qui pecus morbosum aut tignum vitiosum vendidit, si quidem ignorans fecit, id tantum ex empto actione praestaturum, quanto minoris essem empturus, si id ita esse scissem: si vero sciens reticuit et emptorem decepit, omnia detrimenta, quae ex ea emptione emptor traxerit, praestaturum ei: sive igitur aedes vitio tigni corruerunt, aedium aestimationem, sive pecora contagione morbosi pecoris perierunt, quod interfuit id non evenisse erit praestandum. 1. Item qui furem vendidit aut fugitivum, si quidem sciens, praestare debebit, quanti emptoris interfuit non decipi: si vero ignorans vendiderit, circa fugitivum quidem tenetur, quanti minoris empturus esset, si eum esse fugitivum scisset, circa furem non tenetur: differentiae ratio est, quod fugitivum quidem habere non licet et quasi evictionis nomine tenetur venditor, furem autem habere possumus. 2. Quod autem diximus "quanti emptoris interfuit non decipi," multa continet, et si alios secum sollicitavit ut fugerent, vel res quasdam abstulit.

Ulpian in the thirty-second book *On the Edict*:

pr. In the fifteenth book, Julian draws a distinction between a knowing and un-knowing seller with regard to condemnation on purchase. He says that a person who sold diseased livestock or defective timber, if he acted unknowingly, is liable in an action on purchase only for the amount less that I would have purchased for had I known the truth; but if he knowingly kept silent and deceived the buyer, he is liable to him for all losses (*omnia detrimenta*) the buyer sustains from this sale. So if a building collapses because of the defective timber, (he must pay) an evaluation of the building; if livestock perishes through contagion from the diseased livestock, there is liability for the (buyer's) interest in this not having occurred.

1. Likewise, a person who sold (a slave who is) a thief or a runaway, if (he did so) knowingly, should be liable for the buyer's interest in not being deceived. But if he sells unknowingly, with regard to the runaway he is liable for the amount less he would have purchased for had he known he was a runaway; (while) with regard to the thief he is not liable. The reason for the distinction is that he (the buyer) does not obtain the right to hold (*habere licere*) the runaway, and the seller is liable as if on account of eviction; but we can hold the thief.

2. My words, "the buyer's interest in not being deceived," include many things, e.g., if he (the slave) instigates others to run away with him, or steals some property.

Discussion

    1. Julian's Warranty. This text presents the final outcome of the evolution toward buyer protection in Classical Roman Law. Whereas most earlier

juristic holdings turn on the two issues of seller's express warranty or deception, Julian (writing ca. 140 CE) breaks through and requires that, at least in the case of significant and potentially harmful latent defects of the object of sale, the seller impliedly warrants the absence of these defects. Sellers are divided into two classes: those who know of the defects are liable for consequential losses suffered by the buyer, but unknowing sellers are liable only for the difference in price. The rule for knowing sellers may perhaps not represent a major change in the law; that for unknowing sellers does. Julian could have imported this second rule into sales law from the aedicilian remedy discussed in Case 143. Does the final Roman scheme of remedies strike you as satisfactory? Why should so much depend on the seller's knowledge? At the time of the sale, must it be clear to the seller that the buyer values the characteristic? (In the case of contagious livestock, rotten timbers, and thieving slaves, such an evaluation seems self-evident, of course.)

2. Sale of Used Clothing as New. Marcian, D. 18.1.45, discusses a case in which previously used clothing is sold as if it were new; Julian is cited as applying the rule in the present Case. Marcian does not indicate that used clothing would sell for substantially less than new clothing; but can this be presumed? (Ancient clothing was a good deal more substantial and durable than most modern clothing.) What does Marcian's holding indicate about the extent of the seller's implied warranty beyond inherently dangerous objects of sale?

3. Measuring the Buyer's Interest. In the case of a knowing seller, Julian allows the buyer to recover his or her "interest." This measure obviously includes most direct losses the buyer sustains as a result of the latent defect: the collapse of the building because of faulty timbers; the death of other animals because of the diseased herd; and the escape of other slaves, or the theft of buyer's property, because of the runaway slave. Does this measure of damages seem excessive? Can it be reconciled with Case 123? How does this measure differ from expectation damages in Common Law? (The Latin text given in the preceding derives from a famous emendation by Edouard Frankel: *quod interfuit id non evenisse*, "the [buyer's] interest in this not having occurred.")

4. A Slave Who Is a Thief? In section 1, Ulpian distinguishes between sale of a runaway and sale of a thief. Is his argument completely convincing? Can you reformulate it so that the distinction is clearer?

CASE 146: Mistake and the Implied Warranty

D. 19.1.21.2 (Paulus libro trigesimo tertio ad Edictum)

Quamvis supra diximus, cum in corpore consentiamus, de qualitate autem dissentiamus, emptionem esse, tamen venditor teneri debet, quanti interest non esse deceptum, etsi venditor quoque nesciet: veluti si mensas quasi citreas emat, quae non sunt.

Paul in the thirty-third book *On the Edict*:

Although I held above that there is a sale when we agree on the object of sale but disagree about a characteristic (*qualitas*), nonetheless the seller should be liable for the (buyer's) interest in not having been deceived, (and so) even if the seller will also be unaware; e.g., if he buys tables as if they were of citron wood, when they are not.

Discussion

1. **Sale of Citron Wood Tables.** These tables were luxury items, worth a fortune. The original text of Paul appears to have been abridged by the Digest compilers; Paul is likely to have applied the rule in the previous Case, that it is the knowing seller who is liable for the buyer's "interest in not having been deceived," but the unknowing seller only for the difference in price. With this Case, compare Marcian, D. 18.1.45, establishing a similar limited liability if a brass object is unknowingly sold as gold. In what sense are such objects defective? Both Paul and Marcian are late Classical; it certainly looks like Julian's warranty has been expanded, doesn't it?

2. **Mistake Theory.** Reread Cases 88–91 on mistake concerning a characteristic of the object of sale. Those Cases deal with formation of a sale; Ulpian allows the buyer to void the sale if he or she is mistaken about certain fundamental characteristics of the object. But, as Ulpian notes, at least Marcellus wanted to toss out the doctrine of mistake on a characteristic. What is Paul's position? Once Julian's warranty had developed, were problems of buyer mistake on characteristics better handled by upholding the sale and then enforcing the implied warranty?

3. **Sale of a Slave Woman.** In section 11.1 of Case 89, Ulpian voids the sale if a male slave is sold as a female, but upholds it if a sexually experienced woman is sold as a virgin. However, Ulpian, D. 19.1.11.5, holds that if the seller knew the truth about the slave's sexual experience, the buyer can sue on purchase to rescind the sale. Is this an application of Julian's warranty?

CHAPTER V

Other Consensual Contracts

Problems in Execution

Beyond sale, the Urban Praetor's Edict recognized three other "consensual" contracts: lease/hire (*locatio conductio*); partnership (*societas*); and mandate (*mandatum*). All three arise through agreement (*consensus*) alone, without any formality and without the start of performance by either or both parties. Further, all three, like sale, give rise to actions by both parties, and these actions are based on and governed by the concept of good faith, *bona fides*; this concept provides the jurists with leverage for the development of legal rights and duties. The four consensual contracts, taken together, are likely to have accounted for most commercial contracts in the Roman Empire, especially when they were supplemented by stipulation. On the other hand, significant problems remained. The bilateral contract of mandate, in particular, was gratuitous by definition but needed expansion in order to cover situations in which the mandatary acted on a broad commission over an extended period of time (Part C in this chapter; see also Chapter VII.C); and remaining gaps in the list of acceptable contracts had to be filled somehow (Chapter VI). None of this was conceptually easy.

Beyond these jurisprudential problems, the contracts considered in this chapter often raise an additional, very important difficulty. Sale archetypically involves a one-off transaction, a transfer of money in exchange for the transfer of an object of sale. However, many contracts (often, even sales) involve performance over a relatively prolonged period of time, during which one party may be—and very often is—extending credit to the other. Take the easy case of the tenant of a dwelling who, without legal justification, stops paying rent. The landlord obviously has available a legal action to collect the unpaid rent; this is a remedy at law. But legal mechanisms are often slow to work. In the meantime, and for the remainder of the lease term, is the landlord obliged to go on providing shelter to the tenant? It seems obvious that the answer is no, and that the landlord will also, *in addition to the legal remedy of damages for unpaid rent*, be able to expel the tenant from the dwelling—that is, to use nonpayment as a legal basis for ceasing performance of his or her own side of the contract, as a self-help remedy exercised outside the judicial system.

Anglo-American law handles this type of informal self-help remedy through a theory of implied conditions (or interdependent promises): performance by one side becomes a legally implied condition for performance by the other. Conditions such as these can, of course, be express, as part of the contract. But more frequently they operate through implication, as part of a logical sequence of performance between the parties, justifying one party in suspending and ultimately terminating performance because of a material failure in the other's performance. Obviously, this is a tool that a party must use cautiously, since suspending or terminating performance may be a breach of contract in its own right if it is unjustified.

A Casebook on the Roman Law of Contracts. Bruce W. Frier, Oxford University Press. © Oxford University Press 2021. DOI: 10.1093/oso/9780197573211.003.0006

The jurists never developed a generalized theory of material breach, one that is serious enough to justify the other party in suspending its performance, or even, in sufficiently extreme cases, in terminating the contract altogether. But although Roman law appears to lack an explicit doctrine of implied conditions, and instead may treat them just as an aspect of *bona fide* rights and duties, juristic sources nonetheless, as we shall see, often do seem to recognize the underlying difficulty and, at least in some situations, to provide for it.

PART A

Lease/Hire (*Locatio Conductio*)

Although the details are intricate, sale is a relatively simple contract: the exchange of money for an object of sale. By contrast, the contract of lease/hire (*locatio conductio*) is far more convoluted. The starting point is the Latin verb *locare* ("to put into position, to place"; see *locus*), which can be used to describe three quite different legal relationships:

- a person can "place" an object with another who hires its use (*l.c. rei*);

- a person can "place" a job that another party undertakes to perform (*l.c. operis faciendi*); or

- a person can even "place" his or her own labor (*l.c. operarum*).

The "placer" is then called the *locator*, while the other party is the "taker" or *conductor*, with a "fee" (*merces*) that passes between the parties depending on the economic sense of the transaction. Thus, a *locator* who leases out property—in common parlance, the lessor—receives a fee from the *conductor*, a lessee; a *locator* who hires out the performance of a job pays a fee to the *conductor*, who acts as what we would call a contractor; and a *locator* who hires out his own labor receives pay from the *conductor*, in an employment arrangement.

This typology may help to suggest both the origin and ultimate limits of *locatio conductio*, but it has scant relevance to most juristic discussions of the sprawling contract. As sale is the exchange of an object, so *locatio conductio* involves the exchange of a performance for money; and a set "fee" (*merces*) for this performance is as crucial to *locatio conductio* as a set price (*pretium*) is to sale. Beyond this central rule, however, Roman legal sources all but ignore general problems in the contract of lease/hire. They focus, instead, on particular contractual "subtypes," such as lease of a dwelling or a farm, the hire of objects or slaves, or the performance of a job by a building contractor, a transporter, or an artisan. Such contracts obviously have massive social and economic significance.

For each contractual "subtype," the jurists concentrate on developing a set of dispositive rules designed to govern the normal manner and standards for rendering performance, although the parties can usually vary these rules by express agreement. Since, unlike delivery in sale, a performance almost always takes place over a period of time, disputes may often arise between the two parties. Accordingly, legal rules for performance must take account of an intricate balance of interests.

SECTION 1. Lease of a Dwelling

CASE 147: Grounds for Expelling the Tenant

C. 4.65.3 (Imp. Antoninus A. Flavio Callimorpho)

Diaetae, quam te conductam habere dicis, si pensionem domino insulae solvis, invitum te expelli non oportet, nisi propriis usibus dominus esse necessariam eam probaverit aut corrigere domum maluerit aut tu male in re locata versatus es.

The Emperor Caracalla to Flavius Callimorphus (214 CE):

If you pay to the building's owner rent for the lodging that you claim you hold under lease, you should not be unwillingly expelled, except if the owner proves that it is required for his own use, or he wishes to repair the house, or you have behaved wrongly in the leasehold.

The Problem

    Under what circumstances can a landlord expel a tenant from an urban lease-hold prior to the expiration of the lease?

Discussion

    1. The Contract. The emperor's rescript to Flavius Callimorphus (otherwise unknown) assumes that Flavius has a valid lease with the building's owner and is already in residence. Rules for the formation of *locatio conductio* were said to bear a family resemblance to those for sale (Gaius, *Inst.* 3.142, 145; Justinian, *Inst.* 3.24 pr.-5); for instance, the parties must set a money "fee" (*merces*) that is comparable to the price in sale, although Ulpian accepts paying in kind (D. 19.2.19.3; also Gaius, D. 19.2.25.6: sharecropping). The *merces* must be real (Ulpian, D. 19.2.46, 41.2.10.2; Paul, D. 19.2.20.1), but need not be equivalent in value (Case 83).

    2. Justifications for Expulsion. Caracalla lists four grounds that, as it appears, would justify Flavius being expelled from his lodging before the lease term ends: (i) the tenant's failure to pay rent in a timely fashion; (ii) the building owner's personal need for the lodging; (iii) the owner's wish to repair the house; and (iv) the tenant's misbehavior in the lodging. The first and fourth of these reasons are, as it seems, in the nature of implied conditions imposing duties on the tenant, with violation justifying expulsion and thus allowing the owner to cease performance under the contract. Timely payment of rent is a fairly obvious duty; see also Paul, D. 19.2.54.1, and Hermogenianus, D. 39.4.10.1 (both of a tenant farmer), and the following Case. Tenant misconduct is much less easy to understand, although other legal sources show particularly intense concern about the peril of city fires (e.g., Ulpian, D. 1.15.3.3–4 and 4), a danger about which tenants were at times expressly cautioned (Ulpian, D. 19.2.11.1). It is unclear what sorts of lesser misconduct might lead to justified expulsion. Possibly

serious damage to the leasehold? "Immoral or illegal conduct"? "Disorderly conduct"?

What is interesting is that these two reasons are blended with two others that do not represent tenant conduct, but instead the owner's permissible desires within the contract: either his wish to rehabilitate the building (see also Alfenus, D. 19.2.30 pr., and Africanus/Servius, D. 19.2.35 pr.), or his needing the leasehold for his own use. Does it seem right to you that the tenant should have to bear the risk of such things? Would the landlord have to be acting reasonably, according to an objective test? The mixture, in any case, strongly indicates that the Romans are not thinking in terms of the reciprocal contractual rights and duties of the two parties, but rather of what sorts of events might trigger the contract being justifiably terminated by the owner. See also Cases 149–150 for the tenant's remedies, which have a similar construction.

Had the jurists been challenged as to the doctrinal basis for their construction of this law, they would probably have sheltered beneath the opaque umbrella of *bona fides*. Is that explanation adequate here? For instance, can *bona fides* provide a rationale for preferring the housing interests of the landlord over those of the tenant?

3. **Justified and Unjustified Expulsion.** The general rule was that either the owner or the landlord of a leased dwelling could, with legal irreversibility, expel a sitting tenant at any time, with no requirement of reasonable prior notice or specification of grounds. The effects of an expulsion—whether or not it can be justified—are that the tenant can consider the lease terminated (Labeo/Javolenus, D. 19.2.60 pr.) and seek an alternative dwelling. If the tenant believes the expulsion is unjustified, he can also sue the landlord for damages; see the following Case. The surviving texts suggest that the landlord would be obliged to prove the justification; e.g., "except if the owner proves" in this Case.

The rule on expulsion will certainly seem extraordinary to any modern student of Anglo-American law, who may well assume that tenants have always enjoyed some degree of property rights. But the Romans insist that the landlord's most basic duty was only to allow the tenant to "enjoy" the leasehold (*frui licere*), to "dwell" there (*habitare licere*). See, e.g., Labeo, D. 19.2.60 pr.; Gaius, D. 19.2.25.1 (Case 156); Ulpian, D. 19.2.9 pr. (Case 154) and 15.8; Paul, D. 19.2.7. The rights that a tenant derives from this duty are defined by contract, not by property law; tenants (both urban and farm) do not legally possess their leaseholds, but only physically "hold" them (*detinere* or *tenere*). See Gaius, *Inst.* 4.153 (Case 63); Ulpian, D. 43.16.1.22. On a tenant's absence of possession, see, for instance, Pomponius, D. 41.2.25.1; Ulpian, D. 43.26.6.2; also Alexander, C. 7.30.1

(230 CE). It is worth devoting a good deal of thought to the implications of the Roman legal position on this question. Can a tenant be adequately protected on the basis of contract alone?

On what happens when an owner-landlord sells a dwelling that is under lease to a tenant, see the Discussion on Case 156.

4. Interest. Note that, after default (*mora*), the landlord is entitled to interest on overdue rent: Paul, D. 19.2.54 pr., 22.1.17.4; Diocletian, C. 4.65.17 (290). As Diocletian observes, this is normal for money debts in actions based on good faith.

CASE 148: Damages for Unjustified Expulsion

D. 19.2.28.2 (Labeo libro quarto Posteriorum epitomatorum a Iavoleno)

. . . Sed si locator conductori potestatem conducendae domus non fecisset et is in qua habitaret conduxisset, tantum ei praestandum putat, quantum sine dolo malo praestitisset. Ceterum si gratuitam habitationem habuisset, pro portione temporis ex locatione domus deducendum esse.

Labeo in the fourth book of his *Posthumous Writings,* as Epitomized by Javolenus:

. . . If the lessor did not provide the tenant with the power to hold the house under lease, and he rented (another dwelling) in which to live, he (Labeo) thinks he must be provided with as much as he (the lessor) would have provided in the absence of deceit (*sine dolo malo*). But if he (the lessee) had obtained a free dwelling, reduction from the lease of the house should be in proportion to this period.

Discussion

1. Damages. Here the assumption is that the landlord has failed in his duty to provide the tenant with a dwelling; the tenant has, in effect, been unjustifiably expelled (see the reference to deceit, *dolus malus*), and so he sought alternative housing. This is one of the rare texts that tries to describe what the tenant can obtain as damages. How clear is it? Suppose that the substitute dwelling was substantially identical, but ten percent more expensive than the rent for the original one; what would the damages be? Does it look like they would cover any other consequential damages, such as the cost of moving? If the lessee is offered a free dwelling and declines to accept it, would damages be lower?

CASE 149: Justified Abandonment Because of Fear

D. 19.2.27.1 (Alfenus libro secundo Digestorum)

Iterum interrogatus est, si quis timoris causa emigrasset, deberet mercedem necne. Respondit, si causa fuisset, cur periculum timeret, quamvis periculum vere non fuisset, tamen non debere mercedem: sed si causa timoris iusta non fuisset, nihilo minus debere.

Alfenus in the second book of his *Digests*:

Again, he (Servius) was asked whether or not someone owes rent if he moved out (of the leasehold) because of fear. He responded that if there was a cause (*causa*) why he feared danger, he owes no rent even if there was not danger in fact; but if there was no legitimate cause (*causa iusta*) for fear, he owes it nonetheless.

Discussion

1. Unjustified Abandonment. In a fragment that the Digest compilers somewhat coarsely amalgamated so as to cover both urban and farm lease, Paul (D. 19.2.24.2) says: "If a house or a farm is leased for rent for five years, the owner can sue them at once if either the urban tenant abandons the dwelling, or the tenant farmer the cultivation of the land." This rule, in its highly condensed form, seems to presume that the tenants were not justified in abandoning their leaseholds. It therefore allows their landlords to bring a lawsuit at once against the tenants, so also effectively terminating the lease. Do you see how this is the reciprocal of the tenant's right to bring suit if unjustifiably expelled?

2. Fear and Other Causes. Alfenus' position in this text is rather more remarkable than it may seem. The tenant is justified in abandoning the leasehold because of fear (*timoris causa*) if there was a "legitimate cause" for fear; but otherwise not. So what is a legitimate cause? Is it presumed the tenant is acting rationally? The Digest has some arresting opinions on the subject, but none more so than Ulpian, D. 19.2.13.7, which deals with a tenant who abandons a leasehold in the face of an approaching (and not necessarily hostile) army, which then proceeds to strip the dwelling of windows and other furnishings. The landlord, of course, wants compensation. Ulpian approvingly cites Labeo as holding that the tenant is liable "if he could resist and did not"; and Ulpian adds that, even if he abandons justifiably, he must inform the lessor and is liable unless "he was unable to inform him." A tenant may also justifiably abandon the leasehold if he reasonably fears the collapse of a neighboring building (Ulpian, D. 39.2.28), or of his own if the problem arises during the lease term (Ulpian, D. 39.2.13.6, 33; Paul, D. 39.2.34); and likewise if a neighbor's construction darkens the windows of his dwelling, thereby significantly reducing the leasehold's comfort (Case 150; see also Ulpian, D. 39.2.37).

Striking about these sources is that it seems to make no real difference whether the landlord is at fault for the circumstances, or even could have prevented them from arising. The landlord presumably did not bring about the invading army, or the neighbor's construction, although he may be responsible for the tenant's building being about to collapse. Why do the jurists assign primary importance to the continued comfort and security of the tenant?

CASE 150: Tenant Remedies If Dwelling Deteriorates

D. 19.2.25.2 (Gaius libro decimo ad Edictum Provinciale)

Si vicino aedificante obscurentur lumina cenaculi, teneri locatorem inquilino: certe quin liceat colono vel inquilino relinquere conductionem, nulla dubitatio est. De mercedibus quoque si cum eo agatur, repudiationis ratio habenda est. Eadem intellegemus, si Ostia fenestrasve nimium corruptas locator non restituat.

Gaius in the tenth book on the Provincial Edict:

If the windows of an apartment are darkened by a neighbor's construction, (a jurist held) that the lessor is liable to the tenant. Indeed, there is no doubt that the tenant of a farm or dwelling may leave the leasehold. Also, if he is sued about the rent, estimate should be made of the offset. We construe the same result if the lessor did not repair doors or windows that were too broken down.

The Problem

A tenant occupies a dwelling with large windows admitting sunshine and fresh air. The windows are subsequently darkened by construction by a third party on neighboring property. Can the tenant move out or reduce rent payments, even if the landlord was not responsible for the construction?

Discussion

1. Remedies Less than Abandonment. Gaius deals with two situations: the darkening of the tenant's windows by a neighbor's construction, and also the landlord's failure to repair doors or windows. Abandonment is an option, evidently if the loss of amenity is sufficiently severe. But even if the tenant remains in the dwelling, in the event the landlord sues for unpaid rent, the tenant is entitled to an offset as compensation for the reduced comfort. Does this rule follow easily from the previous Case? Ulpian, D. 39.2.37, indicates that, if the neighbor was not entitled to build, the building's owner may be able to obtain consequential damages (under an action protecting neighbor rights, the *actio damni infecti*), including loss of rent because the tenants either abandoned their dwellings or could not dwell as comfortably (this latter a reference to the offset).

2. DIY. What happens if the tenant takes matters into his own hands and replaces the broken doors or windows himself? See Case 158.

CASE 151: Deduction from Rent

D. 19.2.27 pr. (Alfenus libro secundo Digestorum)

Habitatores non, si paulo minus commode aliqua parte caenaculi uterentur, statim deductionem ex mercede facere oportet: ea enim condicione habitatorem esse, ut, si quid transversarium incidisset, quamobrem dominum aliquid demoliri oporteret, aliquam partem parvulam incommodi sustineret: non ita tamen, ut eam partem caenaculi dominus aperuisset, in quam magnam partem usus habitator haberet.

Alfenus in the second book of his *Digests*:

The occupants, if their use of some part of the apartment is a bit less comfortable, must not immediately make deduct from their rent. For (Servius held) that an occupant is subject to the condition that, if something adverse occurred on account of which the owner had to raze something, he should experience a small part of the inconvenience—but not to the extent that he (the owner) had laid bare a part of the apartment in which the occupant had much of his use.

Discussion

1. **A Bit Less Comfortable.** This is a remarkable Case, for all that the Digest compilers fairly clearly condensed and mangled the original. (This is evident from the uncouth Latin wording.) As it stands, the late Republican jurist Alfenus states that an urban tenant may not deduct from rent payments (*deductio ex mercede*) for minor reductions in a dwelling's amenities, and that it is implicit in the contract (a condition, *condicio*!) that the tenant may be inconvenienced so long as his overall use is not substantially impaired. Alfenus therefore appears to acknowledge that the situation would be different if the inconvenience were greater; and he suggests (with the word *statim*, "immediately") that the tenant need not wait indefinitely even for minor impairments of use. In the case of such impairments, the tenant is entitled, as a self-help remedy, to deduct from the rent an amount that is left undefined, but would presumably be roughly proportional to the reduction in amenity. If the landlord disagrees, he would then have the burden of bringing suit. Somewhat similar is Labeo, D. 19.2.28 pr.-1: "If the lessee's use of a dwelling in a home is unchanged, he (Labeo) thinks that rent is owed even for that part of the home which became defective."

   Think about deduction from rent as a self-help remedy. What conception of urban lease does it rely upon? Is it fair to both sides in the contract? How would a deduction operate in practice?

CASE 152: The Tacit Pledge of Furnishings

D. 43.32.1 pr.-1 (Ulpianus libro septuagensimo tertio ad Edictum)

pr. Praetor ait: "Si is homo, quo de agitur, non est ex his rebus, de quibus inter te et actorem convenit, ut, quae in eam habitationem qua de agitur introducta importata ibi nata factave essent, ea pignori tibi pro mercede eius habitationis essent, sive ex his rebus est et ea merces tibi soluta eove nomine satisfactum est aut per te stat, quo minus solvatur: ita, quo minus ei, qui eum pignoris nomine induxit, inde abducere liceat, vim fieri veto." 1. Hoc interdictum proponitur inquilino, qui soluta pensione vult migrare: nam colono non competit.

D. 20.2.4 pr. (Neratius libro primo Membranarum)

Eo iure utimur, ut quae in praedia urbana inducta illata sunt pignori esse credantur, quasi id tacite convenerit: in rusticis praediis contra observatur.

Ulpian in the seventy-third book *On the Edict*:

The Praetor states: "If the slave in question is not included in the property concerning which the plaintiff and you agreed that what was introduced or brought into the dwelling, or born or made there, would be a pledge for your rent for this dwelling, or (if the slave) is included in that property and your rent has been paid or satisfaction given to you on this account, or you are responsible for its nonpayment: I forbid use of force to prevent the person who brought him in as a pledge from leading him out." 1. This interdict is established for an urban tenant who has paid the rent and wishes to move; for it does not apply to a farm tenant.

Neratius in the first book of his *Parchments*:

Our law is that things brought or conveyed into urban properties are treated as a pledge, as though they (landlord and tenant) had tacitly agreed on this. In rural properties the opposite rule is in force.

Discussion

1. And Now, a Major Complication. By the interdict on moving out (*interdictum de migrando*), the Praetor orders a landlord to allow the tenant to remove property (e.g., a slave) if: (i) the tenant did not take the property into his dwelling as a pledge for the rent; or (ii) the tenant did bring in the property for this purpose, but the tenant has paid his rent or given satisfaction, or the landlord has prevented him from doing so. This tightly written language, typical of much of the Praetor's Edict, is intended to deal with a situation in which the landlord is using a practice called "preclusion" (*praeclusio*), which literally refers to his barring the entrance to the dwelling; see Paul, D. 20.2.9. If the amount of the rent was in dispute (for instance, because the tenant had deducted from the rent, as in the previous Case), probably the dispute had to be settled or litigated before this

interdict could be used. The pledge covered not just rent already due, but also future rent (Ulpian, D. 43.32.1.4, citing Labeo).

2. **Agreement on the Pledge of Furnishings.** As the interdict says, the landlord may only prevent removal of property (not just furnishings in our sense, but also even the tenant's slaves) that the two parties have tacitly agreed will be pledged. We are expressly told that, for instance, temporarily introduced property was not included (Pomponius, D. 20.2.7.1), and also, in most cases, the property of other people (Alexander, C. 4.65.5 (223); but see Gaius, D. 43.32.2; Ulpian, D. 43.32.1.5). In addition, prior to preclusion, the tenant could manumit tacitly pledged slaves (Ulpian, D. 20.2.6; Paul, D. 20.2.9).

During preclusion, the landlord was obliged to protect the property he had effectively seized: Paul, D. 39.2.34.

3. **The Tacit Agreement.** By the end of the first century CE, as the Neratius passage shows, the agreement referred to in the interdict had been implied tacitly into all urban leases (except, most probably, where the parties expressly provided the opposite). Neratius also extends the doctrine to outbuildings on the same property (D. 20.2.4.1). After this, the doctrine of tacit pledge appears in other authors: Ulpian, D. 20.2.6, see also D. 24.3.7.11; Paul, D. 2.14.4 pr. The assumption underlying the tacit pledge is perhaps that it was so common as to be considered unexceptionable.

It is worth thinking about the desirability of a pledge of this type. Clearly, the pledge of furnishings provided the landlord with major leverage in the settling rent disputes; even ordinary Romans recognized this (see Martial, 12.32). But it should be observed that preclusion was originally another self-help mechanism deployed without direct official intervention, in a situation that might easily be the source of contention or even violence. By the end of the Classical period, however, the Prefect of the Watch at Rome was using his court to virtually replace the interdict, indicating that preclusion had been subjected to official oversight; see Ulpian, D. 43.32.1.2, and also Paul, D. 20.2.9 (commenting on the duties of the Prefect). Was this move a real improvement?

4. **Contrast with Farm Lease.** As Neratius and Ulpian note, farm tenants were not subject to a tacit lease of things they brought into the leasehold (including their slaves); instead, the pledge had to result from express agreement with their landlords. The farm tenant's pledge was actionable through a special Praetorian action called the *actio Serviana*, which created *in rem* rights and was later extended to all real securities. See Case 75.

CASE 153: Tenant's Liability for Damaging the Dwelling

D. 20.2.2 (Marcianus libro singulari ad Formulam Hypothecariam)

Pomponius libro quadragesimo variarum lectionum scribit: non solum pro pensionibus, sed et si deteriorem habitationem fecerit culpa sua inquilinus, quo nomine ex locato cum eo erit actio, invecta et illata pignori erunt obligata.

Marcian in his monograph *On the Formula for Hypothecation*:

In book 40 of *Various Readings*, Pomponius writes: the (urban tenant's) furnishings will be obligated as a pledge not only for rental payments, but also if the tenant worsens the dwelling through his fault (*culpa*), on which account there will (also) be an action on lease against him.

Discussion

1. **Damage to the Leasehold.** Pomponius, quoted by Marcian, extends the tacit pledge of furnishings to cover tenant's damage to the leasehold. This ruling is somewhat complementary to the tenant's right to deduct from the rent if the level of contracted-for amenity declines (Case 150). The extension presumes that the tenant has a contractually imposed duty of care with regard to the landlord's property (so also Ulpian, D. 19.2.11.2), with the standard of care measured by the tenant's "fault" (*culpa*). The standard is an objective one, measured through reference to a reasonable person. Its application is illustrated by Ulpian, D. 19.2.13.7 (discussed at Case 149), where the early Classical jurist Labeo holds a tenant liable for failure to offer reasonable resistance to a marauding army. Still, there is no indication that the tenant was liable for ordinary wear and tear. Beyond this default rule, however, the tenant can also assume additional liability through lease provisions; e.g., Ulpian, D. 19.2.11.1 (prohibition of fire); Ulpian/ Hermogenianus, D. 19.2.11.4–12 (prohibition of a haystack, presumably a fire hazard).

2. **Liability for Others.** Although a tenant may be liable for his or her personal damage to the leasehold, it is far less clear that tenants also assumed contractual liability for damage done by persons they introduce into the leasehold, especially their families, guests, and slaves. The major surviving juristic text that deals with the subject, Ulpian, D. 19.2.11 pr., has been rather drastically abbreviated, but seems to give it as a rule that the tenant might have contractual liability for their acts if introducing them was somehow blameworthy. A second text, Ulpian, D. 9.2.27.11 (the first part of which is also preserved in a pre-Justinianic version, *Collatio* 12.7.9), is no more helpful, but probably comes to much the same conclusion. So at least some contractual vicarious liability was probably imposed by the late Classical period. What might the obstacles have been, in Roman legal thinking?

The general legal theory here was in later ages called *culpa in eligendo*, "carelessness in choosing," the idea being that a tenant (or someone in a comparable position) might become liable for carelessness in having selected the actual culprit. It is not a common form of liability in Roman law, but you should be alert when other sources seem to pick up the idea.

CASE 154: Mitigation of Damages

D. 19.2.9 pr. (Ulpianus libro trigesimo secundo ad Edictum)

Si quis domum bona fide emptam vel fundum locaverit mihi isque sit evictus sine dolo malo culpaque eius, Pomponius ait nihilo minus eum teneri ex conducto ei qui conduxit, ut ei praestetur frui quod conduxit licere. Plane si dominus non patitur et locator paratus sit aliam habitationem non minus commodam praestare, aequissimum esse ait absolvi locatorem.

Ulpian in the thirty-second book *On the Edict*:

If someone leased to me a house or a farm that he had purchased in good faith (*bona fide*), and he was evicted through no deceit and fault on his part (*sine dolo malo culpaque eius*), Pomponius says that he is nonetheless liable on hire to the renter, in order that he furnish him the right to enjoy what he rented. Obviously, if the owner does not allow (him to remain), but the lessor is ready to provide another dwelling that is no less comfortable, he says it is fairest that the lessor be absolved (by the *iudex*).

Discussion

1. Mitigation. The general principle is that, after a contract has been breached, the aggrieved party ought not to run up damages at the expense of the breaching party. In this case, the landlord leased property (a house or farm) that, as it turned out, he unknowingly and faultlessly had no right to lease; and a true owner then evicted him as well as his tenant. Nonetheless, the landlord's contractual duty to the tenant remains intact despite the eviction, meaning that the tenant can sue for unjustified expulsion; but Ulpian goes on to hold that the landlord can escape liability if he offers an equivalent substitute dwelling to the tenant.

   In this Case, some of the advantages of treating lease from a contractual (rather than a property) perspective become clear. The tenant is seeking a dwelling with a certain level of comfort (*commoditas*), and cannot be heard to reject the proffered substitute because the original contract concerned a particular piece of property. However, the principle is broader still, as a glance back at Case 148 shows: when no adequate substitute dwelling is on offer, but the unjustifiably expelled tenant somehow obtains a free dwelling from someone else (say, a generous relative), the landlord is not liable for the time when the rent was free.

   The issue here, you see, really concerns limiting damages. Surviving texts indicate that the Roman jurists rarely thought very deeply about such issues, but the present Case is the main source indicating a concern. The tenant's duty to mitigate is still very limited, isn't it—restricted only to situations in which the landlord is entirely faultless. Nor is it clear that the same rule would hold if the offer of a substitute dwelling came from a third party and not from the landlord; nor that the tenant was obliged to look for an equivalent substitute.

Further, mitigation appears not to apply in the converse situation, where a tenant abandons without just cause. Several texts indicate that a landlord becomes entitled to seek, not damages, but all outstanding rent (see Labeo, D. 19.2.28.2; Ulpian, D. 43.32.1.4; Paul, D. 19.2.24.2; but also Paul, D. 19.2.55.2, for farm lease, where the last clause is probably Justinianic); but no text indicates he could not then keep rent both from the departing tenant and from a new substitute tenant he has found. Can this acceleration of rent be justified?

SECTION 2. Lease of a Farm

CASE 155: Duties of the Landlord

D. 19.2.15 pr.-1 (Ulpianus libro trigesimo secundo ad Edictum)

pr. Ex conducto actio conductori datur. 1. Competit autem ex his causis fere: ut puta si re quam conduxit frui ei non liceat (forte quia possessio ei aut totius agri aut partis non praestatur, aut villa non reficitur vel stabulum vel ubi greges eius stare oporteat) vel si quid in lege conductionis convenit, si hoc non praestatur, ex conducto agetur.

Ulpian in the thirty-second book *On the Edict*:

pr. The lessee has the action on the hire (*ex conducto*). 1. It lies for reasons such as these: for instance, if he is not permitted to enjoy the thing he rented because, e.g., possession of all or part of the land is not provided to him; or the farmhouse is not repaired, or a stable or the place where his herds must shelter; or, if they agree on something in a clause of the lease, he may sue on hire if this is not provided.

Discussion

1. Farm Lease and Commercial Lease. Leases of property in which both parties are seeking economic gain naturally become more complex than housing leases. In farm lease, which the jurists seem to use as the archetypal example of commercial leases, the property owner is anticipating rent income while the tenant farmer seeks profit beyond expenses including rent payments. To judge from agricultural writers such as Columella, farm lease was fairly common in the Empire; and other forms of the typical private law lease are widely found in the provinces.

   In addition to lease of farms, legal sources also mention lease of barns and storerooms (*horrea*: Labeo, D. 19.2.60.6, 9; Paul, D. 19.2.55 pr.) and pastures (Cases 161 and 163; see also Cato, *Agr.* 149.2). In urban settings, Ulpian, D. 5.1.19.2, mentions leases of shops, stalls, and workplaces; compare, e.g., Ulpian, D. 8.5.8.5 (a cheese factory at Minturnae), and Alfenus, D. 19.2.30.1, and Africanus, D. 20.4.9 pr. (baths).

2. What Must the Parties Do? As Ulpian indicates in this Case, the landlord's basic duty is to provide the leasehold physically, which implies a contractual duty to protect the tenant from unjustified expulsion; see the following Case. The lease might also impose specific duties on him. But the default rule is that he furnish his tenant with a farm that is and remains in good operating order, with the farm buildings and all durable equipment ready to produce the anticipated crop (Ulpian, D. 19.2.19.2, citing Neratius); and he is responsible if his equipment falls into disrepair except because through the tenant's fault. Two sources indicate that landlords could provide this equipment "with an appraisal" (*aestimatum*), meaning that the tenant had either to return it in good condition (he was liable for virtually

all damage to it) or to pay its previously agreed-upon worth (Pomponius, D. 19.2.3 [citing Proculus]; Paul, D. 19.2.54.2). Failing such a lease clause, the landlord probably bore the loss for normal wear and tear (*vetustas*; compare Alfenus, D. 19.2.30.4 [a lease clause], with Cato, *Agr.* 144.2).

For his part, the tenant must provide all else, including, e.g., the seed in the case of cereal cultivation (Ulpian, D. 19.2.15.2 and 7, citing Servius) or new cuttings to replace exhausted vines in the case of viticulture (see Ulpian, D. 19.2.15.5, citing an imperial rescript). It appears that the tenant also supplied farm animals (see section 1 in this part); and jurists regularly describe tenants as using their own slaves as a labor force: Alfenus, D. 19.2.30.4; Ulpian, D. 9.2.27.11 (citing Proculus; = *Collatio* 12.7.9), 9.2.27.9 (citing Neratius; = *Collatio* 12.7.11); Julian, D. 43.33.1 pr.; see also Labeo, D. 7.8.12.6. For farm tenants' further duties, see Case 157.

What do these sources suggest about the economics of tenant farming in the early Roman Empire? Alternatively, and perhaps more to the point, what do they suggest about the interrelationship between law and the economy during this period?

CASE 156: Justified and Unjustified Expulsion

D. 19.2.25.1 (Gaius libro decimo ad Edictum Provinciale)

Qui fundum fruendum vel habitationem alicui locavit, si aliqua ex causa fundum vel aedes vendat, curare debet, ut apud emptorem quoque eadem pactione et colono frui et inquilino habitare liceat: alioquin prohibitus is aget cum eo ex conducto.

Gaius in the tenth book *On the Provincial Edict*:

A person who leases to another the enjoyment of a farm or a dwelling, if for some reason he sells the farm or house, should take care that also with the buyer, by the same agreement, both the tenant farmer is permitted to enjoy (the farm) and the urban tenant to dwell. Otherwise, he (the tenant), if forbidden (to remain), may sue him on the hire (*ex conducto*).

The Problem

Apronius sells to Calpurnia a house that he owns, in which Domitia is currently residing as his tenant. Can Calpurnia expel Domitia from the leasehold?

Discussion

1. "**Sale Breaks Lease.**" This famous maxim (*emptio tollit locatum*), which is of medieval origin, does not mean quite what it seems to mean. When the owner of leased property sells it, the buyer may, if he or she so wishes, assume ownership and then, as the owner, expel any current tenants (with whom he or she has no contractual relationship). The leases of these tenants are not thereby "broken"; but they have no possessory remedy (since they do not have possession), nor any contractual one, against the buyer. All that they have is a contractual remedy against their original landlord, in this Case also the leasehold's former owner. What Gaius is advising is that the landlord/owner include in the contract of sale a provision making the buyer liable for the tenant's unjustified expulsion: liable, that is, to the seller, who will undoubtedly cede his right of action to the tenant. But this is of only modest help to the tenant, who still cannot prevent the expulsion. The same rule is given also by Alexander, C. 4.65.9 (234 CE); see also Ulpian, D. 19.1.13.30 (citing Servius). (However, Marcellus, D. 43.16.12, and Papinian, D. 43.16.18 pr., seem to provide the tenant farmer with limited access to a possessory remedy if the buyer uses force to expel the tenant.)

   In principle, all of this was a straightforward application of the more general rule that the lease relationship was a matter of contract, not of property law. But the results are so very harsh that subsequent Roman-derived legal systems have regularly found legal ways to better protect tenants in this sort of situation.

2. Expropriation. In a highly controversial fragment, Africanus (D. 19.2.33, 35 pr.) discusses a situation in which a farm has been confiscated (*publicatus*) by the government. Africanus' teacher, the great jurist Julian, had argued that the landlord owed the tenant his "interest" stemming from the breach: "that you (the lessor) be liable on hire for letting me enjoy (the leasehold), even though you were not responsible for your not providing it" (*teneri te actione ex conducto, ut mihi frui liceat, quamvis per te non stet, quo minus id praestes*). Has the landlord therefore impliedly warranted that the land would not be expropriated at some point in the future?

But Africanus, apparently rejecting Julian's view, argues that the landlord owes his tenant only return of any prepaid rent, not also the tenant's "interest." Africanus sees this situation as comparable to one in which the landlord expels an urban tenant in order to repair or demolish his dwelling (see Case 147): the expulsion is treated as justified. As Africanus says, "what is the difference whether the landlord of a building is forced to remodel it on account of its age, or the lessor of a farm is forced to suffer outrage from someone whom he cannot stop?" How inevitable does this logic seem to you? Africanus admits an exception only if the lessor has leased the property knowing it belonged to someone else.

Other texts (especially Ulpian/Tryphoninus, D. 19.2.7–8, discussing the same hypothetical) incline to the same result, seeming almost to reflect a general tendency, toward the end of the Classical period, to release an innocent landlord from damages whenever a tenant was expelled by a third party not subject in some legal sense to the landlord's authority. This may help you to understand the background of the present Case.

3. A Farm Left As a Legacy. By a well-established principle (called *separatio*), crops belong to the owner of the land after their harvest, unless another person, such as a tenant, has a right to them on the basis of a contract or otherwise. Ulpian, *Frag. Vat.* 44 (= D. 30.120.2), discusses a hypothetical in which a deceased man had a contract with a tenant farmer; in his will, the landlord left the farm as a legacy to a third party, who, after the will entered into force, harvested and took ownership of the crops that the tenant had planted. Can the tenant sue, and, if so, whom?

Compare Julian, D. 19.2.32: the landlord dies after leasing a farm to a long-term tenant; the landlord's heir cannot compel the tenant to cultivate (why not?), but if the tenant wishes to do so and an heir or legatee prevents this, the tenant can sue the heir for damages. Explain this holding.

D. 19.2.25.3–5 (Gaius libro decimo ad Edictum Provinciale)

3. Conductor omnia secundum legem conductionis facere debet. Et ante omnia colonus curare debet, ut opera rustica suo quoque tempore faciat, ne intempestiva cultura deteriorem fundum faceret. Praeterea villarum curam agere debet, ut eas incorruptas habeat. 4. Culpae autem ipsius et illud adnumeratur, si propter inimicitias eius vicinus arbores exciderit. 5. Ipse quoque si exciderit, non solum ex locato tenetur, sed etiam lege Aquilia et ex lege duodecim tabularum arborum furtim caesarum et interdicto quod vi aut clam: sed utique iudicis, qui ex locato iudicat, officio continetur, ut ceteras actiones locator omittat.

Gaius in the tenth book *On the Provincial Edict*:

3. The lessee should do everything in accord with the terms of the lease. Above all, the farm tenant should be careful to do farm work in proper season, so that he not diminish the farm's value by his unseasonable cultivation. Further, he should take care of the farmhouses so that he keeps them in good condition.

4. But it is also counted as his fault (*culpa*) if a neighbor cuts down trees because of quarrel with him. 5. Likewise, if he (himself) cuts them down, he is liable not only on the lease, but also under the Lex Aquilia (on wrongful damage to property) and under the Twelve Tables on furtively felling trees and by the interdict against stealth or force. But in any case it is part of the discretion of a *iudex* in a trial on lease that the lessor give up the other actions.

Discussion

1. Basic and Implied Duties. Unmentioned by Gaius, and so obvious that they presumably did not need spelling out, are the duties to pay rent (see Case 49, and the Discussion on Case 147; also Scaevola, D. 19.2.61 pr. [the following Case], and Ulpian, D. 33.4.1.15, both of farm lease; Ulpian, *Frag. Vindob.* 1.2, holding that the duty to pay rent arises from the Law of Nations) and to surrender the farm at the end of the lease term (see Case 160). In section 3, Gaius lists three additional duties. Observing the lease seems equally obvious; see, e.g., Alfenus, D. 19.2.29 (tenant not to cut down trees); Ulpian, D. 19.2.11.1 (tenant not allowed to have a fire) and 11.4 (no haystack in a *villa urbana*). Cultivating in timely fashion is, in Gaius' wording, more intended to preserve the farm's value than to obtain profit. A closely similar list of duties is given in a postclassical work (*Pauli Sent.* 2.18.2), which specifies failure to cultivate (*cultura non exercitata*) as actionable; Paul, D. 19.2.24.2 and 54.1 (= Case 49), states that such a failure allows a landlord to terminate the lease and sue at once. As Reinhard Zimmermann observes, the imposition of an implied duty accords with "the official policy of preventing soil-exhaustion and deterioration into wasteland" (*Obligations* 375); see Gellius, 4.12, and Columella, 1.7.1. Gaius also

requires a farm tenant to keep the farm buildings, and by implication other equipment provided by the landlord, in good condition; see the preceding Case. This duty is substantially higher than that imposed on urban tenants (Case 150).

The overriding principle here is rather vaguely stated by Ulpian, D. 19.2.11.2: "the tenant should see to it that he not somehow make the legal or physical condition of the property worse, or allow it to become so" (*Item prospicere debet conductor, ne aliquo vel ius rei vel corpus deterius faciat vel fieri patiatur*). Similar: Marcian in Case 153, which has the most dramatic extension of this general principle: the tenant's liability for third parties in the leasehold.

2. Fault (*Culpa*). Most of the specific default duties that are associated with tenant farming were presumably developed as aspects of the doctrine of *bona fides*. However, as time passed, violation of them came increasingly to be generalized as "fault" (*culpa*), not only when the leasehold was worsened through the tenant's act, but also through his failure to act, in violation of a contractual duty. See, e.g., Ulpian, D. 13.6.5.2 (Case 64) *in fine*: "When the advantage of both parties is involved, . . . as in lease, . . . both deliberate malice and non-deliberate fault (*et dolus et culpa*) are tendered." Think about the differences between the two doctrines, *bona fides* and *culpa*. Is the distinction between them only a minor linguistic matter, or are there potential practical consequences?

CASE 158: Useful Expenses

D. 19.2.61 pr. (Scaevola libro septimo Digestorum)

Colonus, cum lege locationis non esset comprehensum, ut vineas poneret, nihilo minus in fundo vineas instituit et propter earum fructum denis amplius aureis annuis ager locari coeperat. Quaesitum est, si dominus istum colonum fundi eiectum pensionum debitarum nomine conveniat, an sumptus utiliter factos in vineis instituendis reputare possit opposita doli mali exceptione. Respondit vel expensas consecuturum vel nihil amplius praestaturum.

Scaevola in the seventh book of his *Digests*:

Although it had not been included in the terms of the lease that he set out vines, a tenant farmer nonetheless planted vines on the farm; because of their fruits, the land started being leased for ten gold coins more per year. The question arose whether, if the owner expels this farm tenant and sues him because of unpaid rent, he (the tenant) can counterclaim by interposing the defense of deceit (*exceptio doli*) for expenses usefully made in planting the vines. He (Scaevola) responded that either he will obtain his expenses or he will owe nothing further.

The Problem

The tenant has invested in the leasehold by planting vines, something not envisaged in his lease. The vines resulted in both greatly increased productivity and rent increases, with which the tenant was unable to keep up. As a result, the landlord justifiably expelled him. Has the tenant any recourse to get compensation for his expenditure?

Discussion

1. Improvements. Under Roman law, the vines, once implanted, belonged to the land's owner (see, e.g., Gaius, *Inst.* 2.74–75). The tenant therefore has, in principle, no direct claim for recompense even though his expenditure is conceded to be useful (*utilis*). But when the landlord sues him for unpaid rent, he can use the *exceptio doli* in order to get an offset for them. (It's not clear why this is necessary, but perhaps a stipulation is involved; see Cases 35–36.) *Pauli Sent.* 2.18.4 (= D. 19.2.55.1), which dates from ca. 300 CE, allows the tenant to sue directly for necessary or useful expenses; this was probably an equitable postclassical development of Classical law. Our sources do not, however, think of this situation in terms of depreciation and recovery of investment. Should they have?

2. Fixtures. The outcome changes if the alterations are more or less easily removable from the land or its buildings (what in Anglo-American law are called "fixtures"). Ulpian, D. 19.2.19.4, dealing with urban lease, describes a tenant who adds a door or windows to a building. He cites Labeo for

the view that the tenant may sue on the hire to get the landlord to allow their removal, so long as doing so does not damage the building and it can be restored to its prior condition. (The right to removal is called the *ius tollendi*; the sources for it provoke controversy.) If removal is too costly because of resulting damage, the tenant's ownership lapses, but it will revive if the fixtures are later removed; see Julian, D. 6.1.59. How realistic is this solution?

CASE 159: Remission of Rent

D. 19.2.15.2–3, 5, 7 (Ulpianus libro trigesimo secundo ad Edictum)

2. Si vis tempestatis calamitosae contigerit, an locator conductori aliquid praestare debeat, videamus. Servius omnem vim, cui resisti non potest, dominum colono praestare debere ait, ut puta fluminum graculorum sturnorum et si quid simile acciderit, aut si incursus hostium fiat: si qua tamen vitia ex ipsa re oriantur, haec damno coloni esse, veluti si vinum coacuerit, si raucis aut herbis segetes corruptae sint. . . . 3. Cum quidam incendium fundi allegaret et remissionem desideraret, ita ei rescriptum est: "si praedium coluisti, propter casum incendii repentini non immerito subveniendum tibi est." . . . 5. Cum quidam de fructuum exiguitate quereretur, non esse rationem eius habendam rescripto divi Antonini continetur. Item alio rescripto ita continetur: "novam rem desideras, ut propter vetustatem vinearum remissio tibi detur." . . . 7. Ubicumque tamen remissionis ratio habetur ex causis supra relatis, non id quod sua interest conductor consequitur, sed mercedis exonerationem pro rata: supra denique damnum seminis ad colonum pertinere declaratur.

Ulpian in the thirty-second book *On the Edict*:

2. In the event of the power of catastrophic weather, let us consider whether the lessor should provide anything to the tenant. Servius says that the owner should be liable to the tenant farmer for all force that cannot be resisted, such as that of rivers, jackdaws, starlings, and if some similar thing occurs, or if there is an enemy invasion; but if some defects stem from the object itself, this is the tenant's loss, for instance if wine goes sour, (or) if standing crops are destroyed by worms or weeds. . . .

3. When someone alleged a conflagration on the farm (he had rented) and claimed remission (of rent), he received this rescript: "If you cultivated the property, you are not undeserving of aid on account of the accident of a sudden conflagration." . . .

5. When someone complained about small crop yield, a rescript of the deified Antoninus (Pius) held that no consideration should be taken of this (claim). Likewise, another rescript holds: "You claim something novel (i.e., unacceptable), that remission be given to you because of the age of your vines." . . .

7. But whenever remission is evaluated for the reasons given above, the lessee obtains not his interest (*id quod sua interest*), but a prorated abatement of the rent; in addition, loss of the seed is held to fall on the tenant farmer.

Discussion

1. Remission. Although this remedy may have had an earlier history (as the reference to the late Republican jurist Servius shows), its late Classical form, emerging through imperial intervention, somewhat parallels the much older deduction from rent in urban lease (Case 151). The remedy seems to have

originated as a purely social practice to counter catastrophic crop losses; see, e.g., Columella 1.7.1, and Pliny, *Ep.* 10.8.5, both of whom speak of it as the sort of generosity that should be avoided. Our few sources indicate that it was quite difficult to separate agricultural catastrophes from ordinary fluctuations in yield (what distinguishes irresistible force from defects arising from the object itself?). But most genuine catastrophes would not be confined to single farms, and the imperial officials who grant remissions (which are apparently not part of ordinary lease law) would doubtless see a good many similar tenant claims from a single region. The remedy, it should be noted, is only a rent abatement. Is this a good solution to the problem of agricultural catastrophes? How does the solution differ from deduction in urban lease? Can remission be explained from the standpoint of economics?

CASE 160: Holdover

D. 19.2.13.11 (Ulpianus libro trigesimo secundo ad Edictum)

Qui impleto tempore conductionis remansit in conductione, non solum reconduxisse videbitur, sed etiam pignora videntur durare obligata. . . . Quod autem diximus taciturnitate utriusque partis colonum reconduxisse videri, ita accipiendum est, ut in ipso anno, quo tacuerunt, videantur eandem locationem renovasse, non etiam in sequentibus annis, etsi lustrum forte ab initio fuerat conductioni praestitutum. Sed et si secundo quoque anno post finitum lustrum nihil fuerit contrarium actum, eandem videri locationem in illo anno permansisse: hoc enim ipso, quo tacuerunt, consensisse videntur. Et hoc deinceps in unoquoque anno observandum est. In urbanis autem praediis alio iure utimur, ut, prout quisque habitaverit, ita et obligetur, nisi in scriptis certum tempus conductioni comprehensum est.

Ulpian in the thirty-second book *On the Edict*:

When someone remained on the leasehold after the term of his lease expired, not only will he be held to have re-hired, but his pledges are also held to be obligated. . . .

As for my ruling that the tenant farmer is regarded as having re-hired because of the silence of both parties, this should be interpreted to mean that they are held to have renewed the same lease for the year in which they were silent, but not for following years even if, e.g., five years had initially been provided for the lease. But also if nothing contrary is done in the second year after the five-year term ends, the same lease is regarded as having persisted in that year (as well); for they seem to have agreed by the very fact that they were silent. And this should then be observed in each (succeeding) year.

But for urban properties we use a different rule, that each person is obligated (only) for as long as he remains in occupancy, except if a definite term was fixed in writing for the lease.

Discussion

1. Tacit Renewal. It is not at all unusual for tenants to remain in a leasehold, with the landlord's express or tacit consent, after its original term comes to an end. How would such consent be manifested? Simply by failure to expel the tenant? In any case, Ulpian draws a clear distinction between farm tenants, who are held to "renew" on a year-by-year basis, and urban tenants, who hold on what appears to be an "at will" basis. How does the economic distinction between the two forms of lease help to explain this difference?

Note that the respective tenants' pledges for the rent are also simultaneously renewed: Valerian and Gallienus, C. 4.65.16 (260).

A tenant who remained on the leasehold against the owner's express will would commit theft by harvesting any crops: Celsus, D. 47.2.68.5; Ulpian, D. 12.1.4.1. Further, Ulpian, D. 19.2.14, indicates that the landlord must at least have been competent to express his will in the matter.

CASE 161: Lessor's Warranty against Defects

D. 19.2.19.1 (Ulpianus libro trigesimo secundo ad Edictum)

Si quis dolia vitiosa ignarus locaverit, deinde vinum effluxerit, tenebitur in id quod interest nec ignorantia eius erit excusata: et ita Cassius scripsit. Aliter atque si saltum pascuum locasti, in quo herba mala nascebatur: hic enim si pecora vel demortua sunt vel etiam deteriora facta, quod interest praestabitur, si scisti, si ignorasti, pensionem non petes, et ita Servio Labeoni Sabino placuit.

Ulpian in the thirty-second book *On the Edict*:

If someone unknowingly leases out defective storage casks and wine then flows out of them, he will be liable for the interest (of the lessee), nor will his lack of awareness be excused; so Cassius wrote as well. And it is otherwise if you leased a grazing pasture in which poisonous weeds grew; for if livestock either died or even lost value here, the (lessee's) interest is owed if you knew (about the weeds); (but) if you were unaware, you may not claim rent, a view that Servius, Labeo, and Sabinus also adopt.

Discussion

1. Defective Pots; Poisonous Weeds. Ulpian describes two situations. First, the lessor has unknowingly (*ignarus*) leased out large containers that turned out to be leaky, and the lessee's wine was lost; the lessor is liable for the lessee's "interest" in this not happening, i.e., obviously at least the value of the lost wine; and the lessor's lack of knowledge is no excuse. Second, the lessor leases out a pasture containing poisonous weeds that cause the lessee's livestock to sicken or die; the lessor is liable for the lessee's "interest" if he knew of the weeds, but if he did not, for no more than loss of rent.

   How are these two situations different? As you may recall (from Case 142), for the sale of containers the Augustan jurist Labeo ruled that, unless the parties expressly provided otherwise, the seller impliedly warranted their soundness (as we would say, their merchantability), so that the seller was liable for the buyer's consequential damages if the containers were unsound; and Sabinus extended Labeo's ruling to leased casks as well. But according to this Case, the same jurists went on to hold that the lessor of pastureland was not liable (beyond loss of future rent) if the lessee suffered consequential damages from the poisonous weeds, so long as the lessor was unaware of the problem. The problem here is the extent of a lessor's liability for latent defects. Put another way, did the jurists extend the implied warranty against defective containers, and, if so, how far? Unfortunately, our sources largely fail us in answering these questions.

   Scholars have expended much ink in trying to puzzle out at least a theoretical answer. If the two rulings are regarded as the extremes of a spectrum, the murky line between them may include: defects in movables as against immovables; the defect's gravity and ubiquity; the reasonability of saying, in each case, that the lessor *should* have known of the defect, particularly owing to the likelihood of it having been previously detected; the likely extent of the lessor's previous personal knowledge of the leased object; the relative ability of each party to discover the defect; whether the object can serve for its ordinary purposes; whether the defect is inherent to the object, or superficial to it; and so on. Work out your own answer, always remembering that proof of a lessor's knowledge of a defect may be hard to come by.

CASE 162: Leasing a Slave as a Muleteer

D. 19.2.60.7 (Labeo libro quinto Posteriorum a Iavoleno epitomatorum)

Servum meum mulionem conduxisti: neglegentia eius mulus tuus perit. Si ipse se locasset, ex peculio dumtaxat et in rem versum damnum tibi praestaturum dico: sin autem ipse eum locassem, non ultra me tibi praestaturum, quam dolum malum et culpam meam abesse: quod si sine definitione personae mulionem a me conduxisti et ego eum tibi dedissem, cuius neglegentia iumentum perierit, illam quoque culpam me tibi praestaturum aio, quod eum elegissem, qui eiusmodi damno te adficeret.

D. 9.2.27.34 (Ulpianus libro octavo decimo ad Edictum)

Si quis servum conductum ad mulum regendum <habens> commendaverit ei mulum <et> ille ad pollicem suum eum alligaverit de loro et mulus eruperit sic, ut et pollicem avelleret servo et se praecipitaret, Mela scribit, si pro perito imperitus locatus sit, ex conducto agendum cum domino ob mulum ruptum vel debilitatum, . . .

Labeo in the fifth book of his *Posthumous Writings,* as epitomized by Javolenus:

You hired my slave, through whose carelessness (*neglegentia*) your mule perished. If he leased himself out, I (Labeo) hold that I will be liable to you up to the value of his *peculium* or the benefit I took (from this transaction). But if I (myself) leased him out, I will be held responsible to you for no more than the absence of my deceit and fault (*dolus malus et culpa*). If you hired a muleteer from me without specifying the particular person and I gave you the man through whose carelessness the mule died, I think that I will be held responsible to you for fault in that as well, since I chose the one who caused you the loss in question.

Ulpian in the eighteenth book *On the Edict*:

Someone puts a leased slave in charge of driving a mule, and he (the slave) ties the mule by its rein to his thumb; the mule breaks away, thereby ripping off the slave's thumb and hurling itself down. Mela writes that if an unskilled slave was leased as a skilled one, the (slave's) owner may be sued on the lease because the mule was harmed or disabled. . . .

The Problem

A leased slave, whom the lessee placed in charge of driving the lessee's mule, tied the mule's rein to his thumb (a very, very stupid thing to do); the mule bolted, tore off the slave's thumb, and harmed itself, perhaps fatally. Can the lessee (the owner of the mule) collect damages for the loss?

Discussion

1. A **Careless Muleteer**. Labeo sketches three situations: (i) the slave leased himself out, acting independently of his master (for self-leasing by a slave, see also Papinian, D. 33.2.2); (ii) the slave's master leased him out, in which case the master is personally liable for deliberate or faulty (i.e., negligent) conduct; or (iii) the master chose the slave, in which case he may be liable also for fault in the choice.

   The first scenario, although it may seem surprising, is fairly easy; the slave himself is the wrongdoer, and the master's liability for the slave's misconduct is accordingly limited in effect to loss of the value of the slave (see Chapter VII.A). The harder task is to distinguish the second and third scenarios. A lessor's contractual responsibility is described in terms of *dolus* and *culpa* (also, e.g., Ulpian, D. 19.2.9.pr., 3; *dolus* alone: Labeo, D. 19.2.28.2). But unless the lessor realized that the lessee wished to use the leased slave as a muleteer, it may be hard to pin the loss on the lessor's fault; and it should be noted that in the second fragment, at least, it is the lessee who assigns the slave to drive the mule. However, when the intended purpose of the slave's responsibilities is initially made known, and it is the lessor who picks the slave, the situation changes substantially; as we would say, the lessor warrants fitness for purpose. This form of fault (called *culpa in eligendo*) recurs in a variety of texts; we have already seen it, for instance, in the Discussion on Case 153.

2. A **Thieving Slave**. I lease to you a slave that you wish to use in your shop (*taberna*), and the slave steals from you. Paul, D. 19.2.45.1, maintains it is unclear "whether the action on hire suffices (for the lessee), the theory being that it is not in accord with good faith for us to have arranged that you suffer any loss because of the thing you took on lease." He goes on to favor instead a charge of theft lying "outside the sphere of hire" (*extra causam conductionis*), with a distinct cause of action—in this case, presumably an action on the slave's *peculium*. Can such an outcome be explained in terms of the theory of this Case? Under what circumstances would the contractual action be more suitable?

SECTION 4. Performance of a Job; Employment

CASE 163: Duties of the Contractor

D. 19.2.51.1 (Iavolenus libro undecimo Epistularum)

Locavi opus faciendum ita, ut pro opere redemptori certam mercedem in dies singulos darem: opus vitiosum factum est: an ex locato agere possim? Respondit: si ita opus locasti, ut bonitas eius tibi a conductore adprobaretur, tametsi convenit, ut in singulas operas certa pecunia daretur, praestari tamen tibi a conductore debet, si id opus vitiosum factum est: non enim quicquam interest, utrum uno pretio opus an in singulas operas collocatur, si modo universitas consummationis ad conductorem pertinuit. Poterit itaque ex locato cum eo agi, qui vitiosum opus fecerit. Nisi si ideo in operas singulas merces constituta erit, ut arbitrio domini opus efficeretur: tum enim nihil conductor praestare domino de bonitate operis videtur.

Javolenus in the eleventh book of *Letters*:

I leased out the performance of a job (*opus faciendum*) with the provision that I pay the contractor a fixed daily fee for the job. The job was defective. Can I sue on the lease (of the job)?

He responds: If you leased out the job on condition that the contractor demonstrate its quality to you, then even if it was agreed that a fixed amount be paid for each day of work, nonetheless the contractor should be liable to you if his work was defective. For it makes no difference at all whether a job is leased out for a single (overall) price or for single days of work, provided that the contractor is responsible for the entire completion. So he can be sued on the lease (of a job) if he does defective work, but not if the fee was arranged for single days of work in order that the job be done at the owner's judgment; for then the contractor is held to warrant nothing about the work's quality.

Discussion

1. Performance of a Job (*Opus Faciendum*). Roman law, although it continues to use the vocabulary of *locatio conductio*, sharply distinguishes contracts for performance of a job. Normal construction contracts are included in this category: for a home (*domus*: Labeo, D. 19.2.60.3; Javolenus, D. 19.2.59), a building (*aedes*: Alfenus, D. 19.2.30.3), or apartment block (*insula*: Paul, D. 19.2.22.2); and likewise a water channel (*rivus*: Labeo, D. 19.2.62) or a wall (*ILS* 5317). But also more everyday jobs, such as transporting goods or persons by land or sea (Gaius, D. 19.2.25.7; Papinian, D. 19.5.1.1; Ulpian, D. 19.2.11.3; Paul, D. 14.2.2 pr., 10.2); cleaning or repairing clothes (see the following Case); setting or engraving a jewel (Ulpian, D. 19.2.13.5); pasturing calves (Ulpian, D. 19.2.9.5); harvesting crops (Cato, *Agr.* 144-145); making a ring from the customer's gold (Case 185); or educating a slave (Ulpian, D. 19.2.13.3); even a doctor performing an operation

(see Ulpian/Proculus, D. 9.2.7.8). In each case, the person who "places out" the job is the *locator*, while the contractor who performs it is the *conductor*.

2. **Payment and Supervision**. Javolenus describes two payment methods: for the entire job, or by the day until completion; but these are the basis for classifying the contract. What is crucial, rather, is the extent to which "the contractor is responsible for the entire completion," rather than working under the customer's closer supervision; and the contractor's work is certified after the fact by the customer's "approval" (*adprobatio*). Why is this so important?

3. **A Public Contract**. There survives a remarkable inscription recording a public contract for construction of a wall in the port city of Puteoli, 105 BCE: *CIL* 10.1781 (= ILS 5317, FIRA 3.153). Besides giving elaborate specifications for the wall, the contract prescribes the process for approval upon completion by the local council, the date for completion, payment for the job (including a progress payment), and a list of the contractors.

CASE 164: Moving a Column; Cleaning Clothes

D. 19.2.25.7–8 (Gaius libro decimo ad Edictum Provinciale)

7. Qui columnam transportandam conduxit, si ea, dum tollitur aut portatur aut reponitur, fracta sit, ita id periculum praestat, si qua ipsius eorumque, quorum opera uteretur, culpa acciderit: culpa autem abest, si omnia facta sunt, quae diligentissimus quisque observaturus fuisset. Idem scilicet intellegemus et si dolia vel tignum transportandum aliquis conduxerit: idemque etiam ad ceteras res transferri potest. 8. Si fullo aut sarcinator vestimenta perdiderit eoque nomine domino satisfecerit, necesse est domino vindicationem eorum et condictionem cedere.

Gaius in the tenth book *On the Provincial Edict*:

7. A person undertook to transport a column. If it was broken while being removed or carried or repositioned, he is liable for this risk (*periculum*) if it occurred because of some fault (*culpa*) of his own or of the persons whose labor he used; but there is no fault if everything was done which a very careful person (*diligentissimus quisque*) would see to. We would obviously rule the same also if someone undertook to transport containers or timber; and the same rule can also be applied to other property.

8. If a fuller or a clothing-mender lost (a customer's) clothes and gave satisfaction to their owner on this account, the owner must cede to the fuller or cloth-mender) the right to reclaim their ownership and the *condictio* (for theft).

Discussion

1. The Broken Column. This is, of course, a fairly typical example of a job. Columns are large and heavy, hence prone to fracture or chipping as they are manipulated through narrow or crowded city streets. The transporter's liability is defined in terms of *culpa*, which Ulpian, in this case, helpfully defines as requiring a great deal of care not only from the contractor but also from his employees. (It thus appears that the contractor warrants against the fault of his employees.) Ulpian, D. 19.2.9.5, cites Celsus as holding that such care requires also the skill necessary for the job; lack of experience (*imperitia*) is no excuse and is counted as *culpa*.

   These duties become especially heightened when the customer has consigned property for the contractor to work on, as with the column; for instance, a fuller is liable when mice nibble at a customer's clothing, "because he should have guarded against this" (Ulpian, D. 19.2.13.6). Obviously, if the contractor exposes the customer's property to risks not associated with execution of the contract, he is liable for any resulting loss (Ulpian, D. 19.2.13.3); and, indeed, any personal use by him of the property constitutes theft (*Pauli Sent.* 2.31.29, = D. 47.2.83 pr.).

Contractors are normally expected to perform the job themselves, not to delegate its performance to third parties: Ulpian, D. 45.1.38.21, 46.3.31.

2. Stolen Clothing. Along with the high liability a contractor bears for the customer's property goes the duty to protect it against theft or harm by third parties. Fullers treated woolen cloth to make it thicker and non-abrasive, but they also did cleaning. In section 8, the fuller who lost the customer's clothing paid the customer their value. The thief may be impossible to locate, but were that to happen, the customer must cede to the fuller his legal claims against the thief. Gaius, *Inst.* 3.205–206, notes that this rule holds only if the fuller is solvent and able to pay for the clothing; otherwise, the customer's remedies may be only against the thief. (See also Labeo, D. 19.2.60.2.) This high standard of care is frequently described as "safekeeping," *custodia*, meaning liability for any damage or loss unless the contractor can show it to have been caused by a "higher force"; see also Ulpian, D. 47.2.12 pr. (For what happens when the fuller pays for lost clothing that the customer later recovers, see Case 229.)

CASE 165: Timely Completion

D. 19.2.58.1 (Labeo libro quarto Posteriorum a Iavoleno epitimatorum)

In operis locatione non erat dictum, ante quam diem effici deberet: deinde, si ita factum non esset, quanti locatoris interfuisset, tantam pecuniam conductor promiserat. Eatenus eam obligationem contrahi puto, quatenus vir bonus de spatio temporis aestimasset, quia id actum apparet esse, ut eo spatio absolveretur, sine quo fieri non possit.

Labeo in the fourth book of his *Posthumous Writings*, as epitomized by Javolenus:

In the lease of a job a date had not been fixed before which it should be completed; (but) the contractor had then promised (payment of) money equivalent to the lessor's interest if it was not so completed. I think that an obligation is contracted for whatever (time) an honest man (*vir bonus*) would estimate as the time limit, since they obviously arranged that it be finished in the time required for doing it.

Discussion
1. Implying a Time Limit. The parties provided for the contractor's payment of liquidated damages if the work was not completed "on time," but they failed to specify the actual date for completion. Labeo does not prescribe a time (what might inhibit him from doing this?), but instead allows it to be set by the standards of a *vir bonus*, a fictional person who bears resemblance to the Anglo-American "reasonable person." *Arbitrium boni viri*, "the judgment of an honest person," is virtually a catch phrase with the Roman jurists. As Ulpian, D. 50.17.22.1, says, it is also the standard to which a party must adhere when a contract requires him or her to determine a contract term (as when a fee for services is left to the judgment of the contractor or the customer). See also Paul, D. 19.2.24 pr.

In D. 17.2.76 and 78, Proculus discusses situations where the parties expressly refer a contract term to the judgment of a third party. As Proculus states, there are two kinds of arbitrators (*arbitri*): in some cases, the parties are agreeing to accept the arbitrator's judgment as a final settlement, regardless of whether it is fair or unfair; in others, the judgment must conform to that of an honorable man, i.e., it must be objectively reasonable. In the event of doubt, Proculus prefers the second interpretation for *bona fides* contracts, and Paul, D. 17.2.77, applies this preference to contracts for the performance of a job, in cases where the customer decides on whether to approve the work.

In what circumstances might such an objective standard be inappropriate?

CASE 166: Approval and Risk

D. 19.2.62 (Labeo libro primo Pithanon)

Si rivum, quem faciendum conduxeras et feceras, antequam eum probares, labes corrumpit, tuum periculum est. Paulus: immo si soli vitio id accidit, locatoris erit periculum, si operis vitio accidit, tuum erit detrimentum.

D. 19.2.36 (Florentinus libro septimo Institutionum)

Opus quod aversione locatum est donec adprobetur, conductoris periculum est: quod vero ita conductum sit, ut in pedes mensurasve praestetur, eatenus conductoris periculo est, quatenus admensum non sit: et in utraque causa nociturum locatori, si per eum steterit, quo minus opus adprobetur vel admetiatur. Si tamen vi maiore opus prius interciderit quam adprobaretur, locatoris periculo est, nisi si aliud actum sit: non enim amplius praestari locatori oporteat, quam quod sua cura atque opera consecutus esset.

Labeo in the first book of his *Plausible Views*:

If you had contracted to build a water channel and you had completed it, but a land subsidence destroys it before you get it approved, you bear the risk. Paul (comments): No, rather, if this happens because of a defect in the earth, the *locator* (the customer) bears the risk; if it happens due to a defect of the work, the loss will be yours.

Florentinus in the seventh book of his *Institutes*:

When a job is leased out for a lump sum (*aversio*), the contractor bears the risk (*periculum*) until it is approved. But when it is leased so that performance is in feet or (other) measures, the contractor has the risk for as long as it goes unmeasured. In both cases, it will harm the *locator* (who contracted to have the job done) if he is responsible for the job not being approved or measured. Nonetheless, if the work is destroyed by a higher force (*vis maior*) before it is approved, the *locator* bears the risk unless it was otherwise agreed; for no more should be provided to the *locator* than what he would have obtained by his own care and work.

Discussion

1. Approval. As was already mentioned in Case 163, the jurists regularly describe "approval" (*adprobatio*) as the final stage in a job contract. Apart from passage of risk (discussed later), the consequences are not clearly spelled out; but presumably the customer is at least then obligated to pay any outstanding contract price. Disapproval (*improbatio*) is also possible, meaning that the customer would not have an obligation to pay until any problems were remedied; but Labeo, D. 19.2.60.3, holds that if the parties subsequently agreed on changes from the original specifications, "the work is not deemed completed according to the contract terms, but since the change

was willingly made by the *locator*, the contractor should be absolved." Compare Case 104 on modifying a sale.

A particularly odd example of approval is discussed by Labeo and Paul, D. 14.2.10 pr. Ship's passage was arranged for a slave, who died (apparently of natural causes) while the ship was at sea. Labeo holds that the passage fee is not owed, but Paul disagrees, arguing that it depends on whether the fee was imposed upon initial boarding (in which case it is owed) or upon final disembarkation (in which case, not). Sort through the argument here. What should happen if it is unclear what the parties arranged?

2. **Passage of Risk.** *Periculum* should probably be understood loosely. If an earth subsidence (*labes*) destroys Labeo's water channel after its (full or partial) completion, the contractor would bear the risk in the sense that he would receive no pay for his work up to this point (he has not produced the specified result); but if the subsidence occurs after the customer's approval, the contractor is entitled to full payment. So Labeo holds, as it seems, in a decision that places considerable weight on the thoroughness and accuracy of the approval process. Paul's contrary ruling lays more stress on the cause of the water channel's destruction: if prior to approval the destruction results from "a defect in the earth" (*vitium soli*; what is meant?), the *locator* bears the risk and must pay for the work (Africanus, D. 19.2.33, appears to take the same position); but if from "a defect in the work," the contractor does, and so the *locator* is off the hook. Does either Labeo's or Paul's view seem entirely satisfactory? Paul's negative comments on Labeo (a much earlier jurist) often seem excessively pedantic; is that true here, or could a real change have occurred in legal thinking over time?

Florentinus largely concentrates on measurement as a supplement to approval (although it also determines the fee), but in the final sentence he turns to destruction by *vis maior*, here a "superior force," such as an earthquake or a flood, against which "human frailty" is helpless (Gaius, D. 44.7.1.4: *humana infirmitas*); as we might say, an act of God. Is it likely that Labeo's "subsidence" (*labes*) is as catastrophic as an earthquake? Which party should bear the risk if, short of an earthquake, the soil beneath a water channel is too weak to support it?

3. **A Special Case.** Alfenus, D. 19.2.31, raises a related problem. Saufeius owns a ship with a large hold, into which he pours grain from various owners for transport to market; the plan is that, at the end of the voyage, the mingled grain will be offloaded and reapportioned among the various owners. After Saufeius has offloaded and conveyed one owner's grain, the ship sinks. Do the other owners have a claim against either Saufeius or the one owner who received his grain? Servius, Alfenus' teacher, distinguishes

between two ways in which the cargo might have been carried: either in separate compartments, or mixed together in one heap. In the former case, the individual owners retain ownership during the voyage; in the latter, the owners do not, since they are expecting return only of a prorated share of the cargo, of which Saufeius is the owner in the meantime. (This arrangement is described as similar to an "open deposit"; see Case 69.) How does Servius' property analysis affect the outcome? Does it make any difference if the ship sank because of Saufeius' fault? Should distribution to the single owner be regarded as Saufeius' fault?

CASE 167: Cost Overruns

D. 19.2.60.4 (Labeo libro quinto Posteriorum a Iavoleno epitomatorum)

Mandavi tibi ut excuteres, quanti villam aedificare velles: renuntiasti mihi ducentorum impensam excutere: certa mercede opus tibi locavi, postea comperi non posse minoris trecentorum eam villam constare: data autem tibi erant centum, ex quibus cum partem impendisses, vetui te opus facere. Dixi, si opus facere perseveraveris, ex locato tecum agere, ut pecuniae mihi reliquum restituas.

Labeo in the fifth book of *Posthumous Writings*, as epitomized by Javolenus:

I gave you a mandate to estimate how much you would want to build a villa. You notified me that your estimate of the expense was two hundred (thousand sesterces). I leased out the job to you for a fixed fee, and later learned that the villa could not be completed for less than three hundred. One hundred had (already) been paid to you; when you had spent part of it, I forbade your doing the job (any further).

I held that if you continue to do the job, you can be sued on the lease that you return to me the remainder of the money (paid to you).

Discussion

1. Paying the Price. If, as in the previous Case, a job is let out to a contractor at a fixed fee per day, and the job is poorly done, what recourse does the customer have? Javolenus, D. 19.2.51.1, distinguishes: if the job was let out such that its quality (*bonitas*) was subject to the customer's approval, then, even if payment had been made daily, the customer may sue *ex locato* for damages if the work as an entirety is defective. However, if the wage was established for single workdays (*operae*, see the following Case) and effected under the customer's supervision, the worker does not warrant the quality of the job. How clear is this distinction?

2. The Estimate. Here the contractor gave an estimate that turned out to be grossly low. There is no sign that the estimate was given in bad faith or that the ensuing work was faulty, however, and the customer made one payment (what we would call a progress payment) before realizing—presumably because the contractor was pressuring him for an increase in the fee—that the final cost would be far higher than the estimate. Under these circumstances, the customer is legally entitled to order the contractor to stop work, and he can also recover any unspent portion of the payment. (Presumably, a more modest cost overrun would not have had a similar drastic result.) The customer is thus left with a partially completed villa, which he can perhaps complete using a less up-market contractor. How satisfactory is this outcome?

Professionals in the broader construction trade were expected to show considerable diligence. The Praetor's Edict established a special action against surveyors whose report was faulty (Case 184), although only if his deceit, *dolus malus*, was involved; but gross negligence was interpreted as deceit, at least according to our source, which also says that the customer bears the risk if the surveyor is insufficiently experienced (Ulpian, D. 11.6.1.1). The surveyor was also liable if he delegated the job to a third party who acted fraudulently (Paul, D. 11.6.2.1). Ulpian, D.11.6.7.3–4, citing an imperial rescript, recommends an analogous extension of this action to deceitful architects, bookkeepers, and public contractors. Would this seem justified?

CASE 168: "Lease" of One's Own Labor

D. 19.2.38 pr.-1 (Paulus libro singulari Regularum)

pr. Qui operas suas locavit, totius temporis mercedem accipere debet, si per eum non stetit, quo minus operas praestet. 1. Advocati quoque, si per eos non steterit, quo minus causam agant, honoraria reddere non debent.

Paul in his monograph on *Rules*:

pr. A person who leases out his own labor (*operae suae*) should receive pay (*merces*) for the entire time if he is not responsible for not providing the labor. 1. Likewise, advocates, if they are not responsible for not pleading a case, should not return their honoraria.

Discussion

1. **Wage Labor.** The Roman Empire had, of course, a vast multitude of wage laborers, both free and slave (working for third parties; see Case 162). Even in official sources such as statutes or the Edict, the worker is said to "lease out his own labor" (*locare operas suas*: e.g., Ulpian, D. 3.1.1.6, and Paul, D. 38.1.37 pr.), or even to "lease out himself" (*locare se*: Ulpian, *Collatio* 9.2.2). Such a wage laborer is often described as a *mercenarius* (e.g., Pomponius, D. 8.6.20; Ulpian, D. 43.24.3 pr., 5.11; Paul, D. 47.2.90; Marcian, D. 48.19.11.1), a word which, like its English derivative "mercenary," has a disreputable ring; see, for instance, Cicero, *De Off.* 1.150–151 ("Ignoble and vulgar is the income of all *mercenarii*, whose labor, not skill, is being purchased; for in their case the *merces* itself is the payment for slavery"). Those in "higher occupations" therefore preferred to avoid the impression that they worked for wages (*mercedes*), although a good many of them plainly did: e.g., teachers (Julian, D. 27.2.4; Papinian, D. 39.5.27; etc.), doctors (Ulpian, D. 9.2.7.8, citing Proculus; Gaius, D. 9.3.7), forensic advocates (Ulpian, D. 50.13.1.13), public officials (Labeo, D. 39.5.19.1), and surveyors (Ulpian, D. 11.6.1 pr.). Over time, however, their compensation was increasingly designated an *honorarium* or *salarium* rather than a "wage" (*merces*), thereby implying no explicit *quid pro quo*; and in the late Classical period a claim to this compensation was not actionable *ex locato*, but only through imperial courts; see Case 184, and Ulpian, D. 50.13.1 (listing entitled professions, but ruling out philosophers and law teachers, who ought to "spurn working for hire," *mercenariam operam spernere*: 1.4–5).

   One result of this social prejudice is that Roman employment law is poorly developed, few sources being the probable consequence of few actual lawsuits directly on *locatio conductio operarum*. But this Case, which allows the wage laborer to collect his full pay when he is hired for a number of days but does not work all of them because of some external cause (such as cancellation of the employer's project, or the employer's death; see Ulpian, D. 19.2.19.9–10, citing Papinian), is an exception. (The same rule, it should be noted, is carried over to the advocate's honorarium.) But we have next to no information, except from occasional literary or epigraphic evidence, as to the other legal rights and duties of ordinary employers and employees during their service.

How should law best deal with such social prejudices? See also the Discussion on Case 184.

PART B

Partnership (*Societas*)

In Anglo-American law, partnership is a form of enterprise organization. Roman law, however, constructed the contract of partnership (*societas*) differently, as a kind of informal joint venture, in which two or more parties agree to cooperate and pool resources for a common purpose. Although the purpose may be commercial, it need not be. For instance, the parties may agree to share their entire estates (*societas omnium bonorum*); or, at the other extreme, the parties may have only a limited non-commercial end in view. Thus, several persons who agree to share costs while traveling together are partners (*socii*) with regard to their trip. This results in a very different construction of the legal institution. As Reinhard Zimmermann observes (*Obligations* 451, quoting David Daube), *Socii* "are not bent on getting the utmost out of each other; they are, in the first place, 'friends,' pursuing their common interests against third parties."

The originally non-commercial nature of *societas* produces one of its most striking legal characteristics: to a very considerable extent, the contract of *societas* has effect as between the partners, but not with respect to the outside world. If one of the partners arranges a contract with a third party, that party can enforce the contract only against the single partner, not against the others (no joint and several liability). However, the affected partner remains tied to the others through *societas*, so he or she can usually bring claims for contribution against them (and vice versa) regarding any profit or loss the partnership may incur, as well as for misfeasance in carrying out the partnership's objectives.

Societas, although thought-provoking as a contract, was poorly conceived for business purposes. This was so both with respect to the question just discussed, and also because *societas* was constructed as a transient arrangement. Nonetheless, despite the obstacles, commercial partnerships flourished during the Roman Empire, perhaps largely owing to the absence of more sophisticated enterprise organizations. Legal and literary sources attest them in agriculture (cultivating land; breeding and grazing livestock), engaging in sales (food staples such as oil, wine, and grain; slaves; clothing; jewelry; tombs), providing services (educating or training free children and slaves; leasing dwellings; operating shops; transporting both on land and sea), and so on. Most of these operations were quite small: only a handful of partners, most often just two. They frequently seem also rather short-term.

As with the real contracts (Chapter III) and mandate (Part C in this chapter), the jurists confronted the task of adapting these contracts to make them more commercially viable. They went some distance to achieving this goal, although their efforts seem slight by modern standards. Roman law was more successful for partnerships closely associated with public policy: banking (the *argentarii*) and public contracting operations (*publicani*); for these, some special rules were developed that departed from the individualistic template of *societas*. (This topic will not be explored here, however; in the bibliography, see Andreau and Fleckner.) But more developed enterprise forms, such as private corporations based on separation of stockholders and management, were unknown in Roman commercial law, which in general therefore made little direct contribution to the later development of capitalism.

CASE 169: Contributions, Profit, and Loss

Gaius, *Institutiones* 3.148–150

148. Societatem coire solemus aut totorum bonorum aut unius alicuius negotii, ueluti mancipiorum emendorum aut uendendorum. 149. Magna autem quaestio fuit, an ita coiri possit societas, ut quis maiorem partem lucretur, minorem damni praestet. Quod Quintus Mucius contra naturam societatis esse censuit. Sed Seruius Sulpicius, cuius etiam praeualuit sententia, adeo ita coiri posse societatem existimauit, ut dixerit illo quoque modo coiri posse, ut quis nihil omnino damni praestet, sed lucri partem capiat, si modo opera eius tam pretiosa uideatur, ut aequum sit eum cum hac pactione in societatem admitti. Nam et ita posse coiri societatem constat, ut unus pecuniam conferat, alter non conferat et tamen lucrum inter eos commune sit; saepe enim opera alicuius pro pecunia ualet. 150. Et illud certum est, si de partibus lucri et damni nihil inter eos conuenerit, tamen aequis ex partibus commodum ut incommodum inter eos commune esse; sed si in altero partes expressae fuerint, uelut in lucro, in altero uero omissae, in eo quoque, quod omissum est, similes partes erunt.

Gaius in the third book of his *Institutes*:

148. We normally enter a partnership either for our entire estates (*societas omnium bonorum*) or for some particular transaction, such as buying or selling slaves.

149. But there was (at one time) a major disagreement about whether a partnership could be entered such that one (partner) took a larger share of profit and paid a smaller one of loss. Quintus Mucius (Scaevola) thought this contrary to the nature of partnership. But Servius Sulpicius, whose view has prevailed, not only thought it possible to enter such a partnership, but held entry possible also in the following way, that one person pay for no loss at all, but receive part of the profit, provided that his services are deemed so valuable that it is fair he be admitted to the partnership on these terms. For it is agreed that a partnership can be entered such that one contributes money, the other not, but nonetheless they share profit, since often one's services are as valuable as money.

150. And this (at least) is settled: if they do not agree (specifically) on sharing profit and loss, they share advantage, like disadvantage, in equal shares; but if the shares were expressed for one purpose, e.g., for gain, but omitted for the other, the shares are the same also for that which was omitted.

The Problem

Gaius, a wealthy Roman, and Artemisia, his freedwoman, wish to enter a *societas* in which she will operate a butcher shop. To what extent are they free to set up their partnership in the way most advantageous to themselves?

Discussion

1. **"The Nature of Partnership."** Q. Mucius Scaevola (cos. 95 BCE), the earliest important jurist, disallowed agreements that varied the shares of profit and loss. Can you work out what his reasoning might have been? The eventual default rule (given in section 150) was that, unless the parties agreed otherwise, they would share equally in profit and loss; so also Ulpian, D. 17.2.29 pr. Is this irrespective of the relative size of their contributions to the *societas*? Measuring contributions may have been quite difficult, as Gaius indicates; while most partners may have contributed mainly money and property, contributions of labor (including expertise) were also possible. Thus, for instance, one partner might provide capital but then remain relatively passive, while the other less affluent one operated the partnership on the basis of previously acquired skill and knowledge. See Proculus, D. 17.2.80; Ulpian, D. 17.2.5.1 ("A *societas* can be validly formed between persons of unequal means, since often the poorer one supplies in work what he lacks in comparative wealth. A *societas* is not acceptably entered into as a gift."), 29 pr.; Paul 17.2.30; Justinian, *Inst.* 3.25.2. Do you see the reasoning that led Servius Sulpicius Rufus (cos. 51), Q. Mucius' gifted successor, to relax the constrictive ruling of his teacher?

   In Classical law, the parties had considerable legal freedom to shape their partnership as they wished. They could arrange for differing allotments of profit and of loss, and even that the profit be shared while the loss falls only on one partner, provided that this partner primarily contributes his effort (Ulpian, D. 17.2 29 pr.-1; Paul, D. 17.2.30). They could also leave it to a third party to determine their shares (Pomponius, D. 17.2.6: he must use "the judgment of an honest man," *boni viri arbitrium*). However, the jurists draw the line when one partner takes all the profit and the other bears all the loss (Ulpian, D. 17.2.29.2); this is a so-called leonine partnership, after a fable of the Roman poet Phaedrus (1.5). Ulpian describes such a partnership as "exceedingly inequitable" (*iniquissimum*). Can you formulate a better objection?

2. **Profit and the *Societas Omnium Bonorum*.** It is worth noting that, although Roman partnerships need not be aimed at profit, the jurists usually assume that profit is their primary goal. Ulpian, D. 17.2.7, indicates that, unless partners had specified otherwise, "profit" includes "everything stemming from their business" (*universorum quae ex quaestu veniunt*), including any income from sales or leases; see also Paul, D. 17.2.8. But, absent an express agreement to the contrary (Paul, D. 17.2.3.2), partners could still keep for themselves what they received outside the partnership, e.g., by way of inheritance, bequests, or gifts: Ulpian, D. 17.2.9 (citing Sabinus); see also Pomponius, D. 17.2.60.1; Ulpian and Paul, D. 17.2.10–13. Ulpian,

D. 17.2.71.1, gives a case in which two freedmen with the same former master and patron formed "a partnership for profit, business, and income" (*societas lucri, quaestus, compendii*); when their patron's will then left his estate to one freedman and a legacy to the other, neither partner was obliged to share. A similar ruling by Julian, D. 29.2.45.2.

However, profit is probably not the normal motive in one particular form of partnership that Gaius mentions in section 148, in which two or more persons merge all their property (*omnia bona*, a concept widely construed: Paul, D. 17.2.3.1) into a joint ownership. Although in the Roman Empire such a merger may well have been rare, the institution has a long history, and may, in fact, have been the original form of partnership. A fragment of Gaius' *Institutes* (3.154a–b), known only from an Egyptian parchment first discovered in 1933 and published a year later, describes an archaic partnership in which the heirs of a deceased *paterfamilias* by tacit agreement remain together on their undivided familial property; this is called *consortium ercto non cito* ("community in an undivided inheritance"). Scholars widely suppose that this institution, which Gaius treats as obsolete and is only passingly mentioned in other sources, nonetheless had, through *societas omnium bonorum*, a considerable influence on the later (2nd cent. BCE?) development of Classical *societas*, although that contract has a far more individualistic cast.

3. The Action on Behalf of a Partner (*pro Socio*). The model *formula* for the action ran approximately as follows: "Whereas the plaintiff entered a partnership (for all their property) with the defendant, this being the matter under litigation, whatever on this account the defendant ought to give to or do for the plaintiff in accord with good faith (*ex fide bona*), let the *iudex* condemn the defendant to the plaintiff for this; if it does not appear, let him absolve" (Lenel, *EP*³ 297). The action, brought by one partner against another, has the effect of dissolving the partnership: Ulpian, D. 17.2.63.10; Paul, D. 17.2.65 pr. (But see Paul, D. 17.2.65.15, noting an exception for public contractors.) As discussed in the following Cases, the action covered any claim rising out of the *societas*. Condemnation led to the ex-partner being branded with *infamia*; see Discussion 3 on Case 62.

CASE 170: The Common Fund

D. 17.2.58 pr.-1 (Ulpianus libro trigensimo primo ad Edictum)

pr. Si id quod quis in societatem contulit exstinctum sit, videndum, an pro socio agere possit. Tractatum ita est apud Celsum libro septimo digestorum ad epistulam Cornelii Felicis: cum tres equos haberes et ego unum, societatem coimus, ut accepto equo meo quadrigam venderes et ex pretio quartam mihi redderes. Si igitur ante venditionem equus meus mortuus sit, non putare se Celsus ait societatem manere nec ex pretio equorum tuorum partem deberi: non enim habendae quadrigae, sed vendendae coitam societatem. Ceterum si id actum dicatur, ut quadriga fieret eaque communicaretur tuque in ea tres partes haberes, ego quartam, non dubie adhuc socii sumus. 1. Item Celsus tractat, si pecuniam contulissemus ad mercem emendam et mea pecunia perisset, cui perierit ea. et ait, si post collationem evenit, ut pecunia periret, quod non fieret, nisi societas coita esset, utrique perire, ut puta si pecunia, cum peregre portaretur ad mercem emendam, periit: si vero ante collationem, posteaquam eam destinasses, tunc perierit, nihil eo nomine consequeris, inquit, quia non societati periit.

Ulpian in the thirty-first book On the Edict:

pr. If property that one person contributed to the partnership is lost, let us see whether he can sue on partnership. Celsus, in the seventh book of his *Digests*, handled the matter thus in responding to a letter from Cornelius Felix: You have three horses and I have one. We enter a partnership for you to take my horse and sell a four-horse team, and (then) to return to me a fourth of the price. If my horse then dies before the sale, Celsus says that he does not think the partnership continues, nor is a share owed (to you) from the price of your horses, since the partnership was not formed to have a four-horse team, but to sell it. But if the arrangement is said to have been that a four-horse team be created and shared, with you to have a three-quarter share in it and me a quarter, we are undoubtedly still partners (after my horse dies).

1. Celsus also discusses (this problem): if we had contributed money for purchasing goods and my money had been lost, who bears this loss? He says that, if the money is lost after its contribution (to the common fund), which would not occur unless the partnership had been formed, both bear the loss; e.g., if money, when it is carried abroad for buying goods, is lost. But if it is lost before its contribution but after you set it aside (for this purpose), you will get nothing on this account, he (Celsus) says, because it was not the partnership that suffered loss.

Discussion

    1. A Four-Horse Team. This contract is typical of the one-off partnerships mentioned by Gaius in Case 169 (section 148: *societas . . . unius alicuius negotii*); see also Ulpian, D. 17.2.52.7 and 12–13; Paul, D. 17.2.65.2, 71 pr.

The partners' premise here is that a quadriga, sold as a team, will be more valuable than the four horses sold separately; see, e.g., Paul, D. 9.2.22.1.

Although there is no requirement that partnerships have a "common fund," *res communis*, that comprises money or material property contributed by the partners, such a fund seems to have occurred quite often (Ulpian, D. 17.2.14, 45, 47 pr.; Paul, D. 17.2.38.1; et al.), and doubtless almost invariably when a business partnership was capitalized. When I add my horse to your three horses, Celsus, whom Ulpian follows, holds that, if my horse dies (presumably of natural causes and not owing to any fault of yours) before the quadriga can be sold, I bear the loss because our aim was only to sell the team, not to use it, e.g., for chariot racing in the Circus. Does this effectively mean that, because of our intent to sell the team, my horse and yours were not melded into a common fund despite the horses being grouped together for purposes of the sale? Reconstruct, if you can, Celsus' reasoning. Did he get it right?

2. **Contributions of Money.** Celsus' example here illustrates the different treatment given to money. Here, so long as the money is being used for partnership purposes (and, as we shall see, so long as the partner handling it acts with reasonable care), its loss is apportioned to the partners; the money must, however, have been actually contributed, and not just committed for this purpose. (See further Case 174.) Money is a standard example of a fungible, and its passage into the common fund evidently results in the contributing partner's loss of ownership; it becomes common property, out of which all partnership debts can be paid (Case 173). Ulpian, D. 17.2.14, indicates that an agreement between partners barring division of the common fund before an agreed date is ineffective if, for whatever reason, their partnership is subsequently dissolved before that date.

During the partnership, the partners each have "ownership of the entirety, undivided (and) *pro parte*" (Ulpian, D. 13.6.5.15, citing Celsus). Upon dissolution, partners have available, besides the action on partnership, an action for dividing common property, the *actio communi dividundo*: Paul, D. 10.3.1, 17.2.17 pr. Division, which is largely discretionary with the *iudex*, is based upon the actual property held in common, any damage it has sustained, and any loss or gain a partner has had from the common fund: Ulpian, D. 10.3.3 pr. For the jurists' efforts to separate the concept of common property from *societas*, see Paul and Gaius, D. 17.2.31–34.

CASE 171: The Standard of Conduct for Partners

D. 17.2.52.1–3 (Ulpianus libro trigensimo primo ad Edictum)

1. Venit autem in hoc iudicium pro socio bona fides. 2. Utrum ergo tantum dolum an etiam culpam praestare socium oporteat, quaeritur. Et Celsus libro septimo digestorum ita scripsit: socios inter se dolum et culpam praestare oportet. Si in coeunda societate, inquit, artem operamve pollicitus est alter, veluti cum pecus in commune pascendum aut agrum politori damus in commune quaerendis fructibus, nimirum ibi etiam culpa praestanda est . . . Quod si rei communi socius nocuit, magis admittit culpam quoque venire. 3. Damna quae imprudentibus accidunt, hoc est damna fatalia, socii non cogentur praestare: ideoque si pecus aestimatum datum sit et id latrocinio aut incendio perierit, commune damnum est, si nihil dolo aut culpa acciderit eius, qui aestimatum pecus acceperit: quod si a furibus subreptum sit, proprium eius detrimentum est, quia custodiam praestare debuit, qui aestimatum accepit. Haec vera sunt, et pro socio erit actio, si modo societatis contrahendae causa pascenda data sunt quamvis aestimata.

Ulpian in the thirty-first book *On the Edict*:

1. In the lawsuit on partnership (*pro socio*), at issue is good faith (*bona fides*). 2. Question arose whether a partner should be liable just for deceit (*dolus*) or also fault (*culpa*). Celsus wrote in book 17 of his *Digests* as follows: partners should be liable between themselves for deceit and fault. If, he says, in entering a partnership, one person promised a skill or services—e.g, when we give a herd for common grazing, or land to a cultivator for joint raising of crops—obviously here there is liability also for *culpa*. . . . But if a partner harmed common property, he (even) more allows that *culpa* is at issue here.

3. Partners are not forced to bear losses that are unforeseeable, i.e., unavoidable losses. And so if a flock is given along with an assessment (of its value) and it perishes through brigandage or conflagration, the loss is shared if this does not occur by the *dolus* or *culpa* of the person receiving the flock with an assessment. But if it was stolen by thieves, the loss falls on the person who ought to provide safekeeping (*custodia*) and took it with an assessment. These rules are correct and there will be an action on partnership, provided that the animals, although with an assessment, were given for pasturing on the basis of a partnership contract.

Discussion

1. **Liability for Deceit and Fault.** It is certain that a partner was liable at least for *dolus*, deceitful conduct: Paul, D. 2.13.9 pr., apparently referencing the Praetor's Edict; also Pomponius, D. 17.2.59.1. Gaius, D. 17.2.72, also describes a liability for *culpa*, "i.e., idleness and carelessness" (*desidia atque neglegentia*), but not "extreme carefulness" (*exactissima diligentia*). Other late sources, including this Case, support this view: see Paul, D. 17.2.65.9; *Pauli Sent.* 2.16 (postclassical); Justinian, *Inst.* 3.25.9 (from Gaius). However, also

as in this Case, these sources concentrate on potential harm to common property or to the material interests of other partners: a common herd, land given over to joint cultivation, and so on. So it may be that a higher duty was imposed only when such property was involved. Recall the general "Benefit Principle" discussed in Case 64, where *societas* is mentioned. To some extent, for instance, a bailment element is present when one partner's property is consigned to another. What should the Classical rule have been with regard to such property? It's worth noting that a partner who harmed common property might also be liable in delict for wrongful loss: Ulpian, D. 17.2.47.1.

If this limitation is correct, a partner's liability for *culpa* may not have extended to, for instance, conduct of partnership business with third parties. Should it have? See the following Case. Is it fair to say (as Gaius does in the fragment cited earlier) that: "Anyone who takes on a less than diligent partner has only himself to blame"?

2. Liability for *Custodia*? The logic in section 2 of this Case may strike you as more than a bit strange. Ulpian starts out by deriving from Celsus a partner's liability for *dolus* and *culpa*. Then he goes on to say that if "one person promised a skill or services . . . obviously here there is liability also for *culpa*" (*nimirum ibi etiam culpa praestanda est*). But what does the "also" mean, if the partner is already liable for *culpa*? And the following sentence ("But if a partner harmed common property, he [even] more allows that *culpa* is at issue here.") has the same problem. Romanists have long supposed that Justinian's compilers altered this text, and that Ulpian established an even higher liability for *custodia*, namely that a partner in these two situations was liable for all property loss short of unavoidable force; the compilers then replaced *custodia* with *culpa*, in line with their general view that this should be the limit on liability (see Justinian, *Inst.* 3.25.9). What do you think? Should one partner be liable to the others for lack of skill if he holds himself out as having that skill, or for enhanced responsibility if he deals with common property?

3. Liability and *Bona Fides*. At least in this fragment as it is preserved, Ulpian, without further explanation, links the personal liability of partners to the good faith action on partnership. What is the legal connection between the two ideas?

4. Limits on Liability. The liability of *socii omnium bonorum* was restricted to what they could afford, with no account taken of money owed to them but still unpaid: Ulpian, D. 42.1.16. However, Ulpian, D. 17.2.63 pr., citing Sabinus, restricts the liability of all types of partners "to what they are able

to do, or to what they do not deceitfully obstruct their own ability to do," i.e., their liability is usually restricted to their means to pay. Ulpian justifies this by arguing that: "*societas* has a certain inherent law of brotherhood, *ius fraternitatis*." Is this justification sufficient?

CASE 172: Liability for One's Slaves

D. 17.2.23.1 (Ulpianus libro trigesimo ad Sabinum)

Idem quaerit, an commodum, quod propter admissum socium accessit, compensari cum damno, quod culpa praebuit, debeat, et ait compensandum. Quod non est verum, nam et Marcellus libro sexto digestorum scribit, si servus unius ex sociis societati a domino praepositus neglegenter versatus sit, dominum societati qui praeposuerit praestaturum nec compensandum commodum, quod per servum societati accessit, cum damno: et ita divum Marcum pronuntiasse, nec posse dici socio: "Abstine commodo, quod per servum accessit, si damnum petis."

Ulpian in the thirtieth book *On Sabinus*:

He (Pomponius) asks whether the profit accruing because a partner has been admitted should be offset by the loss he causes through his fault (*culpa*). He says it should be offset, but that is incorrect. For Marcellus also writes, in book 6 of his *Digests*, that if one partner's slave was set in charge of the partnership by his owner and (then) acted carelessly, the owner who set him in charge is liable to the partnership, nor should the profit accruing to the partnership through the slave be offset by the loss; and so, too, the deified Marcus (Aurelius) determined. Nor can a partner be told: "If you claim (compensation for) loss, surrender (through offset) the profit that accrued through the slave."

Discussion

1. **Offset of Gains with Losses.** Although the situation described by Marcellus is not entirely clear, the likeliest scenario is that a number of free persons formed a partnership and one partner then placed his slave in charge of partnership business. The slave made money for the partnership (the profit), but also caused it some loss through his carelessness (*neglegentia*). (The nature of the loss, *damnum*, is unfortunately indeterminate, but it probably involved damage to common property.) The question raised by Marcellus, and partially answered also by the pronouncement of Marcus Aurelius, is this: If the other partners seek their shares of the profit, must this profit be offset by the loss the slave caused?

   The answer is no. The slaveowner must make up the loss, thereby replenishing the common fund; and afterward the other partners can take their shares. The implication is that the slaveowner is liable for his slave's act, ostensibly because it was he who picked the slave for this role (*culpa in eligendo*); compare Discussion 2 on Case 153, and also Ulpian, D. 17.2.19, 21. Do you get the logic behind this decision? How does this logic carry over into the hypothetical posed by Pomponius, in which a partner himself causes the loss through his *culpa*? Compare Paul and Ulpian, D. 17.2.25–26.

CASE 173: Compensation for Partnership Debts

D. 17.2.27 (Paulus libro sexto ad Sabinum)

Omne aes alienum, quod manente societate contractum est, de communi solvendum est, licet posteaquam societas distracta est solutum sit. Igitur et si sub condicione promiserat et distracta societate condicio exstitit, ex communi solvendum est: ideoque si interim societas dirimatur, cautiones interponendae sunt.

Paul in the sixth book *On Sabinus*:

All debt that was contracted while the partnership continued must be paid from the common fund (*de communi*), even if it has to be paid after dissolution of the partnership. Therefore if he (a partner) promised under a condition and the condition occurred after the partnership was dissolved, it must be paid from the common stock; and so, if a partnership is dissolved in the meantime, guarantees (*cautiones*) should be interposed (for eventual payment of the debt).

Discussion

1. "Debt." Ulpian, D. 50.16.213.1: "Debt (*aes alienum*) is what we owe to other people." In this Case, Paul intends all the legitimate debts owed by the partnership to third parties, even if they were arranged by individual partners. As he says, these debts remain the partnership's even if they do not become due until after its dissolution. In practical terms, the third-party creditor who became entitled to collect when the condition occurred would seek it from the partner who made the promise, and, if payment was declined, would sue that partner, not the partnership as an entity, nor other partners individually. But the debt would ultimately be paid from the partnership's common fund, which might well require contributions from the other partners or, if the common fund had already been distributed, from the ex-partners. In this sense, the common fund can have a "virtual" existence even while the partnership lasts (see Discussion on Case 170) and extending beyond it.

2. Some Examples. In D. 17.2.65.14, Paul describes a partnership in which the common fund consists of money held by one partner, while a second holds none of it. So Paul determines, a third partner who sues *pro socio* must direct his suit only against the partner holding the money. After the claimant is paid (assuming his claim is legitimate), "all the partners can sue for what is owed to each from the remainder." That is, the third partner's claim for recompense has priority over all the partners' claims to their shares. Is this consistent with the present Case?

   What happens if the holder of the common fund makes use of it for non-partnership purposes? Paul, D. 17.2.67.2, discusses a partner who lends common fund money at interest to a third party. If he lent it on behalf of the partnership, he must share the interest from the loan; but if on his own account, he can keep the interest but bears the risk of the principal being lost. Does this outcome make sense? Compare Pomponius, D. 17.2.59.1: "Any loss a partner sustains from gambling or adultery he will not recover from the common fund. If, indeed, a partner incurs some loss through our deceit (*dolo nostro*), he may reclaim it from us."

After the partnership's dissolution, a partner's contribution to the common fund cannot be recovered by an action *pro socio* because there is no longer a partnership; but the partner can use the action for division of property: Paul, D. 17.2.65.13; see also D. 10.3.1.

CASE 174: Compensation for Expenses

D. 17.2.52.4: (Ulpianus libro trigensimo primo ad Edictum)

4. Quidam sagariam negotiationem coierunt: alter ex his ad merces comparandas profectus in latrones incidit suamque pecuniam perdidit, servi eius vulnerati sunt resque proprias perdidit. Dicit Iulianus damnum esse commune ideoque actione pro socio damni partem dimidiam adgnoscere debere tam pecuniae quam rerum ceterarum, quas secum non tulisset socius nisi ad merces communi nomine comparandas proficisceretur. Sed et si quid in medicos impensum est, pro parte socium agnoscere debere rectissime Iulianus probat. Proinde et si naufragio quid periit, cum non alias merces quam navi solerent advehi, damnum ambo sentient: nam sicuti lucrum, ita damnum quoque commune esse oportet, quod non culpa socii contingit.

Ulpian in the thirty-first book *On the Edict*:

Some men formed a cloth business. One of them, while traveling to buy goods, met up with brigands and lost his own money; his slaves were wounded, and he lost his own property (as well). Julian says that the loss is shared, and so by the action on partnership (*pro socio*) the (other) partner should take responsibility for half of the money and also of.other things that the partner would not have taken with him had he not traveled to buy goods on the common account. But also if there was some expense on doctors, Julian quite rightly approves the (other) partner taking responsibility for a share. Hence if something was lost in a shipwreck, both (partners) experience loss if the goods were not usually conveyed except by ship. For just as profit must be shared, so too (must) such loss as does not occur because of a partner's fault (*culpa*).

Discussion

1. The Victim of Brigandage. Gangs of brigands (*latrones*) the jurists treat as a form of *vis maior*, "higher force," that individuals cannot successfully resist: e.g., Gaius, D. 13.6.18 pr.; Maecian, D. 35.2.30 pr.; so also the emperor Alexander, C. 4.34.1 (234). (It is reasonable to infer that this was an enduring problem in the Roman empire.) The cloth buyer who was waylaid lost his own property, including money presumably intended for the purchase as well as for travel expenses, as well as other personal property; and his slaves were also wounded in the attack. Ulpian, citing Julian, makes the other partner liable to the victim for half of all of these losses, including the slaves' medical expenses. Is Julian presuming that the partners had agreed on an even division of losses? What is the meaning of "things that the partner would not have taken with him had he not traveled to buy goods on the common account"? Is the test here simply a "but for" one, such that, for instance, the victim's baggage is included? Or must the property be clearly related to the partnership?

Pomponius, D. 17.2.60.1, citing Labeo, posits that a partner in a slave-trading venture was wounded when the slaves attempted to escape and the partner resisted. Labeo's view is that the partner cannot charge his medical expenses to the partnership "because the expenditure, although made because of the partnership, is not for the partnership" (*quia id non in societatem, quamvis propter societatem impensum sit*). Here, it seems, "but for" causation is not enough. Is this holding consistent with the present Case? Could the partner argue that his attempt to stop the escape was essential to the partnership's goals?

Compare Ulpian, D. 17.2.52.15 (a partner traveling on partnership business can receive compensation for the cost of fares and for hotel or stable outlays, plus the hire of pack animals and carts for himself, his baggage, and his goods); Paul, D. 17.2.67.2 (he also is compensated for interest paid on necessary loans, or the interest lost if he pays with his own money).

CASE 175: Ending a Partnership

Gaius, *Institutiones* 3.151–154

151. Manet autem societas eo usque, donec in eodem <con>sensu perseuerant; at cum aliquis renuntiauerit societati, societas soluitur. sed plane si quis in hoc renuntiauerit societati, ut obueniens aliquod lucrum solus habeat, ueluti si mihi totorum bonorum socius, cum ab aliquo heres esset relictus, in hoc renuntiauerit societati, ut hereditatem solus lucri faciat, cogetur hoc lucrum communicare; si quid uero aliud lucri fecerit, quod non captauerit, ad ipsum solum pertinet. mihi uero, quidquid omnino post renuntiatam societatem adquiritur, soli conceditur. 152. Soluitur adhuc societas etiam morte socii, quia qui societatem contrahit, certam personam sibi eligit. 153. Dicitur etiam kapitis deminutione solui societatem, quia ciuili ratione kapitis deminutio morti coaequatur; sed utique si adhuc consentiant in societatem, noua uidetur incipere societas. 154. Item si cuius ex sociis bona publice aut priuatim uenierint, soluitur societas. . . .

Gaius in the third book of his *Institutes*:

151. A partnership lasts so long as they continue with the same agreement. But if one (partner) renounces the partnership, it is dissolved. Obviously, if one renounces the partnership in order that he alone have some impending profit— e.g., if a partner in entire estates (*socius totorum bonorum*), when he has been left as heir from someone, renounces his partnership with me so that he alone profits from the inheritance—he is forced to share the profit with me. But if he otherwise profits, he alone acquires what he does not obtain (deceitfully). But whatever is acquired after the partnership is renounced is allotted to me alone.

152. Additionally, a partnership is also dissolved by a partner's death, since a person contracting a partnership chooses a specific person for himself. 153. It is also said that a partnership is dissolved by change in citizen status (*capitis deminutio*), since by Civil Law reasoning a change in citizen status is equivalent to death; still, if the parties still agree on the partnership, a new partnership is held to arise (in that event). 154. Likewise, if one partner's property is publicly or privately sold, the partnership is dissolved. . . .

Discussion

1. **Renunciation.** Paul, D. 17.2.1 pr.: "A *societas* can be entered either permanently, i.e., for their lifetime, or for a period of time or from a time or under a condition." However, during its existence it is terminated, as Paul indicates, by a partner's death (see later discussion), but also by one partner "renouncing" the partnership. (On opportunistic renunciation, see the following Case.) In section 151 Gaius ties renunciation closely to cessation of the agreement, *consensus*, on the basis of which the partnership was originally formed; so also Diocletian and Maximian, C. 4.37.5 (294); Justinian, *Inst.* 3.25.4. However, if the partnership involved more than two

persons, would Gaius allow for its more or less automatic renewal through the agreement of the remaining partners (see 153)? Renunciation cannot be barred through the terms on which the *societas* was formed, and it is effective even when it is made at an inopportune time, although it may result in liability: Ulpian, D. 17.2.14, citing Pomponius; Paul, D. 17.2.65.3–6. Obviously, a partnership is also dissolved if the partners fall into irreconcilable disagreement, *dissensus*: Paul, D. 17.2.65.3.

Renunciation is not a formal legal act; it may be accomplished fairly casually, for instance through one's representative such as a *procurator* (see Chapter VII.C): Paul, D. 17.2.65.7–8.

2. Death. Paul, D. 17.2.65.9, elaborates Gaius' point: "By one partner's death a *societas* is dissolved even though it was formed with everyone's *consensus* and the other partners survive, unless they agreed otherwise in forming the *societas*. A partner's heir does not succeed him; but subsequent gain from the common fund must be provided to the heir, who is also liable for (the decedent's) deceit and fault (*dolus et culpa*) in prior acts." (The "unless" clause is probably interpolated.) Are you convinced by Gaius' rationale for this rule, that the other partner or partners chose the decedent for himself? Why should the death of one partner automatically lead to the dissolution of the entire partnership? Partners were actually barred from agreeing that the eventual heir of one of them could join the partnership: Pomponius, D. 17.2.59 pr.; Ulpian, D. 17.2.35.

What might be thought of as a partner's "civil death"—his loss of freedom or citizenship, or his bankruptcy—has the same consequence; see also Modestinus, D. 17.2.4.1. Ulpian, D. 17.2.58.2, citing Julian, has an interesting discussion of the possible complexities that can arise from a change in a partner's status. A partnership is also ended if one partner sued another *pro socio*: see Discussion 3 on Case 169.

The abiding question, in this long list of ways in which partnerships could come to an untimely end (see also Ulpian, D. 17.2.63.10), is whether the Roman law of *societas* founders on its overt, highly individualistic voluntarism, the belief that individual resolve should be the fundamental, or at least the dominant, factor in constructing the law. The counterargument is mainly one of practicality, that business organizations are thereby rendered transient and vulnerable to chance. What do you think?

CASE 176: Untimely Renunciation

D. 17.2.65.3–5 (Paulus libro trigensimo secundo ad Edictum)

3. Diximus dissensu solvi societatem: hoc ita est, si omnes dissentiunt. Quid ergo, si unus renuntiet? Cassius scripsit eum qui renuntiaverit societati a se quidem liberare socios suos, se autem ab illis non liberare. Quod utique observandum est, si dolo malo renuntiatio facta sit, veluti si, cum omnium bonorum societatem inissemus, deinde cum obvenisset uni hereditas, propter hoc renuntiavit: ideoque si quidem damnum attulerit hereditas, hoc ad eum qui renuntiavit pertinebit, commodum autem communicare cogetur actione pro socio. Quod si quid post renuntiationem adquisierit, non erit communicandum, quia nec dolus admissus est in eo. 4. Item si societatem ineamus ad aliquam rem emendam, deinde solus volueris eam emere ideoque renuntiaveris societati, ut solus emeres, teneberis quanti interest mea: sed si ideo renuntiaveris, quia emptio tibi displicebat, non teneberis, quamvis ego emero, quia hic nulla fraus est: eaque et Iuliano placent. 5. Labeo autem posteriorum libris scripsit, si renuntiaverit societati unus ex sociis eo tempore, quo interfuit socii non dirimi societatem, committere eum in pro socio actione: nam si emimus mancipia inita societate, deinde renunties mihi eo tempore, quo vendere mancipia non expedit, hoc casu, quia deteriorem causam meam facis, teneri te pro socio iudicio. Proculus hoc ita verum esse ait, si societatis non intersit dirimi societatem: semper enim non id, quod privatim interest unius ex sociis, servari solet, sed quod societati expedit. Haec ita accipienda sunt, si nihil de hoc in coeunda societate convenit.

Paul in the thirty-second book *On the Edict*:

3. I held that partnership is dissolved by disagreement; this is true if they all disagree. But what if (only) one person renounces it? Cassius wrote that a person who renounces a partnership does indeed free his partners from himself, but does not free himself from them. This should be the rule, in any case, if the renunciation was made deceitfully (*dolo malo*); for instance, if we created a partnership of our entire estates (*omnium bonorum societas*) and an inheritance came to one person, on account of which he renounced. And so if in fact the inheritance brings loss, it is borne by the person who renounced; but by the action on partnership he is forced to share (any) profit. But if he acquired it after the renunciation, it will not have to be shared, since there is no *dolus* in this.

4. Likewise, if we enter into a partnership to buy something, and you then decide to buy it alone and therefore renounce the partnership in order to buy it alone, you will be liable for the extent of my interest. But if you renounce it because you disliked the purchase, you will not be liable even if I buy it, since there is no fraud here. This is Julian's view as well.

5. But in his *Posthumous Writings*, Labeo wrote that if one partner renounced a partnership at a time when (another) partner had an interest in the partnership's not

being dissolved, he is liable in an action on partnership. For if we create a partnership to buy slaves, and you then renounce it to me at a time when it is inconvenient to sell slaves, in that case you are liable in an action on partnership because you made my situation worse. Proculus says that this is correct if there was a partnership interest in their partnership not dissolving. For what is always protected is not the private interest of one partner, but the benefit to the partnership. These rules should be accepted unless they (the partners) agreed (otherwise) about this matter in forming the partnership.

Discussion

1. Opportunism and Continuing Liability. Paul gives two examples. The first concerns a *societas omnium bonorum* in which the partners share their entire estates; one partner learns that he has received, although he has not yet accepted, a fat inheritance, and he repudiates the partnership so he can keep it all for himself. If the inheritance is in fact profitable, he is obliged to share it even though the partnership has already ended; but if the inheritance is overburdened with debt, he bears the loss himself. How does this illustrate Cassius Longinus' maxim that: "a person who renounces a partnership does indeed free his partners from himself, but does not free himself from them"? Is the partnership also dissolved as to the remaining partners?

   The second and more telling example involves a partnership to buy something (say, a work of art being sold at auction), where one partner then repudiates in order to buy it for himself; his conduct is treated as fraud (*fraus*) and he is then liable for the other party's interest. But this would not be true if the partner simply had second thoughts about the desirability of the purchase—in which case, of course, presumably he would not then buy it. The central question, therefore, is whether the repudiator's conduct can be described as *dolus*, a deceitful attempt to seize advantage that properly belongs to the partnership. As elsewhere Julian is also cited as observing, much here may depend on whether the original agreement to cooperate is interpreted as an actual *societas*, rather than just a casual coalescence of desires: Ulpian, D. 17.2.52 pr.

   In many circumstances, however, a partner may be justified in pursuing his own interests when renouncing the partnership. Some examples are given by Ulpian and Pomponius, D. 17.2.14–16 pr.: failure of a condition for the partnership; the injurious conduct of another partner; not receiving enjoyment of the benefit that the partnership was formed to provide; or the necessity of going abroad on state business.

2. Ill-Timed Renunciation. Even when renunciation is justified, it may come at a time when the erstwhile partnership was already executing its plan

in reliance on the repudiating partner's participation, so that the other partners suffer loss as a consequence. In section 5, Paul, citing Labeo and Proculus, requires the repudiator to pay compensation for this loss, so long, at any rate, as a "partnership interest" in repudiation not occurring can be identified; the interests of the partnership take priority over those of individual partners. Likewise, if the partnership had a definite term and a partner renounced before the term had expired, the repudiator receives no subsequent profit but is responsible for his share of any resulting loss unless his renunciation arose out of some necessity; Paul, D. 17.2.65.6. Paul suggests that this early repudiation is deceitful (*dolus*) unless justified.

PART C

Mandate (*Mandatum*)

A mandate (*mandatum*) is, in principle, a request by one party (the mandator) that another party (the mandatary) perform a gratuitous act on the mandator's behalf. If the mandatary agrees to perform, the contract becomes binding on both parties. At least in theory, the performance has to be gratuitous, in the sense that the mandatary does not receive pay for the service (which would be *locatio conductio*). However, the parties understand, at least tacitly, that the mandatary will be reimbursed for any expenses in carrying out the service, and that the mandator will have a right to the proceeds from the service, as well as a claim if the service is not rendered or is performed unacceptably. Thus the contract is bilateral, although it does not result from a true exchange in the way that the other consensual contracts normally do.

The essentially gratuitous nature of mandate meant that it normally arose from an agreement between friends, who were most commonly social equals; and this theme of friendship, *amicitia*, is often emphasized (e.g., Cicero, *Rosc. Amer.* 111; Paul, D. 17.1.1.4). Many of the legal rules for mandate closely reflect this presumption of friendship and social equality. However, the jurists gradually broadened the concept of mandate until it came to include what we would describe as professional employment, where a highly skilled professional (e.g., a teacher, lawyer, or doctor) received, not pay, but an "honorarium" that in theory is only incidentally connected to the service rendered. In late Classical law the emperors even allowed the professional to bring suit for this payment, although not under the action on mandate. Since such a professional acts not only on the mandator's behalf, but also on his or her own behalf, the required standard of performance is correspondingly raised. The gratuitous contract of mandate has little significance in modern law, although it still survives in Civil Law systems. It had, however, long-lasting influence on legal conceptions of professional employment.

The gradually widening concept of mandate was also instrumental in the later juristic recognition of the *procurator* as a mandatary; see Chapter VII.C.

CASE 177: "On the Mandator's Behalf"

Gaius, *Institutiones* 3.155–156, 162

155. Mandatum consistit, siue nostra gratia mandemus siue aliena; itaque siue ut mea negotia geras siue ut alterius, mandauerim, contrahitur mandati obligatio, et inuicem alter alteri tenebimur in id, quod uel me tibi uel te mihi bona fide praestare oportet. 156. Nam si tua gratia tibi mandem, superuacuum est mandatum; quod enim tu tua gratia facturus sis, id de tua sententia, non ex meo mandatu facere debes; itaque si otiosam pecuniam domi tuae <te> habentem hortatus fuerim, ut eam faenerares, quam<uis> iam ei mutuam dederis, a quo seruare non potueris, non tamen habebis mecum mandati actionem. Item si hortatus sim, ut rem aliquam emeres, quamuis non expedierit tibi eam emisse, non tamen tibi mandati tenebor. et adeo haec ita sunt, ut quaeratur, an mandati teneatur, qui mandauit tibi, ut Titio pecuniam faenerares. Seruius negauit: non magis hoc casu obligationem consistere putauit, quam si generaliter alicui mandetur, uti pecuniam suam faeneraret. <Sed> sequimur Sabini opinionem contra sentientis, quia non aliter Titio credidisses, quam si tibi mandatum esset. . . . 162. In summa sciendum <est, si faciendum> aliquid gratis dederim, quo nomine si mercedem statuissem, locatio et conductio contraheretur, mandati esse actionem, ueluti si fulloni polienda curandaue uestimenta <dederim> aut sarcinatori sarcienda.

Gaius in the third book of his *Institutes*:

155. A mandate (*mandatum*) arises if we give a mandate on our own behalf or on that of a third party (*nostra gratia sive aliena*). So if I give a mandate that you administer either my affairs or a third party's, an obligation of mandate is contracted, and we will both be liable to each other for what I must provide to you, and you to me, in good faith (*bona fides*).

156. If I give you a mandate on your own behalf (*tua gratia*), the mandate is superfluous, since what you do on your own behalf you should do based on your own belief, not on my mandate. So if you had money lying idle at home and I urged you to lend it at interest, you will not have an action on mandate against me even if you lent it to someone from whom you cannot recover it. Likewise, if I urged you to buy something, I will not be liable to you on mandate even if it does not profit you to have bought it.

To such an extent is this true that question arises whether someone is liable on mandate if he gives you a mandate to make an interest-bearing loan to Titius. Servius said no; he thought that no more obligation arises in this case than if a general order is given that he lend money at interest. But we adopt the contrary view of Sabinus, because you would not have lent to Titius unless you received the mandate. . . .

162. In conclusion it should be noted that whenever I give the performance of something without pay, as to which, if I had set a wage, lease and hire (*locatio*

conductio) would be contracted, there is an action on mandate, e.g., if I give clothing to a fuller for cleaning or tending, or to a cloth-mender for mending.

The Problem

I'm moving from one apartment to another, and I ask for your unpaid help with the move. You agree, but you then either fail to show up on moving day (you forgot), or you do show up but carelessly damage my furniture while moving it. Are you liable to me in either case?

Discussion

1. **The Basic Model.** Gaius notes a number of characteristics of traditional mandate: (i) it takes the form of an "order" (often directly called a *iussum*, e.g., Case 183) coming from the mandator who directs it to the mandatary; (ii) the order instructs the mandatary to do something; (iii) this act benefits the mandator; (iv) the mandatary accepts the order (Gaius omits this step, but *consensus* is obviously required; see Paul, D. 17.1.1 pr. 22.11); (v) thereby a bilateral contract is created (the reciprocal duties are spelled out in subsequent Cases); and (vi) the mandatary's performance is gratuitous, "without pay" (*gratis*) beyond, as we shall see, compensation for the mandatary's expenses in executing the order. The order can encompass almost any act (even one granting discretion to the mandatary: Neratius, D. 17.1.35; Celsus, D. 17.1.48.1–2; Paul, D. 17.1.3.1, 59.6), but the jurists most frequently speak of selling or buying for the mandator, or of supporting his or a third party's financial transactions as a surety or otherwise.

   Before going further, it is worth pausing to consider this model closely. Why would the Romans have made mandate a major consensual contract? What sort of social and economic system does it imply? (For instance, does it seem likely that mandate arose in a world where markets were still weak, and where persons therefore often depended on help from friends? See Paul, D. 17.1.1.4.) Note also the very sharp distinction Gaius draws in section 162 between mandate and *locatio conductio operarum*: often the very same act may be involved, but the crucial difference between the two contracts is the presence or absence of "a fee" (*merces*). See also Case 168 for a possible explanation. But numerous problems obtrude. For instance, is Gaius assuming that the fuller will clean your clothes for free?

   After you puzzle all this out, go on to think about how the jurists could proceed if they wished to adapt this contract to the needs of a more sophisticated and complex economy.

2. **"My Interest" and "Your Interest."** Gaius' model uses an analysis of the "interest" underlying a contract. In principle, the mandate will usually be

in the "interest" of the mandator, even if it does not materially benefit him (this concept of "interest" is much broader than Anglo-American consideration as a contract requirement). In a fuller analysis from a later edition of his *Institutes,* Gaius (D. 17.1.2.1) gives examples: I order you to manage my affairs, or buy a farm for me, or go surety on my debt. In each case, the mandate, if accepted, produces a binding contract.

On the other hand, a mandate that is solely in "your interest" (e.g., that the mandatary should invest money in buying land rather than lending at interest, or vice versa: Gaius, D. 17.1.2.6; Justinian, *Inst.* 3.26 pr.-6) does not lead to a binding contract; the mandate is treated as simple "advice" (*consilium*), which, so long as it is not offered maliciously, results in no liability for the mandator, since, as Gaius explains, "everybody is free to examine for themselves whether advice is advantageous to them." Deceitful advice, however, may result in an action on the delict of *dolus*: Ulpian, D. 4.3.9.1, 50.17.47 pr. Even without *dolus,* Ulpian, D. 17.1.6.5, suggests that "my interest" is present if you would not have acted except for my advice.

More complicated is a third situation where the mandate is in the interest of a third party (*gratia aliena*): for instance, a mandate to buy a farm for that person (Gaius, D. 17.1.2.2). In this situation the third-party beneficiary cannot enforce the contract (compare Case 10 on stipulation; also Q. Mucius, D. 50.17.73.4, for contracts generally). But the jurists regularly treat the arrangement as at least binding between mandator and mandatary (e.g., Ulpian, D. 17.1.6.4), meaning that the mandatary can recover any expenditures. Ulpian, D. 17.1.8.6, states that the action on mandate will only lie when the mandator also begins to have an interest in the mandate—an interest that might possibly arise only after the mandate is given. Conversely, says, Ulpian, if the mandator's interest lapses, so too does the action. In general, then, it looks like the mandator's interest is required for the action, even if this interest overlaps with that of the mandatary or a third party. Thus, for example, the mandate will be binding if, for instance, I order you to lend money at interest to a third party who needs it to complete a transaction with me: Gaius, D. 17.1.2.4.

3. **Problem.** Ulpian, D. 17.1.16, citing Celsus, gives the following problem: Aurelius Quietus was accustomed to spend part of every year at the Ravenna country estate of his doctor. Quietus gave the doctor a mandate to build, on the doctor's Ravenna estate and at the doctor's expense, a ball court, a sauna, and other aids to health. If the doctor carries out this mandate, can he recover his expenses from Quietus? Must the doctor deduct any increase in the estate's value?

CASE 178: The Duty to Perform the Mandate

D. 17.1.6.1–2 (Ulpianus libro trigensimo primo ad Edictum)

1. Si cui fuerit mandatum, ut negotia administraret, hac actione erit conveniendus nec recte negotiorum gestorum cum eo agetur: nec enim ideo est obligatus, quod negotia gessit, verum idcirco quod mandatum susceperit: denique tenetur et si non gessisset. 2. Si passus sim aliquem pro me fideiubere vel alias intervenire, mandati teneor et, nisi pro invito quis intercesserit aut donandi animo aut negotium gerens, erit mandati actio.

Ulpian in the thirty-first book *On the Edict*:

1. If someone is given a mandate that he manage affairs, he will be liable through this action (on mandate), nor is suit properly brought against him on (unauthorized) administration of affairs (*negotiorum gestio*). For he is not obligated (only) because he administered affairs, but because he undertook a mandate; and so he is liable also if he failed to administer them.

2. If I allowed someone to be a surety (*fideiussor*) for me or otherwise to assume liability (by taking on my obligations), I am liable on mandate, and, unless someone assumes liability for an unwilling person either with a donative intent or by managing his affairs (without authorization), there will be an action on mandate.

Discussion

1. Executing the Mandate. Once the mandate has been accepted, the mandatary is expected to fulfill it promptly, and, as Ulpian says in section 1, failure to do so may result in liability; see also Paul, D. 17.1.22.11. Further, as Paul, D. 17.2.20 pr., observes, the mandate must be carried out in its entirety: "From the mandate, nothing (of the profit) must remain with the mandatary, just as he should not suffer loss if (e.g.) he cannot collect money he loaned (on the basis of the mandate)." However, so long as the mandatary uses best efforts, he need not actually succeed in carrying out the request: Papinian, D. 17.1.56.4.

The mandator's duty is distinguished from unauthorized administration of affairs (*negotiorum gestio*), in which the administrator acts without an order (or subsequent ratification) from the beneficiary; Roman law treats this as non-contractual, a form of what came to be called quasi-contract; see Chapter VIII.A. The distinction here is, it appears, largely the work of later Classical jurists, who clarified what had earlier been a significant ambiguity in legal procedure.

It should be stressed, once again, that the mandatary is not an agent for the mandator. When a mandatary purchases on behalf of a mandator, for instance, the sale produces in itself no legal relationship between the seller and the mandator, but only one between the seller and the mandatary; and this is so even if the seller was aware that the mandatary was acting at the mandator's request. As we shall see, ways were eventually found to circumvent most of the awkwardness of this legal construction, but it remained an obstacle to economic complexity.

2. **Suretyship.** On going surety (usually by stipulation), see Cases 41–46. There is a considerable difference here from Gaius' basic model in the preceding Case, in that the mandator is described as passively "allowing" (*patior*) the mandatary to act as a surety, with no mention of his giving a direct order (only his awareness is presumed). Accordingly, Ulpian's attention shifts to the mandatary's motives, which, so long as his intent was not to make a gift to the principal or to aid him without an order, result in a binding contract of mandate; compare Papinian, D. 17.1.53 (the mandator "is present and does not object"). Can an order be implied simply from the circumstances of a relationship?

3. **Lapse of a Mandate.** Time may intervene between issuance of a mandate and its execution by the mandatary. During this interval, so long as "the matter is still fresh" (*re integra*; i.e., neither party has relied as of yet), the mandate may lapse without further liability on either side if, e.g., the mandator revokes it, the mandatary renounces it, or either party dies: Gaius, *Inst.* 3.159–160; Ulpian, D. 17.1.12.16 (citing Marcellus); Paul, D. 17.1.22.11; *Pauli Sent.* 2.15.1. To be sure, the mandatary might already have acted while unaware of the mandator's revocation or death, but the jurists permit a reliance claim in this situation; see Gaius, 3.160, as well as Paul, D. 17.1.26 pr.

Under limited conditions, a mandatary might renounce a mandate even after the matter was no long "fresh," e.g., in the event of ill health, or if the mandator brings a frivolous lawsuit against him, or for some other just cause: Hermogenianus and *Pauli Sent.*, D. 17.1.23–25. If unjustified, however, the mandatary's abandonment of performance is a breach of contract, resulting in liability for the mandator's interest; but, if the mandatary finds he cannot perform, he must still inform the mandator as soon as possible so that substitute performance can be arranged; Gaius, D. 17.1.27.2.

CASE 179: The Standard of Performance

D. 17.1.8.9–10 (Ulpianus libro trigensimo primo ad Edictum)

9. Dolo autem facere videtur, qui id quod potest restituere non restituit: 10. Proinde si tibi mandavi, ut hominem emeres, tuque emisti, teneberis mihi, ut restituas. Sed et si dolo emere neglexisti (forte enim pecunia accepta alii cessisti ut emeret) aut si lata culpa (forte si gratia ductus passus es alium emere), teneberis. Sed et si servus quem emisti fugit, si quidem dolo tuo, teneberis, si dolus non intervenit nec culpa, non teneberis nisi ad hoc, ut caveas, si in potestatem tuam pervenerit, te restituturum. Sed et si restituas, et tradere debes. Et si cautum est de evictione vel potes desiderare, ut tibi caveatur, puto sufficere, si mihi hac actione cedas, ut procuratorem me in rem meam facias, nec amplius praestes quam consecuturus sis.

Ulpian in the thirty-first book *On the Edict*:

9. A person who does not deliver up what he can deliver appears to act deceitfully (*dolo*). 10. So if I gave you a mandate to buy a slave, and you made the purchase, you will be liable to me for delivering him (to me). But also if you deceitfully (*dolo*) failed to buy him—e.g., if you accept money to let a third party buy him—or if (you acted) with gross fault (*lata culpa*)—e.g., if you are influenced by a third party to let him buy him—you will be held liable.

But also if the slave you bought then fled, you will be liable if (this occurred) through your *dolus*. If *dolus* is not involved, nor fault (*culpa*), you will not be held liable except for giving a guarantee (*cautio*) that you will deliver him (to me) if he comes (again) into your power.

Further, if you deliver him, you should also hand him over (to me); and if a guarantee is given (by the seller) about eviction, or you can seek that the guarantee be given to you, I think it suffices if you cede (the guarantee) to me through this action (on mandate), so that you make me a *procurator* for my own business; nor will you be liable for more than you would obtain (if you yourself had sued).

Discussion

1. Liability for Deceit (*Dolus*). Because mandate is a gratuitous contract, one might expect that, as with deposit (Case 64), the conduct expected of a mandatary would be set quite low, at avoidance of deliberate misconduct (*dolus*). Even in the late Classical period, there are sources that take this default position: Modestinus, *Collatio* 10.2.3 ("But a trial on mandate involves *dolus*, not also fault, *culpa*"); so also Alexander, C. 2.12.10 (227 CE). However, some juristic holdings, like this one from Ulpian, indicate particularly egregious fault could be counted as *dolus*. Compare Ulpian, D. 17.1.29 pr., arguing that "lax carelessness (*dissoluta neglegentia*) is tantamount to deceit" when a surety is sued and fails to plead an exculpatory defense.

2. Liability for Non-Deliberate Fault (*Culpa*). Some situations, however, seem to cry out for more rigorous conduct from the mandatary. Paul, D. 17.1.22.11, discusses a hypothetical in which the mandatary is to buy something and fails to do so "through his own fault (*culpa*), not that of a third party"; the mandatary is liable, since, if he was merely inconvenienced by having to execute the mandate, he could have begged off. Similarly, Papinian, D. 20.1.2, of a possibly misbehaving surety. Whether Classical jurists ever proceeded to impose on mandataries a general standard of *culpa* (as Ulpian, D. 50.17.23, states) remains uncertain, since it is quite possible the Digest compilers have altered Classical texts. What is your view on what a mandatary's liability should be?

3. The Guarantee against Eviction. The seller normally gives this express warranty through a stipulation; see Case 47. At the end of this fragment, the mandatary (and not the mandator) is treated as the purchaser who either receives the warranty or should receive it, but who has no personal interest beyond the confines of the mandate. In later Classical law a third party in this intermediate position quite frequently "cedes" the right to the warranty to the principal through a process called *cessio*; see Case 215. Here this is accomplished when the mandatary appoints the mandator as his judicial representative "for his (the mandator's) own benefit" (*in rem suam*), meaning that the mandator can then bring the claim more or less directly: *Fragmenta Vaticana* 317. See Cases 212–213.

CASE 180: Overstepping the Mandate

Gaius, *Institutiones* 3.161

Cum autem is, cui recte mandauerim, egressus fuerit mandatum, ego quidem eatenus cum eo habeo mandati actionem, quatenus mea interest inplesse eum mandatum, si modo implere potuerit; at ille mecum agere non potest. Itaque si mandauerim tibi, ut uerbi gratia fundum mihi sestertiis C emeres, tu sestertiis CL emeris, non habebis mecum mandati actionem, etiamsi tanti uelis mihi dare fundum, quanti emendum tibi mandassem; idque maxime Sabino et Cassio placuit. Quod si minoris emeris, habebis mecum scilicet actionem, quia qui mandat, ut C milibus emeretur, is utique mandare intellegitur, uti minoris, si posset, emeretur.

Gaius in the third book of his *Institutes*:

If I gave a valid mandate to someone who overstepped the mandate, I have an action on mandate against him for the extent of my interest in his fulfilling the mandate, provided he could fulfill it; but he cannot sue me (for expenses). So if I gave you a mandate to buy, e.g., a farm for one hundred thousand sesterces, and you bought it for one hundred fifty thousand sesterces, you will not have an action on mandate against me even if you wish to give the farm to me for as much as I gave you the mandate to buy it for; and this was the view especially of Sabinus and Cassius.

But if you buy for less, you will obviously have an action against me, since someone who mandates to buy for one hundred thousand is in any case understood to give a mandate to buy for less if possible.

Discussion

1. Sticking to the Mandate. Paul, D. 17.1.5 pr.-1 is emphatic: "The boundaries of the mandate must be carefully maintained; for a person who has exceeded them seems to have done something else and is liable if he does not fulfill what he undertook." The example he gives (D. 17.1.5.2) is a mandate to you to purchase Seius' house for 100,000 sesterces; if you instead purchase Titius' house, which is worth a great deal more, for 100,000 or even less, you are not held to have fulfilled the mandate. The mandatary's guess about what the mandator would want, had he known of this unusual opportunity, is not good enough; the mandatary cannot substitute his own judgment. In practice, however, this simple rule causes difficulties.

2. A Mandated Purchase. The mandatary was ordered to purchase a farm for 100,000, and purchased it for 150,000. No one whatsoever will require the mandator to compensate him for the full purchase price. But what if the mandatary only seeks recompense for 100,000? Gaius' discussion in this Case reflects a school controversy in the early Empire (reported by Justinian, *Inst.* 3.26.8). The Sabinians, Gaius' own school, stuck strictly to

the letter of the mandate and disallowed an action when the mandate had been violated. But, as Gaius, D. 17.1.4, shows, he was also aware of, and may even have come to approve, the "more liberal" Proculian view that allowed the mandatary to recover up to the set price. Is this the right outcome? Justinian thought so. But Paul, D. 17.1.3.2, points to a problem with the Proculian view: it is unfair that the mandator does not have an action against a mandatary who is unwilling to give up the difference, but does have one with him if he is willing to do so. Gaius, D. 17.1.41, proposes a solution: "An action on mandate can be just one-sided; for if a mandatary exceeds the mandate, he himself has no action on mandate, but the mandator has one against him." Convinced?

If the mandatary gets a better price than the mandator had set, the problem appears to vanish, since the mandator benefits; so also Paul, D. 17.1.5.5. How is this situation different from the previous hypothetical, where the mandatary buys a different but better house for the mandated price or even less?

3. **A Mandated Sale.** Suppose that I give you a mandate to sell my farm for 100,000 sesterces, but you sell it for 90,000 and convey the farm to the buyer. Can I recover the farm? Paul, D. 17.1.5.3, indicates that I can get it back unless the mandatary makes up the difference to me and holds me completely harmless. But *Pauli Sententiae* 2.15.3 (postclassical) takes a different view: "by the action on mandate the amount of the price will be made whole (by the mandatary); for the view that the sale is dissolved did not prevail." This text has been much discussed; does it give the preferable view? What if the mandatary is bankrupt?

4. **Varying the Mandate.** Julian, D. 17.1.33, has the following problem: A person is asked to go surety for the debt of a mandator. The mandatary accepts, but (by stipulation) guarantees less than the full amount of the debt. Julian says that he is nonetheless liable at least for the smaller sum. He contrasts a situation in which the mandatary accepts for a larger sum than he had been asked to do. In that event, "the mandator is deemed to have relied on his credit (only) up to the amount that was asked for." Is this distinction in accord with other sources cited in this Case?

5. **Shame (*Infamia*).** Condemnation in mandate led to a mandatary being branded with *infamia*; see Discussion 3 on Case 62.

CASE 181: Claims of the Mandatary

D. 17.1.12.9 (Ulpianus libro trigensimo primo ad Edictum)

Si mihi mandaveris, ut rem tibi aliquam emam, egoque emero meo pretio, habebo mandati actionem de pretio reciperando: sed et si tuo pretio, impendero tamen aliquid bona fide ad emptionem rei, erit contraria mandati actio: aut si rem emptam nolis recipere: simili modo et si quid aliud mandaveris et in id sumptum fecero. Nec tantum id quod impendi, verum usuras quoque consequar. Usuras autem non tantum ex mora esse admittendas, verum iudicem aestimare debere, si exegit a debitore suo quis et solvit, cum uberrimas usuras consequeretur, aequissimum enim erit rationem eius rei haberi: aut si ipse mutuatus gravibus usuris solvit. Sed et si reum usuris non relevavit, ipsi autem et usurae absunt, vel si minoribus relevavit, ipse autem maioribus faenus accepit, ut fidem suam liberaret, non dubito debere eum mandati iudicio et usuras consequi. Et (ut est constitutum) totum hoc ex aequo et bono iudex arbitrabitur.

Ulpian in the thirty-first book *On the Edict*:

If you give me a mandate that I buy something for you, and I buy it with my own money, I will have an action on mandate to recover the price. But also if (I buy it) with your money, but spend something in good faith (*bona fide*) in order to buy the object, a counteraction on mandate will lie; and likewise, if you refuse to accept the purchased object. And similarly if you give some other mandate and I have expenses on it.

I will obtain not only what I spent, but interest (on it) as well. But (a jurist held) that interest should be granted not just after default (*mora*); the *iudex* should assess (interest) if he (the mandatary) collects (money) from his own debtor and pays (it to a third party in executing the mandate), when he could obtain high interest (by not collecting from the debtor), since it will be very fair to take account of this. Likewise, if he paid after borrowing at high interest.

Further, I do not doubt that he should also obtain interest through a suit on mandate if he did not release the principal debtor (the mandator) from interest, but does not himself receive the interest; or if he did release (the mandator) from interest at a lower rate but himself took a loan at a higher rate. As has been laid down (by the emperor), the *iudex* will decide all this in accord with what is right and proper (*aequum et bonum*).

Discussion

1. Duties of the Mandator. As Ulpian says, the mandator is generally expected to accept the mandatary's satisfactory performance and to assume the rights that were created for him; see, e.g., *Pauli Sent.* 2.15.2 (absent timely revocation, it is immaterial that the mandator no longer wants performance; compare Case 178). Certainly the mandator's principal duty is to compensate

the mandatary for his expenses. In the case of a mandate to buy something, for instance, the mandatary may have *bona fide* expenses in arranging and executing the sale. Gaius, D. 17.1.27.4, notes that it is irrelevant that the mandator could have saved money by arranging the transaction himself. But surely the mandatary's expenses ought at least to be commercially reasonable, no?

Ulpian, D. 17.1.29.1, discusses a situation in which the mandatary (as a surety) pays off the mandator's alleged debt because the mandator had not informed him that the supposed debt never actually arose. What outcome if the mandatary sues the mandator for compensation?

2. **Raising Money to Execute the Mandate.** The mandatary was not necessarily on his own; the mandator might initially give him all or part of the required funds. But the legal sources do suggest that otherwise mandataries did occasionally face problems arranging the finances. In Ulpian's scenario, the mandatary either (i) calls in a debt and uses the proceeds for the mandate, thereby forgoing interest from the debt; or (ii) borrows the money at interest; or (iii) uses his own money to pay and thereby loses interest on it, but has not freed the mandator from paying interest to him on this amount; or (iv) has in fact freed the mandator from paying interest to him, but borrows money at a still higher rate, the liability being for the difference. As is evident, these "expenses" mainly involve lost opportunities, and the law gives a *iudex* discretion to impose interest on them not only for when a mandator is in default for non-payment of expenses, but from when they were incurred.

What if executing the mandate is simply beyond the mandatary's means? In a bravura passage, Paul, D. 17.1.45 pr.-5, goes off from this hypothetical: You buy a farm on my mandate; can you sue me to get me to pay you before you yourself have paid the farm's price? Paul says yes; the action can compel me as the mandator to assume the payment obligation directly to the seller, in return for your ceding to me any actions on purchase against the seller. (All this is necessary because of the absence of agency.) The same is true if you are managing the mandator's affairs and make a promise to one of the mandator's creditors. As the passage continues, Paul gives a different answer when, on my mandate, you undertake a lawsuit for me; then you must await the outcome. What explains this difference?

CASE 182: Limits on the Mandatary's Claims

D. 17.1.26.6–7 (Paulus libro trigensimo secundo ad Edictum)

6. Non omnia, quae impensurus non fui<sse>t, mandator<i> imputabit, veluti quod spoliatus sit a latronibus aut naufragio res amiserit vel languore suo suorumque adpraehensus quaedam erogaverit: nam haec magis casibus quam mandato imputari oportet. 7. Sed cum servus, quem mandatu meo emeras, furtum tibi fecisset, neratius ait mandati actione te consecuturum, ut servus tibi noxae dedatur, si tamen sine culpa tua id acciderit: quod si ego scissem talem esse servum nec praedixissem, ut possis praecavere, tunc quanti tua intersit, tantum tibi praestari oportet.

Paul in the thirty-second book *On the Edict*:

6. He will not claim from the mandator all that he would not have spent (if he had not received the mandate): e.g., that he was robbed by bandits or lost property in a shipwreck, or paid something when he was overcome by his own illness or that of his household; for these things should be ascribed more to accident (*casus*) than to the mandate. 7. But when you bought a slave on my mandate and he stole from you, Neratius says that in an action on mandate you will obtain the slave's noxal surrender to you, provided that this occurred without your fault (*culpa*). But if I knew the slave was like this and gave no warning so that you could take precautions, then (you will obtain) the extent of your interest.

Discussion

1. **The Unlucky Mandatary.** A mandatary undertakes travel in order to execute a mandate, and on the way is robbed by bandits or is shipwrecked. Can the resulting losses be recovered from the mandator? Paul says no, but how sound is his reasoning? Why should it not matter that the losses would not have occurred except for the mandate? The sense seems to be that truly accidental losses should be borne by the person on whom they first fall; but the list of such accidents seems quite broad. Ulpian, D. 50.17.23, reasons as follows: "Accidents and the deaths of animals occurring without (anyone's) *culpa*, the flights of slaves who are not normally kept under guard, robberies, uprisings, conflagrations, floods, and pirate attacks are no one's responsibility." Is this convincing?

   Paul, D. 46.1.67, gives an even more startling example. A mandatary, litigating on behalf of a mandator, loses a lawsuit because of a judge's clearly erroneous decision. The mandatary cannot recover the adverse judgment from the mandator, "for it is fairer that the injustice done to you remain with you rather than being transferred to another." Is an incompetent judge like a conflagration?

2. The Theftuous Slave. Section 7 gives what seemed to the jurists a more difficult problem: a mandatary, acting on the mandate, purchases a slave who steals from him. If the mandator was unaware of his propensity to steal, Neratius gives the mandatary a "noxal" action against the mandator on the slave's misdeed, meaning that the mandator must either pay to the mandatary the damages for theft or surrender the slave (mandator's choice); of course, if the damages are higher than the slave's worth, the mandator will surrender the slave, meaning that the mandatary will not be fully compensated.

Africanus, D. 47.2.62.5, reports his teacher Julian's views on this hypothetical. Julian holds that the innocent mandator should be fully (not just noxally) liable, on the ground that the mandatary "would not have incurred the loss had he not undertaken the mandate" (i.e., just the logic rejected in the previous example). Julian concedes it may seem unfair to burden the mandator for the acts of his purchased slave; nonetheless, he thinks it "still more unfair that a duty causes loss to someone who undertook it on behalf of a contractual partner, not for his own benefit."

CASE 183: Training a Slave

D. 17.1.26.8 (Paulus libro trigensimo secundo ad Edictum)

Faber mandatu amici sui emit servum decem et fabricam docuit, deinde vendidit eum viginti, quos mandati iudicio coactus est solvere: mox quasi homo non erat sanus, emptori damnatus est: Mela ait non praestaturum id ei mandatorem, nisi posteaquam emisset sine dolo malo eius hoc vitium habere coeperit servus. Sed si iussu mandatoris eum docuerit, contra fore: tunc enim et mercedem et cibaria consecuturum, nisi si ut gratis doceret rogatus sit.

Paul in the thirty-second book *On the Edict*:

On a mandate from a friend, an artisan bought a slave for ten (thousand sesterces) and taught him a craft; he then sold him for twenty, which he was forced to pay (to the mandator) in an action on mandate. Soon thereafter, he was condemned to pay the buyer because the slave was unhealthy. Mela says that the mandator will not be liable to him for this unless, without his deceit (*dolus malus*), the slave began to have this defect after he bought him. But if he (the craftsman) taught him on the mandator's order, the opposite will be true; for then he will obtain a fee (*merces*) as well as the cost of (the slave's) board, unless he was asked to teach for free.

Discussion

1. A Curious Decision. The facts are a good deal less than clear, perhaps because of later abridgement. The artisan (*faber*) received a mandate from a friend and, based on it, purchased a slave for 10,000 sesterces. This mandate must have been in the mandator's interest, since the artisan was later condemned in an action on mandate (Case 177). Perhaps the slave was a sort of investment, but he remained for a time with the artisan, who taught him a craft and then sold him for double the initial purchase price, with the increase in value presumably stemming from the slave's training. In the lawsuit that followed, the artisan must have asserted at least a right to the "value added" (the 10,000), while the mandator sought the full resale price. Is the mandator's position justified?

   The answer appears to depend on whether the mandator had requested the training, and, if so, whether it was supposed to be for free or not. If the training was requested and not gratis, then the artisan is entitled to a fee (*merces*) for his training and also to basic board for the slave during the time the artisan was holding him. Is this ruling consistent with the two previous Cases on compensation? The implication of the final sentence, however, is that the teaching was actually not requested and so the mandatary has no claim to the increase in the slave's value; it accrues to the mandator, like a gift. (But the mandatary may perhaps sue on unauthorized administration of affairs, see Chapter VIII.A, since the training was plainly useful.)

All this is further complicated by the discovery, after the mandatary's resale, that the slave was unhealthy, with the result that the slave's buyer sought a remedy from the mandatary (see Cases 143–144). The mandatary has already restored the 20,000 repurchase price to the mandator; can he now get recompense from the mandator for this further charge? Paul cites the Augustan jurist Fabius Mela as ruling against the mandatary unless the defect arose after the original purchase, and even then only if it did not result from the mandatary's deliberate misconduct (*dolus*). So if the slave was defective already at the time of the original purchase, the mandator bears that risk as against the mandatary. Why is the mandatary's liability confined to *dolus*?

See if you can straighten out the finances. Does Paul assume, e.g., that the artisan used the mandator's money to pay for the initial purchase?

CASE 184: The Honorarium

D. 11.6.1 pr. (Ulpianus libro vicensimo quarto ad Edictum)

Adversus mensorem agrorum praetor in factum actionem proposuit. A quo falli nos non oportet: nam interest nostra, ne fallamur in modi renuntiatione, si forte vel de finibus contentio sit vel emptor scire velit vel venditor, cuius modi ager veneat. Ideo autem hanc actionem proposuit, quia non crediderunt veteres inter talem personam locationem et conductionem esse, sed magis operam beneficii loco praeberi et id quod datur ei, ad remunerandum dari et inde honorarium appellari: si autem ex locato conducto fuerit actum, dicendum erit nec tenere intentionem.

D. 50.13.1.10 (Ulpianus libro octavo de omnibus tribunalibus):

In honorariis advocatorum ita versari iudex debet, ut pro modo litis proque advocati facundia et fori consuetudine et iudicii, in quo erat acturus, aestimationem adhibeat, dummodo licitum honorarium quantitas non egrediatur: ita enim rescripto imperatoris nostri et patris eius continetur. . . .

Ulpian in the twenty-fourth book *On the Edict*:

Against a land surveyor, the Praetor established an action on the facts (*in factum*). We ought not to be deceived by this person; for it is in our interest not to be deceived in the declaration of a land measure, should, say, either a dispute arise about boundaries, or a buyer or seller wish to know the measure of land being sold. Therefore he established this action because the Republican jurists did not believe there was a lease and hire (*locatio conductio operarum*) with such a person; rather, his work is provided as a favor (*beneficii loco*), and what is given to him is given as recompense (*ad remunerandum*), and so it is called an honorarium. Further, if suit were brought on lease and hire (*ex locato conducto*), it must be held that the claim fails.

Ulpian in the eighth book on *All Tribunals*:

As regards the honoraria of advocates, the *iudex* should pay attention to setting the amount according to the type of lawsuit, the advocate's skill, and the custom of the venue and court in which he will bring suit, so long as the amount does not exceed the permitted honorarium. This is contained in a rescript of our emperor and his father (Caracalla and Septimius Severus, 198–212). . . .

The Problem

   Sempronia asks Cassius to represent her as her advocate in an upcoming trial. Preparation will take substantial amounts of time and effort, but Cassius is unwilling to accept a fee because he regards paid advocacy as demeaning. Can the two parties arrive at some legally binding arrangement whereby Sempronia can pay Cassius without it being seen as a fee?

Discussion

1. **Must Mandate Always Be Gratuitous?** High and late classical sources repeatedly insist that mandate must be gratuitous: Javolenus, D. 17.1.36.1; Gaius, *Inst.* 3.162 (Case 177); Paul, D. 17.1.1.4 ("A mandate is void unless gratuitous."); and this remains the view of Justinian, *Inst.* 3.26.13. But other sources, all from the late Classical period, speak of mandataries receiving a form of compensation, usually called an *honorarium* or *salarium* apparently to distinguish it from the fee (*merces*) associated with *locatio conductio operarum* (see Case 168): Papinian, D. 17.1.7 (Case 207); Severus and Caracalla, C. 4.35.1 (198–211 CE); Ulpian, D. 17.1.6 pr.; and Paul, D. 17.1.26.8 (the previous Case). Most importantly, the mandatary had a legal right to this agreed-upon honorarium and is described as seeking it not through an action on mandate, but *extra ordinem*, that is, in imperial courts that operated outside the ancient courts of the Praetor and other traditional magistrates. All these sources can probably be reconciled if we suppose that the older Republican courts, by not enforcing a claim to compensation within the action on mandate, maintained the illusion that mandate was entirely gratuitous.

2. **The "Higher Professions."** However, it is unlikely that all workers were able to use this dodge. Ulpian, D. 50.13.1 pr.-8, lists a variety of professions that are allowed to seek compensation through imperial courts: the teachers of the liberal arts, including rhetoricians, grammarians, and geometers (but not teachers of philosophy); doctors, obstetricians, ear and throat specialists, and dentists (but not witch doctors or exorcists); and, by custom, elementary school teachers, archivists, stenographers, accountants, and secretarial aides (but not other ordinary workers or craftsmen). This list probably grew by accretion. Already the emperors Marcus Aurelius and Verus (161–169 CE; in Ulpian, D. 50.13.1.9) had ordered imperial officials to accord all these professions the same consideration.

   To this list must be added courtroom advocates, *advocati*, who ever since the early Empire had usually been allowed to charge (Tacitus, *Ann.* 11.5–7). Ulpian in this Case sets down the criteria imperial judges are to use in determining their honoraria. Advocates may not, however, take a share in a damage award: Ulpian and Papinian, D. 17.1.6.7, 7; Ulpian, D. 50.13.1.12. (Professors of law, by contrast, are excluded altogether from seeking pay: D. 50.13.1.5.)

   Finally, there is the case of surveyors (*mensores agrorum*), on whom Romans heavily relied for settling boundaries; through the Praetor they had established a cause of action, including a lawsuit for compensation, independent of *locatio conductio*. In the first passage, Ulpian explores the logic and social values behind this lawsuit, which probably influenced later law in other areas.

Although the general course of this development is relatively clear, much less certain is whether practitioners of these various professions were actually treated as mandataries. The clearest source suggesting that they were is Ulpian, D. 17.1.6 pr.: "If an honorarium is given as recompense, there will be an action on mandate." (*Si remunerandi gratia honor intervenit, erit mandati actio.*) The wording is admittedly obscure, but indicates, at the very least, that the two means to recovery stood side by side, one on mandate and one for the fee, as in a rescript of Severus and Caracalla, C. 4.35.1 (198–211 CE). Scholars therefore usually assume that the practitioners of these professions entered a contract of mandate with their clients, and certainly that is a reasonable inference.

It remains puzzling, though, that surviving legal sources never unequivocally describe any of these professionals as suing or being sued in mandate. On the contrary, Ulpian, D. 9.2.7.8, citing Proculus, states that a doctor who operates unskillfully on a slave may be sued either on the delict (under the Lex Aquilia) or on the lease of a job (*ex locato*), with no mention of mandate; and Gaius, D. 9.3.7, holds that when a free person is injured by something dropped or poured from an upper-story window, damages include not just medical expenses, but also "the wages paid to doctors" (*mercedes medicis praestitae*), again probably pointing to *locatio conductio*. The deeper question, then, is whether, if a doctor administered care with no fixed fee but at most just a strong tacit expectation of an honorarium, there was any contractual action if he failed to carry through or misperformed.

What confuses the situation still further is that, for their part, in the late Classical period *procuratores* were definitely considered mandataries, although they could also sue for compensation *extra ordinem*; see Chapter VII.C. Both Papinian, D. 17.1.7 (Case 207), and C. 4.35.1 clearly refer to *procuratores*, not to practitioners of the higher professions. No entirely convincing explanation has been devised for this discrepancy.

Whatever the answer, the idea that "higher professions" can work without their compensation being contractually linked to their work has a long subsequent life in the law. Still today, for instance, professors are often invited to give lectures in exchange for honoraria, without any supposition that this is a direct wage. Similarly, ministers officiate at marriages or funerals and are compensated by honoraria. Such payments are today regularly treated as wages for tax purposes. Is this just a holdover from an earlier patriarchal era?

CHAPTER VI

Filling in the Gaps

Contracts Created Through One Party's Performance

The Roman system of recognized contract types was clearly inadequate to catch many agreements deserving of legal protection. Although the jurists construed the recognized contracts as broadly as possible, some agreements did not receive legal protection even under their analysis. Part A of this Chapter presents two Cases in which the jurists discuss "boundary problems"—agreements that are difficult to fit into the recognized system. We have encountered similar discussions in earlier Cases.

Case 186, at least as it is preserved to us (it has signs of later alteration), suggests one possible solution to this problem: the creation of new contract types through the Praetor's Edict. However, after the beginning of the Roman Empire, Praetors were, it seems, increasingly reluctant to create new causes of action. Instead, they granted limited protection, on a case-by-case basis, to plaintiffs deemed particularly worthy. The Praetors did so through what are called actions "on the facts," *actiones in factum*. Because the *formulae* for such actions contained a brief "preamble" describing the particular circumstances, they are also called actions "with a preamble," *actiones praescriptis verbis*.

As it appears (although the details are obscure and still very controversial), by the end of the first century CE the jurists, making use of the theory of *causa* originally devised for stipulation, had formed a generalized theory governing many such anomalous agreements. If an informal agreement involving exchange between two parties fell outside the system of recognized contract types, and one party had already performed while the other had not, the performing party was given a procedural choice: either to demand back the rendered performance (through a theory of unjustified enrichment; see Chapter VIII.B), or, in the alternative, to claim his interest in the defendant's unrendered counter-performance. Because this second claim was treated as effectively valid in Civil Law, the pertinent action at least eventually came to be called an *actio civilis in factum* ("Civil action on the facts"), and it was no longer considered to be dependent on the Praetor's discretion. Many of the rules developed for recognized contracts were applied by analogy to these anomalous agreements of exchange.

The result, to be sure, is far less than satisfactory, in that it protects the performing party only after its own performance has been fully rendered. But the historian of Common Law will recognize a similarity between this Roman remedy and the early Common Law action on debt, which paved the way for the generalized Anglo-American theory of contract. For the jurists, the next step would presumably have been to allow one party to an exchange agreement to bring suit not only if he or she had already performed, but also if performance had only been tendered. Unfortunately, Roman law never quite reached this position.

A Casebook on the Roman Law of Contracts. Bruce W. Frier, Oxford University Press. © Oxford University Press 2021. DOI: 10.1093/oso/9780197573211.003.0007

PART A

Boundary Problems in Roman Contract Law

CASE 185: Sale or Lease?

Gaius, *Institutiones* 3.145–147

145. Adeo autem emptio et uenditio et locatio et conductio familiaritatem aliquam inter se habere uidentur, ut in quibusdam causis quaeri soleat, utrum emptio et uenditio contrahatur an locatio et conductio, ueluti si qua res in perpetuum locata sit. quod euenit in praediis municipum, quae ea lege locantur, ut, quamdiu [id] uectigal praestetur, neque ipsi conductori neque heredi eius praedium auferatur; sed magis placuit locationem conductionemque esse. 146. Item si gladiatores ea lege tibi tradiderim, ut in singulos, qui integri exierint, pro sudore denarii XX mihi darentur, in eos uero singulos, qui occisi aut debilitati fuerint, denarii mille, quaeritur, utrum emptio et uenditio an locatio et conductio contrahatur. et magis placuit eorum, qui integri exierint, locationem et conductionem contractam uideri, at eorum, qui occisi aut debilitati sunt, emptionem et uenditionem esse; idque ex accidentibus apparet, tamquam sub condicione facta cuiusque uenditione aut locatione. iam enim non dubitatur, quin sub condicione res ueniri aut locari possint. 147. Item quaeritur, si cum aurifice mihi conuenerit, ut is ex auro suo certi ponderis certaeque formae anulos mihi faceret et acciperet uerbi gratia denarios CC, utrum emptio et uenditio an locatio et conductio contrahatur. Cassius ait materiae quidem emptionem uenditionemque contrahi, operarum autem locationem et conductionem; sed plerisque placuit emptionem et uenditionem contrahi. atqui si meum aurum ei dedero mercede pro opera constituta, conuenit locationem conductionem contrahi.

Gaius in the third book of his *Institutes*:

145. Purchase and sale (*emptio venditio*) and lease and hire (*locatio conductio*) seem to have so great a degree of kinship between them that in some cases question often arises whether the contract is sale and purchase or lease and hire: for instance, if a property is leased out in perpetuity. This occurs with the property of municipalities, which is leased out on terms that the property not be taken away from the tenant or his heir so long as the land tax (*vectigal*) is paid.

146. Likewise, if I supply gladiators to you on terms that for their toil I receive twenty denarii per man for those who come out unharmed, but one thousand denarii for those killed or disabled, question arises whether the contract is purchase and sale or lease and hire. The more prevailing view is that the contract is lease and hire for those who come out unharmed, but sale for those who were killed or disabled. This emerges from what happens, as though a sale or lease of each man was made under a condition. For there is now no doubt that a thing can be sold or leased under a condition.

147. Question also arises if I agree with a goldsmith that he make me rings, of a specified weight and form, from his own gold, and that he receive, e.g., two hundred denarii: is the contract purchase and sale or lease and hire (of labor)? Cassius says that the contract is purchase and sale of the material, but lease and hire of the labor (*operae*). But most jurists hold that the contract is purchase and sale. However, if I gave him my own gold and set a fee (*merces*) for his labor, it is agreed that the contract is lease and hire (of labor).

Discussion

1. Mixed Contracts. This Case discusses three instances where it can be problematic whether a plaintiff should sue on the basis of a sale or a lease (*locatio*). As Gaius indicates, difficulty can arise at the time of contract formation in three ways: the contract is either sale or lease depending on its details (the gold rings); or it is then legally indeterminate, with its handling determined by a future event (the gladiators); or it is nominally a lease but effectively a sale, unless the buyer defaults on future agreed-upon payments, in which case it reverts to being a lease (the lease of public land in perpetuity). Make sure that you understand the difference between these three situations.

   When a goldsmith made rings from his own gold, Cassius Longinus, writing ca. 50 CE, apparently remained alone in his thoroughly misguided attempt to divide a *bona fides* contract into two parts; see Gaius, D. 19.2.2.1; Pomponius/Q. Mucius, D. 34.2.34 pr. The early Byzantine jurist Theophilus (3.24.4, page 359.13–15 Ferrini) reconstructs Cassius' reasoning: the action on purchase would lie if the gold was defective; the action on hire of labor, for defects in workmanship. Why might other jurists have resisted such a view? (Still odder is Cassius' understanding of this contract as for labor, *operae*, rather than for a job, *opus*; see Chapter V.A.4, especially Case 168. A goldsmith, *aurifex*, is a skilled artisan.) The general principle is carried over also into building construction: Paul, D. 19.2.22.2 (the contractor, in the process of building, conveys the materials to the landowner; one contract).

2. Rent to Own (Hire-Purchase). Javolenus and Paul (D. 19.2.20.2 to 22 pr.) deal with another type of mixed contract that is still much in use today. A would-be buyer takes the object of sale under the condition that he will rent it until the price has been fully paid. Such an arrangement has the advantage of giving the buyer/lessee the object in the interim—something he or she may perhaps require in order to make the payments. The jurists treat this contract as a lease that ripens into a sale upon full payment; so, if the tenant or lessee defaults on the rent, the sale never materializes and the seller/lessor can reclaim the object. But there is one big difference: it can be inferred from Ulpian, D. 43.26.20 (which actually deals with *precarium*,

see Case 70) that, so long as the buyer/lessee kept up payments, the seller/ lessor could not eject him from the leased property, i.e., the buyer/lessee had a sort of property right. This is different from the rule in an ordinary lease; see Cases 147–148. What explains the difference in treatment?

3. Other Informal Promises. A few other informal promises were made enforceable by the Urban Praetor even though they lay outside the contract system, usually for reasons of practicality. Here are the main examples:

- *Constitutum debiti*: An informal promise to pay a debt that was already in existence, whether one's own debt (effectively novating one's prior obligation, whatever the source) or the debt of another (an informal suretyship). The main sources are in D. 13.5 and C. 4.18.

- *Receptum*: Three unilateral undertakings were made actionable, apparently because they involved likely reliance by the promisees. They are a promise by a private arbitrator to settle a dispute (*receptum arbitri*; see D. 4.8, C. 2.55); a formal promise by a banker to pay a client's debt on a certain date (*receptum argentarii*; see Justinian, C. 4.18.2 pr. (531)); and an implied promise of safeguard when a shipowner or an innkeeper accepted custody or transport of goods (*receptum nautae, cauponis*; see D. 4.9).

- *Compromissum*: A bilateral agreement to submit a dispute to an arbitrator, if accompanied by reciprocal stipulations that the losing party would pay a penalty if the judgment went unfulfilled. See D. 4.8, esp. Ulpian, 4.8.11.4.

CASE 186: Brokerage

D. 19.3.1 (Ulpianus libro trigesimo secundo ad Edictum)

pr. Actio de aestimato proponitur tollendae dubitationis gratia: fuit enim magis dubitatum, cum res aestimata vendenda datur, utrum ex vendito sit actio propter aestimationem, an ex locato, quasi rem vendendam locasse videor, an ex conducto, quasi operas conduxissem, an mandati. Melius itaque visum est hanc actionem proponi: quotiens enim de nomine contractus alicuius ambigeretur, conveniret tamen aliquam actionem dari, dandam aestimatoriam praescriptis verbis actionem: est enim negotium civile gestum et quidem bona fide. Quare omnia et hic locum habent, quae in bonae fidei iudiciis diximus. 1. Aestimatio autem periculum facit eius qui suscepit: aut igitur ipsam rem debebit incorruptam reddere aut aestimationem de qua convenit.

Ulpian in the thirty-second book on the Edict:

pr. The action on brokerage (*aestimatum*) was set up to remove doubt. For when an appraised object was given for sale, great doubt once arose as to whether there was an action on sale (*ex vendito*) because of the appraisal, or on lease (*ex locato*) on the theory that I am held to have let out the selling of the object (as a job), or on hire (*ex conducto*) on the theory that I hired labor (*operae*), or on mandate (to the broker).

It (therefore) seemed better to set up this action. For whenever there is uncertainty about the name of a contract, but agreement that an action be given, an action with a preamble (*actio praescriptis verbis*) on brokerage should be given, since this transaction was arranged in good faith (*bona fides*) under the Civil Law (*negotium civile*). Therefore everything I have held concerning the good faith actions is relevant here as well.

1. After appraisal, the person who undertook it (the broker) bears the risk (*periculum*); therefore he must return either the object intact or the appraised value they agreed upon.

The Problem
Aurelius has decided to sell his silver platter, but prefers not to do so directly, so he entrusts it to Mucius, a broker, who is instructed to find a buyer at a minimum price with Mucius to keep any additional price. On the way to market Mucius inadvertently loses the platter. Can Aurelius sue him, and, if so, for how much?

Discussion
    1. *Aestimatum*. In this contract, a person who wishes to sell something without himself making the sale entrusts it to a broker, who undertakes to return either the object or an agreed-upon appraisal (*aestimatio*) of its value. If all goes well, the broker will sell it for more than the appraised value and keep

any profit for himself. But, of course, the object may perish or be stolen before the broker can sell it. The broker accepts this risk, according to this Case. But Ulpian, D. 19.5.17.1, citing Labeo, distinguishes: if the owner initiated the transaction with the broker, then the owner bears the risk; if the broker, he bears it; if neither (they just agree), the broker is liable only for *dolus* and *culpa*. Is this solution better? (The owner also accepts a certain additional risk, of course, that the broker may vanish or may turn out to be judgment-proof.)

As Ulpian says, such an arrangement occasions difficulty because, while it is entirely unobjectionable in itself, it cannot easily be given a pigeonhole within the classical system of contracts. It is likely that the jurists debated the issue, with this Case giving only the outcome of the debate ("It seemed better"). Do any of the four alternatives in the *principium* seem completely plausible? In D. 19.5.13 pr., Ulpian canvasses yet another possibility, that the parties had formed a partnership (*societas*); he rejects this because the original owner and the broker do not share any profit. But at D. 17.2.44 he takes a more positive view of the *societas* possibility.

The outcome of this confusion was, as it seems, the creation of a separate action on brokerage, but the new action had many of the procedural characteristics of the exchange contracts discussed in the following Part. Indeed, it may well have served as a model for them.

2. A Related Problem. Ulpian, D. 19.5.19 pr., sets the following hypothetical: You request that I loan you money, but I lack the cash and instead give you property to sell and use the price as the loan. You either fail to sell the property, or you do sell it but do not take the money as a loan. What action should I bring?

PART B

Half-Executed Contracts of Exchange

CASE 187: Exchange and the Theory of *Causa*

D. 2.14.7 pr.-2, 4, 5 (Ulpianus libro quarto ad Edictum)

pr. Iuris gentium conventiones quaedam actiones pariunt, quaedam exceptiones. 1. Quae pariunt actiones, in suo nomine non stant, sed transeunt in proprium nomen contractus: ut emptio venditio, locatio conductio, societas, commodatum, depositum et ceteri similes contractus. 2. Sed et si in alium contractum res non transeat, subsit tamen causa, eleganter Aristo Celso respondit esse obligationem. Ut puta dedi tibi rem ut mihi aliam dares, dedi ut aliquid facias: hoc συνάλλαγμα esse et hinc nasci civilem obligationem. Et ideo puto recte Iulianum a Mauriciano reprehensum in hoc: dedi tibi Stichum, ut Pamphilum manumittas: manumisisti: evictus est Stichus. Iulianus scribit in factum actionem a praetore dandam: ille ait civilem incerti actionem, id est praescriptis verbis sufficere: esse enim contractum, quod Aristo συνάλλαγμα dicit, unde haec nascitur actio. . . . 4. Sed cum nulla subest causa, propter conventionem hic constat non posse constitui obligationem: igitur nuda pactio obligationem non parit, sed parit exceptionem. 5. . . . Idem responsum scio a Papiniano, et si post emptionem ex intervallo aliquid extra naturam contractus conveniat, ob hanc causam agi ex empto non posse propter eandem regulam, ne ex pacto actio nascatur. Quod et in omnibus bonae fidei iudiciis erit dicendum. Sed ex parte rei locum habebit pactum, quia solent et ea pacta, quae postea interponuntur, parere exceptiones.

Ulpian in the fourth book on the Edict:

pr. Of the agreements (*conventiones*) arising from the Law of Nations (*ius gentium*), some result in actions and some (only) in defenses.

1. Those that result in actions do not remain with their own (general) name ("agreements"), but pass under the name proper to the contract (*contractus*), e.g., purchase and sale, lease and hire, partnership, loan for use, deposit, and other such contracts.

2. However, even if a transaction does not pass as another contract, so long as it has an underlying cause (*causa*), Aristo elegantly responded to Celsus that there is an obligation (*obligatio*). For instance, I gave you something so that you give me something else, or I gave it so that you do something: this is an exchange (συνάλλαγμα), and from it there arises a Civil Law obligation (*civilis obligatio*).

And so I think that Mauricianus rightly criticized Julian in the following case: I gave you Stichus in order that you manumit Pamphilus; you manumitted (Pamphilus), and Stichus was (then) evicted (by his true owner). Julian writes that the Praetor should give an action on the facts (*in factum*); but he (Mauricianus) says that there is available a Civil action for an indefinite amount (*civilis incerti actio*), i.e., with a preamble (*praescriptis verbis*). For (he says) this is a contract, what Aristo calls an exchange (συνάλλαγμα), out of which an action arises. . . .

4. But when there is no underlying *causa*, it is agreed that an obligation cannot be established on the basis of the agreement. So a bare pact (*nuda pactio*) gives rise not to an obligation, but to a defense (*exceptio*). 5. . . . I know the same response (was given) by Papinian, that also if, at some time after a sale, something beyond the contract's nature is agreed, for this *causa* there is no action on purchase on account of the same rule, so that no action arises from a (bare) agreement. This must be held also in all *bona fides* trials. But on the defendant's side the agreement is relevant because those agreements that are later interposed also usually give rise to defenses.

Discussion

1. **The Contractual Hierarchy: Contracts Proper.** In this important Case (which, it is true, has often been suspected of postclassical manipulation), Ulpian distinguishes the legal effects of three types of "agreements" (*conventiones*). The highest category are agreements that belong within the traditional set of contracts (*contractūs*), contracts in the strict sense, that are specifically actionable as such. These are no longer just agreements, but "pass under the name proper" to the individual contract. Ulpian appears to be thinking mainly of informal contracts, but stipulations and other formal contracts, although embodied in outward trappings of ceremony, would undoubtedly also meet the test.

2. **Informal Exchange Agreements That Are Not Treated as True Contracts.** Ulpian's interest is primarily centered on this second class of agreements, to the extent that they are not technically contracts. If such agreements are bilateral (e.g., I promise to give X to you, and you promise to give Y to me), the reciprocal promises are said each to have *causa*, a "reason" or "cause" that, by the early second century (although the idea was still then controversial, as the disagreement between Aristo and Celsus shows), could make them enforceable as obligations (*obligationes*). The requirement of reciprocal *causae* distinguishes these bilateral agreements both from unilateral contracts like stipulation and from gratuitous contracts like mandate.

   But this enforcement was limited to situations where something more than just an exchange of promises had occurred. In Julian's example, one party has actually executed his promise (to manumit a slave), and it is only thereafter that he can demand performance or damages from his counterpart (see Paul, D. 19.5.5.3). In such circumstances, Julian permitted just a fact-specific discretionary action (*actio in factum*), but his contemporary Junius Mauricianus went further, calling the agreement a "contract" (note how loosely this word can be used) because of its robust exchange element; he refers to Aristo's use of the Greek word *sunallagma*, which the jurists understood as a bilateral agreement in which each party undertakes to provide something to the other. On this basis, Mauricianus, like later jurists, accorded to the aggrieved plaintiff a full-blown "Civil action" (*actio civilis*), with a formula expressing the basis of the claim through a preamble (*agere praescriptis verbis*). But the claim was no longer being treated as subject to the Praetor's discretion. (The terminology remained unstable, but Neratius, D. 19.5.6, and later jurists seem to prefer *actio civilis incerti*, "Civil action for an indefinite amount." "Innominate real contracts," the modern Romanist designation for such contracts, is both misleading and surpassingly ungainly.)

By this process, which seems to have taken place over about a half century, bargained-for exchange was finally given the legal recognition it deserves; for an effort at typology, see Paul, D. 19.5.5. By the end of the Classical period, however, the development was still rather constrained, especially, as we shall see, as to remedies. But make sure that you understand what happened. Why did the jurists require performance from one party before enforcement?

It is worth noting that barter, the exchange of an object for an object (Cases 77, 79), since it does not qualify as a contract of sale, is treated under Roman law through the rules for informal exchange agreements. See Case 191.

3. Informal Pacts (*Pacta*). We have already dealt with this subject in discussing sale: Cases 102–104. The general rule is stated by Ulpian in section 4–5 (and see also Ulpian, D. 19.5.15; Alexander, C. 2.3.10 [227 cE]): a pact that is "naked," in the sense of not being "clothed" with a *causa* justifying its enforcement (e.g., a purely donative promise), does not create an obligation. At best, such an agreement can only be used, if appropriate, as a defense against a claim.

CASE 188: Excavating Clay; Sowing a Field

D. 19.5.16 pr.-1 (Pomponius libro vicesimo secundo ad Sabinum)

pr. Permisisti mihi cretam eximere de agro tuo ita, ut eum locum, unde exemissem, replerem: exemi nec repleo: quaesitum est, quam habeas actionem. Sed certum est civilem actionem incerti competere: si autem vendidisti cretam, ex vendito ages. Quod si post exemptionem cretae replevero nec patieris me cretam tollere tu, agam ad exhibendum, quia mea facta est, cum voluntate tua exempta sit. 1. Permisisti mihi, ut sererem in fundo tuo et fructus tollerem: sevi nec pateris me fructus tollere. Nullam iuris civilis actionem esse Aristo ait: an in factum dari debeat, deliberari posse: sed erit de dolo.

Pomponius in the twenty-second book on Sabinus:

pr. You allowed me to excavate clay from your land, on condition that I refill the excavation; I excavated but did not refill. The question was: what action do you have? But it is settled law that a Civil action for an indefinite amount (*civilis incerti actio*) lies; and if you sold the clay (to me), you will sue on sale. But if, after excavating the clay, I refilled and you did not let me remove the clay (from your land), I may then sue for production (of the clay), since it became my property on being excavated in accord with your wish.

1. You gave me permission to sow on your farm and remove the crop; I sowed, but you did not let me remove the crop. Aristo says there is no action at Civil Law (*iuris civilis actio*), and that it can be debated whether one should be given on the facts (*in factum*). But there will be one for deceit (*dolus*).

Discussion

1. Can You Distinguish? Admittedly, the two situations look a lot alike: (i) A arranges with B to excavate clay from B's land, and promises to refill the excavation but does not do so; B is given an action for an indefinite amount (presumably, in the main, the cost of refilling); (ii) A arranges with B to sow crops on B's land and remove them (meaning harvest and carry them away); B does not permit A's removal of the crops; A does not have this action.

   There are a number of possible ways to explain the difference in outcome. In the first situation, it is A who does not fully perform his end of the bargain; in the second, it is B. Again, in the first situation B may perhaps gain some material benefit from the clay being removed and his land then restored; but in the second B does not share in any profit, so the arrangement looks decidedly more gift-like. And yet again, in the first situation A has already physically separated the clay from B's land, while in the second the crops are evidently still attached to B's land (see Javolenus, D. 33.2.42). Is A's sowing of the crop insufficient to create an obligation on B's part?

Without a stipulation, placing a binding condition on a gift (if that is what these two situations amount to) may have been difficult in Classical law, but an early postclassical constitution of Diocletian, C. 8.53.9 (293 CE), does allow for an action *praescriptis verbis* if such a condition goes unfulfilled after the gift is executed; see also Diocletian, C. 4.64.8 (294) and 8.53.22.1 (294).

The last sentence of the Case's *principium* appears to indicate that separation from the soil is important; the suit for production (*actio ad exhibendum*) required a defendant to produce in court movable property that was subject to litigation. But before their separation from the land, crops belong to the landowner; see, e.g., Paul, D. 41.1.48 pr. What would be the obstacle, in this unusual situation, to giving at least a discretionary action on the facts?

2. Alternatives. A's position, in the second situation, is not entirely desperate. Of course, in this case there can be no question of return to the status quo ante, as in Case 191, since the crops have long since been sown at A's expense. Aristo favors A suing on B's deceit (*actio de dolo*) in deliberately depriving A of the bargain's benefit. As W.W. Buckland correctly observes (*Text-Book* 522), "Neither of these remedies was enforcement. They undid what had been done, putting the parties, so far as might be, in the position in which they would have been if the agreement had never been made. What was needed was to put them, so far as might be, in the position in which they would have been had the bargain been completed." This latter was the aim of the *actio civilis incerti*: A should get the value of the harvested crops, not the value of the seed.

CASE 189: Approval; Sharing Oxen

D. 19.5.17.2–3 (Ulpianus libro vicesimo octavo ad Edictum)

2. Papinianus libro octavo quaestionum scripsit, si rem tibi inspiciendam dedi et dicas te perdidisse, ita demum mihi praescriptis verbis actio competit, si ignorem ubi sit: nam si mihi liqueat apud te esse, furti agere possum vel condicere vel ad exhibendum agere. Secundum haec, si cui inspiciendum dedi sive ipsius causa sive utriusque, et dolum et culpam mihi praestandam esse dico propter utilitatem, periculum non: si vero mei dumtaxat causa datum est, dolum solum, quia prope depositum hoc accedit. 3. Si, cum unum bovem haberem et vicinus unum, placuerit inter nos, ut per denos dies ego ei et ille mihi bovem commodaremus, ut opus faceret, et apud alterum bos periit, commodati non competit actio, quia non fuit gratuitum commodatum, verum praescriptis verbis agendum est.

Ulpian in the twenty-eighth book on the Edict:

2. In the eighth book of his *Questions*, Papinian wrote: "If I gave you something to inspect and you say you lost it, I have the action with a preamble (*actio praescriptis verbis*) as long as I do not know where it is; for, if I am sure it is in your house, I can bring an action for theft, or a *condictio* (on theft), or an action for production." On this view, if I gave someone a thing to inspect either for his own benefit or for both of us, I hold that, because of the (flow of) benefit (*utilitas*), there should be liability for both deceit and fault (*et dolus et culpa*), but not for risk (*periculum*). But if it was given solely for my benefit, (there is liability) only for *dolus*, since this is virtually a deposit.

3. My neighbor and I each had an ox. We agreed that, for ten days apiece, we would each lend the other an ox to do work (as a team); and an ox (then) perished while with one of us. The action on loan for use (*commodatum*) is unavailable since the loan was not gratuitous. But an action *praescriptis verbis* should be brought.

Discussion

1. Approval. In fragment 2, it appears that the recipient of the property was considering either buying it or, perhaps, just appraising it for a fee—in either case, both parties would have a strong interest in the arrangement. Ulpian analyzes the situation according to the usual rules on flow of benefit; see Chapter III.B in this volume. When the recipient "lost" the property (the infinitive *perdidisse* could also mean "destroyed"), Ulpian, after considering the possibility of theft, establishes the recipient's liability for deliberate or careless destruction. This would be the ordinary situation; try to construct circumstances in which only the giver or only the recipient would have an interest. (As to the latter, see Case 64 on deposit.) It is usually assumed that the *actio praescriptis verbis* is the same thing as the *actio civilis incerti*.

Ulpian, D. 19.5.20 pr., addresses a problem that he takes from Labeo: I have horses for sale and give them to you on a trial basis for three days; during the trial period, you use the horses in a horse race and win, but then decline to buy them. Labeo may have recommended an action on the particular facts (see Papinian, D. 19.5.1.1, where *civilem* is probably Justinianic), but Ulpian says it is more correct (*verius*) to sue *praescriptis verbis*. If the recipient returns the horses unharmed, what justifies his liability? How should it be measured?

2. **The Ox Team**. Two neighbors, each with an ox, agree to join them into a team they will use in alteration. One ox perishes while in the hands of its non-owner. Under what circumstances can the ox's owner succeed with an action *praescriptis verbis*? Why isn't the action on partnership (Chapter V.B) available?

CASE 190: A Complex Loan

D. 19.5.24 (Africanus libro octavo *Quaestionum*)

Titius Sempronio triginta dedit pactique sunt, ut ex reditu eius pecuniae tributum, quod Titius pendere deberet, Sempronius praestaret computatis usuris semissibus, quantoque minus tributorum nomine praestitum foret, quam earum usurarum quantitas esset, ut id Titio restitueret, quod amplius praestitum esset, id ex sorte decederet, aut, si et sortem et usuras summa tributorum excessisset, id quod amplius esset Titius Sempronio praestaret: neque de ea re ulla stipulatio interposita est. Titius consulebat, id quod amplius ex usuris Sempronius redegisset, quam tributorum nomine praestitisset, qua actione ab eo consequi possit. Respondit pecuniae quidem creditae usuras nisi in stipulationem deductas non deberi: verum in proposito videndum, ne non tam faenerata pecunia intellegi debeat, quam quasi mandatum inter eos contractum, nisi quod ultra semissem consecuturus esset: sed ne ipsius quidem sortis petitionem pecuniae creditae fuisse, quando, si Sempronius eam pecuniam sine dolo malo vel amisisset vel vacuam habuisset, dicendum nihil eum eo nomine praestare debuisse. Quare tutius esse praescriptis verbis in factum actionem dari, praesertim cum illud quoque convenisset, ut quod amplius praestitum esset, quam ex usuris redigeretur, sorti decederet: quod ipsum ius et causam pecuniae creditae excedat.

Africanus in the eighth book of his *Questions*:

Titius gave thirty (thousand sesterces) to Sempronius. They agreed that, from the return on this money, Sempronius would pay the land tax (*tributum*) that Titius was obligated to pay, with interest (on the money) reckoned at six percent; and that, if less was paid in taxes than the amount of this interest, he would return it (the surplus) to Titius, but that if more were paid, this would be deducted from the principal, or, if the total tax exceeded both principal and interest, Titius would pay Sempronius the excess. No stipulation was taken between them on this matter. Titius inquired by what action he could obtain from Sempronius the excess in interest above what he (Sempronius) had paid in taxes.

He (Julian) responded that interest is not owed on money lent unless this was expressed in a stipulation. But in the hypothetical case it should be noted that this should be considered less money lent at interest than a sort of mandate (*mandatum*) contracted between them, except for what he (Sempronius) would obtain beyond the six percent interest. But not even the claim for the principal itself is a claim for money lent, since, if Sempronius, without deceit (*dolus malus*), either lost the money or held it idle (uninvested), it should be ruled that (in a *condictio*) he owed nothing on this account.

So it is safer that an action *praescriptis verbis* on the facts be given, especially since their agreement was that what was paid in excess of the return from the interest be taken from the principal; this oversteps both the law and the nature of lending money.

The Problem

Sex. Caecilius Africanus, a student of Julian, sets out an intricate and absorbing problem. Titius entrusts HS 30,000 to Sempronius, with an informal agreement that Sempronius is to invest it at six percent annual return and use this income to pay Titius' land taxes. If the taxes are less than the six percent interest, Sempronius will pay Titius the excess (interest minus taxes); if the taxes are more than the six percent interest, Sempronius will pay the difference in taxes, but deduct this difference from the principal (which will, of course, probably lower future interest income). If the taxes come to exceed both the principal and the interest combined, Titius will compensate Sempronius for the difference. Had the money in fact been invested at six percent, the parties apparently intended for Sempronius to be acting gratuitously. The problem arose because Sempronius succeeded in getting an interest rate higher than six percent. Who gets the additional return?

Discussion

1. Using a Loan to Pay the Lender's Taxes. Sempronius claimed the additional return for himself, while Titius thought it was his; and the contract was silent on the matter. Julian interpreted the arrangement between Titius and Sempronius as a loan and therefore applied the usual rules on *mutuum* (Case 58); accordingly, he imposes no requirement on Sempronius to use any of the interest income for Titius' benefit. By contrast, Africanus thinks of the arrangement as a gratuitous mandate from Titius to Sempronius (see Chapter V.C). Since both the principal and the six percent income were being used to benefit Titius, Sempronius had a very low level of liability for them (just *dolus*, deliberate deceit); and since mandate is gratuitous, he would not be liable at all for interest above six percent.

   At least in the text as preserved, Africanus ends up supporting a lawsuit *praescriptis verbis*, since this action circumvents the loan issue altogether. But problems remain. Is this really a bilateral exchange, and, if so, what for what? Is it altogether clear that Titius has any claim to interest income over six percent? Is it likely that Titius is better protected at least as to Sempronius' conduct with the principal?

CASE 191: Alternative Remedies

D. 19.5.5.1 (Paulus libro quinto *Quaestionum*)

Et si quidem pecuniam dem, ut rem accipiam, emptio et venditio est: sin autem rem do, ut rem accipiam, quia non placet permutationem rerum emptionem esse, dubium non est nasci civilem obligationem, in qua actione id veniet, non ut reddas quod acceperis, sed ut damneris mihi, quanti interest mea illud de quo convenit accipere: vel si meum recipere velim, repetatur quod datum est, quasi ob rem datum re non secuta. . . .

Paul in the fifth book of his *Questions*:

If I give money to receive property, this is purchase and sale. But if I give property to receive property, because in the prevailing view barter is not sale, there is no doubt that a Civil obligation (*civilis obligatio*) arises. In this action the issue will be, not that you return what you received, but that you be condemned to me for my interest in receiving what was agreed on; or, if I wish to recover my property, what was given may be reclaimed, on the theory that it was given for a purpose not then realized (*ob rem datum re non secuta*). . . .

Discussion

1. **Barter Once Again.** On the sale/barter problem, see Cases 77, 79; after debate, the jurists eventually concluded that barter (*permutatio*) could not be absorbed within the law on sale, and hence that an agreement to barter was not enforceable so long as it remained unexecuted on either side. (This was arguably a considerable hardship because a substantial portion of the Roman economy is believed to have remained non-monetized.) Paul does not expressly state that one party must act before the other becomes liable, but his hypothetical presupposes this.

2. **What Remedy?** Paul proposes two remedies: either the aggrieved plaintiff can sue on the "Civil obligation" and recover his "interest" in the other party having performed (as usual with the jurists, Paul makes no attempt to define the extent of this "interest"). Or he may bring a *condictio* for return of what will eventually be termed the defendant's unjustified enrichment, under a theory examined in Chapter VIII.B in this volume. (Same outcome: Papinian, D. 19.5.7.) In other words, an election of remedies: either expectation damages or restitution, similar to Common Law. The latter remedy was not available to Roman plaintiffs in the recognized contracts, but it is one that modern plaintiffs often prefer if their "interest" is hard to prove or too small. The restitution remedy is justified on the basis that the defendant received property for a particular cause that did not then come to pass. Should the jurists have applied this reasoning more broadly?

CASE 192: Standards of Performance

D. 19.5.5.1–2 (Paulus libro quinto *Quaestionum*)

1. . . . Sed si scyphos tibi dedi, ut Stichum mihi dares, periculo meo Stichus erit ac tu dumtaxat culpam praestare debes. . . . 2. . . . Sed si dedi tibi servum, ut servum tuum manumitteres, et manumissisti et is quem dedi evictus est, si sciens dedi, de dolo in me dandam actionem Iulianus scribit, si ignorans, in factum civilem.

D. 19.4.2 (Paulus libro quinto ad Plautium)

Aristo ait, quoniam permutatio vicina esset emptioni, sanum quoque furtis noxisque solutum et non esse fugitivum servum praestandum, qui ex causa daretur.

Paul in the fifth book of his *Questions*:

1. . . . But if I gave you wine cups so that you give me (the slave) Stichus, Stichus will be at my risk (before delivery) and you ought to be liable only for fault (*culpa*).

2. . . . But if I gave you a slave so that you manumit your slave, and you manumitted (your slave) and the one I gave you is evicted (by a true owner), if I gave him knowingly, Julian writes that an action on deceit (*de dolo*) should be given against me; if unknowingly, a Civil (action) on the facts.

Paul in the fifth book on Plautius:

Aristo says that since barter is akin to purchase, there should also be liability that a slave given for this reason is healthy, free from thefts, and not a runaway.

Discussion

1. Carrying over the Rules on Sale. Compare the rules for sale as to risk prior to delivery (Chapter IV.B.1), implied warranty of title (Chapter IV.B.4), and implied warranty for defects (Chapter IV.B.5). The remedies are, however, somewhat differently constructed than in sale. On eviction for lack of title, see Case 187 in this Chapter, and also Paul, D. 19.4.1.1, and Gordian, C. 4.64.1 (238 CE). In contrast, Sex. Pedius held that when one party lacks title, no barter at all results (Paul, D. 19.4.1.3), in which case the only remedy would presumably be in unjustified enrichment.

CHAPTER VII

Third-Party Rights and Responsibilities

A Casebook on the Roman Law of Contracts. Bruce W. Frier, Oxford University Press. © Oxford University Press 2021.
DOI: 10.1093/oso/9780197573211.003.0008

Part A. Sons and Slaves

The Cases in earlier Chapters usually presumed a contract arrived at between two parties with full legal capacity. In Roman law, such persons are described as *sui iuris*, meaning that they are free and not in the power of a *paterfamilias*. This Part deals with problems that arise when one party to a contract is either a slave or a child in his or her father's power.

In Roman law, children of either sex, even when they reached adulthood, remained in the paternal power (*patria potestas*) of their oldest male antecedent, their *paterfamilias*—usually a father or paternal grandfather.[1] A son, if he was still in his father's power, ordinarily had full capacity to make contracts. But whereas the *paterfamilias* could acquire for himself any proceeds or rights resulting from the contract, the son had no assets of his own and therefore the other party could not effectively sue the son until he was no longer in his father's power—usually, upon the father's death. The position of slaves was broadly similar, except that slaves themselves could neither sue nor be sued under the contract. (Daughters in their father's power did not have independent contractual capacity: Gaius, *Inst.* 3.104.)

To obviate the evident awkwardness of this situation, the Urban Praetor intervened, establishing liability for the father or master on three different theories. First, the father or master was liable if he had specifically authorized or ratified the dependent's transaction, through an "order" (*iussum*). Second, if sons or slaves had separate bookkeeping accounts that were effectively in their own control (*peculia*), the father or master was liable to the extent of these *peculia*; the action on the *peculium* was particularly successful in liberating some of the economic potential of sons or slaves, although the father or master remained in principle its owner. Third, in any case the father or master was liable to the extent he had been enriched as a result of the transactions, by the action on enrichment (*de in rem verso*).

Under all three theories, the father's or master's liability is "added on" to that of the son or slave; the actions devised by the Praetor are therefore described as "adjacent" (*adiecticiae*). In this and other respects, Roman law resists the legal concept of agency: that one person, if authorized to do so, can act for or represent another (loosely termed "the principal") so as to create legal relations directly between the principal and a third party. The reasons for the jurists' resistance to agency are unclear, but may be related to ethical standards prevailing in the ancient world. In most instances, it seemed somehow improper that one person could be obligated through another's actions; see Case 10. As Roman law developed, inroads were made on this moral position, but they remained modest. By contrast, the modern world would scarcely be imaginable without a developed concept of agency.

---

[1] These paragraphs provide only a brief sketch of the legal position of children in a father's power. For more information, consult standard introductions or Frier and McGinn, *Roman Family Law*, especially Chapter III.

CASE 193: Liability of Sons for Their Contracts

D. 5.1.57 (Ulpianus libro quadragensimo primo ad Sabinum)

Tam ex contractibus quam ex delictis in filium familias competit actio: sed mortuo filio post litis contestationem transfertur iudicium in patrem dumtaxat de peculio et quod in rem eius versum est. . . .

Ulpian in the forty-first book *On Sabinus*:

Against a son in his father's power, an action lies from both his contracts and his delicts. But if the son dies after joinder of issue (*litis contestatio*), the trial is transferred to the father up to the extent of the *peculium* or his (the father's) enrichment. . . .

Discussion

1. Sons as Contracting Parties. As Ulpian summarizes the situation, the son can be sued on his contracts (see also Gaius, D. 44.7.39: "A son in his father's power is obligated from all claims just like a *paterfamilias*, and on this basis can be sued like a *paterfamilias*."). But such claims may come up against the legal reality that, with only narrow exceptions, "Those who are in another person's power can physically hold property in their *peculium*, (but) they cannot own or possess it, since possession is a matter not just of physicality but also of law"; Papinian, D. 41.2.49.1. A contractual claim raised directly against a child in power might be honored by his or her *paterfamilias*, and doubtless frequently was, but it did not have to be. One result of the rule was to create intra-familial strains clearly visible in the events allegedly underlying the SC Macedonianum (Case 61). This legal construct was, however, deeply embedded in Roman law, from its very origins: the Twelve Tables of 449 BCE had provided that fathers had "the power of life and death" over children (IV.4.2a, = Papinian, *Collatio* 4.8), and while this power was gradually narrowed as to physical punishment, for property it endured almost unchanged a surprisingly long time. In this respect, it is worth considering the economic consequences of concentrating family property rights in the oldest surviving male antecedent.

   If a son is sued, and he then dies after the Praetor has promulgated a *formula* but before a *iudex* renders judgment, the lawsuit is redirected against the son's *paterfamilias*, whose liability is, however, limited as described in subsequent Cases.

CASE 194: Transactions Ordered by the *Paterfamilias*

Gaius, *Institutiones* 4.70

Inprimis itaque si iussu patris dominiue negotium gestum erit, in solidum praetor actionem in patrem dominumue comparavit, et recte, quia qui ita negotium gerit, magis patris dominiue quam filii seruiue fidem sequitur.

Gaius in the fourth book of his *Institutes*:

Chiefly, if the transaction occurred on the order (*iussum*) of the father or master, the Praetor has devised an action for the entirety (of the debt) against the father or master, and rightly so, since a person who enters such a transaction relies more on the father's or master's credit (*fides*) than on that of the son or slave.

Discussion

1. The Action on an Order (*Quod Iussu*). When a slave or a child in power entered into a contract with a third party in accord with an order from the slave's master or the child's *paterfamilias*, the Praetor allowed the third party to sue the master or father with a special *formula*. In the case of a son, the model wording probably ran: "Whereas on the defendant's order the plaintiff sold a toga to Gaius when he was in the defendant's power, this being the matter at issue, whatever on this matter the son Gaius ought to give or do for the plaintiff in accord with good faith, let him (the *iudex*) condemn the defendant's father to the plaintiff for this; if it does not appear, absolve him" (Lenel, EP³ 278). The *formula* for a slave would be similar. On the nature of an "order," see the following Case. What legal theory does Gaius use in order to explain the liability? Although the father's or master's liability was for the entire debt (*in solidum*; see also *Pauli Sent.* 1.4.6; Justinian, *Inst.* 4.7.1), this is still not agency, since the son remained also liable (see Case 198). The situation of a slave, who lacked capacity and hence could not be sued him or herself, looks a bit more like modern agency, although the underlying institutions are obviously quite different.

2. A Daughter. Paul, D. 15.4.2.1, notes that a free woman subject to the power of her *paterfamilias* could also make him liable if she acted on his order, even though daughters in power lacked contractual capacity in their own right (Gaius, *Inst.* 3.104).

CASE 195: The Nature of an Order

D. 15.4.1.1–2, 6 (Ulpianus libro vicensimo nono ad Edictum)

1. Iussum autem accipiendum est, sive testato quis sive per epistulam sive verbis aut per nuntium sive specialiter in uno contractu iusserit sive generaliter: et ideo et si *sic* contestatus sit: "quod voles cum Sticho servo meo negotium gerere periculo meo", videtur ad omnia iussisse, nisi certa lex aliquid prohibet. 2. Sed ego quaero, an revocare hoc iussum antequam credatur possit: et puto posse, quemadmodum si mandasset et postea ante contractum contraria voluntate mandatum revocasset et me certiorasset. . . . 6. Si ratum habuerit quis quod servus eius gesserit vel filius, quod iussu actio in eos datur.

Ulpian in the twenty-ninth book *On the Edict*:

1. An order (*iussum*) is understood to occur if someone gives an order before a witness or by letter or orally or through a messenger, whether specifically for one contract or generally. (By this message:) "Conduct whatever business you wish with my slave Stichus, at my risk," he seems to have given general authorization unless a specific term forbids something.

2. But I ask whether such an order can be revoked before credit is extended. I think it can be, just as if he had given a mandate and then revoked the mandate by changing his mind (*contraria voluntate*) before a contract (had been executed pursuant to the mandate), and he had informed me (of this revocation). . . .

6. If someone ratifies what his slave or son did, an action on the order is given against them (the master or *pater*).

Discussion

1. Informality. As Ulpian indicates, little stress is laid upon the exact manner in which an order is conveyed, although it must be an actual order and not just a general statement of approval (Honorius and Theodosius, C.Th. 2.31.1 (422); compare Ulpian, D. 15.4.1.5, citing Marcellus). However, both he and Gaius (in the previous Case) appear to indicate that the order must be transmitted to the third party at least indirectly, whether or not also to the son or slave; this is evidently the force behind Gaius' stress on the father's or master's *fides* as the basis for his liability. This point would play out particularly in the case of the general order that Ulpian quotes, which seems to be an extremely open-ended grant of contracting power to Stichus; but it is not the slave himself who is being thereby authorized. (Contrast the *institor* discussed in the following Part.) Still, Ulpian, in section 2, suggests that it was enough if a slave acted with the master's consent (*voluntas*).

Revocation is also easy before the order is carried out. Ulpian notes the broad similarity between this situation and that of mandate (Chapter VI.3), although strictly speaking the third party is not being requested to do anything.

Granted the legal uncertainty of dealings with sons in power or slaves, how likely is it that third parties would frequently have sought the "safe harbor" of such an order?

2. Ratification. As section 6 indicates, a father or master could also ratify a transaction after the event, with ratification construed as the equivalent of an order. Is this holding consistent with Gaius' rationale for liability for transactions that are ordered?

CASE 196: The *Peculium*

Iustinianus, *Institutiones* 4.6.10

Actionem autem de peculio ideo adversus patrem dominumve comparavit praetor, quia licet ex contractu filiorum servorumve ipso iure non teneantur, aequum tamen esset peculio tenus, quod veluti patrimoniam est filiorum filiarumque, item servorum, condemnari eos.

Justinian in the fourth book of his *Institutes*:

The Praetor provided actions on the *peculium* against a father or an owner (of a slave) because, although by (Civil) Law itself they are not liable on the contract of sons or slaves, nonetheless it is fair (*aequum*) that they be condemned up to the value of the *peculium*, which is like the property (*patrimonium*) of sons and daughters or of slaves.

Discussion

1. Defining the *Peculium*. In most historical slave systems, masters have been able, legally, to confer on slaves sums of money, usually small, which they can use to make payments for small daily purchases. The reasons are mainly practical, so that the master not be constantly bothered by having to authorize such payments; the funds resemble the allowances that modern parents frequently give their children in order also to encourage habits of thrift and saving.

   In Rome, however, these allowances, called *peculia* (literally, "petty cash funds") often became in fact quite substantial, even enormous. Essentially, they resemble a separate bookkeeping account that the slave or child manages independently, and they can become major enterprises in their own right, even though the father or master has the legal right to recall them at any time. As Ulpian, D. 15.1.5.4 (citing the late Republican jurist Aelius Tubero), defines it, the *peculium* is "what a slave holds with the owner's permission separate from the owner's accounts, with debts to owner being deducted." The same is true for children in power, especially sons. Inevitably, sons and slaves began extensively contracting on the basis of their *peculia*. By the late Republic, the Urban Praetor had established the action that Justinian describes in his elementary handbook, so as to facilitate a dependent's ability to transact while simultaneously limiting the contractual and other liability of the *paterfamilias* to a *peculium's* value.

2. The Contents of a *Peculium*. It could contain any asset. Ulpian, D. 15.1.7.4–7, mentions "all sorts of property, both movables and land"—even other slaves, who are then called *vicarii*, "deputies"; in addition, any debts owed to the *peculium* as a result of the holder's transactions, including debts owed by the master or father or from the *peculia* of his other slaves.

It should be emphasized that the *peculium*, although an amalgam of tangible and intangible property, is not an object itself. The jurists stress that the owner or master retains ownership, while the slave or child is a mere "holder" (*detentor*; the verb is *tenere*); see Case 193 and Maecian, D. 50.17.93: "A son in a father's power is held not to retain nor recover nor acquire possession of *peculium* property." Just as the *paterfamilias* creates the *peculium* by his own action, so too he is free to dissolve it at any time, except if he does so to defraud its creditors: Ulpian, D. 15.1.4 pr., 15.2.1 pr. (quoting the Edict).

Despite the acknowledged utility of *peculia* in freeing up a degree of independent economic potential within the hierarchical Roman household, the arrangement was confined to those in the household and in principle could not be extended to third parties whether free or slave.

3. **Agency?** The relative independence of the *peculium* holder is still far from modern concepts of agency. The son, in particular, is liable on contracts made through the *peculium*. See Ulpian, D. 15.1.44: "If someone contracts with a son in his father's power, he has two debtors: the son for the entirety and the father for up to the value of the *peculium*." What potential awkwardness does this create, particularly for potential creditors?

4. **Daughters.** Although daughters (like slaves) lacked contractual capacity in their own right, they could contract through a *peculium*; Gaius, D. 15.1.27 pr., citing Julian. Gaius notes that this is especially true if a woman is employed as a tailor or weaver, or she practices some "common skill" (*artificium vulgare*).

CASE 197: The Action on the *Peculium*

Gaius, *Institutiones* 4.72a–73

72a. Est etiam de peculio et de in rem verso actio a praetore constituta. Licet enim negotium ita gestum sit cum filio seruoue, ut neque uoluntas neque consensus patris dominiue interuenerit, si quid tamen ex ea re, quae cum illis gesta est, in rem patris dominive versum sit, quatenus in rem eius uersum fuerit, eatenus datur actio. . . . 73. Cum autem quaeritur, quantum in peculio sit, ante deducitur, quod patri dominoue quique in eius potestate sit, a filio seruoue debetur, et quod superest, hoc solum peculium esse intellegitur. aliquando tamen id, quod ei debet filius seruusue, qui in potestate patris dominiue sit, non deducitur ex peculio, velut si is, cui debet, in huius ipsius peculio sit.

Gaius in the fourth book of his *Institutes*:

72a. The Praetor has established an action on the *peculium* and for benefit received (*de in rem verso*). For although a transaction occurred with a son or slave in such a way that neither the wish nor the agreement of the father or master intervened, if, from the transaction conducted with them, some benefit accrues to the estate of the father or master, an action will be given for the extent of that benefit. . . .

73. When question is raised about the amount of the *peculium*, first there is deducted what the son or slave owes to the father or owner and (to anyone) who is in his power, and only what remains is interpreted as the *peculium*. But sometimes what the son or slave owes to a person who is in the father's or owner's power is not deducted from the *peculium*, e.g., if the person to whom it is owed is in the *peculium* of this very person (the son or slave).

Discussion

1. The Double Nature of the Action. The action on the *peculium* limited the master's or owner's liability to its value, but the Praetor rather awkwardly coupled this cause of action with an exception: he was also liable if his estate had benefited from proceeds of the son's or slave's activity (*in rem versum*). Although the relationship between these two sources of liability is unclear, probably they were independent (no *peculium* was necessary for the enrichment claim), but it was doubtless usually convenient to consider the two causes together.

2. Limits on *Peculium* Liability. The beginning of this Case is heavily reconstructed mainly from Justinian, *Inst.* 4.7.4. Justinian goes on to give an example that illustrates how the action works (the example here substitutes currency values from the Classical period). Suppose that a child or slave with a *peculium* borrows 10,000 sesterces from a third party. If he uses 5,000 of this sum to benefit the *paterfamilias* (for instance, by paying off his creditors or purchasing food for his household), while spending the rest in

some other way, the *paterfamilias* will be liable for the entire 5,000 benefit, plus as much of the remaining 5,000 as can be realized from the assets of the *peculium*. Is the creditor adequately protected? An apprehensive creditor could always seek an order (*iussum*) from the *paterfamilias*. Would you advise this as a safety measure?

3. **Deductions from the *Peculium*.** Section 73 raises what may seem one of the oddest rules: that before *peculium* liability is calculated, the *paterfamilias* is entitled first to deduct from its assets whatever the holder owes to him. Ulpian, D. 15.1.9.2–4, discusses the deduction at length; he cites Pedius to the effect that: "what is owed to the master or father is for this reason no longer in the *peculium* since it is unlikely that the master would let a slave keep in his *peculium* something that is owed to himself." (Ulpian, D. 15.1.9.4.) So the *paterfamilias* becomes, in effect, a preferred creditor. Does this follow automatically from the nature of the *peculium* as a fund initially granted by the *pater* and subsequently subject to his power of withdrawal? How difficult is it likely to have been for a third party, in extending credit to a slave, to determine exactly what the slave's *peculium* owed to a *pater*?

4. **Benefit to the *Paterfamilias*.** The jurists develop this rule casuistically. For instance, if a son or slave spends money on improving the *pater*'s house, this is benefit if it makes the house better or at least not worse; but if the refurbishment was more for decoration than utility, there is no material benefit; Ulpian, D. 15.3.3.2, 4. Likewise, it is benefit if he purchases perfumes for a funeral that the *pater* has an interest in: Ulpian, D. 15.3.7.3; D. 15.3 has many other examples, some of which are quite tricky. For example, Alfenus, D. 15.3.16, deals with a master who leased to his slave a farm along with a team of oxen. The oxen proved unsuitable, and so, with the master's permission, the slave sold them and bought replacements; but the slave then became insolvent without having paid the seller, who subsequently sued the master for the price. There was little or nothing in the slave's *peculium*. Can the owner be said to have benefited from the replacement oxen now in his possession, granted that they had cost him the value of the previous oxen?

CASE 198: Liability Despite a Prohibition to Contract

D. 15.1.47 pr. (Paulus libro quarto ad Plautium)

Quotiens in taberna ita scriptum fuisset "cum Ianuario servo meo geri negotium veto," hoc solum consecutum esse dominum constat, ne institoria teneatur, non etiam de peculio.

Paul in the fourth book *On Plautius*:

Whenever there had been a sign in a shop to this effect: "I forbid conduct of business with my slave Januarius," it is agreed that the master obtained non-liability only on the action concerning a manager (*institor*), not also on the *peculium*.

Discussion

1. Limiting the Powers of a *Peculium* Holder. A *paterfamilias*, in establishing a *peculium*, could also grant a son or slave "free administration" (*libera administratio*) as a separate power allowing him to act almost independently. Paul, D. 15.1.46 ("blanket authorization for everything he would have permitted in particular cases"); Ulpian, D. 6.1.41.1. Such a grant, which had to be made expressly (Ulpian, D. 15.1.7.1), indicated great confidence in the holder's judgment. However, we are also told that a *pater* could limit the free administration given to a child or slave; Marcian, D. 20.3.1.1. For instance, the holder might be forbidden to alienate the *pater*'s property without his consent; if this happened nonetheless, the transaction could be nullified; Proculus, D. 12.6.53; Diocletian, C. 4.26.10.1 (294). So why does the owner have *peculium* liability in Paul's decision in this Case? Gaius, D. 15.1.29.1, has the same outcome ("Even if the master prohibits contracting with a slave, there will be an action on the *peculium* against him"), also without an explanation.

2. Winding Up a *Peculium*. The master can remove property from the *peculium* at will, either physically or by a statement (Ulpian, D. 15.1.7.6; Paul, D. 41.3.4.7). Indeed, he can dissolve the entire *peculium* at will (Paul, D. 15.1.8), without necessarily removing it from the slave's physical supervision. (Reducing the *peculium* to defraud creditors would still raise issues, however: Ulpian, D. 15.2.1 pr., quoting the Edict. Forms of *dolus*: Ulpian, D. 15.1.9.4 and 21 pr.; Paul D. 15.3.19). Such fraud leads to the assets in question being "imputed" to the *peculium*: Ulpian, D. 15.1.21 pr.

Otherwise, if creditors became anxious about the solvency of a *peculium*, they had an additional remedy, an action for its division (*actio tributoria*). In brief, when a *peculium* holder was doing business with all or a portion of it, and he contracted debts with the *pater*'s knowledge, creditors could sue the *pater* if it then became insolvent. This liability effectively forced the *pater* to share out the *peculium*'s business portion among all its creditors, including the *pater* (so his claims therefore received no preference). See D. 14.4; also Gaius, *Inst.* 4.72, 74a.

Part B. The Manager of a Business (*InstStor*)

By the late Republic, the Urban Praetor had introduced another action whereby one person could be made liable for a contract concluded by another person. This was the *actio institoria*, which arose when the owner of a business enterprise (the *dominus*) placed another in charge of operating the business. The manager was called an *institor*, literally a "shopkeeper" or "peddler." The action gave third parties the right to enforce the *institor's* contracts directly against the owner, provided that the contracts were pursuant to the business. For purposes of this action, the juridical status of the *institor* was irrelevant; he or she could be the owner's slave, or a child in power (whether male or female), but also another person's slave who had been hired to run the business, or even a hired free person.

Closely related to the *actio institoria* is another (probably earlier) action whereby the "operator" of a ship, called the *exercitor*, was liable for the contracts of a captain who had been put in charge of the ship. The *actio exercitoria* is referred to in Case 200.

Neither action involves a true agency relationship, since the *institor* or the ship captain is also liable on the contract to the extent permitted by law (this may vary by the status of the person). Further, the two actions run only in one direction, from the third party to the principal; but the principal is not automatically entitled to enforce the contract against the third party. However, some sources (which the Digest compilers may have altered) indicate relaxation of this rule, at any rate in hard cases.

CASE 199: Liability for Contracts of an *Institor*

Gaius, *Institutiones* 4.71

. . . Institoria uero formula tum locum habet, cum quis tabernae aut cuilibet negotiationi filium seruumve suum aut quemlibet extraneum, siue seruum siue liberum, praeposuerit et quid cum eo eius rei gratia, cui praepositus est, contractum fuerit. Ideo autem institoria vocatur, quia qui tabernae praeponitur, institor appellatur. Quae et ipsa formula in solidum est.

Pauli Sententiae 2.8.1–2

1. Sicut commoda sentimus ex actu praepositi institoris, ita et incommoda sentire debemus. Et ideo qui servum sive filium filiamve familias sive ancillam praeposuit negotio vel mercibus exercendis, eorum nomine in solidum convenitur. 2. Si quis pecuniae fenerandae agroque colendo, condendis vendendisque frugibus praepositus est, ex eo nomine quod cum illo contractum est in solidum fundi dominus obligatur: nec interest, servus an liber sit.

Gaius in the fourth book of his *Institutes*:

. . . The *formula institoria* applies when someone places in charge of his shop or any business his son or a slave or any third party whether slave or free, and there was some contract with him related to what he was placed in charge of. It is called the *institoria* because a person placed in charge of a shop is termed an *institor.* This *formula* is also for the entirety (of the debt; *in solidum*).

The second book of *Paul's Sentences*:1. Just as we experience the advantages from the act of a manager (institor) put in charge (of a business), so too we should experience the disadvantages. So if someone places a slave, or a son or daughter in his power, or a slave woman, in charge of a business or the handling of goods, he is liable for the entirety (in solidum) in their respect.

2. If someone is set in charge of lending money, farming land, or storing and selling crops, the farm's owner is obligated for the entirety from the account that is contracted with him (the *institor*); nor does it matter whether he is a slave or free.

Discussion

1. Commerce and Managers. Probably for reasons both social and economic, many Roman owners elected to operate their businesses not themselves but through appointed managers, called *institores*. The action deriving from this relationship (*actio institoria*) made the owner fully liable for debts to anyone transacting with the business, this evidently on the theory that the owner is the real contractual partner in such dealings. The manager could be virtually anyone; as Gaius says, the power of a *paterfamilias* is irrelevant, nor does it matter whether the manager was free or a slave, nor, indeed, whether male or female, or whether of adult age or not (Ulpian/Gaius,

D. 14.3.7.1–2, 8). A slave may even belong to a third party, in which case the slave's owner acquires any rights from transactions but must surrender them to the business owner (Ulpian, D. 14.3.1).

2. **Examples of Managers**. Ulpian, D. 14.3.5.1–9, gives numerous examples of *institores*. Among them:

- A building manager appointed by the owner of an apartment block;
- A person placed in charge of buying grain;
- Someone appointed to lend money, or to run a farm, or to trade in a market, or to undertake building contracts;
- A slave placed in charge of operating a bank;
- Someone whom a tailor appoints to carry around and sell clothing;
- A muleteer placed in charge of a mule team;
- A person operating a stable for its owner;
- Someone whom a shopkeeper appoints to travel abroad for the purpose of buying goods and sending them to him;
- A slave appointed by an undertaker to prepare corpses for burial;
- A slave regularly sent by a baker to sell bread in a particular place.

Such examples vividly illustrate the general character of Roman commerce, and also suggest how frequently ordinary customers are likely to have been dealing with persons whom the law describes as managers (*institores*). Our sources indicate that, at the time of the transaction, a customer did not have to be aware that the other party was actually the manager for a "principal," who might therefore remain undisclosed until after the transaction.

Granted the ubiquity of *institores*, does the Roman failure to develop a generalized law of agency make all that much difference? Possibly. Roman business structures, to the extent we can make them out, often do not seem very deep: a business manager might have employees, but rarely vertical tiers of employees. Would this also have an effect on the complexity and size of businesses?

CASE 200: Liability of the Manager

D. 14.1.1 pr. (Ulpianus libro vicensimo octavo ad Edictum)

pr. Utilitatem huius edicti patere nemo est qui ignoret. Nam cum interdum ignari, cuius sint condicionis vel quales, cum magistris propter navigandi necessitatem contrahamus, aequum fuit eum, qui magistrum navi imposuit, teneri, ut tenetur, qui institorem tabernae vel negotio praeposuit, cum sit maior necessitas contrahendi cum magistro quam institore. Quippe res patitur, ut de condicione quis institoris dispiciat et *sic* contrahat: in navis magistro non ita, nam interdum locus tempus non patitur plenius deliberandi consilium.

Ulpian in the twenty-eighth book *On the Edict*:

No one is unaware of the obvious practicality of this edict (establishing the *actio exercitoria* against shipowners). For since, because of the needs of sailing, we sometimes contract with ship captains (*magistri*) while unaware of their legal status and character, it was fair that the person be liable who put the captain in charge of the ship, just as he is liable who put an *institor* in charge of a shop or business. In fact, the need to contract is greater with a ship captain than with an *institor*. Obviously, one may inquire about the legal status of an *institor* and contract (only) after doing so; it is different with a ship captain, for sometimes place and time do not allow fuller deliberation.

Discussion

1. Dealing with Ship Captains. The Praetor's Edict made ship owners (*exercitores*) liable for the contracts concluded by their appointed ship captains (*magistri*). Ulpian justifies this on the difficulty that travelers and merchants faced in knowing whether captains were reliable contractual partners, which probably indicates that billets or the transport of goods was often a last-minute arrangement. The liabilities of the business owner and the shipowner are largely parallel, with some small differences; for instance, the shipowner was bound not only by the contracts of captains, but also by those persons the captains appointed, even if the owner forbade such appointment; Ulpian, D. 14.1.1.5.

2. The Personal Liability of Captains and Managers. In some respects, the position of these employees starts to look more like agency, especially because they are not necessarily in the legal household of their employers. However, captains and business managers are also personally liable for their contracts if they have independent contractual capacity; Ulpian, D. 14.3.7.1 (who also notes that those without such capacity, like women in a father's power, can still be *institores*). As Ulpian (D. 14.1.1.17) observes, "We can choose whether to sue the ship owner or the captain"; and the same is true for business managers. An additional and very important difference is discussed in Case 202.

CASE 201: Contracts within the Scope of Authorization

D. 14.3.5.11–15 (Ulpianus libro vicensimo octavo ad Edictum)

11. Non tamen omne, quod cum institore geritur, obligat eum qui praeposuit, sed ita, si eius rei gratia, cui praepositus fuerit, contractum est, id est dumtaxat ad id quod eum praeposuit. 12. Proinde si praeposui ad mercium distractionem, tenebor nomine eius ex empto actione: item si forte ad emendum eum praeposuero, tenebor dumtaxat ex vendito: sed neque si ad emendum, et ille vendiderit, neque si ad vendendum, et ille emerit, debebit teneri, idque Cassius probat. 13. Sed si pecuniam quis crediderit institori ad emendas merces praeposito, locus est institoriae, idemque et si ad pensionem pro taberna exsolvendam: quod ita verum puto, nisi prohibitus fuit mutuari. 14. Si ei, quem ad vendendum emendumve oleum praeposui, mutuum oleum datum sit, dicendum erit institoriam locum habere. 15. Item si institor, cum oleum vendidisset, anulum arrae nomine acceperit neque eum reddat, dominum institoria teneri: nam eius rei, in quam praepositus est, contractum est: nisi forte mandatum ei fuit praesenti pecunia vendere. Quare si forte pignus institor ob pretium acceperit, institoriae locus erit.

Ulpian in the twenty-eighth book *On the Edict*:

11. But not every transaction with an *institor* obligates the person who put him in charge, but only if there was a contract related to what he was placed in charge of, i.e., to what he (the owner) placed him in charge of. 12. Therefore if I put someone in charge of selling goods, I will be liable on his account in the action on purchase; likewise, if I happen to put him in charge of buying, I will be liable only in sale. But I should not be held liable if (I put him in charge) of buying and he sold, nor if (I put him in charge) of selling and he bought, a view that Cassius supports.

13. But if someone lent money to an *institor* charged with buying goods, the action on an *institor*'s conduct lies, and so too if (money was lent) to pay rent for his shop. I think this correct unless he was forbidden to borrow. 14. If olive oil was given on loan to a person whom I charged with buying and selling oil, it must be ruled that the action on an *institor*'s conduct lies.

15. Likewise, if the *institor*, when he sold the oil, received a ring as earnest (*arra*) and he does not return it, (a jurist held that) the owner is liable by the *actio institoria*. For this contract is for the purpose he was charged with, unless indeed he was ordered to sell (only) for ready cash. So if, for instance, an *institor* receives a pledge (*pignus*) for the price, the action on an *institor*'s conduct will lie.

Discussion

1. Limits Imposed by the Business Owner. Although the boundaries are rather fuzzy at times, the owner can define the business as he likes, and thereby try to restrict his liability on a manager's contracts. It is easy

enough to see how this works when, as in section 12, a manager appointed to sell goods then buys them, or vice versa. But the situation is more ambiguous if a manager appointed to buy goods then borrows money to pay shop rent (13), or he is charged with buying and selling and he receives a loan of the goods in which he is dealing (14), or he is appointed to sell and receives a pledge for payment of the price (15). As should be clear, at least in the Digest texts as they survive, doubts are usually called in favor of liability unless the questionable action was specifically forbidden. Why is this?

The owner may also restrict business operations in other ways, for instance by forbidding dealings with particular persons, or by requiring that security be provided for performance, or by specifying contract terms (Ulpian, D. 14.3.11.5; Paul, D. 14.3.17.1). Such restrictions can be conveyed either directly to the affected customers or through a posted announcement. Ulpian, D. 14.3.11.2–4, gives elaborate instructions for such a posting in a shop's premises: it must be conspicuous, uninterrupted, and written in a language that customers can understand. Underlying these requirements is an assumption that most customers will be able to read.

2. The Customer's Knowledge. Particularly in the case of limitations on business scope, one salient question is whether a customer, who wishes to sue the owner, is obliged to have known of these limitations; but it seems to be enough if the customer could prove the transaction was related to the business being conducted. Ulpian, D. 14.3.13 pr., citing Julian, develops a hypothetical case in which a person set a slave in charge of two businesses: marketing olive oil in the city of Arles, and borrowing money. The slave received a loan from a customer who thought it was for the olive oil business, but, when he sued the owner, he was unable to prove this as fact. (Julian allows the customer to sue on the other business, by an analogous action.)

This rule could lead to some curious results. Africanus, D. 14.1.7 pr., discusses a parallel case relating to the *actio exercitoria*, in which a ship captain borrows money and guarantees that he will use the loan to repair the ship. Obviously, necessary ship repair would be within the captain's scope of business. The lender now wishes to sue the ship's owner over the loan. He can succeed if the ship was in actual need of repair at the time of the loan, but need not supervise to make sure the money was actually spent for this purpose. But if the loan was grossly more than needed for repairs, the shipowner's liability is restricted to what was necessary; and if the repairs were impossible at the place where the loan was made, the suit may fail altogether. "In short," says the jurist, "the creditor should exercise some caution in this matter." To say the least! Ofilius, a late Republican jurist cited by Ulpian, D. 14.1.1.9, goes even farther: if the captain borrowed the money with the honest intent to make repairs but later converted the loan to his own use, then the lender can sue the shipowner; but if the captain was intending fraud all along, the lender bears the loss. What might justify this holding?

CASE 202: Liability of Third Parties to the Principal

D. 14.3.1 (Ulpianus libro vicensimo octavo ad Edictum)

Aequum praetori visum est, sicut commoda sentimus ex actu institorum, ita etiam obligari nos ex contractibus ipsorum et conveniri. Sed non idem facit circa eum qui institorem praeposuit, ut experiri possit: sed si quidem servum proprium institorem habuit, potest esse securus adquisitis sibi actionibus: si autem vel alienum servum vel etiam hominem liberum, actione deficietur: ipsum tamen institorem vel dominum eius convenire poterit vel mandati vel negotiorum gestorum. Marcellus autem ait debere dari actionem ei qui institorem praeposuit in eos, qui cum eo contraxerint,

D. 14.3.2 (Gaius libro nono ad Edictum Provinciale)

eo nomine, quo institor contraxit, si modo aliter rem suam servare non potest.

Ulpian in the twenty-eighth book *On the Edict*:

It seemed fair to the Praetor that, as we perceive benefit from the action of *institores*, so too we are obligated and are sued on their contracts. But he does not hold the same with regard to the person who appointed the *institor*, that he can sue (the third party). To be sure, if he uses his own slave as an *institor*, he can rest easy since he (automatically) acquires the actions; but if (he uses) another person's slave or even a free man, he will lack an action. Still, he will be able to sue the *institor* himself or his master, either on mandate or for the administration of affairs. But Marcellus says that the person who put the *institor* in charge should be given an action against those who contracted with him (the manager),

Gaius in the ninth book *On the Provincial Edict*:

on the same grounds as the *institor* contracted, (and) provided he cannot otherwise protect his interests.

Discussion

1. Can a Business Owner Sue on an *Institor*'s Contract? Another source of awkwardness was that, while the *actio institoria* allowed the customer to sue the owner, the owner did not necessarily have a reciprocal right, and in principle it was only the *institor* who had standing as a plaintiff. Again, fear of agency seems to be the culprit. Work-arounds were available: if the *institor* was a dependent, the owner might, as Gaius says, acquire the right to sue through being a *pater* or slave owner; if he or she was free, the *institor* could be forced to cede the action to the owner. But problems remained, and they were even worse if the *institor* was the slave of another person.

   By the later Classical period, it appears that Praetors had intervened and allowed an owner to sue directly, "provided he cannot otherwise protect his interests." Paul, D. 46.5.5, gives an example: "when an *institor* is in a situation where, because he is interposed (between owner and customer), the owner of goods will lose his property, e.g., when his (the owner's) estate is sold (for non-payment of debt); for the Praetor should (then) help out the owner." But such an intervention was apparently discretionary and abnormal. What was holding the jurists back from a more equitable solution?

Part C. The Supervisor (*Procurator*)

Procurator can be roughly translated as "supervisor," "general manager," or "overseer." The word derives from *procurare*, "to look after, to attend to." As a title, *procurator* was used for persons set in charge of various, usually relatively complex operations, including provincial government.

In Roman private law, the *procurator*, as a supervisor, occupies a somewhat peculiar place. Already by the late Republic, such *procuratores* were acting as general overseers of all or large portions of personal estates (*procurator omnium bonorum* or *omnium rerum*), or even as representatives for a single matter (*procurator unius rei*); and probably not long thereafter, perhaps as a special type of the *procurator* for a single matter, they were also serving as stand-ins for a party to a lawsuit (*procurator in litem*). For all three types, at least eventually, the legal relationship between a principal and a *procurator* eventually came to be based either upon mandate if the *procurator* was authorized to act, or upon "administration of affairs" (*negotiorum gestio*; see Chapter VIII.A; also Case 212) if he was not. Nonetheless, as we shall see, a *procurator* differs in many ways from the ordinary mandatary discussed in Chapter V.C. The jurists, to some extent, cobbled together mandate and *procuratio* in an awkward amalgam.

The line dividing *procuratores* from *institores* is also not always easy to make out in legal terms, but simpler to understand in social terms: already by the late Republic, the *procurator* was normally not a humble "shopkeeper," but, with increasing frequency, a freestanding general manager who sometimes could have considerable social status (although freedmen also frequently served in this capacity). In Classical law, the *procurator* was eventually accorded wide rights to administer the affairs of the principal; these rights included the ability to acquire property for the principal, and perhaps even to alienate his or her property. In the end, a *procurator* was also even allowed to arrange contracts that bound the principal. The eminent late Classical jurist Papinian reached this result by using analogy to extend the ambit of the action for *institores*.

The *procurator* was as close to a full agent as Classical Roman Private Law came, but in some circumstances was still probably subject to limitations observed in the first two Parts of this Chapter. The same constraints did not apply, however, in the case of *procuratores* operating as imperial delegates; they could make contracts as full agents of the emperor (e.g., Ulpian, D. 1.19.1 pr.; and, for an example, Paul, D. 49.14.50).

CASE 203: The *Procurator*

D. 3.3.1 pr.-1 (Ulpianus libro nono ad Edictum)

pr. Procurator est qui aliena negotia mandatu domini administrat. 1. Procurator autem vel omnium rerum vel unius rei esse potest constitutus vel coram vel per nuntium vel per epistulam: quamvis quidam, ut Pomponius libro vicensimo quarto scribit, non putent unius rei mandatum suscipientem procuratorem esse: sicuti ne is quidem, qui rem perferendam vel epistulam vel nuntium perferendum suscepit, proprie procurator appellatur. Sed verius est eum quoque procuratorem esse qui ad unam rem datus sit.

Ulpian in the ninth book *On the Edict*:

pr. A *procurator* is a person who administers another's affairs on a mandate from the owner (*mandatu domini*; from the principal). 1. A *procurator* can be set up either for all matters (*omnium rerum*) or (just) for a single matter (*unius rei*), (and) either in his (the principal's) presence or by messenger or letter. But, as Pomponius writes in the twenty-fourth book, some do not think that a person who undertakes a mandate for a single matter is a *procurator*, just as a person who undertakes to carry an object or to deliver a letter or message is not properly called a *procurator*. But it is more correct (to hold) that a person who is appointed for a single matter is also a *procurator*.

Discussion

1. Mandate. By the late Classical period, a *procurator* usually served on the basis of a *mandatum* (also called a *iussum*), and his relationship with the other party (often called the *dominus*, owner or principal, similar to the *actio institoria*) was legally handled under the contract of mandate (Chapter V.C), rather than through a special action as with the *institor*. The fit with mandate was precarious, however. In many respects, the *procurator* (especially the *procurator omnium rerum*) had a legal position very different from the ordinary mandatary discussed earlier; he was regularly invested with more discretionary authority, rights, and powers. The law in this area may well have lagged significantly behind social and economic developments, so that, by the time that the jurists came to recognize that procuratorship should be actionable under mandate, the two legal institutions were not easily merged.

   As Ulpian states, there is no prescribed form for a mandate to a *procurator*; it can be oral or in writing (*Pauli Sent.* 1.3.1), so long as it clearly constitutes an order. (For instance, a letter of recommendation is not a mandate; Ulpian, D. 17.1.12.12.) Scaevola, D. 17.1.60.4, quotes an elaborate mandate, in Greek, from an uncle to his nephew; the operative language translates: "I make you the manager of all my affairs, to handle as you see fit, whether you wish to sell or to obligate property as a pledge or to do anything you wish, as master of my affairs. I will ratify whatever you do, nor will I contradict you in any matter." If the nephew, acting under this mandate, uses his uncle's assets to commit fraud, has the uncle waived his right to damages?

Usually, the jurists describe general mandates to *procuratores omnium rerum* as just orders "to administer my business" (*ad negotia gerenda* or *administranda*), under a regime of "free administration" (*libera administratio*). In addition to the specific issues discussed in the following Cases, the general *procurator* can effectively demand and receive payment of debts owed to the principal (Paul, D. 3.3.58, and 12.6.6.2, citing Celsus) and novate or pay off the principal's debts (Celsus, D. 46.3.87; Julian, D. 46.3.34.3; Ulpian, D. 3.5.5.3; Paul, D. 3.3.58), as well as conduct other business if specifically allowed (Ulpian, D. 13.7.11.7: obligate principal's property as security; Gaius, D. 20.6.7.1: consent to the creditor's sale of pledges given by principal).

In order to legitimate such broad grants of discretion as mandates, the jurists had to permit mandates that were indefinite in their scope and allowed the *procurator* to act at will. In high and late Classical jurisprudence, such mandates were clearly enforced: Neratius, D. 17.1.35, and Paul, D. 17.1.3.1 (mandate to purchase a farm for an unspecified price); Paul, D. 17.1.22.7 (mandate to give a third party "what you wish" from a specified sum); Paul, D. 17.1.59.6 (a mandate to take "suitable security" for a transaction, without further specification). These are ordinary mandates, but they also establish the basis for a general mandate to a *procurator omnium rerum*.

2. Scope of Mandate. As Ulpian indicates, in general the principal is the master of the mandate to a *procurator*; a postclassical source states, perhaps too broadly, that the mandate may be "either for a lawsuit, or for every transaction or a part of one, or to administer affairs" (*Pauli Sent.* 1.3.2; compare Ulpian/Paul, D. 3.3.1–2; and see also Case 205). Julian (cited by Ulpian, D. 17.1.6.6), for instance, describes a mandate to a *procurator* that instructs him to take a sum of the principal's money and lend it at interest, with a fixed rate payable to the principal and any excess interest going to the *procurator*; according to Julian, this is effectively a loan to the *procurator* for which he is liable in mandate.

In another decision, Julian (reported by his student Africanus, D. 17.1.34 pr.) considers a *procurator* who, after collecting debts owed to his principal, wrote to the principal that he would hold this money as a loan and pay six percent interest. Julian holds that this is not a loan with interest because such a loan cannot arise from bare agreement (Case 58), but the interest is owed on the basis of mandate.

3. Standard of Care; Compensation for Expenses. In general, *procuratores* were expected to act in accord with *bona fides*; for instance, a *procurator* who purchased a farm on the principal's account was expected both to hand over the farm to the principal and to secure the appropriate warranties; Ulpian and Paul, D. 17.1.8.9–10 pr. Acting in good faith is taken as an implied term of the mandate, one that is not easily waived; Scaevola, D. 17.1.60.4, summarized earlier. Unlike in ordinary mandate, where the standard of care appears to vary according to circumstances (see Case 179), a *procurator* is liable for both *dolus* and *culpa*, or so at least it is held in early postclassical rescripts; Diocletian and Maximian, C. 4.35.11 (293 CE), 13 (294); see also already Alexander, C. 4.35.4 (222–235). What justifies this increase in liability?

So long as he incurs his expenses in good faith, a *procurator* is entitled to recoup them in an action on mandate, regardless whether his efforts were successful: Papinian, D. 17.1.56.4. These expenses include costs of preparation: Ulpian, D. 17.1.12.17.

4. Distinction from the *Institor*. A fuller, traveling abroad, turned over his shop to his apprentices to whom he asked a customer to give his orders. After the fuller's departure, an apprentice took the customer's clothing and fled. Ulpian, D. 14.3.5.10, holds that the fuller is not liable if the apprentice had been left as a *procurator*, but is liable if he was an *institor.* Explain this difference. How would the customer have been able to tell?

5. A Procurator for a Single Matter. What was the concern of "some" jurists who, Pomponius reports, were against allowing mandate to a *procurator* for a single business? How might their concerns have been answered? Other sources indicate that while this issue may still have been controversial in the mid-second century CE when Pomponius wrote, a *procurator unius rei* was generally accepted by the late Classical period.

CASE 204: Acquiring Property for the Principal

D. 41.1.13 (Neratius libro sexto Regularum)

pr. Si procurator rem mihi emerit ex mandato meo eique sit tradita meo nomine, dominium mihi, id est proprietas, adquiritur etiam ignoranti. 1. Et tutor pupilli pupillae similiter ut procurator emendo nomine pupilli pupillae proprietatem illis adquirit etiam ignorantibus.

D. 41.2.42.1 (Ulpianus libro quarto Regularum)

Procurator si quidem mandante domino rem emerit, protinus illi adquirit possessionem: quod si sua sponte emerit, non nisi ratam habuerit dominus emptionem.

Neratius in the sixth book of his *Rules*:

pr. If my *procurator* purchases (something) on my behalf and based on my mandate, and it is handed over to him in my name, ownership, i.e., a property right, is acquired for me even if I am unaware of this. 1. And a guardian of a male or female ward, like a *procurator*, by buying in the name of the ward acquires a property right for them even if they are unaware of this.

Ulpian in the fourth book of his *Rules*:

If, indeed, a *procurator* purchases based on the owner's (i.e., the principal's) mandate, he acquires possession for him at once. But if he buys on his own initiative, not unless the owner ratifies the purchase (will possession pass to him).

Discussion

1. An Exception to the Rule. Gaius, *Inst.* 2.95, writing about 160 CE, states that, as law, we cannot take possession of property through free persons not subject to our power (even as free persons held as slaves in good faith), nor through other people's slaves in whom we have no property interest; this rule is taken to illustrate the more vulgar saying that property cannot be acquired through a stranger (*extranea persona*). But then he adds that question has arisen whether we acquire possession through a *procurator*. These doubts, if they persisted, were gradually overcome. Already Neratius, D. 41.3.41, notes that it was "nearly agreed" that a procurator could take possession for a principal, and so he could thereby start the process to gaining ownership (through usucapion). In an ordinary sale of goods, indeed, taking possession for the principal would usually make the latter the owner outright, as Neratius says in this Case. This exception is refined by Ulpian: If the *procurator* purchased on his principal's mandate, the principal acquired possession immediately upon delivery; but if the *procurator* acted on his own, the owner had to ratify the sale. The exception took hold in later law: *Pauli Sent.* 5.2.2 (describing it as accepted for practical reasons);

and Justinian, *Inst.* 2.9.5, suggests that a constitution of Septimius Severus (193–198 CE) may even have extended it still further, a possibility perhaps supported by Ulpian, D. 41.1.20.2, and Modestinus, D. 41.1.53. What are the "practical reasons" for such an exception?

2. **Alienating the Principal's Property.** Gaius, D. 41.1.9.4, states unequivocally that anyone to whom an owner entrusts "free administration of affairs" (*libera negotiorum administratio*) can sell the owner's property and hand over possession of it to the buyer. This certainly was Justinian's law: *Inst.* 2.1.43. Such a rule would surely include the general *procurator*, but it is doubtful the Classical jurists went this far. Unfortunately, the manuscript of Gaius, *Inst.* 2.64, has a gap at exactly the point where the capacity of the *procurator* to alienate is being discussed. Still, the likeliest restoration of Gaius' text is that the *procurator* could alienate "if specifically permitted to do so" (*si hoc ei concessum est*). See also Case 205; Modestinus, D. 3.3.63 (heavily reworked by compilers); Diocletian and Maximian, C. 2.12.16 (293 CE).

CASE 205: Contracting for the Principal

D. 14.3.19 pr. (Papinianus libro tertio Responsorum)

In eum, qui mutuis accipiendis pecuniis procuratorem praeposuit, utilis ad exemplum institoriae dabitur actio: quod aeque faciendum erit et si procurator solvendo sit, qui stipulanti pecuniam promisit.

D. 3.3.67 (Papinianus libro secundo Responsorum)

Procurator, qui pro evictione praediorum quae vendidit fidem suam adstrinxit, etsi negotia gerere desierit, obligationis tamen onere praetoris auxilio non levabitur: nam procurator, qui pro domino vinculum obligationis suscepit, onus eius frustra recusat.

Papinian in the third book of his *Responses*:

Against a person who placed a *procurator* in charge of receiving money on loan, there will be given an analogous action based on the model of that for an *institor*. This should be done even if the *procurator*, who made a promise to someone who stipulated for it, is (himself) solvent.

Papinian in the second book of his *Responses*:

A *procurator* who guaranteed his own credit (*fides*) regarding eviction from property he sold, even if he ceases to administer (his principal's) affairs, still will not be released from the obligation's burden by the Praetor's help; for a *procurator* who accepts the bond of an obligation for an owner ineffectively rejects its burden.

Discussion

1. A Procurator's Contracts. A *procurator*, placed in charge of taking out loans from third parties, in connection with this charge made a formal promise to someone (presumably for repayment with interest), a promise that was not kept. Since the *procurator* is solvent, the promisee could sue him, but prefers to sue his principal. Although the *procurator's* duties do not exactly amount to a business (and so he is not an *institor*), the Severan jurist Papinian extended the *actio institoria* by analogy to make possible the promisee's lawsuit against the principal.

The extension may seem a small one, but it is highly significant because it palpably expands, beyond the confines of an established and recognizable business, the orbit of persons who can make a principal liable in contract. In order to attain this result, Papinian reached outside the confines of mandate and imported legal conceptions underlying business managers. Ulpian, D. 17.1.10.5, reports another opinion of his regarding a surety who was condemned in a lawsuit after a *procurator*, given a mandate to take out loans, defaulted; same outcome, the surety can sue the principal by an *actio quasi institoria* "because, here as well, he (the principal) is held to have, as it were, placed him (the *procurator*) in charge of taking out loans." See also the following Case.

2. The Procurator's Responsibility. How does the second Papinian fragment help explain why, in the first, Papinian notes the *procurator's* solvency? Contrast Ulpian, D. 3.5.5.3: I lent money to your *procurator* with the intention that he pay off your creditor or redeem your pledge; if the loan is not repaid to me, I can sue you, but not the *procurator*, over management of affairs (*negotiorum gestio*). Why this outcome? Ulpian apparently assumes the money was used for its intended purpose, and that you were unaware of the loan to the *procurator*. But why is the *procurator* not liable himself, even if he gave me a formal promise on repayment? What incentives does Ulpian's decision create?

CASE 206: Liability of Third Parties to the Principal

D. 19.1.13.25 (Ulpianus libro trigesimo secundo ad Edictum)

Si procurator vendiderit et caverit emptori, quaeritur, an domino vel adversus dominum actio dari debeat. Et Papinianus libro tertio responsorum putat cum domino ex empto agi posse utili actione ad exemplum institoriae actionis, si modo rem vendendam mandavit: ergo et per contrarium dicendum est utilem ex empto actionem domino competere.

Ulpian in the thirty-second book *On the Edict*:

If a *procurator* sells (the principal's property) and gives a warranty (*cautio*) to the buyer, it is asked whether an action should be given (either) to or against the owner (the principal). Papinian, in the third book of his *Responses*, thinks there can be an action on purchase (*ex empto*) against the owner, through an analogous action based on that for an *institor*, provided he (the owner) mandated sale of the object. Therefore, conversely (for purchases made by the *procurator* on the owner's behalf), it should be held that the owner has an analogous action on purchase (*ex empto*).

Discussion

1. The Principal's Countersuit. Try to follow the logic of this fragment. The *procurator* has sold his principal's property and given a warranty (probably against eviction) to its buyer, who can bring an *actio quasi institoria* against the principal if the warranty is violated. But what if, instead, the *procurator* bought property from a third party who gives him a warranty? If the warranty is violated, can the principal sue the seller directly, rather than through his *procurator* (by a cession of actions, e.g.)? An analogous action on purchase is almost as daring as the *actio quasi institoria*.

   Ulpian, in Case 202, indicates that it was Marcellus, a generation before Papinian, who suggested this counteraction with regard to the *institor*, although he may not have discovered a procedural vehicle for it. See also Paul, D. 46.5.5.

CASE 207: Compensation

D. 17.1.7 (Papinianus libro tertio Responsorum)

Salarium procuratori constitutum si extra ordinem peti coeperit, considerandum erit, laborem dominus remunerare voluerit atque ideo fidem adhiberi placitis oporteat an eventum litium maioris pecuniae praemio contra bonos mores procurator redemerit.

D. 17.1.10.9 (Ulpianus libro trigensimo primo ad Edictum)

Idem Labeo ait et verum est reputationes quoque hoc iudicium admittere et, sicuti fructus cogitur restituere is qui procurat, ita sumptum, quem in fructus percipiendos fecit, deducere eum oportet: sed et si ad vecturas suas, dum excurrit in praedia, sumptum fecit, puto hos quoque sumptus reputare eum oportere, nisi si salariarius fuit et hoc convenit, ut sumptus de suo faceret ad haec itinera, hoc est de salario.

Papinian in the third book of his *Responses*:

If a suit is brought *extra ordinem* for a stipend (*salarium*) agreed upon for a *procurator*, it will have to be considered whether the owner (the principal) wished to reward him and therefore the agreement must be honored, or (whether instead), contrary to good morals (*contra bonos mores*), the *procurator* purchased the litigation's result for a reward of more money.

Ulpian in the thirty-first book *On the Edict*:

Labeo likewise says, correctly, that this action (on mandate) allows for set-offs as well, and, just as the *procurator* must restore (to his principal) the fruits (profits resulting from the mandate), so he should deduct the expenses he had in collecting the fruits. But also if he had travel expenses for journeying to the (mandatory's) property, I think he should offset these expenses as well, unless he was salaried under an agreement that he pay the travel expenses from his own (pocket), i.e., from his stipend (*salarium*).

Discussion

1. *Salarium*. This word (from which "salary" obviously derives) is most commonly used for the pay of public officials (e.g., Papinian, D. 1.22.4, 6), but in private law it is usually only a near equivalent of *honorarium*, with perhaps a slightly more "official" connotation. In principle, it is meant to cover expenses, but it is often likely to have served as actual pay for services rendered; this ambiguity is reflected in the fragment from Ulpian.

2. Pay for Procurators. The first fragment concerns a *procurator* acting as the principal's representative in a lawsuit (*in litem*), who, in an imperial court (*extra ordinem*), claims an agreed-upon *salarium* for his services. Papinian, following general public policy (Ulpian, D. 17.1.6.7 and 50.13.1.12, both

citing imperial rescripts; Diocletian and Maximian, C. 2.12.15 (293)), rejects this claim if it amounts to purchasing a share in a potential verdict (*quota litis*), but allows it if the payment is independent of the verdict.

The second fragment strongly indicates that other sorts of *procuratores* were accorded *salaria* they could claim in court. The *procurator* described by Ulpian might be a general *procurator* or one appointed for a specific purpose. The parties appear to have broad freedom to set up the arrangement as they wish. Assuming that the *procurator*'s claim would be brought *extra ordinem* (as in the first fragment), the offset (*reputatio*) that Ulpian describes would by his time have taken place, not in a suit in mandate (as in Labeo's day), but rather in an imperial court.

Nevertheless, even during the late Classical period the pay's theoretical "independence" from the mandate was still strongly maintained in principle. Severus and Caracalla, C. 4.35.1 (198–211 CE), allow for a *procurator* to collect money he has spent from his own resources or on loan in executing a mandate, together with interest (Case 181), but then add: "Regarding the *salarium* that he promised, the provincial governor will grant a hearing." The latter proceeding would be *extra ordinem*. Why might the jurists have been reluctant to recognize the salary relationship?

CASE 208: Extension of the Theory

D. 3.5.30 pr. (Papinianus libro secundo Responsorum)

Liberto vel amico mandavit pecuniam accipere mutuam: cuius litteras creditor secutus contraxit et fideiussor intervenit: etiamsi pecunia non sit in rem eius versa, tamen dabitur in eum negotiorum gestorum actio creditori vel fideiussori, scilicet ad exemplum institoriae actionis.

Papinian in the second book of his *Responses*:

A person gave to his freedman or a friend a (written) mandate to borrow money; a creditor, relying on his letter, entered a contract (to give a loan), and a surety (*fideiussor*) guaranteed (repayment). Even if the money did not (actually) benefit him (the mandator), the creditor or the surety will be given an action on administration of affairs (*negotiorum gestio*), obviously based on that for an *institor*.

Discussion

1. His Freedman or a Friend. A man gives a written mandate ordering a person, someone who evidently is not his dependent nor his *procurator* nor the manager of his business (an *institor*), to take out a loan. A creditor, relying on this writing, gives the loan to the mandatary, who promises to repay and is backed up by a surety. If the loan is not repaid, Papinian holds that the lender can sue the mandator by an action constructed on the model of the *institoria*; and likewise, if the surety pays off the lender, he too can sue the mandator—but on administration of his affairs rather than on mandate. This is so even though the principal has not materially benefited from the loan.

   Decide for yourself whether this fragment is fully consistent with what you know of Classical law. The major difficulty is the final clause and the "model" of the *actio institoria* as applied to this situation. Legal sources indicate that the action on administration of affairs may be available against a third party when the plaintiff has relied on that party's mandate to another: e.g., Ulpian, D. 3.5.3.11, 5.6; Ulpian/Papinian, D. 16.1.6–7; Severus and Caracalla, C. 2.18.4 (201 CE); Alexander, C. 2.18.14 (234). But this is really a matter of equity.

PART D

Transfer of Contract Rights and Duties to Third Parties

Delegation (*delegatio*) is a fairly well developed area of Roman law in which one person (the delegator) gives an order to another person (the delegatee) to pay money to or carry out an act for a third party: D. 46.2, C. 8.41. Delegation can be used for a wide variety of purposes, e.g., to make a gift or establish a dowry; but our interest here is only in one important use of delegation: the transfer of a contractual debt—principally, a debt of money—from the original debtor to another person. The counterpart of delegation is what we call assignment: a creditor conveys the right to collect from his debtor.

It helps to make the legal situation more concrete by devising a hypothetical. Say that I am owed money by my debtor D, and I owe money to my creditor C. I may regard it as in my interest to have D pay C directly, without having the money pass into and then out of my hands. There are, in the broadest sense, two ways that I can accomplish this.

First, I can give an order to my debtor D to pay the money not to me, but rather to my creditor C. If the law permits—and Roman law does, although only to a limited extent and under some strict conditions—D's actual payment to C would have the effect of freeing not only D from his debt to me, but me from my debt to C. (Romanists call this *delegatio solvendi*, delegation of paying.) However, if my debtor D, in response to my order, instead promises to pay my creditor C (Romanists call this *delegatio obligandi*, delegation of obligating), C may justifiably be cautious about accepting a new debtor in place of me, and so the law needs to safeguard C's interests.

Second, I can instead give an order to my creditor C to collect my debt from my debtor D. Such an order entitles C to approach D and demand payment directly, and to sue for payment if necessary. If everything goes smoothly, the result is the same as in the preceding example. Here too, however, both my creditor and my debtor may need protection. This cession of actions (*cession actionum*) is broadly similar to what Common Law calls assignment of rights; however, assignment of an entire contract, both rights and duties, seems to be unknown in Roman law.

If this still sounds too abstract, consider the situation in the context of banking. I have an account with a bank where I have deposited money, and therefore the bank is my debtor. Assume that I make a large purchase from an art dealer to whom I promise payment; the art dealer becomes my creditor. I want to pay the art dealer by moving money from my bank account to her. How should I bring this about: by ordering the bank to pay the dealer, or by ordering the dealer (e.g., through a check) to seek payment from the bank? That is the basic problem in the following Part.

Common to both forms of debt transfer is the requirement of an order: *iussum*, or less technically a *mandatum*. It is unilateral and there is no requirement of form; however, all the parties are likely to insist on some sort of accurate record at all stages.

CASE 209: Ordering My Debtor to Pay My Creditor

D. 46.3.64 (Paulus libro quarto decimo ad Plautium)

Cum iussu meo id, quod mihi debes, solvis creditori meo, et tu a me et ego a creditore meo liberor.

Paul in the fourteenth book *On Plautius*:

When, on my order, you pay to my creditor what you owe to me, (simultaneously) you are freed from me and I am freed from my creditor.

Discussion

1. **Payment** (*Solutio*). As Gaius remarks, 3.168, "Obligations are discharged chiefly by payment of what is owed." If the debtor does not tender a cash payment directly to the creditor, Roman law accords the two parties considerable freedom to determine, by agreement, when and how a debt has been paid off. In addition, payment could be made to the creditor's authorized representative, such as a *procurator* or other designated person; e.g., Ulpian, D. 46.3.12 pr.-1. Many other legal rules formed around the process of payment. The creditor's acceptance of full payment could be formally acknowledged with a receipt, *acceptilatio* (Discussion, Case 39).

   The parties could also agree on a substitute performance, such as the debtor conveying property in place of money (*datio in solutum*); and, according to the view that eventually prevailed, full performance then had the effect of discharging the debt: Gaius, *Inst.* 3.168; Diocletian and Maximian, C. 8.42.17 (293); Justinian, *Inst.* 3.29 pr. Partial performance (as where the substituted property proved to be defective) was more doubtful; the jurists debated whether to give the creditor an action on a fictional sale of the substitute (Ulpian, D. 13.7.24 pr.) or instead to revive the original debt (Marcian, D. 46.3.46 pr.).

   The effect of payment was to extinguish not only the debt itself, but also all real and personal securities (Justinian, *Inst.* 3.29 pr.). For a legal fiction used to explain this result, see Ulpian, D. 24.1.3.12–13, citing Celsus and Julian; Africanus, D. 46.3.38.1. See also Cases 45–46 on what happens when a surety pays the debt.

2. **The Effect of the Mandate.** More important for our purposes are the complexities arising when a third party pays off the debt. The jurists affirm the general aphorism that: "A benefit is not given to an unwilling person" (Paul, D. 50.17.69: *Invito beneficium non datur.*), but nonetheless fairly consistently hold that a third party's payment to a creditor extinguishes the debt even if the debtor is unwilling or unaware: Gaius, D. 3.5.38; Pomponius, D. 46.3.17 (so long as the payment is made in the debtor's name). The contradiction here was plainly troubling; what do you think

is the best solution? Labeo, D. 3.5.42 pr., accords the third party an action on unauthorized management of affairs so long as the debtor was benefited (Chapter VIII.A), but elsewhere, D. 46.3.91, gives no release from the debt if the debtor is present (!) and forbids the payment; but two centuries later Paul reverses the latter decision in his note on this passage. What reason might a debtor have for not wanting an unauthorized third party to pay his debt?

The debtor's mandate changes this situation in that when the third party (usually, the debtor of the person issuing the mandate) pays the mandator's debt, both debtors are then released from their respective debts. Paul, D. 46.3.56 ("A person who mandates payment is deemed himself to pay."), 50.17.180. Actual payment is required, not just the debtor's promise of payment.

Papinian, D. 46.3.96 pr., develops a hypothetical in which the debtor of an underage ward, acting on delegation from the guardian, pays money to the guardian's creditor; the result is the release of both debts unless this was part of a fraudulent scheme between the guardian and the debtor. What fraud might have occurred?

CASE 210: Mandate to My Banker to Pay My Debt

D. 2.14.47.1 (Scaevola libro primo Digestorum)

Lucius Titius Gaium Seium mensularium, cum quo rationem implicitam habebat propter accepta et data, debitorem sibi constituit et ab eo epistulam accepit in haec verba: "Ex ratione mensae, quam mecum habuisti, in hunc diem ex contractibus plurimis remanserunt apud me ad mensam meam trecenta octaginta sex et usurae quae competierint. Summam aureorum, quam apud me tacitam habes, refundam tibi. Si quod instrumentum a te emissum, id est scriptum, cuiuscumque summae ex quacumque causa apud me remansit, vanum et pro cancellato habebitur." Quaesitum est, cum Lucius Titius ante hoc chirographum Seio nummulario mandaverat, uti patrono eius trecenta redderet, an propter illa verba epistulae, quibus omnes cautiones ex quocumque contractu vanae et pro cancellato ut haberentur cautum est, neque ipse neque filii eius eo nomine conveniri possunt. Respondi, si tantum ratio accepti atque expensi esset computata, ceteras obligationes manere in sua causa.

Scaevola in the first book of his *Digests*:

Lucius Titius established as his debtor Gaius Seius, a banker with whom he had a tangled account for receipts and payments, and he received a letter from him as follows: "From the bank account that you have with me, up to this day from numerous contracts there have remained with me at my bank 386 (thousand sesterces) plus interest due. The sum of gold coins that you have in secret with me I will refund to you. If any document sent by you, i.e., in writing, for whatever amount from whatever cause has remained with me, it will be considered as void and canceled."

A question arose, when prior to this promissory note (*chirographum*) Lucius Titius had given a mandate to the banker Seius that he return 300 (thousand) to his patron (Titius' former master), whether, on account of the letter's wording whereby it is provided that all obligations from any contract be considered as "void and canceled," neither he himself (i.e., Seius) nor his sons can be sued on this account. I responded that if only an account of receipts and expenses was tallied, the other obligations remained in their legal place.

The Problem
Lucius Titius was a freedman probably indebted to his patron (his former owner). He had a complex account, involving many transactions, with Gaius Seius, a banker; and in addition he had some gold coins on deposit in this bank. Seius sent him a formal letter (later described as a promissory note, *chirographum*) in which he stated the current account balance as 386,000 sesterces resulting from numerous contracts; this balance was held at interest (see Case 69). Seius also stated that any additional written document sent by Titius "for whatever amount

from whatever cause" was now null and void. (He also promised to return on demand the deposited gold coins.)

Before Seius' letter was sent, Titius had given a mandate to Seius to "return" (*reddere*) to Titius' patron the bulk of the money in the account, some 300,000 sesterces—probably as repayment of a loan. Although bankers may often have offered their customers services of this kind, Seius, as it seems, did not execute Titius' mandate, and Titius suffered loss as a result (probably because he had promised timely repayment to his patron). The question of law is whether Seius' letter effectively rendered void Titius' mandate, a declaration that would amount to a mandatary declining to carry out a mandate (see Case 177); or whether the mandate remained valid, in which event Seius (or his sons and heirs if he had died) could be liable for damages for failure to execute a mandate (see Case 178).

The jurist's brief and enigmatic answer is that if Seius' letter or promissory note was just a statement of the current balance, any outstanding obligations that Seius had undertaken were still valid.

Discussion

1. A Complex Case. Although the general situation seems clear enough, many of the details are obscure and controversial. From the wording, it seems likely that Titius had a long-standing bank account with Seius, and that he gave his mandate seeking disbursement from this account. (The mandate operates somewhat like a debit card today.) The banker's motives in writing his subsequent letter are much less clear, and you should try to puzzle them out. It is possible that the Seius is concerned that multiple previously existing instructions could leave Titius' account in overdraft, something that the banker is rightly concerned to avoid if at all possible; that is, he does not necessarily want to honor all previous instructions.

   Scaevola's response (which is written in his characteristically abbreviated style) points to two interrelated questions: first, can Seius' letter be accurately described as just a statement of Titius' current bank balance; and second, with regard to the mandate, what is the meaning and effect of the "void and canceled" language in the letter's third sentence? This response, despite its declaratory nature, is not necessarily meant to decide the hypothetical case; it only states the rule of law that is relevant to it. Work out for yourself how the rule should best be applied. The letter that Scaevola quotes seems to be an authentic bank document (it's written in Big Business Latin), but the text uses "John Doe" names for the parties.

   Note that what is being discussed in this Case is the banker's actual payment to Titius' patron (or more exactly his failure to pay), not a promise to pay, which would be actual delegation. This latter problem is taken up in the following Case.

2. A Promise to Pay a Debt (*Constitutum Debiti*). One problem with this Case
   is its opening words: "Lucius Titius established as his debtor Gaius Seius, a
   banker . . ." This wording could be a reference to *constitutum debiti*, an informal promise to pay money owed by yourself or someone else at a fixed
   time and place; although the original debt remains unaffected, failure to execute the promised payment was actionable (D. 13.5; C. 4.18). The phrase
   does have this sense at Ulpian, D. 2.14.51.1, for instance. But, especially
   given the context, more probably the phrase has no technical meaning here,
   but simply refers to Titius having previously established a bank account
   that "made Seius a debtor"; this is the sense in, e.g., Ulpian, D. 15.3.10.8;
   Paul, D. 46.3.62.

CASE 211: Delegating Obligation for a Debt Owed by Me

D. 46.2.11 (Ulpian libro vicensimo septimo ad Edictum)

pr. Delegare est vice sua alium reum dare creditori vel cui iusserit. 1. Fit autem delegatio vel per stipulationem vel per litis contestationem.

Gaius, *Institutiones* 2.38–39

38. Obligationes quoquo modo contractae nihil eorum recipiunt: nam quod mihi ab aliquo debetur, id si uelim tibi deberi, nullo eorum modo, quibus res corporales ad alium transferuntur, id efficere possum; sed opus est, ut iubente me tu ab eo stipuleris; quae res efficit, ut a me liberetur et incipiat tibi teneri. quae dicitur nouatio obligationis. 39. Sine hac uero nouatione non poteris tuo nomine agere, sed debes ex persona mea quasi cognitor aut procurator meus experiri.

Ulpian in the twenty-seventh book *On the Edict*:

pr. To delegate means to give another debtor in one's place to a creditor or a person he authorizes (to receive payment). 1. Delegation is brought about either by stipulation or through joinder of issue (*litis contestatio*).

Gaius in the second book of his *Institutes*:

38. Obligations, however they are contracted, allow for none of these (previously discussed means of transferring property). For whatever is owed to me by someone, if I want it owed to you, I can bring this about by none of those (means) whereby tangible property is transferred to another person. Rather it is necessary that, on my order, you take a stipulation from him (my debtor); this brings it about that he is freed from me and becomes liable to you. This is called novation of the obligation. 39. Without this novation you will not be able to sue in your own name. Rather, you should sue in my person as my legal counsel (*cognitor*) or my *procurator*.

Discussion

1. Delegating an Obligation. The verb *delegare* can refer simply to the empowerment of a delegated person (e.g., Ulpian, D. 46.2.17: "A person who is unable to speak can delegate his debtor by writing or a gesture."), but more frequently refers to transforming an obligation, and in particular to recasting a trilateral debt relationship (my debtor owes money to me, and I owe money to my creditor) as a bilateral one (my debtor owes money to my creditor). As in this Case, the verb quite often refers to putting a debtor (almost always, my debtor) in my place, so that the debtor owes to my creditor what it was that I had owed him, and my debt is thereby almost always released.

2. How to Delegate. Ulpian mentions two formal ways to delegate, but stipulation is by far the more common. The stipulating parties are (in the preceding

hypothetical), my creditor as the party that puts the question and becomes the promisee, and my debtor as the promissor; I play no direct role in the procedure, although I very likely had initiated it. The stipulation could take two forms: either my debtor promised to pay to my creditor what he owes to me; or he promised to pay what I owe to my creditor. These may be two different amounts, and the legal consequences are also different as far as enforcement is concerned: in the former case, my debtor can raise all the legal defenses he might have raised against me, but not those I might have raised against my creditor (Ulpian, D. 16.1.8.2; Paul, D. 46.2.19); while in the latter case the reverse is usually true (Ulpian, D. 16.1.8.3; Julian, D. 46.1.18). In both cases, however, I can assume the risk that my debtor will not pay (Justinian, *Inst.* 3.26.2; Paul, D. 17.1.22.2, 45.7).

And in both cases the effect is the same: my debtor is substituted for me and, to the extent of the promise, a novation is effected, through which my debt to my creditor is extinguished; on novation, see Case 39. This is the burden of Gaius' comment in the present Case.

3. So Where's the Rub? There are four major problems with this form of *delegatio*. First, it requires the identification of two distinct preexisting debts, which, unless they are clearly denominated (i.e., liquidated), may be hard to integrate. Second, it requires the active cooperation of my creditor, who may be justly concerned about the substitution of a new debtor in place of me; but my creditor is needed to perform the stipulation. Third, my debtor must also cooperate, of course. And fourth, the procedure is, as usual, clumsy and formalistic: the parties must be physically assembled in a single place at a specified time, and the promise must be agreed upon and exactly formulated. The Classical jurists never seem to have found a way around these difficulties. How great do they seem to you? Is Roman law overly protective of a creditor's concerns?

This fragment of Gaius comes at the end of a long passage in which he is considering how to transfer property rights in incorporeal property (*res incorporales*) such as personal and praedial servitudes (2.28–33: e.g., rights of way, usufructs) or inheritances (2.34–37). For them, transfer can be circuitous but is still relatively painless. Not so for obligations. However, at the end of section 39 Gaius suggests another way to solve the problem, a solution to which we turn in the following Cases.

4. Delegating a Duty to Perform. Although virtually all Roman sources describe delegation in terms of a money debt, it could also be used to delegate a performance (Case 234: a freedman's work) or property rights (Ulpian, D. 46.2.4: a usufruct).

CASE 212: Appointing a *Procurator* for a Lawsuit

Gaius, *Institutiones* 4.84

Procurator uero nullis certis uerbis in litem substituitur, sed ex solo mandato et absente et ignorante aduersario constituitur; quin etiam sunt, qui putant eum quoque procuratorem uideri, cui non sit mandatum, si modo bona fide accedat ad negotium et caueat ratam rem dominum habiturum; quamquam et ille, cui mandatum est, plerumque satisdare debet, quia saepe mandatum initio litis in obscuro est et postea apud iudicem ostenditur.

Gaius in the fourth book of his *Institutes*:

On the other hand, a *procurator* for a lawsuit (*in litem*) is substituted by no formal words, on the basis of a mandate alone and with the adversary absent and unaware. Indeed, there are those who think he also is deemed a *procurator* who has no mandate, so long as he approaches the business in good faith (*bona fide*) and gives security that the principal will ratify the act. Yet even a person with a mandate frequently has to give security because often the mandate is unclear at the start of a suit and is (only) made evident afterward before the *iudex*.

Discussion

1. *Procurator in Litem.* On *procuratores*, see Part C of this Chapter, especially its introduction. Roman procedural law began with a general principle denying representation to litigants: Justinian, *Inst.* 4.10 pr. (*nemo pro alio lege agere potest*); see Ulpian, D. 50.17.123 pr. However, this principle came under considerable strain as the Roman legal system grew in complexity, and eventually courts were obliged to accept that representation was inevitable; indeed, the Praetor's Edict itself regulated who was acceptable as a representative (Lenel, *EP*[3] 95–97). The *procurator in litem* was, as Gaius says, informally appointed through a mandate (but even without one, if the representative was acting on behalf of someone lacking legal capacity).

   The *procurator*, however, is unlike a modern judicial advocate in one important respect: the *formula* for the trial states that while the principal is the actual party to the lawsuit, the *procurator* is the person whom the *iudex* should condemn (Gaius, *Inst.* 4.86–87). That is, in Classical procedure the *procurator* is not an agent. Therefore action on the judgment lay against him. Doesn't it make sense, then, that the *procurator in litem* might have to give security that his principal will in fact pay any judgment? In time, though, a *procurator's* position became more transparent; in very late Classical law he was regarded, under many circumstances, as fully representing his client so long as he had been officially appointed and had the "full power of acting," *plena potestas agendi*: Frag. Vat. 317; Alexander Severus, C. 2.12.10 (227).

The *procurator* who intervenes in a lawsuit without a litigant's mandate is usually obliged, in later Classical law, to seek compensation on the basis of quasi-contract (see Chapter VIII.A).

2. Acting in His Own Interests. In principle, a mandate given solely to benefit the mandatary is void: see Case 177. However, as the Cases in Part C show, the application of this general rule became less clear-cut with the acceptance of general *procuratores*, appointed by mandate, who were acting independently and for pay. This may have influenced the procedural development described in the following Case.

CASE 213: Assigning a Debt to Your *Procurator*

D. 3.3.55 (Ulpianus libro sexagensimo quinto ad Edictum)

Procuratore in rem suam dato praeferendus non est dominus procuratori in litem movendam vel pecuniam suscipiendam: qui enim suo nomine utiles actiones habet, rite eas intendit.

D. 2.14.16 pr. (Ulpianus libro quarto ad Edictum)

Si cum emptore hereditatis pactum sit factum et venditor hereditatis petat, doli exceptio nocet. Nam ex quo rescriptum est a divo Pio utiles actiones emptori hereditatis dandas, merito adversus venditorem hereditatis exceptione doli debitor hereditarius uti potest.

Ulpian in the sixty-fifth book *On the Edict*:

When a *procurator* is appointed on his own behalf (*in rem suam*), the principal must not be preferred to the *procurator* in bringing a lawsuit or in receiving money, since he (the procurator) has analogous actions (*utiles actiones*) in his own name and properly brings them.

Ulpian in the fourth book *On the Edict*:

If a pact was made (by a debtor) with the purchaser of an estate and the seller of the estate claims it (the debt), the defense of deceit (*exceptio doli*) is a bar to recovery. For, from when a rescript of the deified Pius (Antoninus Pius, reigned 138–161 CE) specified that analogous actions should be granted to the purchaser of an inheritance, the debtor of an estate can rightly use the defense of deceit against the estate's seller.

Discussion

1. *Procurator in Rem Suam*. As Gaius observed in Case 211, the development of this institution resulted from the awkwardness of delegating a debtor, and it probably occurred as early as the late Republic. As with *procuratores* generally, the debtor gives a mandate (a *iussum*, order) to his creditor to bring a suit "in his own name" (*suo nomine*) against the debtor's debtor; that is, the *procurator* is given the actual plaintiff's claim as his own, and keeps the award. As should be clear, this inverts the procedure of delegating a debtor, but it is much easier because the debtor's cooperation is not required. Still, some obstacles remained. Above all, until his creditor actually sued, the person ceding the action could revoke his order, or he could even sue the debtor himself, or reach a settlement, or release the debt; this problem could only be tackled by the creditor requiring guarantees (Gaius, *Inst.* 2.252: *cautiones*).

   By the late Classical period, the *procurator's* position had been further strengthened, thanks initially to the rescript of Antoninus Pius that Ulpian mentions; initially it concerned only inheritances, but it was quickly extended. The *procurator* now had available, in his own name, analogous actions that were independent of judicial representations. These actions, as Ulpian notes, protected the *procurator* against the grantor's revocation or death (see also Gordian, C. 4.10.1 (242)), and also protected his reliance (see the following Case).

In the second Ulpian passage, a person who owed money to a decedent's estate reached an agreement on the debt with the estate's purchaser; but the seller then tried to recover the debt. Do you see how Antoninus Pius' rescript is relevant to the debtor's defense of deceit? Does the sale of the estate make the buyer into a *procurator in rem suam* for collection of the estate's debts?

CASE 214: Delegation vs. Mandate to a Creditor

C. 8.41.3 (Imp. Gordianus A. Muciano)

pr. Si delegatio non est interposita debitoris tui ac propterea actiones apud te remanserunt, quamvis creditori tuo adversus eum solutionis causa mandaveris actiones, tamen, antequam lis contestetur vel aliquid ex debito accipiat vel debitori tuo denuntiaverit, exigere a debitore tuo debitam quantitatem non vetaris et eo modo tui creditoris exactionem contra eum inhibere. 1. Quod si delegatione facta iure novationis tu liberatus es, frustra vereris, ne eo, quod quasi a cliente suo non faciat exactionem, ad te periculum redundet, cum per verborum obligationem voluntate novationis interposita debito liberatus sis.

The Emperor Gordian, to Mucianus (239 CE):

pr. If there was no delegation of your debtor and therefore the rights of action remained with you, even though you mandated the actions against him to your creditor for payment, still, prior to joinder of issue (*litis contestatio*) or his (the creditor's) receiving some of the debt or his giving notice (demanding payment) to your debtor, you are not forbidden from demanding from your debtor the amount owed, and thereby obstructing your creditor's collection from him.

1. But if a delegation (of the debtor) was made and you were released by the law of novation, you (as the former creditor) needlessly fear that the risk falls on you should he fail to collect as if from his own client, since, through a verbal obligation (the stipulation), with the intent of novation having been interposed, you are freed from the debt.

Discussion

1. Further Protections for the *Procurator in Rem Suam*. Mucianus, the recipient of this imperial rescript, apparently had financial concerns about money owed to his creditor and owing from his debtor. The emperor posits two situations. First, Mucianus has by mandate given his creditor the right to sue his debtor. The emperor does allow Mucianus to revoke his mandate, but only if the creditor has not yet sued or demanded payment. In that event, the creditor takes preference over Mucianus, as in the previous Case.

   Alexander Severus, C. 8.16.4 (225), writes to a veteran soldier who has lent money to a person who gave security in the form of a debt owed to him by X. The veteran can bring an analogous action (*actio utilis*) directly against X; but if X pays veteran's debtor before the latter informs him of the security arrangement, the veteran loses his right to bring the analogous action. If the veteran can sue, how much money can he claim from X? That is, what limits are there on his claim?

2. Delegation and Novation. The emperor's second situation shows the stark contrast when a creditor has delegated a debt to his creditor. As a result of

the novation, the delegating creditor has lost the right to sue his debtor, but also cannot be sued by his creditor.

You should now be in a position to think about what advice you would have given to a creditor in this situation, had you been a Roman lawyer ca. 240 CE. Delegation or mandate?

CASE 215: Cession of Actions against Co-Sureties

D. 46.1.17 (Iulianus libro octagensimo nono Digestorum)

Fideiussoribus succurri solet, ut stipulator compellatur ei, qui solidum solvere paratus est, vendere ceterorum nomina.

D. 46.1.39 (Modestinus libro secundo Regularum)

Ut fideiussor adversus confideiussorem suum agat, danda actio non est. Ideoque si ex duobus fideiussoribus eiusdem quantitatis [cum] alter electus a creditore totum exsolvit nec ei cessae sint actiones, alter nec a creditore nec a confideiussore convenietur.

Julian in the eighty-ninth book of his *Digests*:

Sureties (*fideiussores*) should be helped by the stipulator (creditor) being compelled to sell the accounts of the others (the co-sureties) to the one tendering payment of all (the debt).

Modestinus in the second book of his *Rules*:

An action is not to be granted to a surety bringing suit against a co-surety. And so if, from two sureties for the same amount (of debt), the one chosen by the creditor has paid the whole amount without the actions being ceded to him, the other (surety) will be sued neither by the creditor nor by his co-surety.

Discussion

1. Co-Sureties. On sureties, see Cases 41–46, and especially Case 46, which explains the legal fiction whereby the surety who is about to pay the entire debt to the creditor should require the creditor to cede to him any actions before paying. In this Case, one of a number of co-sureties, who are personally liable on the entire debt (Case 44), has paid off the creditor. Can he demand that the creditor also cede the right of action against the co-sureties? Julian says yes; so also Papinian, D. 46.6.12. But failure to obtain these actions, as Modestinus observes, results in the surety being unable to sue either the debtor or his co-sureties, the theory being that the payment released all the debtor and the co-sureties; see also Alexander, C. 8.40.11 (229).

   On the whole, however, it makes better sense for the surety to demand, before paying the creditor, that his co-sureties chip in, and later Classical law permitted this; see Case 44.

2. Cession of Actions and Subrogation. Although it was never fully developed in Classical law, cession of actions offered a solution to problems such as that presented in the Discussion to Case 156. Tenant A has a multi-year lease with owner/landlord B, who, during the term of lease, sells the

property to buyer C. This buyer then unjustifiably expels A from the lease-hold. Under Roman law, A has no property claim to his leasehold, and he also has no contract claim against C; his main recourse is against B, his landlord and the former owner. But B, if he included in the sales agreement a provision against disturbing the tenant, has a claim on sale against C. If cession is possible, B can cede to A his claim against C, and so let A sue C directly.

Correspondingly, after B's sale to C, if tenant A wrongfully damages the leasehold and cession of the action is possible, B can cede to C the claim against A; for the situation, see Ulpian, D. 19.1.13.30, citing Tubero.

Cession thus had the potential to solve some of the awkwardness associated with privity of contract. However, it appears that cession (in the form of an analogous action) was not extended beyond the purchase of inheritances until the early postclassical period, especially by the emperor Diocletian (284–305): C. 4.39.8 (the purchaser of a debt has a right to pursue pro-perty pledged for that debt); 6.37.18 (294; a legatee has a right to pursue debts in the bequest to him); 4.15.5 (294: right to pursue a claim given by one's debtor as payment for a debt). See also Valerian and Gallienus, C. 4.10.2 (260; a husband has a right to debts assigned as part of his wife's dowry); Justinian, C. 8.53.33 (528: right of an heir to sue on accounts gifted to decedent).

In modern Common Law, one rough equivalent of cession is the equitable remedy of subrogation, the substitution of one party for another as a cred-itor, with the associated transfer of rights and duties; this device is widely used throughout our law.

CHAPTER VIII

Quasi-Contract

In discussing what he calls the law of personal obligations, the jurist Gaius, writing about 160 CE, draws a fundamental divide between contracts where the obligation arises through agreement between two parties, and delicts (*delicta*) where one person inflicts some form of wrongful loss or injury on another (*Inst.* 3.88). He is referencing a long established distinction, going back to fourth-century Greek philosophers.

However, in a passage from what appears to be a later, somewhat expanded version of the *Institutes* (it is called the *Res Cottidianae* or *Aurea*, "Everyday Matters" or "Golden Rules"), Gaius, D. 44.7.5 pr.-3, adds in other sources of personal liability that are not easily incorporated within the contracts/delicts dichotomy, although they may bear some resemblance to one category or the other. Of these sources, two have special historical standing: the action on administration of another's affairs, when someone manages the business of another without that person's prior or subsequent agreement (*actio negotiorum gestorum*); and the *condictio* when it is used to recover a payment or performance made to another by mistake. These two sources ostensibly have little to do with one another, but almost four centuries later Justinian, *Inst.* 3.27, combined them and others in a new category of obligations arising *quasi ex contractu*, "as if from a contract, from quasi-contract." (See Case 216.)

Although the Roman jurists never developed these liabilities with any high degree of precision or analytical abstraction, they did consistently work to expand them beyond their original perimeters, and what they said has proven to be, quite often, not only brilliantly perceptive, but also rich in provocative insights awaiting further development by later scholars, lawyers, and judges, particularly in Civil Law jurisdictions. The one false start, to be sure, was the very name "quasi-contract," particularly if it were falsely taken (as it once frequently was) to imply some sort of actual contract "implied by law" between claimant and recipient. Today the widely preferred name for liabilities of this type is rather "unjustified enrichment" (or, in Common Law jurisdictions, "unjust enrichment").

Common Law countries were slow to recognize unjustified enrichment as an independent source of liability, but over the last half-century it has become firmly established in most of them: in the United States, now above all owing to the *Third Restatement on Restitution and Unjust Enrichment* (2011). The guiding principle of the Restatement, one often repeated with slight variation in many other national codes or legal decisions, is §1: "A person who is unjustly enriched at the expense of another is subject to liability in restitution." This principle is but a more careful version of the jurist Pomponius' famous maxim: *Nam hoc natura aequum est neminem cum alterius detrimento fieri locupletiorem* ("For it is by Nature fair that no one become richer through another's loss": D. 12.6.14, 50.17.206). But the real legal work began, and begins, precisely here, in cutting this lofty but overbroad moral principle down to more manageable size.

A Casebook on the Roman Law of Contracts. Bruce W. Frier, Oxford University Press. © Oxford University Press 2021.
DOI: 10.1093/oso/9780197573211.003.0009

PART A

Unauthorized Administration of Another's Affairs (*Negotiorum Gestio*)

The Praetor's Edict, quoted by Ulpian (D. 3.5.3 pr.), established this liability in the following words: "If someone administers the affairs of another, or what were his affairs at the time of his death, I will give a trial on this account." (*Si quis negotia alterius, sive quis negotia, quae cuiusque cum is moritur fuerint, gesserit: iudicium eo nomine dabo.*)

It is thought likely that the Edictal provision began as a means of handling procedural problems when a lawsuit was brought against an absent defendant whose affairs might be endangered if he went undefended. The defendant could learn of the situation and ask a third party to intervene, through a mandate (*mandatum*; see Chapter V.C); or, on the other hand, a third party might step in voluntarily, without a mandate, as a friendly act. These two situations were thought of as parallel, and accordingly each led to reciprocal actions *ex fide bona*. In the case of the voluntary intervener, the defendant had an action for failure to exercise due care in administration, while the intervener could sue for expenses.

However, the Praetor had phrased his provision broadly, and already by the end of the Roman Republic it was being applied more generally to other situations in which one person had acted to "administer" the non-judicial business of another without that person's knowledge, much less consent. Ostensibly, according a remedy to the intervener in such circumstances, even where the remedy involves only recovery of expenses, seems a direct contradiction of the venerable Common Law dread of the "officious intermeddler," the volunteer who assists or benefits another without contractual authorization or legal duty to do so, but nonetheless wants compensation for these actions. The dread arises from the sense that each person's affairs should be a matter for him or her alone, except under very compelling circumstances. By and large, therefore, benefits nonetheless conferred in this fashion are (somewhat sluggishly) often not considered part of our law of unjustified enrichment.

Roman society generally, and Roman law in particular, are certainly not hostile to individualism. But neither was it the paramount value of, in particular, a Roman citizen, especially an upper-class Roman. As Reinhard Zimmermann (*Obligations* 436) observes, "he felt obliged to help his friends by lending them money, standing surety, or simply giving advice. All this was part of the *officium amici* [a friend's duty], and it could matter little whether such help had been specifically solicited or not. . . . [T]heir lawyers, practical and matter-of-fact, did what was necessary to provide favourable conditions for a behaviour along the accepted ethical lines and to protect the position of both parties."

As we shall see, this creative process involved careful restrictions when a conferred "benefit" was not wanted or needed by the recipient, or when it was actually a burden and no benefit at all.

CASE 216: The Invention of Quasi-Contract

D. 44.7.5 pr., 3 (Gaius libro tertio Aureorum)

pr. Si quis absentis negotia gesserit, si quidem ex mandatu, palam est ex contractu nasci inter eos actiones mandati, quibus invicem experiri possunt de eo, quod alterum alteri ex bona fide praestare oportet: si vero sine mandatu, placuit quidem sane eos invicem obligari eoque nomine proditae sunt actiones, quas appellamus negotiorum gestorum, quibus aeque invicem experiri possunt de eo, quod ex bona fide alterum alteri praestare oportet. Sed neque ex contractu neque ex maleficio actiones nascuntur: neque enim is qui gessit cum absente creditur ante contraxisse, neque ullum maleficium est sine mandatu suscipere negotiorum administrationem: longe [magis] <minus> is, cuius negotia gesta sunt, ignorans aut contraxisse aut deliquisse intellegi potest: sed utilitatis causa receptum est invicem eos obligari. . . .

3. Is quoque, qui non debitum accipit per errorem solventis, obligatur quidem quasi ex mutui datione et eadem actione tenetur, qua debitores creditoribus: sed non potest intellegi is, qui ex ea causa tenetur, ex contractu obligatus esse: qui enim solvit per errorem, magis distrahendae obligationis animo quam contrahendae dare videtur.

Iustinianus, *Institutiones* 3.27 pr.

Post genera contractuum enumerata dispiciamus etiam de his obligationibus, quae non proprie quidem ex contractu nasci intelleguntur, sed tamen, quia non ex maleficio substantiam capiunt, quasi ex contractu nasci videntur.

Gaius in the third book of his *Golden Rules*:

pr. If someone administers the affairs of an absent person, when (he does so) on the basis of a mandate, there clearly arise between them, from the contract (*ex contractu*), the actions on mandate whereby they can sue in turn about what each ought to present to the other in accord with good faith (*ex fide bona*).

But if (he does so) without a mandate, the view has prevailed that they are clearly obligated reciprocally, and on this account there were devised the actions we call "for administered affairs" (*negotiorum gestorum*), whereby they can equally sue in turn for what each ought to present to the other in accord with good faith (*ex fide bona*).

But these actions arise neither from a contract nor from a misdeed (*neque ex contractu neque ex maleficio*), since the administrator is not considered to have previously contracted with the absent person, nor is it any misdeed to take up the administration of affairs without a mandate; (and) far less can the person, whose affairs were administered while he was unaware, be understood either to have contracted or to have done a wrong. But for the sake of practicality (*utilitatis causa*) it was established that they are reciprocally obligated. . . .

3. Likewise a person who receives (payment of) a debt because of the payer's mistake (*error*) is obligated by the same action as debtors to creditors (i.e., the *condictio*). But the person who is held liable for this reason cannot be understood to have been obligated on a contract, since someone who pays by mistake is held to give (the payment) more with the intent of discharging an obligation than of contracting one.

Justinian in the third book of his *Institutes*:

After having listed the various kinds of contracts, let us now also examine obligations that, properly speaking, are not understood to arise from contract (*ex contractu*), but, because they do not come into existence through a misdeed (*ex maleficio*), are held to arise "as if from a contract" (*quasi ex contractu*).

Discussion

1. A New Cause of Action. There is much to look at in these two sources, but for now concentrate on the thread of logic that binds together the Gaius passage, and how the two liabilities are then merged into Justinian's *quasi ex contractu*. Unauthorized administration of affairs may seem at first to have little to do with payments made by mistake, and the remedies in the two situations not only arose wholly independently but also are quite differently structured. Nonetheless, there may be a common idea. See if you can find it. Don't worry if the idea is hard to locate, or seems untenably vague; the Roman jurists themselves never arrived at anything resembling a generalized theory of "quasi-contract" or unjustified enrichment.

   Illustrating this confusion, both Gaius and Justinian list two other alleged forms of quasi-contract: the reciprocal liabilities of a guardian and ward for the guardian's conduct during tutelage; and the liability of an heir to a legatee (D. 48.7.5.2; Justinian, *Inst.* 3.27.2–5, which adds liabilities arising from common property). These liabilities are better explained elsewise, through the law of status, property, and succession; they do not involve the core ideas in this Chapter.

2. Unauthorized Administration of Affairs. It is not known when the Praetor introduced this remedy into his Edict. Formally, the Praetor promises to give an action based on his own authority (*iudicium dabo*, "I will give a trial"); this indicates that the original form of the action was probably based on individual alleged facts (*in factum*), a form that survives in some later texts even as the original form of action was largely superseded by the later one based on *bona fides*—this latter a formulation unlikely to antedate the second century BCE. The good faith actions were, in any case, well established by the late Republic.

Roman legal sources refer to a wide variety of situations in which the actions might be used: not only for emergencies where intervention is urgent (propping up a building that is about to collapse or providing medical care to a sick slave), but also for everyday business like discharging or standing surety for a principal's debt, collecting a debt due to the principal, purchasing farms, selling slaves or livestock, and so on. In each case, the administrator's intervention occurs without the other party's prior or subsequent consent, and almost always without even that party's knowledge. As Gaius says, in Roman law such a unilateral intervention can establish rights and duties on both sides, in accord with good faith (*ex fide bona*).

In modern law, it remains controversial whether a Good Samaritan should be able to claim compensation for expenses, and, if so, whether this claim should be regarded as an instance of unjustified enrichment. Speaking very broadly, Civil Law systems (ultimately based to a considerable extent on Roman law) answer yes to both questions, while Common Law generally discourages liability. See Daniel Visser, "Unjustified Enrichment in Comparative Perspective," in *The Oxford Handbook of Comparative Law* (ed. Mathias Reimann and Reinhard Zimmermann, 2006), 969–1002, at 983–984 ("Is Obtruding a Benefit on Another about Unjustified Enrichment?"). As Visser observes, "The real challenge . . . is to find the appropriate balance between encouraging altruism and protecting personal liability."

CASE 217: The Reason for the Actions on Unauthorized Administration

D. 3.5.1 (Ulpianus libro decimo ad Edictum)

Hoc edictum necessarium est, quoniam magna utilitas absentium versatur, ne indefensi rerum possessionem aut venditionem patiantur vel pignoris distractionem vel poenae committendae actionem, vel iniuria rem suam amittant.

D. 3.5.2 (Gaius libro tertio ad Edictum Provinciale)

Si quis absentis negotia gesserit licet ignorantis, tamen quidquid utiliter in rem eius impenderit vel etiam ipse se in rem absentis alicui obligaverit, habet eo nomine actionem: itaque eo casu ultro citroque nascitur actio, quae appellatur negotiorum gestorum. Et sane sicut aequum est ipsum actus sui rationem reddere et eo nomine condemnari, quidquid vel non ut oportuit gessit vel ex his negotiis retinet: ita ex diverso iustum est, si utiliter gessit, praestari ei, quidquid eo nomine vel abest ei vel afuturum est.

Ulpian in the tenth book *On the Edict*:

This edict is essential because of its great usefulness to absentees, to prevent their suffering, through lack of (judicial) defense, their property being possessed or sold, or a pledge being sold, or the action on forfeiting a penalty, or losing their property wrongfully.

Gaius in the third book *On the Provincial Edict*:

If someone administers the affairs of an absent person, even one who is unaware (of this), nevertheless he has an action on account of whatever he usefully expends on this person's property, or even if he obligates himself to a third party for the absent person's property. And so in this case an action arises on either side, called (the action) on administered affairs. And indeed, just as it is fair that he provide an accounting of his action and on this basis be condemned for whatever either he did not administer as he ought to or (for what) he retains from these affairs, so too conversely it is just, if his administration was useful, that he receive whatever he either lost or will lose on this account.

The Problem

Your house stands on several acres of lawn. While you were away on a month-long vacation, it rained heavily and the grass became very unsightly. I hire a landscaping company to come in and cut your grass. Can I recover for my expenditure?

Discussion

1. Origins. As Ulpian indicates, the Praetor may have devised these actions primarily to benefit defendants who came under judicial assault during their absence (Roman sources frequently mention this situation); while Gaius

frames the edict's purposes much more broadly, in accord with later legal thinking. The Praetor's pronouncement was, in fact, located in the portion of the Edict that dealt with representation in court (Lenel, EP^3 101–105). On Lenel's reconstruction, if the person whose business was administered later sued, the model formula in classical law was:

> Whereas the defendant administered the plaintiff's affairs, this being the matter in question, whatever on this account it is proper that the defendant ought, in accord with good faith, to give to or do for the plaintiff, let the *iudex* of this matter condemn the defendant to the plaintiff; if it does not appear, let him absolve. (Lenel, EP^3 105)

If the administrator sued, the same wording was used, except that, in the "whereas" clause, the wording was changed to "Whereas the plaintiff administered the defendant's affairs." In either formula, the wording was deliberately left quite general, which opened the way for much later juristic development.

2. An Imperfect Bilateral Arrangement. As Gaius says, the administrator is only entitled to expenses for the intervention, while being subjected to liability for lack of due care. Does this balance (or imbalance) seem to encourage the proper level of intervention by third parties in the affairs of others, particularly when the intervention is initiated unilaterally and without the beneficiary's knowledge? The Romans were not unaware of the dangers in promoting such interference; see, for instance, another maxim of Pomponius, D. 50.17.36: "It is fault to involve yourself in a matter not pertaining to you" (*Culpa est immiscere se rei ad se non pertinenti*). But, in an era of slow and erratic communication, the Praetor and the jurists may have been swayed by the weak position of an absent person, not only in litigation but in other vital matters. As you read on, try to determine how well they did in striking the balance.

3. Absence? Many sources insist, as these two fragments do, that the beneficiary must be "absent" (*absens*) if the administrator is to receive compensation for expenses. Presumably, physical absence is meant; the beneficiary physically cannot tend to his or her own affairs, and would presumably have done so were he or she present. But several sources indicate that just lack of awareness (*ignorantia*) was enough; e.g., Paul, D. 3.5.40: "A person who defends my slave in a noxal action when I am unaware (*ignorans*) or absent has the action on administration of affairs with me for the whole amount . . ." This is important because some interventions might be occasioned by the mental incapacity of the beneficiary: too young or insane,

for instance. Clearly, *negotiorum gestio* was available in the case of underage wards (e.g., Paul, D. 3.5.14) and the insane (e.g., Ulpian, D. 3.5.3.5). It seems hard to avoid this extension, doesn't it?

4. The Good Samaritan. A renowned doctor stops to administer medical aid to a victim who has been badly injured in an automobile accident and is unconscious. Assuming that the doctor exercised a high level of skill, does it seem right to you that she receive only her expenses for this intervention, rather than compensation at her regular, very steep fee rates, or at least at going market rates for her profession? In the case of a skilled professional, is the Roman award too low to encourage intervention that is both urgent and socially desirable? Should it matter whether the patient died despite the intervention?

CASE 218: Benefit to the Recipient

D. 3.5.9.1 (Ulpianus libro decimo ad Edictum)

Is autem qui negotiorum gestorum agit non solum si effectum habuit negotium quod gessit, actione ista utetur, sed sufficit, si utiliter gessit, etsi effectum non habuit negotium. Et ideo si insulam fulsit vel servum aegrum curavit, etiamsi insula exusta est vel servus obit, aget negotiorum gestorum: idque et Labeo probat. Sed ut Celsus refert, Proculus apud eum notat non semper debere dari. Quid enim si eam insulam fulsit, quam dominus quasi inpar sumptui deliquerit vel quam sibi necessariam non putavit? Oneravit, inquit, dominum secundum Labeonis sententiam, cum unicuique liceat et damni infecti nomine rem derelinquere. Sed istam sententiam Celsus eleganter deridet: is enim negotiorum gestorum, inquit, habet actionem, qui utiliter negotia gessit: non autem utiliter negotia gerit, qui rem non necessariam vel quae oneratura est patrem familias adgreditur. Iuxta hoc est et, quod Iulianus scribit, eum qui insulam fulsit vel servum aegrotum curavit, habere negotiorum gestorum actionem, si utiliter hoc faceret, licet eventus non sit secutus. Ego quaero: quid si putavit se utiliter facere, sed patri familias non expediebat? Dico hunc non habiturum negotiorum gestorum actionem: ut enim eventum non spectamus, debet utiliter esse coeptum.

D. 17.1.50 pr. (Celsus libro trigesimo octavo Digestorum)

Si is qui negotia fideiussoris gerebat ita solvit stipulatori, ut reum fideiussoremque liberaret, idque utiliter fecit, negotiorum gestorum actione fideiussorem habet obligatum, nec refert, ratum habuit nec ne fideiussor. . . .

Ulpian in the tenth book *On the Edict*:

A person who sues on administration of affairs will not just use this action if he (successfully) accomplishes the matter he administered; it is enough if he acted usefully (*utiliter*), even if he did not accomplish the matter. And so if he propped up an apartment building or took care of a sick slave, he will sue on administration of affairs (even) if the building burned down or the slave died; and Labeo also approves this rule.

But, as Celsus reports, Proculus annotated him (Labeo, as follows): this (the action) ought not always to be given (by the Praetor). For what if he propped up an apartment building that the owner abandoned from not being up to the expense, or that he thought he did not need? In Labeo's view, says Celsus, he burdened the owner, since anyone is allowed to abandon property even because of threatened damage (*damni infecti*; to a neighbor). But Celsus elegantly mocks this view; for, he says, a person who administered affairs usefully has an action on administration of affairs, but someone who undertakes something unnecessary, or that will burden a *paterfamilias*, does not administer affairs usefully.

Related to this is what Julian writes, that a person who propped up an apartment house or cared for a sick slave has an action on administration of affairs if he does this usefully, even if the outcome was unsuccessful. I ask: What if he thought he acted usefully, but it was not benefiting the *paterfamilias*? I hold that this man will not have the action on administration of affairs; for when we do not look to the outcome, it ought (at least) to be started usefully.

Celsus in the thirty-eighth book of his *Digests*:

If a person who was administering a surety's affairs paid a stipulator (creditor) so as to free (both) the principal and the surety (from the debt), and he did this usefully, he has obligated the surety in an action on administration of affairs, nor does it matter whether the surety ratified this or not.

Discussion

1. **Usefulness.** There is general agreement that the administrator's action must be "useful" (*utilis*); see also Alexander Severus, C. 2.18.10 (222 CE): "If you cared for another person's sick slave who was (still) of some use to his master, and you administered the affair usefully (to the master), you can recover your expenses by the appropriate action." However, as this fragment shows, that requirement may be rather difficult to isolate. Ulpian begins by suggesting that the action must be reasonable even if it is not successful; the building may fall down anyway, or the slave may die. So the standard looks to be an objective one: was intervention reasonable?

   But then come the remarks of Proculus, Celsus, and Julian, who veer off in quite a different direction: What if the owner didn't want this building, or couldn't afford to keep it up? (Proculus argues that in such an event the Praetor should not award an action to the administrator in the first place, while Celsus and Julian seem to prefer that the action be awarded but that the administrator be defeated by the absence of benefit. The same destination, different routes.) Here the emphasis seems to be on the putative beneficiary, who, despite the good intentions of the administrator (Julian), may not have actually benefited from the act. This is a much more subjective, case-oriented standard of *utilitas*. Can the two positions be reconciled?

2. **An Equitable Remedy.** One way to reconcile them is to assume that, although in general the administrator is compensated for acting reasonably in light of the impending harm to another's interests, the particular circumstances of a defendant owner may also be taken into consideration, through a process that, in Common Law, would be regarded as essentially equitable, case-oriented, and attentive to potential hardship on all sides. Look again at the rescript of Alexander Severus quoted in the previous note. Why does the emperor insist on the sick slave still being "of some use to his

master"? This certainly looks extremely hard-hearted; but it is possible that a deeper legal point underlies the requirement. Can you spot it?

3. **Celsus's Problem.** In the second passage, a creditor C is owed money by a debtor D, and surety S has guaranteed payment of D's debt. (On suretyship, see Chapter II.F.) Administrator A, intervening in the affairs of S, pays the debt to C, and thereby frees both D and S from further liability to C. S is liable to A for A's expenditures, provided that A acted *utiliter*, usefully. Using the concepts in the Ulpian passage, try to describe circumstances in which A's payment could be regarded as not useful. Note that, according to Celsus, the outcome is not affected by whether or not S has "ratified" (subsequently approved) A's payment. Why not?

4. **Not Useful.** Little survives as to the line between useful and not useful, but Modestinus, D. 3.5.26 pr., describes a case in which two brothers jointly owned a rural property and one built "splendid buildings" (*ampla aedificia*) on it. When the brothers came to divide their property, the builder received no compensation from his brother for buildings constructed "for his enjoyment," *voluptatis causa*, even though the property's market value may have risen as a result.

CASE 219: Benefit the Recipient Does Not Want

C. 2.18.24 (Imp. Iustinianus A. Iuliano pp.)

pr. Si quis nolente et specialiter prohibente domino rerum administrationi earum sese immiscuit, apud magnos auctores dubitabatur, si pro expensis, quae circa res factae sunt, talis negotiorum gestor habeat aliquam adversus dominum actionem. 1. Quam quibusdam pollicentibus directam vel utilem, aliis negantibus, in quibus et Salvius Iulianus fuit, haec decidentes sancimus, si contradixerit dominus et eum res suas administrare prohibuerit, secundum Iuliani sententiam nullam esse adversus eum contrariam actionem, scilicet post denuntiationem, quam ei dominus transmiserit nec concedens ei res eius attingere, licet res bene ab eo gestae sint. 2. Quid enim, si dominus adspexerit ab administratore multas expensas utiliter factas et tunc dolosa adsimulatione habita eum prohibuerit, ut neque anteriores expensas praestet? quod nullo patimur modo: sed ex quo die attestatio ad eum facta est vel in scriptis vel sine scriptis, sub testificatione tamen aliarum personarum, ex eo die pro faciendis meliorationibus nullam ei actionem competere, super anterioribus autem, si utiliter factae sunt, habere eum actionem contra dominum concedimus sua natura currentem.

The Emperor Justinian to Julian, Praetorian Prefect (530 CE):

pr. If anyone intermeddled by administering property when its unwilling owner specifically forbade this, there was doubt among important (juristic) authorities whether such an administrator of affairs would have any action against the owner for expenditures on the property. 1. Some (jurists) promise him a direct or analogous action, while some deny one (altogether), among whom was Salvius Julianus. To decide these questions, We ordain that if the owner objects and prohibits him from administering his property, then in accord with Julian's opinion no counteraction lies against him—that is to say, after the owner transmits a notice to him and does not permit him to lay hands on his property even if he administers the matter well.

2. But what if the owner has watched the administrator making much useful expenditure, and then with deceitful pretense forbids him in order to avoid owing the previous expenditures? In no respect do We allow this. But from the day on which notice (of prohibition) was given to him—either in writing or without writing but with other persons as witnesses—from that day on, no action shall lie for making improvements. But as for prior ones, if they were useful, We allow him to have an action against the owner, (but) one that is by its nature limited in time.

Discussion

1. A Classical Debate, Suppressed. When Justinian's compilers set to work excerpting the writings of the Roman jurists, they were sometimes faced with earlier conflicts of opinion that could only be resolved by calling on the emperor. When Justinian obliged them, the losing juristic views were

then often cut out of the excerpted Digest text, but the emperor's decision survives to attest them indirectly. In this Case, Justinian suggests that some jurists—among them, the acclaimed Julian—declined to allow the administrator to sue for expenses when the owner had "specifically" (*specialiter*) forbidden the administration, while others allowed a lawsuit nonetheless. (On the other hand, the administrator could still be sued if he failed in his duty of care.) Ulpian, D. 3.5.7.3, citing Julian, concurs with him as to a particular case: in a two-person partnership, one partner forbids a third party from administering the partnership's affairs, while the other partner does not; the latter can be sued by the intervener, but a resulting verdict must not harm the former. Paul, D. 17.1.40, adopts a more general rule barring the action, but acknowledges that some jurists favored at least an analogous action (*actio utilis*) in particular cases. What can be said in favor of each of the three positions? In any case, it appears that the beneficiary's prohibition had to be clear, individualized, and, at least in Justinian's law, relatively formal (a simple oral prohibition would not work); so a broad posted ban ("No Trespassing! No Improvements!") would therefore be insufficient.

2. An Attempted Fraud. Section 2 shows the emperor alert to the possibility that his rule might lead a cunning beneficiary to avoid liability by delaying a prohibition. Justinian allows the administrator to seek compensation up to the point of the prohibition, but not thereafter. Notice the presumption here is that the owner is present and aware of the administrator's acts. Is this consistent with Case 217?

CASE 220: Mistake as to the Beneficiary

D. 3.5.44.2 (Ulpianus libro quarto Opinionum)

Titius pecuniam creditoribus hereditariis solvit existimans sororem suam defuncto heredem testamento extitisse. Quamvis animo gerendi sororis negotia id fecisset, veritate tamen filiorum defuncti, qui sui heredes patri sublato testamento erant, gessisset: quia aequum est in damno eum non versari, actione negotiorum gestorum id eum petere placuit.

Ulpian in the fourth book of his *Opinions*:

Titius paid money to the creditors of an inheritance in the belief that his sister had become the testate heir to the deceased. Although he did this with the intent to administer the affairs of his sister, nevertheless in actuality he administered (the affairs) of the decedent's sons, who were the intestate heirs of their father after the will was invalidated. Because it is fair (*aequum*) that he not suffer loss, the view prevailed that he seek this (expenditure) by an action on administration of affairs.

Discussion

1. Inadvertent Administration of Affairs. In a will, Titius' sister was named heir to the decedent's estate, which was burdened with debts that Titius paid off. His act may well have been a simple matter of intra-familial generosity, as in Case 222; in which event, Titius perhaps could not seek compensation from his sister for administering her affairs. But the will was broken, and the true beneficiaries of Titius' payments turned out to be the decedent's sons as heirs upon intestacy, who took an estate no longer burdened with debts. Can Titius sue the sons even though he had no intent to benefit them, and indeed even though he may not originally have wanted compensation at all? Why might the jurists have had doubts on this issue, and why did their position favoring liability ultimately prevail? Note Ulpian's emphasis on "fairness," *aequitas*.

2. A Thieving Slave. Africanus, D. 3.5.48, puts a hypothetical case: I sell a slave who takes with him to the buyer an object that the slave had stolen from me; and the slave's buyer, unaware of the theft, then sells the object. I have an action on administration of affairs against the slave's buyer for the price of the stolen object, even though this buyer, in selling the object, evidently had no intention of benefiting me or indeed anyone but himself. As this text suggests, the jurists seem to place their emphasis on the "utility," *utilitas*, of the benefit conferred, while downplaying "the intent to administer another's affairs," *animus negotia aliena gerendi*. Parallel, but still more surprising, is their handling of a free man who falsely believes himself to be a slave and who is serving a master when he acts (*liber homo bona fide serviens*); after his correct status is vindicated, he may sue or be sued in an action on administration of his putative master's affairs:

Labeo/Paul, D. 3.5.18.2; Ulpian, D. 3.5.5.7; Paul, D. 3.5.35. From this position, it clearly follows that a person who administers affairs which he believes are Titius', when they are actually Sempronius', is liable to Sempronius alone; Ulpian, D. 3.5.5.1.

3. No Mandate. For some reason I thought I had a mandate from you to administer your affairs, but in fact I did not. So of course I cannot sue you on mandate, but I am allowed to bring an action for administration of your affairs; Ulpian, D. 3.5.5 pr. Does it matter what your reason might have been for not giving me a mandate? Should it matter?

CASE 221: Benefit to Oneself

D. 3.5.5.5 (Ulpianus libro decimo ad Edictum)

Sed et si quis negotia mea gessit non mei contemplatione, sed sui lucri causa, Labeo scripsit suum eum potius quam meum negotium gessisse (qui enim depraedandi causa accedit, suo lucro, non meo commodo studet): sed nihilo minus, immo magis et is tenebitur negotiorum gestorum actione. Ipse tamen si circa res meas aliquid impenderit, non in id quod ei abest, quia improbe ad negotia mea accessit, sed in quod ego locupletior factus sum habet contra me actionem.

Ulpian in the tenth book *On the Edict*:

But also if someone administered my affairs with a view not to my profit but to his own, Labeo wrote that he administered his own affair rather than mine—for a person who comes to plunder looks to his own gain, not to my convenience.

But nonetheless, indeed even more so, he will be liable (to me) in an action on administration of affairs. Still, if he spent something on my property, he has a (counter)action against me, not for what he lost, since he undertook my affairs improperly, but for the extent of my enrichment.

Discussion

1. **The Administrator's Benefit.** There reappears here the legal concern about whether the intervenor's acts are oriented to someone else's benefit: a person who administers my affairs with an eye only to his own gain is compared to a looter. Ulpian allows me to sue the administrator for misconduct, but restricts the countersuit for compensation: it must be for the extent of the principal's enrichment, which could, of course, substantially exceed the administrator's costs. Is this decision guided mainly by equity? How easy is it to draw a sharp line between what benefits me and what benefits the administrator? It may help to think up some hypothetical examples: for instance, the Thieving Slave described in the previous Case Discussion.

2. **Altruism.** Zimmermann (*Obligations* 442) observes that: "[N]either the voluntariness of the action on the part of the *gestor* [administrator] nor purely altruistic motive or *amicitia* nor absence of the principal was an essential or a fundamental condition for the *actiones negotiorum gestorum* to arise. . . . We have seen that the recognition of the institution of *negotiorum gestio* was one of the anti-individualistic traits of Roman law; it entailed a certain curtailment of the principal's autonomy. The *utilitas* requirement was the main safeguard to limit the extent of such curtailment." Thinking back on the Cases to this point, do you think this safeguard is entirely sufficient? Do the jurists agree on how strongly the *utilitas* requirement should be enforced?

3. **Common Interests.** Paul, D. 3.5.20 pr., recounts a fascinating case that arose during the Roman Republic. Three Romans were captured and held

for ransom by the Lusitani, a Celtiberian tribe who lived in modern Portugal and were often at war with Rome. One Roman was released on condition that he bring back money for the ransom of all three; but if he did not return, the other two were to come up with the money for him as well. After his release the first man refused to return, but the other two managed to pay the ransom for all three. Can they then sue the first man for compensation? Paul says yes; on what theory? See also Paul, D. 17.1.22.10.

CASE 222: The Intent to Seek Compensation for Expenses

C. 2.18.11 (Imp. Alexander A. Herreniae)

Alimenta quidem, quae filiis tuis praestitisti, reddi tibi non iusta ratione postulas, cum id exigente materna pietate feceris. Si quid autem in rebus eorum utiliter et probabili more impendisti, si non et hoc materna liberalitate, sed recipiendi animo fecisse ostenderis, id negotiorum gestorum actione consequi potes.

The Emperor Alexander Severus to Herrenia (227 CE):

You have no legal basis to demand compensation for support payments (*alimenta*) to your sons, since you were required to do this by motherly devotion to them (*materna pietas*). But if you paid out anything on their affairs usefully and in an acceptable matter, and you show you did this not out of maternal generosity but with the intent to be compensated, you can obtain this (expenditure) by suing on administration of affairs.

Discussion

1. Familial Devotion. The jurists normally presuppose that administrators will want to be paid for their expenses; there is none of the hairsplitting about "volunteers" that characterizes modern law in this area. But the jurists make an exception when one family member administers the affairs of another, for here the intervention is often said to stem from *pietas*, a strong norm of commitment to one's family members even when they are no longer legally joined (as with emancipated children or those given in adoption). Paul, D. 3.5.33, describes a complicated case in which a grandmother administered the affairs of her grandson; after the death of both, the grandmother's heirs sued the grandson's heirs on administration of affairs, in order to receive compensation for expenditures that the grandmother had apparently made on him. Although the grandmother might have been legally compelled to support her grandson if he was indigent (Ulpian, D. 25.3.5 pr.-4), no such order had been issued. As in the previous imperial rescript, this case came to center on the balance between the duty of *pietas* as against whether the grandmother had at the time expressed a clear desire for compensation. Paul holds that this decision is a question of fact, but that doubts should be called in favor of the grandmother's heirs. Similar issues seem to have arisen frequently among family members; see, e.g., Alexander, C. 2.18.12, 13 (both 230); Gordian, C. 2.18.15 (239); etc.

2. Friendship. A person who, out of friendship (*amicitia*) for their deceased father, administers the affairs of his orphaned sons, has no action against them for his expenses; Ulpian, D. 3.5.43. Why? See also Scaevola, D. 17.1.60.1.

CASE 223: Standards of Care in Administering Another's Affairs

D. 3.5.10 (Pomponius libro vicensimo primo ad Quintum Mucium)

Si negotia absentis et ignorantis geras, et culpam et dolum praestare debes. Sed Proculus interdum etiam casum praestare debere, veluti si novum negotium, quod non sit solitus absens facere, tu nomine eius geras: veluti venales novicios coemendo vel aliquam negotiationem ineundo. Nam si quid damnum ex ea re secutum fuerit, te sequetur, lucrum vero absentem: quod si in quibusdam lucrum factum fuerit, in quibusdam damnum, absens pensare lucrum cum damno debet.

Pomponius in the twenty-first book *On Quintus Mucius*:

If you administer the affairs of someone who is absent and unaware, you should be liable for both fault (*culpa*) and deceit (*dolus*).

But Proculus (says) that sometimes (you) should also be liable for accident (*casus*) as well, e.g., if you administer in his name a new affair that the absent person was not accustomed to do; for instance, by buying newly enslaved persons or by initiating some (new) business. For if any loss results from this thing, it falls on you, but profit (goes to) the absent person. But if profit was made in some matters and loss in others, the absent person should offset the profit with the loss.

Discussion

1. The Administrator's Standard of Care. The standard is set relatively high, obviously so as to deter off-the-cuff, ill-considered intervention. The administrator is expected to carry out the intervention fully (Papinian, D. 3.5.30.2), and also to surrender to the principal any profits he receives (Gaius, D. 3.5.2; Case 217): "whatever . . . he retains from these affairs"). In administering, he is obliged to act with conscientiousness (so, at least, a postclassical source, *Pauli Sent.* 1.4.1: "One who administers another's affairs must exhibit both good faith and scrupulous care [*exacta diligentia*] for the affairs of the person for whom he intervenes."). See also Paul, D. 3.5.20.3 (liability for injudiciousness, *imprudentia*, in picking someone to run a third party's affairs), 47.2.54.3 (liability if the principal's property is stolen because of the administrator's fault). The administrator's liability for malfeasance remains even if he intervenes under emergency conditions; Ulpian, D. 3.5.3.10.

   However, the standard can be raised or lowered in appropriate circumstances. Pomponius, citing the earlier jurist Proculus, indicates that when the intervention seems especially officious, the administrator is liable also for *casus*, meaning that if loss results to the principal, the administrator escapes only if it can be shown to have occurred through a "higher force." On the other hand (and somewhat surprisingly), Ulpian (D. 3.5.3.9), citing Labeo, lets the administrator off with a very low standard of *dolus* (liability only for deliberate infliction of loss) if he intervenes because he was "compelled by affection" (*affectione coactus*), such as might occur if one spouse administers the property of the other; see Celsus, D. 24.1.47 ("It is a question of fact, not of law, whether a husband who spends money on his wife's property is managing her affairs or fulfilling a husband's duty; inference as to this is not hard based on the extent and type of the expenditure"; really?). See also Case 222.

CASE 224: Administering the Affairs of a Deceased Debtor

D. 3.5.12 (Paulus libro nono ad Edictum)

Debitor meus, qui mihi quinquaginta debebat, decessit: huius hereditatis curationem suscepi et impendi decem: deinde redacta ex venditione rei hereditariae centum in arca reposui: haec sine culpa mea perierunt. Quaesitum est, an ab herede, qui quandoque extitisset, vel creditam pecuniam quinquaginta petere possim vel decem quae impendi. Iulianus scribit in eo verti quaestionem, ut animadvertamus, an iustam causam habuerim seponendorum centum: nam si debuerim et mihi et ceteris hereditariis creditoribus solvere, periculum non solum sexaginta, sed et reliquorum quadraginta me praestaturum, decem tamen quae impenderim retenturum, id est sola nonaginta restituenda. Si vero iusta causa fuerit, propter quam integra centum custodirentur, veluti si periculum erat, ne praedia in publicum committerentur, ne poena traiecticiae pecuniae augeretur aut ex compromisso committeretur: non solum decem, quae in hereditaria negotia impenderim, sed etiam quinquaginta quae mihi debita sunt ab herede me consequi posse.

Paul in the ninth book *On the Edict*:

My debtor, who owed me fifty (thousand sesterces), died. I undertook to oversee his estate and spent ten (on it); then I placed in my strongbox one hundred received from the sale of inheritance property, and this (money) was lost through no fault of mine. The question arose whether, from the heir who eventually emerged, I can claim either the fifty in money owed or the ten that I spent.

Julian writes that the question turns on our determining whether I had a legitimate reason for separating out the hundred. For if I am obliged to pay both myself and the other inheritance creditors, I will bear the risk not only of the sixty but of the remaining forty; but I will retain what I spent, i.e., only ninety must be restored.

But if there was a legitimate reason for keeping the one hundred apart, e.g., if there was a risk that the property be forfeit to the state, (or) that a penalty on a bottomry loan be increased or that it fall due because of an arbitration agreement (*compromissum*), then I can obtain from the heir not only the ten I spent on the estate's affairs, but also the fifty that were owed to me.

Discussion

1. Creditors of Estates. Because of the vagaries of Roman inheritance law, it was not unusual for a considerable time to elapse before a heir took over an estate, and during this time the estate "lay open" (*hereditas iacens*), to the obvious consternation of the estate's creditors. Therefore the Praetor's Edict on the *actio negotiorum gestorum* (quoted in the introduction to this Part) expressly allowed a creditor to administer the estate in the meantime. Here the creditor, to whom the decedent owed 50,000 sesterces, took control of the estate and sold it at auction for 100,000 after spending 10,000 on it. His

claims therefore amount to a total of 60,000. For a reason that is uncertain, he deposited the 100,000 in his personal strongbox, where it "was lost" (stolen?) through no fault on his part.

Had the money not been lost, he and the other creditors of the estate would have shared it *pro rata*, with any excess, if all of them were satisfied, going to the heir. Work out how Julian and Paul determine the extent of the administrator's liability depending on the reasonability of his decision to place the 100,000 in his strongbox.

PART B

Unjustified Enrichment (The *Condictio*)

It seems extraordinary that the versatile *condictio*, commonly termed a "strict law action" (*actio stricti iuris*), should have come to be the central legal remedy for unjustified enrichment. However, if a *Digest* fragment is to be trusted (though many scholars have doubted this), Roman jurists had already concluded, by the late Roman Republic, that "a *condictio* can be brought for anything held by someone for an unjust cause" (Ulpian, D. 12.5.6: *id, quod ex iniusta causa apud aliquem sit, posse condici*).

Although this fragment may originally have concerned only stolen property that a thief obviously must return to its owner, it already contains the germ of what will be the central insight of Roman law in this area: that the legal claim for restitution of unjustified enrichment is primarily, first, that a benefit has been conferred on its recipient; second, that this conferral occurred at the expense of the claimant; and, third, that the recipient must surrender the benefit to the claimant unless there is a legally acceptable reason for it being retained. The jurists came to stress this last point above all, through an analysis of what they call "cause," *causa*. Of course, we have already encountered the concept of *causa*, for instance in relation to stipulation and half-executed exchange agreements; in fact, you should be able to observe similarities to the use of defenses in stipulation (Chapter II.E). But with unjustified enrichment the concept gradually became central to the law's development.

Causa served the jurists complexly, above all by directing attention to whether the recipient's retention of the benefit can be justified. For this reason, they were less concerned than we tend to be about whether the benefit was conferred "voluntarily" by the claimant (Cases 216, 225); but the jurists seldom inquire about the reasonability, or not, of the "mistake" (*error*).

More remarkably still, despite the "strict law" nature of the *condictio*, the jurists quickly realized that restitution had to be grounded in principles of fairness, *aequitas* or the *aequum et bonum*, broadly similar to what we term "equity." This was because according the claimant too much power to reclaim benefit from the recipient might often be unfair to the latter, a situation particularly poignant when the recipient was entirely faultless in receiving the benefit. Although the jurists never quite reached the point of limiting the claimant's restitution by not leaving the recipient worse off than before the conferral, still their decisions are often imbued with this underlying intuition.

Despite Roman achievements, their law in this area is not nearly so sophisticated and broad in its reach as the modern law of unjustified enrichment in most developed nations.

CASE 225: Payment by Mistake

Gaius, *Institutiones* 3.91

Is quoque, qui non debitum accepit ab eo, qui per errorem soluit, re obligatur; nam proinde ei condici potest "si paret eum dare oportere," ac si mutuum accepisset. unde quidam putant pupillum aut mulierem, cui sine tutore auctoritate non debitum per errorem datum est, non teneri condictione, non magis quam mutui datione. sed haec species obligationis non uidetur ex contractu consistere, quia is, qui soluendi animo dat, magis distrahere uult negotium quam contrahere.

Gaius in the third book of his *Institutes*:

Likewise, a person who received what was not owed (*non debitum*) from someone who paid by mistake (*per errorem*) is obligated by the (transfer of) property (*re*). For the *condictio* can be brought against him "if it appears that he ought to convey," just as if he had accepted a loan for use (*mutuum*).

Therefore some (jurists) think that a juvenile ward or a woman, to whom what was not owed was given by mistake without their guardian's authorization, is not liable under a *condictio*, any more than through the giving of a loan for use. But this type of obligation is not held to arise from a contract, since a person who gives with the intent to pay wants not to contract but to discharge a matter.

The Problem

Apronius, a banker, inadvertently deposited 25,000 sesterces into the account of Caelius, when in fact the money was intended for C. Aelius. Can Apronius recover the deposit? Does it matter that Apronius was negligent in making the deposit? That Caelius, who failed to recognize the mistake, has since spent all of the money on redecorating his house?

Discussion

1. The Basic Elements. Gaius gives a surprisingly thorough summary of what was typically required in order to bring a *condictio* for unjustified enrichment: (i) the transfer of property to a recipient, which (ii) occurs because of a putative transaction such as a payment of a debt, and (iii) is based on a mistake (*error*) by the transferor as to the transaction. The transferor can then reclaim the transferred property, or its value, through a *condictio*; Gaius regards this as roughly similar to reclaiming a loan (where no mistake is involved). The original core idea, therefore, is recovery of a benefit that, because of the claimant's mistake, the recipient is not entitled to retain.

   As the law developed, these typical requirements were often relaxed or even ignored. Just as an example, Pomponius, D. 12.6.22.1, allows a *condictio* (*incerti*) when a landowner conveys a farm but by mistake does not retain a right of way over the farm; the action obliges the transferee to surrender the right of way, which had been implicitly withheld in the farm's conveyance.

2. **Loans to Wards and Women.** Orphans under the age of puberty (by convention, fourteen for boys, twelve for girls) usually require authorization from their guardian (*tutor*) before they can validly receive a loan, since they would thereby incur a contractual obligation (Gaius, *Inst.* 3.107; Case 1). Adult women, if not under a *paterfamilias*, had once been in a similar position (see Cicero, *Caec.* 72), and, although their legal independence steadily increased during the early Empire, may still have been (Gaius, *Inst.* 3.108); their guardian's authorization was, however, just a formality (Gaius, *Inst.* 1.190; Case 5). An unauthorized loan to a juvenile ward or a woman was irrecoverable by the lender. However, as Gaius observes, the balance swings toward the transferor when a mistaken payment is involved; see also Case 227.

3. **Examples.** In which of the following cases would a plaintiff have a *condictio* based on a mistaken payment:

- I promised payment to you, but mistakenly believed that my promise had been to pay either you or Titius; I pay Titius; can I recover the payment from Titius? (Pomponius, D. 12.6.22 pr.; Diocletian and Maximian, C. 4.5.8 (294))

- I promised to give you the slave Stichus, but I mistakenly believe I promised either Stichus or Pamphilus; I give you Pamphilus (who is more valuable than Stichus); can I reclaim Pamphilus and give you Stichus instead? (Pomponius, D. 12.6.19.3)

- I owe you 100, but mistakenly believe I owe you 200; in payment, I make over to you a farm worth 200; can I recover the excess 100? (Ulpian, D. 12.6.26.4–6)

- I made a binding promise to give you 10 or Stichus; by mistake I gave you 5. If I am now willing to give you Stichus instead, can I use the *condictio* to recover the 5? (Ulpian, D. 12.6.26.13. Warning: this one is hard.)

- I think I have promised to pay you a specified sum, and by mistake I pay you with coins belonging to a third party; can I recover the coins if they are not yet mixed with your other money? Does it matter whether my debt was a real one? (Pomponius, D. 12.6.19.2, and Paul, D. 12.6.15.1, disagreeing on the answer)

- Under a will, I as the heir owe you an annuity; I agree with you on a settlement of this debt, and I make the payment. Our settlement is, however, void because of a statute. Can I recover my payment? (Ulpian, D. 12.6.23.2)

- I promised to give you either the slave Stichus or a sum of money, and by mistake I pay you both; can I sue to recover one or the other, and, if so, who gets to make the choice? (Justinian, C. 4.5.10, settling a juristic controversy)

4. **What Justifies Recovery for Unjustified Enrichment?** If you have ever played Monopoly, you will remember the card reading: "Bank Error in Your Favor—Collect $200." But in fact, if a banker inadvertently pays money to you or into your account, our law, like Roman law, requires you to refund it, even if the bank's error was owing to its own negligence. In modern law, safeguards are in place to protect you from unfair treatment, but the principle remains the same. As you read this and subsequent cases, you should think about why banks (like other payers) are afforded such leniency to "call back" their mistakes, and also about what legal protections ought to be afforded to recipients.

CASE 226: Requirements: Mistake

D. 12.6.1.1 (Ulpianus libro vicensimo sexto ad Edictum)

Et quidem si quis indebitum ignorans solvit, per hanc actionem condicere potest: sed si sciens se non debere solvit, cessat repetitio.

D. 22.3.25 pr.-1 (Paulus libro tertio Quaestionum)

pr. Cum de indebito quaeritur, quis probare debet non fuisse debitum? . . . Et ideo eum, qui dicit indebitas solvisse, compelli ad probationes, quod per dolum accipientis vel aliquam iustam ignorantiae causam indebitum ab eo solutum, et nisi hoc ostenderit, nullam eum repetitionem habere. 1. Sin autem is qui indebitum queritur vel pupillus vel minor sit vel mulier vel forte vir quidem perfectae aetatis, sed miles vel agri cultor et forensium rerum expers vel alias simplicitate gaudens et desidia deditus: tunc eum qui accepit pecunias ostendere bene eas accepisse et debitas ei fuisse soltuas et, si non ostenderit, eas redhibere.

Ulpian in the twenty-sixth book *On the Edict*:

And indeed if someone through lack of awareness paid an unowed debt, by this action he recovers it. But if he paid while knowing he did not owe it, restitution fails.

Paul in the third book of his *Questions*:

pr. When question arises about what is not owed, who should prove that it was not owed? . . . And so (the answer is that) he who says he paid unowed (money) is forced to show proof that an unowed debt was paid by him through the recipient's deceit (*dolus*) or some legitimate reason for his lack of knowledge, and, unless he shows this, he will not get restitution. 1. But if the person complaining about an unowed debt is either a juvenile ward or a young person (under twenty-five) or a woman or, perhaps, an adult male (but) either a soldier or farmer and (thus) inexperienced in legal matters, or otherwise enjoying naïveté and given over to idleness, then the money's recipient shows that he received it properly and that what was owed was paid him; and, if he does not show this, he returns it.

Discussion

1. **What Is Meant by Mistake?** Any lawyer will likely be uneasy with a general rule like Ulpian's. What exactly is meant by "lack of awareness" (*ignorantia*) or "mistake" (*error*)? Does it matter how the mistake came about, and in particular if the giver was careless? Are all mistakes equal, or are some more serious than others? Are only mistakes of fact relevant, or do mistakes of law also count? But the classical jurists appear to have left these questions unanswered, so that a *iudex* determined for himself what mistakes invalidated a payment. What can be said in favor of, or against, this strongly case-oriented approach?

2. Justinian Intervenes. From its wording and its style, it is clear that the second passage, although attributed to the jurist Paul, was entirely written by the compilers of the Digest, who imposed on claimants a duty to show that they had paid an unowed debt, while reversing this burden of proof for claimants who, owing to their inexperience, were especially likely to face difficulty in court. At the same time, later law allowed claimants only to allege ignorance of fact, not of law; e.g., Diocletian and Maximian, C. 1.18.10 (294 CE), which was also interpolated by the compilers from a rule once more narrowly applied (Gordian, C. 6.50.9 (238)). However, Justinian allows claimants to show that, despite the appearance of a settlement, they paid because of uncertainty about their legal position: C. 4.5.11 (530). Did the emperor get it right?

CASE 227: Requirements: A Transaction and the Transfer of Property

D. 12.6.33 (Iulianus libro trigensimo nono Digestorum)

Si in area tua aedificassem et tu aedes possideres, condictio locum non habebit, quia nullum negotium inter nos contraheretur: nam is, qui non debitam pecuniam solverit, hoc ipso aliquid negotii gerit: cum autem aedificium in area sua ab alio positum dominus occupat, nullum negotium contrahit. Sed et si is, qui in aliena area aedificasset, ipse possessionem tradidisset, condictionem non habebit, quia nihil accipientis faceret, sed suam rem dominus habere incipiat. Et ideo constat, si quis, cum existimaret se heredem esse, insulam hereditariam fulsisset, nullo alio modo quam per retentionem impensas servare posse.

Julian in the thirty-ninth book of his *Digests*:

If I constructed a building on your site and you possess it, the *condictio* will not lie (against you) because no transaction (*negotium*) was contracted between us. For a person who pays money that is not owed manages a kind of transaction by this very act. But when the owner (of the land) occupies a building placed on his site by a third party, he does not contract a transaction.

But also if he had constructed on another's site and had himself handed over possession, he will not have a *condictio* because he conveys nothing to the recipient; rather, the owner begins to hold his own property. And so it is settled that if someone, thinking he is an heir, propped up an apartment building in the inheritance, he can recover his expenses in no other way than by retention (of the building).

Discussion

1. Construction by a Good Faith Possessor. Assume that I, as the builder, mistakenly construct a building on land that you own. By law, the building accedes to the land (the venerable maxim is *superficies solo cedit*), with the result that you can claim ownership of the building; but this may leave the builder uncompensated. In Julian's view, even if I am entirely blameless (e.g., I was misled by a surveyor), I recover nothing if you have already taken possession of the building, even if I bowed to reality and invited you to do so. My only chance for recovery is if I still retain possession and force you into court, where you will ordinarily be obliged to pay my expenses before you can evict me. The jurists try to mitigate this rule; see, e.g., Celsus, D. 6.1.38, and Gaius, D. 41.1.7.10. But it still seems very harsh, doesn't it? Our law is considerably more evenhanded.

2. A Transaction. Julian argues for his rule by asserting that there is no genuine "transaction" (*negotium*) between the builder and the landowner, so that even a polite handover actually "conveys nothing" but what the

landowner already owns, rather like returning lost property to its rightful owner. How convincing is this? Note Gaius' logic in Case 225: when an unowed payment is made to a juvenile ward without a guardian's authorization, some jurists (Julian quite possibly among them; see Julian, D. 26.8.13) thought the giver could not reclaim the payment, presumably because the "transaction" was void and nonexistent. Gaius rejects this reasoning, but Pomponius, D. 46.3.66, appears to accept it. Which view is correct?

CASE 228: Requirements: Absence of a Basis for Retention of Benefit

D. 12.6.66 (Papinianus libro octavo Quaestionum)

Haec condictio ex bono et aequo introducta, quod alterius apud alterum sine causa deprehenditur, revocare consuevit.

D. 12.7.1 (Ulpianus libro quadragensimo tertio ad Sabinum)

pr. Est et haec species condictionis, si quis sine causa promiserit vel si solverit quis indebitum. Qui autem promisit sine causa, condicere quantitatem non potest quam non dedit, sed ipsam obligationem. 1. Sed et si ob causam promisit, causa tamen secuta non est, dicendum est condictionem locum habere. 2. Sive ab initio sine causa promissum est, sive fuit causa promittendi quae finita est vel secuta non est, dicendum est condictioni locum fore. 3. Constat id demum posse condici alicui, quod vel non ex iusta causa ad eum pervenit vel redit ad non iustam causam.

Papinian in the eighth book of his *Questions*:

This *condictio*, created on the basis of what is right and fair (*ex bono et aequo*), has become the way to reclaim what belongs to one person and is held by another without cause (*sine causa*).

Ulpian in the forty-third book *On Sabinus*:

pr. There is also this type of *condictio* if someone promises without cause (*sine causa*) or if someone pays what is not owed. 1. But also if he promised for a reason (*ob causam*) but the cause did not come to pass, it must be held that the *condictio* lies. 2. Whether the promise was from the start without cause, or there was a cause for the promise which has ended or not come to pass, it must be held that the *condictio* will lie. 3. It is settled that the *condictio* can be brought against someone for that which either did not come to him for a legitimate reason (*ex iusta causa*) or which reverts to an illegitimate reason (*ad non iustam causam*).

Discussion

1. *Causa*. Papinian's terse formulation stresses the equitable character of the *condictio* (see also Celsus, D. 12.1.32; Ulpian, D. 12.4.3.7 [citing Celsus: *naturalis aequitas*]; Paul, D. 12.6.65.4), which justifies restitution when one person holds another's property *sine causa*. The word *causa* is extremely vague in juristic sources, but here it refers to the legal foundation for the recipient's continuing to hold the claimant's property. This foundation can usually be located by examining how the recipient came to hold the property and whether that basis still subsists; so, for instance, if the property were a gift, the object of a sale, a bequest from a deceased person, and so on. If there are no such grounds, then the property is being held

sine causa. This potent idea is not yet highly developed by the jurists, but becomes ever more salient in subsequent legal writing.

2. **Types of Lack of Cause.** In a dense fragment, Ulpian makes out three basic ways in which a recipient may be holding a claimant's property *sine causa:*

   i. The claimant may have conveyed it to the recipient (or even formally promised to pay it, by stipulation) without having a real reason for doing so, as when conveyance is the result of a mistaken belief in a debt (*indebitum*).

   ii. The claimant may have conveyed it in the justified expectation that some event would occur as a consequence, as when a dowry is given in the anticipation of an ensuing wedding; if that event does not occur, a conveyance that originally had a *causa* turns out not to have one (*datio ob causam; causa data, causa non secuta*) and restitution becomes available. (You have already encountered this idea in Chapter VI.B).

   iii. The claimant may have conveyed it on a basis that was entirely valid and unconditional at the time, but which subsequently became invalid (*ob causam finitam*), a category discussed in the following Case.

   In all these ways, a *condictio* may lie against the recipient. As will be obvious, the theory of *causa* helped the jurists move beyond the initial situation of payments made by mistake. The movement forward may have begun ca. 100 CE, as is suggested by Javolenus, D. 12.4.10: A woman who was about to marry gave her husband-to-be a dowry in the form of a receipt for payment of money that he owed her, but the marriage did not come off. Here, no money passed from her to him, but, says Javolenus, she can still bring a *condictio* "because it makes no difference whether the money came to him by being paid out *sine causa*, or through a receipt."

   In later law, as also in the Digest and Codex of Justinian, these various forms of *causa* tend to be presented separately, but in the law of the jurists they were not, it seems. The underlying *condictio*, in any case, is always the same.

3. **Reclaiming a Promise.** Ulpian permits a claimant to recover for a mistake not only when he made a payment, but also when he made a binding promise. Such a promise (usually made through a stipulation) can have value to the promissee in future litigation or just as an asset that can even be sold. The claimant's suit is for release from the promise, or at least for relaxation of it to the extent of the mistake; see Julian, D. 12.7.3, and Alexander, C. 4.30.4.

CASE 229: Subsequent Failure of Cause

D. 12.7.2 (Ulpianus libro trigensimo secundo ad Edictum)

Si fullo vestimenta lavanda conduxerit, deinde amissis eis domino pretium ex locato conventus praestiterit posteaque dominus invenerit vestimenta, qua actione debeat consequi pretium quod dedit? Et ait Cassius eum non solum ex conducto agere, verum condicere domino posse: ego puto ex conducto omnimodo eum habere actionem: an autem et condicere possit, quaesitum est, quia non indebitum dedit: nisi forte quasi sine causa datum sic putamus condici posse: etenim vestimentis inventis quasi sine causa datum videtur.

D. 19.1.11.6 (Ulpianus libro trigensimo secundo ad Edictum)

Is qui vina emit arrae nomine certam summam dedit: postea convenerat, ut emptio irrita fieret. Iulianus ex empto agi posse ait, ut arra restituatur, utilemque esse actionem ex empto etiam ad distrahendam, inquit, emptionem. Ego illud quaero: si anulus datus sit arrae nomine et secuta emptione pretioque numerato et tradita re anulus non reddatur, qua actione agendum est, utrum condicatur, quasi ob causam datus sit et causa finita sit, an vero ex empto agendum sit. Et Iulianus diceret ex empto agi posse: certe etiam condici poterit, quia iam sine causa apud venditorem est anulus.

Ulpian in the thirty-second book *On the Edict*:

If a fuller undertakes to clean clothes, and then, when the clothes are lost, is sued on the contract (*ex locato*) and pays their price to the owner (of the clothes), and the owner later finds the clothes, by what action should he (the fuller) pursue the price he paid? Cassius says not only can he sue on the contract, but he can also bring a *condictio* against the owner (of the clothes). I think that he has the action on the contract in any case; but the question was whether he can also bring a *condictio* because he gave what was not owed. Unless, perhaps, we think he can bring a *condictio* for what was given without cause (*sine causa*), for once the clothes were found the payment is held to be as though without cause (*quasi sine causa*).

Ulpian in the thirty-second book *On the Edict*:

The buyer of wine gave a specified sum (of money) as an earnest (*arra*). Later they had agreed that the sale became void. Julian says action can be on the purchase (*ex empto*) for restitution of the earnest, and, he says, there is an analogous action on the purchase also to discharge the purchase.

I ask this: if a ring was given as an earnest and, after the sale followed and the price was paid and the object of sale transferred, the ring is not returned, by what action should suit be brought: whether a *condictio* on the theory that it was given for a reason (*ob causam*) and the cause has ended, or rather an action on purchase? And Julian would say that action can be brought on the purchase; (but) a *condictio* could also be brought because the ring in now in the seller's hands without cause (*sine causa*).

Discussion

1. The Fuller. On fullers, see Case 164. This fuller lost his client's clothing and then paid compensation when sued on the contract for a job (*ex locato*). The problem arose when the client later recovered his clothing. It clearly seems unfair, doesn't it, that the client can keep both the compensation and the clothing; but how should suit be brought? The jurists allow the fuller to sue on the contract (*ex conducto*) despite the earlier verdict, but also provide him a *condictio*. As to the latter, they differ a little on the theory. Cassius, writing ca. 50 CE, regards the fuller's compensation as "unowed" (*indebitum*) even though, at the time of the first lawsuit, it plainly was owed. Ulpian, with a bit of hesitation, prefers to believe rather that the *causa* for the payment lapsed after the clothing was recovered; this view was made possible by the more advanced *causa* theories of the later jurists.

2. The Wine Buyer. He is not quite in the same situation as the fuller. An earnest payment (*arra* or *arrha*), similar to a modern deposit, was commonly thought to secure a sale even though only the parties' informal agreement was actually required (see Ulpian, D. 14.3.5.15 [Case 205], and Case 78); but a ring might also be used as a token of agreement. If the sale went through, the earnest would be offset against the price, while the ring would normally be returned. The text sets two problems: (i) if the sale agreement becomes void, how can the buyer get the earnest back? (Julian gives an action on sale, compare the Cases in Chapter IV.A.3; but would a *condictio* also be appropriate?); (ii) if the sale goes through but the seller declines to return the ring, what action? In the second case, note that the jurists seem to assume the seller became (temporary) owner of the ring, so they do not consider a property claim. What justifies the *condictio*?

3. Double Payment. Ulpian, D. 17.1.29.3, puts the following problem: A surety for a debt (*fideiussor*; see Chapter II.F) paid the creditor without informing the debtor, who subsequently also paid the creditor for the same debt. Clearly the surety's payment was legitimate when it was made, and he was also negligent not to have informed the debtor of this payment. But can the surety recover what he paid either from the creditor or from the debtor? Ulpian writes: "I believe that if, when he did not inform him when he could have done so, the surety's suit on mandate (against the debtor) should be rebuffed, since it is close to deceit (*dolus*) if he did not inform the debtor after his payment. But by an action on unowed payment (*actio indebiti*) the defendant (debtor) should cede (his action against the creditor) to the surety so that the creditor not receive double payment." The surety's

failure to notify the debtor violated his duty as a mandatary and so he loses that suit; but he still can sue the debtor on unjustified enrichment, since he could have sought reimbursement from the creditor but apparently chose not to. If the opinion's final sentence gives good law, this action results not in the debtor having to pay the surety, but rather in his being forced to surrender his claim against the creditor—a rather extraordinary example of equitable relief.

CASE 230: Misunderstanding about the Basis of a Transaction

D. 12.1.18 (Ulpianus libro septimo Disputationum)

pr. Si ego pecuniam tibi quasi donaturus dedero, tu quasi mutuam accipias, Iulianus scribit donationem non esse: sed an mutua sit, videndum. Et puto nec mutuam esse magisque nummos accipientis non fieri, cum alia opinione acceperit. Quare si eos consumpserit, licet condictione teneatur, tamen doli exceptione uti poterit, quia secundum voluntatem dantis nummi sunt consumpti. 1. Si ego quasi deponens tibi dedero, tu quasi mutuam accipias, nec depositum nec mutuum est: idem est et si tu quasi mutuam pecuniam dederis, ego quasi commodatam ostendendi gratia accepi: sed in utroque casu consumptis nummis condictioni sine doli exceptione locus erit.

Ulpian in the seventh book of his *Disputations*:

pr. If I give money to you as a gift and you receive it as a loan for consumption (*mutuum*), Julian writes that there is no gift. But let us see whether there is a loan. And I think that there is also no loan and further that the coins do not become the recipient's, since he receives them with a different understanding. So if he spends them, although he is liable in a *condictio*, nonetheless he will be able to use the defense of fraud (*exceptio doli*) because the coins were spent in accord with the giver's intent.

1. If I give (money) to you as a depositor and you receive (it) as a loan for consumption (*mutuum*), there is neither a deposit nor a loan. The same is true also if you give money as a loan for consumption (*mutuum*) and I received it as a loan for use (*commodatum*) in order to display it. But in either case, if the coins are spent, the *condictio* will lie without the defense of fraud.

Discussion

1. Agreement (*Consensus*). If the result in the *principium* seems to you absurd, you are exactly right. I intend you to have a gift, and you mistakenly think I am making you a loan. There is no gift; whyever not? But there is also no loan, and the coins, until they are dispersed into commerce, remain mine, so I can bring a property claim; but thereafter I can bring a *condictio* for their value, which you can only defend by interjecting the defense of fraud. Why do the jurists seem to get this situation so wrong? A good starting point is Paul, D. 44.7.3.1, which holds: "But, for an obligation to arise, it is not enough that the coins are the giver's and become the recipient's; (they must) also be given and received with the intent (*animus*) that an obligation be formed. And so if someone gives me his money as a donation, although it both was the giver's and becomes mine, still I am not obligated to him because this was not transacted between us." But is a gift an obligation? What if the situation was reversed: I meant to lend, you thought I made a gift?

Ulpian's holding is not easily reconciled with Julian, D. 41.1.36: ". . . For also if I count out and hand over to you money as a gift, and you take it as a loan, there is agreement (among jurists) that ownership passes to you, nor is it an obstacle that we disagree about the reason (*causa*) for giving and receiving."

2. *Mutuum, Depositum,* and *Commodatum.* The situations in section 1 are a good deal likelier to occur. You leave a sum of money with me for safe-keeping, and for some reason I assume you are allowing me to make use of it, so long as I return the same amount. Or I intended a loan and you thought of it as exhibition material. There is no contract, but, after the identity of the coins is lost, a *condictio* can be brought. Why no defense of fraud?

3. **Celsus' Problem.** You ask both me and Titius for a loan of money. I order my debtor to promise you the money, and he does so; but you think it is Titius' debtor who made the promise. Are you obligated to me? Celsus, D. 12.1.32, sees the difficulty: "My position is unchanged if you have contracted no business (*negotium*) with me. But it is better that I think you are obligated, not because I lent money to you—for this cannot occur except between people who agree—but because my money came to you, and it is right and fair (*bonum et aequum*) that you return this to me." The debtor's payment, on my order, extinguishes his debt to me, and I thereby sustain a loss; but Julian's requirement of a transaction (Case 227) stands in the way, right? Celsus uses equity to steer a path around this requirement and allow for a *condictio.* Is he successful, particularly in evading the issue of intent, *animus*? Why does Celsus refer to the money paid by my debtor as "my money"?

4. **Settling Disputed Claims.** We agree on a payment to settle our dispute. Can the amount that was given be reclaimed if the dispute was in fact unfounded? Paul, D. 12.6.65.1, says no, unless the dispute involved an obviously false claim (*evidens calumnia*). Right solution? What if the claim is false but not obviously so?

CASE 231: Frustration of Purpose

D. 12.4.16 (Celsus libro tertio Digestorum)

Dedi tibi pecuniam, ut mihi Stichum dares: utrum id contractus genus pro portione emptionis et venditionis est, an nulla hic alia obligatio est quam ob rem dati re non secuta? In quod proclivior sum: et ideo, si mortuus est Stichus, repetere possum quod ideo tibi dedi, ut mihi Stichum dares. Finge alienum esse Stichum, sed te tamen eum tradidisse: repetere a te pecuniam potero, quia hominem accipientis non feceris: et rursus, si tuus est Stichus et pro evictione eius promittere non vis, non liberaberis, quo minus a te pecuniam repetere possim.

Celsus in the third book of his *Digests*:

I gave you money in order that you give me (the slave) Stichus. Is this type of contract to some extent a purchase and sale (*emptio venditio*), or is there no obligation here other than for a thing given for a purpose that was not realized (*ob rem dati re non secuta*)? I incline more to the latter view. And so, if Stichus died (before delivery to me), I can reclaim what I gave to you in order that you give me Stichus.

Suppose that Stichus belonged to a third party, but you nevertheless handed him over (without title). I will be able to reclaim the money from you because you did not make the slave the recipient's property. And again, if Stichus is yours and you refuse to give a guarantee against eviction, you will not be freed from my being able to reclaim the money from you.

Discussion

1. **"To Some Extent a Purchase."** Money for a slave: at first glance, this certainly does look like a sale. If it were, the death of Stichus, or the seller's failure to deliver title or to guarantee against eviction by a true owner, would be treated according to the ordinary rules of sale discussed in Chapter IV (especially B.1 and B.4); that is, the buyer would sue on the purchase, *ex empto*, to recover damages, if and to the extent that the law allowed this. Instead, Celsus turns to the rules for half-executed exchange agreements (see especially Case 190) and allows the putative buyer the option of seeking restitution of the price he paid. Does the jurist's move here present a problem? Observe that, especially in the case when Stichus died of natural causes before delivery, usually the buyer bore that risk (Cases 110–111, 113), meaning that the seller was still entitled to the price unless he was somehow at fault for the slave's death. Was Celsus doing an end run around this rule? (In truth, though, this fragment has been the subject of extensive scholarly debate; it remains quite unclear what Celsus was up to.)

CASE 232: Dowry for an Incestuous Marriage

D. 12.7.5 (Papinianus libro undecimo Quaestionum)

pr. Avunculo nuptura pecuniam in dotem dedit neque nupsit: an eandem repetere possit, quaesitum est. Dixi, cum ob turpem causam dantis et accipientis pecunia numeretur, cessare condictionem et in delicto pari potiorem esse possessorem: quam rationem fortassis aliquem secutum respondere non habituram mulierem condictionem: sed recte defendi non turpem causam in proposito quam nullam fuisse, cum pecunia quae daretur in dotem converti nequiret: non enim stupri, sed matrimonii gratia datam esse. 1. Noverca privigno, nurus socero pecuniam dotis nomine dedit neque nupsit. Cessare condictio prima facie videtur, quoniam iure gentium incestum committitur: atquin vel magis in ea specie nulla causa dotis dandae fuit, condictio igitur competit.

Papinian in the eleventh book of his *Questions*:

pr. A woman who was about to marry her maternal uncle gave (him) money for a dowry, but (in the end) did not marry him. It was asked whether she can reclaim it.

I held that, when money was paid because of an immoral cause (*ob turpem causam*) both of giver and recipient, the *condictio* fails and the (current) possessor prevails when the wrong is the same on both sides. Now someone who accepts this reasoning might perhaps respond that the woman will (therefore) not have a *condictio*. But the correct reply is that in the hypothetical case the cause (*causa*; for the payment) was not immoral, but nonexistent, since the money that was given cannot be turned into a dowry; it was given not for an improper sexual relation but for a marriage.

1. A stepmother gave money as a dowry to a stepson, or a daughter-in-law to a father-in-law, and (each of them) did not then marry. The *condictio* seems on its face to fail since, by the Law of Nations (*ius gentium*), incest is committed. However, the better view in this case is that there was no basis (*causa*) for giving a dowry; therefore the *condictio* lies.

Discussion

1. **Immorality and Restitution.** The proposed marriage clearly violated Roman rules on incestuous marriages (*Tituli Ulp.* 5.6–7; Justinian, *Inst.* 3.6), and would therefore have been void. The problem was the woman's dowry payment; is she entitled to reclaim it through a *condictio*? Papinian's initial response suggests that since both the woman and her uncle were participating in the illegality, the payment stays with the recipient. They are, as the Romans say, *in pari turpitudine*, equally reprehensible, and so a court will not intervene—a potentially harsh legal rule also enforced in Common Law. (Paul, D. 12.5.8, gives the explanation.) Clear examples are a litigant paying a judge for a verdict (Ulpian, D. 12.5.2.2; Paul, D. 12.5.3)

or a thief paying hush-money to a witness (Ulpian, D. 12.5.4.1). Payments for sexual offenses produce the same result: Ulpian, D. 12.5.4 pr. (*stuprum* or adultery).

But it may seem unfair (particularly if the social context is considered) to leave the matter there. Clearly the case was contentious, but Papinian reasons that since marriage could not result, her payment lacks *causa* and therefore she can reclaim it. Is this reasoning correct? (Or is he just being solicitous of the woman?) With regard to the dowry payment, how would the legal situation change if the couple had attempted to carry out the marriage?

What is interesting in this fragment is how the jurists manipulate the concept of *causa* in the interests of equity.

2. Immorality of the Giver. In determining whether a payment for an immoral cause can be reclaimed, it is really only the giver's innocence that is crucial. Thus, a *condictio* lies for money extorted from me by force (Pomponius, D. 12.5.7) or threat (Ulpian, D. 12.5.2 pr.-1, 4.2); but not if the immorality is mine alone (Paul, D. 12.5.1 pr.) or shared by both parties. This leads to a famous, highly sophistical opinion by the jurists: "What is given (as payment by a customer) to a prostitute cannot be reclaimed, as Labeo and Marcellus write, but with novel reasoning: because what is involved is not the baseness of both parties, but only that of the giver, since she acts basely because she is a prostitute, but does not take money basely because she is a prostitute." (Ulpian, D. 12.5.4.3).

CASE 233: Extent of Recovery and Change of Position

D. 12.6.65.5–8 (Paulus libro septimo decimo ad Plautium)

5. Ei, qui indebitum repetit, et fructus et partus restitui debet deducta impensa. 6. In frumento indebito soluto et bonitas est et, si consumpsit frumentum, pretium repetet. 7. Sic habitatione data pecuniam condicam, non quidem quanti locari potuit, sed quanti tu conducturus fuisses. 8. Si servum indebitum tibi dedi eumque manumisisti, si sciens hoc fecisti, teneberis ad pretium eius, si nesciens, non teneberis, sed propter operas eius liberti et ut hereditatem eius restituas.

Paul in the seventeenth book *On Plautius*:

5. After deducting expenses, both fruits (*fructus*) and offspring should be restored to a person reclaiming an unowed payment. 6. In the case of unowed grain that was paid, he will also reclaim its price if he (the recipient) consumed the grain.

7. So, when the right to dwell (*habitatio*) is given, my *condictio* is for the money: not, indeed, for as much as it could have been leased for, but for as much as you would have rented it for.

8. If I gave an unowed slave to you and you manumitted him, if you did this knowingly, you will be liable for his price; if unknowingly, you will not be liable, except for the services (*operae*) of this freedman and for restoring the (right of) inheritance from him.

Discussion

1. **Problems with Restitution.** Restitution is an easy enough idea to understand, but often difficult to implement, in our law no less than in Roman. The original ambit of the *condictio* was for a specific amount of money (or of other fungibles, such as grain) or of a specific object (*certa res*); and the aim of restitution was just to put claimants back into their position before the conferral. So, assuming that the conferral itself could not be returned (the money may have been spent, or the object lost), a judgment was in most cases simply for the amount or for an object's price, with adjustments for the claimant's lost profit and the recipient's expenses in the meantime.

   But as a more equitable understanding of *condictio* emerged, the original measures began to seem unfair particularly to a recipient who may have changed position. In section 8, I mistakenly gave you a slave whom you freed without knowing of my mistake; is it fair to ask you to return the slave's price, or indeed anything beyond the legal claims you as an ex-master have against the freed slave? (Paul's holding here seems inconsistent with that in section 6, doesn't it, unless we assume that the recipient consumed the grain while knowing of the claimant's mistake.) In other words, the jurists began to move, with agonizing slowness, toward a fairer solution.

The most intricate situation is in section 7, where, apparently owing to a mistake (doubtless as the consequence of estate settlement), the recipient gets the right to dwell for free in a building (*habitatio*) and does so. The claimant (no doubt the heir) now wants rent money, but this claim is limited: not the market value of a lease, but an amount that takes into account the recipient's circumstances. Here the aim starts to be to remove the benefit from an innocent recipient but without leaving him or her in a worse position, even if this results in some loss to the claimant: a new and very powerful idea. Do you see why? But this development is highly uneven in our sources.

2. **Pomponius' Problem.** A juvenile ward (*pupillus*) cannot become obligated without a guardian's authorization. Pomponius, D. 46.3.66, puts the case of a ward who owes money to a creditor and who, without his guardian's authorization, orders a third party, whom he wrongly takes to be his debtor, to pay the money to the creditor. After the payment, what is the mistaken debtor's position? Technically, the debtor cannot bring a *condictio* against the ward, since the latter is not obligated owing to the missing authorization from the guardian; nor can he seek restitution from the ward's creditor since he acted on the basis of the ward's order and thereby freed the ward from liability to the creditor. So what is to be done? Pomponius: "But the ward will be liable in an analogous action (*actio utilis*) to the extent he became wealthier because he was freed from the debt." This invention of a *condictio* based on the factual situation is a purely ad hoc solution to the legal dilemma, arising out of equity, but the outcome is nonetheless important for incorporating into law the idea of surrendering unjustified enrichment.

CASE 234: Unowed Services by a Freedman

D. 12.6.26.12 (Ulpianus libro vicensimo sexto ad Edictum)

Libertus cum se putaret operas patrono debere, solvit: condicere eum non posse, quamvis putans se obligatum solvit, Iulianus libro decimo digestorum scripsit: natura enim operas patrono libertus debet. Sed et si non operae patrono sunt solutae, sed, cum officium ab eo desideraretur, cum patrono decidit pecunia et solvit, repetere non potest. Sed si operas patrono exhibuit non officiales, sed fabriles, veluti pictorias vel alias, dum putat se debere, videndum an possit condicere. Et Celsus libro sexto digestorum putat eam esse causam operarum, ut non sint eaedem neque eiusdem hominis neque eidem exhibentur: nam plerumque robur hominis, aetas temporis opportunitasque naturalis mutat causam operarum, et ideo nec volens quis reddere potest. Sed hae, inquit, operae recipiunt aestimationem: et interdum licet aliud praestemus, inquit, aliud condicimus: ut puta fundum indebitum dedi et fructus condico: vel hominem indebitum, et hunc sine fraude modico distraxisti, nempe hoc solum refundere debes, quod ex pretio habes: vel meis sumptibus pretiosiorem hominem feci, nonne aestimari haec debent? Sic et in proposito, ait, posse condici, quanti operas essem conducturus. Sed si delegatus sit a patrono<, an teneatur alii exhibere> officiales operas, apud Marcellum libro vicensimo digestorum quaeritur. Et dicit Marcellus non teneri eum, nisi forte in artificio sint (hae enim iubente patrono et alii edendae sunt): sed si solverit officiales delegatus, non potest condicere neque ei cui solvit creditori, cui alterius contemplatione solutum est quique suum recipit, neque patrono, quia natura ei debentur.

Ulpian in the twenty-sixth book *On the Edict*:

In the (false) belief that he owed them, a freedman rendered services (*operae*) to his patron. In the tenth book of his *Digests*, Julian wrote that he cannot bring a *condictio* even though he paid under the belief he was obligated, since by Nature a freedman owes services to his patron. But also if the services were not rendered to the patron, and instead, when his duty (*officium*) was requested, he arranged for and paid a monetary equivalent to his patron, restitution is also impossible.

But if, in the (false) belief he owes them, he renders to his patron services that are not duteous but craftsmanly (*non officiales, sed fabriles*), such as painting or the like, consider whether he can bring a *condictio*. Celsus, in the sixth book of his *Digests*, thinks it is the nature of services that they differ in kind and with respect to the giver and to the recipient. For often a person's strength, age, and the natural circumstances change the nature of services, and so he cannot render them even willingly. Still, he says, (the value of) these services can be estimated.

And sometimes, he says, although we proffer one thing, we bring a *condictio* for another. For instance, I gave you an unowed farm and I bring a *condictio* for the fruits. Or (I gave you) an unowed slave, and you, without fraud, sold him for a low price; surely you need only refund what you (still) have from the price. Or I made the slave more valuable by my expenditures; shouldn't they (the expenditures) be estimated? So also, in the hypothetical case (above), he says a *condictio* can be brought for the amount I (the patron) would have rented these services for.

But question is raised by Marcellus, in the twentieth book of his *Digests*, whether he (a freedman) who was delegated by his patron is liable to render duteous services (*officiales operae*) to a third party. Marcellus says that he is not liable except if, perchance, they consist in a skill (*artificium*), since those can also be rendered to a third party on a patron's order. But if after being delegated he renders duteous ones, he can bring a *condictio* neither against the creditor to whom he rendered them, since they were rendered to him with a view to (satisfying) another person and he (the creditor) receives (only) what is his; nor against his patron, because they were owed to him by Nature.

Discussion

1. **Services.** In freeing their slaves, masters often imposed on them certain duties, called *operae*, conceived as "workdays." By law, they were not to be excessive and, as Celsus indicates, had to be suitable to the age, status, and training of the freedperson: Ulpian, D. 38.1.2; Paul, D. 38.1.16.1. The slave promised to provide them just before being freed; and this promise was later, somewhat anomalously, made legally enforceable. Because they usually stem from the ex-slave's "duty" (*officium*), they are called *officiales*, and they are owed only to the ex-master patron and his or her descendants, so they are non-transferable to third parties.

   These highly personal services are distinguished from "craftsmanly services" (*operae fabriles*), which are essentially those that can be purchased on the open market and hence have a monetary value. These the patron can order the freedperson to perform for third parties: Ulpian, D. 38.1.6, 9.1.

   Trace out how Celsus, Julian, Marcellus, and Ulpian go about handling these two types of services when a freedperson performs them under the mistaken belief that he must do so. On delegation, see Case 211.

2. **Damages.** In the third paragraph of the translation, Celsus is cited (more than a little off-point) as amplifying the general principles for calculating damages that are given in the previous Case. Note, in particular, the slave who is delivered by mistake to an innocent recipient who then sells the slave for a price lower than market value; only the proceeds of the sale can be reclaimed.

CASE 235: Tracing the Benefit

C. 4.26.7 pr.-1, 3 (Impp. Diocletianus et Maximianus AA. et CC. Crescenti)

pr. Ei, qui servo alieno dat mutuam pecuniam, quamdiu superest servus, item post mortem eius intra annum de peculio contra dominum competere actionem vel, si in rem domini haec versa sit quantitas, post annum etiam esse honorariam non est ambigui iuris. 1. Quapropter si quidem in rem domini versa pecunia est, heredes eius convenire potes de ea summa, quae in rem ipsius processit. . . .

3. Alioquin si cum libero rem agente eius, cuius precibus meministi, contractum habuisti et eius personam elegisti, pervides contra dominum nullam te habuisse actionem, nisi vel in rem eius pecunia processit vel hunc contractum ratum habuit.

The Emperors Diocletian and Maximian to Crescens (293 CE):

pr. It is not doubtful law that a person who lends money to someone else's slave has available an action on the (slave's) *peculium* against his owner, for as long as the slave survives and also within one year after his death; or, if the amount has been turned to the owner's benefit (*in rem domini versa*), that he also has a Praetorian (*honoraria*) action after the year. 1. Therefore if indeed the money has been turned to the owner's benefit, you can sue his heirs for the amount that passed into his property. . . .

3. For the rest, if you had a contract with a free person who was conducting the business of the person you mentioned in your petition, and you chose (to do business with) his person (*eius persona*), you realize that you had no action against the principal (*dominus*) unless either the money passed into his property or he ratified this contract.

Discussion

1. "Turned to the Owner's Benefit." The Introduction to Chapter VII.A notes that, when a dependent son or slave makes a contract, the liability of the *paterfamilias* is normally limited by the value of the dependent's *peculium*, a fund held more or less independently of the assets of the father or master. But this limit can be breached in two ways: (i) if the father or master gave an order (*iussum*) allowing the contract, or (ii) if the proceeds of the contract were turned to his material benefit (*in rem versa*). Suppose, for example, that I buy a horse from your son and pay for it, but he does not then deliver the horse; if my payment ends up in your hands, then you may be held liable, above and beyond your son's *peculium*. This form of enrichment is quite different from the *condictio*, but it is worth pausing on it because of what follows in section 3, which has a later historical importance out of all proportion to its length.

2. A Contract with a Free Person. Several third-century sources suggest that the jurists were experimenting with extensions of the action *de in rem verso*

beyond the situation of dependent sons and slaves. For instance, Papinian, D. 17.2.82, discusses partnership (*societas*), in which one partner is not liable for another partner's debts; but the jurist makes an exception if the proceeds from a partner's contract come into the common fund. See also Ulpian, D. 12.1.27 (a city); Emperors Severus and Antoninus, C. 8.15.1 (194; the principal of a *procurator*). However, section 3 of this Case is much the boldest of these sources, even though the circumstances of Crescens' petition are uncertain. Apparently without authorization the free person (*liber*, neither subject to another's power nor a *procurator*) was managing the affairs of a third party and made the contract with the would-be plaintiff; this person may have disappeared or become insolvent. Being able to sue the person's principal could therefore be very important, right? What theories do the emperors use to justify a possible lawsuit?

Glossary

Definitions for Roman legal terms rely heavily on Adolf Berger, *Encyclopedic Dictionary of Roman Law* (1953), which readers are encouraged to consult for further authoritative information.

acceptilatio: a receipt formally discharging a debt.

actio: an "action," a lawsuit or the claim upon which it is based. A "cause of action" is a recognized legal basis for a lawsuit. In Roman private law, the Praetor's Edict listed the available causes of action; see "Edict" and *"formula."* Among the main actions referred to in this Casebook are the *actio ex stipulatu*, the action stemming from a stipulation (Chapter II; see also *condictio*); the *actio empti* and *actio venditi*, the actions on purchase and sale (Chapter IV); and so on. An *actio in personam* is one directed to a particular person, as opposed to a property action *in rem*. An *actio contraria* is a counterclaim. An *actio praescriptis verbis* (action with a preamble) is a special action used for contractual claims falling outside the usual system of contracts (Chapter VI.B). An *actio utilis* (also often called an *actio in factum*) is an analogous action based on those in the Praetor's Edict; an *actio civilis in factum* is a non-discretionary used for half-executed contracts of exchange (Chapter VI.B). See also *cessio actionum*.

addictio in diem: sale subject to rescission within a stated time (Case 105).

administratio libera: the unrestricted right of a dependent to manage his or her *peculium*. See Cases 198, 204.

adprobatio: approval; see Case 166. Opposite: *improbatio*, disapproval.

adstipulatio: a stipulation that adds a secondary creditor for a debt (Case 40).

Aediles: annual magistrates under the Republican constitution, next below the Praetors. Their Edict governed market sales of slaves and farm animals (Cases 143–144).

aequitas or bonum et aequum: fairness or impartiality, often as distinguished from *ius*.

aestimatum: an appraised value of an object, agreed upon by parties. Also, the contract on brokerage (Case 186).

agent, agency: a person acting with authorization in another's stead, or the actor's status. This concept is not wholly present in Roman law, but see Chapters V.C, VII.B–D.

agreement: see *consensus*.

animus: intention or will of a legal actor.

arbitrium boni viri: the judgment of a "good person," i.e., a reasonable person.

arr(h)a: an earnest given at the conclusion of a contract.

auctoritas: authorization, as by a guardian. In sales law, an implied warranty that the seller will stand behind the buyer in the event a third party seeks to evict him (Case 137).

bona fides: good faith, a central contract requirement embracing both fidelity to the terms of the contract and due consideration for a contractual partner; see Introduction, Part E. Also used for actions when the *formulae* carry the phrase *ex fide bona*, "in accord with good faith"; opposite of actions *stricti iuris*, "in strict law."

bottomry loan: a form of marine insurance; see Case 33.

calumnia: trickery, particularly in bringing a vexatious lawsuit.

casus fortuitus: unavoidable accident.

causa: in contract law, the reason why a promise was made. See Introduction, Part F. On *causa turpis*, immoral cause, see Cases 19, 232. See also *condictio*.

cautio: a guarantee, often in the form of a stipulation.

certum or certa res: see *incertum*.

cessio actionum: cession of actions, the grant to another of one's right to sue on a claims against a third party (Cases 46, 215).

commodatum: a contract of loan for use, e.g., a loan of an object where the parties intend that the same property be returned to the lender; see Chapter III.B. Contrast *precarium*.

compromissum: a bilateral agreement to submit a dispute to arbitration (Case 185).

condicio: a condition, resulting in suspension of a promise until an event occurs; see Chapter II, Part C.

condictio: a claim for a specific sum of money or amount of a fungible, or for a specific piece of property; later, also a claim for an initially uncertain amount (a *condictio incerti*). The *condictio* was widely used in Roman contract law. See Introduction, Part B. Sources on unjustified enrichment break up the forms of *condictio* based on the absence of a *causa* for retaining a benefit (Cases 228–231).

consensus: in private law, contractual agreement between two or more parties. See Introduction, Part D. *Consensus contrarius*: a bilateral counteragreement to call off a contract. Tacit agreement occurs when contract terms are implied by law.

consideration: in Common Law, something that a promisor bargains for and receives from the promisee, as part of an exchange.

constitutum debiti: an informal promise to pay a preexisting debt (Cases 185, 210).

contra stipulatorem: a principle of contract interpretation whereby ambiguous stipulations should be interpreted against the promisee; see Case 12. In modern law, *contra proferentem*.

contractus: a contract. Although the jurists never exactly define this concept, it is often limited to a closed list of promissory agreements that the Praetor had recognized as resulting in possible liability. They also sometimes use the word more generally to refer to any promissory agreement that may result in personal liability. On the jurists' typology of contracts, see Introduction, Part C.

conventio: a general term for agreement; see *consensus*.

creditum: credit, the counterpart of debt.

culpa: "fault," particularly non-deliberate carelessness (by contrast with *dolus*, intentional infliction of harm). *Culpa* is used in a wide variety of contexts in Roman law, but it often refers to the legal duty of one individual to exercise reasonable care in protecting someone else or that person's property. *Culpa in eligendo*, "fault in choosing," is a post-Roman term used when a defendant is held liable for carelessly selecting a third party who commits a delict.

curator: guardian of the economic interests of a *sui iuris* person under age twenty-five. *Curatores* were also appointed to protect the insane, *furiosi*, and spendthrifts, *prodigi*.

custodia: safekeeping; in contract law, often a standard of care imposing on the holder of another's property responsibility for all damage except what was unpreventable.

damnum: loss, especially loss recoverable by a lawsuit. *Damnum iniuria datum*: "loss wrongfully inflicted" to another's property, which gives rise to an action under the lex Aquilia of the early third century BCE establishing liability when one person wrongfully damages property belonging to another person.

debitum: a debt, both an obligation owed to another person and the obligatory tie between creditor and debtor. See Introduction, Part G.

default: see *mora*.

delegatio: an arrangement whereby one's debtor pays one's creditor; see Cases 209–211.

delictum: delict, a civil wrongdoing (similar to a tort) that results in a defendant's liability.

denuntiatio: formal legal notice.

depositum: a contract in which a depositor entrusts property to a depositary's safekeeping, with the parties' intent that the depositary not use the object and return it upon demand; see Chapter III.B. *Depositum irregulare* ("irregular deposit," not a Roman term) results when the depositary is meant to return not the property deposited but its equivalent; see Case 69.

detention: in property law, when one person physically holds property on behalf of another, but without owning or possessing the property; from *detinere*, to hold or detain.

dies: a date on which a debt comes due, a deadline for performance.

diligentia: carefulness, especially in handling another's property. Opposite: *neglegentia*.

dolus or dolus malus: deceit, the intent to inflict loss or hurt on another person. Some actions require that a defendant have exhibited *dolus*; but more usually *dolus* is used with *culpa* to indicate a general liability for both intentional and careless fault. The *actio doli* (or *de dolo*) makes deceit actionable as a delict.

dominium: ownership; see *possessio*.

dos: dowry, property entrusted by the bride's family to the groom's during a marriage. *Dotis dictio* is a formal promise of dowry by a bride-to-be, her father, or her debtor (Case 50).

Edict: A list of causes of actions, issued by a Praetor at the start of his year in office. The Roman jurists often organize their legal writings as commentaries on the Edict. During the early Empire, the contents of the Edict gradually became fixed, and a final "permanent" version (the Edictum Perpetuum) was issued under the Emperor Hadrian (reign: 117–138 CE). The "Provincial Edict" was issued by governors in Roman provinces. See Introduction, Part A. The Edict of the Curule Aediles governed market sales of slaves and farm animals.

emancipatio: emancipation, the voluntary release of a child from paternal power.

emptio venditio: purchase and sale; see Chapter IV.

error: mistake, as by one or both parties in the formation of a contract (Chapter IV.A.2). *Error in substantia* is mistake as to a characteristic (Cases 89–91).

evictio: eviction, a claim of property by its true owner.

exceptio: a legal defense; see Chapter II.E. An *exceptio doli* is a defense based on the other party's deceit either in a transaction or through abuse of judicial procedure. An *exceptio non numeratae pecuniae* expresses the defendant's objection that he did not receive money which the plaintiff seeks in restitution. An *exceptio pacti* is a defense based on an agreement that effectively delays or blocks a cause of action.

exercitor: the operator of a ship; see Chapter VII.B.

extra ordinem: trial in an imperial court, outside the "order" of the Praetor's Edict.

fideiussio: suretyship, a guarantee that a debtor will pay or perform. The surety is a *fideiussor*; see Cases 41–46.

fides: fidelity to the terms of a contract; creditworthiness. See also *bona fides.*

fiducia: a form of real security in which the debtor surrenders ownership to the creditor, with the understanding that the property's title will be restored upon payment (Case 76).

formula: a written document by which, in a civil trial, the Praetor appoints a *iudex* and authorizes him to condemn the defendant if certain factual or legal circumstances are proven, or to absolve the defendant if this is not the case. The *formula*, settled upon during the initial portion of the trial (*in iure*), defines the basic issues, including especially the plaintiff's cause of action; it provides a basis for parties' subsequent argument in the second portion of the trial (*apud iudicem*). "Formulary procedure" was the normal method of bringing private lawsuits during the Classical period of Roman law. See Introduction, Parts A–B. *Formulae* can be phrased either *in factum* (X happened, therefore D is liable) or *in ius* (the law establishes D's liability if X happens); see Case 62.

fraus: fraud, or the consequence of a fraudulent infliction of harm. See *dolus.*

fructus: literally, "fruits," including natural proceeds such as the produce of agriculture and the offspring of animals, but also income from legal transactions such as leases.

furiosus: an insane person.

gestio negotiorum: management of another's affairs, especially if unauthorized; see Chapter VIII.A.

honorarium: a grant given for services, but ostensibly independent of them (Case 184).

hypotheca: property the debtor gives as security for a debt, often despite retaining possession; see Chapter III.C.

Idus: the thirteenth or fifteenth day of the month, depending on the month.

impensae: expenses, as on property being held for another (Case 67).

incertum: an unliquidated debt. Antonym: *certum* or *certa res.*

infamia: "infamy," a public shaming that results from condemnation in some contract actions having a strong fiduciary element. *Infamia* carries with it not only loss of public esteem, but also some legal disabilities.

infans: a young child (a legal infant); see Case 1.

institor: a manager appointed by an owner to run a business; see Chapter VIII.B. On the *actio quasi institoria*, see Cases 206–207.

interesse: literally to "differ," hence (in expressions like *id quod interest*) a means to express the extent of a litigant's stake in a lawsuit, as damages.

iudex: a "judge" in a private trial (*iudicium*), appointed by the Praetor to listen to the parties to a specific lawsuit and then to decide the case on the basis of the *formula*. *Iudices* were either appointed by the parties' agreement or drawn from the Praetor's *album*. See Introduction, Parts A–B.

ius: law, irrespective of its source. *Ius civile*: the Civil Law, specific to Roman citizens (*cives*); but this term is often used for Roman law generally. *Ius gentium*: the Law of Nations, the general legal practice observed in human communities. *Ius naturale*: the Law of Nature, often assimilated to the *ius gentium*.

iussum: an order; see *mandatum*. On the *actio quod iussu*, see Cases 194–195.

jurist (iurisconsultus, iuris peritus): an expert in Roman private law.

kalendae: the first day of the month.

laesio enormis: huge inequality of exchange (Case 83).

legatum: a bequest out of an inheritance.

lex : a statute passed by an assembly of the Roman people. The Lex Aquilia is an early third-century BCE statute giving a remedy for wrongful damage to another's property. A *lex* can also be a term of a contract.

lex commissaria: a contract term allowing a seller to rescind a sale if the buyer does not pay by a deadline (Case 106).

"literal" contract: *contractus litteris*, a formal contract arranged through bookkeeping entries (Case 51).

litis contestatio: joinder of issue, the point in a trial when a *iudex* has been named, the *formula* has been settled, and the Praetor submits the case for decision by a *iudex*.

locatio conductio: "lease/hire," a sprawling contract that comprises most exchanges of a performance for a money fee (*merces*); see Chapter V.A. Specific types are *l.c. rei* (V.A.1–3), *operis faciendi* and *operarum* (V.A.4). Rules are developed specific to each form of contract, and the *merces* flows from party to party according to the sense of the contract.

mandatum: an informal contract whereby one person instructs another to perform some act; see Chapter V.C. A mandator gives the order, a mandatary accepts it.

merces: a fee for performance, in *locatio conductio*. A *mercennarius* is a person who works for a wage (Case 168).

merx: property both movable and immovable, the object of a sale.

metus: duress, or fear of harm.

mora: delay or default, failure to perform or pay a debt that has become due; see Cases 30–31, 116.

mutuum: a contract of loan for consumption, e.g., a loan of money or of grain or wine, where the parties intend that an equivalent amount be returned. See Chapter III.A.

neglegentia: carelessness; see *diligentia*.

negotiorum gestio: the conduct of another's business, especially if unauthorized; see Chapter VIII.A.

novatio: novation, the recasting of an existing debt into a new form: Case 39.

obligatio: obligation, a duty to pay or act that derives, in most instances, either from a contract or a delict (a civil wrong). An *obligatio naturalis* ("natural obligation") is an obligation that cannot be enforced by an action, but that is irreversible if carried out. See Introduction, Part G, and Case 3.

operae: "workdays" that a freedman has promised to an ex-master and patron (Cases 50, 234).

pactum: an informal agreement, especially one that is not enforceable as a contract. See especially Chapter IV.A.5. Covenants on use of an object of sale: Case 109. On "naked" pacts, Case 187.

parol evidence: in Common Law, evidence extrinsic to a written contract; in many instances, it is inadmissible to contradict, or even to explain or supplement, the wording of the contract.

paterfamilias: the male head of family descended from him through the male line (agnates), plus adopted children but less emancipated children. A *diligens paterfamilias* is one who is a model of caution and prudence.

patria potestas: a father's power over his unemancipated agnatic descendants.

patrimonium: a person's estate.

peculium: a fund of property or cash set aside by a *paterfamilias* for the exclusive use of a child-in-power or a slave. For the *actio de peculio*, see Cases 196–198.

perfectio: in one meaning, completion. When all elements of a sale are known and there are no outstanding conditions, the sale is said to be complete (*perfecta*). See Chapter IV.B.1.

periculum: the risk, especially that property will be damaged or destroyed.

permutatio: barter, the exchange of an object for an object; see Cases 77–79, 191.

pignus: a contract in which a debtor consigns property to a creditor as security for the debt; see Chapter III.C.

poena: a penalty arranged by contract (Cases 48–49) or imposed by law.

pollicitatio: a charitable promise to a municipality (Case 52).

possessio: possession: in Roman law the physical control of an object with the intent to possess it. Possession is defensible through Praetorian interdicts. But possession is sharply distinguished, in property law, from ownership (*dominium*).

Praetor: in the late Republic and the early Empire, one of several annual magistrates next in rank, in the Republican hierarchy, below the Consuls. Praetors had a wide range of duties, but were particularly charged with overseeing the courts. The Urban Praetor (*praetor urbanus*) headed the court that handled private disputes between Romans, which he channeled by establishing causes of action in his Edict. The Peregrine Praetor (*praetor perigrinus*) presided over a court for private lawsuits between Romans and non-citizen residents, or between non-citizens. Other Praetors handled criminal courts. See Introduction, Part A.

praeclusio: preclusion, when a landlord bars a tenant's entry into a leasehold (Case 152).

precarium: holding another's property on sufferance; see Case 70.

pretium: price, normally as set by parties. *Pretium iustum* or *verum*: true price, apparently in relation to property's market value.

principal: in modern law, a natural or legal person who authorizes another to act as his or her agent. Roman law lacks this concept explicitly, but often recognizes it tacitly. See *reus*.

Proculiani: a prominent juristic "school" of the early Empire, distinguished for their more flexible development of Roman law. Their origin was traced to the Augustan jurist Labeo, but they owe their name to the later Julio-Claudian jurist Proculus. See also *Sabiniani*.

procurator: in private law, the overseer or superintendent of a principal's estate; see Chapter VII.C. *Procurator* is also used more generally to refer to appointed subordinate managers. On the *procurator in litem*, who handles a lawsuit for a principal, see Cases 212–213.

privity of contract: the rule that a contract cannot confer rights or impose obligations upon anyone who is not a party to the contract. See Introduction, Part G, and Case 10.

pupillus: a ward, below the age of adulthood; see Case 1.

quaestio facti: a question of fact, left for determination by a *iudex*. Opposite: a *quaestio iuris*, question of law, in principle determined by jurists. But this distinction is perhaps too formalistic.

quasi ex contractu: quasi-contract, a Justinianic category for liability that is not contractual but "contract-like" in some respects; see Chapter VIII, especially Case 216.

quanto minoris: a contract remedy for the difference in value between the object of sale as warranted and the object as it is; see Chapter IV.B.5.

quod actum est: "what was transacted," a basis for interpreting contracts; see Case 11.

receptum: "receipt" of property taken for safekeeping; see Case 65. See also Case 185 for other forms of *receptum*.

redhibitio: a contract remedy that rescinds a sale and restores the parties to their prior position; see Chapter IV.B.5.

remissio mercedis: remission of rent, to a tenant farmer after catastrophic crop failure; see Case 159.

res: property. *Res mancipi*: certain forms of property (land, slaves, large farm animals, etc.) that require a special procedure (called mancipation) for conveyance of title. *Res communes* is the common fund in *societas* (Case 170)

responsum: a jurist's legal answer to an inquiry about a question of law.

reus: a principal debtor.

Sabiniani or Cassiani: a prominent juristic "school" of the early Empire, noted mainly for their stricter interpretation of legal norms. Their name comes from the Julio-Claudian jurists Massurius Sabinus and Cassius Longinus. See also *Proculiani*.

Senatus consultum: a decree of the Senate, a form of early imperial legislation. On the SC Macedonianum, see Case 61.

servitutes: servitudes, which, like modern easements, limit an owner's property rights in favor of a neighboring "dominant" property (as by a right of way or a right to convey water). Praedial servitudes attach to both the dominant and the servient property, and they regularly remain with the respective properties when either property changes ownership.

sestertius: a Roman coin equal to one-quarter of a denarius; the most common unit of valuation in Roman law.

severance: the separation of complex promises into their constituent elements (Case 7).

societas: partnership; see Chapter V.B. A *societas omnium bonorum* merges two or more estates.

stipulatio: stipulation, a formal unilateral promise made in a question-and-answer arrangement; in principle, it becomes valid because of its form. From the verb *stipulari*, "to put a question." See Chapter II. An Aquilian stipulation consolidates all parties' existing debts to the same creditor (Case 12). The *stipulatio duplae* is a penalty in the event of eviction (Case 134).

stuprum: gross sexual misconduct in violation of law.

sui iuris: for free persons, not subject to *patria potestas*, the power of a paterfamilias; also used more generally: under one's own authority. The antonym is *alieno iuri subiectus*, subject to the power of a *paterfamilias*.

surety: see *fideiussor*.

traditio: handover of property, often thereby conveying possession and ownership. For extended forms of *traditio* (*longa manu, brevi manu*), see Cases 55, 68.

tutor: guardian of a *sui iuris* minor (a *pupillus* or *pupilla*). Also, the guardian of an adult *sui iuris* woman.

Twelve Tables: Rome's earliest attempt at a comprehensive statement of its law; promulgated in 449 BCE.

usucapio: a means to acquire ownership of property through legal possession for a period prescribed by law (two years for immovables, one year for movables). Usucapion was used mainly when *res mancipi* had been conveyed without the owner passing title through a formal ceremony. It is not similar to adverse possession in Common Law.

usurae: interest on debt. Usury statutes limited interest rates.

utilitas: benefit to individuals or to a community (*utilitas publica*). See especially Case 64. The adjective *utilis* is also used for analogous actions under the Praetor's Edict. The jurists also describe some useful rules, which seem to defy ordinary legal logic, as being introduced *utilitatis causa*, "for the sake of practicality."

vir bonus: an honest person, often equated to a "diligent *paterfamilias*"; very broadly similar to a reasonable person in modern law.

vis maior: "higher force," which cannot be averted by human action; the category includes not just acts of God, but unavoidable events like the natural death of a slave.

voluntas: wish or intention, usually expressed in action or writing.

warranty: a contractual guarantee that something is or will be true (Case 47). See especially Chapter IV.B.4–5.

Short Biographies of the Jurists

AFRICANUS. Sextus Caecilius Africanus was a student of Julian; in his nine books of *Questions* he generally seems to follow and comment on Julian's decisions. The *Digest* contains 130 fragments or citations of his writings.

ALFENUS. Publius Alfenus Varus, Consul in 39 BCE and a student of Servius, wrote 40 books of *Digests* that were excerpted and commented on by Paul in the late classical period. He is the only preclassical jurist whose writings are represented by numerous excerpts (81 fragments) in the *Digest*; they frequently report views of Servius.

ARISTO. Titius Aristo was a member of Trajan's council in the early second century CE, but held no public office. He wrote annotations on several earlier jurists, including Labeo.

CAELIUS SABINUS. A Flavian jurist, Consul in 69 CE, who belonged to the Sabinian "school."

CASSIUS. C. Cassius Longinus, descended from an eminent Republican family, was Consul in 30 CE, later proconsul and legate in Asia and Syria, but in 65 he was banished to Sardinia by Nero (reign: 54–68 CE); he died soon after his recall in 69. A pupil of Sabinus, he helped found the school that is also called Cassian. His major work, a commentary on the *ius civile*, is known mainly from excerpts commented on by Javolenus.

CELSUS. Publius Juventius Celsus (Praetor in 108 CE, Consul for the second time in 128, Governor of Thrace and Asia, a member of Hadrian's Council) is one of the most prominent juristic personalities of the high Classical period. His acuteness and originality were accompanied, at times, by aggressive polemics. Although along with Neratius he headed the Proculian "school," Celsus appears to have contributed to overcoming school controversies. Of special note are his abstract statements on the sources of law and the methods of legal interpretation. Celsus' major work, the *Digests* in 39 books, follows the order of the Edict (books 1–27) and a standard list of statutes and decrees of the Senate (279 fragments). His son, also a jurist, is cited as Celsus the Younger (Celsus Adulescens).

FLORENTINUS wrote the *Institutes*, a fairly comprehensive introductory work in 12 books, apparently no earlier than the reign of Marcus Aurelius (161–180 CE)

GAIUS (his family name and origin are unknown) was an outsider in Classical jurisprudence; he was a teacher of law, probably without the *ius respondendi*. His writings (some 20 in number, dating from ca. 150–180 CE) were intended mainly to instruct (e.g., the material is carefully organized) and also show an interest in legal history (e.g., his commentary on the Twelve Tables); but they avoid casuistic discussion of legal problems. Perhaps for this reason Gaius was not considered worthy of citation by his contemporaries, but he came to be recognized as a major jurist in the postclassical period and is frequently cited in the *Digest* (521 fragments). His main significance lies in the area of abstract doctrine and system-building.

Gaius' 30 books on the Provincial Edict are an extended commentary on the model Edict for the Provinces; the Emperor Hadrian (reign: 117–138 CE) had ordered the Provincial Edict to be edited along with the Urban Praetor's Edict, and the two closely resembled each other. Governors were required to proclaim the Provincial Edict unchanged. Gaius' commentary was perhaps written as a basis for law courses in a provincial city.

Gaius' *Institutes*, a beginner's text in four books, was used as the basis for Justinian's *Institutes*, which have profoundly influenced Continental legal education and codification down to modern times. Gaius' *Institutes* is the only work of classical jurisprudence that survives to us in approximately its original form. The single manuscript (a palimpsest, in which the text of Gaius was overwritten with the letters of Saint Jerome) was rediscovered by the historian B. G. Niebuhr in Verona in 1816, and identified by the legal historian F. C. von Savigny soon thereafter.

Gaius also prepared an expanded seven-book edition of the Institutes, which he called the *Res Cottidianae* or *Aurea*. Scholars today believe that the preserved fragments from this work contain some postclassical additions.

GALLUS. Gaius Aquilius Gallus, a student of Quintus Mucius Scaevola, was Praetor in 66 BCE and one of the major jurists of his day. He apparently wrote nothing, and his opinions are mainly transmitted through Servius.

HERMOGENIANUS is an early postclassical jurist who wrote six books of *Legal Excerpts* under Diocletian (reign: 284–305 CE); he probably also compiled the Hermogenian Code, a collection of Diocletian's rescripts, between 291 and 294.

JAVOLENUS. Lucius Javolenus Priscus, head of the Sabinian "school" and Julian's teacher, wrote during the late first and early second centuries CE; he was Consul in 86 CE, and later Governor in Upper Germany, Syria, and Africa, as well as a member of Trajan's Council (reign: 98–117 CE). The *Digest* contains 72 excerpts from his most important work, the *Letters* (14 books), the longer fragments of which preserve the response format. He also prepared critical editions of several earlier jurists (Labeo, Cassius, Plautius).

JULIAN. Publius Salvius Julianus, a student of Javolenus, enjoyed a brilliant career during the reigns of Hadrian (117–138 CE), Antoninus Pius (138–161 CE), and Marcus Aurelius (161–180 CE), to whose Council he belonged. "Because of his extraordinary learning" (so an honorary inscription tells us) the young Julian's pay as Quaestor was doubled by Hadrian, who later entrusted to him the final edition of the Praetor's Edict. Julian reached the Consulate in 148 and served as Governor in Lower Germany, Nearer Spain, and Africa.

Besides his major juristic work, the *Digests* (90 books), he also wrote four books commenting on Urseius Ferox and six books of excerpts from Minicius (an otherwise unknown jurist of the late first century CE. Julian is praised especially for his clarity, elegance, intuition, and the concrete vividness and realistic persuasiveness of his decisions. He seldom cites other jurists, basing his decisions instead on virtuosic reasoning from case to case; nor does he hesitate to overstep doctrinal boundaries in order to obtain fair results. The late classical jurists, especially Ulpian, cite him as a towering authority. In the *Digest* the compilers include more than 900 direct excerpts or citations from Julian's work.

LABEO. Marcus Antistius Labeo was a student of Trebatius; because of his creative originality, he is considered the preeminent figure in early Classical jurisprudence. He allegedly declined the consulate because of his dislike for the Emperor Augustus (reign: 31 BCE–14 CE). Labeo taught law extensively—the Proculian juristic "school" is traced back to him—and also wrote at length. Labeo's voluminous works (over 400 books) are known to us only through two abbreviated versions: the jurist Javolenus epitomized and commented on Labeo's posthumous writings (in 10 books), and Paul later did the same for the *Pithana* (*Arguments*, in 8 books).

LICINIUS RUFINUS. Marcus Gnaeus Licinius Rufinus, very likely a student of the jurist Paul, wrote a work in 12 books on *Rules* (*Regulae*).

MAECIAN , a respected member of the imperial bureaucracy and a teacher of Marcus Aurelius, wrote a 16-book work on testamentary trusts (*fideicommissa*).

MARCELLUS. Ulpius Marcellus, a high classical jurist, belonged to the Councils of Antoninus Pius (reign: 138–161 CE) and Marcus Aurelius (reign: 161–180). His major work is 31 books of *Digests*, a collection of problems influenced by Julian's *Digests*. Justinian's *Digest* contains 292 fragments of his writings.

MARCIAN. Aelius Marcianus, one of the last of the late Classical jurists, wrote a lengthy *Institutes* in 16 books, as well as a collection of *Regulae* (*Rules*) and some monographs, mainly on criminal procedure, most likely in the reigns of Elagabalus (218–222) and Alexander Severus (222–235).

MAURICIANUS. Junius Mauricianus wrote an extensive commentary on the *lex Iulia et Papia*, the Augustan marriage legislation, under Antoninus Pius (reign: 138–161).

MELA. Fabius Mela is thought to have written during the reign of Augustus (31 BCE–14 CE).

MODESTINUS. Herennius Modestinus, a student of Ulpian, is the last securely datable late Classical jurist. Modestinus was Prefect of the Watch under Alexander Severus (reign: 222–235) and/or one of his successors. He composed *Responsa* in 19 books as well as *Differentiae* (*Controversial Questions*), *Regulae* (*Rules*), and—in Greek— *Excusationes*, a work dealing with grounds for exemption from guardianship.

NERATIUS. Lucius Neratius Priscus (Consul in 98 CE, later Legate in Pannonia) headed the Proculian "school" after the elder Celsus; he belonged to the Imperial Council of Trajan (reign: 98–117) and Hadrian (117–138). His major works are collections of case law (*Responses, Letters, Rules of Law, Parchments*). He is well represented by 188 fragments or citations in the *Digest.*

NERVA. Marcus Cocceius Nerva (Consul in 21 or 22 CE) was a close advisor of the Emperor Tiberius (reign: 14–37). Along with Proculus, he led what was later called the Proculian "school" of jurists. Although later jurists often cite him, the titles of his writings are unknown. His son was also a jurist, and his grandson was the Emperor Nerva (reign: 96–98).

OFILIUS. A. Ofilius was a student of Servius and a friend of Julius Caesar; no excerpts from his work survive in the Digest, but he is cited by other jurists more than 50 times.

PAPINIAN. Aemilius Papinianus rose to the summit of the imperial bureaucracy. In 198 CE Papinian appears to have headed the Office of Petitions (*a libellis*), which drafted rescripts for the Emperor Septimius Severus (reign: 193–211) and his son, co-ruler, and successor Caracalla (198–217); Ulpian, who served as Papinian's clerk (*adsessor*), often refers to Severus' rescripts in his writings. From 203 to 211 Papinian served as Praetorian Prefect, with Paul and Ulpian probably acting as his clerks (*adsessores*) during part of this period. Papinian was executed in 211 or 212, allegedly because he objected to Caracalla's murder of his brother and co-ruler Geta.

Papinian's works (especially his 37 books of *Questions* and 19 books of *Responses*) preserve casuistry in its highest form. Despite their difficult style and their frequent extreme brevity of expression, Papinian is fascinating because of the richness of his thought and the sureness of his handling. The compilers of the

Digest regarded him highly and made numerous excerpts from his writings (only Ulpian and Paul are used more frequently); and still today he is rightly regarded as one of the greatest Roman jurists.

PAPIRIUS JUSTUS may have held an equestrian post in the imperial bureaucracy; he collected the constitutions of Marcus Aurelius and Lucius Verus (joint reign: 161–169 CE), and those of Marcus from his sole reign (169–176). He is the only jurist known to have edited imperial constitutions in their original text, without commentary.

PAUL. The late classical jurist Julius Paulus was a student of Cervidius Scaevola. Like Ulpian, he began his bureaucratic career as a clerk (*adsessor*) to the Praetorian Prefect Papinian. Along with Ulpian, he then served on the Council of Septimius Severus (reign: 193–211 CE); and under Alexander Severus (222–235) he may have become Praetorian Prefect, the highest imperial office. Paul is considered more original than his slightly younger contemporary Ulpian, who seems to have inclined more strongly toward consolidating legal conceptions through dogma, thereby obscuring their original elasticity.

Despite his undoubtedly difficult and time-consuming official duties, Paul was astonishingly productive (notes on Neratius, Julian, Marcellus, and Scaevola; 16 books on Sabinus; 26 books on *Questions*; 23 books on *Responses*; dozens of monographs on specialized topics). Paul's commentary on the Praetor's Edict is a monumental work in 80 books, in which classical case law is critically assembled, examined, and presented from a relatively systematic viewpoint. The compilers of the *Digest* made numerous excerpts from his writings, amounting to about one-sixth of the entire *Digest*; but in the process they usually struck out Paul's extensive citation of earlier jurists and his reports of controversies.

The *Sentences* (*Pauli Sententiae*), attributed to Paul, are a collection of edited excerpts from the writings of Classical jurists; the collection was assembled in the late third century CE. Until fairly recently the *Sentences* were considered a genuine and important work of Paul; as such, they had a major influence on medieval law. Today the *Sentences* are valued mainly because they preserve much Roman law in an evolved postclassical, but pre-Justinianic form.

PEDIUS. Sextus Pedius is known only through citations by Paul and Ulpian. He wrote a wide-ranging commentary on the Praetor's Edict and was probably a contemporary of Julian.

PLAUTIUS , an adherent of the Proculian "school," wrote during the Flavian period (69–96 CE). The writings of Plautius were regarded as highly as Sabinus' Civil Law; they were annotated by Neratius and Javolenus; Pomponius (7 books) and especially Paul (18 books) wrote commentaries on his work.

POMPONIUS. Sextus Pomponius, a contemporary of Gaius, like him represents an academic tendency in Roman jurisprudence. Nonetheless, he had great influence as the author of wide-ranging commentaries (39 books on Quintus Mucius; an exhaustive commentary on Sabinus in 35 books; his commentary on the Praetor's Edict may have reached the impressive length of 150 books). Pomponius is frequently cited, especially by Ulpian, and there are numerous excerpts from him in the *Digest* (861 fragments or citations).

PROCULUS. The early classical jurist Proculus wrote in the first half of the first century CE. Probably in 33 he took over direction of the "school" that was later named for him.

The *Digest* contains 33 fragments from his main work, the *Letters*. This work discusses legal problems in the question-and-answer format of responses; but the actual case is less prominent than its theoretical extensions. Proculus' numerous distinctions give the work a didactic schematism.

QUINTUS MUCIUS. Quintus Mucius Scaevola (the Pontifex), Consul in 95 BCE, is considered the most important preclassical jurist. He came from an aristocratic family that boasted many jurists, and his father Publius Mucius Scaevola was one of the founders of Roman legal science. According to Pomponius, Quintus Mucius was the first jurist to present the *ius civile* in systematic classifications. His 18 books on the *ius civile* were still commented on by Pomponius in the second century CE.

SABINUS. Masurius Sabinus was an early classical jurist to whom the Emperor Tiberius (reign: 14–37 CE) gave the *ius respondendi*; Sabinus was the first member of the equestrian order to have that right. The Sabinian "school" of jurists was founded by him. His most significant work, three books on the *ius civile*, was widely used throughout the classical period; Pomponius, Paul, and Ulpian wrote enormous commentaries on it.

SCAEVOLA. Quintus Cervidius Scaevola was Paul's teacher and an advisor of Marcus Aurelius (reign: 161–180 CE). His casuistic writings (6 books of *Responses*, 20 of *Questions*, 40 of *Digests*) contain brief, precise descriptions of cases, often without justifications. His writings are well represented by 344 excerpts or citations in the Digest.

SERVIUS. Servius Sulpicius Rufus, Consul in 51 BCE, was one of the most prominent and versatile jurists of the later Republic. He taught a large number of students; Cicero also praised his eloquence as an advocate. Servius wrote, among other things, the first commentary on the Praetor's Edict. After his death a comprehensive collection of his responses was published by his students Aufidius and Alfenus.

TREBATIUS. Gaius Trebatius Testa, a friend and protégé of Cicero, also served as a legal advisor to Julius Caesar and Augustus. His opinions are known mainly through his student Labeo.

TRYPHONINUS. Claudius Tryphoninus was a member, along with Papinian, of the Council of Septimius Severus (reign: 193–211). He wrote a lengthy (21 books) casuistic work, *Disputationes*, and is credited with a collection of *Annotations* (*Notae*) to the work of Cervidius Scaevola.

TUBERO. Q. Aelius Tubero, from an old senatorial family, was a student of Q. Ofilius and evidently the first in his family to reach the consulate in 11 BCE.

ULPIAN. The late classical jurist Domitius Ulpianus was a student of Papinian; like Paul, Ulpian served as clerk (*adsessor*) when Papinian was Praetorian Prefect. Ulpian later became a member of the Imperial Council; under Alexander Severus (reign: 222–235 CE) he finally reached the office of Praetorian Prefect. In 223 he was murdered during a riot of the Praetorian Guard.

Ulpian's 83-book commentary on the Praetor's Edict had virtually the same breadth as Paul's; it contained extensive discussion of the views of earlier jurists. Ulpian's commentary on the *ius civile* (51 books on Sabinus), a second edition, breaks off at the discussion of vindication; we do not know whether it was left incomplete at his death or a part has been lost. He also wrote numerous monographs and collections of legal opinions.

The compilers of the *Digest* drew more extensively on Ulpian's writings than on those of any other classical jurist; more than 40 percent of the *Digest* comes from his work. Although Ulpian is often considered less brilliant than his slightly older contemporary Paul, the compilers were evidently attracted by the comprehensive character of Ulpian's writing, as well as by his open-minded willingness to entertain divergent views of earlier jurists.

The *Tituli ex Corpore Ulpiani* ("Excerpts from Ulpian's Writings"), falsely attributed to Ulpian, actually derive from a Classical introductory work dating to ca. 180 CE.

VENULEIUS. Venuleius Saturninus wrote extensive monographs on private and public law during the reigns of Antoninus Pius (138–161 CE) and Marcus Aurelius (161–180).

Suggested Further Reading

(This short bibliography concentrates mainly on scholarship in English. An asterisk indicates works that are especially recommended.)

Primary Sources in English Translation

Bruce W. Frier, general ed., *The Codex of Justinian* (3 vols., 2016).J. B. Moyle, *The Institutes of Justinian* (5th ed., 1913), with J. B. Moyle, *Imperatoris Iustiniani Institutionum Libri Quattuor* (5th ed., 1912).

Alan Watson, general ed., *The Digest of Justinian* (4 vols., 1985), with corrected translation (revised ed. 2009).

Francis de Zulueta, *The Institutes of Gaius* (2 vols., 1946).

General Roman Law

Ulrike Babusiaux, Christian Baldus, Wolfgang Ernst, Franz-Stefan Meissel, Johannes Platschek und Thomas Rüfner, eds., *Handbuch des Römischen Privatrechts* (forthcoming).

*Adolf Berger, *Encyclopedic Dictionary of Roman Law* (1953).

W. W. Buckland, *The Roman Law of Slavery* (1908).

W. W. Buckland, *Equity in Roman Law* (1911).

*W. W. Buckland, *A Text-Book of Roman Law from Augustus to Justinian* (3rd ed. by Peter Stein, 1966).

W. W. Buckland and Arnold D. McNair, *Roman Law and Common Law: A Comparison in Outline* (2nd ed., 2008).

*Paul J. Du Plessis, *Borkowski's Textbook on Roman Law* (6th ed., 2020).

Paul J. Du Plessis, Clifford Ando, and Kaius Tuori, eds., *The Oxford Handbook of Roman Law and Society* (2016).

Bruce W. Frier and Thomas A. J. McGinn, *A Casebook on Roman Family Law* (2004).

Bruce W. Frier and Dennis P. Kehoe, "Law and Economic Institutions," in *The Cambridge Economic History of the Greco-Roman World* (ed. R. Saller, I. Morris, and W. Scheidel; 2007), 113–143.

Heinrich Honsell, *Römisches Recht* (8th ed., 2015).

*David Johnston, *Roman Law in Context* (1999).

*David Johnston, ed., *The Cambridge Companion to Roman Law* (2015).

*H. F. Jolowicz and Barry Nicholas, *Historical Introduction to the Study of Roman Law* (3rd ed., 1972).

*Max Kaser, *Das Römische Privatrecht* (2 vols., 2nd ed., 1971, 1975).

*Max Kaser, *Roman Private Law* (trans. Rolf Dannenbring; 3rd ed., 1980).

*Max Kaser and Karl Hackl, *Das Römische Zivilprozessrecht* (2nd ed., 1996).

*Wolfgang Kunkel, *An Introduction to Roman Legal and Constitutional History* (2nd ed., 1973; transl. J. M. Kelly from *Römische Rechtsgeschichte*, 6th ed., 1972).

Otto Lenel, *Das Edictum Perpetuum* (3rd ed., 1927).

Ernest Metzger, ed., *A Companion to Justinian's Institutes* (1998).

George Mousourakis, *The Historical and Institutional Context of Roman Law* (2015).

Barry Nicholas, *An Introduction to Roman Law* (revised ed. by Ernest Metzger, 2008).

A. Arthur Schiller, *Roman Law: Mechanisms of Development* (1978).

Fritz Schulz, *Principles of Roman Law* (transl. Marguerite Wolff; 1936).

Fritz Schulz, *Classical Roman Law* (1951).

Law and the Roman Economy

*Jean Andreau, *The Economy of the Roman World* (2016).

Alan Bowman and Andrew Wilson, eds., *Quantifying the Roman Economy: Methods and Problems* (2009).

*Giuseppe Dari-Mattiacci and Dennis P. Kehoe, eds., *Roman Law and Economics* (2 vols., 2020).

Peter Garnsey and Richard P. Saller, *The Roman Empire: Economy, Society and Culture* (2nd ed., 2014).

Dennis P. Kehoe, *Law and the Rural Economy in the Roman Empire* (2007).

Walter Scheidel, ed., *The Cambridge Companion to the Roman Economy* (2012).

Walter Scheidel, Richard P. Saller, and Ian Morris, eds., *The Cambridge Economic History of the Greco-Roman World* (2007).

Andrew Wilson and Alan Bowman, eds., *Trade, Commerce and the State in the Roman World* (2018).

Obligations (esp. Contracts)

Vincenzo Arangio-Ruiz, *Responsabilità Contrattuale in Diritto Romano* (1958).

Emilio Betti, *La Struttura dell'Obbligazione Romana e il Problema della Sua Genesi* (1955).

*Peter Birks, *The Roman Law of Obligations* (2014).

Cosimo Cascione, Consensus: *Problemi di Origine, Tutela Processuale, Prospettive Sistematiche* (2003).

György Diósdi, *Contract in Roman Law: From the Twelve Tables to the Glossators* (transl. J. Szabó, 1981).

Herbert Hausmaninger and Richard Gamauf, *Casebook zum Römischen Vertragsrecht* (7th ed., 2012).

*Heinrich Honsell, *Quod Interest im Bonae-Fidei-Iudicium: Studien zum Römischen Schadenersatzrecht* (1969).

Philip L. Landolt, *"Naturalis Obligatio" and Bare Social Duty* (2000).

Ernest G. Lorenzen, "*Causa* and Consideration in the Law of Contracts," *Yale Law Journal* 28 (1919): 621–646.

Thomas A. J. McGinn, ed., *Obligations in Roman Law: Past, Present, and Future* (2013).

Peter Stein, *Fault in the Formation of Contract in Roman Law and Scots Law* (1958).

Alan Watson, *The Law of Obligations in the Later Roman Republic* (1965).

Sven Erik Wunner, *Contractus: Sein Wortgebrauch und Willensgehalt im Klassischen Römischen Recht* (1964).

*Reinhard Zimmermann, *The Law of Obligations: Roman Foundations of the Civilian Tradition* (1996).

Stipulation

Malte Dobbertin, *Zur Auslegung der Stipulation im Klassischen Römischen Recht* (1987).

Rolf Knütel, "Zur Auslegung und Entwicklung der Stipulation im Klassischen Römischen Recht," in Martin Avenarius et al., eds., *Ars Iuris: Festschrift für Okko Behrends zum 70 Geburtstag* (2009), 223–257.

Barry Nicholas, "The Form of the Stipulation in Roman Law," *Law Quarterly Review* 69 (1953): 233–252.

Salvatore Riccobono, *Stipulation and the Theory of Contract* (transl. J. Kerr Wylie; revised and edited by B. Beinart, 1957).

The "Real" Contracts

Barbara Berndt, *Das "Commodatum": Ein Rechtsinstitut im Wandel der Anschauungen* (2005).

Byoung-Ho Jung, *Darlehensvalutierung im Römischen Recht* (2002).

Dieter Nörr, "Die Entwicklung des Utilitätsgedankens im Römischen Haftungsrecht," *Zeitschrift der Savigny-Stiftung*, Rom. Abt. 73 (1956): 68–119.

Tom Walter, *Die Funktionen der Actio Depositi* (2012).

Sale (Emptio Venditio)

Barbara Abatino, *Alle Radici delle Obbligazioni Generiche: Le "Emptiones Venditiones" di "Res Quae Pondere Numero Mensura Constant"* (2012).

Vincenzo Arangio-Ruiz, *La Compravendita in Diritto Romano* (2 vols., 1987, 1990).

Martin Bauer, *Periculum Emptoris: Eine Dogmengeschichtliche Untersuchung zur Gefahrtragung beim Kauf* (1998).

David Daube, ed., *Studies in the Roman Law of Sale: Dedicated to the Memory of Francis De Zulueta* (1959).

Wolfgang Ernst, *Rechtsmängelhaftung* (1995).

Luigi Garofalo, *La Compravendita e l'Interdipendenza delle Obbligazioni nel Diritto Romano* (2 vols., 2007).

Eva Jakab and Wolfgang Ernst, eds., *Kaufen nach Römischem Recht: Antikes Erbe in den europäischen Kaufrechtsordnungen* (2008).

Martin Pennitz, *Das Periculum Rei Venditae: Ein Beitrag zum 'Aktionenrechtlichen Denken' im Römischen Privatrecht* (2000).

*Francis De Zulueta, *The Roman Law of Sale: Introduction and Selected Texts* (1949).

Lease/Hire (*Locatio Conductio*)

Luigi Capogrossi Colognesi, *Remissio Mercedis: Una Storia tra Logiche di Sistema e Autorità della Norma* (2005).

P.W. De Neeve, *Colonus: Private Farm-Tenancy in Roman Italy during the Republic and Early Principate* (1984).

Paul J. Du Plessis, *A History of Remissio Mercedis and Related Legal Institutions* (2003).

Paul J. Du Plessis, *Letting and Hiring in Roman Legal Thought: 27 BCE–284 CE* (2012).

Bruce W. Frier, *Landlords and Tenants in Imperial Rome* (1980).

Susan Dunbar Martin, *Building Contracts in Classical Roman Law* (1981).

Carsten H. Müller, *Gefahrtragung bei der Locatio Conductio: Miete, Pacht, Dienst- und Werkvertrag im Kommentar Römischer Juristen* (2002).

Mandate

Dennis P. Kehoe, "Mandate and the Management of Business in the Roman Empire," in Dari-Mattiacci and Kehoe, eds., *Roman Law and Economics*, vol. I (2020), 307–338.

Salvo Randazzo, *Mandare: Radici della Doverosità e Percorsi Consensualistici nell'Evoluzione del Mandato Romano* (2005).

Tobias Rundel. *Mandatum Zwischen Utilitas und Amicitia: Perspektiven zur Mandatarhaftung im Klassischen Römischen Recht* (2005).

Alan Watson, *Contract of Mandate in Roman Law* (1961).

Partnership (*Societas*)

Jean Andreau, *La Vie Financière dans le Monde Romain. Les Metiers de Manieurs d'Argent (IVe siècle av. J.-C.–IIIe siècle ap. J.-C.)* (1987).

Vincenzo Arangio-Ruiz, *La Società in Diritto Romano* (6th ed., 1982).

David Daube, "*Societas* as Consensual Contract," *Cambridge Law Journal* 6 (1938): 381–493.

Geneviève Dufour, *Les Societates Publicanorum de la République Romaine: Ancêtres des Sociétés par Actions?* (2012).

Andreas M. Fleckner, *Antike Kapitalvereinigungen: Ein Beitrag zu den Konzeptionellen und Historischen Grundlagen der Aktiengesellschaft* (2010).

Andreas M. Fleckner, "Roman Business Associations," in Dari-Mattiacci and Kehoe, eds., *Roman Law and Economics*, vol. I (2020), 233–272.

Max Kaser, "Neue Literatur zur 'Societas,'" *Studia et Documenta Historiae et Iuris* 41 (1975): 278–338.

Franz-Stefan Meissel, *Societas: Struktur und Typenvielfalt des römischen Gesellschaftsvertrages* (2004).

Half-Executed Exchange Agreements

Michael Artner, *Agere Praescriptis Verbis: Atypische Geschäftsinhalte und Klassisches Formularverfahren* (2002).

Hans-Peter Benöhr, *Das Sogenannte Synallagma in den Konsensualkontrakten des Klassischen Römischen Rechts* (1965).

Luigi Pellecchi, *La Praescriptio: Processo, Diritto Sostanziale, Modelli Espositivi* (2003).

Third Parties

Barbara Abatino and Giuseppe Dari-Mattiacci, "Agency Problems and Organizational Costs in Slave-Run Businesses," in Dari-Mattiacci and Kehoe, eds., *Roman Law and Economics*, vol. I (2020), 273–306.

Barbara Abatino, Giuseppe Dari-Mattiacci, and Enrico C. Perotti, "Depersonalization of Business in Ancient Rome," *Oxford Journal of Legal Studies* 31 (2011): 365–389.

Piero Angelini, *Il Procurator* (1961).

Jean-Jacques Aubert, *Business Managers in Ancient Rome: A Social and Economic Study of Institores, 200 B.C.–A.D. 250* (1994).

Axel Claus, *Gewillkürte Stellvertretung im Römischen Privatrecht* (1973).

Wolfgang Endemann, *Der Begriff der Delegatio im Klassischen römischen Recht* (1959).

Andreas Fleckner, "The Peculium: A Legal Device for Donations to *Personae Alieno Iuri Subiectae*," in *Filippo Carlà and Maja Gori, Gift Giving and the "Embedded" Economy in the Ancient World* (2014), 213–239.

Dennis P. Kehoe, "Agency, Roman Law, and Roman Social Values," in Dennis P. Kehoe and Thomas A.J. McGinn, eds., *Ancient Law, Ancient Society* (2017), 105–132.

Aaron Kirschenbaum, *Sons, Slaves, and Freedmen in Roman Commerce* (2005).

Luuk De Ligt, "Legal History and Economic History: The Case of the Actiones Adiecticiae Qualitatis," *Tijdschrift voor Rechtsgeschiedenis* 67 (1999): 206–226.

Andrea Di Porto, *Impresa Collettiva e Schiavo "Manager" in Roma Antica (II sec. a.C.–II sec. d.C.)* (1984).

Lucia Zandrino, *La Delegatio nel Diritto Romano. Profili Semantici ed Elementi di Fattispecie* (2010).

Lucia Zandrino, *La Delegatio nel Diritto Romano. Effetti Giuridici e Profili di Invalidità* (2014).

Quasi-Contract

John P. Dawson, *Unjust Enrichment: A Comparative Analysis* (1951).

Susanne Hähnchen, *Die Causa Condictionis: Ein Beitrag zum Klassischen Römischen Kondiktionenrecht* (2003).

Jan Dirk Harke, *Geschäftsführung und Bereicherung* (2007).

Jeroen Kortmann, *Altruism in Private Law: Liability for Nonfeasance and Negotiorum Gestio* (2005).

Max Radin, "The Roman Law of Quasi-Contract," *Virginia Law Review* 23 (1937): 241–258.

Elto J. H. Schrage, *Unjust Enrichment: The Comparative Legal History of the Law of Restitution* (1999).

Index of Passages Cited

Reference is to the Cases in which each passage is cited. Numbers in bold are the Cases or to the Casebook's Introduction. The texts of most Roman legal sources can be found online at *The Roman Law Library*, https://droitromain.univ-grenoble-alpes.fr/.

I. Pre-Justinianic Legal Sources

Collatio Mosaicarum et Romanarum Legum
- 4.8   193
- 9.2.2   168
- 10.2.4   62
- 10.2.1   64
- 10.2.3   179
- 10.2.5   67; 69, 74
- 10.2.6   66
- 10.2.7   62
- 10.7.3   62
- 10.7.9   68
- 12.7.9, 11   153, 155

Duodecim Tabulae
- IV.4.2a   103
- VII.11   121
- VI.3   127, 134

Fragmenta Vaticana
- 2   119
- 4   106
- 9   73
- 11   120
- 12   119, 129
- 16   87, 112
- 44   156
- 266   36
- 317   179, 212

Fragmentum Vindobonense
- 1.2   157

Codex Theodosianus
- 2.31.1   195

Gaius, *Institutiones*
- 1.119   127
- 1.173   5
- 1.190–191   5
- 1.196   1

- 2.28–37   211
- 2.38–39   211; 39, 234
- 2.60   76
- 2.64   204
- 2.74–75   158
- 2.77–79   85
- 2.80   5
- 2.84   2
- 2.95   204
- 2.252   213
- 3.88 Intro.
- 3.91   225; 29, 227
- 3.92–93   6
- 3.96   50
- 3.97–97a, 99   24
- 3.98   18
- 3.100   19
- 3.102   7
- 3.103–103a   10; 48, 177
- 3.104   194
- 3.105–106   6
- 3.106–109   1; 225
- 3.110–111   40
- 3, 113, 126   42
- 3.115–126   41
- 3.117   39
- 3.121–122   44; 215
- 3.124–125   44
- 3.127   45
- 3.128–130, 134   51; Intro.
- 3.135–137, 139   78; 229
- 3.140   81
- 3.142, 145   147
- 3.141   79
- 3.145–147   185; 85, 163
- 3.148–150   169; 170, 175
- 3.151–154   175
- 3.154a–b   169
- 3.155–156, 162   177; 183, 184, 212

Gaius, *Institutiones (cont.)*
  3.159–160 178
  3.161 **180**
  3.163–167 Intro.
  3.168 209
  3.168–181 Intro.
  3.169–172 39
  3.176–177 **39**; 12, 50, 72, 211
  3.179 36
  3.204–206 64, 76, 164
  4.47 **62**; 67, 71, 169, 180
  4.49–50 Intro.
  4.53–53b 59
  4.53–60 Intro.
  4.56 59
  4.70 **194**
  4.71 **199**
  4.72, 74a 198
  4.72a–73 197
  4.84 **212**; 179
  4.86–87 212
  4.115–116b 36
  4.119 35
  4.126 36
  4.126a 78
  4.131a 127
  4.136–137 **34**; Intro, 23
  4.153 **63**; 147
  4.182 62

Gaius, *Institutionum Epitome*
  2.9.3–4 50

Pauli Sententiae
  1.3.1–2 203
  1.4.1 223
  1.4.6 194
  2.3 6
  2.4.2 64
  2.5.2 72
  2.8.1–2 **199**
  2.13.4 72
  2.14.1 102
  2.15.1 178
  2.15.2 181

  2.15.3 180
  2.15.16 42
  2.16 171
  2.17.1–3 **137**; 134
  2.17.3 127
  2.17.4 138
  2.18.2 157
  2.18.4 150, 158
  2.31.24 **53**
  2.31.29 164
  3.4a.5 1
  3.8.4 30
  4.9.1–9 5
  5.2.2 204
  5.7.2 9
  5.7.4 28

Tituli ex Corpore Ulpiani
  5.6–7 232
  11.25 4
  11.28 28

II. The *Corpus Iuris Civilis* of Justinian

Institutiones
  1.21 pr. 1, 2
  2.1.41 121
  2.1.43 204
  2.9.5 204
  2.14.10 18
  2.20.16 27
  3.6 232
  3.13 pr. Intro.
  3.14.2 **54**; 68
  3.14.4 71
  3.15.1 6
  3.16 40
  3.19.3–4, 21 10
  3.20 pr.-3 41
  3.23.1 81
  3.23.3 111
  3.24 pr.-5 147
  3.25.2 169
  3.25.4 175
  3.25.9 171

3.26 pr.-6   177
3.26.2   211
3.26.8   180
3.26.13   184
3.27 pr.   **216**; 71
3.27.2–5   216
3.29 pr.   209
4.6.7   75; 15
4.6.10   **196**; 101
4.6.33   59
4.7.1   194
4.7.4   197
4.10 pr.   212

Codex
1.18.10   226
2.2.10   179
2.3.10   187
2.3.13   102
2.12.10   212
2.12.15   207
2.12.16   204
2.18.4   208
2.18.10   218
2.18.11   **222**; 220
2.18.12–13, 15   222
2.18.14   208
2.18.24   **219**
2.19.3–5   92
2.55.1   48
3.25.9   171
4.2.8   56
4.2.11   54
4.5.8, 10–11   225
4.10.1   213
4.18   185, 210
4.18.2 pr.   185
4.26.7 pr.-1, 3   **235**
4.26.10.1   198
4.28.1, 3   61
4.30.3   **38**
4.30.4   38
4.30.7   38
4.32.3,   11, 23 58

4.34.1   174
4.35.1   184, 208
4.35.4, 11, 23   203
4.37.5   175
4.44.2, 8   83
4.48.4   **125**; 117
4.54.3–4   106
4.55.1–2   109
4.56.1   109
4.64.1   192
4.64.8   188
4.65.3   **147**; 49, 156, 157, 185
4.65.5   152
4.65.9   156
4.65.16   160
4.65.17   147
6.23.28.1–3   6
6.50.9   226
7.30.1   147
7.47.1   123
8.15.1   235
8.16.4   214
8.26.1.2–3   72
8.27.4   73
8.27.20   73
8.32.1   38
8.33.1–2   73
8.37.1   **9**
8.37.10   6
8.37.11   19
8.38.3 pr.   10
8.40.1   42
8.40.2   46
8.40.5   42
8.40.11   215
8.41.3   **214**
8.42.17   209
8.53.9   188
8.53.22.1   188

Digesta
Const. Tanta 10 Intro.
1.15.3.3–4, 4   147
1.22.4, 6   207

Digesta (cont.)

2.11.10.1   21, 31
2.13.9 pr.   171
2.14.1.3 Intro., 8
2.14.4 pr.   152
2.14.4.3   11
2.14.7 pr.-2, 4, 5   **187**; 192
2.14.7.5   **102**; 58, 69, 96, 138, 187
2.14.7.6   **104**; 166. 187
2.14.7.12   9
2.14.16 pr.   **213**; 179
2.14.17 pr.   58
2.14.21.5, 22   43
2.14.47.1   **210**
2.14.51.1   **210**
2.14.57 pr.   60
2.14.58   104
2.15.5   12
3.1.1.6   168
3.2.1   62
3.3.1 pr.-1   **203**
3.3.55   **213**; 179
3.3.58   203
3.3.63   204
3.3.67   **205**; 204
3.5.1–2   **217**; 219, 223
3.5.3 pr.   224
3.5.3.4   3
3.5.3.5   217
3.5.3.9–10   223
3.5.3.11   208
3.5.5 pr.-1   **220**
3.5.5.3   203, 205
3.5.5.5   **221**
3.5.5.6   208
3.5.5.7   220
3.5.9.1   **218**
3.5.10   **223**
3.5.12   **224**
3.5.14   217
3.5.18.2   220
3.5.20 pr.   221
3.5.20.3   223
3.5.26 pr.   218

3.5.30 pr.   **208**
3.5.30.2   223
3.5.33   222
3.5.35   220
3.5.38   209
3.5.40   217
3.5.42 pr.   209
3.5.43   222
3.5.44.2   **220**
3.5.48   220
4.2.1, 6   92
4.2.14.11   125
4.3.7.3   27, 114, 127
4.3.9 pr.   **92**; 82
4.3.9.3   62
4.3.9.1   177
4.4.1   4
4.4.39.1   4
4.8   185
4.8.11.4   185
4.9   185
4.9.5.1   65
5.1.57   **193**
6.1.15.3   125
6.1.38   227
6.1.41.1   198
6.1.59   158
6.30.18 pr.   1
7.8.12.6   155
8.3.30   **99**
8.6.20   168
9.2.7.8   163, 168, 184
9.2.11.9   65
9.2.22.1   170
9.2.27.11   153, 155
9.2.27.34   **162**
9.3.7   168, 184
10.3.1   170, 173
10.3.3 pr.   170
10.4.12.4   167
11.6.1 pr.   **184**; 167, 168
11.6.2.1   167
11.6.7.3–4   167
12.1.1.1   54

12.1.2 pr.-2   54; 68
12.1.2.3, 3   54
12.1.4 pr.   56, 68
12.1.4.1   160
12.1.5   116
12.1.7–8   60
12.1.9.4   57
12.1.9.8   55
12.1.9.9, 10   68; 55, 56
12.1.11 pr.   56
12.1.11.1   58; 55, 61
12.1.13 pr.-1   54
12.1.15   55
12.1.18   230; 54
12.1.19.1   54
12.1.22   60
12.1.27   235
12.1.32   88, 228, 230
12.1.40   57
12.4.3.7   228
12.4.10   228
12.4.16   231
12.5.1 pr.   232
12.5.2.2–4   232
12.5.7–8   232
12.6.1.1   226
12.6.6.2   203
12.6.10   29; 36
12.6.15.1   225
12.6.16 pr., 17   29; 36
12.6.19.2–3   225
12.6.22 pr.-1   225
12.6.23.2   225
12.6.26 pr.   58
12.6.26.3   36
12.6.26.4–6   225
12.6.26.12   234
12.6.26.13   225
12.6.33   227
12.6.40 pr.   44
12.6.47   41
12.6.53   198
12.6.65.1   230
12.6.65.4   228

12.6.65.5–8   233; 27, 211
12.6.66   228
12.7.1   228
12.7.2   229; 164
12.7.3   228
12.7.5   232; 19
13.3.4   60
13.5   19, 185, 210
13.5.24   39
13.6.1.1   62
13.6.3 pr.   3
13.6.5.2–3   64; 67, 157, 171, 179, 189
13.6.5.5–8, 10   64
13.6.5.12   62
13.6.5.14   66
13.6.5.15   170
13.6.12.1   64
13.6.13.1   66
13.6.18 pr.   64, 174
13.6.18.2–4   67
13.6.19   65
13.7.3   74
13.7.4   73
13.7.8 pr.   74
13.7.9.3, 5, & 10   72; 121
13.7.10   72
13.7.11.1–2   72, 89
13.7.11.5   72
13.7.11.7   203
13.7.13.1   71
13.7.16.1   74
13.7.20.2   72
13.7.24 pr.   209
13.7.25   74
13.7.31   67, 74
13.7.36 pr.   74
14.1.1 pr.   200
14.1.1.5, 17   200
14.1.1.9   201
14.1.7 pr.   201
14.2.2 pr., 10.2   163
14.2.10 pr.   166
14.3.1–2   202; 200, 206
14.3.5.1–9   199

Digesta (cont.)

14.3.5.10 203
14.3.5.11–15 **201**; 229
14.3.7.1 200
14.3.11.2–5 201
14.3.13 pr. 201
14.2.17.1 201
14.3.19 pr. **205**
14.4 198
14.5.2.1 53
14.6.1 pr. **61**
14.6.3 pr., 3 61
14.6.7 pr.–1, 3 61
14.6.7.15 61
14.6.9.2 61
14.6.9.3–4, 11 61
14.6.14 61
15.1.7.1, 4–7 198
15.1.8 198
15.1.5.4 196
15.1.9.2–4 197
15.1.9.4 198
15.1.21 pr. 198
15.1.27 pr. 196
15.1.29.1 198
15.1.44 196
15.1.46 198
15.1.47 pr. **198**; 194
15.2.1 pr. 198
15.3 197
15.3.3.2,4 197
15.3.7.3 197
15.3.10.8 210
15.3.16 197
15.3.19 198
15.4.1.1–2, 6 **195**
15.4.1.5 195
15.4.2.1 194
16.1.1 44
16.3.1.5 66
16.1.6–7 208
16.1.8.2–3 211
16.3.1.8 64
16.3.14.1 125

16.3.1.23–25 66
16.3.1.34 68
16.3.1.35 64
16.3.5.1–2 62
16.3.6 62
16.3.7.2–3 69
16.3.16 63
16.3.17.1 62
16.3.23 **67**
16.3.24 **69**; 62, 64, 102, 166
16.3.25.1 69
16.3.28 102
16.3.31 pr.-2 Intro., 64
16.3.32 177
17.1.1 pr. 177, 184
17.1.1.4 177, 203
17.1.2.1–2, 4, 6 177
17.1.3.1 177, 203
17.1.3.2 180
17.1.4 180
17.1.5 pr.-1, 3, 5 180
17.1.6 pr. 184
17.1.6.1–2 **178**; 45, 181, 210
17.1.6.2 **45**; 41
17.1.6.4–5 177
17.1.6.7 184, 207
17.1.7 **207**; 184
17.1.8.6 177
17.1.8.9–10 pr. **179**; 203
17.1.10.4 55
17.1.10.5 205
17.1.10.9 **207**; 184
17.1.12.9 **181**; 207
17.1.16 177
17.1.22.11 178
17.1.12.12 203
17.1.12.16 178
17.1.12.17 203
17.1.20 pr. 177
17.1.22.2 211
17.1.22.7 203
17.1.22.10 221
17.1.22.11 177, 178, 179
17.1.23–26 pr. 178

17.1.26.6–7 **182**
17.1.26.8   177, 183, 184
17.1.27.2   178
17.1.27.4   181
17.1.29 pr.   179
17.1.29.1   181
17.1.29.3   229
17.1.33   180
17.1.34 pr.   55
17.1.35   177, 203
17.1.36.1   184
17.1.40   219
17.1.41   180
17.1.45 pr.-5   181
17.1.45.7   211
17.1.48.1–2   177
17.1.50 pr.   **218**
17.1.53   178
17.1.56.4, 6   178, 203
17.1.60.1   223
17.1.60.4   203
17.2.1 pr.   175
17.2.3.1–2   169
17.2.4.1   175
17.2.7–8   169
17.2.5.1, 6, 9, 10–13   169
17.2.14   170, 175
17.2.14–16 pr.   176
17.2.17 pr.   170
17.2.19, 21   172
17.2.23.1   **172**
17.2.25–26   172
17.2.27   173; 170
17.2.29 pr.-2   169
17.2.30   169
17.2.31–34   170
17.2.35   175
17.2.38.1   170
17.2.44   186
17.2.445, 47 pr.   170
17.2.47.1   171
17.2.52 pr.   176
17.2.52.1–3   **171**
17.2.52.4   174; 170

17.2.52.7, 12–13   170
17.2.15   174
17.2.58 pr.-1   **170**
17.2.58.2   175
17.2.59 pr.   175
17.2.59.1   170, 173
17.2.60.1   169, 174
17.2.63 pr.   171
17.2.63.10   169, 175
17.2.65 pr.   169
17.2.65.2   174
17.2.65.3–5   **176**; 175
17.2.65.6   176
17.2.65.7–8   175
17.2.65.9   170, 175
17.2.65.13–14   173
17.2.65.15   169
17.2.67.2   174
17.2.71 pr.   9, 170
17.2.71.1   169
17.2.72   235
17.2.76–78   165
17.2.80   169
17.2.82   235
18.1.1 pr.   77; 112, 187, 191
18.1.1.1   79; 77, 187, 191
18.1.3   107
18.1.4–6 pr.   94
18.1.7 pr.   108
18.1.7.1–2   **81**
18.1.8   **86**; 95, 110, 122, 129, 131, 133
18.1.9 pr.-1   **88**; 78
18.1.9.2, 11   **89**; 91, 146
18.1.13.14   122
18.1.14   **90**
18.1.15 pr.   95
18.1.15.1   **91**; 89
18.1.15.2   94
18.1.16 pr.   94
18.1.19   **121**
18.1.20   **85**; 87, 110, 111
18.1.21   99
18.1.25.1   **127**; 114, 132, 134, 137
18.1.28   94

Digesta (cont.)

18.1.29 100	18.1.80.2 **96**
18.1.33 99	18.1.80.3 129
18.1.34 pr. **88**	18.2.2 **105**
18.1.34.1 **84**	18.2.4.3, 6 105
18.1.34.2-3 94; 84	18.2.6.1 105
18.1.34.6 110	18.3.2 **106**
18.1.34.7 84	18.3.4 pr., 2 106
18.1.35 pr. 78	18.3.7 106
18.1.35.1 81	18.4.4–5 129
18.1.35.2 83	18.4.7–13 129
18.1.35.4 113; 110	18.4.7–10, 12 86
18.1.35.5–6 **87**; 110, 112	18.4.21 125
18.1.35.7 **112**	18.5.2–3 104
18.1.35.8 139	18.5.7.1 **2**
18.1.36 82	18.6.1 pr. 139
18.1.37 79	18.6.4.1 **108**
18.1.38 **82**;=	18.6.1.3 **118**
18.1.39.1 86, 96	18.6.1.4 118
18.1.40.2 97	18.6.2 pr. 118
18.1.40.1, 3 98	18.6.4 pr. 108
18.1.41 pr. 97	18.6.3 112
18.1.41.1 89	18.6.4.2 **117**
18.1.43 **138**	18.6.5 37
18.1.44 95	18.6.7 pr. 111
18.1.45 145, 146	18.6.8 pr. **110**; 112
18.1.50 22	18.6.9 140
18.1.53 121	18.6.10 110
18.1.56 **109**	18.6.13–14 118, 128
18.1.57 pr. 95	18.6.15.1 128
18.1.58 95	18.6.16 **139**; 108
18.1.61 94	18.6.17 112
18.1.62.1 93	18.6.18 **126**; 37
18.1.65 85	18.6.19.1 119
18.1.66 pr. 129	18.6.20 **119**
18.1.66.1 **141**	18.7.9 109
18.1.66.2 100	19.1.1 pr. **122**; 127
18.1.70 93, 94	19.1.1.1 **131**; 92, 129
18.1.72 pr. **103**	19.1.3.1 128
18.1.74 128	19.1.3.3–4 **124**; 116, 117
18.1.77 **98**	19.1.6.1–2 80
18.1.78 pr. 100	19.1.6.4 **142**; 161
18.1.79 **80**	19.1.6.9 131
18.1.80.1 96	19.1.9 117
	19.1.11.1 119, 138

19.1.11.2   122
19.1.11.5   89, 140, 146
19.1.11.6   **229**; 78
19.1.11.8–9   136
19.1.11.13   **128**
19.1.11.15–18   129, 131
19.1.11.15   134
19.1.11.18   **133**; 131, 136
19.1.12   86, 122
19.1.13 pr.-2   **145**; 140
19.1.13.3–4   **140**; 138
19.1.13.8   78
19.1.13.10–18   122
19.1.13.10–11, 13   **101**
19.1.13.22   **115**
19.1.13.25   **206**
19.1.13.29   2
19.1.13.30   156
19.1.13.12   110
19.1.13.30   215
19.1.13.31, 15   100
19.1.17 pr.   100
19.1.21.1   131
19.1.21.2   **146**; 89
19.1.21.3   **123**; 145
19.1.21.4   80
19.1.21.6   99
19.1.25   38, 96
19.1.27   142
19.1.28   **48**; 31
19.1.29   137
19.1.30.1   **132**; 137
19.1.31 pr.   113
19.1.31.1   111, 122
19.1.38.1   117
19.1.38.2   **100**
19.1.41   92
19.1.43, 45 pr.-1   130
19.1.47   31
19.1.48 pr.   122
19.1.51   126
19.1.54 pr.   **114**; 111, 127
19.1.55   24
19.2.2.1   185

19.2.3   155
19.2.7–8   147, 156
19.2.9 pr.   **154**; 147, 162
19.2.9.3   162
19.2.9.5   163, 164
19.2.11 pr.   153
19.2.11.1   147, 153, 157
19.2.11.2   1
19.2.11.3   153, 157
19.2.11.4–12   163
19.2.13.3   153, 157
19.2.13.5   164
19.2.13.6   163
19.2.13.7   149
19.2.13.11   **160**; 157
19.2.14   160
19.2.15 pr.-1   155
19.2.15.2–3, 5, 7   **159**; 155
19.2.15.8   147
19.2.19.1   **161**; 142, 155
19.2.19.2   155
19.2.19.3   147, 163
19.2.19.4   158
19.2.19.9–10   168
19.2.21 Intro.
19.2.20.1   82, 147
19.2.20.2–22 pr.   185
19.2.22.2   85, 163, 185
19.2.22.3, 23   **83**; 147
19.2.24 pr.   165
19.2.24.2   149, 153, 157
19.2.25.1   **156**; 49, 147
19.2.25.2   **150**; 147, 149, 153, 157
19.2.25.3–5   **157**; 155
19.2.25.6   147
19.2.25.7–8   **164**; 163
19.2.27 pr.   **151**; 159
19.2.27.1   **149**; 147
19.2.28.2   154, 162
19.2.29 pr.-1   151, 157
19.2.28.2   **148**; 185
19.2.30 pr.   147
19.2.30.3   163
19.2.30.4   155

Digesta (cont.)

19.2.31   69, 166
19.2.32   156
19.2.33   113, 156
19.2.35 pr.   147, 156
19.2.36   **166**
19.2.38 pr.-1   **168**; 177, 184
19.2.41   **65**
19.2.45.1   162
19.2.46   82, 147
19.2.51.1   **163**; 166, 167
19.2.52   88
19.2.54 pr.   155
19.2.54.1   **49**; 21, 147, 157
19.2.54.2   155
19.2.55 pr.   155
19.2.55.1   158
19.2.55.2   153
19.2.58.1   **165**
19.2.59   163
19.2.60 pr.   147
19.2.60.2   164
19.2.60.3   163, 166
19.2.60.4   **167**; 229
19.2.60.6   155
19.2.60.7   **162**
19.2.61 pr.   **158** 150, 157
19.2.62   **166**
19.3.1   **186**; 56, 94
19.4.1 pr.   127
19.4.1.1, 3   192
19.4.2   **192**
19.5.1.1   163, 189
19.5.5   187
19.5.5.1-2   **191**; 188
19.5.5.3   187
19.5.6   80, 187
19.5.7   191
19.5.13 pr.   185
19.5.15   53, 187
19.5.16 pr.-1   **188**
19.5.17.1   186

19.5.17.2-3   **189**
19.5.18   62
19.5.19 pr.   186
19.5.20 pr.-1   **107**; 189
19.5.24   **190**; 58
20.1.1.2   72
20.1.2   179
20.1.11.1   72
20.1.16.9   73, 82
20.1.29.1   72
20.2.2   **153**; 112, 157, 162, 172
20.2.4 pr.   **152**
20.2.4.1, 6, 7.1, 9   152
20.3.1.1   198
20.6.3   195, 107
20.6.7.1   201
21.1   144
21.1.1-2   **143**; 47. 135. 145. 183
21.1.1.7   144
21.1.1.8, 4.4   **144**; 135, 183
21.1.14.10   143
21.1.17.20   138, 143
21.1.18-19 pr.   138
21.1.28   143
21.1.31.20   96, 135
21.1.31.22-23   107
21.1.38 pr.   122, 143
21.1.48.8   143
21.1.59 pr.   119
21.2.1   134
21.2.2   136
21.2.3   122
21.2.6   **135**
21.2.8   **130**; 137
21.2.9   137
21.2.11 pr.   113
21.2.18   134
21.2.51.1   131
21.2.16.1   **134**; 103, 137
21.2.31   **47**; 179
21.2.33   134
21.2.37 pr.-1   **136**

21.2.53.1 130
21.2.55 130, 134
21.2.56.2 134
21.2.56.3 130
21.2.60 **129**; 137
21.2.61 134
21.2.68 pr. 131
21.2.74.3 86
21.2.75 138, 141
22.1.17.4 147
22.1.21–24 116
22.1.32 pr.-2 **116**; 30
22.2.8 **22**
22.2.9 **22**
22.3.25 pr. **226**
22.3.25.4 20
23.3.14–15 125
23.3.21–23 **20**
23.3.25 50
24.1.1–3 pr. 82
24.1.3.12–13 209
24.1.5.5 82
24.1.47 223
24.1.57 9
24.3.7.11 152
24.3.9 37
24.3.66.4 8
25.3.5 pr.-4 222
26.7.28.1 116
26.8.1 pr. 3
26.8.5 pr.-1 3
26.8.9.5 2
26.8.13 227
27.2.4 168
29.1.9 1
29.2.45.2 169
30.120.2 156
32.79.3 25
33.2.2 162
33.4.1.15 157
34.2.33 14
34.2.34 pr. 185

34.5.26 12
35.2.30 pr. 174
38.1.2 50, 234
38.1.6 234
38.1.7.2 50
38.1.9.1 234
38.1.16.1 234
38.1.37 pr. 50, 168
39.2.13.6 149
39.2.28 149
39.2.33–34 149, 152
39.2.37 149, 150
39.4.10.1 147
39.5.1 pr. 60
39.5.19.1 168
39.5.27 168
39.6.39 27
41.1.7.10 227
41.1.9.4 204
41.1.9.6 128
41.1.13 **204**
41.1.20 pr. 127
41.1.20.2 204
41.1.31 pr. 127
41.1.36 230
41.1.48 pr. 188
41.1.53 204
41.2.3.1 128
41.2.25.1 147
41.2.42.1 **204**
41.2.49.1 193
41.3.4.7 198
41.3.41 204
4.2.16 171
43.16.1.22 147
43.16.12, 18 pr. 156
43.24.3 pr., 5.11 168
43.26 69
43.26.1 70; 185
43.26.6.2 147
43.26.20 185
43.32.1 pr.-2 152

Digesta (cont.)

43.32.1.4–5   152, 153
43.32.1.5–2   152
43.33.1 pr.   155
44.1.7 pr.   43
44.1.19   43
44.4.2.3   35; 29, 26, 33, 54
44.4.2.6   60
44.7.1.4   166
44.7.1.5   64
44.7.3 pr. Intro.
44.7.3.1   54, 230
44.7.3.2   6
44.7.5 pr., 3   216
44.7.23   22
44.7.39   193
44.7.44.6   48
44.7.46   3
44.7.52 pr., 3   57
45.1.1 pr.-2   6; 21
45.1.1.3–5   7
45.1.1.6   6
45.1.5 pr.   136
45.1.8   21
45.1.12   7
45.1.22   17; 89
45.1.29 pr.   7
45.1.32   8
45.1.33   26
45.1.35.2   38
45.1.37   26
43.1.38 pr.-5   133
45.1.38.17   10
45.1.38.18   12
45.1.38.20, 22–23   10
45.1.38.21   164
45.1.41 pr.   13; 14
45.1.41.1–2   13
45.1.61   19
45.1.68   57
45.1.75 pr.-2, 5   23; 16, 87
45.1.80   13; 14
45.1.81 pr.-1   10

45.1.82.1   28
45.1.83.1   8
45.1.83.2–3   7
45.1.83.5   25
45.1.84   32
45.1.86   7
45.1.91 pr., 2   27; 32, 127
45.1.91.3   28; 30, 125
45.1.97.2   19
45.1. 99 pr.-1   12; 14, 21, 39, 99
45.1.105   37; 35
45.1.106   16
45.1.107   19
45.1.109   7
45.1.110.1   14
45.1.111   15; 7
45.1.113 pr.   31
45.1.113.1–114   30; 28. 32
45.1.115.2   31
45.1.122.1   33; 9, 58
45.1.126.2   10
45.1.126.2   57
45.1.134 pr.   19
45.1.134.2   9
45.1.137 pr.   6
45.1.137.1   8; 17
45.1.137.2   32
45.1.137.3   32; 21, 30
45.1.137.4   24
45.1.137.6   18
45.1.138 pr.   15
45.1.140 pr.-1   7, 9
45.1.141.4   24
45.2.2   39
45.2.6.3   6
45.2.24.2   69
46.1.8.7   42
46.1.15 pr.   43
46.1.17   215; 46, 179
46.1.18   42
46.1.26, 28   44
46.1.36   46; 215
46.1.39   215; 179

46.1.42   42
46.1.47 pr.   41
46.1.56.2   54
46.1.67   182
46.2.4   211
46.2.6.1, 7   57
46.2.11   211
46.2.17, 19   211
46.3.5.2   58
46.3.12 pr.-1   209
46.3.17   209
46.3.31   164
46.3.34.3   203
46.3.38.1   209
46.3.46 pr.   209
46.3.56   209
46.3.62   219
46.3.64   209; 39
46.3.66   227, 233
46.3.72 pr.   37
46.3.72.1   39
46.3.79   55
46.3.87   203
46.3.91   209
46.3.96 pr.   209
46.3.98.8   25
46.3.102.3   58
46.3.107   27
46.5.5   202, 206
46.5.11   48; 21, 31
46.6.12   211
46.8.13 pr.   30
47.2.12 pr.   164
47.2.14 pr.   110
47.2.54.3   223
47.2.60   67
47.2.62.5   182
47.2.68.5   160
47.2.83 pr.   164
47.2.90   168
47.8.2.23   69
47.10.19   42
48.7.5.2   216

48.19.11.1   168
50.12.1 pr.-2, 4   52
50.12.2, 13.1   52
50.13.1   168, 184
50.13.1.4–5   168, 184
50.13.1.12–13   184
50.13.1.13   168
50.13.1.9   184
50.13.1.10   184
50.16.11 Intro.
50.13.1.12   207
50.16.108 Intro.
50.16.213.1 Intro., 173
50.17.22.1   165
50.17.23   179, 182
50.17.34   11; 13, 23, 96
50.17.36   217
50.17.47 pr.   177
50.17.60   45
50.17.69   209
50.17.73.4   177
50.17.93   196
50.17.123 pr.   211
50.17.161   22
50.17.180   209

III. Non-Legal Sources

Aristotle
   Politics 1.8–10   77

Cato Maior, *de Agricultura*
   144–145   163
   144.2   155
   149.2   155

Cicero
   pro Caecina 54   127
   72   225
   de Officiis 1.150–151   168
   3.70 Intro.
   Topica 66 Intro.

Columella, *de Re Rustica*
   1.7.1   157, 159

Corpus Inscriptionum Latinarum
    10.1781   163
    15.2.7194   53

Fontes Iuris Romani Anteiustiniani
    III no. 132   47

Aulus Gellius, *Noctes Atticae*
    4.12   157

Isidore, *Etymologiae*
    5.25.21–24   76

Martial
    12.32   152

Phaedrus, *Fabulae*
    1.5   169

Pliny the Younger, *Epistulae*
    10.8.5   159

Tacitus, *Annales*
    11.5–7   184